Learning and Instruction

Richard E. Mayer
University of California, Santa Barbara

Upper Saddle River, New Jersey
Columbus, Ohio

Library of Congress Cataloging in Publication Data

Mayer, Richard E.
Learning and instruction / Richard E. Mayer.
p. cm.
Includes bibliographical references and index.
ISBN 0-13-098396-9
1. Educational psychology. 2. Teaching. 3. Learning. I. Title.

LB1051.M3913 2003
370.15'23—dc21

2002141562

Vice President and Publisher: Jeffery W. Johnston
Executive Editor: Kevin M. Davis
Editorial Assistant: Autumn Crisp
Production Editor: Mary Harlan
Production Coordination: Cindy Miller, Clarinda Publication Services
Design Coordinator: Diane C. Lorenzo
Cover Design: Andrew Lundberg
Cover Art: © 1998 C. Herscovici, Brussels/Artists Rights Society (ARS), New York
Illustrations: Clarinda Publication Services
Production Manager: Laura Messerly
Director of Marketing: Ann Castel Davis
Marketing Manager: Amy June
Marketing Coordinator: Tyra Cooper

This book was set in Berkeley by The Clarinda Company. It was printed and bound by R. R. Donnelley & Sons Company. The cover was printed by Phoenix Color Corp.

Credits and Acknowledgments: Credits and acknowledgments begin on p. 504.

Pearson Education Ltd.
Pearson Education Australia Pty. Limited
Pearson Education Singapore Pte. Ltd.
Pearson Education North Asia Ltd.
Pearson Education Canada, Ltd.
Pearson Educación de Mexico, S.A. de C.V.
Pearson Education—Japan
Pearson Education Malaysia Pte. Ltd.
Pearson Education, *Upper Saddle River, New Jersey*

10 9 8 7 6 5 4 3 2
ISBN 0-13-098396-9

Dedicated to

Beverly

PREFACE

How do people learn? How can we promote their learning? If these questions interest you, then you should read this book. These seemingly simple questions have interested educators and researchers for more than 100 years, but significant advances in answering them have been occurring recently. Although I am not able to give you a complete answer to these questions in this book, I try to show you some of the exciting progress that has been made.

The scientific study of education began about 100 years ago, when the world's first educational psychologist, E. L. Thorndike, initiated his 40-year-long research program at Columbia University in 1901. Then, as now, researchers and educators sought to understand how students learn and how to design instruction that would promote their learning. During the last quarter century the pace and productivity of educational research has accelerated, yielding exciting advances in our understanding of school learning and instruction. In particular, the two most significant breakthroughs involve *psychologies of subject matter*—that is, how students learn school subjects such as reading, writing, mathematics, science, and history—and *cognitive process instruction*—that is, research on how to help students use appropriate cognitive processes on specific academic tasks, such as how to abstract the theme of a passage or how to identify needed and unneeded information in an arithmetic story problem. My goal in writing this book is to introduce you to some of the exciting research on school learning and instruction. If you are interested in what research has to say about school learning and instruction, then this book is for you.

I do not assume that you have any previous background in education or psychology. I do assume that you prefer to focus on research about learning and instruction rather than opinions and unsubstantiated claims. This book is appropriate for courses in education or psychology that focus on learning and instruction. I created it by merging and updating two recently published books: *The Promise of Educational Psychology, Volume I: Learning in the Content Areas* and *The Promise of Educational Psychology, Volume II: Teaching for Meaningful Learning. Learning and Instruction* also represents an up-to-date revision and extension of my earlier book, *Educational Psychology: A Cognitive Approach.*

This book is based on several fundamental values that I have developed over the years as an author and teacher. First, in each chapter I prefer to focus clearly on a few big ideas rather than to mention everything there is to say on a topic. If you somehow miss the big ideas, I summarize them at the end of each chapter. I would prefer for you to understand a few exemplary ideas deeply than to learn about a list of topics superficially. My approach is focused rather than encyclopedic. Second, I prefer to base my conclusions on scientific research rather than on the opinion of experts. When I present an exemplary research study, I try to give you enough detail so you can see what was done (method), what was found (results), and what it all means (conclusion). I prefer for you to be able to see how educational practice can be informed by research rather than ask you to "trust me." My approach values solid research over well-intentioned opinions. Third, I prefer to convey an understanding of what is known about how to help people learn rather than give you a list of specific prescriptions for immediate classroom practice. My approach values understanding the learning/teaching process rather than memorizing a set of classroom procedures. When I present instructional implications, I try to help you see how they follow from research and theory. Fourth, I value clear organization so I provide a chapter outline that is keyed to the headings I use throughout the chapter. Fifth, I value active learning so I try to engage you in tasks that are directly relevant to the theme of a chapter or section, and I write in a conversational style in which I address you directly. Sixth, I value meaningful learning so I try to provide clear definitions and concrete examples of key concepts. Overall, rather than simply presenting information, my approach values conciseness, research-based conclusions, theory-based recommendations, clear structure, empathy, and concreteness.

Preparing this book has reminded me of the exciting progress researchers have made in understanding how students learn in subject areas and how instruction can promote meaningful learning. I hope that you enjoy reading this book as much as I have enjoyed writing it. If it conveys this sense of progress and if it makes sense to you, then I will consider this book a success. Please feel free to contact me with any comments or suggestions (at mayer@psych.ucsb.edu).

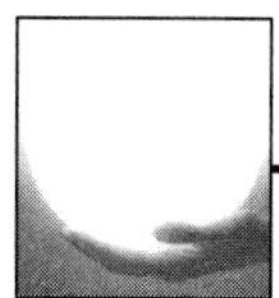

ACKNOWLEDGMENTS

I am indebted to my publisher, my teachers, my colleagues, my students, and my family. I thank Kevin Davis and his associates at Merrill/Prentice Hall for their patience and support during the course of this project. This text is a combination and updating of two currently published books: *The Promise of Educational Psychology: Learning in the Content Areas* and *The Promise of Educational Psychology, Volume II: Teaching for Meaningful Learning*. I wish to thank the reviewers of these two works for their helpful critques: Thomas Anderson, University of Illinois; Carol Anne Kardash, University of Missouri–Columbia; Kenneth Kiewra, University of Nebraska; Kathryn W. Linden, Purdue University; John R. McClure, Northern Arizona University; Michael S. Meloth, University of Colorado; Otherine Neisler, Yale University; Gary Phye, Iowa State University; and Paul R. Pintrich, The University of Michigan. I also appreciate the production services of Clarinda Publication Services. I am grateful to my mentors at the University of Michigan (where I received my Ph.D. in 1973), including James Greeno and Bill McKeachie. I also learned much from my colleagues at Indiana University (where I served from 1973 to 1975) and at the University of California, Santa Barbara (where I have served since 1975), as well as colleagues around the nation and the world. I have been fortunate to be able to work with an outstanding group of graduate students and postdoctoral scholars over the years, and I appreciate the many helpful suggestions of undergraduate students in my educational psychology course. I am grateful to my parents, who were my first teachers, and whose memory is now never far from my thoughts. I thank my children, Ken, Dave, and Sarah, for reminding me to keep the book interesting, and for keeping my life so interesting. I particularly wish to thank my wife, Beverly, for her unwavering support and encouragement, and just for bringing so much happiness into my life. I dedicate this book to her with love.

Richard E. Mayer
Santa Barbara, California

BRIEF CONTENTS

CHAPTER 1: Introduction to Learning and Instruction 1

SECTION I: LEARNING 29

CHAPTER 2: Learning to Read Fluently 30

CHAPTER 3: Learning to Read for Comprehension 72

CHAPTER 4: Learning to Write 112

CHAPTER 5: Learning Mathematics 146

CHAPTER 6: Learning Science 190

SECTION II: INSTRUCTION 237

CHAPTER 7: Teaching by Giving Productive Feedback 238

CHAPTER 8: Teaching by Providing Concreteness, Activity, and Familiarity 274

CHAPTER 9: Teaching by Explaining Examples 306

CHAPTER 10: Teaching by Guiding Cognitive Processes During Learning 326

CHAPTER 11: Teaching by Fostering Learning Strategies 360

CHAPTER 12: Teaching by Fostering Problem-Solving Strategies 398

CHAPTER 13: Teaching by Creating Cognitive Apprenticeship in Classrooms 428

CHAPTER 14: Teaching by Priming Students' Motivation to Learn 456

CONTENTS

CHAPTER 1: Introduction to Learning and Instruction 1

Wild Boy, 2
What Is Educational Psychology? 4
A Brief History of the Relationship Between Psychology and Education, 9
A Closer Look at the Learner-Centered Approach, 14
How to Foster Meaningful Learning, 19
What Is the Promise of Educational Psychology? 24
Chapter Summary, 26

SECTION I: **LEARNING** **29**

CHAPTER 2: Learning to Read Fluently 30

The Problem of Reading a Word, 32
Recognizing Phonemes, 36
Decoding Words, 43
Accessing Word Meaning, 55
Sentence Integration, 62
Chapter Summary, 69

CHAPTER 3: Learning to Read for Comprehension 72

Effort After Meaning, 74
Schema Theory, 77
Using Prior Knowledge, 80
Using Prose Structure, 87
Making Inferences, 95
Using Metacognitive Knowledge, 100
Building a Reading Comprehension Program That Works, 109
Chapter Summary, 110

CHAPTER 4: Learning to Write 112

The Storytelling Problem, 114
Cognitive Processes in Writing, 116
Planning, 120
Translating, 125
Reviewing, 133
Building a Writing Program That Works, 138
Chapter Summary, 144

CHAPTER 5: Learning Mathematics 146

What Do You Need to Know to Solve Math Problems? 148
Problem Translation, 152
Problem Integration, 157
Solution Planning and Monitoring, 169
Solution Execution, 179
Chapter Summary, 188

CHAPTER 6: Learning Science 190

The Intuitive Physics Problem, 192
Recognizing Anomalies: Discarding a Misconception, 194
Initiating Conceptual Change: Constructing a New Conception, 205
Developing Scientific Reasoning: Using a New Conception, 213
Building Scientific Expertise: Learning to Build and Use Scientific Knowledge, 226
Chapter Summary, 234

SECTION II: **INSTRUCTION** **237**

CHAPTER 7: Teaching by Giving Productive Feedback 238

A Response Learning Task, 240
The Law of Effect, 242
How Do Classroom Management Techniques Affect Classroom Behavior? 246
How Do Rewards Affect Classroom Activities? 252
How Does Feedback Affect Response Learning? 256
How Does Feedback Affect Concept Learning? 260
How Does Feedback Affect Skill Learning? 267
Chapter Summary, 271

CHAPTER 8: Teaching by Providing Concreteness, Activity, and Familiarity 274

The Parallelogram Problem, 276
Concrete Methods, 278
Discovery Methods, 287
Inductive Methods, 298
Chapter Summary, 303

CHAPTER 9: Teaching by Explaining Examples 306
Introduction, 308
Worked-Out Examples, 309
Case-Based Learning, 319
Chapter Summary, 323

CHAPTER 10: Teaching by Guiding Cognitive Processes During Learning 326
How to Improve a Textbook Lesson, 328
Cognitive Theory of Instruction, 329
Adjunct Questions, 332
Signaling, 338
Advance Organizers, 348
Chapter Summary, 358

CHAPTER 11: Teaching by Fostering Learning Strategies 360
How to Turn a Passive Learning Task into an Active Learning Task, 362
Mnemonic Strategies, 364
Structure Strategies, 370
Generative Strategies, 386
Chapter Summary, 395

CHAPTER 12: Teaching by Fostering Problem-Solving Strategies 398
Can Problem-Solving Skills Be Taught? 400
What Makes an Effective Problem-Solving Program? 401
Productive Thinking Program, 413
Instrumental Enrichment, 417
Project Intelligence, 421
The Case for Improving Problem-Solving Skills Instruction, 424
Chapter Summary, 426

CHAPTER 13: Teaching by Creating Cognitive Apprenticeship in Classrooms 428
Introduction 430
Learning in and out of School, 434
Traditional and Cognitive Apprenticeship, 437
Reciprocal Teaching, 440
Cooperative Learning, 444
Participatory Modeling, 450
Chapter Summary, 454

CHAPTER 14: Teaching by Priming Students' Motivation to Learn 456

Introduction, 458
Motivation Based on Interest, 461
Motivation Based on Self-Efficacy, 469
Motivation Based on Attributions, 475
Chapter Summary, 481

REFERENCES 483

CREDITS 504

AUTHOR INDEX 508

SUBJECT INDEX 511

CHAPTER 1 Introduction to Learning and Instruction

CHAPTER OUTLINE

Wild Boy

What Is Educational Psychology?

A Brief History of the Relationship Between Education and Psychology

A Closer Look at the Learner-Centered Approach

How to Foster Meaningful Learning

What Is the Promise of Educational Psychology?

Chapter Summary

After exploring a classic educational study, this chapter defines educational psychology, summarizes the history of the educational psychology, explores the role of educational psychology, explains how to foster meaningful learning, and examines how educational psychology can help to answer questions about educational practice. It also provides an organization for the rest of the book.

WILD BOY

Suppose a child was freed completely of all social interaction with other humans. Suppose this child was allowed to develop without any social contact with other people. This experiment could be viewed as providing a child with the ultimate in educational freedom. What would happen to such a child? What would the child be like? Is society needed in order to help children develop to their fullest potential as human beings? Take a moment to provide some predictions in Figure 1–1.

These questions were at the heart of an historic educational experiment that began in 1800 in Paris. The experiment involved only one student, an adolescent boy named Victor, and his teacher, a physician named Dr. Jean-Marc Itard. Victor had been discovered living in the forests of Aveyron in France. Apparently, the boy had grown up in the forest, without any human contact. When captured, the boy was completely naked, dirty, and inarticulate. He seemed insensitive to temperature and pain, and was incapable of maintaining attention. He ate his food raw, using only his hands. Although physically healthy, he was totally unsocialized. The public showed great interest in the boy, and he become popularly known as the "enfant sauvage de l'Aveyron"—that is, the "wild boy of Aveyron." Dr. Itard was convinced that the boy, whom he named Victor, could be taught to become a civilized member of French society. For the next five years, Dr. Itard worked with his student, often having to develop new materials and instructional techniques.

Dr. Itard's educational program was based on several principles. First, he believed that the needs and characteristics of the student should dictate the educational program, an approach that can be called *learner-centered.* Instead of letting the curriculum determine what students would learn, in lock-step fashion, the teacher must be free to shape instruction to suit the needs of the student. Second, he believed that education depends on the student having had certain experiences (i.e., most educational programs assume that the child has acquired "readiness skills" through natural interactions with the physical and social environment). For example, a student needs experiences with objects before learning the language names for them. If a student lacks appropriate sensory experiences, then these experiences must be provided as prerequisites to more academic components of an educational program. Third, he believed that the student had to be motivated to learn. According to Dr. Itard, Victor successfully learned to cope in the wild because his survival depended on it. Now, Dr. Itard introduced new needs for Victor so that Victor would be motivated to learn social skills. Finally, Dr. Itard believed that instruction often requires the development of new instructional devices and techniques. Many of the materials and techniques of behavior modification that Dr. Itard developed became the basis for subsequent programs to teach special education students.

How far did Victor progress during the five years of instruction? He learned basic social skills, such as dressing himself, sleeping in bed without wetting, and eating with utensils. He learned to make use of his senses including sight, sound, and taste. He learned to show affection and to try to please others. Although he never learned to speak effectively, he did learn to communicate using written language. However, Victor did not reach full self-sufficiency, and spent the rest of his life under the supervision of a caretaker. The lack of complete success has been attributed to many causes including the lack

FIGURE 1–1

What would it be like for a child to grow up without any human contact?

Suppose that a child grew up from birth to age 12 in a forest, without any human contact. What do you think the child would be like at age 12? For each pair of attributes listed below, place a check next to the one you think would apply.

_____ physically weak and unhealthy	_____ physically strong and healthy
_____ attentive to stimuli	_____ unattentive to stimuli
_____ responsive to pain	_____ unresponsive to pain
_____ responsive to temperature	_____ unresponsive to temperature
_____ interested in other people	_____ uninterested in other people
_____ enjoyed a broad variety of food tastes	_____ restricted to a very few food tastes
_____ had developed a form of oral language	_____ hadn't developed a form of oral language
_____ had developed a form of gesturing language	_____ hadn't developed a form of gesturing language
_____ had developed a form of written language	_____ hadn't developed a form of written language
_____ had developed basic arithmetic skills	_____ hadn't developed basic arithmetic skills
_____ had invented many useful tools	_____ hadn't invented useful tools
_____ was well mannered with people	_____ wasn't well mannered with people
_____ longed for human affection	_____ was not interested in human affection
_____ would be able to learn basic social skills swiftly	_____ wouldn't be able to learn basic social skills swiftly
_____ would be able to learn basic language skills swiftly	_____ wouldn't be able to learn basic language skills swiftly

of appropriate stimulation during critical periods of development, the limitations of Itard's methods (including his insistence than Victor use spoken rather than sign language), and the possibility that Victor was born with brain damage. Thus, you would have been correct in your predictions in Figure 1–1 if you had checked each of the attributes on the right-hand side and none on the left side of Figure 1–1.

As we leave the "wild boy," let's consider what this case demonstrated about the nature of education. Some of the broader educational issues addressed by Itard were (Lane, 1976, p. 129):

1. Society (including formal instruction) is crucial for human development. "The moral superiority said to be natural to man is only the result of civilization . . . [and without society, man] pitifully hangs on without intelligence and without feelings, a precarious life reduced to bare animal functions."

2. People learn in order to satisfy their needs. "In the most isolated savage as in the most highly civilized man, there exists a constant relation between ideas and needs."
3. Instructional programs should be based on science. "The progress of education can and ought to be illuminated by the light of modern medicine, which of all the natural sciences can help most powerfully toward the perfection of the human species."
4. Instructional programs should take into account the individual characteristics of each student. "[Progress will be made] by detecting the organic and intellectual peculiarities of each individual and determining from there what education ought to do for him."

The conclusions of Itard, written 200 years ago, can serve as a starting point for this book on the promise of educational psychology's future. Like Itard's research, this book is based on a *learner-centered approach* in which the learner is at the heart of all learning (Lambert & McCombs, 1998). In taking a learner-centered approach, the first overarching goal is to understand the cognitive processes and knowledge used by learners in carrying out academic tasks. What are the cognitive processes that a skilled reader engages in while reading a textbook lesson? What are the cognitive processes that a skilled writer engages in while composing an essay? What are the cognitive processes that a skilled mathematician engages in while solving a mathematics problem? What are the cognitive processes that a skilled scientist uses in investigating a new phenomenon? These kinds of cognitive questions are addressed in the first section of this book on learning. In short, I seek to understand what skilled readers, writers, mathematicians, and scientists know.

The second overarching goal is to understand how to help students to develop the processes used by skilled practitioners to perform academic tasks. How can we help a beginning reader to know what a skilled reader knows? How can we help an aspiring writer to know what a skilled writer knows? How can we help novice mathematics and science students to have the knowledge needed to think like skilled mathematicians and scientists? These kinds of instructional questions are addressed in the second section of this book on instruction. In short, I seek to understand the kinds of learning experiences that foster cognitive growth in learners.

In summary, this book takes a learner-centered approach to learning and instruction. In particular, I examine the learning issue of what students need to learn to accomplish academic tasks and the instructional issue of how to help students achieve meaningful learning. The remainder of this chapter explores some of the basic issues in educational psychology.

WHAT IS EDUCATIONAL PSYCHOLOGY?

DEFINITIONS

What is educational psychology? Based on the learner-centered perspective described in the previous section, educational psychology can be defined as a branch of psychology concerned with understanding how the instructional environment and the characteristics of the learner interact to produce cognitive growth in the learner. In particular, educational psychology focuses on the scientific study of techniques for manipulating human cognitive processes and knowledge states. There are three major components in this definition:

1. Educational psychology is a science, namely a branch of psychology.
2. Educational psychology investigates the instructor's manipulation of the environment (i.e., instruction).
3. Educational psychology investigates resulting changes in the learner's cognitive processes and knowledge structures (i.e., learning).

In short, educational psychology studies how instruction affects learning.

What is instruction? Educational psychology stands between instruction and learning (i.e., between the instructional manipulations provided by the teacher and the changes in knowledge and behavior created in the learner). Instruction refers to the teacher's construction of environments for the student, where such environments are intended to foster changes in the learner's knowledge and behavior. For example, Gagne (1974, p. vii) defines instruction as "the arrangement of external events to activate and support the internal processes of learning." Thus, the definition of instruction has two main components:

1. Instruction is something the teacher does.
2. The goal of instruction is to promote learning in the student.

This definition of instruction is broad enough to include lectures, discussions, educational games, textbooks, research projects, and Web-based presentations.

What is learning? If the goal of education is to promote learning, it is worthwhile to understand what learning is. Learning refers to lasting changes in the learner's knowledge, where such changes are due to experience. Thus, learning is defined as a relatively permanent change in someone's knowledge based on the person's experience. This definition has three parts:

1. Learning is long-term rather than short-term, such as learning how to use a word-processing program. A change that disappears after a few hours does not reflect learning.
2. Learning involves a cognitive change that is reflected in a behavioral change, such as changing from not knowing to knowing the procedure for erasing a word in a word-processing program. If there is no change, then no learning occurred.
3. Learning depends on the experience of the learner, such as reading a word-processing manual. A change that occurs solely because of a physiological state—such as being tired, hitting one's head, or taking a mind-altering drug—is not an example of learning. Furthermore, it depends not on what is done to the learner, but rather on how the learner interprets what happens, that is, on the learner's personal experience.

Although two of the components of the definition of learning (learning is permanent and experience-based) have remained consistent for a century, the issue of what is changed (or what is learned) has been more controversial (Mayer, 1992a, 2001a). Does learning involve a behavioral change or a cognitive change? This question reflects the classic tension between behaviorist and cognitive approaches to learning. In this book, I take a cognitive approach by defining "what is learned" as a cognitive change that is reflected in a behavioral change.

Overall this definition of learning is broad enough to include everything from how children learn to talk when they are toddlers to how they eventually learn to read, write, and compute, to how they come to be able to navigate in the social world.

In his classic textbook, *Principles of Teaching,* E. L. Thorndike (1913, p. 1) recognized that the central theme in education is an externally manipulated change in the learner:

> The word *education* is used with many meanings, but in all its usages it refers to changes. No one is educated who stays as he was. We do not educate anybody if we do nothing that makes any difference or change in anybody. . . . In studying education, then, one studies always the existence, nature, causation or value of change of some sort.

In summary, teaching and learning are inevitably connected processes that involve the fostering of change within the learner.

In his provocative little book *Experience & Education,* John Dewey (1938, p. 25) described the relationship between teaching—providing students with useful experiences—and learning, or the acquisition of knowledge. "All genuine education comes about through experience," Dewey argued. However, he added an important warning that "all experiences are not genuinely or equally educative." Unfortunately, many instructional manipulations are what Dewey calls "mis-educative":

> Some experiences are mis-educative. Any experience is mis-educative that has the effect of arresting or distorting the growth of further experiences. . . . Every experience lives on in further experiences. Hence the central problem of an education based on experience is to select the kind of present experiences that live fruitfully and creatively in subsequent experiences.

In summary, instructional manipulations result in changes in the learner's knowledge. Because all learning involves connecting new information to existing knowledge, it is crucial to help students develop knowledge structures that can support the acquisition of useful new information. If students have not acquired knowledge, then information cannot be successfully connected with it.

RESEARCHING INSTRUCTION AND LEARNING

How can we tell whether instruction affects learning? In short, how can we tell whether one way of teaching is better than another at helping students learn? In this section I explore three ways of conducting research on instructional methods: behaviorist approaches, which focus on whether one method is better than another; cognitive approaches, which focus on how instructional methods affect underlying learning processes and learning outcomes; and contextual approaches, which focus on how instructional methods are used in real classroom settings.

BEHAVIORIST APPROACH The traditional approach to instructional research has been to conduct some instructional manipulation (such as presence versus absence of an outline on the blackboard before the start of a lecture) and then measure the performance of students who learned under each method. Thus the goal of research is to determine the effects of some observable manipulation on some observable behavior. This approach is summarized in the top panel of Figure 1–2, which shows only two observable variables. In general, the results of such studies may be summarized as "method A is better than method B."

COGNITIVE APPROACH One problem with the behaviorist approach is that it does not provide an understanding of why or how method A is better than method B. A teacher could make better use of instructional methods by understanding the general principles that mediate between instruction and test performance. The cognitive approach to instruction seeks to determine how instructional procedures influence internal information-processing events and the acquired cognitive structure. For example, we might be interested in how various methods of instruction affect how a learner selects relevant information, organizes it into a coherent cognitive structure, and integrates it with existing knowledge. This approach is shown in the middle portion of Figure 1–2; in addition to the two observable variables, internal cognitive processes and learning outcomes have been added. Instead of focusing simply on how much is learned, our focus shifts to what is learned, that is, to qualitative differences in the learner's cognitive processing during learning and in the resulting learning outcome.

FIGURE 1–2 Three approaches to research on instructional methods

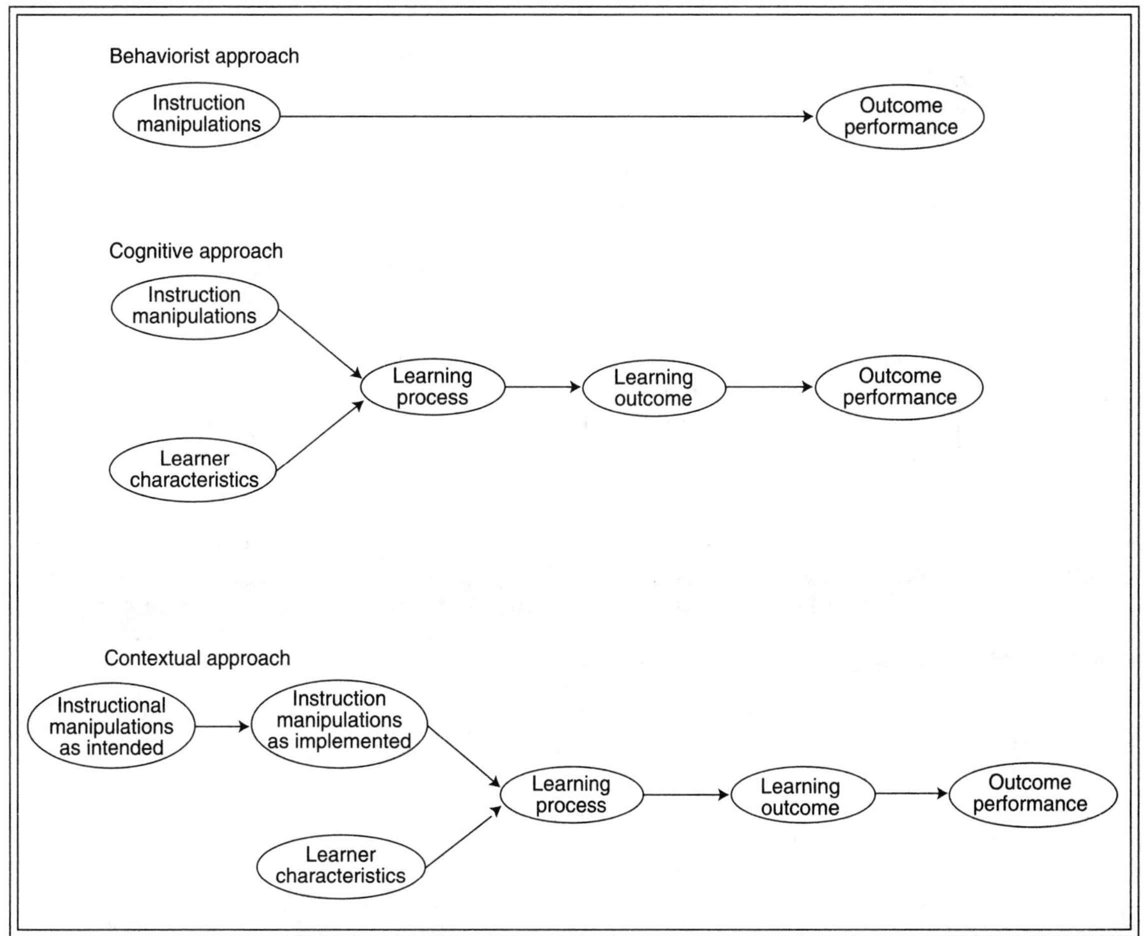

CONTEXTUAL APPROACH Although the cognitive approach offers a deeper picture of teaching for transfer than does the behaviorist approach, the picture is still not complete. According to the contextual approach, instructional methods cannot be separated from the context in which they are used—including the social and cultural background of the students, the classroom, the school, and educational system at large. Using method A versus method B may mean different things for different teachers, different students, and in different classrooms. Thus, an increasingly important aspect of instructional research concerns how instructional programs are actually implemented in real classrooms. This approach is represented in the bottom of Figure 1–2.

Each of the three approaches offers something useful, and you will find all three in this book. As you read research studies on instructional methods, you may be able to tell whether the authors are taking a behaviorist, cognitive, or contextual approach.

However, I focus somewhat on the cognitive approach because I think it offers advantages over the older behaviorist approach and because research on the newer contextual approach is not yet well developed.

FACTORS IN THE TEACHING/LEARNING PROCESS

Table 1–1 summarizes some examples of factors that might be involved in the teaching/learning process. The factors are as follows:

Instructional manipulations: the sequence of environmental (i.e., external) events including the organization and content of instructional materials and the behaviors of the teacher. The instructional manipulations include both what is taught and how it is taught, and depend on the characteristics of the teacher and on the curriculum.

Learner characteristics: the learner's existing knowledge, including facts, procedures, and strategies that may be required in the learning situation, and the nature of the learner's memory system, including capacity and mode of representation in memory.

Learning context: the social and cultural context of learning, including the social structure of the classroom and school.

*Learning processes:*the learner's internal cognitive processes during learning, such as how the learner selects, organizes, and integrates new information with existing knowledge.

TABLE 1–1 Examples of factors in the teaching/learning process

Instructional Manipulations	**Learning Context**	**Learner Characteristics**	**Learning Processes**	**Learning Outcome**	**Outcome Performance**
Repeating a lesson	Social and cultural context	Existing knowledge	Selecting information	Rote learning	Retention
Providing examples		Existing information-processing strategies	Organizing information	Meaningful learning	Transfer
Asking questions			Integrating information		

Adapted from Mayer (1984)

Learning outcome: the cognitive changes in the learner's knowledge or memory system, including the newly acquired facts, procedures, and strategies.

Outcome performance: the learner's performance (i.e., behavior) on tests, such as retention or transfer to new learning tasks.

As you can see, the cognitive approach involves several factors that are internal to the learner: learner characteristics, learning processes, learning outcomes. Thus the cognitive approach is clearly learner centered.

Because these factors are not directly observable, they can only be inferred from the learner's behavior. Thus a major challenge of the cognitive approach is to devise methods of study that allow us to make correct inferences about internal processes and states in the learner.

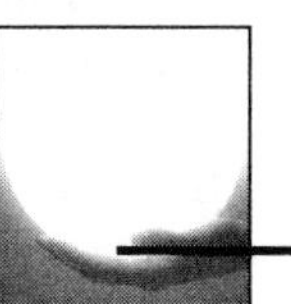

A BRIEF HISTORY OF THE RELATIONSHIP BETWEEN PSYCHOLOGY AND EDUCATION

What is an effective relationship between psychology and education? How does the psychologist's view of learning affect the educator's approach to instruction? In this section we explore the historical evolution of three views of the role of psychology in education, and of three views of learning and instruction.

THREE ROADS FOR PSYCHOLOGY IN EDUCATION

Psychology involves the study of how people learn and develop, whereas education involves helping people to learn and develop. What do you think should be the relation between psychology and education? Check one of the following answers:

_____Psychologists should conduct laboratory research about learning and development and explain the resulting theories to educators; educators should apply this scientific research to their instruction.

_____Psychologists should conduct laboratory research about learning and development without concern for educators; educators should develop instruction that meets the practical needs of their students without examining irrelevant psychological theories.

_____Psychologists should study how people learn and develop in real educational situations, basing their research on the challenges of educators; educators should base their instructional decisions on psychological theories of how students learn and develop.

If you chose the first answer, you opted for a one-way street that runs from psychology to education. If you chose the second answer, you selected a dead-end street in which psychology and education do not meet. If you chose the third answer, your path lies on a two-way street that runs from psychology to education and from education to psychology.

These three kinds of paths represent three phases in the history of psychology in education (Mayer, 1992a, 1996). By the 1890s psychologists, who had recently given birth to what Gardner (1985) called "the mind's new science," were struggling to keep their infant science alive. At the same time, educators, who faced the daunting task of providing universal compulsory education, were struggling to professionalize the practice of teaching. The rise of both psychology and education at the end of the 1800s suggested the question of what should be the proper relation between psychologists and educators. In short, what should be the path between the science of psychology and the practice of education? The answer to this question passed through three major phases: (1) a one-way street—a phase of naive optimism during the early 1900s in which psychological advances would be applied directly to improving education; (2) a dead-end street—a pessimistic phase during the mid-1900s in which the paths of psychology and education failed to cross; and (3) a two-way street—the rebirth of optimism during the latter part of the 1900s in which educational issues shape psychological research and psychological research informs educational practice. These three paths are summarized in Table 1–2.

PHASE 1: ONE-WAY STREET FROM PSYCHOLOGY TO EDUCATION At the start of this century, educational psychologists were optimistic that psychological science could improve educational practice. They viewed educational psychology as the "guiding science of the school" (Cubberly, 1920, p. 755), a discipline that borrowed its research methods from psychology and its research agenda from education. In his classic book, *The Principles of Teaching Based on Psychology,* E. L. Thorndike (1906, p. 206) proclaimed:

> The efficiency of any profession depends in large measure upon the degree to which it becomes scientific. The profession of teaching will improve (1) in proportion as its members direct their work by the scientific spirit and methods, that is by honest, open-minded consideration of facts, by freedom from superstitions, fancies, and unverified guesses, and (2) in proportion as the leaders in education direct their choices of methods by the results of scientific investigation rather than general opinion.

As the first editor of the *Journal of Educational Psychology* in 1910, Thorndike envisioned that educational psychologists would apply the exact methods of science to the problems of education. Thus began this 100-year-old vision that the "proper application of psychological findings might lead the way to better instruction in all schools" (Woodring, 1958, p. 6).

TABLE 1–2

Three paths for psychology and education

Phase	Direction of Relation	Period	Emotional Tone	Vision for Psychology and Education
Phase 1	One-way street	Early 1900s	Naive optimism	Psychology is applied to education; education is recipient of psychology
Phase 2	Dead-end street	Mid-1900s	Pessimism	Psychology ignores education; education ignores psychology
Phase 3	Two-way street	Late 1900s	Cautious optimism	Education shapes psychological research; psychology shapes educational practice

Yet, even during the optimism of the early 1900s, educational psychologists recognized that psychology was not likely to be able to satisfy the needs of educators. In his famous lectures on psychology for teachers, which he later published as *Talks to Teachers*, the great American psychologist William James (1899/1958, p. 22) admitted his doubts as follows:

> The desire of the schoolteachers for a completer professional training, and their aspiration toward the professional spirit in their work, have led more and more to turn to us for light on fundamental principles. . . . You look to me . . . for information concerning the mind's operation, which may enable you to labor more easily and effectively in the several classrooms over which you preside. . . . Psychology ought certainly to give the teacher radical help. And yet I confess that, acquainted as I am with the height of your expectations, I feel a little anxious lest, at the end of these simple talks of mine, not a few of you may experience some disappointment at the net results.

James acknowledged two obstacles blocking the application of psychology to education. First, James (1899/1958) correctly observed that the psychology of the late 1800s lacked a sufficient database, and that much work needed to be done to test psychological theories. Second, James warned that psychological research results and theories would not necessarily translate directly into prescriptions for classroom practice: "You make a great, a very great mistake, if you think that psychology, being a science of the mind's laws, is something from which you can deduce definite programmes and schemes and methods of instruction for immediate classroom use" (p. 23).

PHASE 2: DEAD-END STREET FOR PSYCHOLOGY IN EDUCATION Despite the aspirations of early educational psychologists, the discipline of educational psychology was in serious trouble by the mid-1900s. Educators and psychologists became pessimistic concerning whether educational psychology would be able to assume its role as the guiding science of education. Psychologists busied themselves by studying the learning of laboratory animals, such as rats running in mazes, or human learning of senseless material in rigid laboratory settings, such as memorizing lists of nonsense syllables—issues that seemed far removed from the world of education. Educators focused on practical issues, such as whether one method was better than another for teaching a given skill, while failing to base educational decisions on a coherent theory of how students learn.

Grinder (1989) identified three reasons for the decline of educational psychology in the mid-1900s:

Withdrawal: Educational psychologists lost interest in contributing to educational policy.
Fractionation: Educational psychologists failed to achieve a coherent theoretical perspective.
Irrelevance: Educational psychologists focused on research issues far removed from the problems of schooling.

In short, during this dead-end phase, psychology and education became disconnected.

PHASE 3: TWO-WAY STREET BETWEEN PSYCHOLOGY AND EDUCATION Something happened in the late 1950s and early 1960s that brought a new phase of optimism to educational psychology. That something was the "transition from behavioral to cognitive psychology" (DiVesta, 1989, p. 39), or what Scandura et al. (1981, p. 367) called the "shift from S-R [stimulus-response] to information processing" theories. The cognitive revolution in educational psychology highlighted "the learner as an active participant in the learning process" (DiVesta, 1989, p. 54). It encouraged research that examines how real students learn in real classroom settings, with a particular focus on the individual learning strategies that students use when faced with learning school material such as reading or writing or arithmetic. This view allowed the discipline of educational psychology to overcome the withdrawal, fractionation, and irrelevance that previously plagued it.

In a recent historical review, Mayer (1992a) asked: "Can educational psychology regain its position as the guiding science of education?" (p. 406). In many ways, this book provides the latest installment in educational psychology's quest to become the place where psychology and education meet. During the first part of the century, educational psychology failed largely because it lacked the research tools and database necessary to improve education. During the middle part of this century, educational psychology failed because of its unwillingness to build theories that were relevant to improving education. In the last part of this century, however, educational psychology acquired both research tools and theories relevant to improving education. After nearly 100 years, there again is cause for optimism reviving the vision of educational practice based on scientific theory as well as psychological theory based on real human learning.

The road between psychology and education has become a two-way street. The road runs from education to psychology: By providing the research agenda, education challenges psychology to develop theories about real people in real situations rather than theories that are limited to how people learn contrived tasks in artificial laboratory settings. The road runs from psychology to education: By developing useful theories of human learning and cognition and development, psychology provides the basis for making informed decisions about educational practice. In summary, "educational psychology—rather than being the place solely to apply psychological theories that have been developed elsewhere—is an exciting venue for shaping and testing the dominant psychological theories of the day" (Mayer, 1993a, p. 553).

THREE METAPHORS OF LEARNING

If I asked you to complete the following sentence, how would you respond?

Learning is like:

_____ strengthening a connection (i.e., adding new behaviors to your repertoire).
_____ adding files to a file cabinet (i.e., adding new facts and skills to your knowledge base).
_____ building a model (i.e., understanding how to fit pieces of information together).

If you chose the first answer, you seem to view *learning as response strengthening*—the idea that learning involves adding new responses to an ever-growing collection. If you chose the second answer, you view *learning as knowledge acquisition*—the idea that learning involves transferring knowledge from the teacher's head to the student's head. If you chose the third answer, you view *learning as knowledge construction*—the idea that students actively create their own learning by trying to make sense out of their experiences.

These three views of learning represent three persistent metaphors developed over the history of psychology in education—metaphors invented by psychologists and applied by educators. Examining your personal metaphor of learning is worthwhile because educational practice can be influenced by the educator's underlying metaphor of learning. Table

TABLE 1–3
Three metaphors of learning

Learning	The Learner	The Teacher	Typical Instructional Methods
Response strengthening	Passive recipient of rewards and punishments	Dispenser of rewards and punishments	Drill and practice on basic skills
Knowledge acquisition	Information-processor	Dispenser of information	Textbooks, workbooks, and lectures
Knowledge construction	Sense-maker	Guide for understanding academic tasks	Discussion, guided discovery, and supervised participation in meaningful tasks

1–3 summarizes three common metaphors for learning: learning as response strengthening, learning as knowledge acquisition, and learning as knowledge construction.

LEARNING AS RESPONSE STRENGTHENING The first metaphor to gain broad acceptance in psychology is learning-as-response-strengthening, which evolved throughout the first half of the twentieth century and was based largely on research on laboratory animals. According to this view, learning is a mechanical process in which successful responses to a given situation are automatically strengthened and unsuccessful responses to the situation are weakened. In this way, learning is like strengthening or weakening the association between a stimulus (S) and a response (R). Thus, the term "response strengthening" includes the idea of both strengthening and weakening of responses, or more properly, of stimulus-response (S-R) associations. For example, in reading, a to-be-strengthened S-R association may be between the printed word "cat" and its corresponding sound; in writing between the spoken word "cat" and its corresponding spelling "c-a-t"; and in arithmetic, between "4 + 4 = " and "8." According to this metaphor, the learner becomes a passive recipient who is completely shaped by reinforcements in the environment, and the teacher becomes a feedback dispenser who delivers rewards and punishments.

The learning-as-response-strengthening view suggests educational practice in which the teacher creates situations that require short responses, the learner gives a response, and the teacher provides the appropriate reward or punishment. For example, the teacher may ask, "What is 750 divided by 5?" If the student responds with the correct answer ("150") the teacher says, "Right, good job." If the student responds with an incorrect answer ("250"), the teacher may say, "No, you need to review the worksheet." As you can see, drill-and-practice is a popular method of instruction that is consistent with the learning-as-response-strengthening metaphor. When they accept the learning-as-response-strengthening metaphor, educators emphasize teaching of basic skills in reading, writing, and arithmetic.

LEARNING AS KNOWLEDGE ACQUISITION The second metaphor, learning-as-knowledge-acquisition, developed during the 1960s and 1970s as research shifted from studying animal learning in laboratory settings to studying human learning in laboratory settings. According to this view, learning occurs when information is transferred from a more knowledgeable person (such as a teacher) to a less knowledgeable person (such as a student). In this way, learning is like filling a void, that is, like pouring information into a student's memory. Within this metaphor, the learner becomes an processor of information and the teacher becomes a dispenser of information. Information is a commodity the teacher gives to the student.

The learning-as-knowledge-acquisition view suggests educational practice in which the teacher presents new information for the student to learn. For example, the teacher may ask students to read a section in their science textbooks on how electricity flows in a circuit, and then test them on the material. As you can see, the goal of instruction is to increase the amount of knowledge in the learner's memory, so textbooks and lectures offer popular methods of instruction. When educators call for covering material in the curriculum, they are working under a learning-as-knowledge-acquisition metaphor.

LEARNING AS KNOWLEDGE CONSTRUCTION The third metaphor is learning-as-knowledge-construction, the idea that learners actively build their own mental representations as they attempt to make sense out of their experiences. This view grew out of research on human learning in realistic settings conducted since the 1970s and 1980s. Learning occurs when people select relevant information, organize it into a coherent structure, and interpret it through what they already know. Resnick (1989, p. 2) expresses this view as follows: "Learning occurs not by recording information but by interpreting it." According to this view, the learner is a sense maker and the teacher is a guide who assists students as they seek to understand how to perform academic tasks. The focus is on the learner and on helping the learner to build cognitive strategies for academic learning tasks.

The educational practices suggested by the learning-as-knowledge-construction view include group discussions and supervised participation in meaningful academic tasks. For example, in learning how to write, students may discuss how they plan out what to say and the teacher may offer suggestions along the way. Instead of emphasizing the learning products—such as how much is learned—this view emphasizes the learning processes, such as strategies for how to learn and understand. When educators take a "learner-centered" approach, they are consistent with the learning-as-knowledge-construction metaphor.

There is merit in each of these metaphors and in the instructional methods they suggest (Mayer, 1996a). However, in this book, I rely most heavily on the learning-as-knowledge-construction metaphor because I think it offers the most potential benefit for improving education; that is, it seems most likely to promote the promise of educational psychology. By emphasizing knowledge construction, I do not mean to diminish the value of learning basic skills, such as facts and procedures. However, according to the knowledge-construction metaphor, basic skills should be learned in the context of larger academic tasks rather than in isolation. For example, learning Ohm's Law could occur as part of project involving the design of a real electrical circuit rather than memorizing the formula in isolation.

A CLOSER LOOK AT THE LEARNER-CENTERED APPROACH

This book is concerned mainly with influencing the intellectual growth of the learner. More specifically, this book focuses on understanding how instructional manipulations affect changes in the learner's knowledge, including changes in learning strategies and the structure of memory. As you can see, the learner's construction of knowledge is at the center of the educational process. Helping change the learner's knowledge—manifested in changes in academic, motor, social, and personal behavior—is what education is all about.

KINDS OF KNOWLEDGE

Educational and cognitive psychologists generally distinguish among several different kinds of knowledge, including the following (Anderson et al., 2001; Mayer, 1992):

Semantic knowledge refers to a person's factual knowledge about the world. Examples include being able to answer the questions, What is the capital of California? or How many sides does a square have?

Conceptual knowledge refers to a person's representation of the major concepts in a system. Examples include being able to answer questions such as, "What is the difference between the units-column and the tens-column in two-column addition problems such as 39 + 45 = _____?"

Schematic knowledge refers to a person's knowledge of problem types such as being able to distinguish between word problems that require the use of a time-rate-distance formula and those requiring a formula for computing interest.

Procedural knowledge refers to an algorithm, or list of steps, that can be used in a specific situation. An example is being able to use the procedure for long division in order to solve the problem, 234234 ÷ 13 = _____. Other examples are being able to classify objects, such as different geometric shapes, into categories, or being able to change a word to plural form using the rule "Add s."

Strategic knowledge refers to a general approach for how to learn or remember or solve problems, including the self-monitoring of progress in the use of the strategy. Examples include being able to design and monitor a plan for how to compose an essay, or being able to decide on a technique for how to memorize a list of definitions.

In subsequent chapters, we explore how each kind of knowledge is related to school tasks. Other kinds of knowledge include affective, motoric, personal, or social knowledge. However, this book focuses mainly on the kinds of knowledge noted in the preceding list because they represent the areas in which most of the research has been carried out.

KINDS OF MEMORY STORES AND LEARNING PROCESSES

If knowledge construction is at the center of educational psychology, then the learner's memory system is where the action is! Figure 1–3 describes the basic architecture of the memory system. As you can see, there are three main components indicated as rectangles:

Sensory memory. Incoming information is accepted by the sense receptors and is held briefly in a sensory memory store. According to the classic model, the capacity of sensory memory is unlimited, the mode of representation is sensory, the duration is brief (e.g., one half second for visual information), and loss occurs due to time decay.

Short-term memory. If you pay attention to the incoming information before it decays, you may be able to transfer some of that information to short-term memory (STM).

FIGURE 1–3 An information-processing model of the memory system

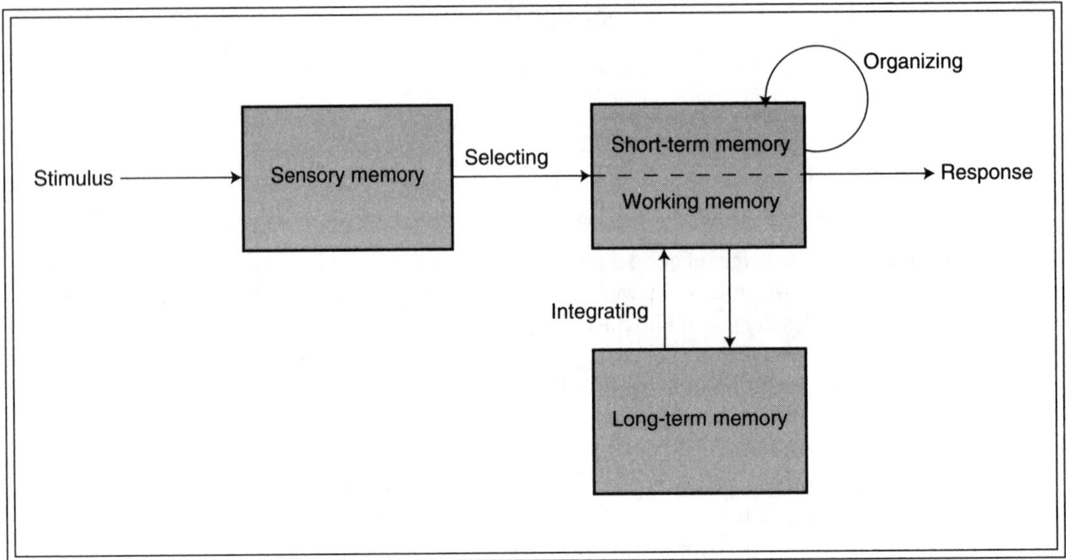

You can think of STM as that part of memory corresponding to your active consciousness or awareness. According to the classic model, the capacity of short-term memory is extremely limited (e.g., you can actively think about only five or so different things at one time), the mode is acoustic or some other modification of the sensory input, the duration is temporary (e.g., items are lost after about 18 seconds unless you actively rehearse), and loss is due to new information displacing the items in STM. In addition, a portion of STM can be used for performing mental manipulations such as mental arithmetic—this portion is referred to as working memory.

Long-term memory. If you encode the information from STM into long-term memory, then some of that information may be retained permanently. Long-term memory has unlimited capacity including the five kinds of knowledge listed previously, can retain information for long periods of time, and loses information when other information interferes with retrieving the target information.

In addition to these three components, the arrows in the figure represent basic learning processes:

Selecting involves focusing attention on the relevant pieces of the presented information and adding them to STM, as indicated in Figure 1–3 by the arrow from SM to STM. In paying attention to some of the information that enters through your eyes and ears, you are selecting pieces of information for further processing in STM. Sternberg (1985) refers to this process as *selective encoding* and defines it as "sifting out relevant from irrelevant information" (p. 107).

Organizing involves constructing internal connections among the incoming pieces of information in STM, as indicated in Figure 1–3 by the arrow from STM to STM. In constructing internal connections, the learner is "organizing the selected information

. . . into a coherent whole" (Mayer, 1984, p. 32). Sternberg (1985) refers to this process as *selective combination* and defines it as "combining selectively encoded information in such a way as to form an integrated . . . internally connected whole" (p. 107).

Integrating involves constructing external connections between the newly organized knowledge in STM and existing relevant knowledge that the learner retrieves from LTM, as indicated by the arrow from LTM to STM. This process involves "connecting the organized information to other familiar knowledge structures already in memory" (Mayer, 1984, p. 33). Sternberg (1985) referred to integrating as *selective comparison,* and described it as "relating newly acquired or retrieved knowledge . . . to old knowledge so as to form an externally connected whole" (p. 107).

As you can see, the learner uses selecting, organizing, and integrating processes to construct new knowledge in short-term memory. Knowledge constructed in STM is transferred to LTM for permanent storage, via the process of *encoding,* which is represented by the arrow from STM to LTM.

COGNITIVE CONDITIONS FOR MEANINGFUL LEARNING

Now that we have briefly explored the kinds of knowledge and the architecture of the memory system, let's return to the foundational theme of this book—the promise of educational psychology. For example, let's suppose that we ask students to read a short lesson on how lightning occurs. Then we give them a retention test to measure how much of the presented information they remember, and a transfer test, to measure how well they can creatively apply what they learned to solve new problems. The retention test could include items such as, "A lightning flash lasts about _____ microseconds" or "The amount of electrical potential in a lightning flash is _____ volts." The transfer test could ask, "How could you decrease the intensity of lightning?"

Some students will not remember much from the lesson and will not be able to answer transfer questions. These students could be called nonlearners. Some students will remember much of the information but will not be able to creatively use the information to solve problems or make explanations. These students could be called nonunderstanders (or rote learners). Finally, some might be able to remember information and to use that information creatively in solving novel problems. They are understanders. Table 1–4 summarizes the differences in the performance among these three types of learners.

TABLE 1–4

Three kinds of learners

Type of Learner	Retention Performance	Transfer Performance
Nonlearner	Poor	Poor
Nonunderstander	Good	Poor
Understander	Good	Good

Adapted from Mayer (1984)

What conditions of learning create each of these kinds of outcomes? Gagne (1974) made a useful distinction between two distinct conditions of learning: internal conditions refer to the cognitive processes that are activated inside the learner at the time of learning; external conditions refer to the instructional events that occur outside of the learner.

Mayer (1996b, 2001b) suggested that three major internal conditions must be met for instruction to foster meaningful learning: instruction must help the learner to select relevant information, organize information, and integrate information, as summarized in Figure 1–4. As you can see, three scenarios can be generated:

Nonlearning: If the first condition is not met, nothing will be learned. Thus, even when a student may be actively thinking about all he or she knows about lightning, nothing will be learned if the student fails to carefully read the passage. This result is indicated by poor retention and poor transfer performance.

Nonunderstanding: If the first condition is met, but the second or third condition is not met, then the student will learn in a nonmeaningful way. For example, in reading a passage on lightning, the second condition would be lacking if the learner fails to create a cause-and-effect chain among events in the process of lightning. Similarly, the third condition would be missing, if the learner does not possess or activate relevant existing knowledge (e.g., the ideas of temperature imbalance and electrical imbalance),

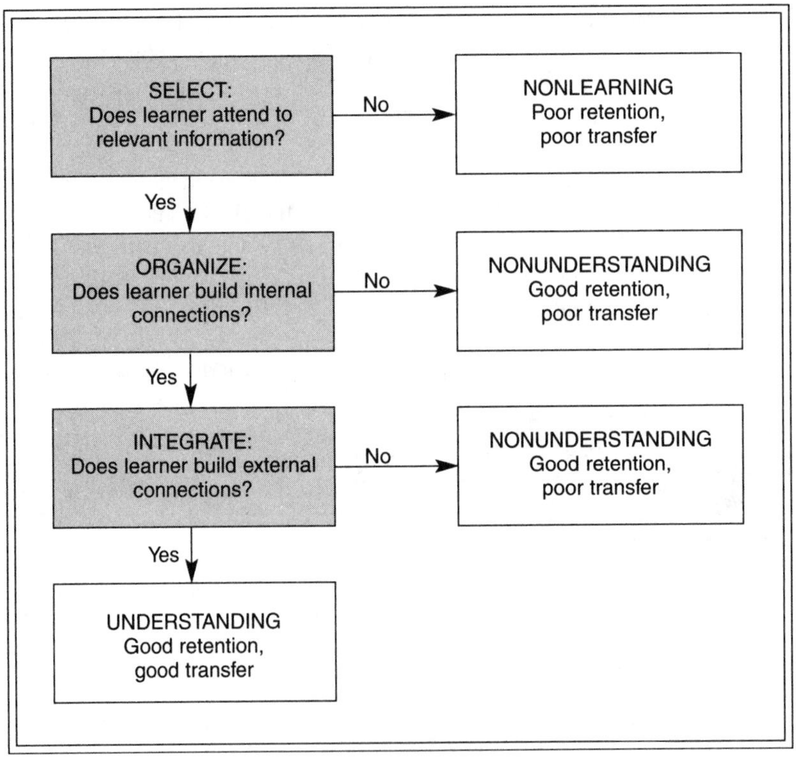

FIGURE 1–4 The three major conditions of meaningful learning

so the material is not well integrated with existing knowledge. This result is indicated by good retention and poor transfer performance.

Understanding: If all three conditions are met, then the student will learn in a meaningful way. For example, the new information about lightning will be organized into a coherent cause-and-effect structure and integrated with existing knowledge about temperature and electrical imbalances. The result is manifested in good retention and transfer performance.

Although these distinctions are much too vague to qualify as a theory of instruction, they do provide a framework for describing different kinds of learning situations. The main theme, of course, is that meaningful learning depends on active cognitive processing during learning, that is, on the active construction of knowledge.

In addition, three external conditions required for instruction to foster meaningful learning are that the material is potentially meaningful, the learner needs help, and the test evaluates meaningful learning. If the material is not understandable—such as a random list of unconnected facts—no type of instruction can help the learner make sense out of it. If the learner already knows how to select, organize, and integrate information in a lesson, then instruction aimed at inducing the learner to use these processes is not needed. Finally, if the test simply measures overall amount retained, it is not possible to show that meaningful learning occurred.

HOW TO FOSTER MEANINGFUL LEARNING

Perhaps the central goal of education is to promote meaningful learning—that is, learning in which the learner engages in active cognitive processing that leads to transfer. If your goal is to teach in ways that enable transfer, it is useful to explore the nature of transfer and its somewhat disappointing history in education.

WHAT IS TRANSFER?

Transfer is the effect of previous learning on new learning or problem solving. This definition yields two types of transfer—transfer of learning and problem-solving transfer. *Transfer of learning* (or learning transfer) is the effect of previous learning on new learning. It occurs successfully when a person uses knowledge from previous experience to help learn something new. *Problem-solving transfer* is the effect of previous learning on new problem solving. Problem-solving transfer occurs successfully when a person uses knowledge from previous experience to devise a solution to a new problem (Mayer & Wittrock, 1996). In this book, I focus mainly on problem-solving transfer, that is, the ability to use what you have learned when you are faced with a new problem.

Transfer can be positive, negative, or neutral. Positive transfer occurs when previous learning helps new problem solving or learning; negative transfer occurs when previous learning hurts new problem solving or learning; and neutral transfer occurs when previous learning has no effect on new problem solving or learning. Figure 1–5 shows one way to test

FIGURE 1–5

Testing for transfer

Group	*Learning Task*	*Transfer Task*
Experimental group	A	B
Control group	—	B

Type of Transfer	*Performance on Transfer Task*
Positive transfer	Experimental group outperforms control group
Negative transfer	Control group outperforms experimental group
Neutral transfer	Experimental and control groups are equivalent

for transfer in which some people learn A and then are asked to solve problem B (experimental group) whereas other people do not learn A and then are asked to solve problem B (control group). If the experimental group outperforms the control group on B, positive transfer occurred; if the control group outperforms the experimental group on B, then negative transfer occurred, and if the two groups perform similarly on B, then there is neutral transfer. For example, you might expect positive transfer if someone learns how to use a word processor and then needs to use it to write a business letter. You might expect some negative transfer if a person learned to use one kind of word processor and then had to write a business letter using a different kind. My focus in this book, of course, is on how to promote positive transfer.

Transfer can be specific, general, or mixed as shown in Figure 1–6. Specific transfer means that elements in A are identical to B; for example, you learn how to add and subtract single-digit numbers, and then you try to solve some two-digit addition and subtraction problems. Some of the steps are the same in both procedures, such as knowing that 2 + 2 is 4. Although specific transfer has been demonstrated in many experiments, it offers a somewhat circular view of teaching for transfer: The only way to help students be able to solve new problems is to teach them how to solve them in advance. General transfer means that although no elements are identical, the general experience of knowing A is somehow related to B; that is, learning A somehow improves one's mind so that taking on a new task such as B is affected. For example, some scholars have claimed that learning a foreign language such as Latin may instill mental discipline that helps you solve logic problems—a claim we investigate later in the "Historical Overview" section. Unfortunately, researchers have not been able to produce much evidence for general transfer, so the implications for teaching for transfer are disappointing: It may not be possible to provide learning experiences that improve the mind in general. Finally, mixed transfer refers to specific transfer of a general principle or strategy; it occurs when a general principle or strategy used in A is also used in B. For example, learning the general strategy of how to critique psychology experiments in a course on social psychology may help you critique experiments in a course on educational psychology even though none of the experiments are the same. In this book, my primary focus is on mixed transfer, that is, helping students learn general principles or strategies that are specifically relevant to important academic tasks.

FIGURE 1–6

Three views of transfer

View of Transfer	*Definition*	*Example*	*Instructional Implication*
Specific transfer	Specific transfer of specific behaviors	Thorndike's theory of transfer by identical elements	Teach specific behaviors by drill and practice
General transfer	General transfer of general skills	Doctrine of formal discipline	Improve the mind by teaching Latin
Mixed transfer	Specific transfer of general principles or strategies	Katona's learning by understanding	Teach principles and strategies to explain solution behavior

HISTORICAL OVERVIEW

Teaching for transfer is a classic goal of education but the history of such efforts is somewhat disappointing. The twentieth century is littered with failed attempts to teach for transfer, yielding an "elusive search for teachable aspects of problem solving" (Mayer, 1987, p. 327). As an example, consider the well-documented case of Latin schools, which was the first to be tested in educational psychology.

When the curtain rose on the twentieth century, the dominant view of transfer was the doctrine of formal discipline—the idea that certain school subjects (such as Latin and geometry) improve learners' minds. In short, the doctrine of formal discipline was a theory of general transfer. Proponents claimed, for example, that learning Latin promoted proper habits of mind, including mental discipline and orderly thinking. According to this view, these general skills would transfer to all other academic tasks, even those completely unrelated to Latin. Rippa (1980) shows that in the eighteenth and nineteenth centuries, the curriculum of the Boston Latin School—the oldest in the United States—included being able to read, write, and speak Latin, as well as have some knowledge of Greek and geometry.

E. L. Thorndike is widely recognized as the first educational psychologist, and in the early 1900s he set his sites on testing the doctrine of formal discipline in scientific experiments (Mayer, in press). In short, he and his colleagues were the first to test for any evidence of general transfer in which learning one thing (e.g., Latin) would help students perform other tasks that had no elements in common (Thorndike & Woodworth, 1901; Thorndike, 1906). For example, in well-controlled laboratory studies, learning to perform one kind of task (such as estimating the length of lines .5 to 1.5 inches long) did not strongly affect performance on other tasks (such as estimating the length of lines 6 to 12 inches long). In classroom studies, students who took Latin did not perform better on tasks within in new school subject than did students who took more mundane classes. In an exhaustive series of studies, Thorndike found that learning to perform one cognitive task resulted in improvements on a different task, only to the extent that the two tasks shared many elements in common.

Thorndike rejected the doctrine of formal discipline (with its emphasis on general transfer) and replaced it with his theory of transfer by identical elements (with its emphasis on specific transfer). According to Thorndike (1906): "One mental function or activity improves others in so far as and because they are in part identical with it, because it contains elements in common to them" (p. 243). For example, "knowledge of Latin gives increased ability to learn French because many of the facts learned in the one case are needed in the other" (Thorndike, 1906, p. 243). In rejecting the concept of general transfer, Thorndike offered a conception of the mind as a collection of domain-specific skills: "the mind is a host of highly particularized and independent abilities" (Thorndike, 1903, p. 39). The idea that learning and cognition are domain-specific is still an important theme in cognitive science today (Mayer, 1999).

The results of Thorndike's research helped to demolish the doctrine of formal discipline and the conception of general transfer on which it is based. Educators could no longer find scientific justification for teaching general skills such as mental discipline that were supposed to transfer to new tasks. Consistent with Thorndike's monumental research on transfer, the search for teachable aspects of general transfer has not been very successful.

Is the only alternative, then, for educators bent on teaching for transfer to accept a theory of specific transfer, such as Thorndike's theory of transfer by identical elements? If so, the only way to teach for transfer is to know in advance every transfer problem the student would encounter and to teach the behaviors needed to solve those problems. In short, if all transfer is specific, then preparing students for completely novel problems is impossible. If this is true, then I can stop writing this book now, because my goal is to examine instructional methods that prepare students to solve problems they have never seen before.

There is an important alternative to theories of general transfer, which have been largely discredited, and to theories of specific transfer, which really don't allow for much problem-solving transfer. That alternative is what I have called specific transfer of general principles or strategies. According to this theory of mixed transfer, it is possible to learn certain general principles or strategies that are specifically applicable to new tasks.

Consider the following test of a mixed theory of transfer. Young boys are taught to shoot darts at an underwater target that is submerged 12 inches. When they are tested later on targets that are submerged only 4 inches, they make many errors. This result, you might say, is consistent with a theory of specific transfer because the boys seem to have learned behaviors that are appropriate only for the situation they learned about. However, suppose that for some of the boys, we provide brief instruction in the theory of refraction so they can understand how water level affects the apparent location of the target. In this case, practice with the 12-inch deep target transferred to learning how to hit the 4-inch-deep target. Apparently, the boys learned a general strategy that applied to both situations. When Judd found these results in 1908, he offered an important compromise between theories of general transfer and theories of specific transfer.

The Gestalt psychologists (Katona, 1940; Wertheimer, 1959) compared two methods of teaching: learning by memorizing (which is based on a theory of specific transfer of specific behaviors) and learning by understanding (which is based on a theory of specific transfer of general principles). For example, consider a card problem in which you begin with a deck of eight cards, half red and half black:

> I take the top card and place it on the table. It is a red card. Then I take the next card and put it at the bottom of the deck without determining what it is. I place the third card on the

table. It is a black card. The following card I place undetermined below the others; while the next card, which is red, I put on the table. The procedure of alternatively placing one card on the table and one at the bottom of deck was continued until all the cards of the deck were placed on the table; the cards appeared in this order: red, black, red, black, red, black, red, black. Then said the experimenter, "It is a nice trick, I suppose you would like to learn how to do it. I will teach you." (Katona, 1940, pp. 34–35)

Figure 1–7 shows two methods for teaching students how to solve this problem—learning by memorizing and learning by understanding. In learning by memorizing, students memorize a chain of behaviors that generates the answer. In learning by understanding,

FIGURE 1–7

Two instructional methods for the card trick problem: Learning by memorizing and learning by understanding

LEARNING BY MEMORIZING

To achieve this goal, you must take in your hand first, two red cards; then, one black card; then, two red cards; and last, three black cards. [The experimenter writes the sequence on a blackboard, repeats it aloud three times, and asks the student to repeat it until the student recites it twice without error.]

LEARNING BY UNDERSTANDING

? ? ? ? ? ? ? ?	. . . We put eight question marks on the blackboard. The first question mark represents the first card, the second question mark represents the second card, and so forth . . .
R ? B ? R ? B ?	The first card should be a red card. The second card should be placed below the others; since we do not know what it is, it is represented by a question mark. The third card must be a black card, while the fourth is unknown (a question mark), and so forth. The four cards that are designated by letters on the blackboard are supposed to be on the table. The four cards designated by question marks are still in my hand . . .
R ? B ?	The next card (that is, the first of the remaining question marks) must therefore be a red card. The following card, represented by the following question mark, has to be placed below the others and remains a question mark. Then, follows a black card and lastly a question mark.
R ?	Two question marks remain. . . . The first one must be a red card, while the next one remains a question mark.
B	This one being the last card, following a red card, must be black.
R R B R R B B B	Now we are ready to add up our findings: red, red, black, red, red, black, black, black.

Adapted from Katona (1940, pp. 263–264)

students learn a general principle or strategy that can apply to a wide variety of card problems.

On a retention test, in which students are asked to solve the same problem, both groups perform about the same—42% percent correct for the memorizing group and 44% for the understanding group. What happens on a transfer test in which students are asked to solve a new problem (same description except you put two cards on the bottom of the deck after each card you place on the table)? According to a theory of specific transfer (such as Thorndike's identical elements), both groups should perform poorly; but according to a theory of specific transfer of general principles or strategies (as suggested by Judd), the understanding group should perform better. The results show that the memorizing group performs poorly (8% correct) but the understanding group performs quite well (40% correct). Katona (1940) concludes that "learning by memorizing is a different process from learning by understanding" (p. 53). In learning by understanding, students discover a generalizable principle or strategy that makes sense to them and can be applied in a variety of problems that depend on the same principle or strategy. In this classic example lies the essence of what it means to teach for transfer.

WHAT IS THE PROMISE OF EDUCATIONAL PSYCHOLOGY?

From today's vantage point—200 years after Itard's valiant efforts to teach Victor using learner-centered methods and 100 years after the beginnings of the scientific discipline of educational psychology—the future of educational psychology looks promising once again. Although education and psychology experienced a rocky relationship in the past, today's educational psychology holds great potential for improving educational practice and advancing psychological theory.

What is the promise of educational psychology? The theme of this book is that the two most promising contributions of educational psychology are:

Psychologies of subject matter: A focus on developing, learning, teaching, and thinking within the context of specific subject areas.

Cognitive process instruction: A focus on fostering cognitive processing that leads to meaningful learning.

Thus, this book represents a sort of progress report covering recent advances in the cognitive psychology of subject matter and the cognitive psychology of instructional methods.

The first promising contribution of educational psychology is a focus on psychologies of subject matter. In contrast to traditional experimental psychology's focus on developing general theories of how people learn or develop or think, today's educational psychology seeks to build domain-specific theories within each subject area. For example, instead of asking domain-general questions such as, "How do people learn?" "How do people develop?" or "How do people think?" we can ask, "How do people learn to solve mathematics problems?" "How do people develop mathematical competence?" or "How do people think mathematically?" By examining cognition in the context of real academic tasks rather than in contrived laboratory tasks, we can develop more realistic theories of how people learn, develop, and think. Although sporadic interest in psychologies of subject matter popped up throughout the twentieth century—such as Huey's (1908/1968) *Psychology and Pedagogy of Reading* or Thorndike's (1922) *Psychology of Arithmetic*—the groundbreaking consensus to focus on specific subject domains occurred only within the last 20 years (Shulman & Quinlan, 1996). In the first section of this book, I explore five promising paths to the study of learning in the content areas:

Learning to read fluently (Chapter 2)—in which students learn how to read printed words.
Learning for reading comprehension (Chapter 3)—in which students learn how to make sense of printed text.
Learning to write (Chapter 4)—in which students learn how to produce written essays.
Learning mathematics (Chapter 5)—in which students learn how to solve mathematics problems in fields such as arithmetic, algebra, and geometry.
Learning science (Chapter 6)—in which students learn how to explain how scientific systems work in fields such as physical, biological, and earth sciences.

In addition there is much promising research on learning in other subject areas such as history (Carretero & Voss, 1994; Leinhardt, Beck, & Stainton, 1994; Wineburg, 1996).

The second promising contribution of educational psychology is a focus on instruction for meaningful learning. No single instructional method is guaranteed to promote meaningful learning. Although researchers and teachers have discovered several roads that can lead to learning for transfer, each must be crafted to fit the needs of the learner, the requirements of the learning task, and the personal skills of the teacher. In the second section of this book, I explore eight promising paths to promoting meaningful learning.

Teaching by giving productive feedback (Chapter 7)—in which teachers critique student performance.
Teaching by providing concreteness, activity, and familiarity (Chapter 8)—in which teachers allow guided exploration.
Teaching by explaining examples (Chapter 9)—in which teachers allow students to learn from examples of how to accomplish academic tasks.
Teaching by guiding cognitive processes during learning (Chapter 10)—in which teachers encourage students to engage in appropriate cognitive processing as they learn.
Teaching by fostering learning strategies (Chapter 11)—in which teachers help students learn how to learn.
Teaching by fostering problem-solving strategies (Chapter 12)—in which teachers provide help as students learn how to think.
Teaching by creating cognitive apprenticeship in classrooms (Chapter 13)—in which teachers allow students to learn by participating in academic tasks with others.
Teaching by priming students' motivation to learn (Chapter 14)—in which teachers try to motivate students to work harder.

In this book, I examine the research base concerning the effectiveness of each of these ways of teaching for meaningful learning.

Educational psychology has a unique and central role to play within the fields of education and psychology. To education, educational psychology can contribute a theoretical account of how the human mind works in academic settings including how students learn, remember, and use academic knowledge. By constructing cognitive theories of academic learning, educational psychologists enable the development of more effective methods of instruction. In short, educational psychology offers an alternative to education's unproductive proclivity for basing instructional practice on undocumented fads. To psychology, educational psychology can contribute an ecologically valid context for generating and testing cognitive theories. By challenging psychologists to develop theories that can account for academic learning, educational psychologists ensure the authenticity of cognitive theories. In short, educational psychology offers an alternative to psychology's unproductive record of developing precise theories of artificial learning tasks.

CHAPTER SUMMARY

The example of the Wild Boy of Aveyron raises issues concerning the role of education in human development. A boy raised in the wild without human guidance failed to reach his full potential as a human being. This example suggests that natural experience—everyday interactions with the environment—must be supplemented by manipulated experience in the form of instructional sequences designed by teachers. The example is important because it was one of the first to emphasize a learner-centered view of education.

Educational psychology is a branch of psychology concerned with understanding how the instructional environment and the characteristics of the learner interact to produce cognitive growth in the learner. Instruction refers to manipulations intended to foster learning. Learning refers to a relatively permanent change in a person's knowledge based on experience. Thorndike and Dewey both recognized that the central theme in education is an externally manipulated change in the learner. The definition of educational psychology requires a distinction between the behaviorist approach, which focuses solely on external conditions of learning such as instructional manipulations and outcome performance; the cognitive approach, which adds internal conditions of learning such as learner characteristics, learning processes, and learning outcomes; and the contextualist approach, which also considers the social and cultural context of learning.

The history of the relationship between psychology and education includes three phases: (1) a one-way street in which educators were supposed to apply what psychologists created, (2) a dead-end street in which psychology and education went their separate ways, and (3) a two-way street in which psychology and education mutually enrich one another. In addition, the history of psychology and education includes the progression of three metaphors: learning as response strengthening, learning as knowledge acquisition, and learning as knowledge construction.

The learned-centered approach is based on the idea that instruction helps learners to bring about change in their knowledge. Five kinds of knowledge are semantic, conceptual, schematic, procedural, and strategic knowledge. The architecture of the memory system includes memory stores—sensory memory, short-term memory, and long-term memory—and the memory processes of selecting, organizing, and integrating. Instructional manipulations may result in no learning, nonunderstanding, or understanding. Understanding, or meaningful learning, requires that the learner pay attention, that the learner possess appropriate prerequisite knowledge, and that the learner actively organize and integrate the new information with existing knowledge.

Transfer is an important educational goal. Three theories of transfer are specific, general, and mixed.

The remainder of this book examines what researchers have discovered about how students learn various academic tasks and how to promote meaningful learning.

SUGGESTED READINGS

Berliner, D. & Calfee, R. (Eds.). (1996). *Handbook of educational psychology.* New York: Macmillan. (Systematically presents everything you ever wanted to know about educational psychology.)

Bransford, J. D., Brown, A. L., & Cocking, R. (Eds.). (1999). *How people learn.* Washington, DC: National Academy Press. (Summarizes research on how people learn.)

Dewey, J. (1938). *Experience and education.* New York: Collier. (Provides a dose of Dewey's "child-centered" educational philosophy.)

Lambert, N. M., & McCombs, B. L. (Eds.). (1998). *How students learn.* Washington, DC: American Psychological Association. (Examines research on learning in educational settings.)

Section I
Learning

The first section of this book examines learning in the content areas—namely, reading, writing, mathematics, and science. In particular, I focus on the cognitive processes needed to accomplish basic academic tasks such as reading a word, comprehending a passage, writing an essay, solving a story problem, or explaining a scientific phenomenon. In Chapter 2, I explore the cognitive processes involved in reading words, including recognizing the 42 sound units of English, converting printed words into spoken sounds, recognizing the meaning of printed words, and integrating printed words into a meaningful sentence. In Chapter 3, I explore the cognitive processes involved in comprehending passages, which include using your existing knowledge, analyzing the organization of the passage, making necessary inferences, and keeping track of your level of understanding. In Chapter 4, I explore the cognitive processes involved in writing an essay, including planning what you want to say, putting words on paper, and revising what you have written. In Chapter 5, I explore the cognitive processes involved in solving a story problem, which include translating each sentence into a mental representation, integrating the information into a coherent mental representation of the problem situation, devising a step-by-step solution plan, and carrying out the plan. In Chapter 6, I explore the cognitive processes involved in explaining a scientific phenomenon, which include recognizing that your current theory is flawed, inventing a new theory, and using the new theory to make predictions. Importantly, in each chapter I also examine research on how to teach students to engage in the cognitive processes needed to carry out these basic academic tasks.

Learning to Read Fluently

CHAPTER OUTLINE

The Problem of Reading a Word

Recognizing Phonemes

Decoding Words

Accessing Word Meaning

Sentence Integration

Chapter Summary

Learning to read is a fundamental national goal, because academic and economic success often build on the ability to read words quickly and effortlessly. Unfortunately, one out of five adults in the United States is functionally illiterate, and these people account for 75% of the unemployed and 60% of the prison population (Adams, 1990). This chapter is concerned with early reading instruction. In particular, this chapter focuses on four processes involved in learning to read: recognizing the sound units that comprise words, decoding the symbols on the page into pronounced words, accessing the meaning of each word in long-term memory, and integrating the words into a coherent sentence. I explore research and instructional implications for each of these topics.

THE PROBLEM OF READING A WORD

Let's consider the task of reading words from a printed page, as you are doing now. How much time do you think that it takes you to read a typical word? The answer is that competent adult readers can read a word in a fraction of a second, usually less than one-quarter of a second (Crowder & Wagner, 1992; Just & Carpenter, 1982; Rayner & Pollatsek, 1989). The act of reading a word may seem so rapid and so automatic that it could not possibly involve much cognitive processing. However, in this introduction, I will try to convince you that the seemingly simple act of reading a word may indeed involve many cognitive processes.

WHAT COGNITIVE PROCESSES ARE INVOLVED IN READING A WORD?

First, say aloud each of the four words in the first row of Figure 2–1. Based on the sounds in the words, circle the word that lacks a sound that is present in the other three words. Now, follow this same procedure for each set of four words. This is a test of *phonological awareness,* that is, the ability to recognize that words are made up of component sounds. For example, in the first row of Figure 2–1 the sound unit (*or phoneme*) common to three words is /ng/, so the correct answer is "pain." The other answers are "fan," "treat," and "light." When Bradley and Bryant (1978) used a similar task to evaluate students' ability to recognize sound units in words, they found that good readers were successful but that poor readers often were not. It thus appears that an important process in reading is recognizing the separate phonemes that make up words as separate sound units.

Second, try to pronounce each "word" in Figure 2–2. If you are like most adult readers, you used a variety of pronunciation strategies and made errors on about one-tenth of the

FIGURE 2–1 Which word does not belong?

For each set of four words, circle the word that does not belong:

1. song long pain wrong
2. hit pit fan kit
3. boat treat bank bunk
4. shoe light ship sheet

FIGURE 2–2 Can you pronounce these words?

caws	fign
saif	shud
wight	phrend
hought	blud
frish	nal
ait	

words (Baron, 1977). Some possible strategies are sounding out the letters and blending them together, finding a real word that rhymes with the nonsense word, and pronouncing a real word that is similar to the nonsense word. This word-pronunciation task highlights an aspect of reading referred to as *decoding,* which is the process of translating printed symbols into sounds.

Now, let's try another task related to reading. You will need a pencil and a watch with a second hand (to record your starting time and ending time for this task). Remembering to record your times, circle each word in Figure 2–3 that is a member of the category "animal." If you are like most readers, you were able to accomplish this task without too much difficulty. For those of you who like to keep score, the list contains seven animals, and it takes school children about 1 second per word to make decisions like the ones you made (Perfetti & Lesgold, 1979). This word-recognition task requires decoding as well as the process known as *meaning accessing.* Meaning accessing refers to searching long-term memory for the meaning of a word.

Let's try one more reading task, using Figure 2–4. Read each sentence, and then pick the one that is the easiest and the one that is the hardest to read. Sentence 1 is an excellent candidate for the hardest, because it requires moving your eye many times in order to read the words. Sentence 4 is an excellent candidate for the easiest, because it is presented in the most familiar format. However, you probably could learn to read sentences presented as words or phrases, such as sentences 2 and 3.

As this task demonstrates, reading involves moving your eye across the page to take in information. In addition to using the processes of decoding and accessing meaning, you must also put all the information in each sentence together. Figure 2–4 shows that the integration process may be easier if presentation formats allow the eye to take in a lot of information on each glance. The process of joining all of the words of a sentence into a coherent idea is known as *sentence integration.*

The four tasks you just tried represent four kinds of processes in reading words: recognizing phonemes, decoding words, accessing meaning, and integrating sentences. In this chapter, a brief historical and theoretical overview are presented, followed by an examination of each of these four kinds of processes.

FIGURE 2–3 Circle each animal word

house	mountain	zebra
rabbit	elephant	belt
tree	dog	deer
shoe	lamp	cloud
horse	bed	basket
table	shirt	mouse

Adapted from Baron (1977)

WHAT IS READING?

Any serious discussion of reading must confront the problem that reading means different things to different people. For example, reading researchers make a fundamental distinction between *learning to read* and *reading to learn* (Adams, 1990; Chall, 1979; Singer, 1981; Weaver & Resnick, 1979). Learning to read involves learning how to translate printed words into another form, such as pronouncing and understanding words. Developing automaticity in this translation process is a dominant focus of reading instruction in grades K-3. Although many students may achieve reading fluency by the third grade, other children may complete junior high school without mastering basic reading skills (Singer, 1981). The present chapter deals with this phase of reading, which can be called *reading fluency.*

Reading to learn involves the use of reading as a tool for gaining specific knowledge in some subject domain. This activity includes comprehension and evaluation of entire passages. The acquisition of specific knowledge from reading is a dominant focus of reading instruction in grade 4 and thereafter. Chapter 3 examines techniques for improving students' success in extracting useful knowledge from text, which is called *reading comprehension.*

A HISTORY OF READING RESEARCH

In the early days of educational psychology, the question of how people learn to read was a fundamental research issue. In his classic book *The Psychology and Pedagogy of Reading,* Huey (1908/1968) summarized the importance of understanding the reading process:

> And so to completely analyze what we do when we read would almost be the acme of a psychologist's achievement, for it would be to describe very many of the most intricate workings of the human mind, as well as to unravel the tangled story of the most remarkable specific performance that civilization has learned in all its history. (p. 6)

Unfortunately, the early enthusiasm for experimental research on reading did not find a comfortable home in the psychology of the early 1900s. The behaviorist movement, which

FIGURE 2–4

Which sentence is the easiest and which is the hardest to read?

SENTENCE 1

R	e	c	e	n	t						
r	e	s	e	a	r	c	h				
h	a	s		s	h	o	w	n			
t	h	a	t		s	a	c	c	a	d	e
l	e	n	g	t	h		i	s			
a	b	o	u	t		o	n	e		o	r
t	w	o		w	o	r	d	s,			
w	h	i	c	h							
c	o	r	r	e	s	p	o	n	d	s	
t	o		a	b	o	u	t				
e	i	g	h	t		l	e	t	t	e	r
p	o	s	i	t	i	o	n	s			
p	e	r		f	i	x	a	t	i	o	n.

SENTENCE 2

One
educational
implication
of
this
work
is
that
students
can
read
faster
if
they
can
be
taught
to
increase
their
saccade
length.

SENTENCE 3

Training in speed reading
can increase reading rates
from less than 300 words a minute
to more than 900 words a minute.

SENTENCE 4

However, many research studies have shown that there can also be a corresponding drop in readers' performance on tests of comprehension.

swept across the scene during the first half of the twentieth century, was not consistent with the study of underlying cognitive processes in reading. As Kolers points out in his introduction to a reissued version of Huey's book in 1968, "remarkably little empirical information has been added to what Huey knew" (p. xiv).

The rebirth of cognitive psychology in the 1960s brought with it a renewed interest in the psychological study of reading. During the past decades, many models have been proposed to describe the processes by which people understand written language. Although a review of all of the proposed models is beyond the scope of this book, most include the basic cognitive processes of recognizing phonemes, decoding words, accessing word meaning, and integrating sentences.

RECOGNIZING PHONEMES

WHAT IS PHONOLOGICAL AWARENESS?

Phonological awareness refers to knowledge of the sound units (phonemes) used in a language, including the ability to hear and produce separate phonemes. Following initial work by Mattingly (1972), Wagner and Torgesen (1987) define phonological awareness as "awareness of and access to the phonology of one's language" (p. 192). Similarly, Blachman (2000, p. 483) defines phonological awareness as "awareness of the phonological segments in speech," and Ehri et al. (2001, p. 253) refer to the "ability to focus on and manipulate phonemes in spoken words." Some researchers use the term *phonemic awareness* to refer to awareness of the smallest sound units (phonemes) and *phonological awareness* to refer to awareness of all sound units (including phonemes, syllables, and words), but for purposes of our discussion I use the terms interchangeably to refer to awareness of phonemes.

Phonological awareness involves knowing that words are composed of sound units and that sound units can be combined to form words. For example, the spoken word "hat" consists of three phonemes: /h/, /a/, and /t/. Phonological awareness refers to (1) the process of breaking a spoken word into its sound units—such as being able to discriminate the sounds /h/, /a/, and /t/ when the word "hat" is spoken—and to (2) the process of producing and blending sound units to form spoken words—such as being able to produce and blend these three sounds when one wants to say the word "hat."

If you looked at a spectrogram showing the speech stream for a sentence such as "The cat in the hat is back," you would not see a series of neatly separated sound units. Instead, you would see continuous waves representing acoustic energy. Acoustic speech entering our ears comes as a continuous flow. The apparent segmentation that we hear is based on our cognitive processing, rather than on the acoustic properties of the utterance. The ability to segment a continuous flow into discrete sound units requires learning by the listener.

Standard American English contains approximately 42 basic sound units (i.e., "phonemes"), as summarized in Table 2–1, although regional differences in pronunciation and dialect can create more units. Interestingly, there are more than 26 phonemes in English because some letters can produce more than one sound. For example, "c" can be hard as in "cat" or soft as in "cent." Phonological awareness of English does not focus on

TABLE 2–1 Common sound units for English words

Character	Common Spellings	Examples
b	b	back
c or k	c, k	cat, kitten
ch	ch, _tch	chief, catch
d	d	dog
f	f, ph	fit, elephant
g	g	give
h	h	help
j	j, _dge, ge, gi, gy	just, fudge, age, giant, gym
l	l	lion
m	m	milk
n	n, kn	no, know
ng	ng	sing
p	p	pot
r	r, wr	right, write
s	s, c	sent, cent
sh	sh, _t_, _c_	shoe, nation, special
t	t	ten
th	th	thin
t̄h̄	th	that
v	v	voice
w	w	way
wh	wh_	white
y	y	yes
z	s, _s	zebra, nose
zh	_s_	vision
a	a, a_e, ai_, -ay, ea, -ey	able, cape, train, day, steak, they
e	e, ee, e_e, ea, _y, _i_	equal, feet, eve, each, baby, babies
i	i, i_e, igh, _y, _ie, ai	I, bite, high, sky, pie, aisle
o	o, o_e, oa, _ow, _oe	go, phone, boat, low, toe
u	u, ue, you, u_e, _ew	using, cue, youth, use, few
ā	a, au, ai	hat, aunt, plaid
ah	a, al, o	father, calm, on
aw	a, aw, au, o	tall, law, caught, soft
ē	e, ea	bed, bread
ī	i, ui, u, ea, ee, ie	sit, build, busy, dear, deer, pierce
ū	u, o, ou, a, e, o	cup, some, couple, alone, loaded, wagon
oo	oo, u, ew, ue, ou, o	too, rule, new, due, group, do
o͞o	oo, u	book, full
oi	oi, -oy	oil, toy
ow	ow, ou	owl, ouch
ar	ar	park, car
ur	ur, ir, er, or, ear	hurt, stir, term, word, earn

Note: *This table does not include separate listings for q (as in queen) or for changes in sounds in unaccented syllables. Pronunciation guides vary in listing from 41 to 45 sounds.*

awareness of the relation between letters and sounds (that skill is covered in the next section on decoding), but rather consists of representing these sound units in long-term memory.

What are the sounds in "cat"? What word is /s/ /k/ /u/ /l/? What is "smile" without the /s/? All are examples of tests of phonological awareness (referred to respectively as phoneme segmentation, phoneme blending, and phoneme deletion). Students are classified as phonologically aware if they are able to break a word such as "cat" into its three constituent sounds; to combine the /s/, /k/, /u/, and /l/ sounds to create the spoken word "school"; and to say "mile" when asked to delete the /s/ sound from "smile." An alternative test of phoneme segmentation is to tap out the number sounds in a spoken word (such as giving 3 taps for "hat"). Other common tests include phoneme isolation (e.g., Tell me the first sound in "paste."), phoneme identity (e.g., Tell me the sound that is the same in "bike," "boy," and "bell."), phoneme categorization (e.g., Which word does not belong: "bus, bun, rug."), and phoneme substitution (e.g., For "ball" change the /b/ to /k/.).

RESEARCH ON PHONOLOGICAL AWARENESS

How does phonological awareness develop? To answer this question, Liberman and colleagues (Liberman, Shankweiler, Fischer, & Carter, 1974) tested four-, five-, and six-year-olds on their ability to segment words into phonemes and syllables. Figure 2–5 indicates a developmental trend in which almost none of the four-year-olds recognized phonemes but almost all six-year-olds did. However, half of the four- and five-year-olds and almost all of the six-year-olds could break words into syllables. These results demonstrate that phonological awareness tends to develop in children in the years leading up to the primary grades.

FIGURE 2–5 The development of phonological awareness

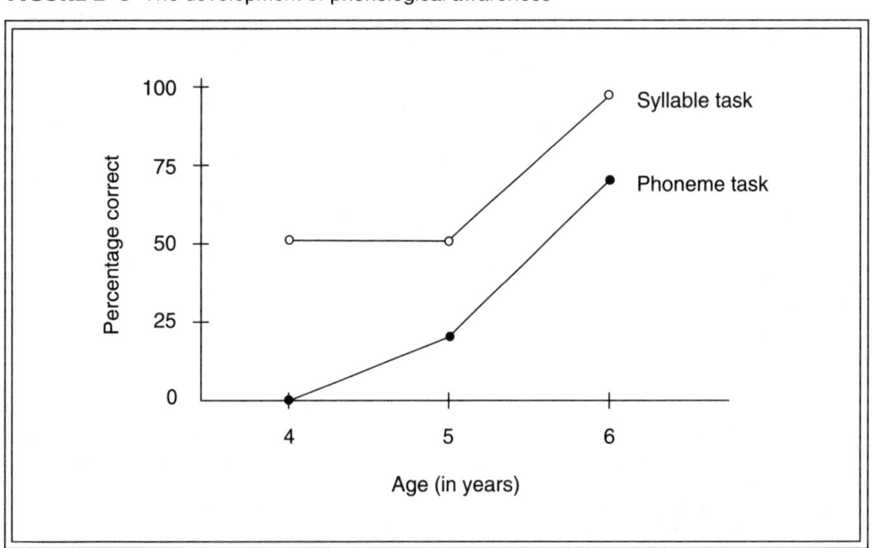

Adapted from Liberman, Shankweiler, Fischer, and Carter (1974)

TABLE 2–2

A test of phonological awareness

Task	Tester Says:	Child Says:
Segmentation	Say "no." What are the two sounds in "no"?	/n/ /o/
Blending	Say /n/, /i/, /s/. What word is /n/ /i/ /s/?	"nice"
Deletion of first phoneme	Say "top." Now say "top" without the /t/.	"op"
Deletion of last phoneme	Say "same." Now say "same" without the /m/.	"sa" (as in "say")
Substitution of first phoneme	Say "ball." Instead of /b/, begin the new word with /k/.	"call"
Substitution of last phoneme	Say "park." Instead of /k/, end the word with /t/.	"part"

Adapted from Juel, Griffin, and Gough (1986)

Similar results were obtained when Juel, Griffin, and Gough (1986) tested the phonological awareness of a group of 80 children at several points across the first and second grades. Table 2–2 shows some of the items included on the phonological awareness test they used. Children correctly answered 35% of the items in fall of the first grade, 73% in spring of the first grade, 83% in fall of the second grade, and 86% in spring of the second grade. These results are consistent with the idea that phonological awareness increases across the primary school years.

What is the relation between phonological awareness and learning to read? Phonological awareness is a prerequisite for learning to read, so that students who lack skills in phonological awareness are likely to have difficulty in learning to read. This claim, which can be called the *phonological awareness hypothesis,* has been subjected to rigorous study (Adams, 1990; Ehri, 1991; Rieben & Perfetti, 1991; Wagner & Torgesen, 1987). In particular, let's examine two straightforward predictions of the phonological awareness hypothesis.

First, in comparing groups of good and poor readers, the phonological awareness hypothesis predicts that students who have difficulty in reading tend to have difficulty on tests of phonological awareness. Bradley and Bryant (1978) measured the phonological awareness of younger good readers and older poor readers by asking them to identify which of four words lacked a sound contained in the other words (e.g., answering "rag" for the set "sun, sea, sock, rag," or answering "man" for the set "cot, hut, man, fit") and to produce a word that rhymed with a target word (e.g., saying "fun" for the target word "sun"). As predicted by the phonological awareness hypothesis, in spite of having had more exposure to reading, the older poor readers performed more poorly than the younger good readers on both measures of phonological awareness. Similarly, other researchers also found that children who have difficulty in learning to read in elementary school often lack skill in phonological awareness (Nation & Hulme, 1997; Pennington, Groisser, & Welsh, 1993; Stanovich, 1991). Although these results suggest that lack of phonological awareness is related to reading difficulties, group comparisons such as these do not allow us to tell whether phonological awareness has a causal relation with reading achivement. For this reason longitudinal studies are useful in determining whether a child's phonological awareness at an early age is related to his or her reading achievement at a later age.

Second, in longitudinal studies the phonological awareness hypothesis predicts that a child's level of phonological awareness at an early age is related to his or her level of reading performance in primary grades. For example, Bradley and Bryant (1985) tested four- and five-year-olds on phonological awareness tasks and retested them three years later on a standardized test of reading achievement. The correlation was strong ($r = .5$) providing support for the phonological awareness hypothesis.

In a more focused study, Juel et al. (1986) tested students at several points during their first and second grade school years on phonological awareness (as exemplified in Table 2–2) and reading skills (such as pronouncing a printed word and writing a spoken word). Phonological awareness correlated strongly with children's ability to pronounce printed words at the end of the first grade ($r = .8$) and at the end of the second grade ($r = .5$), and phonological awareness correlated strongly with children's ability to write spoken words at the end of the first grade ($r = .8$) and at the end of the second grade ($r = .6$). Even after the effects of intelligence were statistically removed from the analysis, phonological awareness strongly influenced year-end performance on basic reading skills.

In a review of longitudinal studies, Wagner and Torgesen (1987) found 20 instances in which measures of phonological awareness at an early age correlated strongly with later reading achievement, even when the effects of general cognitive ability were taken into account. They concluded that "phonological awareness and reading are related independent of general cognitive ability" (p. 202). Of course, many factors other that phonological awareness may be related to a child's reading level, but this research demonstrates that phonological awareness may be one important contributing factor.

Although these results are consistent with the phonological awareness hypothesis, you might ask whether they prove it. These results seem to be consistent with several possible relations between phonological awareness and reading skill: (1) phonological awareness might cause reading skill (i.e., as claimed by the phonological awareness hypothesis); (2) reading skill might cause phonological awareness; and (3) both phonological awareness and reading skill might be caused by a third factor (such as general intelligence). A useful way of distinguishing among these three possibilities is to conduct a training study in which prereaders who are equated on basic characteristics are taught phonological awareness skills and later tested on their level of reading achievement. This approach is taken in the next section.

IMPLICATIONS FOR INSTRUCTION: PHONOLOGICAL AWARENESS TRAINING

If the phonological awareness hypothesis is correct, then teaching students how to recognize phonemes will improve their ability to learn to read. In addition to providing an important theoretical test of the hypothesis, training studies offer practical implications for early reading instruction. Based on the kinds of results reported in the previous section, Juel et al. (1986) argue for the practical need to provide instruction in phonological awareness:

> These findings suggest the need for oral phonemic awareness training for entering-first grade children with poor phonemic awareness. Without special training, children with poor phonemic awareness appear disadvantaged in learning to read and write. . . . [S]uch children are frequently minority children. It may be that training in oral phonemic awareness should be a routine precursor to reading instruction. (p. 249)

Does phonological awareness training help students learn to read? To answer this question, Bradley and Bryant (1983, 1985, 1991) provided phonological awareness training to five- and six-year-olds through 40 10-minute sessions spread over a two-year period (phoneme-trained group). The training involved recognizing phonemes in words presented as pictures or as spoken words. For example, in some sessions, the child was shown a picture of a bus and asked to select the picture of a word starting with the same sound in a set of pictures. In other sessions, the child was given a set of pictures and asked to select the one that started with a sound different from the others. In yet other sessions, the child was given a large array of pictures and asked to classify them based on shared sounds while stating which sound each group had in common. In sessions involving spoken words, the child was asked to determine whether two spoken words rhymed, whether two spoken words began with the same sound, which of several spoken words ended in a sound different from the others, and so on. In contrast, a control group received 40 lessons involving the same words, but in which the task was to categorize words based on semantic category (such as grouping pictures of a cat, bat, and rat together because they are all animals). By the end of the training period, the phoneme-trained group scored almost one year ahead of the control group on a standardized test of reading performance. Importantly, the advantage of the phoneme-trained students persisted so that five years later the phoneme-trained group still scored higher than the control group on reading performance.

In a shorter-term study, some kindergarteners received instruction in phonological awareness during 28 20-minute sessions over a 7-week period in the winter (phoneme-trained group), whereas an equivalent group received no intervention beyond regular classroom instruction in reading (control group). For example, phoneme-trained students were taught to repeat a word spoken by the teacher and then to say each phoneme in the word. Other activities were like those used by Bradley and Bryant (1983, 1985) as well as letter-naming tasks.

The left two columns in Table 2–3 show that the training seems to have a strong effect on children's phonological awareness: Although both phoneme-trained and control students scored at the same level on a pretest of phonological awareness, the phoneme-trained group showed a large improvement on a posttest, whereas the control group improved only slightly. More importantly, the right two columns of Table 2–3 show that the training had a positive effect on children's reading skills: On a word-reading posttest administered after the training, phoneme-trained students were able to correctly pronounce printed words containing two or three phonemes much better than the control students. In addition, on a word-spelling posttest, phoneme-trained students performed much better on phonetic spelling of spoken words than did control students. Finally, according to a standardized reading test administered at the end of the school year, 35% of

TABLE 2–3

Percentage correct on four tests for phoneme-trained and control students

Group	Phonological Awareness		Word Reading	Word Spelling
	Pretest	Posttest	Posttest	Posttest
Phoneme-trained	40%	72%	52%	46%
Control	40%	45%	10%	25%

Adapted from Bradley and Bryant (1983)

the phoneme-trained group could be classified as readers compared to only 7% of the control group.

These results, like those of other training studies (Ehri et al., 2001; Cunningham, 1990; Lundberg, Frost, & Peterson, 1988), provide evidence that explicit instruction in phonological awareness can facilitate early reading skill. Indeed, they offer reason to suspect that the benefits of phonological awareness in young children extend beyond initial learning of basic reading skills. For example, Stanovich (1986) has shown how teachers may be initiating "a causal chain of escalating negative side effects" (p. 364) if they fail to provide phonological awareness instruction to beginning readers with poor phonological skills. The negative effects begin when students with poor phonological skills have more difficulty in learning to read words, thus limiting the amount of text they are exposed to, which in turns reduces opportunities to develop automaticity in decoding. Without automated decoding skills, students must pay attention to the process of decoding words rather than to comprehending the meaning of what they are reading. The consequence is a more limited vocabulary and knowledge base compared to those acquired by more skilled readers. Research on phonological training suggests that it may be possible to break this chain before it starts.

Although phonological awareness does not develop naturally in some children, there is encouraging evidence that it can be taught. In reviewing research on phonological training, Spector (1995) concludes that "the research to date provides clear evidence that phonemic awareness training works" (p. 47). Based on this research base, Spector (1995) recommends engaging "children in activities that direct their attention to the sounds in words . . . at the preschool level" (p. 41). This advice includes teaching students both to segment (i.e., analyze words into their constituent sounds) and to blend (i.e., to combine sounds into words) in addition to offering instruction in letter-sound relations.

More recently, several reviews of published studies have produced consistent support for phonological awareness training (Blachman, 2000; Bus & van IJzendoorn, 1999; Ehri et al., 2001; Snow, Burns, and Griffin, 1998). For example, a review of 36 published research studies found that, on average, phonological awareness training had a strong effect on improving phonological awareness and reading skills. Bus and van IJzendoorn (1999, p. 411) conclude: "The training studies settle the issue of the causal role of phonological awareness in learning to read: Phonological training reliably enhances phonological and reading skills." In short, "phonological awareness is an important but not a sufficient condition for learning to read" (Bus & van IJzendoorn, 1999, p. 412).

In a more recent review of 52 published research studies, Ehri et al. (2001) found strong and consistent evidence that 5 to 18 hours of phonological awareness training improved children's performance on tests of phonological awareness and, more importantly, on word reading and on reading comprehension. The researchers concluded that "phonemic awareness instruction is effective . . . in helping children acquire phonemic awareness and in facilitating transfer of phonemic awareness skills to reading" (Ehri et al., 2001, p. 260). The effects of instruction on learning to read were stronger for at-risk students than for normally progressing students and were stronger when instruction focused on helping students master one or two phonological skills rather than exposing them to multiple skills. Overall, the preponderance of evidence shows that phonological awareness is "a skill essential to becoming a proficient reader" (Blachman, 2000, p. 495).

Goswami and Bryant (1992) provide a useful summary of the instructional implications of phonological awareness research:

> There can be little doubt that phonological awareness plays an important role in reading. The results of a large number of studies amply demonstrate a strong (and consistent) relationship between children's ability to disentangle and to assemble the sounds in words and their progress in learning to read. . . . There is also evidence that successful training in phonological awareness helps children learn to read. . . . [P]honological awareness is a powerful causal determinant of the speed and efficiency of learning to read. . . . However, it is only the first step. (p. 49)

The next step seems to be the development of cognitive processes for decoding words, which is examined in the next section.

DECODING WORDS

WHAT IS DECODING?

Decoding refers to the process of translating a printed word into a sound. This is a rather restricted process, for it involves being able to pronounce (or name) printed words rather than being able to explain what they mean. In this section, we explore the long-standing debate over how to teach decoding, some major research findings related to decoding, and instructional research on decoding training.

THE GREAT DEBATE

One of the great debates (Adams, 1990; Chall, 1979, 1983; Pressley, 1998) in the teaching of reading concerns whether to use a *phonics* or a *whole-word* approach. The phonics (or *code-emphasis*) method involves teaching children to be able to produce sounds for letters or letter groups, and to blend those sounds together to form words. Adams (1990) notes that the central component in phonics instruction is "teaching of correspondences between letters or groups of letters and their pronunciations" (p. 50). For example, Table 2–1 lists 42 basic sounds in spoken English and gives examples of letters that correspond to the sounds. Readers learn to associate the appropriate sound with the appropriate letter(s). Figure 2–6 shows a picture of a flat tire (making the "sssss" sound) along with letters that can correspond to this sound.

In contrast, the whole-word method involves teaching children to "sight read" words, that is, to be able to pronounce a whole word as a single unit. For example, an early reading program may concentrate on introducing a few hundred words. Figure 2–7 shows some typical first words to be learned by beginning readers. Over time, new words are systematically added to the reader's repertoire. The whole-word approach is generally part of a *meaning-emphasis method,* in which determining the meaning of each word is a major goal.

The history of reading research in the United States documents several swings between the phonics and whole-word approach (Adams, 1990; Singer, 1981). In the beginning, during the 1700s, the phonics method was emphasized. The standard textbook was *The New England Primer,* originally published in 1690. First, children learned the alphabet; then, they learned to read two-letter combinations (*ab, ac, ad, af,* and so on) and consonant-vowel syllables (*ba, da, ca,* and so on); next, children were asked to read words containing up to five syllables. Students were drilled on the correct pronunciation for each syllable and the correct spelling of words until they could spell and read short words by sight. Finally, children orally read sentences and stories and afterward answered comprehension questions.

The phonics tradition was heavily used through the early 1800s, when the dominant textbook was *The American Spelling Book.* Published in 1790, this book, like *The New*

FIGURE 2–6 Phonics instruction involves associating sounds with letters or letter groups

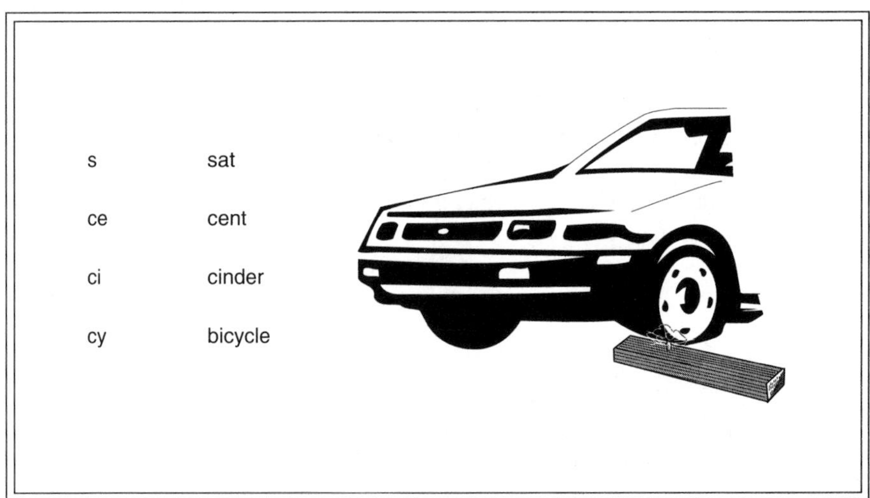

Adapted from Open Court Phonics Kit *(1979)*

FIGURE 2–7 Whole-word instruction involves associating word names with printed words

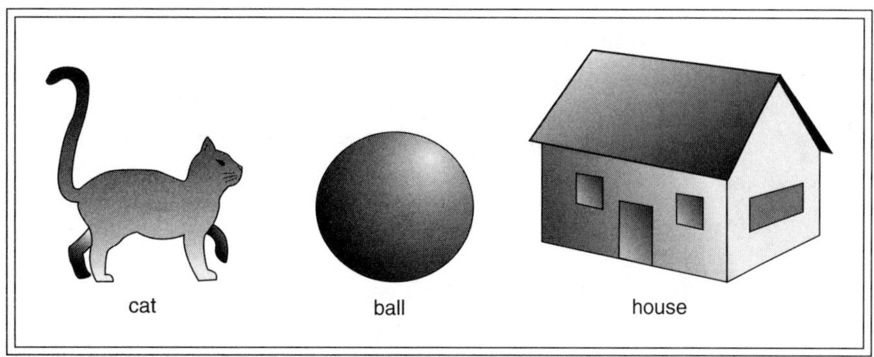

England Primer, progressed from alphabet to syllables to words. However, whereas *The New England Primer* focused on religious material, *The American Spelling Book* focused on national loyalty and traditions.

During the mid-nineteenth century, there was a swing to the whole-word method. The dominant textbooks were *McGuffey Readers,* which appeared between 1836 and 1844. They systematically introduced a new word by letting the student see the word, hear the word, see a picture or sentence referring to the word, and later spell the word (or break it into sounds). Unlike previous texts, *McGuffey Readers* were a graded series that allowed for children to be grouped by age and achievement.

By the 1880s emphasis was placed on the reading of fine literature, prompting a return to the phonics method of instruction. The scientific alphabet was introduced in 1902; it consisted of 44 phonemes along with 44 corresponding symbols. Students learned to write sentences phonetically, using these symbols. Other techniques involved teaching students to sound out words before giving any hints with pictures or sentence context.

By the early 1900s scientific research in education was influencing reading instruction. In schools, silent reading rather than oral reading was stressed. For example, as an introductory lesson a teacher might write "Come here" on the blackboard; students would then carry out the commands as written. Emphasis was also placed on getting the meaning out of stories; teachers would question children about their experiences before asking them to read a story. Students learned to recognize whole words before they learned how to break them into parts.

Since the end of World War II, the dominant reading textbooks in American schools have been basal readers. Like *McGuffey Readers,* the modern basal readers are an integrated and graded series of reading books and activities, with each successive book in the series requiring more sophisticated and difficult reading skills. Most basal readers employ aspects of both the whole-word and phonics approach, but according to many critics (Singer, 1981; Flesch, 1955), more attention is given to whole-word methods. For example, Flesch's (1955) famous book *Why Johnny Can't Read and What You Can Do About It* called for a shift back to the phonics method of instruction.

Deciding which method is best for teaching beginning reading has become "the most politicized topic in the field of education" (Adams, 1990, p. 13). Fortunately, the debate is informed by a large and fairly consistent research base. In her classic book *Learning to Read: The Great Debate,* Chall (1967) reviewed the research literature and concluded that children should learn the relation between sounds and letters before they learn to read for content and meaning. In a more recent review of research, Adams (1990) came to the same conclusion: "programs that include some explicit, systematic phonic instruction tend to produce better word reading skills than those that do not" (p. 93). Although today's reading programs attempt to balance phonics and whole-word approaches, the preponderance of research shows that children need to develop fast and automatic word decoding processes before they can become proficient in reading comprehension. In other words, children must first learn to read (code emphasis) before they can successfully read to learn (meaning emphasis).

As you can see, there has been a sort of battle in American reading instruction between a phonics method that progresses from letters to syllables to words to sentences on one side and a whole-word approach that progresses from meaningful context to words to parts on the other. What is the current status of the "great debate" concerning the merits of phonics and whole-word instruction? In recent years, the alternative to the phonics approach changed somewhat from the whole-word approach to the whole-language philosophy—that is, the idea that students learn best by reading and writing (Williams, 1994)—but the same debate remains. Williams (1994, p. 61) aptly summarizes the state of the research as follows: "(a) phonics instruction should be incorporated prominently into beginning reading instruction, and (b) it should by no means be considered the entirety of any reading program." Based on a review of research, Pressley (1998, p. 265) concludes that ". . . balanced elementary instruction—that is, balancing of whole-language and skills components—seems more defensible than instruction that is only immersion in reading and writing, on the one hand, or predominantly skills driven, on the other."

Similarly, in a review of research comparing traditional reading programs that emphasize phonics skills and whole-language programs that emphasize reading authentic literature, Stahl, McKenna, and Pagnucco (1994) found a slight advantage for traditional programs on word reading and a slight advantage for whole-language programs on reading comprehension. Yet, the majority of studies exhibited no differences, perhaps because most of the whole-language programs included some teaching of phonics skills and most traditional programs included some exposure to authentic literature. Based on their analysis of existing programs, Stahl et al. (1994) call for an "eclectic reading program" that includes "a great deal of attention to decoding especially in the early grades" and "greater emphasis to the reading of interesting and motivating texts" (p. 182).

The next section explores research on three important aspects of the great debate about decoding: (1) automaticity effects, involving how people learn to decipher symbols, (2) word superiority effects, involving how people identify letters, and (3) pronunciation effects, involving how people put letters together to make words.

RESEARCH ON DECODING

AUTOMATICITY EFFECTS As a historical introduction to the great debate, consider the following scene. The story begins in the fall of 1895. The place is the Western Union telegraph office in Brookville, Indiana. The characters are an 18-year-old young man named Will Reynolds and a 17-year-old young woman named Edyth Balsley. Both have come to learn to become telegraph operators under the tutelage of the telegraph office's operator, Mr. Balsley. They are bright and eager learners, so by June of 1896, both can send and receive ordinary business letters over the main line. More importantly, during this period both have agreed to be tested once a week on how fast they can send and receive telegraph messages. In doing so, Will and Edyth enter the annals of educational psychology history by becoming participants in what is today widely recognized as the first major psychological study of skill learning (Bryan & Harter, 1897).

To measure their receiving speed, the tester gave them a message in Morse code at a certain rate for a two-minute period; the student's task was to listen to the incoming dots and dashes and write down the message in words. If the student failed to decipher the code correctly, the task was repeated at a slower rate. If the student succeeded, a faster rate was tried. Figure 2–8 shows the number of letters per minute that Will and Edyth could correctly receive on each of the weekly tests from the day they started until they mastered the

FIGURE 2–8 Letters per minute Edyth and Will could receive during their first 36 weeks of learning

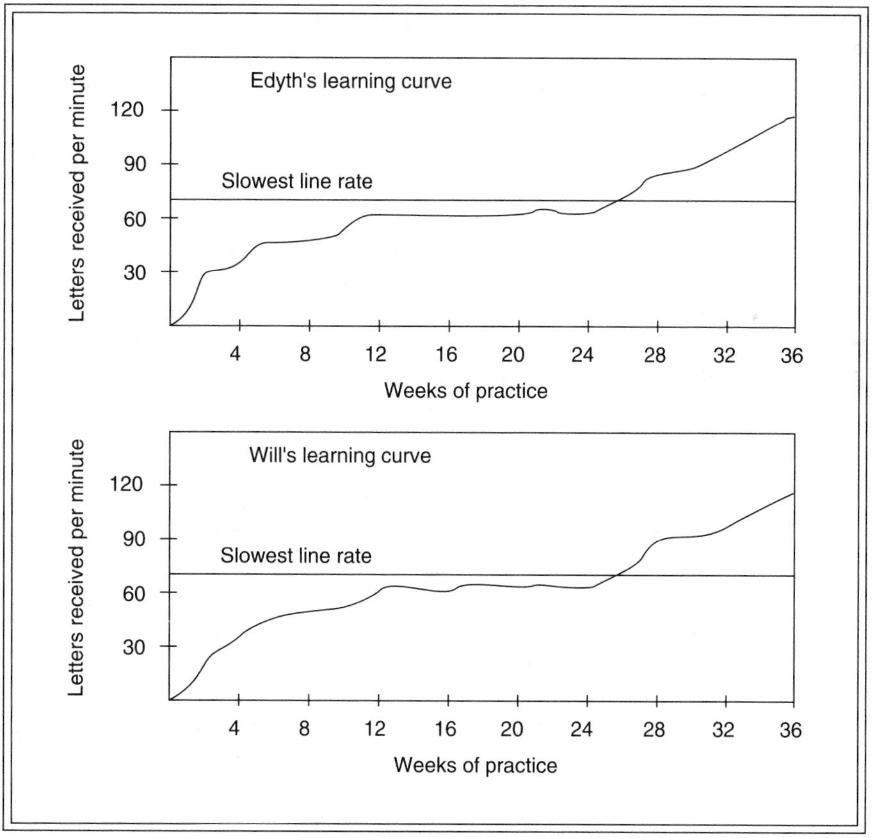

Adapted from Bryan and Harter (1897)

basics. This is a learning curve, in which the *x*-axis indicates the amount of practice and the *y*-axis shows the level of learning.

Bryan and Harter (1897) noted both quantitative and qualitative changes in Will's and Edyth's deciphering skill. These quantitative and qualitative changes constitute an *automaticity effect,* that is, an ability to carry out a task without having to pay attention to each step. First, as you can see in the learning curves, over the course of training both students improved greatly in the speed with which they could decode incoming messages. It took them about six months of practice before they could handle messages coming in at the slowest main line rate (71 letters per minute), but within nine months they could receive 100 words per minute and were on a trajectory of getting faster every week. The increasing speed of the students is evidence that components of their decoding skill were becoming automated, that is, that their conscious attention was not required.

Second, in addition there was also a qualitative change in which the students first translated the code on a letter-by-letter basis, then word-by-word, and finally phrase-by-phrase. According to Bryan and Harter (1897), this qualitative shift is reflected in the observation that both students reached a plateau in the middle of their training—their learning curves became somewhat flat between the 16th and 20th weeks. Bryan and Harter interpreted this pattern as evidence of stages in skill learning: the increase in speed from the first week to the 16th week reflects a phase of increasing skill at decoding individual letters and even short words, the plateau represents a phase of consolidation of letter-decoding skill so that it becomes automatic, and the increase in speed from the 24th week onward represents a shift of focus to decoding by words and phrases. By observing operators as they progressed from novices to experts, Bryan and Harter found that at first they decoded messages letter-by-letter, then after more practice, they began to decode word-by-word, and eventually were able to decode phrase-by-phrase, so that their writing was 6 to 12 words behind the flow of the incoming code. The plateau represents a period in which a component skill—letter-by-letter decoding—reaches its highest speed but is still not completely automatic; once it becomes automatized, it can be used as a component in learning higher-order skills such as decoding words and phrases. Importantly, when novices decoded letter-by-letter, they reported being unaware of the meaning of the message, whereas expert operators who listened to an entire phrase before writing it down stated that they were aware of the meaning of the message.

What can this nineteenth-century study of telegraph operators tell us about how today's children learn to read? When the famous educational psychologist E. L. Thorndike (1913) examined Bryan and Harter's classic study of skill learning, he was struck by the possibility that "in learning to read (first year primary) . . . one's progress is analogous to that of the student of telegraphy" (p. 100). The crucial event in learning to decipher code—whether it is printed words or the sounds of the Morse code—is the development of automaticity of low-level skills. Accordingly, it is crucial that students develop the ability to recognize the relation between a letter (or letter group) and its sound rapidly and automatically, that is, phonological deciphering must become effortless. This goal is accomplished through practice.

Consistent with this view of the development of automaticity of basic skills, many authors propose that students who must consciously monitor their decoding process have less attentional capacity for making inferences and otherwise trying to comprehend the passage (Adams, 1990; Chall, 1967; Perfetti & Lesgold, 1979). In order to investigate this idea, Perfetti and Hogaboam (1975) selected third- and fifth-graders who either scored low in standardized tests of reading comprehension (below the thirtieth percentile) or scored high in reading comprehension (above the sixtieth percentile). Reading comprehension involves being able to answer meaningful questions about a passage you just read. Subjects were asked to participate in a word-pronunciation task: A word was presented on a screen and the subject's job was to say the word as soon as he or she knew what it was. This task requires decoding, but not comprehension.

Some of the words were familiar; as Figure 2–9 shows, skilled and less skilled readers did not differ greatly in their pronunciation times for familiar words. Other words were unfamiliar to the readers; as Figure 2–9 shows, the less skilled readers averaged 1 second longer than the skilled readers. One explanation may be that skilled readers are more familiar with the "unfamiliar" words, perhaps because they spend more time reading more difficult texts. However, Figure 2–9 also shows that the less skilled readers required an average of over 1 second more than the skilled readers to pronounce pseudowords (i.e., nonsense words that could be pronounced). Apparently, skilled readers employ fast and automatic decoding processes, even for words that have no meaning, whereas less skilled readers have great difficulty in decoding words that are not part of their sight-reading vocabulary. These results are consistent with the idea that well-practiced decoding skills allow the reader to use his or her attentional resources to comprehend the passage. In fact,

FIGURE 2–9 Mean pronunciation time for high- and low-skill readers

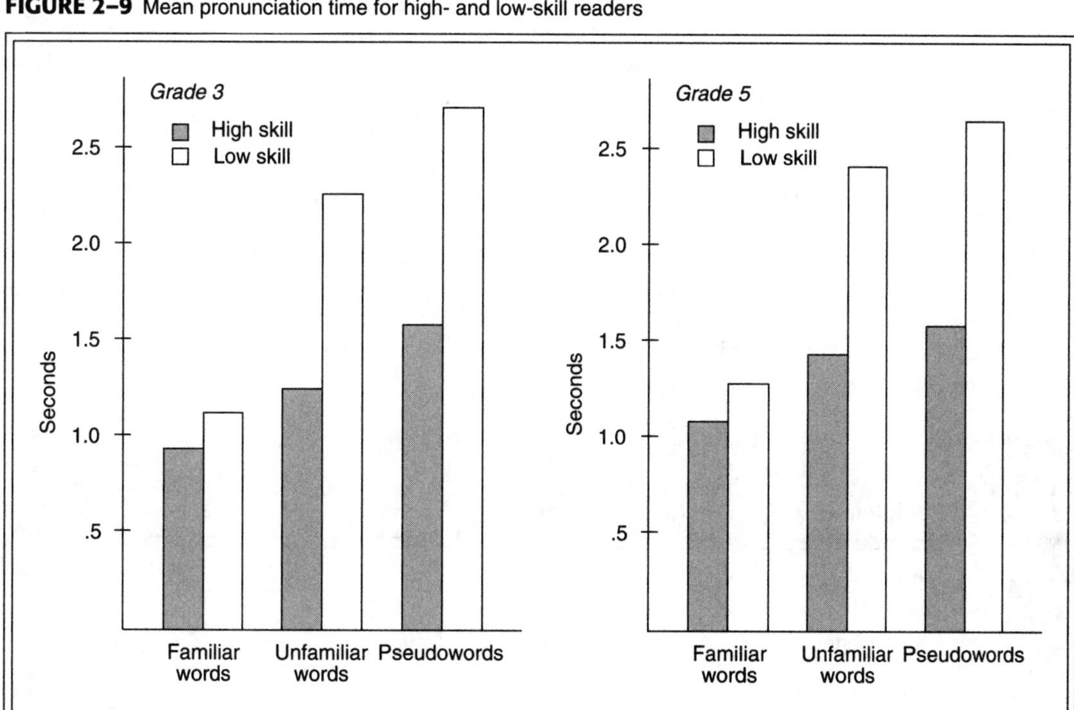

Adapted from Perfetti and Hogaboam (1975)

fluent readers may be so well practiced in decoding that they are unaware of the rules of pronunciation (Calfee, Chapman, & Venezky, 1972). Apparently, learning efficient decoding skills is a prerequisite for learning efficient comprehension skills.

WORD SUPERIORITY EFFECTS One way to provide more detailed information concerning the great debate over decoding is to determine how skilled readers, such as normal adults, read letters in words. For example, we might ask: Do people read each letter and put these parts together to form a word, as would be suggested by a phonics approach to reading? Alternatively, do people read the whole word first and then recognize each letter?

The second alternative may sound odd, because common sense seems to tell us that you must recognize the parts before you recognize the whole. However, some early research may surprise you. For example, Cattell (1886) found that letters can be perceived more accurately when they are part of a word than when they are not. In experiments, if unrelated letters were flashed on the screen for very brief exposures, people could correctly perceive about three letters; however, if the letters formed simple three-letter words, subjects correctly perceived about six letters. This phenomenon—that people can read letters faster and more accurately when they are parts of words—has been called the *word superiority effect* (Baron, 1978; Kreiger, 1975; Reicher, 1969; Smith & Spoehr, 1974).

The word superiority effect is one of the oldest and best-established facts in experimental psychology. As an example of research on the phenomenon, let's consider an experiment by Johnston (1978, 1981). Subjects were asked to watch a screen, and to be ready to report the letters that were flashed on a screen. Table 2–4 shows that a word (such as "COIN"), a letter string (such as "CPDT"), or a letter (such as "C") was presented briefly (e.g., for 30 milliseconds); then a mask (such as "XXXXX") was flashed to blot out any afterimages; finally, subjects were asked to take a forced choice test concerning one of the letters (e.g., Was the first letter of the word "C" or "J"? or Was the letter that you saw a "C" or "J"?). Subjects were not told in advance which letter in a word or letter string would be the one they would be tested on. As Table 2–4 indicates, subjects more accurately recognized letters when they were parts of words (such as the "C" in "COIN") than when they were presented singly (such as "C" alone) or in nonsense strings. In Johnston's experiment, the word superiority effect represents a difference of about 13 percentage points in accuracy.

The word superiority effect has been used as a rationale for teaching reading by the whole-word method (Singer, 1981), because it seems to imply that readers perceive words

TABLE 2–4

The word superiority effect

Treatment	Example of Stimulus	Mask	Forced Choice Test		Proportion Correct
Word	COIN	XXXXX	COIN	JOIN	.845
Letter string	CPDT	XXXXX	CPDT	JPDT	.686
Single letter	C	XXXXX	C	J	.710

Adapted from Johnston (1981)

more easily than individual letters. However, you need to be suspicious of this conclusion. The word superiority effect is not a theory; it is just a well-established empirical fact. What is needed is a theory of how people read and how they learn to read. Educational practice should be based on our understanding of the reading process (i.e., a unified theory of reading) rather than single facts.

Johnston (1981) suggested three different ways to interpret the word superiority effect. Theory 1 says that the visual shape of the word provides information that is not present for single letters. However, in contrast to this theory, the word superiority effect still is obtained when the word is presented all in capital letters (such as "COIN"), in alternating letters (such as "CoIn" or "cOiN"), or with irregular spacing (such as "CO IN"). Theory 2 argues that the word provides cues about what the letters can be; for example, if you know that the last three letters of a four-letter word are "NOB," you can limit your hypotheses concerning the first letter to "S" and "K." However, in contrast to this theory, words that constrain the possible first letters to one of three letters (such as "-RIP") do not provide better word superiority effects than words that constrain the possible first letter to one of nine possible letters (such as "-ATE"). Theory 3 states that the word allows for better retention through the mask. However, this theory is inadequate because it cannot explain why the code for a word should be easier to remember than the code for a letter. In short, Johnston (1981) concludes that all of the popular theories for the word superiority effect should be rejected.

What causes the word superiority effect? Johnston and his colleague (1981; Johnston & McClelland, 1980) offer a theory based on the idea that a word is analyzed on several levels. When a word such as "COIN" is presented, the reader begins to form and test hypotheses about the word on each of the following levels:

Feature detectors, which determine whether the lines of the letters are curved or straight and the orientation of lines for each position.

Letter detectors, which determine the letter that is present at each position, based partly on information from the feature detectors.

Word detectors, which determine the word that is present, based partly on information from the letter detectors.

However, as soon as the mask is presented, the feature and letter detectors are erased. Thus the only level of analysis that survives the mask is the word level. If the stimulus is a letter or a letter string, no word-level analysis can take place, and thus the mask is more likely to damage performance. Thus Johnston and his colleague seem to be able to explain the word superiority effect by assuming that readers analyze words by their parts; if this theory is correct, the word superiority effect does not suggest that the whole-word method of instruction is better than the phonics method for beginning readers.

PRONUNCIATION STRATEGY EFFECTS As another source of research information, let's return for a moment to the pronunciation task shown in Figure 2–2. Baron (1977) presented pronouncable nonsense words like these to adults, who were asked to pronounce each one and to tell how they decided on the pronunciation.

The results indicated that Baron's subjects tended to use three distinct pronunciation strategies. With the similarity strategy, they pronounced a nonsense word so that it sounded exactly the same as a familiar real word. For example, "BLUD" was pronounced "blood." With the analogy strategy, subjects pronounced the nonsense word so that it partially rhymed with a real word. For example, "ROTION" was pronounced to rhyme with "motion." With the corresponding strategy, subjects used phonetic rules to sound out each part of the word and then blended the sounds together. For example, "SHUD" was pronounced as "sh" for "SH," "ah" for "U," and "d" for "D," yielding "sh-ah-d."

In Baron's study, the most commonly used strategy was the corresponding strategy, in which the word was sounded out. This strategy corresponds to the phonics method of reading instruction in which students learn the relation between letters and sounds. In contrast, the similarity strategy corresponds somewhat to the whole-word method of reading instruction. Finally, the analogy approach seems to involve a compromise that deals with sounds of word parts (phonics) and whole words. An analysis of subjects' errors in pronunciation tended to favor the analogy strategy as the most effective.

To test the merits of the analogy strategy, Baron (1977) provided explicit training to some subjects in how to use the analogy strategy to pronounce nonsense words. Subjects given such analogy strategy training showed a large improvement in pronunciation performance, with errors dropping from 9% to 4%. Baron also showed that training in the analogy strategy can be applied successfully to children as young as four years old. For example, students can be taught to pronounce three-letter words ending in "IN" and "AX," such as "TIN" and "TAX," or "PIN" and "WAX," by using rhymes.

There is increasing evidence that beginning readers who have not yet fully mastered phonological decoding are able to read words by analogy (Goswami, 1986; Goswami & Bryant, 1990). In one study, beginning readers received a sheet with a clue word on top, such as "beak," followed by other words and nonwords such as "bean," "beal," "peak," "neak," "lake," and "pake." The teacher pronounced the clue word and then asked the child to read aloud the other words on the sheet. Children performed better in reading words that rhymed with the target, such as "peak" and "neak," than words that shared some word parts, such as "bean" and "beal," or that had little in common with "beak," such as "lake" and "pake." In a follow-up study, Ehri and Robbins (1992) provided additional evidence that "reading unfamiliar words by analogy to known words . . . can be executed by beginners more readily than reading unfamiliar words by phonologically recoding the words" (p. 22).

A first step in building automaticity in English letter-sound combinations is to learn the 42 major sounds in English (as summarized in Table 2–1) and the 26 letters of the alphabet. Next, a student must learn the rules by which letters are related to sounds, but unfortunately the rules relating letters to sounds are far from regular (Clymer, 1963). For example, Clymer (1963) generated a list of 45 rules, including those selected for Table 2–5, but most had many exceptions. What is the best way to learn phonological decoding in a language such as English? One promising answer to this question grows out of early work on skill learning, which indicates that the path to automatic decoding includes practice.

IMPLICATIONS FOR INSTRUCTION: AUTOMATICITY TRAINING

The major implication of the research previously cited is that readers must become automatic in recognizing letters and sounding out letter groups. In short, a main focus of reading instruction during the first few years of school should be to help students develop

TABLE 2–5

Selected phonics rules for vowels and consonants

Rule	Example	Exception	Percentage Consistent
When there are two vowels, one of which is the final *e*, the first vowel is long and the *e* is silent.	bone	done	63%
When a word has only one vowel, the vowel sound is short.	hid	kind	57%
When there are two vowels side by side, the long sound of the first one is heard, and the second is silent.	bead	chief	45%
When two of the same consonants are side by side, only one is heard.	carry	suggest	99%
Ch is usually pronounced as it is in *chair.*	catch	machine	95%
When *g* precedes *i* or *e*, it sounds like *j* in *jump.*	engine	give	64%

Adapted from Clymer (1963)

decoding skills that are automatic (i.e., that do not require extensive conscious effort by the reader). This section focuses on how to provide training for decoding automaticity.

Stanovich (1980) summarized research on decoding by noting that good readers differ from poor readers mainly in their rapid context-free word recognition. The limited capacity of the memory system requires that if some processes demand a great deal of attention, there will not be adequate attention available for other processes. For example, LaBerge and Samuels (1974) proposed that fluent readers are able to decode text automatically, which means that they have attention available for comprehension processes. In contrast, beginning readers' attention must be devoted mainly to decoding, leaving relatively little processing capacity available for comprehension processing. Perfetti and Hogaboam (1975) summarize this idea as follows: "To the extent that decoding is a mainly automatic process, it does not make great demands on the readers' higher comprehension processes" (p. 466).

LaBerge and Samuels (1974) proposed three stages in the development of automaticity:

1. ***Nonaccurate stage,*** in which the reader makes errors in word recognition.
2. ***Accuracy stage,*** in which the reader can recognize words correctly but must use great attention to do so.
3. ***Automatic stage,*** in which the reader can recognize words correctly without requiring attention.

How can we teach students to gain automaticity in decoding? Samuels (1979) suggested a technique called the *method of repeated readings.* According to this technique, a student

FIGURE 2–10 Improving decoding fluency by repeated readings

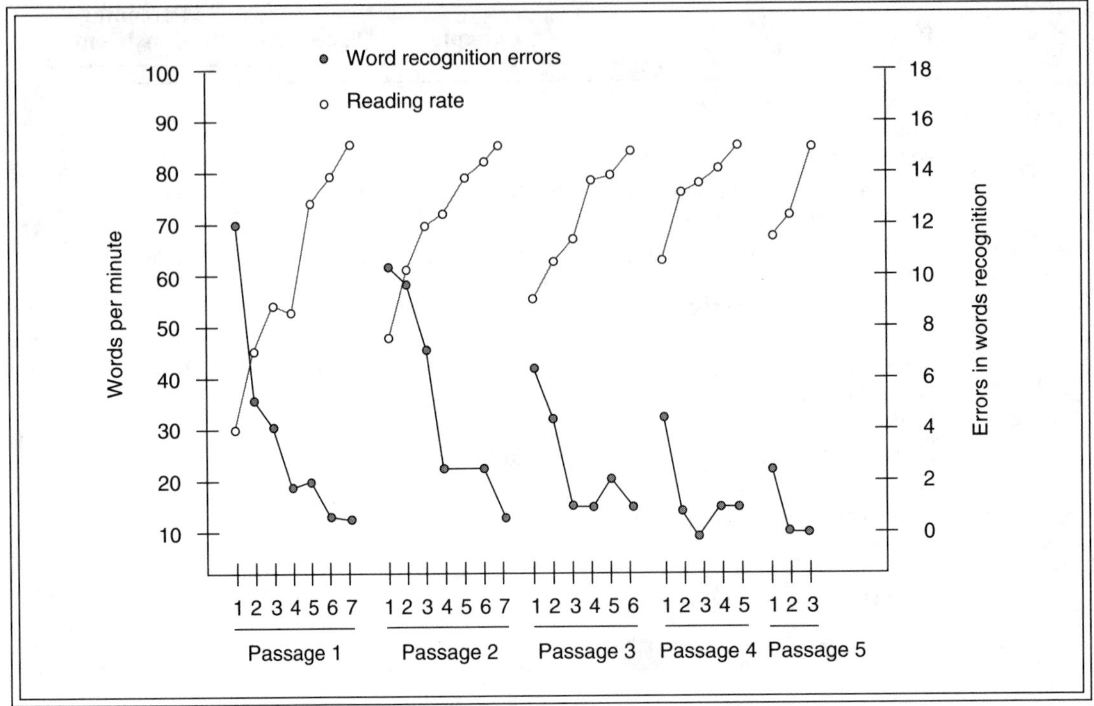

Adapted from Samuels (1979)

reads a short, easy passage over and over again until a satisfactory level of fluency is reached. This procedure is repeated for another passage, and so on. Figure 2–10 shows the changes in reading and word-recognition rate as a student read five different passages using the method of repeated readings. Two findings are particularly interesting. First, for each passage, the fluency improves greatly with repetition. Second, fluency tends to improve from one passage to the next, even though the words are different.

What is the best way to increase word recognition automaticity? Samuels (1967) proposed the *focal attention hypothesis,* which holds that visual attention should be focused on the printed word rather than the context. Thus word-recognition training that relies on context such as pictures and sentences is seen as distracting the reader from focusing on the printed word. For example, Ehri and Roberts (1979) asked first-graders to learn to read 16 words using flash cards. For some students, each card contained just one word; for others, each card contained a target word within the context of a sentence. As expected, students in the word-only condition could sight-read the words faster (averaging 10.9 seconds) than could students in the context condition (averaging 15.7 seconds). Students in the word-only condition, as compared to the context condition, remembered more about the orthographic characteristics of the words, such as the correct spelling, but less of the semantic characteristics of the words needed to generate a sentence. Similarly, Nemko (1984) asked first-graders to learn to read 16 words using flash cards, with each word presented either individually or in the context of a sentence. The test involved reading each word either individually or within a sentence. The best performance was for students who learned and were tested with individual words.

Samuels (1979) argued that as readers become more fluent, their comprehension improves, for "as less attention is required for decoding, more attention becomes available for comprehension" (p. 405). Unfortunately, the idea that training in decoding automaticity will improve reading comprehension is not universally supported. Fleisher, Jenkins, and Pany (1979) gave decoding training to poor readers in the fourth and fifth grades. First, students in the trained group practiced by rapidly reading single words from flash cards, while students in the control group received no training. Then, all students took a criterion test in which they were asked to read a randomly ordered list of the words that the trained group had practiced reading. Students in the trained group reached a level of automaticity in which they made nearly no errors and read at least 90 words per minute; in contrast, the control students read at half the rate and made many more errors. Next, all students read two passages containing the practice words and took a twelve-item comprehension test. Although the trained group read the passage faster than the control group (91 words per minute versus 61 words per minute, respectively), there were no significant differences between the groups in comprehension test performance. A reasonable conclusion to draw from this study is that automatic decoding is a necessary but not sufficient condition for improved comprehension. Rapid decoding skill may help to reduce the bottleneck (or demands on memory processes), but a skilled reader also needs to know how to use comprehension strategies.

In a recent review, Dowhower (1994) concluded "because of the strong evidence of the effectiveness of repeated reading . . . this procedure should be integrated into the fabric of daily literacy instruction" (p. 343). Based on current research, Dowhower argued that students benefit from unassisted repeated-reading procedures in which they read and reread aloud on their own, and from assisted repeated-reading procedures in which they read and reread along with a teacher. If both methods are used, Dowhower suggests beginning with the assisted procedure and subsequently introducing the unassisted procedure for each passage. Koskinen and Blum (1986) developed a modified version of repeated reading in which children work in pairs as they take turns reading 50-word passages three times to each other. The ultimate goal of the method of repeated readings and other forms of automaticity training is for children to be able to decode words without having to pay conscious attention to the decoding process.

ACCESSING WORD MEANING

WHAT IS MEANING ACCESS?

The two preceding sections highlight two cognitive processes involved in being able to read a printed word: being able to recognize the sound units that make up words (e.g., when hearing the word "cat," being able to recognize that it is composed of the three sounds /k/, /a/, and /t/), and knowing which sounds go with the printed letters that make up words (e.g., knowing that in the printed word "cat," the letter "c" goes with the sound /k/). Being able to recognize the phonemes in spoken words and being able to decode printed letters into phonemes are two essential cognitive skills for reading, but they are not enough. As an example, please read the following sentence aloud: "Ismam stog kopob amjut metula ildat." This sentence is not a secret message, but rather a collection of pronounceable nonwords. Although you might be able to say each of the words aloud, this exercise is not very meaningful. What is missing from this exercise? The words you read had no meaning to you. When you read a familiar English word, you engage in an important cognitive process that can be called *meaning access,* or finding in your memory a mental representation of the meaning of the word. Thus, meaning access is the third essential cognitive process involved in reading a word.

Meaning access depends on the reader knowing the meanings of many words—what educators call having a *vocabulary* and what linguists call knowing a *lexicon*. For example, when you see the printed word "cat" you not only can pronounce the word aloud but you also can think of a small furry four-legged animal that purrs. In thinking of what "cat" means you are engaging in meaning access. In short, the search for word meaning can be called meaning access.

Nagy and Scott (2000) estimate that young readers need to add at least 2,000 new words to their vocabulary each year. If building a vocabulary is a prerequisite for learning to read, it is useful to ask where children's vocabularies come from and how best to foster this vocabulary growth. Two approaches to fostering growth are immersion and direct instruction. In *immersion,* the child is encouraged to engage in literacy activities such as reading, writing, listening, and speaking. Reading books to young children is an example of an immersion approach. In short, the child is placed in an environment that is rich with words. In *direct instruction,* the child is asked to learn the definitions of specific words as a learning activity. Giving a student a list of words and asking them to learn the definition of each word is an example of the direct instruction approach. A related approach is to teach students skills for how to analyze word meaning, such as understanding of prefixes, suffixes, and core words.

Determining which approach is better constitutes a central issue in research on vocabulary learning. The case for immersion is based on the sheer magnitude of the vocabulary learning task. If a child attends school for 180 days per year, he or she must learn more than 10 new words a day in school to sufficiently build a vocabulary. It is doubtful that there is enough instructional time in the school day to achieve this goal. For this reason, Nagy and Scott (2000, p. 280) conclude that "the high rates of vocabulary growth seen in many children occur only through immersion in massive amounts of rich written and oral language." Pressley and Woloshyn (1995) observe that "the evidence is simply overwhelming (and continues to increase) that children learn new vocabulary by hearing and rehearing stories and other content that are rich in vocabulary, as well as talking about and retelling what they have heard" (p. 102).

The case for direct instruction is that some words need to be explained because students may not be able to master them simply from context. Pressley and Woloshyn (1995) summarize evidence that "students learn quite a bit from simply processing a word and its definition" (p. 103). For example, in Chapter 13, I describe the keyword method, which has been shown to be effective in helping students memorize definitions for vocabulary words. However, students may benefit even more from semantically based techniques such as learning to use new words in sentences (Blachowicz & Fisher, 2000) or from learning word analysis skills based on prefixes, suffixes, and core words (Pressley & Woloshyn, 1995).

This section explores basic research relevant to meaning access (including context effects and vocabulary effects) and instructional studies aimed at improving the process.

RESEARCH ON MEANING ACCESS

CONTEXT EFFECTS *Context effects* are the impact of the context of a word within a sentence on the speed and accuracy of word recognition. Tulving and Gold (1963) reported a landmark study concerning the role of sentence context on word meaning. In the experiment, a word was flashed on the screen and the subjects were asked to read the word aloud. Before the word was flashed, subjects were given a cue such as, "The actress received praise for being an outstanding ______________." As you can see, this cue provides what Tulving and Gold called an *appropriate context* for the target word "performer," but an *inappropriate context* for the target word "potato." The length of the cue given before the target word was either zero (i.e., no cue), one, two, four, or eight words. Longer cues, presumably, provide a stronger context for the target word.

Figure 2–11 summarizes the results of the experiment. The researchers measured the amount of time that a word had to be presented for a subject to be able to read it. When the target word was presented after an appropriate context, subjects were able to read it even when the duration of the flash was short. But when the target word was presented after an inappropriate context, it had to be presented for a longer time. As shown in Figure 2–11, the time needed to read a word that followed a long, appropriate cue was about half as much as the time needed to read a word that followed a long, inappropriate cue. Compared to having no cue, inappropriate contexts tended to inhibit the subject's ability to read a word, whereas appropriate contexts tended to facilitate that ability.

These results demonstrate the role of the reader's knowledge of meaning and syntax in word reading. One explanation is that the context provides syntactic cues (i.e., cues about what part of speech should occur) and semantic cues (i.e., cues about the possible meanings of the word). These cues allow the reader to generate specific hypotheses even before the target word is presented. If the hypotheses are correct, less reading time will be required; if the hypotheses are incorrect, more time will be required to generate and test new hypotheses.

West and Stanovich (1978) extended the Tulving and Gold research method to younger readers. For example, fourth-graders, sixth-graders, and adults were asked to read words that were presented on a screen. Some target words were preceded by a sentence context that was not congruent with the word, some target words were preceded by a sentence context that was congruent, and others were preceded only by "the." West and Stanovich measured the amount of time between presentation of the target word and the subject's pronunciation of the word. Figure 2–12 shows that for all age groups, performance was better for words in congruous sentences; however, the effects of context appear to weaken for older subjects. Apparently, adults are less reliant on context than children. One possibility is that adults search for word meaning in an automatic way, while children are more conscious of the context.

FIGURE 2–11 Time to read a word in an appropriate versus inappropriate sentence context

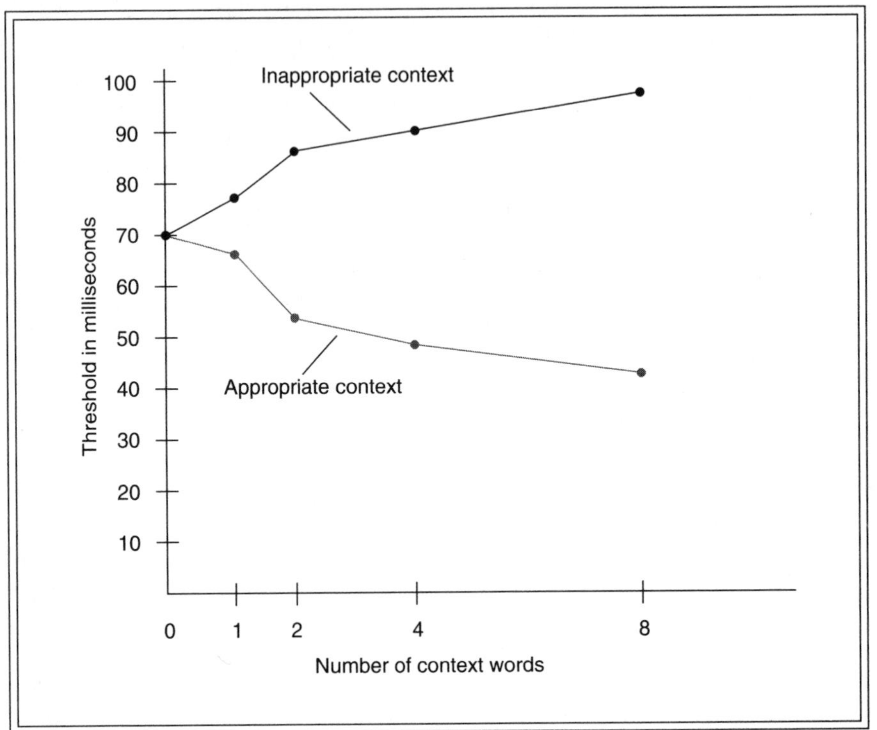

From Tulving and Gold (1963)

In a review of research comparing good and poor readers, Spoehr and Schuberth (1981) found that poor readers were more influenced by context cues than were good readers. For example, in the West and Stanovich study, poorer readers showed a greater context effect than did good readers. Schvaneveldt, Ackerman, and Semlear (1977) found a developmental trend similar to that obtained by West and Stanovich in which younger readers showed a greater context effect than did older readers. These results are consistent with the idea that meaning access becomes automatic in good readers, while the use of context cues is more time-consuming and conscious in poorer or younger readers.

IMPLICATIONS FOR INSTRUCTION: VOCABULARY TRAINING

The foregoing results show that good readers are more efficient than less skilled readers in finding a word's meaning from memory. Let's suppose that improvement in the speed of meaning access (i.e., the time needed to retrieve a word's meaning from long-term memory) is a skill that can be taught. Vocabulary training is a popular technique for increasing the efficiency of readers' meaning-access processes (Pressley, 1990).

FIGURE 2–12 Average time to pronounce a word in a congruous or incongruous context or preceded only by "the"

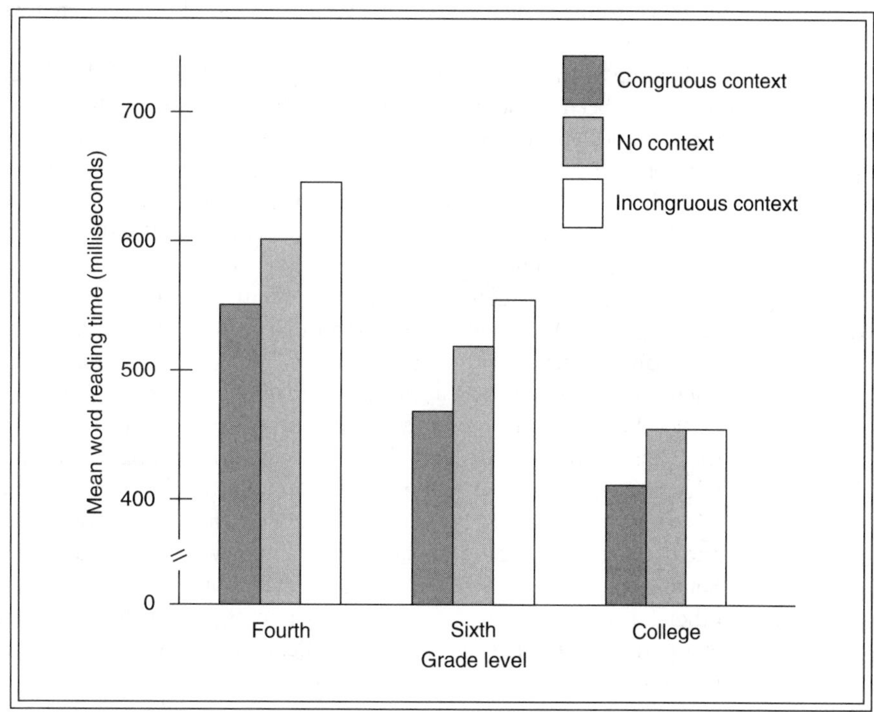

From West and Stanovich (1978)

Not surprisingly, children who have better vocabularies (i.e., knowledge of the meanings of more words) perform better on reading comprehension tests (Anderson & Freebody, 1981). Similarly, changing unfamiliar words in a passage to more familiar synonyms increases children's reading comprehension (Marks, Doctorow & Wittrock, 1974), and word recognition is easier when words are embedded in a familiar rather than unfamiliar context (Wittrock, Marks, & Doctorow, 1975). The explanation for these results is that when the words in a passage are unfamiliar, students must focus their attention on the process of meaning access; in contrast, when the words are familiar, students can access their meaning automatically and use their attention to comprehend the passage.

A straightforward implication of these findings is that reading comprehension will be enhanced if students are given vocabulary training. However, analyses of school reading materials in grades three to nine found that as many as 88,000 distinct word meanings are required, and the average school student acquires as many as 2,000 to 5,000 words per year (Nagy & Anderson, 1984; Nagy & Herman, 1987; Nagy, Herman, & Anderson, 1985; Nagy & Scott, 2000). According to Nagy and his colleagues, the direct instruction of vocabulary words would not be able to produce such large vocabulary growth in students.

Instead, the bulk of new vocabulary words must be learned from context—that is, from reading or listening to or producing prose. Thus, exercises such as silent sustained reading, in which students read books for a certain period of time on a regular basis, may serve as vocabulary training exercises.

In spite of these warnings concerning the limitations of direct vocabulary instruction, there have been numerous studies aimed at teaching vocabulary to young readers. Many of these studies are successful in teaching vocabulary as measured by multiple-choice tests, but not in greatly influencing readers' comprehension (Nagy & Herman, 1987; Pearson & Gallagher, 1983). One reason for the failure of some vocabulary training programs is that much printed material in schools can be understood with a vocabulary of only 4,000 words. Training in new words reaches a point of diminishing returns, because most words outside of this basic core of 4,000 words occur very rarely in school materials. For example, Nagy and Anderson (1984) found that most of the words in school materials occur less than one per million. Learning the meaning of words that occur with such low frequency is unlikely to have a substantial effect on comprehension.

Vocabulary training programs that successfully enhance comprehension tend to be those that help the reader to embed each word within a rich set of experiences and knowledge and that involve test passages containing the just-learned vocabulary words (Kameenui, Carnine, & Freschi, 1982). For example, in a series of studies, fourth-, fifth-, and sixth-graders read a passage and then answered test questions about the passage. Some of the subjects received a passage that contained difficult vocabulary words, while others received a passage where easier synonyms were substituted. The following example is a portion of the passage with the difficult words in italics and the easier synonyms in parentheses:

> Joe and Ann went to school in Portland. They were *antagonists* (enemies). They saw each other often. They had lots of *altercations* (fights). At the end of high school, Ann *maligned* (said bad things about) Joe. Then Ann moved away. Joe stayed in Portland. He got a job as a *bailiff* (worked for a judge). One day Joe was working, and he saw Ann. Ann did not see Joe. Ann looked *apprehensive* (afraid). She was being *incarcerated* (under arrest).

The test included literal questions such as:

Joe and Ann saw each other ______________ in school.
(a) never
(b) not much
(c) frequently
(d) often

In addition, the test included inference questions such as:

Joe works in a ______________.
(a) school
(b) hospital
(c) courthouse
(d) university

Figure 2–13 shows the percentage of correct answers given by students reading the difficult and easy vocabulary versions of the passage on literal and inferential questions. Those

FIGURE 2–13 Percentage correct on literal and inferential questions for three vocabulary treatment groups

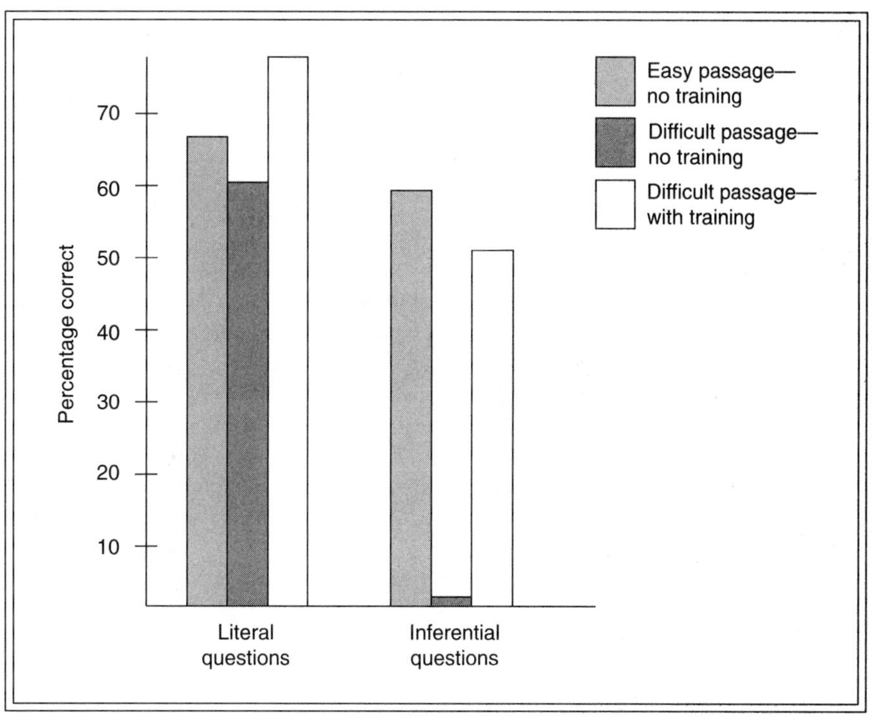

Adapted from Kameenui, Carnine, and Freschi (1982)

who read the easy version performed slightly better on literal questions and much better on inference questions. Apparently, a reader who understands the words has more opportunity to make meaningful inferences about the story.

The most interesting aspect of the study, however, involved an attempt to train some readers in the meanings of the six difficult vocabulary words before they read the passage. The training involved extensive discussions about each word, such as the following dialogue for altercations.

The experimenter placed an index card containing one vocabulary word and its meaning on the desk in front of the subject.

EXPERIMENTER: This word is "altercations." What word is this?

CHILD: "Altercations."

EXPERIMENTER: Correct, "altercations." What does "altercations" mean? [The experimenter points to the meaning given on card.]

CHILD: "Fights."

EXPERIMENTER: Yes, "altercations" means "fights." Listen, do you have altercations with your teacher? [Child responds.] Do you have altercations with a tree? [Child responds.] So what does "altercations" mean?

CHILD: "Fights."

The new vocabulary word is then integrated with the next one. For example, after the experimenter has gone through the same process for "antagonists," the experimenter asks: "Listen, do you have any antagonists? [Child responds.] Do you have any altercations with your antagonists? [Child responds.]"

Does vocabulary training improve reading comprehension? As Figure 2–13 indicates, students who were given vocabulary training before reading the difficult vocabulary version of the passage tended to excel in answering both literal and inference questions. You should note, however, that the training was for words that were specifically required for the passage and that the training forced the reader to connect the vocabulary words with the reader's prior knowledge and experience.

Beck and her colleagues (Beck, Perfetti, & McKeown, 1982; McKeown, Beck, Omanson, & Perfetti, 1983) also developed techniques for helping readers to embed words within their own experiences. Their extensive vocabulary training was successful in increasing readers' comprehension of texts that contain the just-learned words. Again, success seems to be tied to knowledge-based training and tests that involve the specifically taught words (Stahl & Fairbanks, 1986).

Overall, research on vocabulary training shows that certain forms of direct instruction can be effective in improving students' vocabularies but that immersion is essential to foster the amount of vocabulary growth that students need. Thus, instead of asking which approach is best, it makes more sense to craft a program of vocabulary instruction that builds on the best features of both approaches.

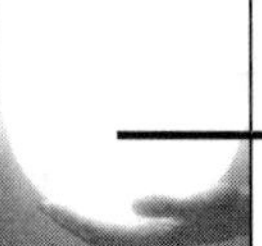

SENTENCE INTEGRATION

WHAT IS SENTENCE INTEGRATION?

The previous sections show that reading a word involves knowing the sounds that form words, knowing how printed words are related to sounds, and knowing the meanings of words. However, reading a text also involves fitting the words together into a coherent sentence structure. This process can be called *integrating sentences* or *sentence integration,* and one way of investigating this process is to observe readers' eyes as they read a passage.

RESEARCH ON SENTENCE INTEGRATION

EYE MOVEMENTS DURING READING Let me ask you to consider what your eyes are doing as you read the words in this paragraph. Does reading seem to involve a smooth and continuous flow of information from the page into your eyes? Does it seem that your eyes move smoothly across the page, taking in information that is analyzed by your brain? If so, your description corresponds to what has been called a "buffer model" of reading—the idea that your eyes smoothly scan each line from left to right, placing information into a short-term buffer so that it can be continuously analyzed.

Although this description of reading may be consistent with the commonsense experiences of skilled readers, it has been subjected to rigorous experimental tests by researchers.

One technique that can provide some information is to observe a reader's eye movements during reading. In the late 1800s, researchers discovered that readers' eyes tend to move in discontinuous jumps rather than in a smooth, continuous flow. You can confirm this observation by carefully watching someone's eyes as the person reads from a book or computer screen.

Research conducted during the last 20 years (Crowder & Wagner, 1992; Rayner & Pollatsek, 1989; Rayner & Sereno, 1994; Reichle, Pollatsek, Fisher & Rayner, 1998) provides clear and consistent evidence of the following aspects of eye movements during reading:

Fixation duration: A reader's eyes typically focus on a point in the text for an average of 200 to 250 milliseconds.

Fixation span: The fixation span of an eye focused on text is about six to eight letters. When the eyes are fixated on some point in the text, the center of the reader's field of vision (which is used for word identification) extends about seven letter positions to the right of this point. Thus, in normal reading a person can identify one medium-sized word or perhaps two short words in a single fixation. In addition, a reader may have some reduced acuity for about four letter positions to the left and up to fifteen letter positions to the right of the fixation point on the line of text being read. Although some useful information can be extracted to help guide the reading process, this additional information is not used for word identification.

Saccade duration: The eyes rapidly jump to another point in the text, with the jump (or saccade) lasting about 15 to 30 milliseconds; no information can be acquired during the jump. Most of the time, readers move to the next important word in the text, but about 10% to 15% of eye movements are *regressions* (or *regressive saccades*) in which readers look back to reread part of the text.

Saccade length: For readers of English, the eyes move from left to right across the page (or return to the beginning of the next lower line) at a rate averaging eight letter positions (or about one and a half words) per move.

The fact that the eyes move in a pattern of fixations and saccades tends to conflict with readers' reports that the information seems to flow smoothly. This experience of smooth processing might result if the eyes moved at a regular rate (i.e., if all fixations averaged about the same time) and at a regular distance (i.e., if all saccade lengths averaged about the same number of spaces). However, many researchers (Crowder & Wagner, 1992; McConkie, 1976; Rayner & Sereno, 1994) have documented that there is great variance within a reader in both the duration of the fixation (ranging from less than 100 milliseconds for simple words to more than 1 second for words at the ends of sentences) and saccade length (ranging from one to fifteen letters, depending on the shape of surrounding words). Thus readers do not sweep their eyes across the page at regular intervals and for regular distances; instead, eye movements seem to be controlled partially by the text.

HOW MUCH IS SEEN IN ONE FIXATION? How can the text control the eye fixations and movements until the reader knows what he or she is reading? In other words, how can you know where to move your eyes until you have looked to see what is ahead? To investigate this question, McConkie and Rayner (1975) asked high school students to read a passage on a computer screen. The computer determined where the reader was fixating on the screen; the computer did not alter the area around the fixation point (called the "window"), but did alter the rest of the text.

On each fixation, the size of the window was 13, 17, 21, 25, 31, 37, 45, or 100 letter positions, so that if a person was reading the line shown in Figure 2–14 with a window of 17 letters, all the letters would be correct for the 8 letter positions before and the 8 after the fixation point. However, beyond this window, each word would be changed to random letters. For some readers, the spaces between words were filled with other letters, whereas for other readers the spaces were retained. (Figure 2–14 shows examples for fixation on "d" in "diagnosis.")

Figure 2–15 shows the median saccade length and average reading time for each window size. As you can see, when the window is artificially restricted, the saccade length drops from about eight letter spaces to six letter spaces, and the reading rate falls. In addition, filling spaces between words with letters also tended to reduce the saccade length, with window sizes up to 25. In a subsequent study, Rayner, Well, and Pollatsek (1980) found that readers are affected only by the size of the window to the right of the fixation point; for example, similar results are obtained for a window of eight letters on either side of the fixation point and for one of eight letters to the right of the fixation point only. These findings suggest that readers focus on about six to eight letters at a time and can look ahead approximately fifteen letters to determine the appropriate length of the next saccade.

WHERE DO READERS' EYES FIXATE? As another example of eye movement research, consider the passage shown in Figure 2–16. Carpenter and Just (1981) asked a college student to read this passage while a computer monitored where and how long the reader's eyes fixated on the text. In Figure 2–16, numbers are given above places in the line on which the eyes fixated; the numbers in parentheses indicate the order of fixations, and the numbers below them indicate the length of the fixations in milliseconds.

What do Carpenter and Just's observations tell us about the reading process? First, the results demonstrate that fixation points are neither randomly nor evenly selected. For example, almost all content words are fixated, while blank spaces between sentences are not heavily fixated. There is also great variability in the length of the jumps from one fixation point to the next, with some saccades spanning just three letters (such as from the 12th to the 13th fixation) and others spanning about 10 letters (such as from the 21st to the 22nd fixation).

FIGURE 2–14

Examples of the reading task used by McConkie and Rayner

ORIGINAL TEXT

Graphology means personality diagnosis from handwriting. This is a

WINDOW SIZE OF 17 WITH PERIPHERAL TEXT FILLED

Hbfxwysyvoctifdlexiblonality diagnosiscabytewfdnehbemedveee clfw

WINDOW SIZE OF 17 WITH PERIPHERAL TEXT SPACED

Hbfxwysyvo tifdl xiblonality diagnosis abyt wfdn hbemedv. Awcl el f

Adapted from McConkie and Rayner (1975)

FIGURE 2–15 Median length of forward saccades and median reading rates for eight windows

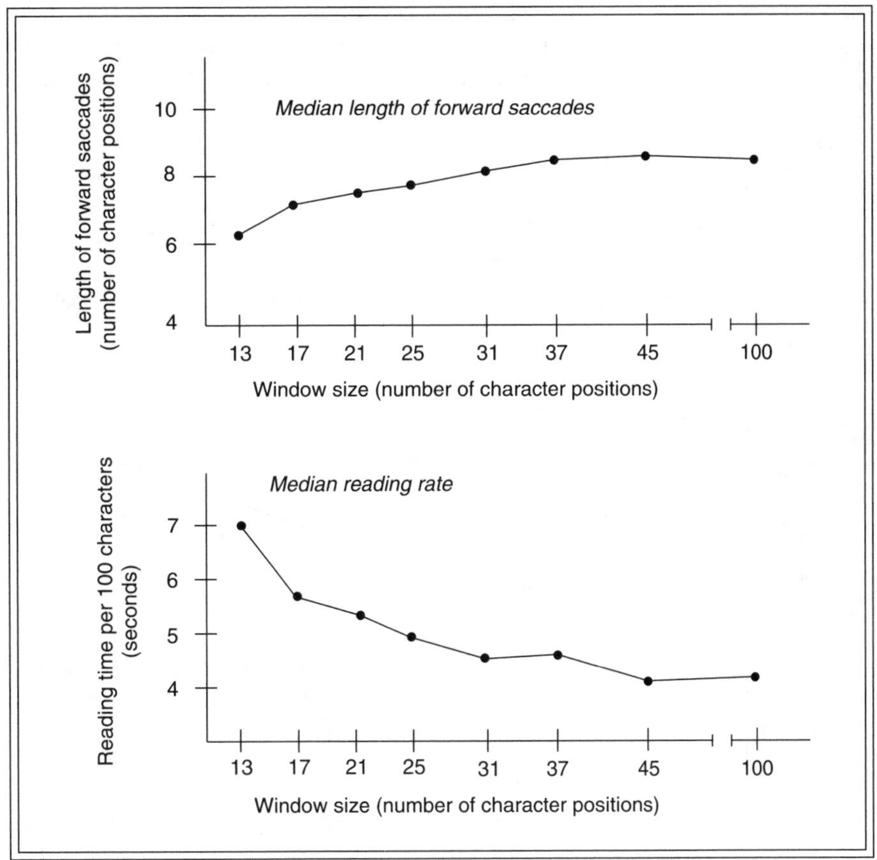

Adapted from McConkie and Rayner (1975)

Second, the findings show that each fixation is not treated equally. For example, the duration of fixations varies greatly with a range from 100 to 683 milliseconds. Unfamiliar words, such as "radioisotopes" and "icons," are fixated for much more time than familiar words. Similarly, other researchers have found that reading a uncommon word, such as "steward," takes an average of 30 to 90 millseconds longer than reading a common word, such as "student," even when both are placed within otherwise identical sentences (Rayner & Duffy, 1986; Rayner & Raney, 1996). These results are inconsistent with the buffer theory (i.e., the idea that the eye moves at a relatively constant rate, taking in information that is analyzed later). Instead, these results suggest that eye movements are guided, in part, by the difficulty of the text.

When readers come to an unfamiliar word, they spend more time looking at it than when they come to a familiar word (Rayner & Raney, 1996). When students come to an unpredictable word based on its context in the sentence, they spend more time on it than

FIGURE 2–16

A reader's eye fixations while reading a passage on radioisotopes

The sequence of fixations within each sentence is indicated by the successively numbered fixations above the word being fixated. The duration of each fixation (in milliseconds) is shown immediately below the fixation number.

(4) (11)
286 466
(1) (2) (3) (5) (6) (7) (8) (9)
166 200 167 299 217 268 317 399
Radioisotopes have long been valuable tools in scientific and medical

(16)
183
(10) (12) (13) (14)(15) (17) (18) (19)(20)
463 317 250 367 416 333 183 450 650
research. Now, however, four nonradioactive isotopes are being produced.

(24) (28)
366 183
(21) (22) (23) (25) (26) (27) (29) (30) (31) (32) (33)
250 200 367 400 216 233 317 283 100 683 150
They are called "icons"—four isotopes of carbon, oxygen, nitrogen, and sulfur.

From Carpenter and Just (1981)

when they come to a predictable word (Rayner, Binder, Ashby, & Pollatsek, 2001). Why? According to Reichle, Pollatsek, Fisher, and Rayner (1998), students seek to understand the meaning of each sentence by looking up the meaning of key words in long-term memory and by forming a structure for the sentence. Thus, by examining the time that readers devote to fixating on each word (i.e., fixation duration), we can gauge the reader's mental effort in making sense of the printed text. Eye movement research provides evidence that reading is a sense-making activity in which reading a word includes figuring out its meaning and place within the sentence.

A third major discovery is that readers seem to be thinking about what they read during the reading process. For example, in Figure 2–16 fixation durations are generally much longer at the end of a sentence, such as for "medical research" in the first sentence and "being produced" in the second. This result suggests that readers may be trying to integrate the information at sentence or major clause boundaries. Since the fixation seems to be much longer than is required to perceive the word, the long fixations at sentence (and clause) boundaries imply that additional cognitive processing is occurring. Carpenter and Just (1981) called this activity *sentence wrap-up*, and suggest that it includes searching for referents, building relations among clauses, drawing inferences, and resolving inconsistencies.

Just and Carpenter (1978) provided an example of how eye fixations may be related to readers' integration of information. In their study, subjects read two-sentence passages. One text was as follows:

> It was dark and stormy the night the millionaire was murdered.
> The killer left no clues for the police to trace.

Other readers received a slightly different passage:

> It was dark and stormy the night the millionaire died.
> The killer left no clues for the police to trace.

As you can see, the noun "killer" in the second sentence is the agent for the verb "murdered" or "died" in the first sentence. In reading the second sentence, the reader must make the inference that the killer is responsible for the death of the millionaire. Just and Carpenter found that readers paused an average of 500 milliseconds longer for the second sentence in the second passage than in the first. The two main places that required extended fixation times were the word "killer" and the word "trace" at the end of the sentence.

As another example of how readers adjust their reading rates to meet the demands of the text, consider the following two sentences:

> Al is a doctor.
> Bill is a doctor, too.

In this case, the two sentences are somewhat independent, so that the information in the first sentence is not needed to help you make sense of the second. However, now read the following two sentences:

> Al is a surgeon.
> Bill is a doctor, too.

To comprehend the second sentence, you need to make a logical inference based on your knowledge that all surgeons are doctors; namely, you need to infer that Al is a doctor. Singer, Revlin, and Halldorson (1990) found that the time needed to read the second sentence was about 500 milliseconds greater when such an inference was required than when no inference was required. These results show that the reader's integration of information can be observed through careful observation of eye fixations and reading times.

IMPLICATIONS FOR INSTRUCTION: SPEED READING

Suppose we ask some 12-year-olds to silently read a text. What determines their reading speeds? That is, what do faster readers do better than slower readers? A recent study (Sovik, Arntzen, & Samuelstuen, 2000) pinpointed three factors: (1) faster readers spend less time on each fixation (i.e., fixation duration); (2) faster readers take in more letters on each fixation (i.e., fixation span); and (3) faster readers look back to previous words less often (i.e., regressive saccades).

The research described in this section has implications for speed reading programs, which generally attempt to teach students how to increase their fixation span (i.e., how many letters they see in one fixation), to decrease their fixation duration (i.e., how long their eyes remain fixated), and to decrease the number of regressions (i.e., how many times they look back to an earlier word). Many speed reading programs claim to be able to increase a person's reading speed without decreasing comprehension. Crowder and Wagner (1992) observed that the following techniques are often used to accomplish these goals:

1. The student is taught to eliminate subvocal speech so that less time is spent on each fixation.
2. The student is encouraged to chunk words visually into meaningful units so that more information can be processed during each fixation.
3. The student is taught to use the index finger as a guide that moves down the page so that fewer fixations will be made.
4. The student is taught to read more actively by making inferences during reading.

How does eye movement research square with these practices and claims? Unfortunately, the research on eye movements would lead us to be cautious in accepting the claims of speed reading advocates. First, the foregoing research shows that pauses in reading (e.g., long fixations at the end of phrases or sentences) may be related to the reader's integration of the information in the phrase or sentence. Thus teaching students to reduce their fixation time could disrupt the integration process. Second, the research also shows that a reader can usually take in only one or two words per fixation, so increasing the saccade length (or decreasing the number of fixations) means that some words may never be seen.

How fast can the visual system work? According to research on eye movements, humans can clearly see no more than two words per fixation and can fixate no more than four times per second, yielding a maximum possible reading rate of about 480 words per minute (wpm). In an admittedly generous analysis, Crowder and Wagner (1992) set the upper limit at 900 wpm by estimating that readers have access to three words per fixation and can fixate five times per second. Thus, there are physiological constraints on the reading rate with estimates ranging from 480 to 900 wpm. Interestingly, the average reading rate for college students falls well within even the lower of these estimates, at about 300 wpm (Crowder & Wagner, 1992).

Can some people read much faster than 900 wpm? To answer this question, Carver (1985) carefully tested exceptionally fast readers, such as graduates of speed reading programs who were touted as having reading rates above 20,000 wpm. In addition, Carver tested college students who performed at the top of the class on reading tests and students who earned perfect scores on the reading sections of the Scholastic Aptitude Test. After three days of well-controlled testing, the results were in: Average rates ranged from 250 to 450 wpm, corresponding to the estimates based on eye movement research.

Can people learn to read faster than 900 wpm? To evaluate the effectiveness of a typical speed reading program, consider the following scenario. A school district decides to hire a speed reading company to improve students' reading rates. The company agrees to provide approximately 50 hours of instruction and practice, and guarantees that at least 75% of the students will quintuple their reading rates and increase their comprehension by 10%. Do you think the program will succeed? A program just like the one described was carried out in a school district in southern California (Crowder, 1982). Students were given reading speed and comprehension tests before and after instruction. The average reading rate rose from 155 wpm before instruction to 657 wpm after instruction, while comprehension scores fell slightly from 35 to 33% correct.

Should you be happy with these results? Crowder (1982) pointed out that the company failed to reach its goal, since only 13% of the students quintupled their reading rates and increased their comprehension by 10%. In addition, Crowder noted that the program contained no comparison group, so we do not know how much improvement would have occurred over the course of the year if students had not received speed reading instruction. In fact, most standardized tests show that students gain in comprehension each year. Finally, Crowder stated that the reading speed test given after training was easier than the test given before training; thus any gains claimed by the speed reading company cannot be accepted as valid.

In summary, this example shows why you should critically examine any claims about speed reading. The good news is that adults with low reading rates (e.g., 100 to 200 wpm) may be able to increase their rates (e.g., closer to the average of 300 wpm for college students) without losing comprehension. The bad news is that readers are unlikely to be able to increase their reading rates beyond 900 wpm without serious losses in comprehension. For example, Carver (1971) showed that speed reading courses that teach people to move their eyes faster often do not help people to comprehend more text. Apparently, readers need some pauses to make inferences, access meanings of unusual words, and integrate the information into a coherent message. The positive features of speed reading training are that students may learn how to skim material effectively, and some students may become more automatic in their decoding skills. The negative features are that when the rate of reading is pushed beyond the physical limits of how fast the eye can move, the reader is forced to skip some material and to spend less time integrating the material, which results in less comprehension.

CHAPTER SUMMARY

A great deal of cognitive processing occurs during the quarter of a second that a reader's eye looks at a word on the printed page. This chapter explored four related processes: recognizing phonemes, decoding words, accessing word meaning, and integrating sentences.

Research on reading is notable for several reasons. First, it represents an old area in psychology that is currently experiencing a welcome revival. Second, an extremely large and rapidly growing body of literature addresses reading. Third, there are many different approaches to the study of reading, ranging from pronunciation tasks to eye movement tasks, and many different theoretical approaches.

Basic research on phonological awareness shows that students need to be able to segment a spoken language into its sound units. Phonological awareness appears to be a readiness skill for reading, so some students who have not acquired it by the primary grades may benefit from direct instruction in how to recognize phonemes.

Some of the basic findings concerning decoding have implications for the decision about whether to use a whole-word or phonics approach in reading instruction. First, there is an automaticity effect in which skilled learners can perform a task without paying attention to what they are doing. Second, there is a word superiority effect in which skilled readers can recognize letters in words more easily than individual letters. Third, skilled readers possess and use pronunciation strategies for combining letters or letter groups into words. The research suggests that skilled readers have automated the processes involved in word decoding, including the use of word context to identify letter sounds and of pronunciation strategies to combine letters. As children's decoding processes become more automatic, they have more attentional capacity to use for comprehending the material. The current consensus of reading researchers is that the best way to help children acquire automatic decoding processes is to rely on the phonics approach.

Some of the research findings concerning meaning access have implications for vocabulary training. Beginning or younger readers tend to rely on the context of the other words in a sentence to recognize the meaning of a word; in contrast, older or more skilled readers are able to access word meaning directly. In order to help children become more automatic in their use of sentence context and in understanding unusual words, students can benefit from vocabulary training. Other forms of vocabulary training include encouraging children to engage in silent sustained reading regularly and providing an environment where children hear spoken language. The ultimate goal of such instruction is to help students automate their meaning accessing processes, so that more attention can be devoted to sentence integration and other comprehension processes.

Some of the research findings concerning sentence integration have implications for speed reading training. First, reading involves eye movements, with each fixation requiring a certain amount of time, during which the reader can take in only a small amount of text. Second, long fixations (or pauses) often occur at the end of a phrase or sentence, suggesting that the reader needs time to integrate the material. Speed reading programs that reduce the fixation time may also reduce the time for integration; similarly, speed reading programs that reduce the number of fixations per page may reduce the amount of information that a reader takes in. Thus while speed reading training may help students learn how to skim, it may also result in poorer comprehension.

In summary, the implications of psychological research on reading are still far from complete; however, based on the current state of our understanding, instruction in reading should: (1) insure that beginning readers possess phonological awareness; (2) emphasize phonics for beginning readers as well as meaning approaches for developing readers; (3) develop automatic word reading skills through practice; and (4) promote increased reading speed only when a reader does not lose comprehension or when skimming is the goal of reading.

SUGGESTED READINGS

Adams, M. J. (1990). *Beginning to read.* Cambridge, MA: MIT Press. (An award-winning review of research on reading and its relevance to reading instruction.)

Crowder, R. G., & Wagner, R. K. (1992). *The psychology of reading: An introduction* (2nd ed). New York: Oxford University Press. (An excellent textbook that summarizes psychological research on the reading process.)

Oakhill, J. & Beard, R. (Eds.). (1999). *Reading development and the teaching of reading: A psychological perspective.* Oxford, UK: Blackwell. (A useful collection of papers by leading researchers in reading.)

Osborn, J. & Lehr, F. (Eds.). (1998). *Literacy for all: Issues in teaching and learning.* New York: Guilford. (A useful collection of papers by leading researchers in reading.)

Snow, C., Burns, M., & Griffin, P. (Eds.). (1998). *Preventing reading difficulties in young children.* Washington, DC: National Academy Press. (A research-based analysis of how to help children learn to read.)

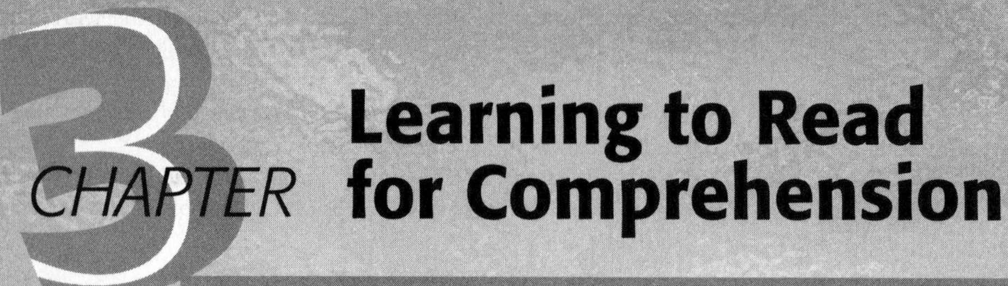

CHAPTER 3 Learning to Read for Comprehension

CHAPTER OUTLINE

Effort After Meaning

Schema Theory

Using Prior Knowledge

Using Prose Structure

Making Inferences

Using Metacognitive Knowledge

Building a Reading Comprehension Program That Works

Chapter Summary

This chapter examines techniques for improving students' comprehension of text. Four kinds of cognitive processing needed for effective reading comprehension are using prior knowledge to relate to the new material, using prose structure to determine important information, making inferences during reading, and monitoring whether one comprehends the material. In particular, this chapter investigates the reading comprehension processes of skilled readers and the degree to which these processes can be taught. Finally, it examines reading programs that attempt to teach one or more of these kinds of knowledge.

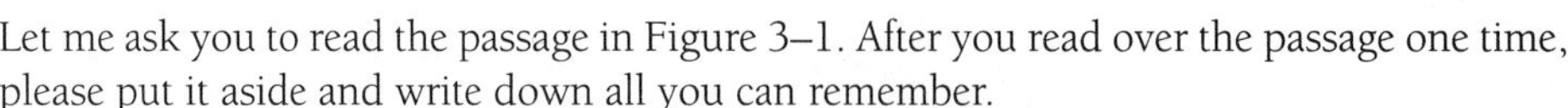

EFFORT AFTER MEANING

Let me ask you to read the passage in Figure 3–1. After you read over the passage one time, please put it aside and write down all you can remember.

This passage was used by Bartlett (1932) in his famous research on how people learn and remember meaningful prose. Bartlett asked British college students to read a folk story from a North American Indian culture, so his readers did not have much prior experience with the ideas in the passage. In Bartlett's study, first one person read the passage twice and then 15 minutes later wrote down all he could remember; the version that the first person had written was then read by a second person, who wrote down all he could remember;

FIGURE 3–1

Original version of "The War of the Ghosts"

THE WAR OF THE GHOSTS

One night two young men from Egulac went down to the river to hunt seals, and while they were there it became foggy and calm. Then they heard war-cries, and they thought: "Maybe this is a war-party." They escaped to the shore, and hid behind a log. Now canoes came up, and they heard the noise of paddles, and they saw one canoe coming up to them. There were five men in the canoe, and they said:

"What do you think? We wish to take you along. We are going up the river to make war on the people."

One of the young men said: "I have no arrows."

"Arrows are in the canoe," they said.

"I will not go along. I might be killed. My relatives do not know where I have gone. But you," he said, turning to the other, "may go with them."

So one of the young men went, but the other returned home.

And the warriors went on up the river to a town on the other side of Kalama. The people came down to the water, and they began to fight, and many were killed. But presently the young man heard one of the warriors say: "Quick, let us go home, that Indian has been hit." Now he thought: "Oh, they are ghosts." He did not feel sick, but they said he had been shot.

So the canoes went back to Egulac, and the young man went ashore to his house, and made a fire. And he told everybody and said: "Behold I accompanied the ghosts, and we went to fight. Many of our fellows were killed, and many of those who attacked us were killed. They said I was hit, and I did not feel sick."

He told it all, and then he became quiet. When the sun rose he fell down. Something black came out of his mouth. His face became contorted. The people jumped up and cried.

He was dead.

From Bartlett (1932)

this version was in turn passed on to the next person; and so on. By the time the story was read and recalled by the last person, it had changed greatly, as shown in Figure 3–2. If you are like the subjects in Bartlett's study, here are some of the changes you made in your recall:

Leveling or flattening: You left out many of the details, such as proper names (e.g., Egulac, Kalama). You lost the verbatim writing style of the writer and instead remembered the general points or gist of parts of the story.

Sharpening: You emphasized a few distinctive details, such as the fact that one Indian was not able to go to fight because he had an old mother at home.

Rationalization: You made the passage more compact, more coherent, and more consistent with your expectations. For example, if you viewed the passage as a story about a fishing trip or a naval battle, you would be less likely to remember references to spirits and ghosts.

As you can see, the main point of this demonstration is that people's memories do not work like computers' memories. We do not tend to remember information in verbatim form. We remember some things, but not necessarily in the form they were presented. We

FIGURE 3–2

What readers remember from "The War of the Ghosts"

VERSION REPRODUCED BY THE FIRST SUBJECT

THE WAR OF THE GHOSTS

There were two young Indians who lived in Egulac, and they went down to the sea to hunt for seals. And where they were hunting it was very foggy and very calm. In a little while they heard cries, and they came out of the water and went to hide behind a log. Then they heard the sound of paddles, and they saw five canoes. One canoe came toward them, and there were five men within, who cried to the two Indians, and said: "Come with us up this river, and make war on the people there."

But one of the Indians replied: "We have no arrows."

"There are arrows in the canoe."

"But I might be killed, and my people have need of me. You have no parents," he said to the other, "you can go with them if you wish it so; I shall stay here."

So one of the Indians went, but the other stayed behind and went home. And the canoes went on up the river to the other side of Kalama, and fought the people there. Many of the people were killed, and many of those from the canoes also.

Then one of the warriors called to the young Indian and said: "Go back to the canoe, for you are wounded by an arrow." But the Indian wondered, for he felt not sick.

And when many had fallen on either side they went back to the canoes, and down the river again, and so the young Indian came back to Egulac.

Then he told them how there had been a battle, and how many fell and how the warriors had said he was wounded, and yet he felt not sick. So he told them all the

(continued)

FIGURE 3–2

(continued)

tale, and he became weak. It was near daybreak when he became weak; and when the sun rose he fell down. And he gave a cry, and as he opened his mouth a black thing rushed from it. Then they ran to pick him up, wondering. But when they spoke he answered not.

He was dead.

VERSION REPRODUCED BY THE TENTH SUBJECT

THE WAR OF THE GHOSTS

Two Indians were out fishing for seals in the Bay of Manpapan, when along came five other Indians in a war-canoe. They were going fighting.

"Come with us," said the five to the two, "and fight."

"I cannot come," was the answer of the one, "for I have an old mother at home who is dependent upon me." The other said he could not come, because he had no arms. "That is no difficulty," the others replied, "for we have plenty in the canoe with us"; so he got into the canoe and went with them.

In a fight soon afterwards this Indian received a mortal wound. Finding that his hour was coming, he cried out that he was about to die. "Nonsense," said one of the others, "you will not die." But he did.

From Bartlett (1932)

often add other elements that were not given as we try to organize our memories in a way that makes sense.

According to Bartlett, when we read a meaningful prose passage we are not passively putting the information into our minds; instead, we are actively trying to understand the passage. Bartlett referred to this active comprehension process as "effort after meaning." In reading a text, humans must assimilate the new information to existing knowledge—or to what Bartlett called "schemas." What a person learns from reading a text does not correspond directly to what is presented, but rather to a combination of what is presented and the reader's schema to which it is assimilated. The reader changes the new information to fit his or her existing concepts, and in the process, details are lost and the knowledge becomes more coherent for that person. For "The War of the Ghosts" passage, for example, most readers lacked the appropriate schema concerning a spirit world. Since learning involves assimilating new material to existing concepts, the readers were at a loss. According to Bartlett (1932), "without some general setting or label as we have repeatedly seen, no material can be assimilated or remembered" (p. 172). Because mystical concepts were not a major factor in the readers' culture, these aspects of the story were not well remembered; as a result, the passage was changed into a more common "war story."

Bartlett also proposed that recalling a story involves an active "process of construction" rather than straightforward retrieval. During recall, we use a general schema—such as a war story—to help generate details that fit with it. Memory is not detailed but rather is schematic, that is, based on general impressions. Although recall produces specific details that seem to be correct, many are, in fact, wrong.

Bartlett's work, although done more than 70 years ago, is concerned with many of the same issues raised by modern cognitive psychologists. Of particular interest is Bartlett's view of the reader as actively engaged in an "effort after meaning," that is, in an effort to make sense out of the text by relating it to his or her existing knowledge.

SCHEMA THEORY

WHAT IS A SCHEMA?

Bartlett was one of the first psychologists to address the question of how people learn from meaningful prose. Bartlett's main theoretical concept was the *schema*—a person's existing knowledge that is used both to assimilate new information and to generate recall of information. For example, in reading "The War of the Ghosts," you must construct an appropriate schema (such as a war story), assimilate facts from the passage to the schema (such as being mortally wounded), and then use the schema to construct a recalled version that includes inferences consistent with the theme.

What is a schema? In a sense, answering this question is a major goal of modern cognitive psychology. Although each theorist offers a slightly different interpretation of what a schema is, a general definition would contain the following points (Mayer, 1992):

General: A schema may be used in a wide variety of situations as a framework for understanding incoming information.
Knowledge: A schema exists in memory as something that a person knows.
Structure: A schema is organized around a theme.
Comprehension: A schema contains "slots" that are filled by specific information in the text.

Thus a schema is a reader's general knowledge structure that serves to select and organize incoming information into an integrated, meaningful framework.

SCHEMAS FOR NARRATIVE PROSE Several authors have proposed story *grammars* that readers might use to understand narrative prose, that is, text that tells a story (Mandler & Johnson, 1977; Rumelhart, 1975; Thorndyke, 1977). For example, Mandler and Johnson (1977) suggested that most folk stories can be divided into two main parts: *story* = *setting* + *episode(s)*. An episode in turn can be split into two parts: *episode* = *beginning* + *development*. The development of an episode contains two parts: *development* = *response* + *ending*. A response can consist of two simple parts: *response* = *simple reaction* + *action*, or it can be more complex: *response* = *complex reaction* + *goal path*. A goal path is composed of two parts: *goal path* = *attempt* + *outcome*. Figure 3–3 shows how "The War of the Ghosts" can be broken into a setting and five episodes according to Mandler and

FIGURE 3–3

Analysis of "The War of the Ghosts" using story grammar

Setting	1	One night two young men from Egulac went down to the river to hunt seals,
	2	and while they were there it became foggy and calm.
		Episode 1
Beginning	3	Then they heard war-cries,
Complex reaction	4	and they thought: "Maybe this is a war-party."
Attempt	5	They escaped to the shore,
	6	and hid behind a log.
	7	Now canoes came up,
Ending	8	and they heard the noise of paddles,
	9	and then saw one canoe coming up to them.
		Episode 2
Setting	10	There were five men in the canoe,
Beginning	11	and they said: "What do you think? We wish to take you along.
	12	We are going up the river to make war on the people."
Attempt	13	One of the young men said: "I have no arrows."
Outcome	14	"Arrows are in the canoe," they said.
	15	"I will not go along.
Attempt	16	I might be killed.
	17	My relatives do not know where I have gone.
	18	But you," he said, turning to the other, "may go with them."
Outcome	19	So one of the young men went,
	20	but the other returned home.
Ending	21	And the warriors went on up the river to a town on the other side of Kalama.
		Episode 3
Beginning	22	The people came down to the water,
	23	and they began to fight,
	24	and many were killed.
	25	But presently the young man heard one of the warriors say: "Quick, let us go home; that Indian has been hit."

(continued)

FIGURE 3–3

(continued)

Simple reaction	26	Now he thought: "Oh, they are ghosts."
	27	He did not feel sick,
Action	28	but they said he had been shot.
Ending	29	So the canoes went back to Egulac,
		Episode 4
Beginning	30	and the young man went ashore to his house, and made a fire.
	31	And he told everybody and said: "Behold I accompanied the ghosts, and we went to fight.
	32	Many of our fellows were killed,
Action	33	and many of those who attacked us were killed.
	34	They said I was hit,
	35	and I did not feel sick."
	36	He told it all,
Ending	37	and then he became quiet.
		Episode 5
Beginning	38	When the sun rose he fell down.
	39	Something black came out of his mouth.
	40	His face became contorted.
Action	41	The people jumped up and cried.
Ending	42	He was dead.

From Mandler and Johnson (1977)

Johnson's story grammar. Episode 1 is followed by Episode 2, which is followed by Episode 5; Episodes 3 and 4 are subepisodes connected to Episode 2. Within each episode, a beginning event is usually followed by some reaction that results in an outcome or ending.

When a reader is given a story to read or listen to, the reader will have expectations that the story will have a structure, such as is indicated in Mandler and Johnson's story grammar. For example, readers expect episodes in which some beginning event is followed by attempts to respond to it that result in an ending. Graesser (1981), Gernsbacher (1990), and others point out that younger readers often lack appropriate schemas to understand prose. For example, Whaley (1981) found that third-graders are far less able than sixth-graders to predict what will come next in a story. Presumably, younger readers are not as aware of story grammars as older readers. Thus learning to read involves learning to fill in each general part of the structure (such as the beginning, action, and ending of each episode) with specifics from the story.

WHAT SKILLS ARE NEEDED FOR READING COMPREHENSION?

This chapter is concerned with the process of reading comprehension and in particular with understanding the skills that underlie a reader's "effort after meaning." What are these skills? In a review of five major basal reading series, Rosenshine (1980) found that all emphasized the following eight skills: (1) locating details, (2) identifying the main idea, (3) recognizing the sequence of events, (4) developing conclusions, (5) recognizing cause-and-effect relationships, (6) understanding words in context, (7) making interpretations, and (8) drawing inferences from the text. However, Rosenshine found no evidence that all basal series taught these skills in the same order and sequence. Similarly, Pearson and Fielding (1991) noted that reading comprehension instruction often teaches students how to activate background knowledge, to use text structure, or to summarize text. Brown and Palinscar (1989; Palinscar & Brown, 1984) identified four major reading comprehension skills: (1) generating questions that are answered by the text, (2) identifying words that need to be clarified, (3) summarizing text, and (4) predicting what will come next in a text. Although these skills have long been part of reading comprehension programs taught to millions of students, we are just beginning to understand how these skills are related to the process of reading comprehension.

In this chapter, we explore three kinds of knowledge suggested by Brown, Campione, and Day (1981), which a reader might use in the process of "effort after meaning":

Content knowledge refers to information about the subject domain of the passage and is discussed in the section "Using Prior Knowledge."

Strategic knowledge refers to the reader's collection of procedures for learning more effectively. These procedures are discussed in the sections "Using Prose Structure" and "Making Inferences."

Metacognitive knowledge refers to the reader's awareness of her own cognitive processes and whether she is successfully meeting the demands of the task. These skills include comprehension monitoring, which is explored in the section "Using Metacognitive Knowledge."

In particular, we focus on the cognitive processes of using prior knowledge, using prose structure, making inferences, and using metacognitive knowledge.

USING PRIOR KNOWLEDGE

WHAT IS THE READER'S PERSPECTIVE?

One of the most persistent findings in the literature on adult prose learning is that people's prior knowledge about the topic of a passage influences what they remember from that passage. The reader's perspective includes the prior knowledge that the reader uses to understand the passage. What is remembered seems to depend both on what is presented in the passage and on what perspective the reader brings to the reading task.

RESEARCH ON DIFFERENCES IN READERS' PRIOR KNOWLEDGE

DIFFERENCES IN THE AMOUNT OF PRIOR KNOWLEDGE As an example of the role of prior knowledge, consider the passage shown in the top of Figure 3–4. Bransford and Johnson (1972) asked college students to read this passage, to rate its comprehensibility (1 is low and 7 is high), and to recall it. Some students were given a title ("Washing Clothes") for the passage before they read the passage, other students were given the title after they had read the passage, and still others were given no title at all. The table at the bottom of Figure 3–4 shows the performance of the three groups on the recall and comprehension rating tasks. The group that had the title before reading had a much higher comprehension score and recalled about twice as much as the other groups. Apparently, giving students the title of the passage allowed them to relate the new information to their prior knowledge about washing clothes; providing the title after reading or not at all left the reader without a way of meaningfully relating the new information to prior knowledge during reading.

Figure 3–5 presents another passage for you to read. Suppose I asked you to read the passage from the perspective of a potential home buyer. Alternatively, suppose I asked you to read it from the perspective of a burglar. Would what you remembered from the passage

FIGURE 3–4

The "Washing Clothes" passage

THE PASSAGE

The procedure is actually quite simple. First you arrange items into different groups. Of course one pile may be sufficient, depending on how much there is to do. If you have to go somewhere else due to lack of facilities, that is the next step; otherwise, you are pretty well set. It is important not to overdo things. That is, it is better to do too few things at once than too many. In the short run this may not seem important, but complications can easily arise. A mistake can be expensive as well. At first, the whole procedure will seem complicated. Soon, however, it will become just another facet of life. It is difficult to foresee any end to the necessity for this task in the immediate future, but then, one never can tell. After the procedure is completed, one arranges the materials into different groups again. Then they can be put into their appropriate places. Eventually they will be used once more, and the whole cycle will then have to be repeated. However, that is part of life.

COMPREHENSION AND RECALL SCORES FOR THE PASSAGE

	No Topic	*Topic After*	*Topic Before*	*Maximum Score*
Comprehension ratings	2.29	2.12	4.50	7.00
Number of idea units recalled	2.82	2.65	5.83	18.00

From Bransford and Johnson (1972)

FIGURE 3–5

"The House" passage

The two boys ran until they came to the driveway. "See, I told you today was good for skipping school," said Mark. "Mom is never home on Thursday," he added. Tall hedges hid the house from the road so the pair strolled across the finely landscaped yard. "I never knew your place was so big," said Pete. "Yeah, but it's nicer now than it used to be since Dad had the new stone siding put on and added the fireplace."

There were front and back doors and a side door which led to the garage, which was empty except for three parked 10-speed bikes. They went in the side door, Mark explaining that it was always open in case his younger sisters got home earlier than their mother.

Pete wanted to see the house, so Mark started with the living room. It, like the rest of the downstairs, was newly painted. Mark turned on the stereo, the noise of which worried Pete. "Don't worry, the nearest house is a quarter of a mile away," Mark shouted. Pete felt more comfortable observing that no houses could be seen in any direction beyond the huge yard.

The dining room, with all the china, silver, and cut glass, was no place to play so the boys moved into the kitchen, where they made sandwiches. Mark said they wouldn't go to the basement because it had been damp and musty ever since the new plumbing had been installed.

"This is where my Dad keeps his famous paintings and his coin collection," Mark said as they peered into the den. Mark bragged that he could get spending money whenever he needed it since he'd discovered that his Dad kept a lot in the desk drawer.

There were three upstairs bedrooms. Mark showed Pete his mother's closet, which was filled with furs, and the locked box which held her jewels. His sisters' room was uninteresting except for the color TV, which Mark carried to his room. Mark bragged that the bathroom in the hall was his since one had been added to his sisters' room for their use. The big highlight in his room, though, was a leak in the ceiling where the old roof had finally rotted.

From Pichert and Anderson (1977)

be influenced by your perspective—home buyer versus burglar—while reading the passage? Pichert and Anderson (1977) asked students to read the house passage from the perspective of a potential home buyer or burglar or with no perspective instructions. Students' recall of details from the passage was greatly influenced by their perspective while reading. For example, details such as where the father keeps the coin collection were better recalled by the students who had read with the burglar perspective. Again, these results show that what is learned from reading depends on both the passage and the reader's perspective.

Similar results have been obtained in studies using younger readers. Pearson, Hansen, and Gordon (1979) asked second-graders to read a modified basal passage on spiders. Although all of the children were classified as good readers based on their scores on standardized reading comprehension tests, half of the students knew a lot about spiders and half did not. After reading the spider passage, the children answered text-explicit questions that dealt with information specifically presented in the passage, such as, "What does Webby bite insects with?" and text-implicit questions that required inferences, such as "What part of Webby's body is nearly the same as part of a snake's body?" Figure 3–6 shows that the high-knowledge readers scored almost three times better than the low-knowledge readers on questions requiring inference and about 25% better on questions requiring retention of facts. These results are consistent with the idea that good reading skill is not the sole determinant of what is learned from reading a passage. In addition, the knowledge that the reader brings to the reading situation seems to influence heavily the reader's ability to make inferences about the material.

Marr and Gormley (1982) also found evidence that prior knowledge tends to enhance readers' inference-making performance more than simple retention of facts. Fourth-graders were asked to read either familiar or unfamiliar passages, and then asked to retell the story and to answer some questions. Examples are given in Figure 3–7. Responses were scored as "textual" if they referred to material in the text and as "scriptal" if they involved inferences. As you can see in Figure 3–7, the differences between the familiar and unfamiliar texts were not great for textual responses on the retelling and question-answering tasks; however, the familiar texts generated considerably more scriptal responses as compared to the unfamiliar text for both the retelling and question-answering tasks. Again, it appears that prior knowledge has its strongest effects on helping readers make useful inferences rather than on simply retaining facts.

DIFFERENCES IN THE KINDS OF PRIOR KNOWLEDGE In a better controlled study, Lipson (1983) varied the background knowledge of readers who were all given the same passages to read. The subjects were Jewish and Catholic students in grades four,

FIGURE 3–6 Effects of background knowledge on reading comprehension and retention

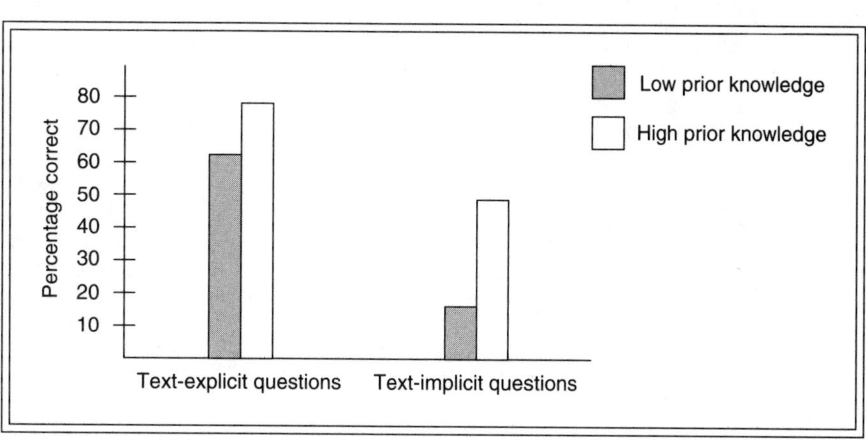

Adapted from Pearson, Hansen, and Gordon (1979)

FIGURE 3–7

Effects of familiar and unfamiliar passages on reading comprehension and retention

A FAMILIAR SPORTS PASSAGE

Baseball is a summer game. Usually it is played outdoors on a field. Baseball is a team sport that has nine players. A baseball has a rubber center that is covered with both string and leather. The pitcher winds up and throws the baseball to the batter. Then the batter tries to hit the ball out of the baseball field. A run is made each time a baseball batter hits the ball, runs all three bases, and touches home plate. A game is won by the team scoring the most runs. This game is an exciting sport.

AN UNFAMILIAR SPORTS PASSAGE

Curling is a winter game. Usually it is played indoors on the ice. Curling is a team sport that has four players. A curling stone is a round rock that has a handle on the top. The curler slides the stone down the ice toward colored circles. The team captain or skip stands at the end with these circles. A point is scored each time the curling stone is thrown, aimed toward the skip, and stops on a colored circle. A game is won by the team scoring the most points. This game is an unusual sport.

NUMBER OF TEXTUAL AND SCRIPTAL RESPONSES ON TWO TESTS

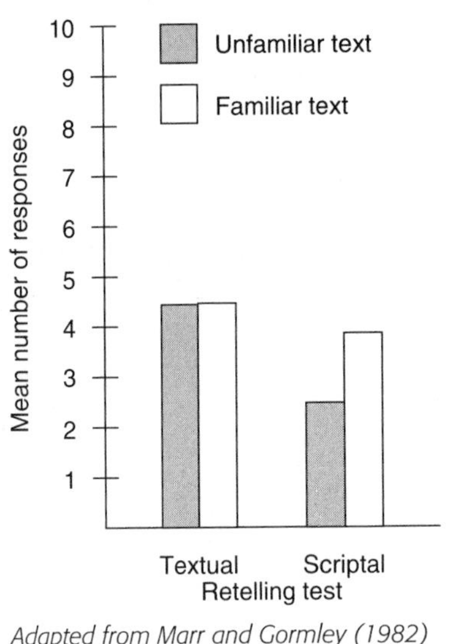

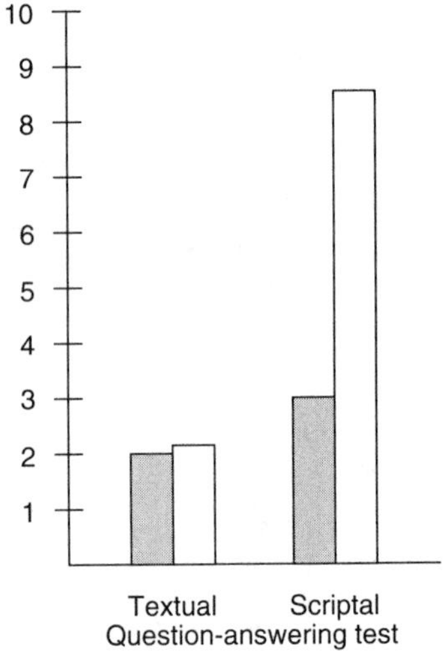

Adapted from Marr and Gormley (1982)

five, and six. All were classified as good readers, but they differed in their knowledge of Jewish and Catholic ceremonies. The passages included one entitled, "Bar Mitzvah" and one entitled, "First Communion." Students were asked to read and recall the material in the passages. As expected, the Jewish students read the Bar Mitzvah passage faster than the Catholic students, while the Catholic students read the First Communion passage faster than the Jewish students. Figure 3–8 summarizes the number of pieces of information correctly recalled (text-explicit recall), the number of correct inferences (inference recall), and the number of errors (error recall). As you can see, readers recalled more text-explicit information, made more inferences, and made fewer errors on passages for which they possessed a large amount of prior knowledge than on passages for which they did not.

IMPLICATIONS FOR INSTRUCTION: PROVIDING PRIOR KNOWLEDGE

The main theme of this section of the chapter is that readers of all ages seem to use their prior knowledge to help them understand what they are reading. The foregoing examples demonstrate that a passage may be difficult to comprehend when the reader lacks an appropriate perspective or has a perspective different from that of the writer. Overall, research on the role of prior knowledge in reading comprehension has consistently "demonstrated strong effects of knowledge on comprehension" (Roller, 1990, p. 83). In summary, reading comprehension depends partly on the content knowledge that the reader brings to the task.

For example, consider what happens when elementary school students read a text on events leading to the Revolutionary War from their textbook on American history. Beck, McKeown, Sinatra, and Loxterman (1991) examined a textbook lesson that began with the following sentence: "In 1763 Britain and the colonies ended a seven-year war with the

FIGURE 3–8 How different perspectives affect what is remembered from the same passage

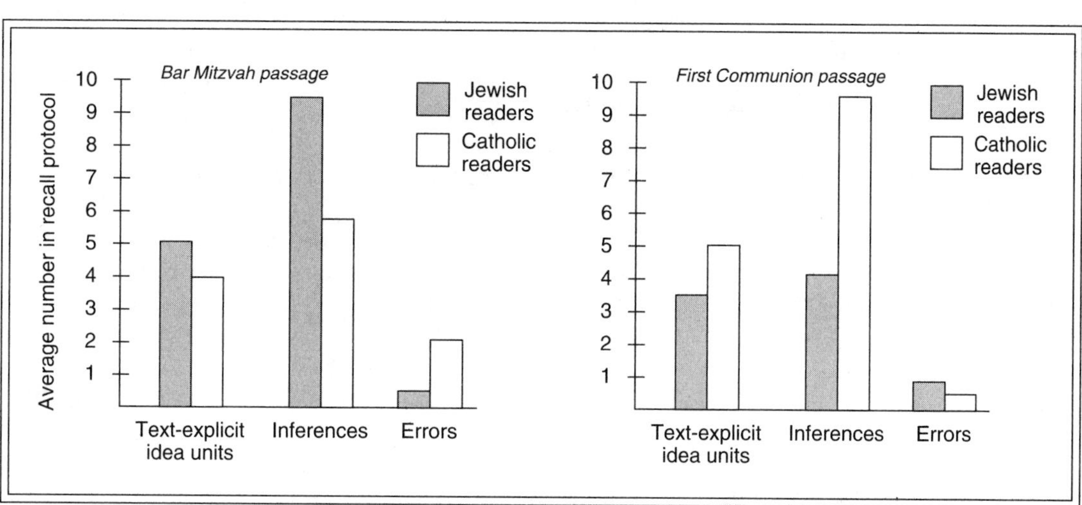

Adapted from Lipson (1983)

French and Indians" (p. 257). What prior knowledge does a fourth- or fifth-grade student need to make sense of this statement? Some of the things they need to know are that about 250 years ago both Britain and France claimed the same land in North America, just west of the 13 American colonies; that the American colonies belonged to Britain, so the colonists fought on the same side as Britain; that many Indians fought on the same side as the French; and that the war that resulted was called the French and Indian War because Britain and the American colonies were fighting against the French and Indians.

Do students come to such a reading task with appropriate prior knowledge? To answer this question, McKeown and Beck (1990) interviewed elementary school children before they took a course in American history. Although their textbooks assumed that the readers possessed adequate background knowledge, McKeown and Beck found that the students had only a small part of the needed background knowledge and that this knowledge was not well interconnected.

To examine the role of providing background knowledge in aiding comprehension, Beck et al. (1991) rewrote the passage on the French and Indian War to contain appropriate background knowledge. For example, the original first sentence in the text was replaced with the following seven sentences:

> About 250 years ago, Britain and France both claimed to own some of the same land, here, in North America. This land was just west of where the 13 colonies were. In 1756, Britain and France went to war to see who would get control of this land. Because the 13 American colonies belonged to Britain, the colonists fought on the same side as Britain. Many Indians fought on the same side as France. Because we were fighting against the French and Indians, the war has come to be known as the French and Indian War. The war ended in 1763. (Beck et al., 1991, p. 257)

As you can see, the first sentence is intended "to activate a conflict schema in the reader's mind" (Beck et al., 1991, p. 257), so the reader can understand that the motive for the war was that two parties wanted to possess the same object. Activating this schema can help the reader see how the pieces of information fit together. The first and second sentences also set the time and place for the conflict episode in a way that is familiar to the reader. The third sentence explicitly shows how the war was a result of the conflict introduced in the first sentence. The next sentences explain who fought on which side and why, and how the war got its peculiar name.

The next sentences in the original text were "As a result of this war France was driven out of North America. Britain would now rule Canada and other lands that had belonged to France" (Beck et al., 1991, p. 258). According to Beck et al. (1991), the problem with this text is that it begins by talking about the loser and uses the unfamiliar wording "driven out of North America." To activate appropriate prior knowledge, they revised the passage as follows: "Britain won the war. Now Britain had control of North America, including Canada. The French had to leave North America" (Beck et al., 1991, p. 259). This wording is intended to activate an important slot in the child's conflict schema, namely the "winner." The children can use their knowledge about winning a conflict to understand that Britain won control of a part of North America and that France had to give up control of North America.

Beck et al. (1991) asked fourth- and fifth-grade students to read either the original or revised versions of four American history lessons, including one on the French and Indian

War. When they were asked to recall the information in the lessons, students who had read the original lesson remembered 44% of the key facts in the original lesson, whereas students who had read the revised lesson remembered 58%. On an open-ended question-answering test covering the material in the original lesson, students who read the original lesson had 30% correct, whereas those who read the revised lesson had 49% correct.

In a follow-up study using the same text, McKeown, Beck, Sinatra, and Loxterman (1992) found that students who read some background information (e.g., material emphasizing the idea of Britain as the owner of the colonies) were better able to remember and answer questions about the original passage than were students who had not received the background information. Taken together, these results provide strong evidence that students learn better when they can use their background knowledge to understand a text. An important educational implication is that the teacher should play a central role in helping students use appropriate background knowledge for making sense out of text. However, Beck and McKeown (1994) pointed out that "many teachers need assistance, because, at the elementary level, few have the background in subject matter that allows them to easily take stock of the texts and provide students with the kind of enhanced information they need" (p. 254).

The implications of these findings for instruction include making sure that reading material is appropriate for the interests and experience of the child. This recommendation is particularly important when children are reading either far above or below their grade level. For example, a student who reads books intended for children who are three or four years older may be able to decode each sentence, but may lack the necessary prior knowledge to appreciate the theme of the material. Similarly, a student who is reading books intended for children three or four years younger may be bored with the immature theme of the material.

A related implication is that reading should be integrated with other subject areas. For example, if a topic such as the Mayan Indians in Mexico is covered in social studies, then it might be appropriate to read a folk story about the life of Mayan children. The material learned in the social studies unit could provide the prior knowledge students need to appreciate the folk story.

Finally, classroom discussion and activity can also provide the prior knowledge readers need for comprehending a passage. This kind of prereading activity can help to turn unfamiliar passages into familiar ones.

USING PROSE STRUCTURE

DOES THE READER REMEMBER IMPORTANT INFORMATION?

Another persistent finding in the literature on adult learning from prose is that important information from a passage is remembered better than unimportant information (Gernsbacher, 1994; Johnson, 1970; Kintsch, 1976; Mayer, 1992; Meyer, 1975; Meyer & McConkie, 1973). This research suggests that skilled readers know about the macrostructure of the passage—that is, about how the passage may be broken down into ideas and how the ideas may be related in a hierarchical outline.

As an example, suppose that we broke a typical story passage into idea units—sentences or phrases that convey one event or action. Then suppose that we asked some skilled adult readers to point out one-fourth of the idea units as the least important (rated 1), one-fourth as the second least important (rated 2), one-fourth as the second most important (rated 3), and one-fourth as the most important (rated 4). Now, let's ask some other skilled adult readers to read this story in its normal form and then recall the information. Do you think that they will show a preference for recalling the important information over the unimportant information? Figure 3–9 summarizes the results of just such a study carried out by Brown and Smiley (1978). As shown, the recall of important information is much better than the recall of unimportant information. This pattern, obtained in many studies, can be called a *levels effect,* because the level of importance of an idea unit influences its probability of being recalled.

RESEARCH ON DIFFERENCES IN CHILDREN'S USE OF PROSE STRUCTURE

AGE-RELATED DIFFERENCES IN THE USE OF PROSE STRUCTURE There is some evidence that more able and older readers have a better awareness of the structure of passages that they read as compared to less able or younger readers. Awareness of structure would be reflected in recognizing and paying attention to information that is important to the theme of the passage. For example, Brown and Smiley (1977) conducted a study using short stories called "The Dragon's Tears" and "How to Fool a Cat." First, they broke the story down into idea units and asked a group of skilled adult readers to identify one-quarter of the idea units as least important (rated 1), one-quarter as second least important (rated 2), one-quarter as second most important (rated 3), and one-quarter as most important (rated 4). Then, Brown and Smiley asked third-graders, fifth-graders, seventh-graders, and college students to rate the importance of each idea unit, using a procedure similar to that just described. Figure 3–10 gives the average rating for each category by age group. As you can

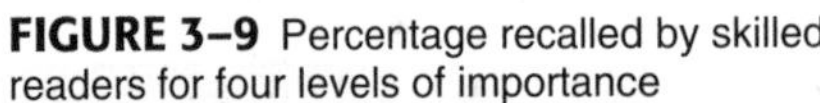

FIGURE 3–9 Percentage recalled by skilled readers for four levels of importance

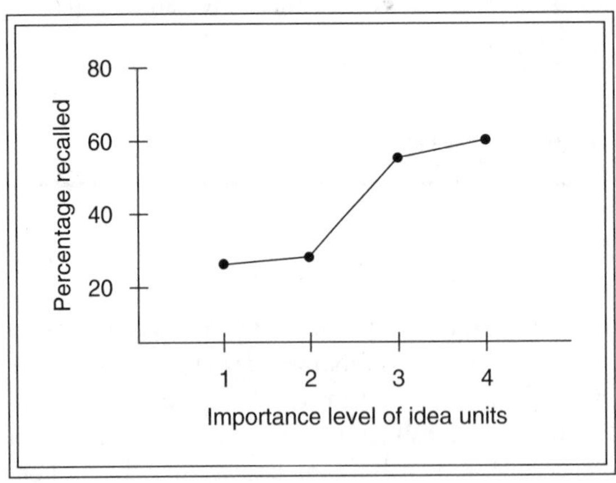

Adapted from Brown and Smiley (1978)

FIGURE 3–10 Average importance ratings for text given by students at four age levels

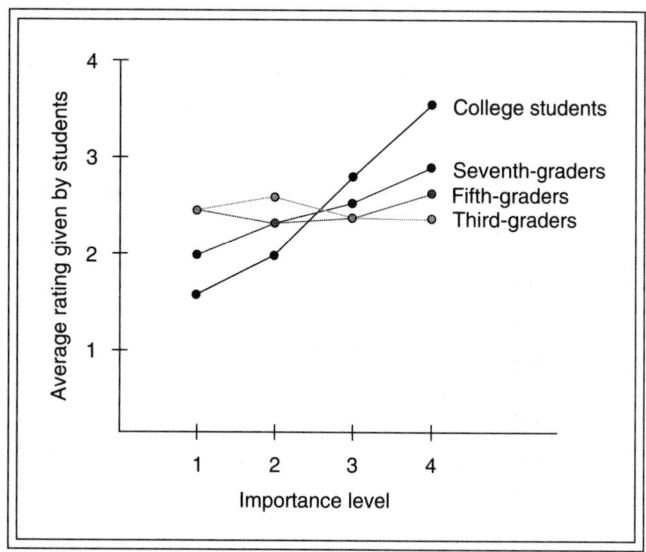

Adapted from Brown and Smiley (1977)

see, the third- and fifth-graders were not able to recognize which of the idea units are important and which are unimportant; they tended to rate the most important idea units about the same as the least important ones. However, seventh-graders and to a greater extent college students displayed an awareness of the relative importance of idea units; they tended to give high ratings to important idea units and low ratings to unimportant ones. In follow-up studies, older readers were better able to summarize text—such as identifying the important points—than were younger readers (Brown & Day, 1983).

ABILITY-RELATED DIFFERENCES IN THE USE OF PROSE STRUCTURE Meyer (1975) devised a technique for determining whether readers use the *top-level structure* of a passage, which is a sort of skeleton outline of the main topics. Use of this top-level structure would be indicated if students recall the main superordinate ideas before they recall the subordinate ideas. If more mature readers are more sensitive to top-level structure, their recall protocols should be organized around this structure and recall should be enhanced mainly for the superordinate rather than the subordinate information in a passage.

Taylor (1980) asked good fourth-grade readers, poor sixth-grade readers, and good sixth-grade readers to read and recall a short passage. As expected, on delayed recall, 59% of the good sixth-grade readers used top-level structure in recalling the material compared to only 18% of the poor sixth-grade readers and 12% of the good fourth-grade readers. If skilled readers focus more on top-level structure, we would expect them to excel particularly in the recall of superordinate ideas. As expected, on delayed recall, the good readers in the sixth grade recalled about 75% more of the superordinate information than the poor readers in the sixth grade, but only 30% more of the subordinate information than the poor readers. These results are summarized in Figure 3–11.

FIGURE 3–11 Recall of superordinate and subordinate information by three groups

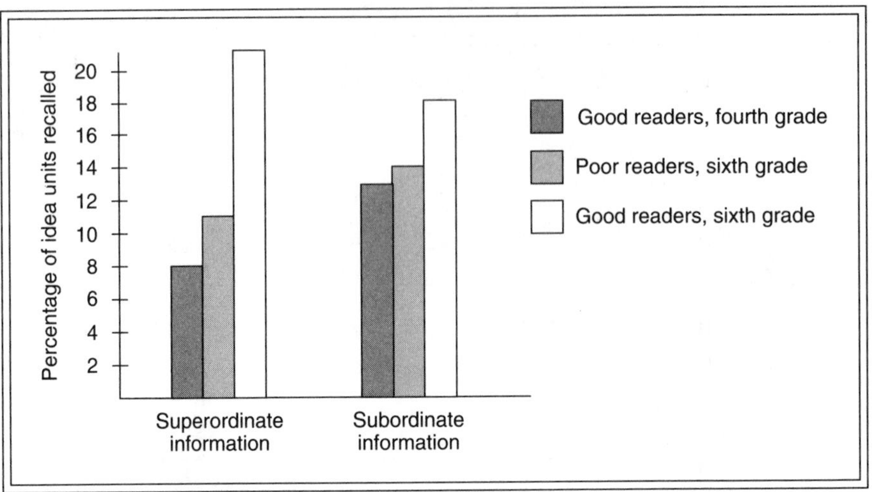

Adapted from Taylor (1980)

AGE-RELATED DIFFERENCES IN SENSITIVITY TO TOPIC SHIFTS If skilled readers are more sensitive to prose structure, we would expect them to pay more attention to topic sentences. Gernsbacher (1990) showed how reading a text involves a process of structure building in which "the goal of comprehension is to build a coherent mental representation or structure of the information being comprehended" (p. 1). Gernsbacher argues that the first step in building a structure is to lay a foundation, a process that presumably takes time. To study this process, skilled readers were asked to read a passage that was presented one sentence at a time on a computer monitor. When readers finished reading a sentence, they pressed a button to see the next sentence. In a series of research studies, Gernsbacher found that skilled readers spent more time reading the initial sentence in a passage than subsequent sentences. According to Gernsbacher (1990), "comprehenders slow down on the initial sentences of paragraphs because they use those initial sentences to lay a foundation for mental structures representing paragraphs" (p. 5).

For example, consider the story shown in the left portion of Table 3–1. According to a structural analysis by Haberlandt (1984), the story consists of a statement of the setting followed by two episodes and an ending. An episode consists of a beginning, reaction, goal, attempt, and outcome. These components are labeled in the second column in the table. If students use the first sentence of an episode to lay the foundation for representing the episode, we would expect their reading time to be longer for the first sentence than for the other sentences in the episode. The right-hand column of the table shows the mean reading times by skilled readers for each sentence in the two episodes. Consistent with the predictions of structure-building theory, the first sentence took much more time to read than the other sentences.

Interestingly, when the story shifts from the first episode to the second, the readers' reading time increases. This increase indicates that the readers are sensitive to the topic shift, as

TABLE 3–1

How much time does it take to read each sentence in a story?

Sentence	Type	Reading Time (Seconds)
Mike and Dave Thompson lived in Florida.	Setting	
They lived across from an orange grove.		
There was a river between their house and the grove.		
One Saturday they had nothing to do.	Beginning	3.1
They were quite bored.	Reaction	2.3
They decided to get some oranges from the grove.	Goal	2.1
They took their canoe and paddled across the river.	Attempt	2.2
They picked a crate full of oranges.	Outcome	2.1
While they were paddling home the canoe began to sink.	Beginning	2.6
Mike and Dave realized that they were in great trouble.	Reaction	2.1
They had to prevent the canoe from sinking further.	Goal	1.8
They threw the oranges out of the canoe.	Attempt	2.1
Finally the canoe stopped sinking.	Outcome	2.5
Now all the oranges were gone.		
Their adventure had failed after all.	End	2.4

Adapted from Haberlandt (1984)

skilled readers are aware of text structure. In a recent review, Hyona (1994) found consistent evidence for a "topic-shift effect" in which skilled readers devote "increased processing time for the sentence that introduces a new topic in the text" or in which "sentences located at episode boundaries are allocated more reading time than within-episode sentences" (p. 77).

Are skilled adult readers more sensitive than children to topic shifts? To examine this question, Hyona (1994) asked fifth-graders and adults to read a story, "Life at the Market Square," that was presented one sentence at a time on a computer monitor. The reader was told to read each sentence, pressing a button to go on to the next, and to be prepared for a test on the passage. A portion of the story is presented in Figure 3–12, with the topic-shift sentences underlined. The results showed that both adults and children devoted more time to topic-shift sentences than to other sentences, but that adults showed a stronger topic-shift effect than did children, especially when more difficult expository texts were used. Apparently, children are most able to build coherent structures when they are reading relatively easy stories.

FIGURE 3–12

Portion of "Life at the Market Square"

What is happening at the market square? You can join me to get a feeling of life at the square on a typical autumn day.

I buy an ice cream at a stand and go sit on a bench. Peach ice cream—yum, yum. I enjoy my ice cream while watching the people at the square. The square is full of life. There are shouting salesmen, crying kids, fighting drunkards, couples in love, grim-looking elderly ladies, and crazy pigeons.

There comes a strong smell of vomit from somewhere. Two drunkards have fallen asleep on the ground. One of them is surrounded by vomit. I begin to feel sick when watching them.

I go to a fish stand to look for some herring. The little stand is just in the middle of the square. The fish seller advertises his fish to me. I don't want to buy his fish, because they look old. On the ground, in front of the fish stand, there are scales of fish that stick to my shoes.

The pigeons seem to be having their meal. Besides me, there is a whole bunch of them rushing around. The pigeons are permanent customers of the market. In front of me, a pigeon couple fights for a herring that has fallen from the fish stand. Other pigeons join in the fight.

A man gets in front of a microphone. People at the square are clearly amazed. They start to gather around the man. The place is getting crowded.

Note: underlining added.
Adapted from Hyona (1994)

IMPLICATIONS FOR INSTRUCTION: SUMMARIZATION TRAINING

What can be done to help readers learn to pay attention to the top-level structure (or superordinate information) in a passage? Brown and Smiley (1978) provide some evidence concerning the potential trainability of structure-based reading strategies. For example, fifth-, seventh-/eighth-, and eleventh-/twelfth-graders were asked to read along as the experimenter read a short story such as "The Dragon's Tears" or "How to Fool a Cat." Then subjects were asked to recall the passage, with the results summarized by the solid line in Figure 3–13. The results shown in Figure 3–13 indicate a levels effect for each age group in which students performed better on recall of more important idea units than on less important idea units. After the first recall test, students were given a five-minute study period and told to undertake any activity that would improve recall. Paper, pens, and a copy of the passage (in primary type) were available. Then, a second recall test was administered, with the results summarized by the dotted line in Figure 3–13. The results show that the extra study time did not have much of an effect on the younger students but did improve the performance of the older students, particularly on recall of the more important idea units. Apparently, the older students knew to use the study time in order to focus on important information, while the younger students did not spontaneously use this strategy.

FIGURE 3–13 Percentage correct recall by importance level for three age groups

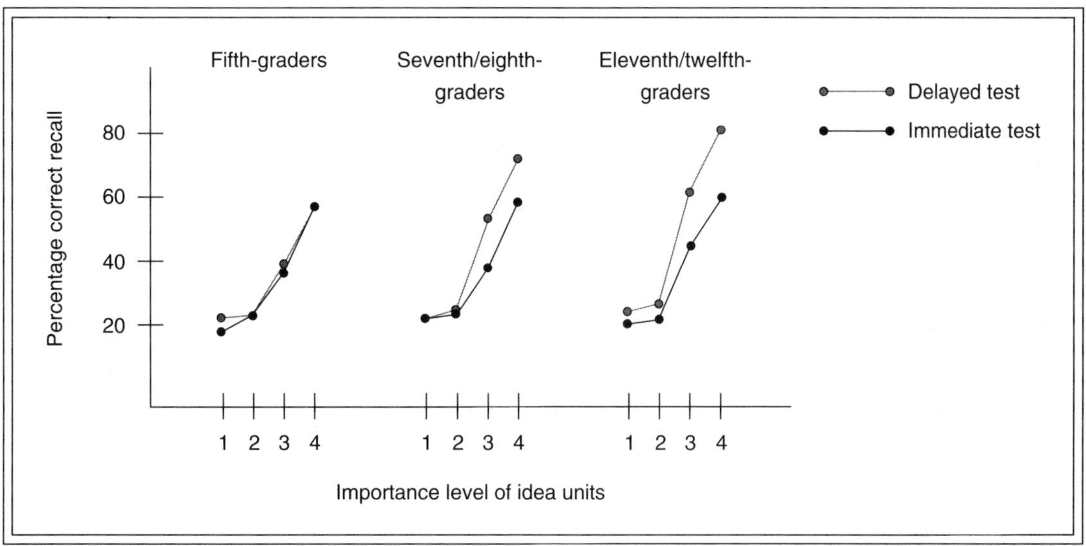

Adapted from Brown and Smiley (1978)

Can the younger students be induced to apply helpful study strategies even if they would not use them spontaneously? To investigate this question, Brown and Smiley (1978) continued the experiment for a second day. The procedure was identical except that during the five-minute study interval students who did not show evidence of actively studying were prompted to engage in study activities such as underlining. Figure 3–14 shows the recall patterns for fifth-graders who underlined spontaneously, fifth-graders who were induced by the experimenter to underline, and fifth-graders who could not be induced to underline during the five-minute study period. Again, the solid line is the recall performance on the second test after the five-minute study period. As can be seen, the students who spontaneously underline without having to be instructed to do so seem to have focused on important information, which is indicated by the improvement in recall of important idea units but not of other information. In contrast, inducing students to underline did not focus their attention on important information, as is indicated by the improvement in recall of unimportant information only. Similar results were obtained for the seventh- and eighth-graders. Apparently, younger readers need practice in effective techniques for recognizing and using the hierarchical organization of a passage.

In a direct training study, Taylor and Beach (1984) taught seventh-graders to use a hierarchical summary procedure for reading social studies texts. For each training passage, the student made a skeleton outline consisting of a thesis statement for the entire passage at the top of the page and a statement of the main idea of each section as indicated by headings. Then the student generated two or three important supporting details for each main idea statement, and wrote superordinate topic headings in the left margin to connect to

FIGURE 3–14 Percentage correct recall by importance level for three groups of fifth graders

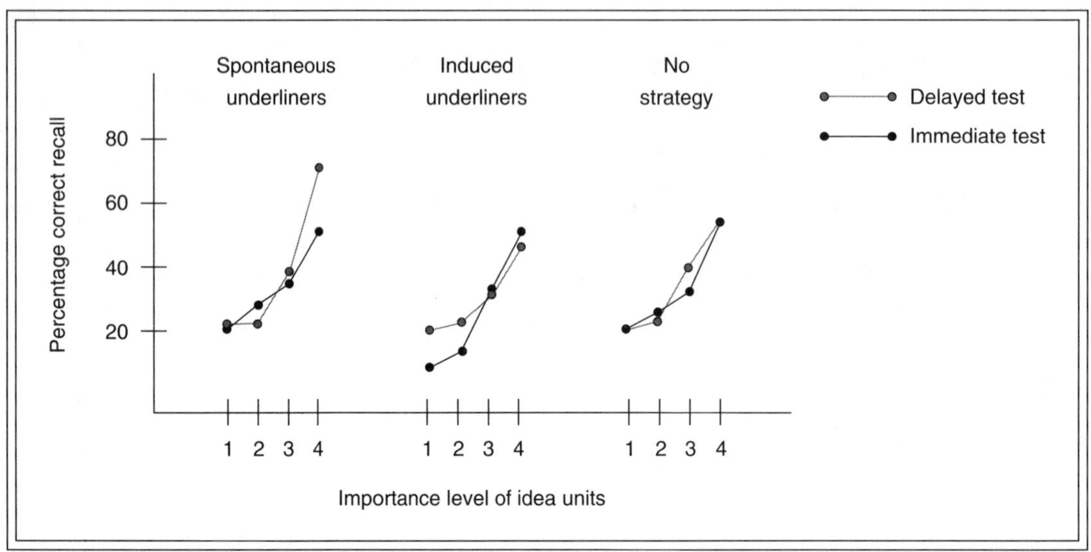

Adapted from Brown and Smiley (1978)

sections of the text. Figure 3–15 gives an example of a hierarchical summary of a three-page social studies text containing one heading and six subheadings. The trained students received no training. To test the effectiveness of the hierarchical summary procedure, students in both groups were given pretests and posttests that involved reading passages and then recalling and answering questions about them. As expected, the trained students showed greater pretest-to-posttest gains in recall and in answering questions than the control group.

What techniques do skilled readers use for summarizing a text, and can these skills be taught to less skilled readers? By analyzing skilled reading processes, Brown and Day (1983) identified the following principles of text summarization: deleting irrelevant information, deleting redundant information, substituting a superordinate term for a list of items, substituting a subordinate term for a series of events, selecting a topic sentence, and inventing a topic sentence if none is given. Over the course of twelve 30-minute sessions, Bean and Steenwyk (1984) taught sixth-grade students to use these principles to summarize a series of paragraphs. In contrast, a control group was told to find the main ideas but was given no explicit instruction. On a subsequent test of summarizing a paragraph, the summarization-trained group obtained a much better score than the control group (17.6 versus 11.0, respectively). Importantly, on a subsequent test of reading comprehension, the summarization-trained students scored 62% correct, whereas the control group scored 47% correct. These results provide additional evidence that summarization skills can be taught and that learning them improves students' reading comprehension.

FIGURE 3–15

A hierarchical summary for a three-page social studies text

I. *Johnson developed many programs to fight injustice and poverty.*

A. *Lyndon Johnson became President of the U.S. after Kennedy was assassinated.*
hard worker, tried to carry out some of Kennedy's programs

Civil Rights

B. *Johnson fought for civil-rights law.*
purpose: to protect blacks from discrimination in hotels and restaurants, blacks had not been allowed in some hotels or restaurants in the South

C. *Johnson persuaded Congress to pass a law ensuring all people the right to vote.*
protected black people's right to vote, literacy tests now illegal

Great Society programs

D. *Johnson started a "war on poverty."*
job training, education for poor people, plans for a "Great Society"

E. *Johnson persuaded Congress to develop a Medicare program.*
for people at least 65 years old, hospital bills paid, doctor's bills paid in part

F. *Johnson persuaded Congress to pass a law giving money to schools.*
purpose: to improve education of children from poor families, $1 billion in aid to schools

From Taylor and Beach (1984)

MAKING INFERENCES

WHAT IS INFERENCE MAKING?

The process of comprehending text often requires the reader to make inferences. For example, consider the sentence "Our neighbor unlocked the door." An inference you might make is that the instrument used to unlock the door was a key (Paris & Lindauer, 1976). As another example, consider the sentence "She slammed the door shut on her hand." An inference you might make is that she hurt her finger (Paris, Lindauer, & Cox, 1977).

Overall, inference making is so important to reading comprehension that "the ability to draw inferences is a cornerstone of reading competence" (Winne, Graham, & Prock, 1993, p. 53). For example, Weaver and Kintsch (1991) estimate that as many as a dozen implicit inferences may be required to understand every explicit statement in a passage fully. Yet, an important educational issue is that young readers are notoriously poor at making inferences during reading (Oakhill & Yuill, 1996).

RESEARCH ON THE DEVELOPMENT OF CHILDREN'S INFERENCE MAKING

Paris and his colleagues (Myers & Paris, 1978; Paris & Lindauer, 1976; Paris et al., 1977; Paris & Upton, 1976) found evidence of a developmental trend in which younger readers are less likely to make inferences during reading than are older readers. For example, kindergartners, second-graders, and fourth-graders listened to eight sentences. The sentences each suggested an implicit inference about the instrument used to carry out the action mentioned in the sentence. For example, "Our neighbor unlocked the door" implies that the instrument is a key. Students were given a cued recall test in which for each sentence the experimenter gave either an explicit cue—the subject, verb, or object of the sentence—or an implicit cue—the instrument. For example, an explicit cue for the preceding sentence is "neighbor," "unlocked," or "door," whereas an implicit cue is "key." Figure 3–16 shows the percentage of correctly recalled sentences when the cue was explicit versus implicit for each age group. For the kindergartners, performance was much better with the explicit cue, but for the second- and fourth-graders implicit cues were just as useful as explicit ones. Apparently, the younger children do not spontaneously go beyond the information given to make and use inferences as well as the older children. Paris et al. (1977) obtained a similar developmental trend using inferences about consequences such as the "door slamming" sentence given earlier.

In a related series of studies, Paris and Upton (1976) examined developmental changes in children's inference making for short paragraphs. Students in each grade K–5 listened to six stories, including the following:

FIGURE 3–16 Age-related differences in children's use of inference

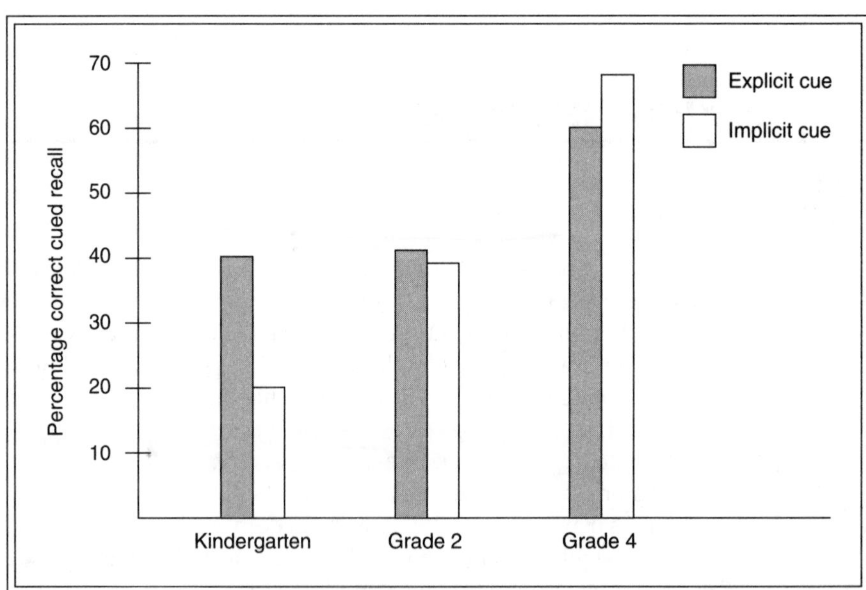

Adapted from Paris and Lindauer (1976)

> Chris waited until he was alone in the house. The only sound he heard was his father chopping wood in the barn. Then he pushed the red chair over to the sink, which was full of dishes. Standing on the edge of the sink, he could just barely reach the heavy jar. The jar was behind the sugar and he stretched until his fingers could lift the lid. Just as he reached inside, the door swung open and there was his little sister.

Students were asked eight questions about each passage. Half of the questions concerned verbatim memory, such as "Was the jar heavy?" or "Was the chair brown?" The other half concerned inferences, such as "Was Chris's father using an ax?" or "Was Chris caught in the act of doing something he was not supposed to do?" Performance on both verbatim and inferential questions improved with age, but there was a larger increase in inference performance. In addition, ability to make inferences was highly correlated with overall amount recalled. These results suggest that as children develop, they become more able to make inferences that give meaning to their reading of the passage.

IMPLICATIONS FOR INSTRUCTION: INFERENCE TRAINING

Inference training is a central feature of most basal reading programs (Pressley, 1990; Rosenshine, 1980) and of many traditional reading programs. However, until recently there has been little empirical research concerning the effectiveness of inference training. For example, Hansen (1981) developed a five-week classroom program for second-graders. Some students were given practice in answering inference questions for each of several practice passages; other students used the same practice passages in class but followed the normal instructional program. On a posttest, all students read new passages and answered some literal and inference questions about the passages. The question-trained group performed 12% better than the control group on literal questions and 26% better on inference questions. However, a group that received training in the use of prereading strategies, such as trying to predict what would happen or relating the story to their own experiences, did not show strong posttest advantages over the control group. Apparently, an effective way to teach students how to answer inference questions is to give them direct instruction and practice in answering inference questions.

In a follow-up study, Hansen and Pearson (1983) provided five weeks of inference training to poor and good fourth-grade readers. The training included prereading strategies such as discussing the reader's own experiences and making predictions about the story. For example, the script for prereading strategies was as follows:

TEACHER: What is it that we have been doing before we discuss each story?

DESIRED RESPONSE: We talk about our lives and we predict what will happen in the stories.

TEACHER: Why do we make these comparisons?

DESIRED RESPONSE: These comparisons will help us understand the stories.

TEACHER: Last week I asked you to think about a social studies lesson on Japan. Today, pretend that you are reading a science article about conservation. What might you be thinking about while you are reading the article?

DESIRED RESPONSE: [Students relate personal experiences with conservation and explain how the experiences would be related to the text.] For example, students talked about how their families heat with wood to conserve oil and stated that they wanted to find out how the Japanese conserve oil.

Training for a story on a man who is embarrassed by his appearance focused on understanding the main ideas:

TEACHER: Sometimes people are embarrassed by their personal appearance. Tell us about a time you were embarrassed about the way you looked.
TYPICAL RESPONSES: I got a short haircut. I wore short pants. I'm too short.
TEACHER: In the next story there is an old man who is embarrassed about the way he looks. What do you think is the thing that embarrasses him?
TYPICAL RESPONSES: Ragged clothes. Cane. Gray hair. Wrinkles.

These prereading scripts led to discussions that lasted approximately 20 minutes. Then students read the passage independently. Students in the control group did not engage in the prereading activities. After reading the story, the class was asked to discuss 10 questions. For the trained group, all the questions required inferences. For example, in a discussion of a basal version of *Charlotte's Web*, the teacher asked, "What kind of person do you think Templeton [the rat] would be if he were human?" The control group discussion involved questions using the ratio of four literal questions for each inference question. This ratio corresponds to the normal pattern of reading discussions. Following the training program, students were tested by asking them to read a passage appropriate for their reading level and to answer both literal and inference questions. Figure 3–17 shows that the training seems to have had no effect on the good readers, presumably because they already possessed good inference strategies. However, Figure 3–17 also indicates that the training greatly enhanced the performance of the poor readers on both inference and literal questions.

Does inference training affect students' reading comprehension performance? To help answer this question Yuill and Oakhill (1988; Oakhill & Yuill, 1996) provided seven 30-minute training sessions to seven- and eight-year-olds who had scored either low or high on a test of reading comprehension. In the training, students read short stories, performed several inference-inducing tasks with them, and then received feedback and discussed their answers. One task was to generate questions based on a short passage, such as shown in Figure 3–18. Some possible questions that students could generate for this story are "Where was Lucy?" "Why was she there?" and "Why couldn't she move?" A second task was to identify words in the story that suggested what a character was like, where the story takes place, and the like. In a third task, part of the text was covered, and students were asked to guess at what was missing.

Students were given a reading comprehension test before and after the training period. For those who had done poorly on the pretest, scores increased greatly for the trained group but not for a control group that received practice in decoding. For those who had done well on the pretest, the trained group did not show large gains, nor did it gain more than the control group. Overall, these results show that inference training has a strong effect on students who scored low in reading comprehension, suggesting that the ability to make inferences is a key component in skilled comprehension.

Although many students develop reading comprehension competence in elementary school, some do not. These students are often labeled as "learning disabled" and receive special pull-out instruction during the academic year. Will inference training help these young readers? Winne et al. (1993) tackled this question by providing nine sessions of inference training to a group of students in grades four through six who had poor compre-

FIGURE 3–17 Effects of inference training on poor and good readers

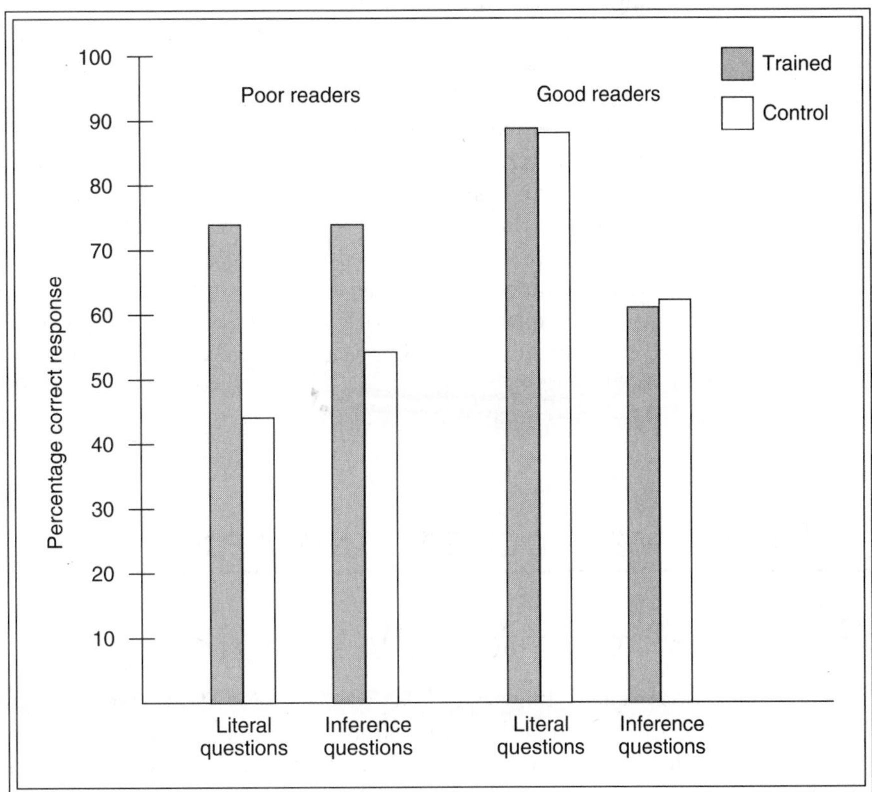

Adapted from Hansen and Pearson (1983)

FIGURE 3–18

An inference-training exercise based on generating a question

Read this text:

Lucy saw the ground below her. It seemed very far away. She heard the cat and tried to move, but she realized it was unsafe. What could she do? Then she saw her father walking toward the house. She called loudly to him. Father looked up and saw Lucy; then he ran toward the tree.

Write some questions that can be answered by the text:

1. ____________________
2. ____________________
3. ____________________

Adapted from Oakhill and Yuill (1996)

hension skills. During the sessions, students worked individually with an adult tutor on answering inference questions about short texts.

For example, in one session the tutor read the summer camping passage in Figure 3–19 and then asked the student to answer a series of questions aimed at promoting inference making, such as those in the bottom of Figure 3–19. The correct answer to the first question is that the boys camped near the pond; this answer can be derived by noting that "the boys decided that their campsite should be near some water" and that only one of the available sites was near water. After each answer, some students received feedback on the correct answer and were shown where in the text it was found (abbreviated feedback group), whereas others received the same feedback along with explanations of how the answer could be derived from the relevant portion of the text (explanatory feedback group). As expected, students in the explanatory feedback group showed more improvement in their inference-making than did those in the abbreviated feedback group. The results suggest that students with poor comprehension skills need practice not only in inference making but also in explaining how the inferences are made.

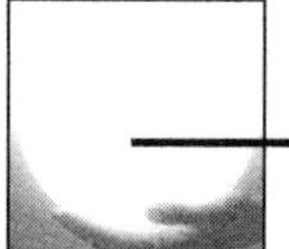

USING METACOGNITIVE KNOWLEDGE

WHAT IS METACOGNITIVE KNOWLEDGE?

Metacognition is knowledge and awareness of one's own cognitive processes. Brown et al. (1981) pointed out that although metacognitive skills are particularly difficult to teach to readers, they are crucial for effective reading. For example, one kind of metacognitive knowledge related to reading is *comprehension monitoring*, which we focus on in this section.

RESEARCH ON DIFFERENCES IN METACOGNITIVE KNOWLEDGE

COMPREHENSION MONITORING Comprehension monitoring is an awareness of whether you understand what you are reading. In essence, a reader with good comprehension monitoring skills is continually asking, "Does this make sense?" For example, Markman (1979) read three short essays to third-, fifth-, and sixth-graders. Each story contained either an explicit or an implicit inconsistency as shown in italics in Figure 3–20. For example, the inconsistency in the fish essay is that there is not enough light at the bottom of the ocean to see colors and that fish see the color of their food at the bottom of the ocean. The experimenter told the students that she was trying to write a children's book and that she needed them to serve as consultants. The children were asked to assess the understandability of the essays and to suggest ways of making them easier to understand. After reading the story twice, the experimenter prompted the students to point out any inconsistencies. The first seven prompts for the passages in Figure 3–20 were:

1. Read the essay.
2. Reread the essay.

FIGURE 3–19

An inference-training exercise based on answering questions

Read this passage:

It was summer at last! John and Peter were going camping. They wanted to find a really good campsite this year. Last summer they were almost two kilometers from the store and ice cream stand.

Both the boys loved camping. John had been a Boy Scout for five years. Peter and his mother had camped in the woods every summer when he was younger. This year, the boys decided that their campsite should be near water.

When they arrived at the campground, the park ranger told them that only two campsites were left. "One site is close to a Dairy Queen store," he said. "There are many beautiful wild flowers nearby. The other site is by a small pond. It is a peaceful camping spot away from other campers. However, there are lots of insects there."

Answer these questions:

1. Where did the boys camp?
   (Answering this question requires making an inference, namely, that the boys camped near a pond.)
2. Why?
   (Answering this question requires remembering a rule—"their campsite should be near some water"—and a critical fact—"the other site . . . by a small pond" was the only available site near water.)
3. What did John and Peter want to find?
   (The answer is "a really good campsite." The reader must notice that this is the problem statement, that is, the main problem in the story.)
4. What sort of a campsite had the boys decided they wanted this year?
   (The answer is one "near some water." The reader must note that it is a rule, that is, a major constraint in the story.)
5. What campsites did the ranger give the boys to choose from?
   (The answer is "one site is close to a Dairy Queen" and "the other site is by a small pond." The reader must determine that these are the important relevant facts in the story.)
6. What was wrong with the campsite by the pond?
   (Although the answer is that "there are lots of insects there," the reader must also realize that this information is not relevant to the boys' decision.)

Adapted from Winne, Graham, and Prock (1993)

FIGURE 3–20

Do young readers recognize inconsistency in prose passages?

A PASSAGE WITH AN EXPLICIT INCONSISTENCY

Many different kinds of fish live in the ocean. Some fish have heads that make them look like alligators, and some fish have heads that make them look like cats. Fish live in different parts of the ocean. Some fish live near the surface of the water, but some fish live way down at the bottom of the ocean. *Fish must have light in order to see. There is absolutely no light at the bottom of the ocean. It is pitch black down there. When it is that dark the fish cannot see anything. They cannot even see colors. Some fish that live at the bottom of the ocean can see the color of their food; that is how they know what to eat.*

A PASSAGE WITH AN IMPLICIT INCONSISTENCY

Many different kinds of fish live in the ocean. Some fish have heads that make them look like alligators, and some fish have heads that make them look like cats. Fish live in different parts of the ocean. Some fish live near the surface of the water, but some fish live way down at the bottom of the ocean. *There is absolutely no light at the bottom of the ocean. Some fish that live at the bottom of the ocean know their food by its color. They will only eat red fungus.*

PERCENTAGE OF CHILDREN WHO RECOGNIZED INCONSISTENCIES IN AT LEAST TWO OF THREE PASSAGES

Grade Level	*Explicit Condition*	*Implicit Condition*
Grade 3	50%	0%
Grade 5	60%	10%
Grade 6	60%	0%

Adapted from Markman (1979)

3. That's it. That's the information about fishes.
4. What do you think?
5. Do you have any questions?
6. Did I forget to tell you anything?
7. Did everything make sense?

Did the children respond to these prompts by referring to the inconsistency in the passage? Figure 3–20 lists the percentage of students at each grade level who recognized the inconsistencies in at least two out of three essays. As you can see, about half the students found the explicit inconsistencies in at least two essays, while almost none found the implicit inconsistencies. Apparently, it is difficult for students to recognize spontaneously that the text they are reading is incomprehensible, especially when inconsistencies are implicit.

CAN CHILDREN BE INDUCED TO MONITOR THEIR COMPREHENSION? To test this question, Markman (1979) conducted a follow-up study on third- and sixth-graders using the same task described above. However, this time half the children were told, "There is something tricky about each of the essays. Something which does not make any sense. Something which is confusing. I would like you to try and spot the problem with each essay, and tell me what it was that did not make any sense." These instructions did not greatly influence the ability of the third-graders to find either implicit or explicit inconsistencies, but it did greatly improve the ability of the sixth-graders to find both. Apparently, the older children are capable of comprehension monitoring but do not engage in this activity spontaneously.

Myers and Paris (1978) interviewed second- and sixth-graders concerning their metacognitive knowledge about reading. Some of the questions focused on comprehension monitoring, such as "Do you ever have to go back to the beginning of a paragraph or story to figure out what a sentence means? Why?" About 60% of the sixth-graders were able to explain why they reread (e.g., to get context cues); in comparison, less than 10% of the second graders were able to explain why they reread. Apparently, younger readers are less aware of the role of comprehension monitoring in reading.

These results suggest that skilled readers are able to focus on inconsistencies in text. To examine this idea, Baker and Anderson (1982) asked college students to read short expository passages, some of which contained inconsistencies. The passages were presented on a computer terminal screen with only one sentence on the screen at a time. The reader pressed the "Next" button to see the next sentence, the "Back" button to see the previous sentence, and the "Lab" button to start over at the beginning of the passage. The results indicate that readers spent much more time reading a sentence that conflicted with previously presented information compared to reading the same sentence in a consistent passage. In addition, skilled readers were far more likely to look back to an inconsistent sentence than to the same sentence when it was in a consistent passage. These results suggest that comprehension monitoring is a characteristic of skilled readers.

WHY DO CHILDREN FAIL TO RECOGNIZE INCONSISTENCIES IN A PASSAGE? There are two major explanations as to why children fail to detect inconsistencies in passages. According to a representational theory, students fail to adequately represent and retain the two inconsistent statements in their working memory. According to a processing theory, students adequately represent the two conflicting statements in working memory but fail to compare them adequately. To test these two theories, Vosniadou, Pearson, and Rogers (1988) asked first-, third-, and fifth-graders to listen to (or read) stories, such as the one partially shown in Figure 3–21. As you can see, the stories contain contradictions, such as the sentence in Figure 3–21 stating that "when you pour spaghetti and water into a strainer, the water passes through the holes and the spaghetti stays in the strainer," and another sentence stating that when Georgette poured the spaghetti and water into the strainer, "the spaghetti passed through the holes of the strainer into the bowl and the water stayed in the strainer." The children were told:

> Listen very carefully to each story because there is something wrong with each one of them, something wrong with the way the author wrote them, something that doesn't make sense. We would like you to listen very carefully to each story and then tell the story back to us and also tell us what it is that does not make any sense. (Vosniadou et al., 1988, p. 30)

FIGURE 3–21

How recall affects detection of inconsistencies in stories

Read this story, then recall it, and point out what does not make sense in the story:

First Georgette filled a pot with water and put it on the stove. She turned on the flame and soon the water was boiling, so she put a boxful of spaghetti into the water. The water boiled again, and Georgette watched it until the spaghetti got soft and looked like it was done. Now she had to think of a way to take the spaghetti out of the water.

Then she remembered that her father had used a strainer to separate spaghetti from water. When you pour spaghetti and water into a strainer, the water passes through the holes and the spaghetti stays in the strainer.

So Georgette looked in the kitchen cabinets and found a strainer. She put the strainer over a bowl. She then poured the spaghetti and water into the strainer. As she did this, the spaghetti passed through the holes in the strainer into the bowl and the water stayed in the strainer. Georgette was glad that the water and spaghetti were separated. She placed the bowl of spaghetti on the counter.

INCONSISTENT STATEMENTS:

1. When you pour spaghetti and water into a strainer, the water passes through the holes and the spaghetti stays in the strainer.
2. As she did this, the spaghetti passed through the holes in the strainer into the bowl and the water stayed in the strainer.

PERCENTAGE OF INCONSISTENCIES RECOGNIZED AND INCONSISTENT STATEMENTS RECALLED BY FOUR GROUPS:

Group	*Recognize Inconsistencies*	*Recall Inconsistencies*
Grade 1 (listen)	35%	35%
Grade 3 (listen)	47%	65%
Grade 3 (read)	27%	51%
Grade 5 (read)	63%	74%

Adapted from Vosniadou, Pearson, and Rogers (1988)

Then, each child was asked to recall the story, to say what about it did not make sense, and to justify the answer.

The left panel of the table in Figure 3–21 shows a developmental trend in which younger readers tended to miss the inconsistencies, whereas older readers were more likely to catch them. In addition, third-graders were more likely to notice the inconsistencies when they listened to the story than when they read it themselves, presumably because they had less attentional capacity available when they had to do the reading. The right panel of the table shows a developmental trend in which younger readers were less successful in remembering the conflicting statements than were older students. The recall data show that younger readers' difficulties in detecting inconsistencies occurred mainly because younger readers were more likely than the older readers to forget the inconsistent information. Vosniadou et al. (1988) concluded that "greater attention should be paid to how children's mental representations of text affect inconsistency detection and comprehension monitoring" (p. 36). According to this view, an important factor in comprehension monitoring is the prior knowledge of the reader, because inconsistent statements are more easily represented (and therefore compared) when they are familiar to the reader.

IMPLICATIONS FOR INSTRUCTION: COMPREHENSION MONITORING TRAINING

When low-skill readers in the third grade were asked to read stories containing inconsistencies, they detected only 13% of the inconsistencies (Rubman & Waters, 2000). What can we do to increase their comprehension monitoring performance? In a recent study, Rubman and Waters (2000) asked third- and sixth-graders to read a story that had an inconsistency such as the fish story used by Markman (in Figure 3–20). Then, some students were asked to read the story again while placing cutouts (such as red fungus plants and fish with big eyes) on a magnetic board. The top of Figure 3–22 shows an example of the picture constructed for the fish story. Other students simply read the story a second time. After the second reading, all students were explicitly asked, "Did everything in the story make sense?" and "Was there anything wrong with the story?" as well specific questions such as, "What color of food do fish eat? How can fish tell what color their food is? Is it light or dark at the bottom of the ocean? Do you think that the fish can see the color of their food in the dark?" The bottom of Figure 3–22 shows the percentage of high-skill readers and low-skill readers in grades three and six who detected inconsistencies in the storyboard construction and read-only treatments. As you can see, students detected more inconsistencies when they constructed a pictorial version of the story, and this effect was particularly strong for the low-skill readers in the third grade.

Why did storyboard construction produce such strong improvements in inconsistency detection? Rubman and Waters propose that low-skill readers may view their task as decoding the words rather than making sense of the passage (that is as learning to read rather than reading to learn). Accordingly, the storyboard construction task "encouraged the less skilled readers to pay attention to the meaning of the text" and "changed the focus of the less skilled readers from pure decoders to more meaningful text processors" (p. 510). Thus, an important step in the promotion of comprehension monitoring strategies is to help students learn how to make sense of text passages.

Can children learn to be more effective comprehension monitors? In a classic study, Markman and Gorin (1981) provided encouraging evidence that students more accurately detect inconsistencies in text when they are given some instruction in how to do so. Eight- and ten-year-olds listened to a series of short stories that either did or did not contain inconsistencies, and then indicated after each story whether it was easy to understand or they had some problem in understanding it. For example, the following story has an inconsistency between the second and final sentences:

> Corn can be served in many ways. I've never met anyone who didn't consider corn, in one form or another, one of their favorite foods. Corn can be steamed and served with melted

FIGURE 3–22

Using storyboard construction to help students make sense of a story

STORYBOARD CONSTRUCTION MATERIALS

Students are asked to place cutouts on a magnetized board as they read the fish story. Here's the final picture that can be constructed:

PERCENTAGE OF INCONSISTENCIES RECOGNIZED BY FOUR GROUPS IN TWO TREATMENT CONDITIONS

Group	*Read-Only Condition*	*Storyboard Construction Condition*
Low-skill third-graders	13%	54%
High-skill third-graders	46%	67%
Low-skill sixth-graders	38%	67%
High-skill sixth-graders	50%	71%

From Rubman and Waters (2000)

butter; mixed with flour and egg to make a bread; or made into popcorn for a favorite snack. The people I know don't enjoy eating corn very much. (p. 322)

Some of the students (instructed group) received brief examples of how to detect inconsistencies, such as the following:

For example, suppose you heard, "John loves to ski" and later you heard, "John hates to ski." Those two sentences do not make sense together. Any time two parts of an essay do not make sense together, that would be confusing. Suppose one part of an essay said, "Suzie is a

> tiny baby," then another part said "Suzie is big enough to walk to school." It would be confusing to have two sentences that do not make sense together. (p. 322)

Other students did not receive these examples (control group).

Figure 3–23 shows the percentages of 8- and 10-year-old students in each group who correctly detected inconsistencies. Those who had received instructions on how to detect inconsistencies performed better than did those who had not. The instructions were particularly helpful for the 10-year-olds, suggesting that they had known the strategy for detecting inconsistencies but had not been fully aware that they should use it in this task before instruction. Markman and Gorin (1981) concluded that "when children are given examples of what types of problems to look for, they are capable of adjusting their standard of evaluation" (p. 325).

In an important extension of this study, Elliot-Faust and Pressley (1986) asked third-graders to listen to four stories, two of which contained inconsistencies such as the following:

> The sea horse is a fascinating fish. Sea horses are found in oceans and seas. Sea horses are very small. Sea horses grow to be twelve centimeters long. The sea horse's head looks like a tiny horse's head. The sea horse has a small body and a long tail. When the sea horse swims it looks like it's standing on its tail. It moves through the water by moving its fins on its head and back. The sea horse is not a very fast swimmer. It makes jerky movements as it swims.

FIGURE 3–23 Percentage of inconsistencies detected by four groups

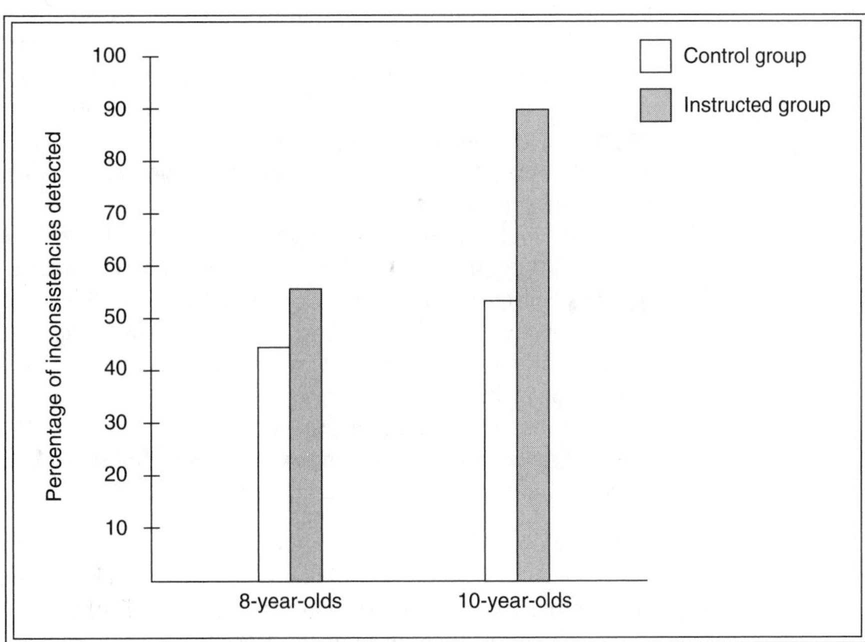

Adapted from Markman and Gorin (1981)

> The sea horse moves slowly through the water. The sea horse escapes enemy fish by swimming quickly away. That is how the sea horse keeps from being eaten by other fish. That's the story about sea horses. (p. 28)

After listening to each story the students were asked, "Did the story make sense?" If they answered no, the experimenter asked, "Why?" and "What part didn't make sense?" In this example, the correct answer is to point out the contradiction between "the sea horse is not a very fast swimmer" and "the sea horse escapes enemy fish by swimming quickly away."

Some students were given examples of inconsistent sentences (instructed group), while others received no training (control group), as in the Markman and Gorin (1981) study. In addition, some students (strategy group) received the same training as the instructed group as well as explicit training in how to use comprehension monitoring strategies for detecting contradictions between sentences. The strategy training included practice in controlling one's use of comprehension monitoring strategies by asking questions such as "What is my plan?" "Am I using my plan?" and "How did I do?" As in the Markman and Gorin study, the instructed group detected more inconsistencies (73%) than the control group (37%). In addition, the strategy group detected more inconsistencies (91%) than either of these groups. These results demonstrate that extended strategy training can greatly improve the comprehension-monitoring skills of young readers.

What can be done to help students develop appropriate metacognitive skills? Based on research on children's comprehension monitoring, Markman (1985) makes the following suggestions:

1. Children should read a "variety of well-organized, tight passages" that involve "simple logical, causal, and temporal relations" (p. 288). Unfortunately, textbooks written for young children often are unstructured, with many paragraphs consisting of lists of descriptive sentences. Thus, they do not offer children practice in determining whether the material makes sense, because the text has often been rewritten to minimize logical, causal, or temporal structure. In addition, children should be asked to predict the next logical event or the actions of a character, to infer the order of events in a causal sequence, to guess the cause of an event, or to infer the motives of a character.
2. Children should be given a set of general questions to ask themselves as they read, such as "Do I understand?" "What is the main point?" "What else do I know that is related?" Self-testing has been successfully used in improving the reading comprehension of developmentally delayed children (Brown, Campione, & Barclay, 1979).
3. Children should be exposed to teachers who model appropriate comprehension-monitoring techniques.
4. Children should practice evaluating explanations of a passage, such as choosing which of several possible explanations makes the most sense.
5. Children should practice detecting inconsistencies or other problems in text.

In summary, children often fail to use appropriate comprehension monitoring and related skills, even though they are capable of doing so. Instruction in using metacognitive knowledge may improve their comprehension performance. Clearly, research is needed to help determine how to apply these recommendations to the needs of individual children.

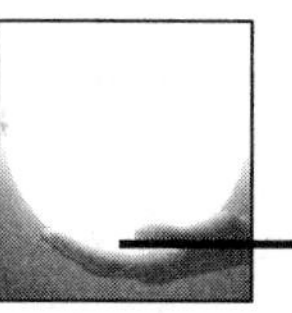

BUILDING A READING COMPREHENSION PROGRAM THAT WORKS

The research on reading comprehension presented in this chapter demonstrates that progress is being made in identifying the strategies that successful readers use and in teaching these strategies to beginning readers. In particular, this chapter focused on four active cognitive processes in reading that can be taught:

Integrating: Using one's prior knowledge to make sense out of text.
Organizing: Identifying important ideas and the relationships among them.
Elaborating: Making necessary inferences while reading.
Monitoring: Evaluating one's comprehension and adjusting one's reading strategy.

Accumulated research evidence from the past 20 years shows that it is possible to help students learn component skills such as how to write a summary of a passage, how to predict what will come next, how to clarify a sentence, how to generate questions, and how to detect inconsistencies (Pearson & Fielding, 1991; Pressley & Woloshyn, 1995). These findings are consistent with Bartlett's (1932) vision of reading comprehension as an active search for meaning.

The task for any effective reading program is to incorporate successful techniques into an integrated reading program for classroom use. As we observed in this chapter, a large body of scientific research addresses how readers use their prior knowledge, make judgments of importance, draw inferences, and monitor their comprehension process. Because school reading comprehension instruction is shaped by a few major basal reader series (Chall & Squire, 1991; Rosenshine, 1980), it would make sense for such programs to be coordinated with research on reading comprehension. An important trend for the future would be for reading programs to be developed in accord with the research on reading and for theories of reading instruction to be tested within the context of real school reading programs. This section briefly examines a traditional reading comprehension program that has a long history—SQ3R.

Suppose we could find a well-established and long-lived program that is widely used in many schools to promote reading comprehension. SQ3R is a reading comprehension program that fits this definition. It was developed long before most of the research cited in this chapter was conducted, but seems consistent with the general theme that reading comprehension is an active process of making sense out of text.

Robinson—1941, 1961 suggested that learners be trained to use five steps in reading a new passage: survey, question, read, recite, and review (SQ3R). During the survey step, the reader skims the material to get an idea of what the passage is about. For example, in reading this chapter, you might read the beginning and concluding sentences and headings of each section. During the question step, the reader formulates a question for each subheading or unit of the passage. For example, for this section of the text you might ask, "What makes an effective reading comprehension program?" In the read step, the student reads the passage with the goal of answering the question for each subheading or part of the passage. In the recite step, the student answers each question in his or her own words. In the review step, the student practices recalling as much information as possible from each section of the passage.

Adams, Carnine, and Gersten (1982) pointed out that since its inception SQ3R has been "widely reported in textbooks and teacher training manuals as being empirically based, though in fact the research literature does not support the claims" (p. 31). For example, Adams et al. (1982) were able to locate only six studies evaluating the effectiveness of SQ3R, but five had serious methodological flaws and the sixth did not use school-aged subjects. Similarly, Shepard (1978) argued that some students fail to use this system because it appears to be too time-consuming. In a more recent review, Pressley and McCormick (1995) noted that "although recommended in many study skills courses, [SQ3R] does not have a track record of exceptional effectiveness" (p. 374).

Adams et al. (1982) developed a four-day training program similar to SQ3R, but with each step based on the current reading comprehension research. Direct instruction was provided in each of the five skills already listed, using sample passages in social studies. Unlike previous studies, the subjects were elementary school children (fifth-graders) who possessed adequate decoding skills but poor study skills. To assess the effectiveness of the training program, students were asked to read a passage and then to retell it and answer some factual questions about it. Students who were given the training scored 47% correct on the questions compared to only 28% correct by students who were not trained. The trained group also remembered more of the important information than the control group, but the difference failed to reach statistical significance. Apparently, students can be taught to read in ways that will enhance their ability to answer factual questions. However, more research is needed to understand when, why, where, and for whom SQ3R affects reading comprehension.

In Chapter 13, I describe a more recent program aimed at improving reading comprehension called *reciprocal teaching* (Palinscar & Brown, 1984; Brown & Palinscar, 1989). This program teaches specific skills such as how to summarize a passage or predict what will come next, and students learn by working in a group to make sense of an academic text. As you will see in Chapter 13, teaching of specific skills within the context of an authentic academic task can be a powerful approach to teaching of reading comprehension.

CHAPTER SUMMARY

This chapter briefly explored the processes by which a reader comes to understand a passage, that is, the processes of reading comprehension. We began by examining Bartlett's (1932) concept of "effort after meaning," the view that reading involves trying to make sense out of what is presented. Then, we explored four cognitive processes involved in reading comprehension: using prior knowledge, using prose structure, making inferences, and engaging in comprehension monitoring.

First, this chapter presented examples of the well-documented evidence concerning prior knowledge. For both adults and children, a reader who has appropriate background knowledge comprehends a passage differently from one who lacks such knowledge. In particular, a reader with rich background knowledge is more likely to make inferences that give coherence to the passage.

Second, this chapter presented examples of the well-documented evidence concerning prose structure. For adults and older children, readers are more likely to remember important information than unimportant information from a passage. However, younger readers are less likely to be able to distinguish between important and unimportant information in the text and are less likely to spend their study time focusing on the important information.

Third, this chapter examined examples of research concerning inference making during reading. Younger readers are much less likely than older readers to make inferences spontaneously. Although answering inference questions can be taught, the general effects of inference training on reading comprehension are not yet clear.

Fourth, this chapter examined the research on metacognitive processes such as comprehension monitoring. Again, some evidence indicates that younger readers are less likely than older readers to monitor their performance or to alter their reading strategy for different tasks.

For each of these cognitive processes in reading comprehension, we explored exemplary research studies in which students could be taught to use the process.

Finally, the chapter examined reading programs that teach comprehension skills. Although this chapter cannot provide many definitive conclusions, it does point to the crucial contribution of the reader's existing knowledge—content, strategic, and metacognitive—in the reading process. Given the emerging research base on teaching reading comprehension processes, it may soon be possible to build an integrated reading comprehension program that develops students' content, strategic, and metacognitive knowledge for reading.

SUGGESTED READINGS

Barr, R., Kamil, M. L., Mosenthal, P., & Pearson, P. D. (Eds.). (1991). *Handbook of reading research* (Vol. 2). New York: Longman. (A collection of papers by leading researchers on reading.)

Bartlett, F. C. (1932). *Remembering*. London: Cambridge University Press. (Presents work that was the forerunner of modern cognitive research on learning from prose.)

Cesare, C., & Oakhill, J. (Eds.). (1996). *Reading comprehension difficulties*. Mahwah, NJ: Erlbaum. (A collection of papers aimed at understanding the cognitive processes underlying reading comprehension difficulties.)

CHAPTER 4 Learning to Write

CHAPTER OUTLINE

The Storytelling Problem

Cognitive Processes in Writing

Planning

Translating

Reviewing

Building a Writing Program That Works

Chapter Summary

This chapter asks the question, What processes are involved in writing a composition? The answer to this question includes planning what to write, translating from the plan to words on the page, and reviewing what has been written. Students need training in each of these component processes in writing.

THE STORYTELLING PROBLEM

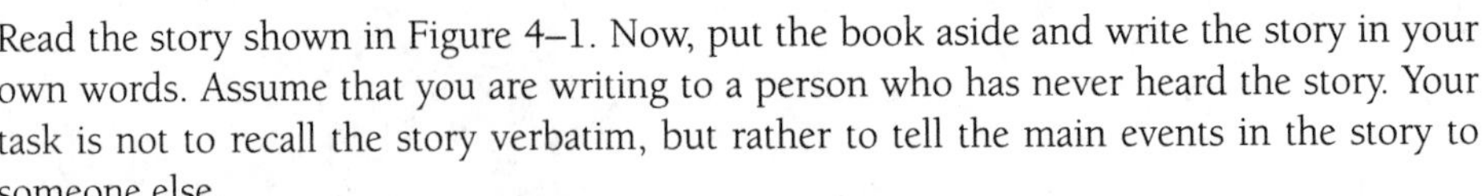

Read the story shown in Figure 4–1. Now, put the book aside and write the story in your own words. Assume that you are writing to a person who has never heard the story. Your task is not to recall the story verbatim, but rather to tell the main events in the story to someone else.

Figure 4–2 shows the main points of the story. Did your version of the story contain all or most of these points? Did you clearly introduce the lady and the fairy (rather than just referring to them as "she")? Could someone else read your story and understand it? Did your story present the events in the proper order?

This story is taken from an early study by Piaget (1926). In the study, a child between the ages of six and eight was asked to listen to the story and was given instructions like these:

FIGURE 4–1

Can you retell this story?

Once upon a time, there was a lady who was called Niobe, and who had twelve sons and twelve daughters. She met a fairy who had only one son and no daughter. Then the lady laughed at the fairy because the fairy only had one boy. Then the fairy was very angry and fastened the lady to a rock. The lady cried for ten years. In the end she turned into a rock, and her tears made a stream which still runs today.

From Piaget (1926)

FIGURE 4–2

The main points in the story

1. Once there was a lady (or Niobe, etc.).
2. She had children (provided they outnumber those of the other character).
3. She met a fairy (or a girl, etc.).
4. This fairy had few children (or none, provided their number is inferior to the first lot).
5. The lady laughed at the fairy.
6. Because the fairy had so few children.
7. The fairy was angry.
8. The fairy fastened the lady to a rock (or a tree, etc.).
9. The lady cried.
10. She turned into a rock.
11. Her tears made a stream.
12. Which flows to this day.

From Piaget (1926)

> Are you good at telling stories? Very well then, we'll send your little friend out of the room, and while he is gone, we'll tell you a story. You must listen carefully. When you have listened to it all, we'll make your friend come back, and then you will tell him the same story. (pp. 96–97)

Some examples of the stories that children told are given in Figure 4–3. As you can see, the children make many mistakes in their retelling of the story. Some of their obvious problems are leaving out crucial pieces of information, such as the reason that the fairy attacked the lady; referring to characters by pronouns that lack clear referents; and ignoring the order of events. Piaget (1926) summarized the performance of his young storytellers as follows: "The words spoken are not thought of from the point of view of the person spoken to" (p. 16). In other words, the children seemed to have trouble taking the listener's point of view, so they behaved as if the listener already knew the story (i.e., young children assume that everyone else knows what they know). In contrast, adults are often able to adjust their stories for different audiences (i.e., adults can often take the listener's perspective into account).

In this chapter, we explore the nature of writing. What does Piaget's storytelling demonstration tell us about writing? His work suggests that one major aspect of speaking and

FIGURE 4–3

How children told the story

Ri (age eight)

There was a lady once, she had twelve boys and twelve girls. She goes for a walk and she meets a fairy who had a boy and a girl and who didn't want to have twelve children. Twelve and twelve make twenty-four. She didn't want to have twenty-four children. She fastened N to a stone, she became a rock.

Gio (age eight)

Once upon a time there was a lady who had twelve boys and twelve girls, and then a fairy a boy and a girl. And then Niobe wanted to have some more sons. Then she was angry. She fastened her to a stone. He turned into a rock and then his tears made a stream which is still running today.

Met (age six)

The lady laughed at this fairy because she only had one boy. The lady had twelve sons and twelve daughters. One day she laughed at her. She was angry and she fastened her beside a stream. She cried for fifty months, and it made a great big stream.

Ce (age six)

There's a lady who was called Morel, and then she turned into a stream . . . then she had ten daughters and ten sons . . . and then after that the fairy fastened her to the bank of a stream and then she cried twenty months, and then after that she cried for twenty months and then her tears went into the stream, and then . . .

From Piaget (1926)

writing is to influence an audience. In speaking, the audience is physically present, but in writing, the audience is not physically present. Thus the requirement of keeping the audience in one's mind as one writes is particularly difficult; adult writing often shows some of the egocentric characteristics and disorganization of Piaget's young storytellers. This demonstration suggests that writing is a skill that depends partly on the writer's ability to understand the perspective of the audience (i.e., of the potential readers).

What does a good writer need to know? In answer to this question, Applebee (1982) identified three kinds of knowledge, each of which is exemplified in Piaget's storytelling study:

1. *Knowledge of language,* such as the grammatical rules of English.
2. *Knowledge of topic,* such as the specific information to be conveyed.
3. *Knowledge of audience,* such as the perspective of the potential readers.

The remainder of this chapter explores how writers use these bodies of knowledge in the writing process, and how the writing process can be improved through instruction.

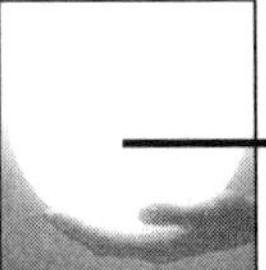

COGNITIVE PROCESSES IN WRITING

ANALYZING WRITING INTO THREE PROCESSES

Suppose that you were asked to write a short biographical story, such as an essay on how a water faucet works or a business letter. What cognitive processes would occur as you wrote? To examine this issue, Flower and Hayes (1981; Hayes & Flower, 1980; Hayes, 1996) gave writing assignments to people and asked them to describe what they were thinking as they carried out the assignment. This procedure is called *thinking aloud,* and the final transcript of everything that the writer says is called a *thinking aloud protocol.*

Based on their analysis of writers' thinking aloud protocols, Hayes and Flower (1980) identified three distinct processes in writing—planning, translating, and reviewing:

Planning involves searching for information from one's long-term memory, from the assignment, and from what has been written so far, and using this information to establish a plan for producing text. Three subprocesses in planning are generating, organizing, and goal setting. *Generating* involves retrieving information relevant to the writing task from one's long-term memory; for example, in writing an essay on the writing process, you might remember that the three major processes are planning, translating, and reviewing. *Organizing* involves selecting the most useful information that you have retrieved and structuring it into a writing plan; for example, in writing an essay on the writing process, you might devote one section to each of the three major processes in the order given earlier. *Goal setting* involves establishing general criteria for guiding the execution of the writing plan; for example, you may decide that since your audience is unfamiliar with the material, your essay on the writing process should be kept simple and free of jargon. To be more consistent with newer taxonomies of planning (Kellogg, 1994, 2000), this chapter includes goal setting under the planning subprocess of *evaluating* (i.e., determining the degree to which planned writing corresponds to the writer's goals).

Translating involves producing text that is consistent with the plan, that is, the act of putting words on the page. For example, the produced text should consist of legible, grammatically correct English sentences that convey the intended information in an effective way.

Reviewing involves improving the written text using the subprocesses of *reading* and *editing*. In reading, the writer detects problems in the text; in editing, the writer attempts to correct the problems. For example, if the first draft contains a sentence that is ungrammatical or that fails to convey the intended meaning the sentence will be rewritten as part of the reviewing process.

Figure 4–4 provides a simplified version of the general model of writing proposed by Hayes and Flower (1980). The three shaded rectangles represent the three major processes in writing. The two unshaded rectangles on the left represent the input into the writing process: the writing assignment (including an understanding of the topic and audience) and the writer's knowledge (including knowledge of the topic, the audience, and written English). The unshaded rectangle on the right represents the output (i.e., the text that is produced). The arrows indicate that the three writing processes interact rather than occur in a fixed order.

More recently, Hayes (1996) offered a revised model that still contains three basic cognitive processes in writing. However, in his model planning is subsumed into a broader process called *reflection*, "an activity that operates on internal representations to produce other internal representations" (p. 13); translating is subsumed into a broader process

FIGURE 4–4 A model of the writing process

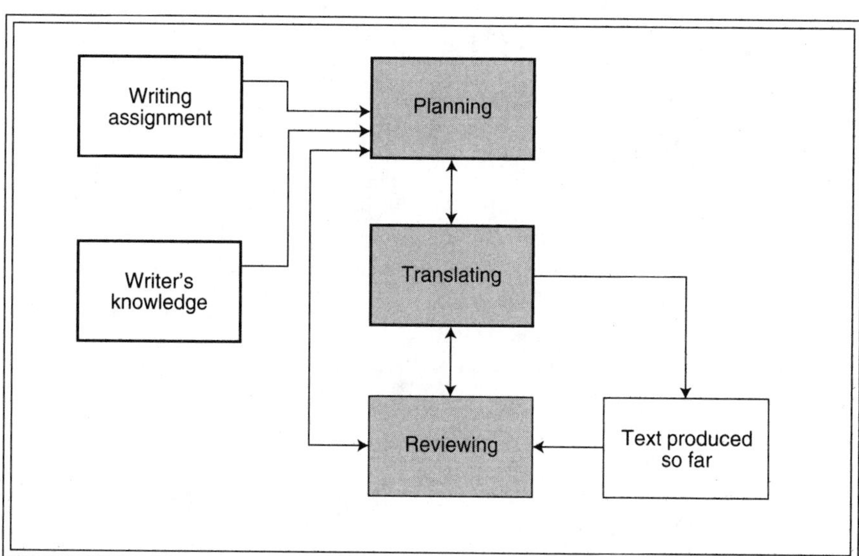

Adapted from Hayes and Flower (1980)

called *text production,* "a function that takes internal representations . . . and produces written, spoken, or graphical output" (p. 13); and reviewing is replaced by *text interpretation,* a process that "creates internal representations from linguistic and graphic inputs" (Hayes, 1996, p. 13). In addition, Hayes's revised model emphasizes the role of working memory in writing, includes visual and spatial representations in writing (such as graphs, tables, and pictures), and acknowledges the role of motivational and social factors in writing.

Similar analyses of the writing process have been proposed by other researchers. For example, Nold (1981) suggests three major processes: planning, transcribing (corresponding to translating), and reviewing. Similarly, Bruce, Collins, Rubin, and Gentner (1982) include the following steps in their model of writing: production of ideas (corresponding to planning), production of text (corresponding to translating), and editing (corresponding to reviewing). Gould (1980) lists four processes: planning, accessing additional information (corresponding to a part of planning), generating (corresponding to translating), and reviewing. In a recent review, Kellogg (1994) concluded that "writing involves four cognitive operations that play a role in all thinking tasks: collecting information, planning ideas, translating ideas into text . . . , and reviewing ideas and text" (p. 16). The first two processes would be considered part of planning in the Hayes and Flower model, whereas the second two correspond to translating and reviewing, respectively. Apparently, there is some consensus that the major writing processes include planning, translating, and reviewing. Furthermore, all the analyses assume that a great deal of interaction occurs among the processes, rather than each process occurring separately.

LOOKING AT STUDENT PROTOCOLS

As evidence to support their model of the writing process, Hayes and Flower (1980) presented an analysis of the thinking aloud protocol of a typical writer. The protocol contained 14 pages covering 458 simple statements or comments made by the writer. The protocol could be divided into three sections. In the first section, consisting of the first 116 comments, the writer seemed to focus on the planning subprocess of generating information, with occasional interruptions to focus on reviewing. Some typical comments made during this section of the protocol were "And what I'll do now is simply jot down random thoughts . . . " and "Other things to think about in this random search are. . . ." In the second section, consisting of the next 154 comments, the writer concentrated on the planning subprocess of organizing the information, with occasional interruptions to focus on reviewing. Typical comments made during this section of the protocol included "Now I think it's time to go back and read over the material and elaborate on its organization." Finally, in the third section, containing the final 188 comments, the writer emphasized the process of translating, with occasional interruptions for generating and reviewing. Examples of typical comments were "Let's try and write something," or "Oh, no. We need more organizing" (p. 10).

Figure 4–5 shows the proportion of comments directed toward generating, organizing, translating, and reviewing for each section of the protocol. These data were derived using only major comments from two writers. As can be seen, the first section of the protocol is devoted mainly to generating ideas, the second mainly to organizing the ideas, and the third mainly to translating the writing plan into acceptable sentences. In addition, the

FIGURE 4–5 What writers do during the writing process

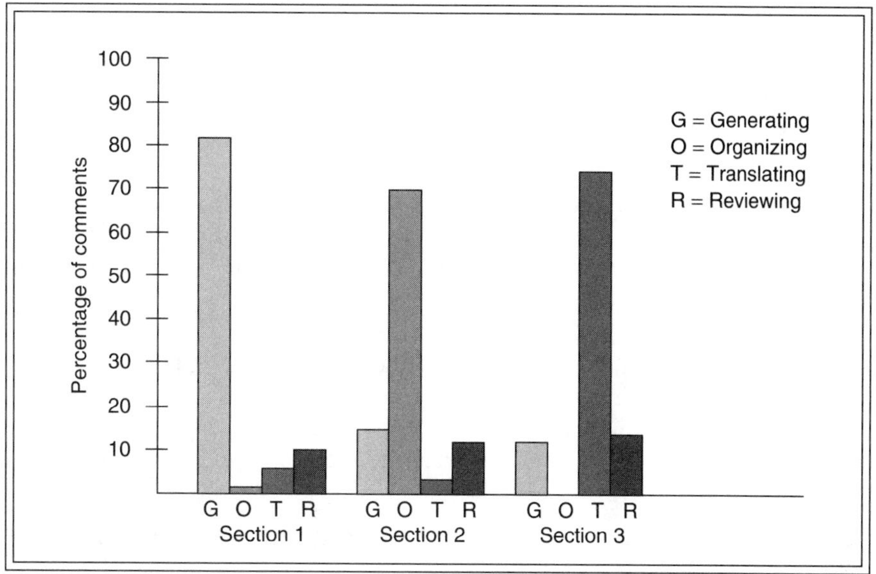

Adapted from Hayes and Flower (1980)

reviewing process (consisting mainly of editing) seems to play a small part in each of the three sections of the protocol.

INSTRUCTIONAL THEMES

As can be seen in the foregoing analysis, the study of writing is in its early stages of development. However, even in this early work on writing, several implications for writing instruction have emerged.

PROCESS VERSUS PRODUCT Much of the emphasis in writing instruction is typically on the final product, including spelling, punctuation, and grammar. An additional focus suggested by the cognitive analysis of writing is that writing instruction should also concentrate on the *process* of writing. In particular, the foregoing analysis suggests that most of the time and effort in writing is devoted to planning rather than to actually producing acceptable text. Steinberg (1980) summarizes this idea as follows: "teaching of writing focuses too much on product, on the written paper that the student submits, and not enough on process, on how to write" (p. 156).

PROBLEM SOLVING VERSUS PROCEDURE APPLICATION Much of the instruction in writing involves teaching procedures for producing sentences properly, such as "Never begin a sentence with 'because,'" or "Each paragraph should have a topic sentence, a summary sentence, and approximately three core sentences." In addition to using such procedures, a writer must also engage in an act of problem solving. For example, Kellogg (1994) shows that "in composing a written text, individuals . . . engage in a special form of thinking—the making of meaning—that may well define one of the most unique characteristics of our species" (p. 3). As in other types of problem solving, the writer must establish goals and work to achieve them. Thus instruction in writing may be viewed as instruction in problem solving. Flower and Hayes (1981) make this argument as follows: "writing is problem solving, and can be analyzed from a psychological view of problem-solving processes" (p. 40).

COMMUNICATION VERSUS COMPOSITION Much of the instruction in writing involves learning to produce a composition that meets stylistic and grammatical requirements. Nystrand (1982a) points out there is an emphasis on "proper talk" and "standardized composition" rather than on writing in a way that influences the audience. In addition to teaching students how to write compositions that conform to "school English," students must learn to be sensitive to the idea that writing is an attempt to communicate with a reader. As Frase (1982) points out, "effective writing is bringing one's own goals in line with the readers' constraints" (p. 130). Similarly, Nystrand (1982a) notes that writers need to develop a "notion of audience as person or persons whom . . . the writer hopes to influence" (p. 2).

KNOWLEDGE TRANSFORMING AND KNOWLEDGE TELLING Bereiter and Scardamalia (1987) distinguished between knowledge transforming, in which a writer selects and organizes ideas into a coherent message, and knowledge telling, in which a writer expresses ideas in the order they are thought of. In knowledge transforming, the writer modifies the knowledge he or she accesses in order to communicate with a reader, whereas in knowledge telling, the writer's goal is to present information to the reader. One of the main differences between knowledge transforming and knowledge telling lies in the role of planning in that knowledge transforming requires more planning than does knowledge telling. According to this analysis, a major goal of writing instruction is to help students progress from a knowledge-telling approach to a knowledge-transforming approach.

In the remainder of this chapter, we examine each of the three major processes in writing—planning, translating, and reviewing—as well as the educational implications of work in these areas.

PLANNING

WHAT IS PLANNING?

As noted in the previous section, planning is a major process in writing. Planning includes generating information from memory, which Hayes and Flower (1980) call *generating*; evaluating that information with respect to criteria for writing, which Hayes and Flower (1980) call *goal setting;* and organizing that information into a writing plan, which Hayes and Flower (1980) call *organizing*.

RESEARCH ON PLANNING

HOW MUCH DO STUDENTS PLAN IN DICTATION? As an example of planning, let's suppose you were asked to dictate a one-page business letter. The dictation rate is potentially 200 words per minute (i.e., a person can speak comfortably at a rate of 200 words per minute). However, Gould (1980) reports that the normal dictation rate is approximately 23 words per minute. Similarly, suppose you were asked to write a one-page business letter. The writing rate is potentially 40 words per minute, yet Gould (1980) reports that the normal writing rate for business letters is 13 words per minute.

These results indicate that people produce text much more slowly than the limits imposed by the output device (writing or dictating). Why do people dictate (or write) at such slow rates? According to research summarized by Gould (1980), most of the speaking or writing time is devoted to planning. For example, by carefully recording pauses that are made during speaking or writing, Gould (1978a, 1978b, 1980) was able to determine that pauses accounted for approximately two-thirds of total composition time in both writing and speaking. These results are summarized in Figure 4–6.

WHEN DO STUDENTS PLAN IN WRITING? Interestingly, Gould's studies revealed that planning pauses occurred during the writing process (as *local planning*) rather than before it (as *global planning*), suggesting that writers rarely plan before they start writing. In a more focused study, Matsuhashi (1982, 1987) carefully observed the pauses made by high school students as they wrote essays. As in the Gould study, Matsuhashi found that

FIGURE 4–6 How much planning time is used in writing or dictating a letter?

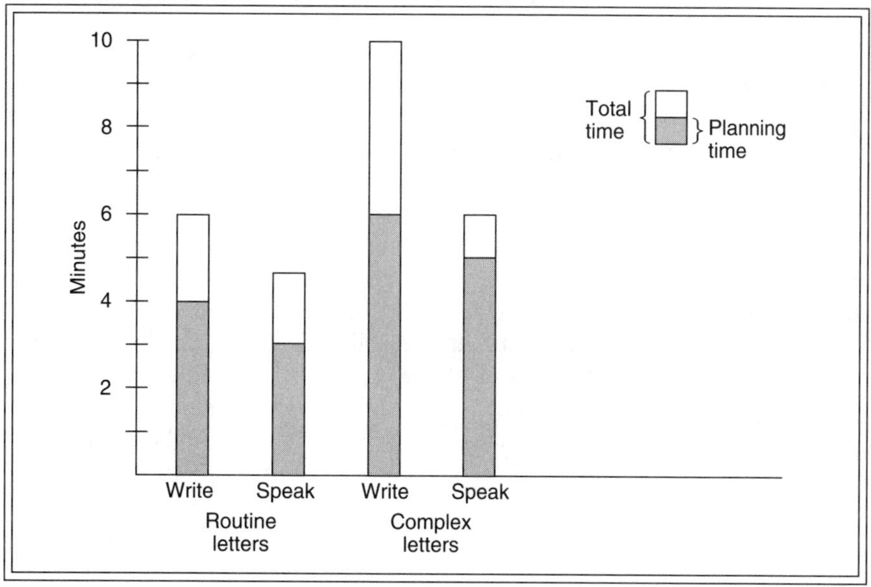

Adapted from Gould (1980)

planning time accounted for approximately one-half to two-thirds of the total writing time. In addition, Matsuhashi found that pauses occurred mainly at the borders between ideas (e.g., at the end of sentences). Figure 4–7 shows the time spent by a high school student in writing an essay; the numbers after each word indicate the length of the pause (in seconds) that occurred before the writer moved on to the next word. As can be seen, the longest pauses are in line 4 (9.7 seconds before going on to a new clause), line 5 (16.6 seconds after the sentence), line 8 (13.3 seconds before the new paragraph), and line 11 (12.8 seconds after the sentence). During some of the longer pauses, the writer removed his pen from the paper and shifted position in his seat. Matsuhashi suggests that the pauses allowed the writer to organize the information mentally and place it within the appropriate context.

HOW FAR AHEAD DO STUDENTS PLAN? Additional evidence concerning the planning process is reported by Scardamalia, Bereiter, and Goelman (1982). For example, in one study elementary school children were asked to write an essay. At various points during the writing process, the teacher would interrupt a student, asking what he or she was going to write. Usually students had the next five or six words in mind and had thought ahead to the end of the clause. Young children (in the primary grades) tended to dictate to themselves, mouthing each word while writing. In contrast, older children (grade 4 and above) rarely vocalized during writing but did vocalize during pauses. Apparently, young children rely on external memory (i.e., self-dictation) in order to keep the next few words in their short-term memory, whereas older children behave as if a memory load of several words does not require external memory.

FIGURE 4–7

Pauses in writing an essay

1 Truly$^{.6}$successful$^{1.1}$person$^{.5}$-to$^{.8}$-person$^{2.3}$communi-
2 $^{1.8}$cation$^{3.5}$is$^{1.9}$difficult$^{1.3}$because$^{6.9}$people$^{.6}$in$^{.9}$general$^{1.1}$are$^{.9}$poor
3 $^{1.0}$listeners. $^{7.0}$They$^{1.0}$would$^{.7}$rather$^{1.4}$listen$^{.5}$to$^{.9}$themselves $^{1.9}$speaking
4 $^{2.1}$than$^{.4}$someone$^{.7}$else$^{.5}$.$^{4.7}$It$^{.9}$is$^{.7}$my$^{.7}$feeling$^{1.9}$that$^{9.7}$this$^{.8}$occurs
5 $^{1.6}$because$^{1.1}$of$^{1.2}$a$^{.8}$basic$^{2.7}$self-centeredness.$^{16.6}$People $^{4.8}$tend$^{1.2}$to
6 $^{1.9}$be$^{.6}$more$^{.5}$interested$^{.7}$in$^{.7}$their$^{.9}$own$^{.7}$lives$^{1.5}$to$^{1.2}$bother$^{1.0}$ exposing
7 $^{1.3}$themselves$^{.7}$to$^{.5}$how$^{.7}$others$^{.8}$live.
8 $^{13.3}$Communication$^{1.2}$is$^{.7}$successful$^{.8}$only$^{.9}$when$^{2.9}$there
9 $^{2.2}$is$^{2.4}$“$^{.5}$give$^{.6}$and$^{.8}$take”$^{1.1}$between$^{3.7}$the$^{.7}$parties$^{1.1}$. $^{3.7}$Each$^{.7}$one
10 $^{1.9}$should$^{.9}$contribute$^{1.2}$equally$^{2.1}$,$^{1.0}$as$^{.8}$well$^{.7}$as$^{2.0}$accepting$^{.7}$the
11 $^{2.2}$contributions$^{5.3}$of$^{.6}$the$^{.7}$others. $^{12.8}$The$^{.6}$situation$^{.7}$I$^{1.0}$have
12 $^{1.8}$described$^{6.6}$above$^{3.2}$leads$^{.6}$to$^{.6}$poor$^{.8}$communication$^{1.7}$,$^{1.0}$since
13 $^{1.9}$everyone$^{.8}$wants$^{.9}$to$^{.6}$“give”$^{1.2}$and$^{.8}$no$^{1.0}$one$^{.6}$wants$^{.9}$to
14 $^{1.2}$“take.”

(Numbers after words indicate pause times, in seconds.)

From Matsuhashi (1982)

DO EXPERIENCED AND INEXPERIENCED WRITERS PLAN DIFFERENTLY? Experienced writers are more likely than inexperienced writers to generate, evaluate, and organize ideas before writing; that is, experienced writers engage in more global planning than do inexperienced writers. For example, Pianko (1979) found that few students—even at the high school and college levels—engage in any planning prior to writing a school assignment. In contrast, professional writers overwhelmingly report creating some sort of written outline before beginning a draft (Stotsky, 1990). When told to write a short story within a time limit ranging from 2.5 to 20 minutes, fifth-grade and tenth-grade students generally began writing immediately, whereas adults were more likely to engage in prewriting planning activities such as writing an outline (Zbrodoff, 1985). When given longer time limits for the assignment, adults, in contrast to elementary and high school students, spent more time planning and produced more detailed outlines (Zbrodoff, 1985). These results suggest that global planning is a hallmark of experienced writers.

Bereiter and Scardamalia (1987) analyzed the ideas generated by students at various ages, and identified three stages of planning activity. First, young children such as those entering elementary school have difficulty generating any ideas at all. Writers at this level have problems with even the most basic planning subprocess—generating ideas. Second, elementary school children (up to approximately 12 years old) engage in knowledge telling—expressing ideas as they are generated without evaluating or organizing them. Writers at this stage seem to have mastered one planning subprocess—generating ideas—but have not mastered other planning subprocesses, such as evaluating and organizing ideas. Third, older writers can engage in knowledge transforming—generating, evaluating, and organizing ideas before expressing them in order to communicate with the reader. This analysis shows how the ability to generate ideas is not enough, because students also need to learn how to evaluate and organize the ideas they have generated.

IMPLICATIONS FOR INSTRUCTION: PLANNING

In summary, this section presented several important findings concerning the planning process: planning is a time-consuming process accounting for most of writing time, local planning seems to occur mainly at sentence and clause boundaries, local planning generally allows the writer to work on one clause or sentence at a time, and inexperienced writers often do not engage in global planning.

Although the ability to generate, evaluate, and organize ideas is central to the writing process, writing instruction does not normally teach students how to plan. The foregoing analysis of planning suggests that students may need instruction and practice in how to generate ideas, how to organize information, and how to evaluate whether that information fits into the organization.

A major finding of the research on planning is that students often fail to engage in global planning; that is, they fail to generate ideas, evaluate those ideas for relevance to the writing goals, and organize the relevant ideas before writing. If writers do not engage in these prewriting activities, they may have to try to generate, evaluate, and organize at the same time that they are engaged in translating. By trying to do two things at once—plan and translate—both processes might suffer, resulting in lower-quality essays. It follows that an important instructional intervention is to encourage students to engage in a range of planning subprocesses—including generating, evaluating, and organizing—before they begin to write.

For example, Kellogg (1994) investigated the hypothesis that asking students to plan before they write would result in better essays. College students were asked to write an essay on the pros and cons of professionals joining an "Anti-Greed" Club, based on the following instructions:

> Imagine that you are a successful professional. An "Anti-Greed" Club has been formed in your neighborhood. All the members of this club are professionals like you (attorneys, physicians, business executives, etc.) who earn over $50,000 per year. Each member pledges to give annual income over $50,000 to poor families in the community. The recipients and amount each receives are decided by chance—that is, by a drawing. Several members of your social club are considering joining the "Anti-Greed" Club and have asked your help in making an objective, rational decision. Write a paper giving the pros and cons of such a move as you see it. Be careful to give fair treatment to both sides of the issue, regardless of how you feel about it personally. (Kellogg, 1987, p. 262)

One group of students was not asked to engage in any prewriting activity (no-prewriting group) so that no planning processes were activated prior to writing. Another group was asked to write down as many ideas as possible without evaluating or organizing them (generating group), so that only the planning subprocess of generating was activated. Another group was asked to generate a list of relevant ideas (listing group), so that the planning subprocesses of generating and evaluating (or goal setting) were activated. Finally, a group was asked to produce an outline containing relevant ideas within a hierarchical structure (outlining group) so that the planning subprocesses of generating, evaluating (or goal setting), and organizing were activated.

How do prewriting activities affect what is written? Judges were asked to rate the quality of each essay on a 10-point scale. Figure 4–8 shows that the average quality ratings of the essays written by the no-prewriting group and the generating group were low, whereas the outlining group wrote the highest-quality essays. According to Kellogg (1994), students in the no-prewriting group and the generating group must try to engage in planning and translating processes at the same time. Given the constraints on how much can be processed in working memory at one time, the quality of their writing was affected. In contrast, when students engaged in intensive planning before writing, as those in the outlining group had done, memory resources could be used mainly for the translating processes during writing, thus allowing for better essays. Similarly, Kellogg (1988) found that students composed better business letters when they were forced to spend 10 minutes generating an outline before writing than when there was no prewriting activity. Kellogg's results are encouraging, because they show that it is possible to teach students to engage in productive planning processes before they begin to write.

Fostering planning skills in students includes helping students learn how to generate, evaluate, and organize ideas. First, training students in how to retrieve information is an important aspect of planning. Students need practice in how to search for needed information, including how to take (and use) notes from sources. A key finding in many writing studies is that students' knowledge of the domain is a crucial determinant of the quality of the writing (Voss & Bisanz, 1985). For example, Caccamise (1987) found that students

FIGURE 4–8 Quality of essays produced after four types of prewriting activities

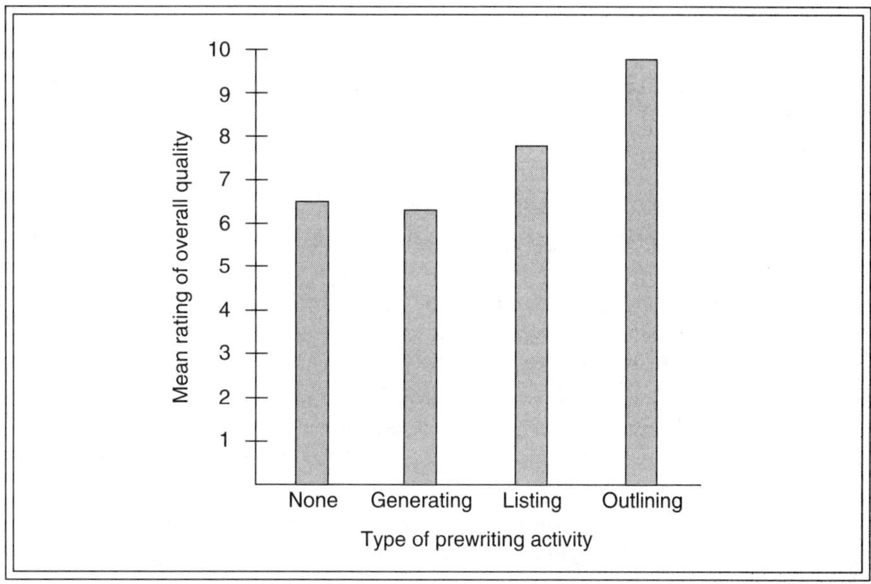

Adapted from Kellogg (1994)

generated far more ideas when writing about a familiar topic than when writing about an unfamiliar one. In short, students need to write about topics that they already know about or have researched. Second, students need practice in establishing goals and evaluating whether the ideas they generate meet their goals, including being able to write for a specific audience and for a specific purpose. Third, learning to organize ideas into a coherent structure is another important aspect of planning, which often involves being able to create and monitor outlines.

TRANSLATING

WHAT IS TRANSLATING?

The next component in the writing process is what Hayes and Flower (1980) call *translating*. This phase involves carrying out the writing plan by actually generating some written text. According to Hayes and Flower, translating is done interactively with planning; in other words, a writer generates a plan, translates a small part of it, then checks the next part of the plan, translates that part, and so on. Research described in the previous section suggests that people may translate one phrase (or simple sentence) at a time.

CONSTRAINTS ON TRANSLATING Suppose that you write by checking your overall writing plan, sentence by sentence. In other words, you check your plan for the first main idea and then try to translate it into a sentence. Then you check your plan for the next main idea and try to translate it into a sentence, and so on. As you move from your writing plan (i.e., your idea of what you want to say) to the production of prose (i.e., the sentence that you actually write), you are constrained by several factors. As listed by Nystrand (1982b), these constraining factors are:

Graphic: The sentences that you generate must be legible for the reader; they must use lettering, penmanship, layout, spacing, indentation, and spelling that are familiar to the reader.

Syntactic: The sentences that you generate must be based on the rules of written English; grammar, punctuation, and sentence organization must be appropriate for the reader.

Semantic: The sentences that you generate must convey the meaning to the reader that you intended; your assumptions about the information that a reader brings to the reading task must be appropriate.

Textual: The sentences that you generate must fit together into a cohesive paragraph and passage.

Contextual: The sentences that you generate must be written in the appropriate style (e.g., sarcasm or understatement).

Each of these types of constraints involves ensuring a correspondence between your written words and the reader's understanding of them. Examples of writers' failures to follow the constraints on writer-reader communication are given in Figure 4–9. Nystrand

FIGURE 4–9

Examples of five errors in writer-reader communication

Graphic Misconstraint
"now here" for "nowhere"

Syntactic Misconstraint
"Your still going to get where your going with a seatbelt on."

Semantic Misconstraint
"The law against drinking is for your own safety." (Written to adults whereas the law against drinking applies only to minors.)

Textual Misconstraint
"I think that the snowmobilers will get used to these new laws, and people will see the laws the government put out are for our protection." (The previous sentences have discussed only automobile seatbelts so the reader has not been prepared to consider snowmobiles.)

Contextual Misconstraint
Asking high school students to read the state laws on drunk driving.

Adapted from Nystrand (1982b)

(1982b) refers to these examples as *misconstraints* (i.e., cases in which the reader is either misled or misinterprets the writer's information).

RESEARCH ON TRANSLATING

REMOVING CONSTRAINTS ON TRANSLATING The translation process may require a great deal of attentional capacity on the part of young writers, because so much of the translation process is not yet automatic to them. One solution to this problem is to ignore the normal constraints on writing, as the following writing from a six-year-old demonstrates:

> WONS A LITOL GIRL WOS WOKIG IN HR GARDIN INTIL SE GOT KOT BIY A ROBR AND TIN SE SKREMD AND TIN HR MON AND DAD KAM OUT AND HLPT HR OWT OV THE ROBRS HANDS AND TIN TAY KOLD THE POLES AND TIN THE POLES TOK KAR OV THE ROBR AN POT HIM IN THE GAOL (Read, 1981, pp. 106–107)

As can be seen, this young writer was able to tell a story without paying great attention to some of the basic rules of spelling, punctuation, grammar, and the like. By freeing herself from the tedious constraints on writing, the young writer was able to produce a story.

Read (1981) suggests that "teachers and parents can look upon early writing in roughly the same way that they regard children's art, as an expression which is created with pleasure and which is not expected to be adult-like" (p. 114). In addition, Read provides evidence that the use of nonstandard spelling during writing does not adversely affect reading; for example, the little girl who wrote this story was able to sight-read words such as "girl" even though she wrote "GROL."

In most school writing tasks, the graphic and syntactic constraints (as well as others) are enforced. If the rules of spelling, grammar, and even penmanship are not yet automatic, then the writer's full attentional capacity must be devoted to the correct production of text rather than to organizational planning. For example, Scardamalia, Bereiter, and Goelman (1982) proposed that since the information-processing capacity of young writers is limited, and since the mechanical and syntactic aspects of writing are not automatic, an emphasis on correctly formed sentences results in poorer overall writing quality. The low-level aspects of writing (such as correct spelling, punctuation, and penmanship) interfere with higher-level planning.

To test this idea, Bereiter and Scardamalia (1987) asked fourth- and sixth-grade children to write an essay, dictate an essay at a normal rate, or dictate an essay at a slow rate. The dictation modes were used because they presumably freed the young writer from some of the mechanical and syntactic demands of translating. As predicted, the dictation modes resulted in about twice as many words being produced and in small increases in judged quality, as compared to writing. However, Gould (1980) notes that dictation does not tend to increase the quality of prose in adults. Apparently, the mechanical processes of handwriting, proper spelling, and punctuation are not automatic in young writers, but, for simple assignments, do eventually become automatic in adults. Thus the act of translating ideas into words may actually disrupt the flow of thinking in young writers.

POLISHED VERSUS UNPOLISHED FIRST DRAFTS There is some potentially important evidence that the quality of adult writing is also hindered when attention must be focused on the mechanics of writing. For example, suppose that you were asked to write a formal business letter in order to persuade your teacher to use a future class period for either a film that is related to the course or for a library reading session. First, you will have 10 minutes to complete a preliminary draft. Then, after a 5-minute rest period, you will have 10 minutes to produce the final draft.

Suppose your goal is to produce a high-quality final draft, containing many persuasive arguments expressed in a coherent way. Would it be better to try to write a polished letter as your first draft—including proper sentence formation, punctuation, and spelling—or would it be better to try to concentrate only on generating arguments in the preliminary draft, with revisions for organization, sentence formation, and mechanics handled in the final draft?

Glynn, Britton, Muth, and Dogan (1982) investigated this question in a controlled experiment in which students were given writing assignments as just described. Some students were told to write a polished first draft:

> On this preliminary draft, you need to be concerned with content (i.e., the production of persuasive ideas), order (i.e., the logical sequence of these ideas), sentence formation (i.e., the incorporation of these ideas into sentences), and mechanics (i.e., compliance with punctuation and spelling rules). Communicate all the ideas that you think may be useful in persuading me to choose one alternative and not the other. More than one persuasive idea can be incorporated into each sentence. (p. 558)

Other students were told to write an unpolished first draft:

> On this preliminary draft you need to be concerned with content (i.e., the production of persuasive ideas). Communicate all the ideas that you think may be useful in persuading me to choose one alternative and not the other. Summarize each of these persuasive ideas using only three or four words, and write them in order. On this draft, do not attempt to work on order (i.e., the logical sequence of persuasive ideas), sentence formation (i.e., the incorporation of these ideas into sentences), or mechanics (i.e., compliance with punctuation and spelling rules). You will be permitted to work on order, sentence formation, and mechanics during the next draft. (pp. 558–559)

For the final draft, all students were told to "produce the best letter you can," including consideration of content, order, sentence formation, and mechanics.

Table 4–1 summarizes the differences between the final drafts produced by the two groups. Students who wrote unpolished first drafts tended to write final drafts containing more persuasive arguments, more arguments per sentence, and fewer mechanical errors, as

TABLE 4–1

Differences in final drafts when preliminary drafts are polished versus unpolished

	Total Number of Arguments	**Arguments per Sentence**	**Mechanical Errors per Sentence**
Polished preliminary draft	2.9	.38	.43
Unpolished preliminary draft	8.0	.85	.23

Adapted from Glynn, Britton, Muth, and Dogan (1982)

compared to students who wrote a polished first draft. Subsequent experiments determined that this pattern was most strongly pronounced for students with average verbal ability as compared to students with low verbal ability. These results suggest that when good writers are forced to express early drafts in complete sentences, the quality of the final draft suffers. Apparently, the heavy load placed on attentional capacity limits the writers' ability to retrieve and organize information. By forcing ideas to be translated prematurely into polished sentences, without allowing time for planning, the result may be a final draft that lacks integrated content.

INDIVIDUAL DIFFERENCES IN TRANSLATING Another approach to the study of the translation process involves comparing older and younger writers, or comparing more skilled and less skilled writers. For example, in one study (Scardamalia, Bereiter, and Goelman, 1982), fourth- and sixth-grade students were asked to write essays on topics such as, "Is it better to be an only child or to have brothers and sisters?" "Should boys and girls play sports together?" or "Should children be allowed to choose what subject they study in school?" When students finished their essays, they were given cues to keep working such as, "You're doing fine. Now I know it's a bit tough, but you can write some more about this."

The results indicated that the cues to keep writing encouraged both fourth- and sixth-graders to add about 50% more to their essays. However, the judged quality of the essays improved only for the fourth-graders. Apparently, the younger writers stopped writing before they were really finished, whereas the sixth-graders continued until they had written a good essay. One implication is that younger children may be using the conventions of oral speech (e.g., needing someone to tell them to go on) while older writers can tell themselves to continue producing text.

When young writers were asked to dictate their essays, the students produced longer essays than when they were asked to write them. However, cues to produce more text resulted in more words being produced but not in increased quality ratings for the essays. Apparently young writers stop too soon when they must physically produce the sentences; however, when they are encouraged to continue or when they are allowed to dictate, they produce more complete, coherent essays.

There is clear evidence that as children grow, the quality and quantity of their writing increase. For example, an analysis of a national child development study revealed that older children write longer and more complex sentences than younger children (Richardson, Calnan, Essen, & Lambert, 1975). In a typical research study, Bartlett and Scribner (1981) asked children in grades three to six to write a story based on the following: "A man leaves his house. His body is found the next morning." As expected, sixth-graders produced longer stories than third-graders (an average of 227 words versus 103 words, respectively); in addition, sixth-graders produced more complex referring expressions (e.g., pronouns) as compared to third-graders. Scardamalia et al. (1982) reported on a study in which fourth- and sixth-graders were asked to write essays. The experimenters measured the length of the longest "coherent string," that is, the longest string of words with no nonfunctional units (such as "you know") and no incoherent orderings. For fourth-graders the average was 4.1 words, and for sixth-graders the average was 6.3, suggesting that older writers produce longer coherent strings.

Scardamalia (1981) compared different levels of sophistication in sentence production. For example, writers using a low level of sophistication state single facts without any integration, as in the following:

> In the state of Michigan the climate is cool. In the state of Michigan the fruit crop is apples. In the state of California, the climate is warm. In the state of California the fruit crop is oranges.

In contrast, writers using a high level of sophistication integrate all of the information into a coherent sentence, such as:

> In Michigan's cool climate they harvest apples, but with California's warm climate, oranges may be grown.

Scardamalia (1981) noted similar differences among levels of sophistication in the essays students wrote on the question "Should students be able to choose what subjects they study in school?" A low level of sophistication is exemplified in the following essay:

> Yes, I think we should. Because some subjects are hard like math. And because the teachers give us a page a day. I think the subjects that we should have is Reading. Because that is easyest one. I think we should't have math, science and social studies. Because in social studies and science we have to write up notes and do experiments. I think math is the worst subject. And I hate spelling to. Because in spelling there are so many words to write and they are all hard. And they waste my time. I think school shouldn't be to 3:45. I think it should be to 2:00. I think school is too long.

As can be seen, the writer simply expressed each idea that came into her head in the order that the ideas occurred to her. This type of writing is called *associative writing* by Bereiter (1980) and *writer-based prose* by Flower (1979).

In the following example from Scardamalia (1981), the writer used a high level of sophistication in the production of sentences (the spelling is original):

> Chose is an important thing but a very tricky thing to fool with. I feel that chose of school subjects should be something that is done carefully. A young child given a chose would pick the easiest subjects with no foresight into his future. But choose in his later years could be very important. To develop his leadership qualities. To follow and develop his interests and charictor to his fillest. So with these facts I come to the conclusion that chose of subjects should not be given until about the age of fifteen. You can not condem or praise what you know little about. Until the age of choise a full and general cericulum should be given. It is not up to the school board to decide your life and until you are old enough to decide it is not your dission either.

This writer is able to express conflicting points of view and weave them into a coherent solution. This type of writing requires holding many different ideas in one's mind at one time and seeing the relationships among them. If a writer's attention is absorbed by the mechanics of writing, it is not possible to hold all of these relations in mind.

One implication of this work is that high-quality writing requires that the writer not have to use much attention for the mechanical aspects of sentence production. Good writing requires that the mechanics of penmanship, spelling, punctuation, and grammar be automatic. Thus, to be a good writer requires much more than having good ideas; it also requires a great deal of well-learned knowledge about the English language.

IMPLICATIONS FOR INSTRUCTION: TRANSLATING

The foregoing review of research on translation makes three points. First, the writer is constrained by many factors, including the mechanics of using proper grammar, spelling, and penmanship. Second, the mechanics of proper sentence writing may overload the writer's attentional capacity, thus interfering with high-level planning and organization. Third, there appears to be a developmental trend in which older writers, who presumably have automated much of the mechanics of writing, are able to write more complex sentences, to integrate the information, and to keep writing until finished.

Writing instruction that emphasizes correct spelling, punctuation, grammar, penmanship, and other mechanics may serve to reduce or eliminate the student's ability to plan. The result can be a mechanically correct composition that lacks coherence. Instead, students may benefit from writing situations in which the mechanical constraints are removed or relaxed (e.g., being free to write rough drafts that may not be mechanically perfect). The promising research on unpolished first drafts suggests that the quality of the final product may be higher if students are not forced to write polished first drafts. Even practice in oral expression—which certainly avoids constraints on spelling and penmanship—may provide needed practice in the translation process. These kinds of relaxations of mechanical constraints seem particularly important for young writers who have not yet automatized many of the mechanical aspects of writing.

Eventually, students need to develop automatic skills in the mechanics of writing such as penmanship (or typing), spelling, grammar, and punctuation. These automatic skills will free their attentional capacity to concentrate on the relations among ideas in the composition.

WRITING WITH WORD PROCESSORS A potentially important instructional intervention that may reduce the drudgery of the translation process is learning to use a word processor. The translation process involves putting words on paper. An obvious question concerns whether this process is influenced by whether the words are produced by typing them on a keyboard versus handwriting them. According to a cognitive theory of working memory, the amount of attentional resources are limited. If using one type of the output device—word processor versus pen—places a greater load on working memory than the other, the quality of the written product would suffer. For example, if students lack experience in using a word processor, they have to devote more attentional resource to the mechanics of typing and less to what they are writing. To test this hypothesis, Kellogg and Mueller (1993) compared the writing of students who were asked to compose by longhand, students who were asked to compose on a word processor but who lacked extensive word-processing experience, and students who were asked to compose on a word processor and who possessed extensive word-processing experience. Figure 4–10 shows that the

FIGURE 4–10 Quality of essays produced by longhand and by word processors

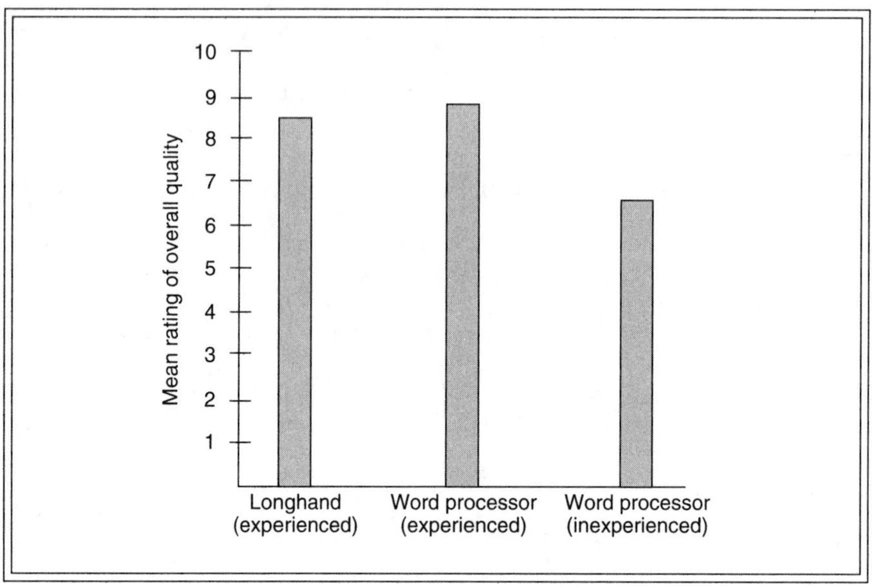

Adapted from Kellogg and Mueller (1993)

rated quality of the essay (on a 10-point scale) was nearly equivalent for longhand writers and experienced word-processor writers, but that inexperienced word-processor writers produced lower quality essays than did longhand writers.

By the same argument, if younger students have difficulty with the mechanics of handwriting, allowing them to use a word processor might enable them to devote more attention to what they are writing. This intervention will work, of course, only if students are well practiced in the use of word processors. In an extensive review of studies comparing writing by longhand and by word processor, Bangert-Drowns (1993) found no significant differences in the quality of writing products in most of the studies. However, overall the word-processing groups had a small advantage. Consistent with the working-memory hypothesis, the advantage of word processing over longhand writing was much greater for elementary school children than for college students, especially when the elementary school students were not highly skilled writers and when they had received extensive practice in using word processors.

These results are consistent with the idea that the translation process is equivalent when writing by pen or by word processor, as long as the writer is skilled in its use. In reviewing research comparing writers who generally possessed these skills, Kellogg (1994) concluded that "word processors and pens are equally effective output devices" (p. 147). However, when a writer lacks skill in using either, the need to focus on correctly using the device detracts from writing a high-quality product. In short, when the translation process requires paying attention to physically writing words, less attention can be paid to what to write.

REVIEWING

WHAT IS REVIEWING?

The third major process in our model of writing is the reviewing process. As Bartlett (1982) points out, this process involves both detecting errors in the text and correcting them.

RESEARCH ON REVIEWING

HOW MANY CHANGES DO STUDENTS MAKE? Gould (1980) presents evidence showing that revision is almost totally absent from adult writing or dictating of simple assignments, such as one-page business letters. Experienced dictators use less than 10% of dictation time on reviewing or revising what they have said. If reviewing is not used often in letter writing, then prohibiting writers from reviewing should not greatly affect their writing performance. To test this idea, Gould (1978b) asked adults to engage in "invisible writing." This invisible writing involved writing with a wooden stylus on a sheet of paper that had carbon paper and another sheet of paper under it so subjects could not see what they had written. Based on the writing of eight business letters, those using invisible writing required about the same amount of time as those using normal writing (10 minutes for invisible writing versus 11 minutes for normal writing), achieved about the same quality ratings from judges (3.0 for invisible writing versus 3.2 for normal writing, with 1 being unacceptable and 5 being excellent), and needed about the same amount of proof-editing changes (almost none for both groups). Similarly, Pianko (1979) reported that college freshmen spent less than 9% of writing time on reading or reviewing what they had written. Apparently, adults often do not review what they have written, especially when the assignment is a fairly short and simple one.

WHAT KINDS OF CHANGES DO STUDENTS MAKE? In a review of the research on revision in writing, Fitzgerald (1987) reported that students mainly make surface and mechanical revisions, suggesting that they generally equate revision with proofreading. In addition, Fitzgerald (1987) found that although teachers rarely ask students to revise what they have written, when they were asked to engage in in-depth revision, their final product was generally improved.

Bartlett (1982) conducted an extensive series of studies of how children in grades three through eight revise text. For example, in one study, fourth- and fifth-graders were asked to revise their own text and text provided by the teacher. Both texts contained syntax errors (such as failure of subject-verb agreement or inconsistent use of verb tense), and referent errors (such as using a pronoun that has an unclear or ambiguous antecedent). Table 4–2 shows that students detected errors in someone else's text much more easily than errors in their own; in addition, students detected syntax errors more easily than referent errors, especially in their own text.

Children have difficulty not only in detecting referent errors but also in making the appropriate correction. For example, Figure 4–11 shows original versions of text along with revised versions suggested by students. As can be seen, the correction strategies

TABLE 4–2

Detecting errors in text

	Percentage of Errors That Were Detected	
	Referent Errors	Syntax Errors
In writer's own text	17%	53%
In other texts	73%	88%

Adapted from Bartlett (1982)

selected were not successful. Bartlett (1982) found that the most commonly used successful strategies for correcting referent errors are the use of pronouns (such as, "One day a man went to the beach. The day was hot and he needed a cool swim.") and use of repetition (such as, "Shortly after Christmas, a young woman moved into the house. The young woman had few possessions and she settled in quickly."). However, in the examples in Figure 4–11 these strategies are not appropriate.

INDIVIDUAL DIFFERENCES IN REVIEWING In another experiment reported by Bartlett (1982), children were given eight paragraphs to revise. Each paragraph included an unusual referent error that could not be corrected by the most common strategies of

FIGURE 4–11

Unsuccessful correction strategies

Original Text
One day a man left his house. Another man was standing outside. The man took out a letter and gave it to him. They talked for a while and then they got into a car. They were both policemen. They were going to catch a thief.

Attempts to Repeat an Antecedent (60% of Unsuccessful Corrections)
The man took out a letter and gave it to the other man. . . .

Attempts to Differentiate Among Characters (25% of Unsuccessful Corrections)
The man that was outside took a letter and gave it to the other man outside. . . .

Introduction of Nondiscriminating New Information (15% of Unsuccessful Corrections)
Joe left his house. Another Joe was standing outside. Joe took out a letter and gave it to the other Joe. . . .

Adapted from Bartlett (1982)

using pronouns or repetition. For example, one of the paragraphs involved what Bartlett called *ambiguous referencing:*

> One day two girls set out for the park.
> She had a bike. . . .

Figure 4–12 summarizes the revision performance of above-average and below-average writers in grades five through seven. As might be expected, above-average writers corrected about twice as many errors as below-average writers, and older writers corrected about twice as many errors as younger writers. However, even the oldest and most able writers successfully corrected only 36% of the referent errors.

Bartlett (1982) also found differences among the correction strategies used by above-average and below-average writers in grades five through seven. Figure 4–13 lists five correction strategies, along with examples of each. Table 4–3 summarizes the proportion of solutions that involved each strategy for above-average and below-average writers. As can be seen, above-average writers tended to rely most heavily on adding descriptive information about both referents or on naming the characters; in contrast, the below-average writers relied on nondefinite referencing or on adding descriptive information about only one referent. In a follow-up study, Bartlett (1982) found that the performance of adults closely paralleled that of above-average fifth-, sixth-, and seventh-grade writers. Apparently, good and poor writers differ with respect to both the quantity and quality of their corrections.

Bartlett's research focused on how children revise text containing referent errors, including comparisons of the general revising behavior of skilled and less skilled writers. Using a similar approach, Stallard (1974) compared the writing performance of skilled twelfth-graders versus a randomly selected control group of twelfth-graders. As expected, the skilled writers took more time than the control writers (41 minutes versus 23 minutes) and

FIGURE 4–12 Detection and correction of referent errors by above- and below-average writers

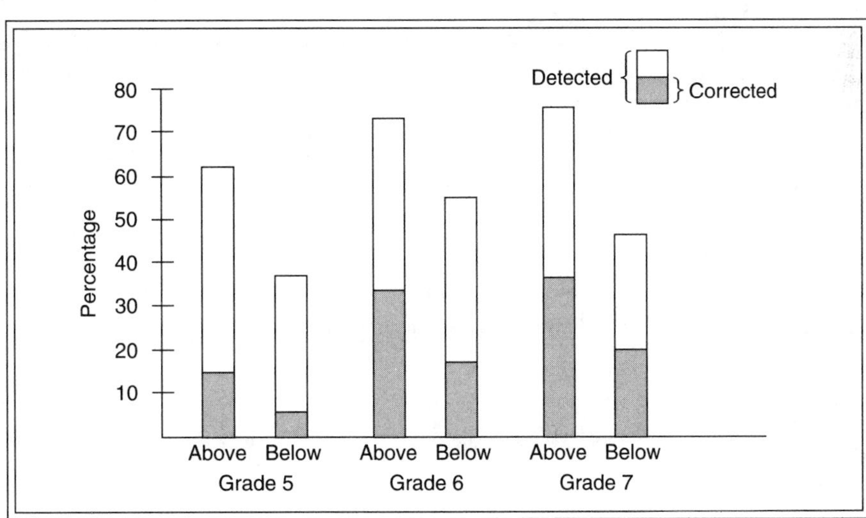

Adapted from Bartlett (1982)

FIGURE 4–13

Successful corrections of a referent error

Original Text

One day two girls set out for the park. She had a bike. . . .

Adding Descriptive Information about Both Referents

One day two girls set out for the park. One was very athletic, and the other hated sports. The athletic one had a bike. . . .

Adding Descriptive Information about One Referent

One day two girls set out for the park. One of the girls was athletic, and she had a bike. . . .

Naming Characters

One day two girls named Sandy and Karen went to the park. Sandy had a bike. . . .

Indefinite Referencing Using Plural Noun

One day two girls went to the park. They had a bike. . . .

Indefinite Referencing Using Singular Noun

One day two girls went to the park. One had a bike. . . .

Adapted from Bartlett (1982)

TABLE 4–3

Differences in correction strategies of good and poor writers

	Percentage of Total Solutions	
Strategy Used	**Above-Average Writers**	**Below-Average Writers**
Adding descriptive information about both referents	33%	9%
Adding descriptive information about one referent	10%	41%
Naming characters	29%	5%
Indefinite referencing using plural noun	23%	27%
Indefinite referencing using singular noun	6%	18%

Adapted from Bartlett (1982)

produced more words (343 words versus 309). However, Stallard also noted that the skilled group conducted three times as many revisions (184 versus 64). In fact, less than half of the control group ever looked back to see what they had written, whereas most of the skilled writers did. Similar differences between the writing processes of skilled and less skilled writers led Hayes and Flower (1986) to conclude that "the more expert the writer, the greater the proportion of writing time the writer will spend in revision" (p. 110).

What can be done to help students during the revision process? Consider the following task. You are an editor for a magazine that publishes accounts of famous people in history. An author has just given you two articles she has written on Christopher Columbus and Margaret Mead. Your job is to read and revise the two articles. She was in a hurry, so there are likely to be several problems that you will have to fix. These problems may range from mechanical errors such as spelling and punctuation to problems with the way that the material is organized.

When this task was given to seventh-graders, they were far more successful in correcting errors in meaning when the text covered a familiar topic (e.g., Christopher Columbus) than an unfamiliar topic (e.g., Margaret Mead), but familiarity did not affect students' correcting of mechanical errors (McCutchen, Francis, & Kerr, 1997). These results, as well as related studies, show that detection and correction of meaning errors depends partly on the knowledge that writers possess (McCutchen, 2000).

In addition, some students were told that an assistant had already done some preliminary editing and had highlighted sentences that need corrections. The highlighting caused seventh-graders to focus on correcting mechanical errors but to ignore some meaning errors. Overall, cueing seems to "focus less sophisticated writers too narrowly and thereby impede meaning-based revision" (McCutchen et al., 1997, p. 667). The negative effects of cueing were confined to young readers. College students were able to make more corrections of both mechanical problems and meaning problems when problem sentences were highlighted. Thus, younger readers seem particularly vulnerable to focusing on mechanical errors at the expense of correcting meaning errors.

IMPLICATIONS FOR INSTRUCTION: REVIEWING

In summary, the foregoing review of research makes several points concerning the review process. First, writers often do not review what they have written. Second, when writers are encouraged to review, they fail to detect most of the errors (especially referent errors), and even when they do detect errors they often fail to correct them properly. Third, older or more skilled writers appear to detect and correct far more errors and use more sophisticated review strategies than younger or less skilled writers. Older or more skilled writers also engage in more review than less skilled or younger writers.

These results suggest that students need to be encouraged to review what they have written. Some instruction may be needed in specific strategies for detecting and correcting errors. Checklists or questions can be used to guide a student's review, although the review process should eventually become internalized. The use of word processors may allow for easier review and revision, since students are freed from the need to write each new draft by hand. The difference between a good writer and poor writer is often not in the quality of the first draft but in the number of drafts generated. Students need to see how revision can turn a poor paper into an excellent one. Some of these ideas are examined more fully below in our discussion of an instructional program aimed at improving the revision process—revision training.

REVISION TRAINING Can students be taught to be more effective reviewers? According to an exemplary study by Fitzgerald and Markman (1987), the answer is yes. In their study, some sixth-grade students received thirteen 45-minute lessons on the process of revision (revision training group), whereas other sixth-graders spent an equivalent amount of time reading good literature (comparison group). The instruction consisted of four three-lesson units on how to make additions, deletions, substitutions, and rearrangements. In the first day of each unit, the teacher defined the target process (e.g., addition), modeled the process, and led the class in revising an example story. On the second day, students worked in pairs on revising a portion of a text, guided by a step-by-step handout. On the third day, students worked individually on revising a story supplied by the teacher and one they had written themselves. After completing all four units, students received an integrative summary in the 13th lesson.

As a final test, students wrote a first draft of a story (stage 1), marked the original paper for changes (stage 2), made changes on the original paper (stage 3), and wrote a final draft on new piece of paper (stage 4). On average, the revision training group made 23 revisions per 100 words over the course of all four stages, whereas the comparison group made only 16 revisions per 100 words. The revision training group produced 61% more additions, 69% more deletions, 27% more substitutions, and 42% more rearrangements than the comparison group. Importantly, the rated quality of the stories improved from stage one to stage four for the revision training group but not for the comparison group. Fitzgerald and Markman (1987) concluded that "our findings support the utility of direct instruction in revision in writing in the classroom" (p. 18).

BUILDING A WRITING PROGRAM THAT WORKS

THE INSTRUCTIONAL METHOD AND CONTENT OF WRITING PROGRAMS

The previous sections explored three important components in the writing process as well as some possible instructional techniques for improving each component. How could you put this information together into a writing program that works? To answer this question, Hillocks (1984, 1986) carefully analyzed experimental studies on writing to determine how and what to teach.

From research on how to teach, Hillocks (1984, 1986) identified three general methods of instruction in writing programs:

Natural process mode: The student dominates by initiating most of the writing activity, working at her or his own pace, and seeking feedback, when needed, from other students or the teacher. This approach involves little guidance from the teacher and is similar to pure discovery methods of instruction.

Presentational mode: The teacher dominates by providing traditional instruction and lectures on how to write, determining the writing topic, and making extensive corrections of student writing. This approach involves much guidance from the teacher and is similar to rule methods of instruction.

Environmental mode: Student and teacher cooperate in discussing the goals, content, and process of writing a composition. Instead of lecturing, the teacher works with small groups on specific writing projects, helping students to support their assertions with evidence, to predict and counter opposing arguments, to generate appropriate assertions from available data, and so on. Instead of beginning with independent free writing, the student works on specific writing tasks under teacher supervision within small groups. This approach involves an intermediate amount of teacher guidance and is similar to guided discovery methods of instruction.

Which method of instruction is most effective? On the average, Hillocks (1984, 1986) found that the environmental mode resulted in three times more improvement than the natural process method and four times more improvement than the traditional presentational method. The environmental method provides enough guidance to ensure that students come in contact with specific skills needed for writing and at the same time allows enough freedom to keep students actively involved in the learning process.

From research on what to teach, Hillocks (1984, 1986) noted differences in the content of instruction in various writing programs, including the following:

Grammar: The teacher focuses on the mechanics of writing, including defining parts of speech, phrasing sentences, and so on. Usually, the teacher marks every error in a student's writing.

Models: Students are asked to study pieces of good writing as models for their own writing.

Free writing: Students are asked to write freely about anything they choose.

Sentence combining: Students are asked to build more complex sentences out of simpler ones.

Scales: Students are given a list of questions or a checklist to apply to their own composition or someone else's. Eventually they should internalize this review process.

Inquiry: Students are asked to discuss their own writing process and to improve their strategies for writing. For example, they might be asked to find details to describe a personal experience vividly.

Which kinds of content result in the most improvement in writing? Focusing on sentence combining, scales, and inquiry are the most effective, presumably because they help students acquire skills that are specifically related to composition writing. Focusing on models and free writing is less effective, presumably because the goal of instruction is unclear; focusing on grammar is the least effective of all the approaches, presumably because it draws attention away from the actual writing process. In fact, Hillocks's (1984; 1986) analysis of the research shows that in some cases heavy emphasis on grammar may actually decrease the quality of writing. This finding is consistent with the research on translation cited earlier in this chapter, which shows that mechanical constraints can interfere with students' attention to planning a coherent composition. Instead of focusing on grammar as a way of teaching writing, Hillocks (1984; 1986) suggests teaching grammar within the context of actual writing.

Hillocks (1984) reports the disturbing fact that the most popular writing programs ignore the available educational research on writing. In spite of findings to the contrary, many writing programs assume that the most effective method of instruction is natural process and that the most effective content is free writing:

> For over a decade, authorities in the field have been caught up in the "writing as process" model, which calls for exploratory talk, followed by free writing, reading by or for an audience of peers, comments from peers, and revision. The teacher's role is simply to facilitate this process—not to make specific assignments, not to help students learn criteria for judging writing, not to structure classroom activities based on specific objectives as in environmental treatments, not to provide exercises in manipulating syntax, not to design activities that engage students in identifiable processes of examining data. In short, this mode . . . studiously avoids the approaches to writing instruction that this report demonstrates to be more effective. (Hillocks, 1984, p. 162)

The approach that Hillocks describes seems to offer too little guidance and may be a sort of reaction against the programs that provided too much guidance in the past. In essence, Hillocks suggests the compromise of using guided discovery methods for teaching writing, in which the teacher provides some scaffolding for students as they learn the basic processes of writing.

COGNITIVE STRATEGY INSTRUCTION IN WRITING

Cognitive Strategy Instruction in Writing (CSIW) is an example of a writing program that seems to follow Hillocks' advice: The method involves some guidance from the teacher and the content involves the basic processes of writing (Englert, Raphael, Anderson, Anthony, & Stevens, 1991). In this chapter, we have seen how each cognitive process in writing—planning, translating, and reviewing—can be taught as a separate component. However, to produce a high-quality essay, writers need to be able to coordinate all three processes. CSIW is a comprehensive program that involves instruction in all of these processes.

The target task in CSIW is to write an essay. For example, suppose you were asked to write an essay explaining how to play a game you know, assuming that the audience does not already know how to play it. Alternatively, suppose you were asked to write a paper comparing how people, places, or things you know are alike and different. These are the kinds of writing assignments that Englert et al. (1991) gave to fourth- and fifth-graders. As you can see, the first one involves an explanation essay, whereas the second one involves writing a compare/contrast essay. Before giving these assignments, however, Englert et al. wanted to use the regular classroom writing time during the academic year to help students improve their writing skills. Based on what you know about cognitive processes in writing, what advice would you give to Englert et al. in preparing students to do well on writing these explanation and compare/contrast essays?

The cognitive model of writing examined in this chapter pinpoints the kinds of cognitive skills that should be part of any writing program. Students need to practice in planning, translating, and revising, as well as in coordinating these processes in actual writing tasks. Because students often fail to engage in appropriate planning (including generating and organizing ideas) and revising processes (including detecting and correcting errors), it is particularly important for students to gain specific experience in how to carry out these processes.

CSIW is a writing program designed to teach students how to use and coordinate five writing strategies: plan, organize, write, edit, and revise (Englert et al., 1991). Plan and organize are parts of the cognitive process of planning, write corresponds to the process of translating, and edit and revise are components of the process of revising. The CSIW program does the following:

1. Promotes self-monitoring in which writers learn to "conduct an inner dialogue about the text and its content, the writing process, and the structure of text" (Englert et al., 1991, p. 338).
2. Provides scaffolded instruction that "prompts . . . strategies for planning, organizing, drafting, editing, and revising" (Englert et al., 1991, p. 340).
3. Transforms writing into a collaborative activity through "participation in a writing community" (Englert et al., 1991, p. 340).
4. Situates skills within specific types of text structures such as writing an explanation or a compare/contrast text.

The program is integrated into the regular classroom activities by the teacher, is comprehensive in that it involves all aspects of the writing process, and is individualized in that the teacher provides necessary guidance to students based on their individual needs.

In CSIW, students learn how to use a series of "think-sheets" while writing explanation or compare/contrast texts. The think-sheets are intended to prompt students to engage in cognitive processes that they might otherwise omit, and include the following types:

Plan think-sheet: The purpose of the plan think-sheet is to help students set criteria and generate ideas. For example, students are prompted to write down answers to questions such as "Who am I writing for?" "Why am I writing this?" "What do I know?" (with a list numbered from 1 to 8), "How can I group my ideas?" (with four boxes), and "How can I organize my ideas?" (with four categories: comparison/contrast, explanation, problem/solution, or other). An example is given in Figure 4–14.

Organize think-sheet: The purpose of the organize think-sheet is to help students organize their ideas into an outline. For example, if students have opted for the explanation organization in the plan think-sheet, in the organize think-sheet they will be prompted to specify the subject of the explanation, the material needed, the setting, and the steps in the explanation.

Write think-sheet: The purpose is to assist students as they write their first draft on the write think-sheet, in which they are encouraged to reread their plan and organize think-sheets, flesh out their ideas by using examples, provide engaging introductions and conclusions, and signal the organization of the text to the reader.

Edit/editor think-sheet: The edit think-sheet guides students through self-editing and the editor work-sheet guides students through peer-editing. Both think-sheets ask students to place stars next to parts of the essay they like, place question marks next to parts that are confusing, and to rate the text on several criteria. This phase includes a face-to-face meeting between the writer and the peer editor as they collaborate on improving the paper.

Revision think-sheet: The purpose is to encourage students to reflect on their editing plans. Students list all the suggested revisions and decide on which ones to implement. By carrying out the revisions, they produce a final draft that is published in a class book.

FIGURE 4–14 A plan think-sheet to help students plan their compositions

PLAN

Name ____________________ Date ____________

Topic: ____________________

Who: Who am I writing for?

____

____

Why: Why am I writing this?

____

____

What: What do I know? (brainstorm)

1. ____________________
2. ____________________
3. ____________________
4. ____________________
5. ____________________
6. ____________________
7. ____________________
8. ____________________

How: How can I group my ideas?

How will I organize my ideas?

_______ Comparison/contrast _______ Problem/solution

_______ Explanation _______ Other

Adapted from Englert, Raphael, and Anderson (1989)

Does CSIW help students to become more effective writers? To answer that question, Englert et al. (1991) compared fourth- and fifth-grade students who participated in the CSIW program throughout the academic year from October to May (treatment group) to equivalent students who participated in the school's regular writing program (comparison group). Students were asked to write essays at the start of the school year as a pretest and toward the end of school year as a posttest. Figure 4–15 shows that the overall quality of the essays (on a three-point scale) improved greatly from pretest to posttest for the treatment group but not for the comparison group. Similarly, ratings of the writer's sensitivity to the reader, the writer's organization of the text, and the number of ideas produced by the writer increased greatly for the treatment group but not for the comparison group. Importantly, these same differences in pretest-to-posttest gains between treatment and comparison students were found for learning disabled, low-achieving, and high-achieving students. Overall, these results show that it is possible to design a writing program that works by providing sufficient guidance in using and coordinating the cognitive processes for writing.

STRATEGY INSTRUCTION IN WRITING

Sawyer, Graham, and Harris (1992) developed another writing program called self-regulated strategy development (SRSD) that is consistent with Hillocks's advice. The program was intended to help elementary school students with learning disabilities to improve their writing of stories. The instruction included preskill development, conferencing, strategy presentation, modeling, and practice. During preskill development, students learned to answer seven questions in writing a story, as listed in Table 4–4. During conferencing the instructor

FIGURE 4–15 Quality of essays produced by treatment and comparison groups on pretest and posttest

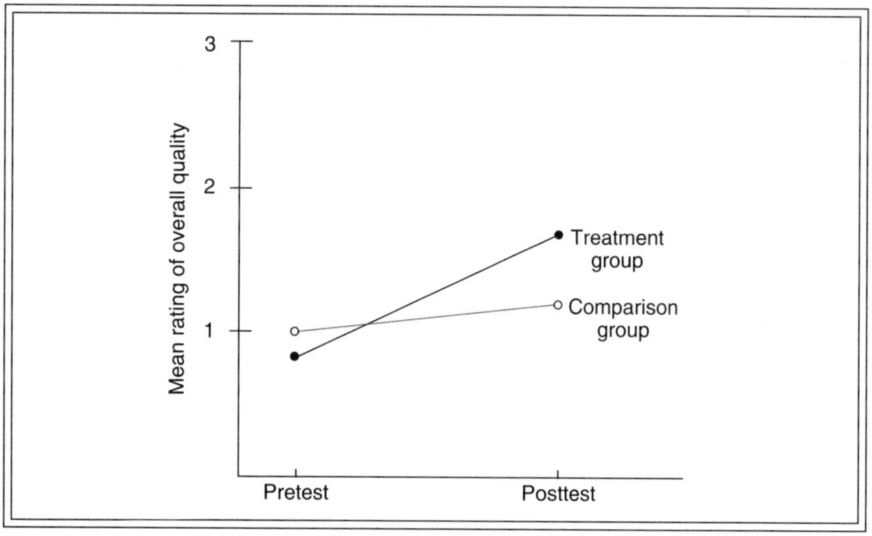

Adapted from Englert et al. (1991)

TABLE 4–4

Seven questions for writing a story

1. Who is the main character? Who else is in the story?
2. When does the story take place?
3. Where does the story take place?
4. What does the main character want to do?
5. What happens when he or she tries to do it?
6. How does the story end?
7. How does the main character feel?

Adapted from Sawyer, Graham, and Harris (1992)

explained that the goal of the lessons was to improve the students' writing of stories, and the instructor reviewed a story the student had written with respect to each of the seven questions in Table 4–4. During strategy presentation, the instructor helped the student develop ways of implementing each of five steps in story writing, including generating, organizing, and evaluating ideas. During modeling, the instructor described her cognitive processes while writing a story. During practice, students worked individually and with peers to write stories based on the strategies presented. Students who received SRSD instruction showed large pretest-to-posttest gains in the quality ratings of their stories, whereas students who simply practiced writing stories did not.

READING-WRITING CONNECTION

What is the relationship between learning to read and learning to write? Both depend on some of the same knowledge and cognitive skills (Fitzgerald & Shanahan, 2000), and there is evidence that reading and writing are connected (Nelson & Calfee, 1998). An important instructional implication is that reading and writing programs should be coordinated.

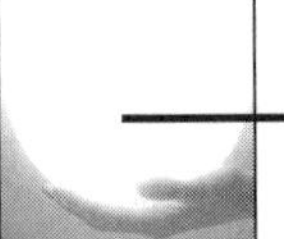

CHAPTER SUMMARY

The research on writing is just beginning to make sense of the writing process. However, even the preliminary research presented in this chapter invites implications for instruction.

First, planning, which includes the development of an organization and the generation of content information, is a major component in writing. Students need explicit and specific training in techniques for organizing compositions, paragraphs, and sentences. Similarly, students need training and practice in how to generate and record information to be used in a composition.

Second, translation is a major writing component that involves converting ideas into words. The translation process relies on mechanical skills, such as handwriting, spelling, punctuation, grammatical sentence construction, and so on. Students need to be freed from the mechanical constraints on translation to concentrate their attentional capacity on planning a coherent composition. For older or more skilled students, the mechanical skills should become automatic; for younger or less skilled students, heavy emphasis on mechanics should not be required in the first draft.

Third, reviewing is a major writing component that involves the detection and correction of errors. The difference between a good composition and a poor composition may depend not on differences in the first draft, but on differences in how subsequent drafts are carried out. Students need explicit and detailed instruction in how to revise, with the ultimate goal of internalizing the revision procedures.

Finally, this chapter explored the characteristics of effective writing programs. The more successful programs use instructional methods that foster the cognitive processes of writing.

SUGGESTED READINGS

Bereiter, C., & Scardamalia, M. (1987). *The psychology of written composition.* Hillsdale, NJ: Erlbaum. (A review of research on writing in school settings.)

Kellogg, R. T. (1994). *The psychology of writing.* New York: Oxford University Press. (A review of research and theory on how people go about the task of writing.)

Levy, C. M., & Ransdell, S. (Eds.). (1996). *The science of writing.* Mahwah, NJ: Erlbaum. (A collection of papers on writing research, including advances in theories of writing.)

CHAPTER 5 Learning Mathematics

CHAPTER OUTLINE

What Do You Need to Know to Solve Math Problems?

Problem Translation

Problem Integration

Solution Planning and Monitoring

Solution Execution

Chapter Summary

This chapter asks, "What does a student need to know to solve mathematics problems?" The answer to this question includes four components. Linguistic and factual knowledge are needed to help the student translate each sentence of the problem into some internal representation. Schematic knowledge is needed to help the student integrate the information into a coherent representation. Strategic knowledge is needed to help the student devise and monitor a solution plan. Procedural knowledge is needed to help the student carry out the computations required in the plan.

WHAT DO YOU NEED TO KNOW TO SOLVE MATH PROBLEMS?

Suppose I asked you to solve the following problem:

> Floor tiles are sold in squares 30 centimeters on each side. How much would it cost to tile a rectangular room 7.2 meters long and 5.4 meters wide if the tiles cost $.72 each?

What skills must you possess to solve this problem? First, you need to be able to translate each statement of the problem into some internal representation. This translation process requires that you understand English sentences (i.e., you need linguistic knowledge). For example, you need to be able to recognize that the problem contains the following facts: each tile is a 30-by-30-centimeter square, the room is a 7.2-by-5.4-meter rectangle, each tile costs 72 cents, and the unknown is the cost of tiling the room. This translation process also requires that you know certain facts, i.e., you need factual knowledge. For example, you need to know that all sides of a square are equal in length and that there are 100 centimeters in a meter. The top portion of Figure 5–1 presents other examples of mathematical tasks that focus on problem translation. Try these problems to exercise your problem translation skills.

Second, you need to be able to integrate each of the statements in the problem into a coherent problem representation. This problem integration process requires that you must be able to recognize problem types (i.e., you need schematic knowledge). For example, you need to recognize that this problem is a rectangle problem requiring the formula *area* = *length* × *width*. Problem integration also involves being able to distinguish between information that is relevant to the solution and information that is not relevant to the solution. The second portion of Figure 5–1 offers examples of mathematical tasks that focus on problem integration. Try these problems to test your problem integration skills.

Third, you need to be able to devise and monitor a solution plan. This solution planning process requires knowledge of heuristics (i.e., strategic knowledge). For example, you need to break the problem into subgoals, such as finding the area of the room, the number of tiles needed, and the cost of those tiles. You also need to be able to monitor what you are doing, such as knowing that when you multiply 7.2 × 5.4, you are finding the area of the room in meters. The third portion of Figure 5–1 gives examples of mathematical tasks that focus on solution planning and monitoring. Try some of these problems.

Finally, a fourth major component involved in answering the title problem is to be able to apply the rules of arithmetic. For example, you must be able to calculate the answer of 7.2 × 5.4 = ___, or .72 × 432 = ___. Accurate and automatic execution of arithmetic and algebraic procedures is based on procedural knowledge. The fourth section of Figure 5–1 presents examples of mathematical tasks that focus on solution execution. Go ahead and select your answers.

As the examples show, solving a problem involves more than just getting the final answer. Our componential analysis of the tile problem suggests that at least four major components are involved in mathematical problem-solving, as summarized in Table 5–1. In this chapter we will take a closer look at each of these four components: (1) translating

FIGURE 5–1

Skills involved in solving math problems

PROBLEM TRANSLATION

Restating the Problem Givens

1. Floor tiles are sold in squares 30 centimeters on each side. How much would it cost to tile a rectangular room 7.2 meters long and 5.4 meters wide if the tiles cost $.72 each?

Which of the following sentences is not true?

a. The room is a rectangle measuring 7.2 meters by 5.4 meters.
b. Each tile costs 30 cents.
c. Each tile is a square measuring 30 centimeters by 30 centimeters.
d. The length of the long side of the room is 7.2 meters.

Restating the Problem Goal

2. Floor tiles are sold in squares 30 centimeters on each side. How much would it cost to tile a rectangular room 7.2 meters long and 5.4 meters wide if the tiles cost $.72 each?

What are you being asked to find?

a. the width and length of the room
b. the cost of each tile
c. the cost of tiling the room
d. the size of each tile

PROBLEM INTEGRATION

Recognizing Problem Types

3. Melons were selling three for $1. How many could Larry buy for $4?

Which of the following problems can be solved in the same way as the preceding problem?

a. There were three books for every four students. How many books were there in a class of twenty students?
b. A car travels 25 miles per hour for 4 hours. How far will it travel?
c. John has 25 marbles. Sue has 12 marbles. How many more marbles does John have than Sue?
d. If balloons cost 10 cents each and pencils cost 5 cents each, how much do three balloons and two pencils cost?

Recognizing Relevant and Irrelevant Information

4. The manager bought 100 cameras for $3,578. The cameras sold for $6,024. How much was the profit?

Which numbers are needed to solve this problem?

a. 100, 6,024, 3,578
b. 100, 6,024
c. 100, 3,578
d. 3,578, 6,024

(continued)

FIGURE 5–1

(continued)

Determining Information That Is Needed for Solution

5. How much longer is the Mississippi River than the Yangtze River?

   What information is needed to answer this question?

a. the length of the Mississippi River and the length of the Yangtze River
b. the location and length of the Mississippi River and the location and length of the Yangtze River
c. the average rainfall for the Mississippi River and the average rainfall for the Yangtze River
d. the length of the Yangtze River

Representing a Problem as a Diagram or Picture

6. Mary Jackson earns $215 a week. She pays 30% of this for housing. How much does she pay for housing each week?

Which diagram best represents the problem?

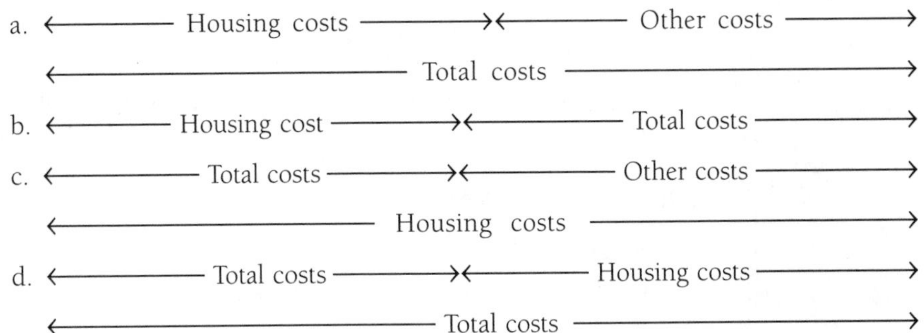

SOLUTION PLANNING AND MONITORING

Representing the Problem as a Number Sentence, Equation, or List of Necessary Operations

7. An insurance agent visited 585 customers. He sold 76 life insurance policies, 97 fire insurance policies, and 208 auto insurance policies. How many policies did he sell in all?

Which number sentence corresponds to this problem?

a. 76 + 97 + 208 =
b. 585 − 76 − 97 − 208 =
c. 585 + 76 + 97 + 208 =
d. 208 − 97 − 76 =

FIGURE 5–1

(continued)

Establishing Subgoals

8. Floor tiles are sold in squares 30 centimeters on each side. How much would it cost to tile a rectangular room 7.2 meters long and 5.4 meters wide if the tiles cost $.72 each?

To answer this question, you need to determine:

a. how many tiles are needed
b. how much longer one side of the room is than the other side
c. how much 100 tiles would cost
d. how much money will be left

Drawing Conclusions

9. The 130 students from Marie Curie School are going on a picnic. Each school bus holds 50 passengers. How many buses will they need?

Rose worked the following problem:

$$\begin{array}{r} 2 \\ 50\overline{)130} \\ \underline{100} \\ 30 \end{array}$$

Look back at the question in the problem. What is the answer?

a. 2 b. 2 R30 c. 2 3/5 d. 3

SOLUTION EXECUTION

Carrying Out Single Calculations

10. 7.2 × 5.4 = ____________

The correct answer is:

a. 38.88 b. 432 c. 311.04 d. 28

Carrying Out Chains of Calculations

11. ((7.2 × 5.4)/(.3 × .3)) × .72 = ____________

The correct answer is:

a. 38.88 b. 432 c. 311.04 d. 28

TABLE 5–1

The four components of mathematical problem-solving

Component	Type of Knowledge	Examples from the Tile Problem
Problem translation	Linguistic knowledge	The room is a rectangle with 7.2-meter width and 5.4-meter length.
	Factual knowledge	One meter equals 100 centimeters.
Problem integration	Schematic knowledge	Area = length × width
Solution planning and monitoring	Strategic knowledge	Find the area of the room in meters by multiplying 7.2 × 5.4. Then, find the area of each tile in meters by multiplying 0.3 × 0.3. Then, find the number of tiles needed by dividing the area of the room by the area of each tile. Finally, find total cost by multiplying the number of needed tiles by $.72.
Solution execution	Procedural knowledge	7.2 × 5.4 = 38.88 0.3 × 0.3 = 0.09 38.88/.09 = 432 432 × .72 = $311.04

each statement of the problem; (2) integrating the information into a coherent problem representation; (3) devising and monitoring a solution plan; and (4) accurately and efficiently carrying out the solution plan. (By the way, the answer for the tile problem is $311.04. The answers for the items in Figure 5–1 are: 1, b; 2, c; 3, a; 4, d; 5, a; 6, a; 7, a; 8, a; 9, d; 10, a; 11, c.)

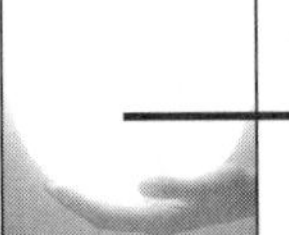

PROBLEM TRANSLATION

WHAT IS PROBLEM TRANSLATION?

The first step in solving the tile problem is to translate each statement into an internal representation. For example, the major statements in the tile problem are: the tiles are squares measuring 30 centimeters by 30 centimeters; the tiles cost 72 cents each; the room is a rectangle measuring 7.2 meters by 5.4 meters, and the cost of tiling the room is unknown. To translate these statements, a problem solver needs some knowledge of the English language (i.e., linguistic knowledge) and some knowledge about the world (i.e., factual knowledge). For example, linguistic knowledge is required to determine that “floor tiles” and “the tiles” refer to the same thing. Similarly, factual knowledge is required to know that a square has four sides of equal length and that 100 centimeters equals 1 meter.

RESEARCH ON PROBLEM TRANSLATION

COMPREHENDING RELATIONAL SENTENCES A growing research base suggests that the translation process can be difficult for students, especially when the problem contains relational statements (i.e., statements that express a quantitative relation between variables). For example, in an analysis of factors that contribute to problem difficulty, Loftus and Suppes (1972) found that the most difficult problems tend to contain relational statements, such as "Mary is twice as old as Betty was 2 years ago. Mary is 40 years old. How old is Betty?"

In another study (Greeno, 1980; Riley, Greeno, & Heller, 1982), children were asked to listen to and then repeat word problems. For example, suppose that the following problem was presented: "Joe has three marbles. Tom has five more marbles than Joe. How many marbles does Tom have?" Children's errors included ignoring the relational statements, such as repeating the problem as follows: "Joe has three marbles. Tom has five marbles. How many marbles does Tom have?"

Adults also seem to have difficulty in translating relational statements. In one study (Soloway, Lochhead, & Clement, 1982), college students were given statements and asked to translate them into equations. For example, suppose the statement was "There are six times as many students as professors at this university." Approximately one-third of the students produced the wrong equation, such as $6S = P$.

In a related study, Mayer (1982a) asked college students to read and then recall eight algebra story problems. The students made approximately three times as many errors in recalling relational statements (29% errors) than in recalling assignment statements (9% errors) which tell the value for a variable. Furthermore, an analysis of the errors revealed that on 20 occasions students converted a relational into an assignment statement, but that there was only one instance of a student converting an assignment into a relational statement. For example, one student changed the relational statement "the steamer's engine drives in still water at 12 miles per hour more than the rate of the current," into the assignment statement "its engines push the boat at 12 miles per hour in still water." These results suggest that some students may lack the appropriate linguistic knowledge to represent relational statements in memory.

Is difficulty in representing relational statements related to problem-solving performance? In a recent study, Hegarty, Mayer, and Monk (1995) asked students to solve 12 word problems, and later gave a recognition test on four of the problems that contained relational statements. For example, one problem was: "At ARCO, gas costs $1.13 per gallon. This is 5 cents less per gallon than gas at Chevron. If you want to buy 5 gallons of gas, how much will you pay at Chevron?" Table 5–2 lists four alternatives for this problem on the recognition test: The correct answer in which the relational statement is in verbatim form, a literal error in which the meaning of the relational statement is retained but the keyword is changed from "less" to "more," and two kinds of semantic errors in which the meaning of the relational statement is changed. Poor problem solvers produced four times as many semantic errors on the recognition test as did good problem solvers (39% versus 9%, respectively). In contrast, good problem solvers produced twice as many literal errors as did poor problem solvers (44% versus 19%, respectively). These results suggest that successful problem solvers are much more able than unsuccessful problem solvers to use their linguistic knowledge to determine the meaning of the relational statements.

TABLE 5–2 Which problem did you solve?	Alternatives	Scored As
	At ARCO, gas costs $1.13 per gallon. This is 5 cents less than gas costs at Chevron. If you want to buy 5 gallons of gas, how much will you pay at Chevron?	Correct
	At ARCO, gas costs $1.13 per gallon. Gas at Chevron costs 5 cents more per gallon than gas at ARCO. If you want to buy 5 gallons of gas, how much will you pay at Chevron?	Literal error
	At ARCO, gas costs $1.13 per gallon. Gas at Chevron costs 5 cents less per gallon than gas at ARCO. If you want to buy 5 gallons of gas, how much will you pay at Chevron?	Semantic error
	At ARCO, gas costs $1.13 per gallon. This is 5 cents more than gas costs at Chevron. If you want to buy 5 gallons of gas, how much will you pay at Chevron?	Semantic error

Adapted from Hegarty, Mayer, and Monk (1995)

USING FACTUAL KNOWLEDGE Factual knowledge is another key component in problem translation. For example, Loftus and Suppes (1972) found that problems involving scale conversion were much more difficult than corresponding problems that did not. Scale conversions require factual knowledge; for example, converting 30 centimeters to .3 meters requires knowing that 100 centimeters equals 1 meter. Bobrow (1968) developed a computer program capable of solving algebra story problems. The program involved two major phases: translation of each statement into an equation and solution of the equations. For the program to translate, a large store of both linguistic and factual knowledge had to be included in the program. For example, the program needed linguistic knowledge, such as "pounds is the plural of pound," and factual knowledge, such as "16 ounces equals 1 pound."

IMPLICATIONS FOR INSTRUCTION: TEACHING PROBLEM TRANSLATION SKILLS

What do successful problem solvers know that unsuccessful problem solvers do not know? The research results suggest that successful problem solvers are more likely than unsuccessful problem solvers to know how to comprehend the sentences in word problems, especially how to comprehend sentences that express a relation between two variables. Apparently, unsuccessful problem solvers may not know how to understand statements such as "the Acme building is 27 feet taller than the Bendex building" or "Elena is 8 centimeters shorter than Andrea." In short, unsuccessful problem solvers may lack problem translation skills.

Can problem translation skills be taught? Lewis (1989) developed a two-session instructional program that teaches students how to represent sentences from word problems. In the first session, the instructor demonstrates how each sentence in a series of nine word problems can be classified as an assignment, a relation, or a question, and then students are given a worksheet in which they practice classifying the sentences in 18 word problems. In the second session, the instructor demonstrates how to diagram each of four sample problems using a simple number-line method, as exemplified in Figure 5–2. For example, the first step is to place the amount Megan saved on the number line, the second step is to determine whether the amount James saved goes to the left or right of Megan, the third step is to check the placement of James, and the third step is to determine what kind of operation to perform. Then, students receive worksheets in which they diagram eight word problems using the number-line diagram. The problems contain relational statements so students receive practice in recognizing relational statements and representing them on a number line.

Does translation training help students solve word problems? To answer this question, Lewis (1989) asked college students to take a pretest that contained two-step comparison problems (such as the gas problem in Table 5–2) and three-step comparison problems. About one-third of the students made errors on some of the two-step problems, so they could be classified as unsuccessful problem solvers. Lewis's goal was to reduce the errors of these unsuccessful problem solvers, so she invited them to remain in the study. Some of these unsuccessful problem solvers (translation-trained group) received approximately 60 minutes of training across two sessions in which they learned how to recognize and diagram relational sentences from two-step word problems using a number line. Others students (control group) spent an equal amount of time working on the same problems, but their task was merely to judge the difficulty of the problems. Then, the translation-trained and control students took a posttest that contained both two-step and three-step problems.

If translation training helps students to translate the sentences of a word problem and if improper translation is the major impediment to successful problem solving, then unsuccessful problem solvers who receive translation training should show a large pretest-to-posttest decline in errors on solving word problems. The left panel of Figure 5–3 shows that the translation-trained group eliminated almost all of its errors on two-step problems on the posttest, whereas the control group did not. Similarly, the right panel of Figure 5–3 also shows that the translation-trained group eliminated most of its errors on three-step problems, whereas the control group did not. These results provide solid evidence that translation training is effective in improving students' problem-solving performance. The improvement occurred both on problems like those presented during training (two-step problems) and on problems that were more complex (three-step problems).

Based on these results, Lewis (1989) concluded that "training aimed at remedying students' erroneous comprehension processes for relational statements can be successful and can result in transfer" (p. 530) to new kinds of word problems. Translation training is consistent with the call for helping mathematics students to build multiple representations of the same problem, such as being able to represent a problem in words, a diagram, and an equation (Grouws, 1992; National Council of Teachers of Mathematics, 1989; Wagner & Kieran, 1989). More recently, Brenner et al. (1997) developed a 20-day program for middle-school prealgebra students that emphasized daily experience in translating among relational sentences, tables, graphs, and equations. Students who participated in the program showed much greater improvements in their ability to understand and solve word problems than did those who received conventional instruction. These results suggest that a

FIGURE 5–2

Worksheet for learning how to translate sentences into diagrams

SAMPLE PROBLEM

Megan has saved $420 for vacation. She has saved one-fifth as much as James has saved. James has been saving for his vacation for six months. How much has he saved each month?

DIAGRAMMING STEPS

1. Draw a number line, and place the variable and the value from the assignment statement in the middle of the line.

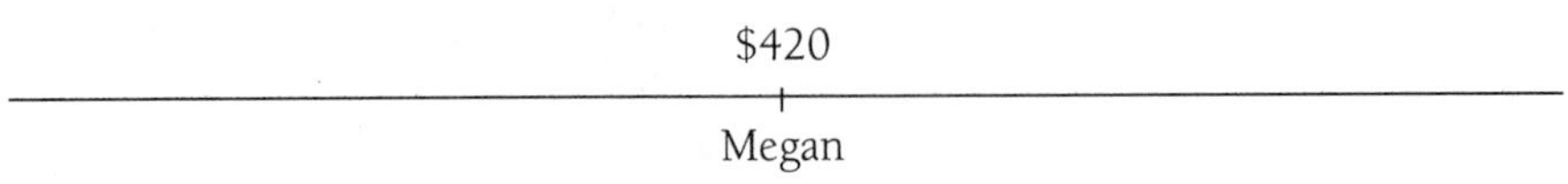

2. Tentatively place the unknown variable (James's savings) on one side of the middle.

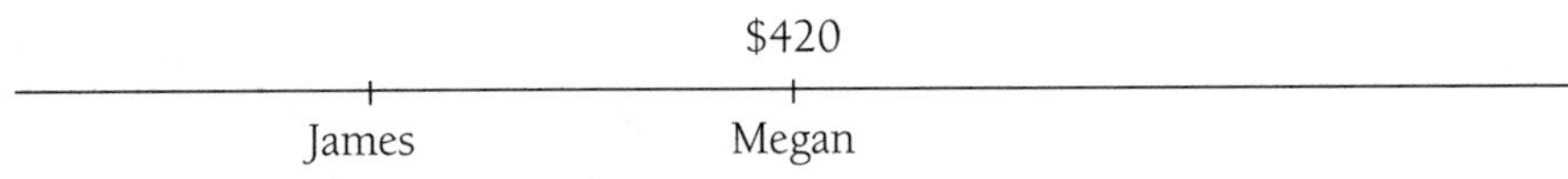

3. Compare your representation with the information in the relation statement, checking to see whether your representation agrees with the meaning of the relation statement. If it does, then you can continue. If not, then try again with the other side.

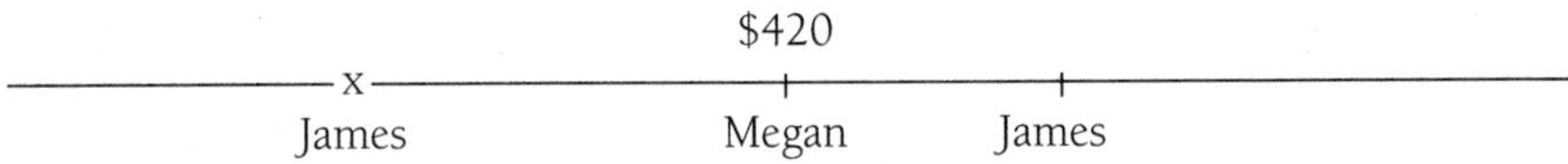

4. Translate your representation into an arithmetic operation. If the unknown variable is to the right of the center, then the operation is an increase, such as addition or multiplication. If the unknown variable is to the left of the center, then the operation is a decrease, such as subtraction or division.

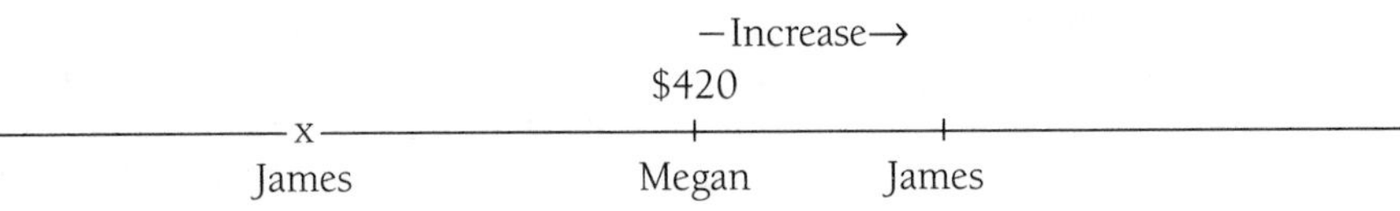

Adapted from Lewis (1989)

FIGURE 5–3 Percentage of errors on pretest and posttest for translation-trained and control students

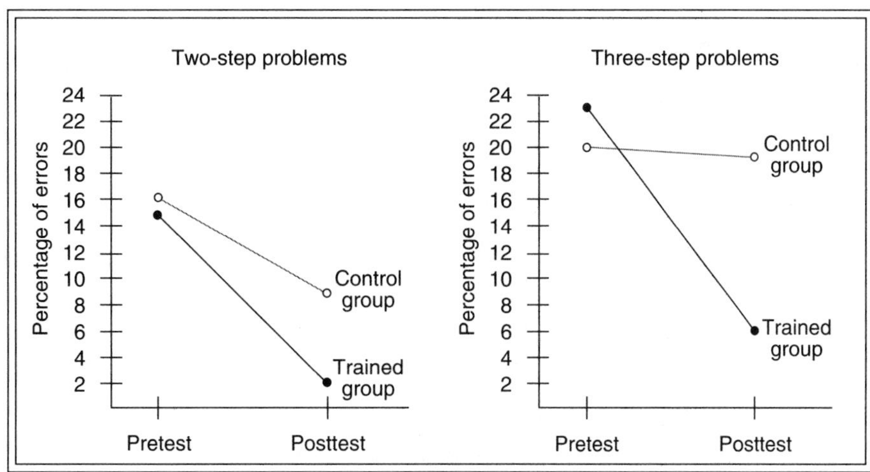

major impediment to successful problem solving may be poor problem translation skills. Although translation skills are not typically emphasized in mathematics curricula, increasing evidence indicates translation training can be helpful.

The research summarized in this section suggests that problem translation may be a major source of difficulty in mathematical problem solving. Apparently, many students come to the problem-solving task lacking the prerequisite linguistic and factual knowledge. One implication of this research is that students may need practice in problem translation, such as paraphrasing statements from the problem.

Let's return to the tile problem described in the introduction to this chapter. The research presented in this section indicates that many students have difficulty in comprehending each major statement in the problem, such as, "Floor tiles are sold in squares 30 centimeters on each side." How can you provide translation training for a problem like the tile problem? Some activities that might encourage the development of translation skills include students restating the problem givens or goals in their own words. In some cases, students could be asked to draw a picture that corresponds to a sentence in the problem, such as the first sentence of the tile problem. Similarly, the first section of Figure 5–1 suggests the use of multiple-choice items to offer practice in recognizing problem givens and goals. These suggestions, of course, are tentative ones that require research verification.

PROBLEM INTEGRATION

WHAT IS PROBLEM INTEGRATION?

The accurate representation of a story problem often requires more than statement-by-statement translation. For example, Paige and Simon (1966) asked students to solve impossible problems such as "The number of quarters a man has is seven times the number of dimes he has. The value of the dimes exceeds the value of the quarters by \$2.50. How many of each coin does he have?" (p. 84) Using factual and linguistic knowledge, a person could translate these statements into equations such as

$$Q = 7D$$
$$D(.10) = 2.50 + Q(.25)$$

where Q is the number of quarters and D is the number of dimes. However, if you try to understand how the two statements fit together to form a coherent problem, you might recognize an inconsistency, namely that having more quarters than dimes is inconsistent with the value of the dimes exceeding the value of quarters. In Paige and Simon's study, both types of approaches were observed: some subjects translated each statement separately, while other subjects tried to understand how the statements related to one another.

As another example of problem integration, consider the following computational problem: $1\frac{3}{4} \div \frac{1}{2} =$ ____. Please write a story problem that corresponds to this computational problem. In short, this task asks you to think of an appropriate situation model—a representation of a concrete situation corresponding to the problem.

Ma (1999) gave this kind of problem to elementary school teachers in the United States and China. If you are like many of the U.S. teachers in Ma's study, you had difficulty in thinking of an appropriate situation model. Ninety-six percent of the U.S. teachers either gave an incorrect model or were unable to describe a model at all. For example, two common errors—summarized in the top of Figure 5–4—are to confuse division by $\frac{1}{2}$ with division by 2 or to confuse division by $\frac{1}{2}$ with multiplication by $\frac{1}{2}$. In contrast, 90% of the Chinese teachers produced correct models, such as summarized in the bottom on Figure 5–4. For example, two correct models approach the problem as finding how many $\frac{1}{2}$s there are in $1\frac{3}{4}$ or finding the number such that half of it is $1\frac{3}{4}$.

This research demonstrates that an important part of mathematics learning is the ability to build a mental representation of a concrete situation that corresponds to a mathematical

FIGURE 5–4

Incorrect and correct situation models for $1\frac{3}{4} \div \frac{1}{2}$

INCORRECT MODELS

Confounding division by $\frac{1}{2}$ with division by 2. "If you have one pie and $\frac{3}{4}$ of another pie to be divided equally between two people, how much pie will each person get?" Confounding division by $\frac{1}{2}$ with multiplication by $\frac{1}{2}$. "If you have one pie and three-quarters of another pie, what is half of the total?"

CORRECT MODELS

Finding how many $\frac{1}{2}$s are in $1\frac{3}{4}$: "If a team of workers constructs $\frac{1}{2}$ kilometer of road per day, how many days will it take them to construct a road $1\frac{3}{4}$ kilometers long?" Finding a number such that $\frac{1}{2}$ of it is $1\frac{3}{4}$. "If $\frac{1}{2}$ of a jump rope is $1\frac{3}{4}$ meters, what is the length of the whole rope?"

Adapted from Ma (1999).

problem. Ma's research shows that even many teachers require more training in how to represent problems, a theme that is echoed in research-based recommendations for the reform of mathematics education (Kilpatrick, Swafford, & Findell, 2001).

The foregoing examples show that another important component in the process of understanding a story problem is to put the statements of the problem together into a coherent representation that can be called a *situation model* (Kintsch & Greeno, 1985; Mayer & Hegarty, 1996; Nathan, Kintsch, & Young, 1992). In order to integrate the information in a problem, the problem solver needs to have some knowledge of problem types (i.e., schematic knowledge). For example, you need to recognize that the tile problem is a rectangle problem based on the formula *area* = *length* × *width.* This knowledge will help you to understand how the statements in the problem fit together; for example, the situation described in the tile problem consists of a rectangular floor that is covered with square tiles.

RESEARCH ON PROBLEM INTEGRATION

STUDENT SCHEMAS FOR STORY PROBLEMS According to the cognitive analysis of mathematical problem solving shown in Table 5–1, successful problem solvers need to possess knowledge of problem categories (or schemas). Hinsley, Hayes, and Simon (1977) studied students' schemas for story problems by asking students who were experienced in algebra to sort a series of algebra story problems into groups. Students were quite proficient at this task and reached high levels of agreement. Table 5–3 shows the 18 categories that the subjects used. Apparently, experienced students come to the problem-solving task with some knowledge of problem types.

Hinsley et al. (1977) also found that students were able to categorize problems almost immediately. For example, as soon as a student has read the first few words of a problem, such as "A river steamer travels 36 miles downstream . . . ," we would expect the student to say, "Oh, it's one of those river current problems." Follow-up studies (Hayes, Waterman, & Robinson, 1977; Robinson & Hayes, 1978) found that students who are experienced in algebra use their schemas to make accurate judgments concerning which information is relevant to a problem and which is not.

Many errors in problem integration occur when a person uses the wrong schema for determining which information is necessary. For example, the following problem used by Hinsley et al. (1977) can be viewed as either a distance-rate-time problem or a triangle problem:

> Because of their quiet ways, the inhabitants of Smalltown were especially upset by the terrible New Year's Eve auto accident which claimed the life of one Smalltown resident. The facts were these: Both Smith and Jones were New Year's babies and each had planned a surprise visit to the other on their mutual birthday. Jones had started out for Smith's house traveling due east on Route 210 just 2 minutes after Smith had left for Jones' house. Smith was traveling directly south on Route 140. Jones was traveling 30 miles per hour faster than Smith even though their houses were only five miles apart as the crow flies. Their cars crashed at the right-angle intersection of the two highways. Officer Franklin, who observed the crash, determined that Jones was traveling half again as fast as Smith at the time of the crash. Smith had been driving for just 4 minutes at the time of the crash. The crash occurred nearer to the house of the dead man than to the house of the survivor. What was the name of the dead man? (p. 102)

TABLE 5–3

Examples of eighteen problem types

Problem Type	Example of Problem
1. Triangle	Jerry walks one block east along a vacant lot and then two blocks north to a friend's house. Phil starts at the same point and walks diagonally through the vacant lot, coming out at the same point as Jerry. If Jerry walked 217 feet east and 400 feet north, how far did Phil walk?
2. DRT	In a sports car race, a Panther starts the course at 9:00 A.M. and averages 75 miles per hour. A Mallotti starts 4 minutes later and averages 85 miles per hour. If a lap is 15 miles, on which lap will the Panther be overtaken?
3. Averages	Flying east between two cities, a plane's speed is 380 miles per hour. On the return trip, it flies 420 miles per hour. Find the average speed for the round trip.
4. Scale conversion	Two temperature scales are established, one, the *R* scale, where water under fixed conditions freezes at 15 and boils at 405, and the other, the *S* scale, where water freezes at 5 and boils at 70. If the *R* and *S* scales are linearly related, find an expression for any temperature *R* in terms of a temperature *S*.
5. Ratio	If canned tomatoes come in two sizes and the radius of one is two-thirds the radius of the other, find the ratios of the capacities of the two cans.
6. Interest	A certain savings bank pays 3% interest compounded semiannually. How much will $2,500 be worth if left on deposit for 20 years?
7. Area	A box containing 180 cubic inches is constructed by cutting from each corner of a cardboard square a small square with sides of 5 inches, and then turning up the sides. Find the area of the original piece of cardboard.
8. Max-min	A real estate operator estimates that the monthly profit p in dollars from a building s stories high is given by $p = -2s^2 + 88s$. What height building would he consider most profitable?

Some students interpreted this problem as a triangle problem. For example, they drew triangles and tried to determine the lengths of the two legs and the hypotenuse. One student misread "4 minutes" as "4 miles" and assumed this was the length of one of the legs; another subject assumed "5 miles apart" referred to the length of the hypotenuse. In contrast, other students interpreted this problem as a distance-rate-time problem. For example, one student said: "It looks like a distance problem. So Jones is going east two minutes after Smith is going west. So it might be an overtake problem." Subjects who interpreted the problem as a distance-rate-time problem initially assumed that one driver was going east and the other driver was going west. Apparently, students use either a triangle schema or a distance-rate-time schema as a template for understanding the problem. In all, Hinsley

TABLE 5–3 (continued)	Problem Type	Example of Problem
	9. Mixture	One vegetable oil contains 6% saturated fats, and a second contains 26% saturated fats. In making a salad dressing, how many ounces of the second must be added to 10 ounces of the first if the percent of saturated fats is not to exceed 16%?
	10. River current	A river steamer travels 36 miles downstream in the same time that it travels 24 miles upstream. The steamer's engines drive in still water at a rate that is 12 miles an hour more than the rate of the current. Find the rate of the current.
	11. Probability	In an extrasensory-perception experiment, a blindfolded subject has two rows of blocks before him. Each row has blocks numbered 1 to 10 arranged in random order. The subject is to place one hand on a block in the first row and then try to place his other hand on the block having the same numeral in the second row. If the subject has no ESP, what is the probability of his making a match on the first try?
	12. Number	The units digit is 1 more than 3 times the tens digit. The number represented when the digits are interchanged is 8 times the sum of the digits.
	13. Work	Mr. Russo takes 3 minutes less than Mr. Lloyd to pack a case when each works alone. One day, after Mr. Russo had spent 6 minutes packing a case, the boss called him away, and Mr. Lloyd finished packing in 4 more minutes. How many minutes would it take Mr. Russo alone to pack a case?
	14. Navigation	A pilot leaves an aircraft carrier and flies south at 360 miles per hour, while the carrier proceeds N30W at 30 miles per hour. If the pilot has enough fuel to fly 4 hours, how far south can he fly before returning to his ship?
	15. Progressions	From two towns 363 miles apart, Jack and Jill set out to meet each other. If Jill travels 1 mile the first day, 3 the second, 5 the third, and so on, and Jack travels 2 miles the first day, 6 the second, 10 the third, and so on, when will they meet?
	16. Progression-2	Find the sum of the first 25 odd positive integers.
	17. Physics	The speed of a body falling freely from rest is directly proportional to the length of time that it falls. If a body was falling at 144 feet per second $4\frac{1}{2}$ seconds after beginning its fall, how fast was it falling $3\frac{3}{4}$ seconds later?
	18. Exponentials	The diameter of each successive layer of a wedding cake is two-thirds the diameter of the previous layer. If the diameter of the first layer of a five-layer cake is 15 inches, find the sum of the circumferences of all the layers.

Adapted from Hinsley, Hayes, and Simon (1977)

et al. identified 18 basic problem schemas and found that these schemas influence how a subject reads a problem.

In a follow-up study, Mayer (1981b) analyzed the story problems in some typical secondary-school algebra textbooks. Approximately 100 problem types were found, including many varieties of the 18 categories that Hinsley et al. (1977) found. For example, there were at least 12 kinds of distance-rate-time (or motion) problems, including overtake (in which one vehicle starts and is followed later by a second vehicle that travels over the same route at a faster rate), closure (in which two vehicles start at different points and travel toward one another), round trip (in which a vehicle travels from point A to B and returns), speed change (in which a vehicle travels at a certain rate for the first leg of a trip and then changes to another rate for the remainder of the trip), and opposite direction (in which two vehicles start at one point and travel in opposite directions). Certain problem types occurred frequently in the textbooks (e.g., more than 25 instances per 1,000 problems), while others were rarely found (e.g., less than 4 instances per 1,000 problems). Table 5–4 lists some common problem types (or categories), with similar types grouped into families. The numbers in parentheses indicate the percentage of problems in textbooks that belonged to the category.

In another study (Mayer, 1982b), students were asked to read and then recall a series of eight story problems. The results indicated that students were far more successful at recall-

TABLE 5–4

Some problem types from algebra textbooks

Family	Category (Percentage of Total)
Amount-per-time family	Motion (13%) Current (5%) Work (11%)
Cost-per-unit family	Unit cost (4%) Coins (7%) Dry mixture (6%)
Portion-of-total family	Interest/investment (12%) Profit/discount (2%)
Amount-per-amount family	Direct variation (16%) Inverse variation (3%) Wet mixture (6%)
Number story family	Part (4%) Age (3%) Consecutive interest (1%)
Geometry family	Rectangle/frame (3%) Circle (1%) Triangle (1%)

Adapted from Mayer (1981b)

FIGURE 5–5 More common problem types are easier to recall

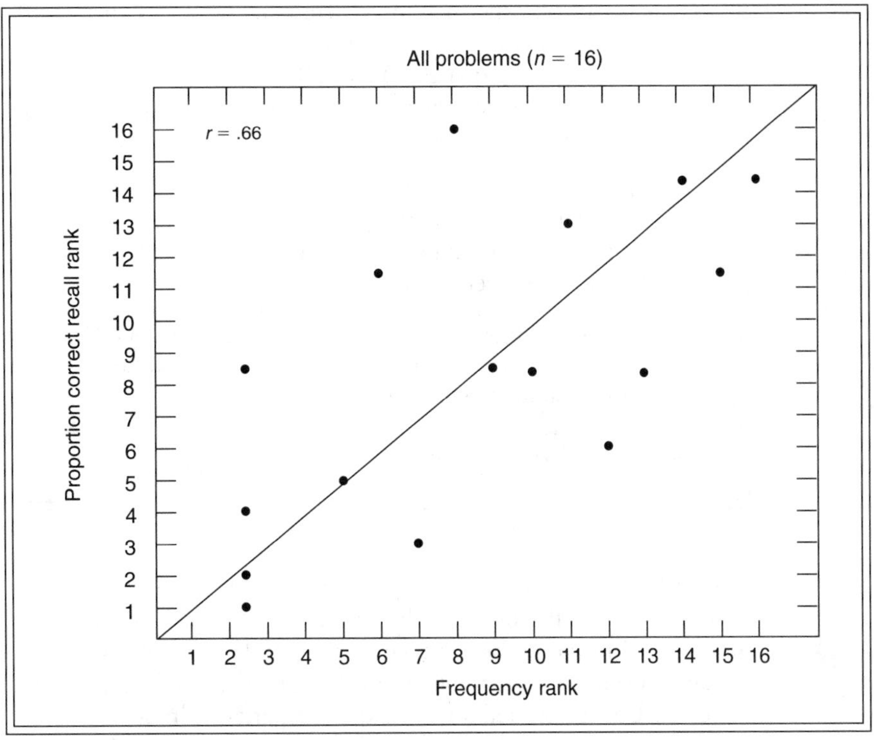

From Mayer (1982b)

ing high-frequency problem types than low-frequency types. Figure 5–5 shows the relationship between the frequency of the problem (i.e., how many times per 1,000 problems this type of problem occurred in typical math books) and the probability of correct recall for the problem. As you can see, the probability that a student will correctly recall a problem is strongly correlated with the frequency with which the problem type is represented in typical math textbooks. In addition, an analysis of errors in recall revealed a tendency for subjects to change a low-frequency problem into a similar problem that occurred with higher frequency; in contrast, no high-frequency problems were changed into low-frequency problems by students. Apparently, students possess schemas for some of the more typical problem types. When students are given a problem for which they do not possess an appropriate schema, representation of the problem is in jeopardy.

EXPERT/NOVICE DIFFERENCES IN STUDENT SCHEMAS. Experienced and inexperienced problem solvers differ in the ways they categorize word problems: Experienced problem solvers are more likely to focus on the structural features of problems, such as the underlying principle or relation, whereas inexperienced problem solvers are more likely to focus on the surface features, such as the objects described in the problem.

For example, Quilici and Mayer (1996) asked students to sort 12 statistics word problems into categories based on similarity, that is, by grouping together problems that could

FIGURE 5–6

Three statistics word problems

1. A personnel expert wishes to determine whether experienced typists are able to type faster than inexperienced typists. Twenty experienced typists (i.e., with 5 or more years of experience) and 20 inexperienced typists (i.e., with less than 5 years of experience) are given a typing test. Each typist's average number of words typed per minute is recorded.
2. A personnel expert wishes to determine whether typing experience goes with faster typing speeds. Forty typists are asked to report how many years they have worked as typists and are given a typing test to determine their average number of words typed per minute.
3. After examining weather data for the last 50 years, a meteorologist claims that the annual precipitation varies with average temperature. For each of 50 years, she notes the annual rainfall and average temperature.

Adapted from Quilici and Mayer (1996)

be solved in the same way. Figure 5–6 shows three of the problems used in the study. If a person sorts the problems based mainly on *surface characteristics,* such as the objects described in the problems, then all the problems involving typists will be placed in the same category, all the problems involving rainfall will be placed in the same category, and so on. College students who had no experience in statistics (i.e., novices) tended to group the problems based on surface features; for example, they would put Problems 1 and 2 together because they both involve typists. In contrast, if a person sorts the problems based on *structural features,* such as how many groups are involved (i.e., one or two) and the nature of the dependent measure (i.e., categorical or quantitative), the person will sort problems requiring computing a *t*-test into one group, problems requiring the computation of a correlation into another group, and so on. Graduate students who had extensive experience in statistics tended to the group the problems based on structural features; for example, they would put Problems 2 and 3 together because they both deal with correlation. Interestingly, students tended to change from sorting mainly by surface features before taking an introductory course in statistics to sorting at least partially by structural features after taking the course. Apparently, experience in a mathematical domain can help students change the way they organize their schematic knowledge of problem types.

Similarly, Silver (1981) asked seventh-graders to sort 16 story problems into groups. Students who performed poorly in solving story problems tended to group the problems based on their cover stories, such as putting together all problems about money. Students who performed well in solving story problems tended to group the problems based on their underlying mathematical structure. Apparently, learning to solve story problems successfully is related to the development of useful schemas for problem types.

DEVELOPMENTAL DIFFERENCES IN STUDENT SCHEMAS. The sophistication of students' schematic knowledge may be related to prior experience with story problems.

For example, Greeno and his colleagues (Greeno, 1980; Riley et al., 1982) identified three types of arithmetic word problems:

Cause/change problems, such as "Joe has two marbles. Tom gives him four more marbles. How many marbles does Joe have now?"

Combination problems, such as "Joe has two marbles. Tom has four marbles. How many marbles do they have altogether?"

Comparison problems, such as "Joe has two marbles. Tom has four more marbles than Joe. How many marbles does Tom have?"

As you can see, all three of these problems involve the same underlying computations (2 + 4 = _____). However, Greeno and his colleagues found that the problems differed greatly in difficulty. Children in grades K–3 all performed well on cause/change problems. However, children in grades K and 1 performed poorly on combination and comparison problems, while children in grades 2 and 3 performed well on them. One way to interpret these data is to say that the younger children have only one schema for word problems (i.e., the cause/change schema) and that they try to apply this schema to all word problems. In contrast, the older children seem to have developed different schemas for different problem types (i.e., they have added schemas for combination and comparison problems). Thus many errors on comparison problems seem to occur because students lack appropriate schemas rather than because students lack appropriate computational skill.

A CLOSER LOOK AT THE PROBLEM INTEGRATION PROCESSES OF SUCCESSFUL AND UNSUCCESSFUL PROBLEM SOLVERS. Lewis and Mayer (1987) proposed that many errors in problem solving occur mainly because of a superficial integration process in which students use key words in problems to determine which arithmetic operations to perform. For example, consider the two versions of the butter problem shown in Figure 5–7. On the top is a consistent version of the butter problem because the key word ("less") primes the appropriate arithmetic operation (subtraction); the other is an

FIGURE 5–7

Consistent and inconsistent versions of the butter problem

CONSISTENT VERSION

At Lucky, butter costs 65 cents per stick.
Butter at Vons costs 2 cents less per stick than butter at Lucky.
If you need to buy 4 sticks of butter,
how much will you pay at Vons?

INCONSISTENT VERSION

At Lucky, butter costs 65 cents per stick.
This is 2 cents less per stick than butter at Vons.
If you need to buy 4 sticks of butter,
how much will you pay at Vons?

Adapted from Hegarty, Mayer, and Monk (1995)

inconsistent version of the butter problem because the key word ("less") primes an inappropriate arithmetic operation (subtraction instead of addition of 65 and 2). In-depth analyses of students' problem solving revealed that students made many errors on inconsistent problems in which focusing on key words led to the wrong answer, but almost no errors on consistent problems in which focusing on key words led to the correct answer (Lewis & Mayer, 1987; Verschaffel, De Corte, & Pauwels, 1992). When students made errors, they tended to perform the arithmetic operation primed by a key word, such as subtracting 2 from 65 and multiplying the result by 4 in the butter problem. These results implicate a faulty problem integration process as a major culprit in producing problem-solving errors.

Successful and unsuccessful problem solvers may engage in quite different processes for representing word problems such as the two versions of the butter problem shown in Figure 5–7 (Hegarty et al., 1995; Lewis & Mayer, 1987; Mayer & Hegarty, 1996). When confronted with a word problem, unsuccessful students may be more likely to use a direct translation approach in which they select numbers from the problem and use key words in the problem to determine which arithmetic operations to perform. Students using a direct translation approach are likely to extract the numbers "65 cents," "2 cents," and "4 sticks." The key word "less" primes the arithmetic operation of subtraction, so the first step is to subtract 2 from 65. The key words "how much" prime the arithmetic operation of multiplication, so the next step is to multiply the result by 4. In contrast, successful students may be more likely to use a problem model approach in which they construct a mental model of the situation that is described in the problem statement. Students using a problem model approach integrate the sentences by determining that "this" refers to butter at Lucky.

To examine more closely differences in how successful and unsuccessful problem-solvers represent word problems, Hegarty et al. (1995) monitored the eye movements of eight successful and eight unsuccessful problem solvers as they read word problems from a computer screen and formulated a solution plan. All students carefully read the four lines of the problem and then went back to reread certain parts of the problem. Unsuccessful problem solvers tended to look back at numbers and key words far more often than did successful problem solvers; in contrast, successful problem solvers tended to frequently reread the variable names (e.g., "Vons" and "Lucky") and other words before rereading the numbers in the problem. These findings indicate that unsuccessful problem solvers are more likely to use a direct translation approach to problem integration, whereas successful problem solvers are more likely to use a problem model approach.

IMPLICATIONS FOR INSTRUCTION: TEACHING PROBLEM INTEGRATION SKILLS

When confronted with a problem, students must determine what information is needed to solve it and then locate that information in the problem. If the problem contains irrelevant information, students must ignore it. If the problem lacks essential information, students must recognize that it cannot be solved.

For example, consider the three problems in Figure 5–8. Determine whether each problem has (1) sufficient information (i.e., enough information to solve the problem); (2) irrelevant information (i.e., information that is irrelevant to the solution); or (3) missing infor-

FIGURE 5–8

Does the problem have sufficient, irrelevant, or missing information?

For each problem indicate whether:

a. It contains enough information to be able to solve the problem,
b. It contains information that is irrelevant for the solution of the problem (if so, please underline the unnecessary information), or
c. It does not contain enough information to be able to solve the problem (if so, please specify the additional information needed to solve the problem).

Problems

1. A rectangular lawn is 12 meters long and 5 meters wide. Calculate the area of a path 1.75 meters wide around the lawn.
2. The length of a rectangular park is 6 meters more than its width. A walkway 3 meters wide surrounds the park. Find the dimensions of the park if it has an area of 432 square meters.
3. The lengths of the sides of a blackboard are in a 2:3 ratio. What is the perimeter (in meters) of the blackboard?

Adapted from Low and Over (1993)

mation (i.e., not enough information to solve the problem). The correct answers are that problem 1 has sufficient information, Problem 2 has irrelevant information, and Problem 3 has missing information. If you are like most of the high school students tested by Low and Over (1989, 1990, 1993; Low, 1989), you made errors on more than half of the problems, such as failing to recognize a piece of irrelevant information or that an additional piece of information was needed.

The type of task exemplified in Figure 5–8—asking a student to judge whether the information presented in a problem corresponds to the information needed to solve the problem—represents a crucial test of a student's schematic knowledge. To make judgments about the relevance of information, a student needs to construct an integrated representation of the problem. Low and Over (1989, 1990, 1993; Low, 1989) found that high school students often are unable to use schematic knowledge about common problem types such as rectangle, interest, and distance problems.

Is problem-solving performance related to the ability to detect whether a problem contains sufficient, irrelevant, or missing information? On some of the problems that Low and Over (1989) presented to students, they were asked to identify information that was missing or what information was not needed; on other problems (which contained sufficient or irrelevant information), the students were asked to compute a solution. As expected, performance on judging whether problems contained missing or irrelevant information correlated highly ($r = .9$) with ability to solve problems, such that students who performed well on solving problems also tended to perform well judging whether problems contained missing or irrelevant information, and those who performed poorly on problems also tended to perform poorly on making judgments. These results support the contention that problem integration skills are an important component in mathematical problem solving.

If the ability to make relevance judgments is highly related to success in solving word problems, and if many high school students perform poorly on making relevance judgments, then teaching students how to judge the relevance of problem information should lead to improved problem-solving performance. This was the premise behind an instructional study involving high school students reported by Low (1989). Some students (relevance-trained group) were given 80 minutes of training in recognizing whether word problems contained sufficient, irrelevant, or missing information, and in specifying which information was irrelevant or missing. In all, students classified each of 27 problems and subsequently received feedback from the teacher concerning how to classify the problems. For example, in modeling her rationale for classifying a problem as having missing information, the teacher would say: "This is an area-of-rectangle problem. Since area equals length multiplied by width and only length is given, the information provided is insufficient for solution." In contrast, other students (conventional group) received 80 minutes of conventional instruction during which they solved problems similar to the sufficient problems given to the relevance-trained group and received feedback from the teacher concerning how to calculate a solution to the problems. Other students (control group) received no instruction.

Does relevance training affect students' ability to solve word problems? To help answer this question, students were given a pretest and posttest in which they were asked to solve word problems that contained either sufficient or irrelevant information. On the pretest, lower-ability students in each group solved about one-fourth of the problems. However, on the posttest, students in the conventional and control groups showed modest gains of about 10 percentage points whereas the relevance-trained group showed a much larger increase of about 25 percentage points. As you can see, training in how to judge the relevance of problem information was more effective than instruction in generating solutions in improving problem-solving performance. These results encourage the idea that students can learn problem integration skills that significantly improve their problem-solving performance.

This section provided some research evidence that errors occur when students lack a schema or use the wrong schema for organizing a problem. How could you provide schema training? Some textbooks organize practice problems so that all problems on a page are solvable by the same procedure. This homogeneous organization fails to give students practice in recognizing different problem types. A greater mixture of problems would encourage students to learn how to discriminate among different types of problems.

Let's return to the tile problem. Some techniques for helping students learn problem types include asking students to draw an integrated diagram of the problem, to sort the problems into categories, or to determine which information is irrelevant. The second part of Figure 5–1 offers multiple-choice items aimed at fostering these skills. As with the suggestions given in the previous section, these suggestions also require research verification.

Schema training is not the same as training students to recognize key words. For example, some students learn to categorize problems on the basis of superficial key words, such as, "If the problem says 'more,' then add the numbers in the problem," and "If the problem says 'less,' then subtract the second number from the first." This system is a poor one because it does not encourage the student to understand and represent the problem. It also can lead to errors such as the one in the inconsistent version of the butter problem in Figure 5–7. Students need to see that key word methods do not always lead to the correct answer. Instead of relying on key words, students should be encouraged to represent the problem in their own words (or pictures).

In summary, when students represent a problem, they must engage in problem translation and problem integration. The foregoing two sections provided examples of how failures in problem solving often occur because of students' lack of schematic, linguistic, or factual knowledge. Instructional techniques that help students acquire such knowledge should be recognized as a crucial aspect of mathematics instruction. One promising sign is that items testing problem representation are beginning to appear on standardized mathematics tests.

SOLUTION PLANNING AND MONITORING

WHAT IS SOLUTION PLANNING AND MONITORING?

The next component in solving a mathematics story problem is to devise and monitor a plan for solving the problem. For example, in the tile problem at the beginning of this chapter, the plan might involve breaking the problem into subproblems: First, find the area of the room by multiplying room length by room width; second, find the area of a single tile by multiplying tile length by tile width; third, find the number of tiles needed by dividing area of the room by the area of one tile; fourth, find the cost of the tiles by multiplying the number of tiles by the cost per tile. As you can see, this solution plan involves four parts; in solving the problem, you must monitor where you are in the plan. In addition, you must be able to make scale conversions where needed, such as converting meters to centimeters or dollars to cents.

DEVISING A SOLUTION PLAN

When you are confronted with a problem you have never seen before, where does the idea for a solution plan come from? In his classic book *How to Solve It,* Polya (1945) offered the following advice for devising a solution plan: "If you cannot solve the proposed problem try to first solve some related problem. Could you imagine a more accessible related problem?" (p. xvii). Once the student finds a related problem that he or she has solved before, Polya (1945) asks: "Could you use it? Could you use its results? Could you use its method? Should you introduce some auxiliary element in order to make its use possible?" (p. xvii). In short, Polya (1945) concluded that "it is often appropriate to start work with the question: Do you know a related problem?" (p. 9). According to Polya (1945), "the main achievement in the solution of a problem is to conceive of the idea of a plan" (p. 8), and the planning process should begin with the question "Do you know a related problem?" (p. 9).

For example, consider the frustrum problem in Figure 5–9. You are given the values of the lower base (b), upper base (a), and height (h) of a frustrum of a right pyramid, and are asked to find the volume of the frustrum. If you are like most students who encountered this problem in Polya's geometry classes, you have never seen this problem before. Do you

FIGURE 5–9

The frustrum problem

Here's a problem to solve:

Find the volume F of the frustrum of a right pyramid with a square base. Given the altitude h of the frustrum, the length a of a side of its upper base, and the length b of a side of its lower base.

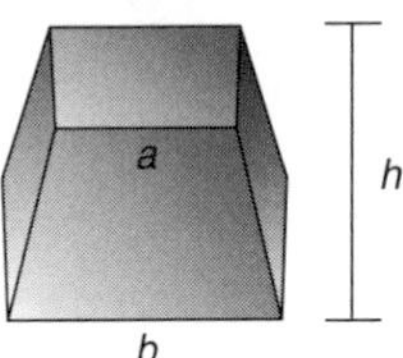

Here's a hint to help you devise a plan:

If you cannot solve the proposed problem, look around for an appropriate related problem. For example, do you know how to find the volume of a pyramid? If so then you know that the procedure for computing the volume of a pyramid is to multiply the area of the base times the height and divide the result by 3.

Here's a flash of insight provoked by the related problem:

To find the volume of the frustrum, subtract the volume of the large pyramid from the volume of the small pyramid.

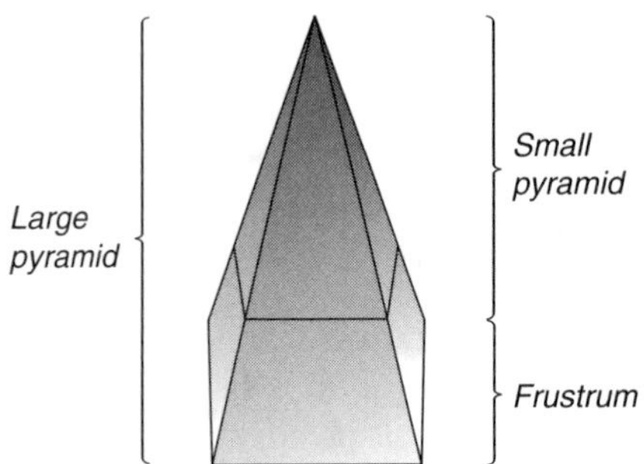

Here's how to develop the plan based on the procedure for a related problem:

The volume of the big pyramid is $b^2(h + x)/3$ and the volume of the small pyramid is $a^2(x)/3$ where b is the base of the big pyramid, a is the base of the small pyramid, x is the height of the small pyramid, and $(h + x)$ is the height of the big pyramid.

Adapted from Polya (1945, 1965)

know how to solve a related problem? Most geometry students know how to find the volume of a right pyramid using the following formula: volume equals one-third of the product of the area of the base and the height of the pyramid. Can you use this related problem to solve the frustrum problem? Imagine completing the pyramid as shown in the bottom of Figure 5–9. Because you already know how to use the formula to find the volume of the big pyramid (with *a* as its base) and the small pyramid (with *b* as its base), you can find the volume of the frustrum by subtracting the volume of the small pyramid from the volume of the large pyramid. Now your plan is taking shape: Find the volume of the large pyramid, find the volume of the small pyramid, and subtract the smaller from the larger to get the volume of the frustrum.

As you can see, this process of devising a plan depends on several heuristics: (1) finding a related problem; (2) restating the problem; and (3) breaking the problem into subgoals. In the frustrum problem, a related problem you know how to solve is finding the volume of a right pyramid. Before you can use the formula, however, you must restate the problem as: "Find the difference between the volume of the big pyramid and the small pyramid." Finally, you need to break your solution to subgoals—such as finding the volume of the large pyramid, finding the volume of the small pyramid, and subtracting the volume of the small pyramid from the volume of the large pyramid. To accomplish these goals, you need to break each down further into finding the values for base and height, and plugging them into the formula for volume.

Although Polya's ideas have been influential, especially among some mathematics educators, you might wonder whether there is any evidence that problem-solving heuristics for planning can be taught. To help answer this question, Schoenfeld (1979, 1985) taught students how to use problem-solving heuristics, including finding a related problem, restating the problem, and breaking the problem into subgoals. Students who received practice in using these kinds of heuristics improved from 20% correct on a pretest to 65% on a posttest, whereas control students who received practice in solving problems without heuristics training averaged 25% correct on both tests. Although the sample size was small in this study, the results suggest that it is possible to help people improve the way they devise plans for solving mathematics problems.

USING WORKED-OUT EXAMPLES. Polya's suggestion, based on his practical experience in teaching mathematics, corresponds to current cognitive theories of analogical transfer. When a student is confronted with a mathematics problem that she has never seen before, how does she figure out how to solve it? Where does a creative solution plan come from? According to analogical transfer theory, a student solves a new problem (called a *target*) by remembering another problem (called a *base*) that she can solve, by abstracting a solution method from the base, and then by mapping that solution method to the target. The process of analogical transfer requires three steps:

1. ***Recognition:*** A student identifies a related problem (called a *base*) that can be solved.
2. ***Abstraction:*** A student abstracts a solution method or principle from the base.
3. ***Mapping:*** A student applies that method or principle to the target.

The most commonly used technique in mathematics textbooks for helping students acquire a useful collection of base problems is to provide worked-out examples (Mayer, Sims, & Tajika, 1995). For example, consider the worked-out distance-rate-time problem

FIGURE 5–10

A short worked-out example and an equivalent test problem

Here's a (short) worked-out example:

PROBLEM:

A car traveling at a speed of 30 miles per hour (mph) left a certain place at 10:00 a.m. At 11:30 a.m., another car departed from the same place at 40 mph and traveled the same route. In how many hours will the second car overtake the first car?

ANSWER:

The problem is a distance-rate-time problem in which distance (D) = rate $(R) \times$ time (T). Because both cars travel the same distance, the distance of the first car (D_1) equals the distance of the second car (D_2). Therefore $D_1 = D_2$, or $R_1 \times T_1 = R_2 \times T_2$, where $R_1 =$ 30 mph, $R_2 = 40$ mph, and $T_1 = T_2 + 3/2$ hr. Substituting gives the following:

$$30 \times (T_2 + 3/2) = 40 \times T_2$$
$$30\,T_2 + 45 = 40\,T_2$$
$$T_2 = 4.5 \text{ hr}$$

Can you solve this problem?

A car travels south at the rate of 30 mph. Two hours later, a second car leaves to overtake the first car, using the same route and going 45 mph. In how many hours will the second car overtake the first car?

Adapted from Reed, Dempster, and Ettinger (1985)

in the top of Figure 5–10. Do you think that studying this example will help students solve an equivalent test problem, such as the one shown at the bottom of Figure 5–10?

To examine this question, Reed, Dempster, and Ettinger (1985) asked students to solve some word problems after they had studied both equivalent and unrelated worked-out examples. Students who studied equivalent examples performed poorly (25% correct) on the test problems, even though the test problems could be solved using the same solution method as in example problems they had just studied; unsurprisingly, students who studied unrelated examples also performed poorly (18% correct).

Why did students in the equivalent-example group often fail to transfer their learning of example problems to the solution of a new equivalent problem? Two major obstacles get in the way of problem-solving transfer. The first obstacle is that students may not be able to abstract the solution method from the worked-out example. To overcome this obstacle, Reed et al. (1985) provided an expanded version of the worked-out example that included a verbal explanation for each step in the solution processes. The second obstacle is that students might not realize that the worked-out example is relevant to solving the test problem. To overcome this obstacle, Reed et al. (1985) presented the corresponding worked-out example along with each test problem so students could refer to the example as they solved the test problem. In this situation, students given equivalent worked-out examples performed well (69% correct), but students given unrelated examples did not (17%).

Students also have difficulty knowing how a particular worked-out example (i.e., base problem) is related to a new test problem (i.e., target problem). For example, how would you go about solving the following grocer problem:

> A grocer mixes peanuts worth \$1.65 a pound and almonds worth \$2.10 a pound. How many pounds of each are needed to make a mixture worth \$1.83 a pound?

If you are like most students in a study conducted by Reed (1987), you were not able to solve this problem. However, now study the worked-out solution of the nurse problem in Figure 5–11. Do you see the connections between the nurse problem and the grocer problem? To help you map the correspondences between the two problems, fill in the blanks in

FIGURE 5–11

A worked-out example of the nurse problem

A nurse mixes a 6% boric acid solution with a 12% boric acid solution. How many pints of each are needed to make 4.5 pints of an 8% boric acid solution?

The problem is a mixture problem in which two quantities are added together to make a third quantity. The two component quantities are the 6% and 12% solutions.

The total amount of acid in the combined solution must equal the total amount of acid in the two component solutions. The amount of acid is found by multiplying the percentage of acid in a solution by the quantity of the solution. If we mix p pints of 6% solution with $4.5 - p$ pints (since we want a total of 4.5 pints) of 12% solution, the 6% solution will contribute $.06 \times p$ pints of acid. The 12% solution will contribute $.12 \times (4.5 - p)$ pints of acid. The first two lines of the table show this information.

Kind of Solution	*Quantity of Solution (Pints)*	*Percentage of Acid*	*Quantity of Acid (Pints)*
6% acid	p	6%	$.06 \times p$
12% acid	$4.5 - p$	12%	$.12 \times (4.5 - p)$
8% acid	4.5	8%	$.08 \times 4.5$

The bottom line shows that the combined solution consists of 4.5 pints of 8% acid, or $.08 \times 4.5$ pints of acid. Since the total amount of acid in the combined solution must equal the total amount in the two component solutions:

$$.06 \times p + .12 \times (4.5 - p) = .08 \times 4.5$$

Solving for p yields:

$$.06p + .54 - .12p = .36$$

$$.18 = .06p$$

$$p = 3 \text{ pints of 6\% solution}$$

1.5 pints of 12% solution

Adapted from Reed (1987)

TABLE 5–5 Can you map the nurse problem onto the grocer problem?

Mapping Test: Fill in the Corresponding Values and Expressions

Nurse Problem	Grocer Problem
1. 6% acid	1. ________
2. 12% acid	2. ________
3. 8% acid	3. ________
4. 4.5 − *p* pints	4. ________
5. 4.5 pints	5. ________
6. 4.5 pints × 8% acid	6. ________

Correct Answers for Mapping Test

Nurse Problem	Grocer Problem
1. 6% acid	1. $1.65
2. 12% acid	2. $2.10
3. 8% acid	3. $1.83
4. 4.5 − *p* pints	4. 30 − *A*
5. 4.5 pints	5. 30
6. 4.5 pints × 8% acid	6. 30 × $1.83

Note: Solution equation for the grocer problem is: $1.65 × A + $2.10 × (30 − A) = $1.83 × 30. (A = pounds of peanuts.)

Adapted from Reed (1987)

Table 5–5. If you are like most students in Reed's (1987) study, you were able to solve the grocer problem after studying the worked-out nurse problem.

Catrambone (1995) investigated another technique for making worked-out examples more effective—explicitly labeling the subgoals in the worked-out example. For example, consider the briefcase problem:

> A judge noticed that some of the 219 lawyers at City Hall owned more than one briefcase. She counted the number of briefcases each lawyer owned and found that 180 of the lawyers owned exactly one briefcase, 17 owned two briefcases, 13 owned three briefcases, and 9 owned four briefcases. Use the Poisson distribution to determine the probability of a randomly chosen lawyer at City Hall owning exactly two briefcases.

Catrambone taught college students how to solve this problem by giving them six worked-out examples showing each of the steps in the solution (including using the formula for the Poisson distribution). For some students, the main subgoals were labeled: (1) find the total number of briefcases owned [e.g., 180 (1) + 17 (2) + 13 (3) + 9 (4) = 289], (2) find the average number of briefcases owned per lawyer (289 ÷ 219 = 1.32), and (3) find the probability that a lawyer has two briefcases (by plugging the numbers 2 and 1.32 into the formula for the Poisson distribution). For other students, the main subgoals were not labeled. On a posttest, the labeled and unlabeled groups both performed well on solving problems that were very similar to the training problems—achieving scores of 2.9 and 2.8 (out of 3), respectively. However, on posttest problems that required altering the solution procedure, the labeled group scored much higher than the unlabeled group—achieving scores of 2.2 and 1.3 (out of 3), respectively. Apparently, students benefit more from worked-out examples when the instructor includes commentary describing the major subgoals.

Overall, the research on worked-out examples continues to demonstrate the persistent finding that the road to problem-solving transfer is a rocky one (Salomon & Perkins, 1989). In particular, students need help in learning how to abstract a solution from a worked-out example, and how to make connections between an example and a new problem (Reed, 1999). Teaching by explaining examples is highlighted in Chapter 9.

ATTITUDES FOR MATHEMATICAL PROBLEM SOLVING. Student attitudes about problem solving may also influence the way they plan a method for reaching a solution. Perhaps the most destructive belief concerning the planning process is the idea that math problems must be solved by applying meaningless procedures. Schoenfeld (1992) summarizes this belief as follows: "Ordinary students cannot expect to understand mathematics; they expect simply to memorize it and apply what they have learned mechanically and without understanding" (p. 359). For example, Lester, Garofalo, and Kroll (1989) reported that many third-graders believed that "all story problems could be solved by applying the operations suggested by the key words present in the story (e.g., *in all* suggests addition, *left* suggests subtraction, *share* suggests division)" (p. 84). As a consequence of this belief, these students "did not bother to monitor their actions or assess the reasonableness of their answers because they saw no need to do so" (Lester et al., 1989, p. 84). Where did such a bizarre belief come from? According to Lester et al. (1989), such a belief was well-founded because "most of the story problems to which these children had been exposed could be answered correctly by applying their key-word method" and in many cases "teachers had taught them to look for key words" (p. 84).

Another common belief that prevents students from using productive planning processes is the idea that "students who have understood the mathematics they have studied will be able to solve any assigned problem in five minutes or less" (Schoenfeld, 1992, p. 359). The effect of this attitude is that students will give up on a problem if they are unable to solve it within a few minutes. For example, when Schoenfeld (1988) asked high school students how long it should take them to solve a typical homework problem, the average estimated time was two minutes. When he asked them how long they would work on a problem before giving up, the average estimated time was twelve minutes. The belief that all math problems can be solved quickly is based on students' experience in mathematics classes: "Students who have finished a full twelve years of mathematics have worked thousands upon thousands of 'problems'—virtually none of which were expected to take the students more than a few minutes to complete" (Schoenfeld, 1988, pp. 159–160). In monitoring their problem solving, students are likely to quit when they reach a major obstacle even though they might have solved the problem if they had persevered.

One of the basic components of mathematical proficiency is *productive disposition*, which is the "habitual inclination to see mathematics as sensible, useful, and worthwhile, coupled with a belief in diligence and one's own efficacy" (Kilpatrick, Swafford, & Findell, 2001, p. 5). One source of information about productive disposition comes from surveys of student attitudes. For example, the National Assessment of Educational Progress—a nationwide assessment given to U.S. students—reported that 54% of the fourth-graders and 40% of the eighth-graders thought that mathematics was mostly a set of rules and that mathematics learning means memorizing the rules (Silver & Kenney, 2000). In general, girls have more negative attitudes about mathematics than do boys, and girls' attitudes about mathematics decline with age more than they do for boys (Leder, 1992; Silver & Kenney, 2000).

Observations of student problem solving also provide information about productive disposition. Students often solve mathematics problems by manipulating symbols without understanding; that is, by combining numbers in the problem to produce an answer. For example, consider the problem: "John's best time to run 100 meters is 17 seconds. How long will it take him to run 1 kilometer?" When this problem was given to middle school students, almost all of them (i.e., 97%) proceeded to carry out computations such as $10 \times 17 = 170$ seconds (Verschaffel, Greer, & De Corte, 2000). Yet, if you give one moment of thought to this problem you will realize that a runner cannot keep up the same pace for 1,000 meters as for just 100 meters. Schoenfeld (1991) found that students learn to engage in a "suspension of sense-making" when they solve mathematics problems: "suspending the requirement that the problems . . . make sense" (p. 316). Overall, there is convincing evidence that students need help in developing a productive disposition concerning mathematics.

IMPLICATIONS FOR INSTRUCTION: TEACHING FOR PLANNING

When confronted with a new word problem, some students do not know what to do, even though they may know how to carry out the required arithmetic. Not knowing what to do reflects a lack of strategic knowledge, and in particular, a failure in planning. National assessments of mathematics achievement show that conventional instruction in word-problem solving is not equipping students with the planning skills they need (Dossey et al., 1988; Silver & Kenney, 2000).

How can we help students to develop appropriate planning skills? A team of researchers called the Cognition and Technology Group at Vanderbilt developed a video-based program for helping students learn how to plan solutions to mathematics problems (Bransford et al., 1996; Cognition and Technology Group at Vanderbilt, 1992; Van Haneghan et al., 1992). The materials consist of a series of video episodes of *The Adventures of Jasper Woodbury,* each lasting 15 to 20 minutes. In each episode, the character is faced with a challenge that requires mathematical problem solving, such as planning a trip, generating a business plan based on statistics, and using geometry meaningfully. Working in small groups, the students in the class solve the problem and then see another video showing how the character solved the problem.

For example, in the episode "Rescue at Boone's Meadow," Jasper's friend Larry teaches Emily how to fly an ultralight airplane in a scene that provides information about the plane's payload, fuel capacity, fuel consumption, speed, and landing capabilities. Later, in a restaurant, Jasper tells Emily and Larry about his planned fishing trip to Boone's Meadow, noting that a landing strip is located next to where he plans to park his car and that the hiking distance to Boone's Meadow is 18 miles. On the way from the restaurant, Emily and Larry stop to weigh themselves. Jasper is next seen happily fishing at Boone's Meadow when he discovers a wounded bald eagle and through a radio is able to get this information to Emily. In the final scene, Emily is in a veterinarian's office, where she learns about eagles and consults a map on the wall showing that no roads lead to Boone's Meadow. The problem is how to save the eagle.

Working in groups to solve the problem, students must consider a range of possibilities and variables. For example, the ultralight aircraft needs to fly a greater distance than normal to get to the rescue site; to fly a greater distance, more fuel must be added, but this would increase the overall weight, which in turn would require a change in pilots. Although students can usually generate an answer within about 30 minutes, they are encouraged to work longer to develop a better solution. In the process of problem solving, they often review parts of the video to check or gather information. They also work on alternative versions of the problem. In all, they spend about a week on each episode.

Does participating in the Jasper series affect students' planning skills? To examine this question, 10 classrooms of fifth- and sixth-graders (Jasper-trained group) received instruction in three or four Jasper adventures for three to four weeks, whereas 10 matched classrooms (control group) received their regular instruction, which focused on word problems. To measure their planning skills, all students took a planning test before and after instruction, consisting of problems such as shown in Figure 5–12. As you see, the test included questions about how to plan a solution to a word problem (Question 1) and how to break a problem into parts (Question 2). Although both the Jasper-trained group and the control group scored about the same on the pretest (i.e., achieving scores of approximately 20% correct), the Jasper-trained group performed much better than the control group on the posttest (i.e., achieving approximately 40% correct compared to 25% for the control group). These results show that training with the Jasper adventures resulted in a large improvement in students' planning performance, whereas conventional training in word problems did not.

Why does the Jasper series improve students' planning skills? *The Adventures of Jasper Woodbury* is based on three principles that distinguish it from conventional mathematics programs:

Generative learning: Students learn better when they actively construct their own knowledge rather than when they passively receive information from the teacher.

Anchored instruction: Students learn better when material is presented within an interesting situation rather than as an isolated problem.

Cooperative learning: Students learn better when they communicate about problem solving in groups rather than when they work individually.

Although it is not possible to isolate the features of the Jasper series that are responsible for its effectiveness, the program is based on a combination of generative, anchored, and cooperative methods of teaching and learning. In summary, as one reviewer noted, the Jasper series "uses videodisc computer technology as a vehicle for changing the fabric of instruction, away from transmission and toward active problem solving in realistic contexts" (Lehrer, 1992, p. 287). Additional research is needed, but this promising project encourages the development of other programs based on the same instructional principles.

FIGURE 5–12

Can you devise a solution plan for this problem?

JILL'S TRIP PROBLEM

Jill lives in Carson City. She wants to drive her car from her house to a friend's house in Meridien. As shown on the map, Jill can take the road from Carson City to Johnstown and Johnstown to Meridien. Her car is filled with gasoline and ready to go. Gas stations are located in Carson City, Ceymore, and Meridien, but not in Johnstown. Jill plans to leave on her trip at 8:00 in the morning.

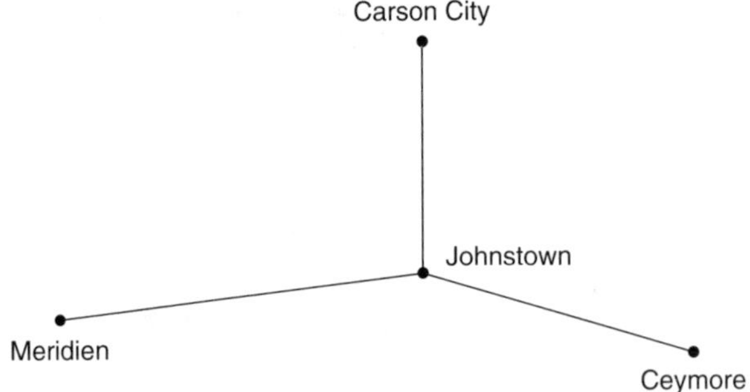

Question 1: What does Jill need to think about to figure out how long it will take her to make the trip?

Question 2: Jill divides the distance from Carson City to Meridien (120 miles) by the speed she will drive (60 miles per hour). Why does she do this?

Adapted from Cognition and Technology Group at Vanderbilt (1992)

This section examined both heuristics that help students devise solution plans and obstacles that may impede successful planning. Heuristics for planning include using a related problem, restating the problem, and breaking the problem into subgoals. Obstacles to planning include difficulties in finding a related problem, reliance on meaningless solution procedures, and a failure to persevere. How can you provide strategy training? It is important for students to recognize that there may be more than one right way to solve a problem and that finding a solution method can be a creative activity. Students need to be able to describe their solution methods and to compare their methods with those used by other students. Some researchers have been successful in explicitly teaching strategies for problem solving, such as asking students to write a list of operations (or a number sentence) necessary for solving a problem, to list the subgoals needed in a multistep problem, or to draw a conclusion based on the partial completion of a solution plan. Sample multiple-choice items are given in the third section of Figure 5–1.

In summary, devising and monitoring a solution plan are crucial components in mathematical problem solving. Students and teachers should pay as much attention to process (i.e., their solution strategy) as to product (i.e., the final numerical answer). Research is needed to verify the preceding suggestions for improving students' strategic planning skills in mathematics.

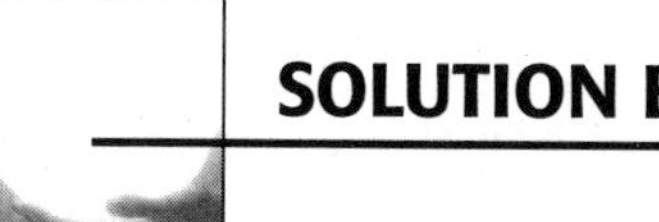

SOLUTION EXECUTION

WHAT IS SOLUTION EXECUTION?

Once you understand the tile problem presented at the beginning of this chapter and devise a plan for solving it, the next major component is to carry out your plan. For a problem like the tile problem, you need to be able to carry out arithmetic operations such as $7.2 \times 5.4 = \_\_\_$ or $.72 \times 432 = \_\_\_$. As you can see, problem execution requires procedural knowledge (i.e., knowledge about how to carry out procedures such as addition, subtraction, division, or multiplication).

The acquisition of computational procedures involves a progression from naive procedures to more sophisticated procedures, and from tedious application of procedures to automatic application. In summary, as children gain experience, their procedures become more sophisticated and automatic. With experience students develop a collection of procedures that can be selected for various computational problems.

RESEARCH ON SOLUTION EXECUTION

DEVELOPMENT OF EXPERTISE FOR SIMPLE ADDITION. As an example of the development of expertise in computation, let's consider a child's procedure for solving single-column addition problems of the form,

$$m + n = \_\_\_$$

where m and n are single-digit positive integers whose sum is less than 10.

Fuson (1982, 1992) has identified four major stages in the development of computational expertise: counting-all, counting-on, derived facts, and known facts. The counting-all procedure involves setting a counter to 0, incrementing it m times, and then incrementing it n times. For the problem $2 + 4 = \_\_\_$, the child might put out one finger and say "1," put out another finger and say "2," pause, put out a third finger and say "3," put out a fourth finger and say "4," put out a fifth finger and say "5," and put out a sixth finger and say "6."

The counting- on procedure involves setting a counter to m and incrementing it n times. For the problem $2 + 4 = \_\_\_$, the child might put out two fingers and then say "3, 4, 5, 6," as each of four additional fingers was put out. One version of this approach is what Groen and Parkman (1972) call the "min model," which involves setting a counter to the larger of m or n and then incrementing the counter by the smaller number. For the problem $2 + 4 = \_\_\_$, the child might put out four fingers and then say "5, 6," as each of two additional fingers is put out.

The derived facts procedure involves using one's knowledge of number facts to figure out answers for related problems. For example, the first number facts that a child learns are usually the doubles, such as $1 + 1 = 2$, $2 + 2 = 4$, $3 + 3 = 6$, and so on. For the problem 2 + 4 = ___, a student might say: "I can take 1 from the 4 and give it to the 2. That makes 3 + 3, so the answer is 6." In this example, the child knew that the sum of 3 plus 3 is 6, but did not directly know the answer for 2 plus 4.

The known facts procedure, also called retrieval, involves having a ready answer for each number fact. For example, drill and practice with flash cards is generally aimed at helping students acquire rapid responses for a set of basic facts. For the problem 2 + 4 = ___, the child would say "6."

As you can see in this progression, the child's early procedures for single-digit addition are based on counting. The child can treat addition as if it were an extension of what the child already knows about counting. With more experience, the counting procedures can become more efficient, such as the use of a counting-on procedure instead of a counting-all procedure. With even more experience, some of the facts become automatic, and eventually all may become automatic.

What evidence is there for stages in the development of computational expertise? One method for studying students' solution procedures is to observe carefully what children do as they solve addition problems; in particular, we should listen to what they say and watch their fingers. Another method is to measure the time it takes to solve addition problems. Figure 5–13 summarizes the counting-all and counting-on (min version) procedures, with boxes representing actions and diamonds representing decisions. For example, we could make the following predictions concerning response times for each procedure. For the counting-all procedure, response time should be a function of the sum of $m + n$. For the problem 2 + 4 = ___ or 4 + 2 = ___, the child must increment a counter six times. For the min version of the counting-on procedure, response time should be a function of the smaller number (m or n). For the problem 2 + 4 = ___ or 4 + 2 = ___, the child must increment two times. For the derived facts procedure, response time should be fastest for the problems that are already known. Thus doubles (like 2 + 2 = ___ or 3 + 3 = ___) should yield the fastest response times when they become memorized. For the known facts procedure, response time should be the same for all problems since the child is simply "looking up" the answer in memory.

To determine which procedures children use as they begin formal instruction in computation, Groen and Parkman (1972) asked first-graders to answer a series of single-column addition problems. Their response time performance could best be described by the min model of the counting-on procedure. Figure 5–14 shows the response time for problems that the min model says require 0 increments (such as 1 + 0 = ___ or 5 + 0 = ___), 1 increment (such as 5 + 1 = ___ or 6 + 1 = ___), 2 increments (such as 5 + 2 = ___ or 6 + 2 = ___), 3 increments (such as 5 + 3 = ___ or 6 + 3 = ___), and 4 increments (such as 5 + 4 = ___ or 4 + 5 = ___). As shown, response time generally increases by about one-third second for each additional increment in the value of the smaller number. Thus most problems seem to be solved by setting a counter to the larger number and incrementing it by the smaller number. However, you might note that there is some evidence that doubles (0 + 0 = ___, 1 + 1 = ___, 2 + 2 = ___, and so on) were answered rapidly regardless of the number of increments; this suggests that doubles might already be well-memorized number facts (requiring a known facts procedure), while other problems require a counting procedure.

Parkman and Groen (1971) also found that a min model best fit the performance of adults. However, the time needed for an adult to make an increment was one-fiftieth

FIGURE 5–13 Counting-all and counting-on (min) procedures for simple addition

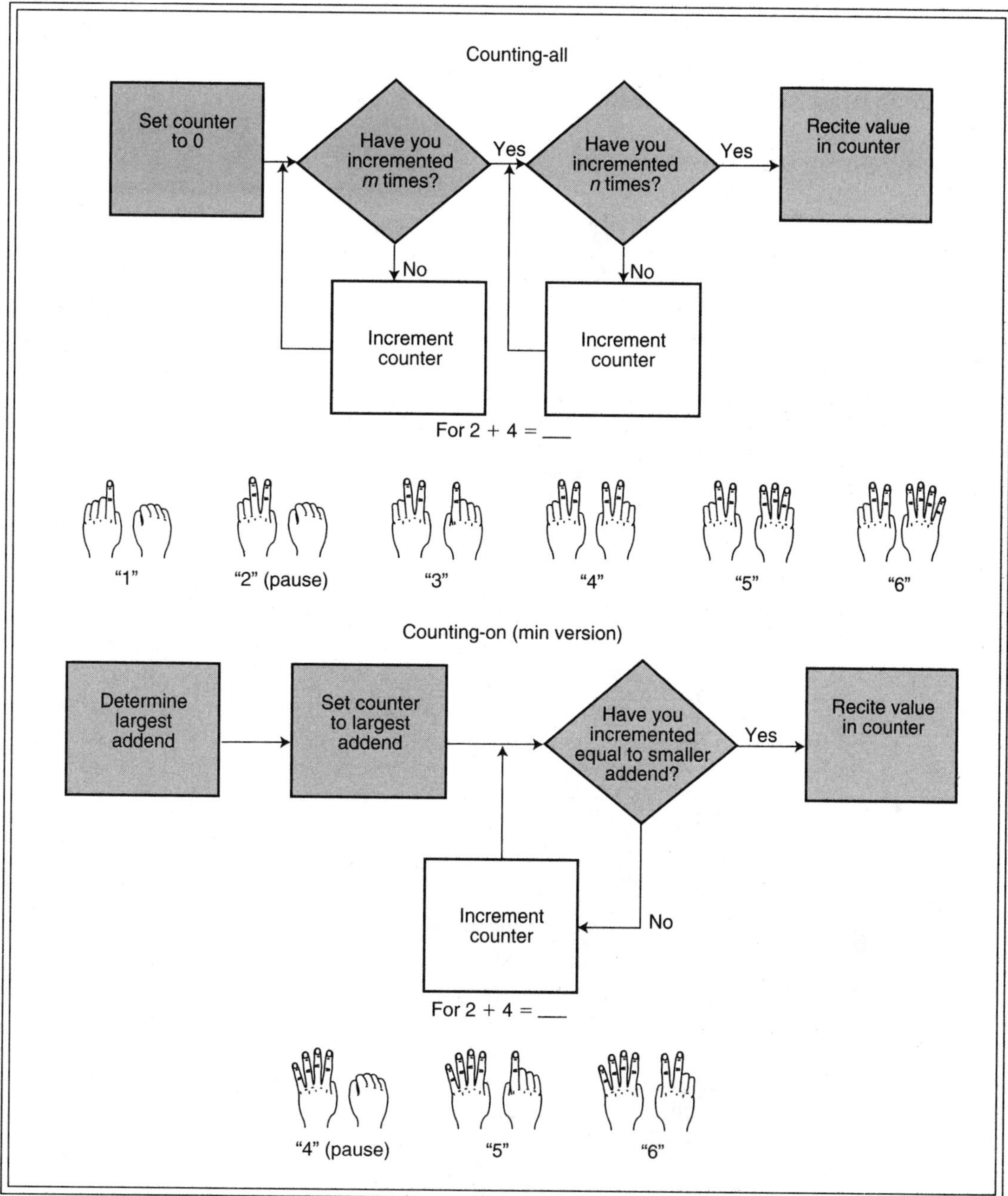

Adapted from Mayer (1992)

FIGURE 5–14 Response time depends on the number of increments required by the min model

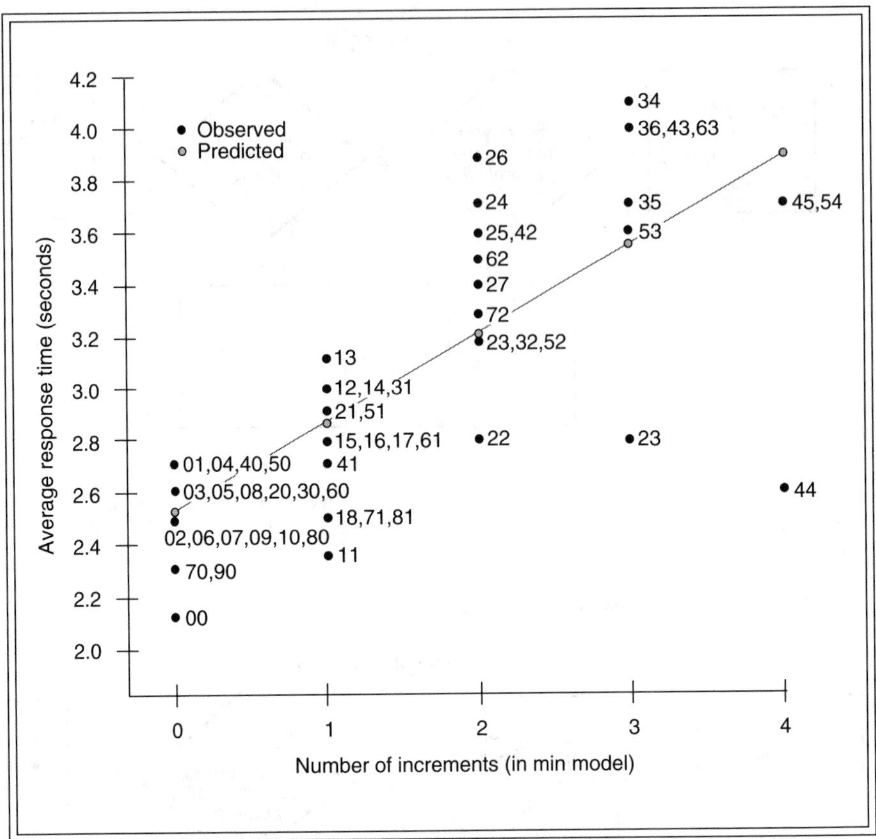

From Groen and Parkman (1972)

second, compared to one-third second for first-graders. Because it is unlikely that a person can count silently at a rate of fifty increments per second, Parkman and Groen (1971) offered an alternative explanation: For almost all problems, adults have direct access to the answer in their memories (i.e., on most problems, adults use a known facts approach), but on a few problems they fall back to a counting procedure. Ashcraft and Stazyk (1981) accounted for the performance of adults by assuming that they must "look up" answers in a complicated network. Thus adults apparently use some version of a known facts approach, while first-graders seem to be using some version of a counting approach.

SELECTION OF ADDITION PROCEDURES. Students seem to progress through a series of mathematical discoveries, inventing progressively more efficient procedures for solving simple arithmetic problems. Does a child's procedural knowledge consist mainly of the more efficient methods that have replaced the earlier ones or of an ever-increasing collection of procedures ranging from the least to the most mature? To answer this question,

Siegler (1987) asked kindergartners, first-graders, and second-graders to solve 45 addition problems, such as "If you had 8 oranges and I gave you 7 more, how many would you have?" and "What is 8 plus 7?" After giving each answer, the students were asked to describe verbally how they solved the problem.

Children reported using five kinds of procedures: guessing (or not responding), counting-all, counting-on (min version), derived facts, and known facts. Table 5–6 shows the percentage of time students at each grade level used each of the procedures. Most children reported using at least three procedures, and at no age was one procedure used most of the time. Did the children accurately describe their solution procedures? Siegler (1987) found that on problems for which children reported using a counting-on procedure, the min model was a good predictor of their solution times, but on problems for which they reported using other strategies, the min model was not a good predictor. In reviewing these results, Siegler and Jenkins (1989) concluded that "these and a variety of other data converged on indicating that children used the strategies they reported using and that they employed them on those trials where they said they had" (p. 25).

Overall, these results suggest that students build an arsenal of addition procedures and choose procedures independently for different addition problems. Interestingly, children use a known-facts approach (which can also be called *retrieval*) for easy problems, but for hard problems they rely on what Siegler and Jenkins (1989) call "back-up strategies" (such as derived facts or counting). In deciding whether to use counting-all or counting-on (min version), students are more likely to use counting-on (min version) when one of the addends is smaller, such as 9 + 2, than when the two addends are close in value, such as 5 + 6. As you can see, this choice makes sense, because it is easier to use a counting-on (min version) when one addend is smaller. Siegler and Jenkins (1989) argue that rather than using a single procedure for all addition problems, children "behave adaptively . . . in choosing among alternative . . . strategies" (p. 29).

COMPLEX COMPUTATIONAL PROCEDURES. Once a child has achieved some level of automaticity in carrying out simple procedures (e.g., single-column addition or subtraction), these procedures can become components in more complex computational procedures. For example, solving a three-column subtraction problem such as

$$456 - 321 = \_\_\_\_$$

TABLE 5–6

Percentage of time that kindergartners, first-graders, and second-graders use each of five procedures for simple addition

	Addition Procedure				
Grade	**Guessing**	**Counting-All**	**Counting-On**	**Derived Facts**	**Known Facts**
K	30%	22%	30%	2%	16%
1	8%	1%	38%	9%	44%
2	5%	0%	40%	11%	45%

Adapted from Siegler (1987)

requires the ability to solve single-digit subtraction problems such as $6 - 1 =$ ___, $5 - 2 =$ ___, and $4 - 3 =$ ___. The procedure for three-column subtraction is summarized in Figure 5–15, where the boxes represent processes, the diamonds represent decisions, and the arrows show where to go next. As shown, one of the skills required to use this procedure is the ability to carry out single-column subtraction (e.g., see step 2c).

Figure 5–15 diagrams the procedure that children are supposed to acquire; however, some students acquire a flawed version. For example, a student may have a procedure for three-column subtraction that contains one small "bug" (i.e., one of the steps in the student's procedure might be different from the corresponding step of the procedure in Figure 5–15). A student who uses such a "buggy" procedure (i.e., a procedure with one or more bugs in it) may be able to answer some problems correctly but not others.

Consider the following problems:

$$\begin{array}{r} 564 \\ -472 \\ \hline 112 \end{array} \quad \begin{array}{r} 722 \\ -519 \\ \hline 217 \end{array} \quad \begin{array}{r} 821 \\ -431 \\ \hline 410 \end{array} \quad \begin{array}{r} 954 \\ -233 \\ \hline 721 \end{array} \quad \begin{array}{r} 349 \\ -123 \\ \hline 226 \end{array}$$

As you can see, the student who solved these problems obtained correct answers for two out of the five. A more precise way of characterizing the student's performance is to say that the student is using a procedure that has a very common "bug" in it: At steps 2a, 2b, and 2c, the student subtracts the smaller number from the larger number, regardless of which one is on top in the problem statement. Brown and Burton (1978) have argued that a student's knowledge of subtraction procedures can be described by listing which bugs (if any) are found in the student's processes. This example involves a very common bug, which Brown and Burton call "subtract smaller from larger."

According to Brown and Burton (1978), errors in subtraction may occur because a student consistently uses a flawed procedure, not because a student cannot apply a procedure. To test this idea, Brown and Burton gave a set of 15 subtraction problems to 1,325 primary-school children, and developed a computer program called "BUGGY" to analyze each student's subtraction procedure. If all the student's answers were correct, BUGGY would conclude that the student was using the correct procedure (shown in Figure 5–15). If the student made errors, BUGGY would attempt to find one bug that could account for them. If no single bug could be identified, BUGGY would evaluate all possible combinations of bugs that could account for the errors. Table 5–7 shows some of the most common bugs; for example, 54 of the 1,325 students behaved as if they had the "smaller-from-larger" bug.

Although the BUGGY program searched for hundreds of possible bugs and bug combinations, it was able to find the subtraction procedure (including bugs) for only about half of the students. The other students seemed to be making random errors, were inconsistent in their use of bugs, or may have been learning as they took the test. Thus Brown and Burton's (1978) work allows for a precise description of a student's procedural knowledge—even when that knowledge is flawed.

IMPLICATIONS FOR INSTRUCTION: TEACHING FOR EXECUTING

How can we help students to build a useful base of procedural knowledge? For nearly 100 years, drill-and-practice has been the dominant instructional method for teaching arithmetic

FIGURE 5–15 A procedure for three-column subtraction

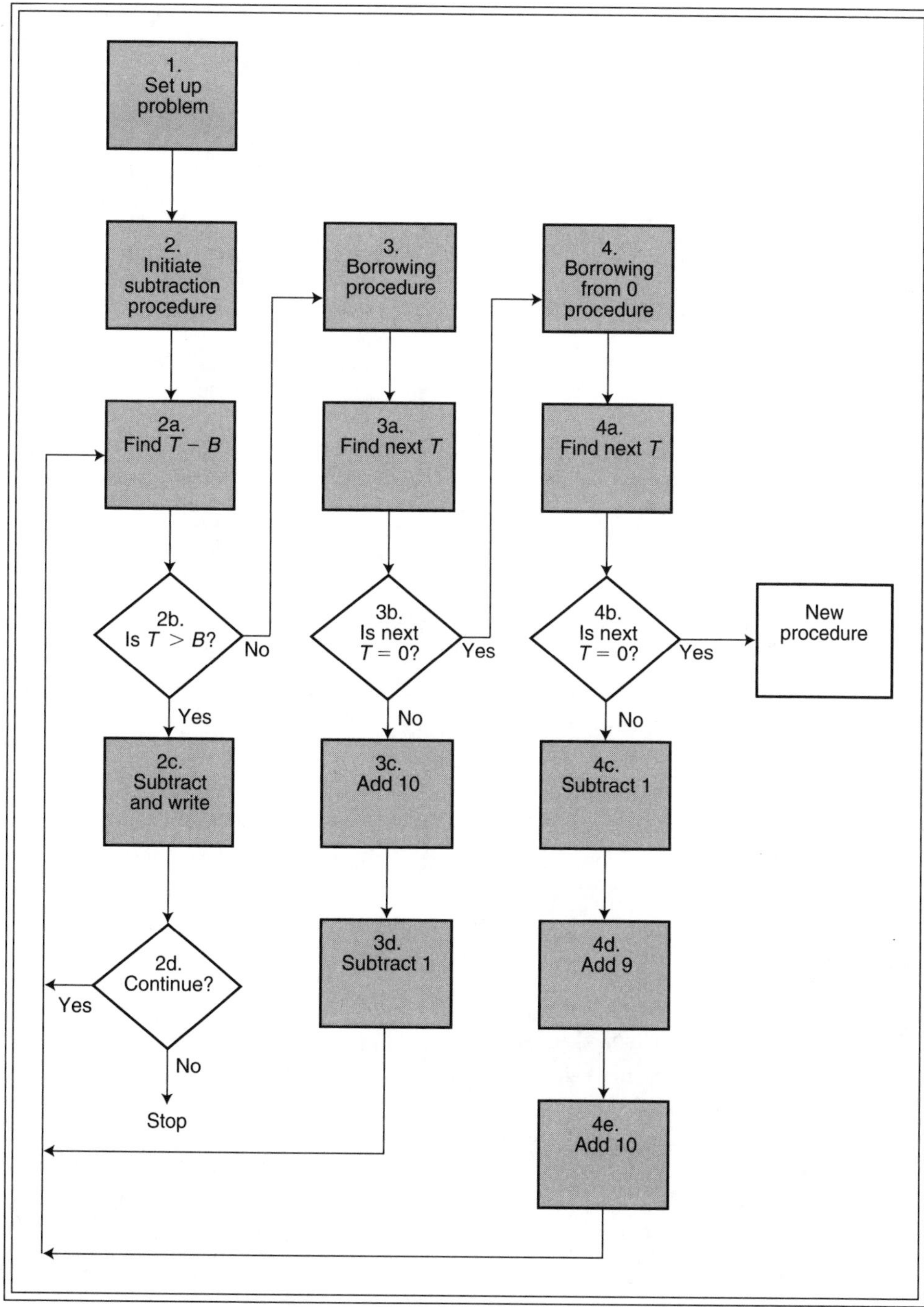

From Mayer (1981a)

TABLE 5–7 Some subtraction bugs

Number of Occurrences in 1,325 Students	Name of Bug	Example	Description
57	Borrow from 0	103 − 45 158	When borrowing from a column whose top digit is 0, the student writes 9, but does not continue borrowing from the column to the left of 0.
54	Smaller from larger	253 − 118 145	The student subtracts the smaller digit in each column from the larger, regardless of which one is on top.
10	$0 - N = N$	140 − 21 121	Whenever the top digit in a column is 0, the student writes the bottom digit as the answer.
34	$0 - N = N$ *and* move over zero	304 − 75 279	Whenever the top digit in a column is 0, the student writes the bottom digit as the answer. When the student needs to borrow from a column whose top digit is 0, he or she skips that column and borrows from the next one.

Adapted from Brown and Burton (1978)

procedures. In drill-and-practice, a student is given a simple problem and asked to give a response, such as, "What is 2 plus 4?" If the student gives the correct response, the student receives a reward, such as the teacher saying, "Right!" If the student gives the wrong response, the student receives a punishment, such as the teacher saying, "Wrong!" When you use flash cards, with the question on one side and the answer on the other, you are learning by drill-and-practice. When you sit in front of a computer screen that presents problems and gives feedback, you are learning by drill-and-practice. When you answer a series of exercise problems in a textbook and then check your answers, you are learning by drill-and-practice.

Although drill-and-practice can be an effective method for teaching procedural knowledge, it may not be the only worthwhile method. A major problem is that learning procedural knowledge (such as how to add and subtract) can become isolated from conceptual knowledge (such as what a number is) so that mathematics becomes a set of meaningless procedures for students.

Case and his colleagues (Case & Okamoto, 1996; Griffin, Case, & Capodilupo, 1995; Griffin, Case, & Siegler, 1994) argued that the learning of basic arithmetic procedures must be tied to the development of central conceptual structures in the child. According to this view, the most important conceptual structure for learning arithmetic procedures is a mental number line. Case and his colleagues developed a test of students' knowledge of a mental number line that included their ability to compare two numbers, to visualize the number line, to count, and to determine the magnitude specified by number words. When they gave the test to six-year-olds of low socioeconomic status (SES), only 32% demonstrated an acceptable knowledge of the number line; however, 67% of high-SES six-year olds demonstrated such knowledge. More importantly, 25% of the low-SES children and 71% of the high-SES children could solve simple addition problems, such as 2 = 4 = ___.

Why do some students have difficulty with simple addition? According to Case and his colleagues, the source of the difficulty is that students lack a representation of a mental number line. If this premise is true, the instructional implication is clear: Teach students to construct and use mental number lines as a prerequisite for learning arithmetic procedures. This is the approach taken in a math readiness program called "Rightstart" (Griffin & Case, 1996; Griffin et al., 1994, 1995). The program consists of 40 half-hour sessions in which students learn to use a number line by playing a series of number games. For example, in one game two students each roll a die and must determine who rolled the higher number. The student who rolled the higher number then moves his or her token along a number-line path on a playing board. The first student to reach the end of the path wins. These games promote skills such as comparing the magnitude of two numbers, counting forward and backward along a number line, and making one-to-one mapping of numbers onto objects when counting.

Does number-line training help students learn arithmetic procedures? To answer this question, researchers (Griffin & Case, 1996; Griffin et al., 1994, 1995) gave one group of low-SES first-graders the Rightstart training (treatment group), whereas another group of similar children received their regular mathematics instruction (control group). First, there was overwhelming evidence that number-line training helped students build conceptual knowledge of number lines. On a posttest of number-line knowledge, 87% of the treatment group and 25% of the control group demonstrated skill on number-line tasks such as determining which of two numbers was smaller. Second, there was evidence that number-line training helped students learn arithmetic procedures. On a posttest with simple addition, 82% of the treatment group and 33% of the control group gave correct answers. Third, treatment students were more successful than control students in learning mathematics in school: 80% of the treatment group and 41% of the control group mastered first-grade mathematics units on simple addition and subtraction. Griffin and Case (1996) noted that "a surprising proportion of children from low-income North American families—at least 50% in our samples—do not arrive in school with the central cognitive structure in place that is necessary for success in first grade mathematics," so "their first learning of addition and subtraction may be a meaningless experience" (p. 102). However, they argued that this problem can be overcome with a relatively modest instructional program aimed at promoting the conceptual knowledge that underpins arithmetic procedures.

In reviewing the Rightstart program, Bruer (1993) argued for the importance of connecting procedural and conceptual knowledge:

> Without this understanding [of the mental number line], [students'] basic number skills remain recipes, rather than rules for reasoning. If they don't understand how number concepts and structures justify and support these skills, their only alternative is to try to understand school math as a set of arbitrary procedures. Why arithmetic works is a mystery to them. . . . For mathematics to be meaningful, conceptual knowledge and procedural skills have to be interrelated in instruction. (p. 90)

Number-line training is an important demonstration of the value of helping students to make connections between arithmetic procedures and number concepts.

What can you do to improve training in computational procedures? This question was addressed early in the history of educational psychology by Thorndike (1922), who argued for the importance of practice with feedback, as exemplified in the last portion of Figure 5–1. Thus, to acquire skill in solving computation problems, students need practice in solving computation problems. In addition, students need feedback on whether their answers are correct. This advice has become well accepted in educational psychology and is amply supported by research. However, more recent research shows that students tend to develop new arithmetic procedures by using their previously learned procedures and conceptual knowledge of numbers. For example, Resnick (1982) argued that procedural knowledge should be tied to a learner's conceptual knowledge by making computation more concrete. This approach is explored in Chapter 8.

CHAPTER SUMMARY

Let's return one final time to the tile problem described at the opening to this chapter. To solve that problem, a person needs several kinds of knowledge: linguistic and factual knowledge for problem translation, schematic knowledge for problem integration, strategic knowledge for solution planning and monitoring, and procedural knowledge for solution execution.

A review of mathematics textbooks and achievement tests reveals that procedural knowledge is heavily emphasized in school curricula (Mayer, Sims, & Tajika, 1995). For example, students are given drill-and-practice in carrying out computational procedures. In this chapter, we refer to this type of instruction as solution execution. However, systematic instruction in how to translate problems, how to make meaningful representations of problems, and how to devise solution plans is not always given.

Problem translation involves converting each statement into an internal representation, such as a paraphrase or diagram. Students appear to have difficulty in comprehending simple sentences, especially when a relationship between variables is involved, and students often lack specific knowledge that is assumed in the problem (e.g., the knowledge that a square has four equal sides). Training in how to represent each sentence in a problem is an important and often neglected component of mathematics instruction.

Problem integration involves putting the pieces of information from the problem together into a coherent representation. Students appear to have trouble with unfamiliar problems for which they lack an appropriate schema. Training for schematic knowledge involves helping students to recognize differences among problem types.

Solution planning and monitoring involve devising and assessing a strategy for how to solve the problem. Students appear to have trouble describing the solution procedure they are using, such as spelling out the subgoals in a multistep problem. In addition, students often harbor unproductive attitudes, such as the idea that a problem has only one correct solution procedure. Strategy training is needed to help students focus on the process of problem solving in addition to the product of problem solving.

These three types of training complement the fourth component in mathematics instruction, solution training in which students learn to carry out procedures. All four components are needed for students to become productive mathematical problem solvers.

Although this chapter focused on just one type of mathematics problem, many of the concepts apply to other kinds of mathematics problems as well. The tile problem was selected as an example because it is representative of the type of story problems found in secondary-school mathematics courses. A major theme of this chapter is that there is more to mathematics than learning to get the right answer (i.e., more than learning number facts and computational procedures). This chapter provided examples of the important role played by linguistic and factual knowledge, schematic knowledge, and strategic knowledge, as well as procedural knowledge.

SUGGESTED READINGS

Kilpatrick, J., Swafford, J., & Findell, B. (Eds.). (2001). *Adding it up: Helping children learn mathematics.* Washington, DC: National Academy Press. (A review of research on mathematics learning along with research-based recommendations for improving mathematics education.)

Reed, S.K. (1999). *Word problems.* Mahwah, NJ: Erlbaum. (A review of research on how students learn to solve arithmetic word problems along with implications for how to improve mathematics education.)

Sternberg, R. J., & Ben-Zeev, T. (Eds.). (1996). *The nature of mathematical thinking.* Mahwah, NJ: Erlbaum. (A description of various research programs on mathematical thinking.)

CHAPTER 6 Learning Science

CHAPTER OUTLINE

The Intuitive Physics Problem

Recognizing Anomalies: Discarding a Misconception

Initiating Conceptual Change: Constructing a New Conception

Developing Scientific Reasoning: Using a New Conception

Building Scientific Expertise: Learning to Build and Use Scientific Knowledge

Chapter Summary

According to the conceptual-change approach to science education, science learning involves helping learners change their existing conceptions rather than solely add new information to their memories. What cognitive processes are involved in learning a new scientific principle? In this chapter we explore four cognitive processes in science learning: recognizing that one's current conception is inadequate to explain one's observations, inventing a new conception that better fits the observed data, applying one's conception to solve a new scientific problem, and developing expertise in scientific reasoning. In addition, this chapter examines techniques for fostering each of these four processes.

THE INTUITIVE PHYSICS PROBLEM

Figure 6–1 shows a bird's-eye view of a curved metal tube. A metal ball is put into the end indicated by the arrow. The ball is then shot through the tube at a high speed, so that it comes out the other end of the tube. Your job is to use a pencil to draw the path that the ball will follow after it comes out of the tube. (You can ignore the effects of air resistance.)

Instructions and diagrams like these were used in a study by McCloskey, Caramazza, and Green (1980). They found that college students tended to give two kinds of answers to the problems. Some students drew a curved line, as shown at the left side of Figure 6–2.

FIGURE 6–1 Where will the ball go?

You are looking down on the curved metal tube shown below. Assume that a metal ball is put in the end with the arrow, and that the ball is shot through the tube at a high rate of speed. Your task is to draw a line corresponding to the path that the ball will follow once it leaves the tube.

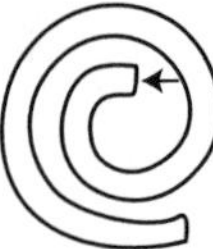

Adapted from McCloskey et al. (1980)

FIGURE 6–2 Two possible answers to the tube problem

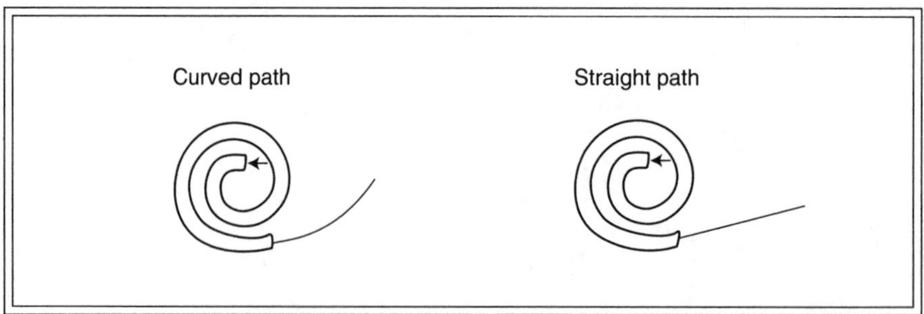

Adapted from McCloskey et al. (1980)

Others drew a straight line, as shown at the right of Figure 6–2. Does your answer correspond to either of these drawings?

Now consider the two explanations shown in Figure 6–3. The first explanation states that the ball acquires a "force" or "momentum" as it moves through the curved tube, and that this force causes the ball to continue its curved path for some time after it emerges from the tube. In contrast, the second explanation states that the ball will continue at a constant speed in a straight line until some force acts on the ball. Choose the explanation that corresponds most closely with your conception of motion.

If you drew a curved line, as shown in the left side of Figure 6–2, your answer is consistent with that given by the majority of college students in the McCloskey et al. (1980) study. Similarly, if you selected the first explanation in Figure 6–3, you are in agreement with a student who had completed one year of high school physics and one year of college physics. However, this answer is incorrect and seems to be based on a medieval conception of motion called the "theory of impetus"—the idea that when an object is set into motion it acquires a force or impetus that keeps it moving, at least until the impetus gradually dissipates. For example, this idea was popular in the fourteenth century writings of Buridan (cited in McCloskey, et al. 1980). In contrast, the correct answer, based on modern Newtonian conceptions of motion, is the straight path shown on the right-hand side of Figure 6–2 and the second explanation in Figure 6–3. The Newtonian concept is that an object in motion will continue until some external force acts upon it.

The point of this demonstration is not to show that people don't understand physics but rather that students approach learning and thinking in physics, or any science, with certain preexisting conceptions. An important educational implication of this demonstration is that instruction should take into account the fact that students already possess intuitions or conceptions about science. Thus, instruction cannot be viewed as providing knowledge about an entirely new topic; rather, instruction involves beginning with the learner's existing "intuitive physics" (or "intuitive science") and trying to change or build upon those conceptions.

FIGURE 6–3

Two possible explanations for the tube problem

Student A

"The momentum that is acquired as it went around here [through the tube], well, the force holding it has given it angular momentum, so as it comes around here [out of the tube], it still has some momentum left, but it loses the momentum as the force disappears."

Student B

"The ball will continue to move in a line away from here [end of tube]. It will keep going until some force acts on the ball. If no force acts on the ball, it will just continue."

Adapted from McCloskey et al. (1980)

CONCEPTUAL-CHANGE THEORY

Research on science education has encouraged a shift from a traditional to a conceptual-change view of learning (Carey, 1986; Posner, Strike, Hewson, & Gertzog, 1982; Strike & Posner, 1985, 1992). According to a traditional view, learning involves adding more and more facts to one's memory. In contrast, the conceptual-change view is that learning occurs when one's mental model (or naive conception) is replaced by a new one. According to *conceptual-change theory*, learning involves three steps:

Recognizing an anomaly: Seeing that your current mental model is inadequate to explain observable facts; that is, realizing that you possess misconceptions that must be discarded.

Constructing a new model: Finding a more adequate mental model that is able to explain the observable facts; that is, replacing one model with another.

Using a new model: When confronted with a problem, using your new model to discover a solution; that is, being able to operate your new model mentally.

As you can see, mental models are at the heart of conceptual-change theory. A mental model is a cognitive representation of the essential parts of a system as well as the cause-and-effect relations between a change in the state of one part and a change in the state of another part (Gentner & Stevens, 1983; Halsford, 1993; Mayer, 1992). For example, you are using a mental model—albeit a discredited one—when you think of force as a sort of constant pushing that keeps an object moving. If you find that this model fails to generate correct predictions on problems such as the ones you just tried, then you need to find a new mental model, such as the idea that force is like a single kick that changes the speed of an object by a certain amount.

This chapter explores four aspects of how students learn science. First, students must overcome their misconceptions that conflict with school science, that is, they may need to discard their existing mental models. Second, students must replace their misconceptions with new conceptions; that is, they must find new mental models. Third, students must develop skills for thinking scientifically; that is, they need to use their new mental models. Fourth, students must acquire content knowledge that will allow them to begin to change from being novices to being experts.

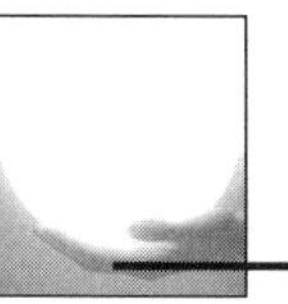

RECOGNIZING ANOMALIES: DISCARDING A MISCONCEPTION

THEORY: KNOWLEDGE AS DESCRIPTION VERSUS EXPLANATION

Historians of science have distinguished between two goals of science—*description* versus *explanation* (Bronowski, 1978; Kearney, 1971; Westfall, 1977). According to the traditional view, the goal of science is to describe the natural world, including descriptions of the relations among variables that can be stated as laws, such as *force* = *mass* × *acceleration*. It follows that the goal of science education is to help students learn facts about the natural universe. To accomplish this goal, science books and encyclopedias keep growing in length.

In contrast, according to the conceptual-change view, the goal of science is not only to describe but also to explain the natural universe, including the mechanisms underlying the descriptive laws. For example, to understand Newton's laws of motion, one's conception of motion must change from seeing rest as the natural state of objects to seeing movement at a constant velocity as the natural state. The study by McCloskey et al. (1980) shows that students may enter the learning situation with certain preexisting conceptions (or misconceptions) of science, so the first step in science education should be to help students recognize the inadequacies of their conceptions.

In their theory of conceptual change, Posner et al. (1982) point to detection of anomalies as the first step in science learning.

> There must be dissatisfaction with existing conceptions. [S]tudents are unlikely to make major changes in their concepts until they believe that less radical changes will not work. . . . [A]n individual must have collected a store of . . . anomalies and lost faith in the capacity of his current concepts to solve these problems. (p. 214)

The first step toward meaningful learning is to recognize that one's current conceptions are unable to explain the available data.

In this section, let's pursue the second view of science education by focusing on learning explanations rather than solely on learning descriptions. In particular, additional examples of misconceptions of physics are presented, and educational implications are drawn.

RESEARCH ON LEARNERS' MISCONCEPTIONS OF PHYSICS

THE CLIFF PROBLEM. Consider a cartoon character who runs over a cliff and falls into the valley below, as shown in Figure 6–4. With a pencil, draw the path that the falling body will follow. Figure 6–5 shows four possible answers:

FIGURE 6–4 How does a moving object fall over a cliff?

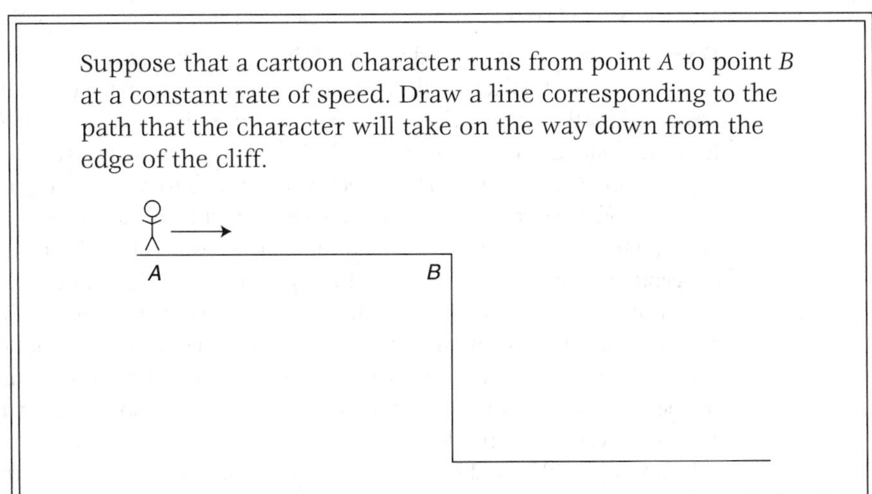

FIGURE 6–5 Four possible paths for a falling body

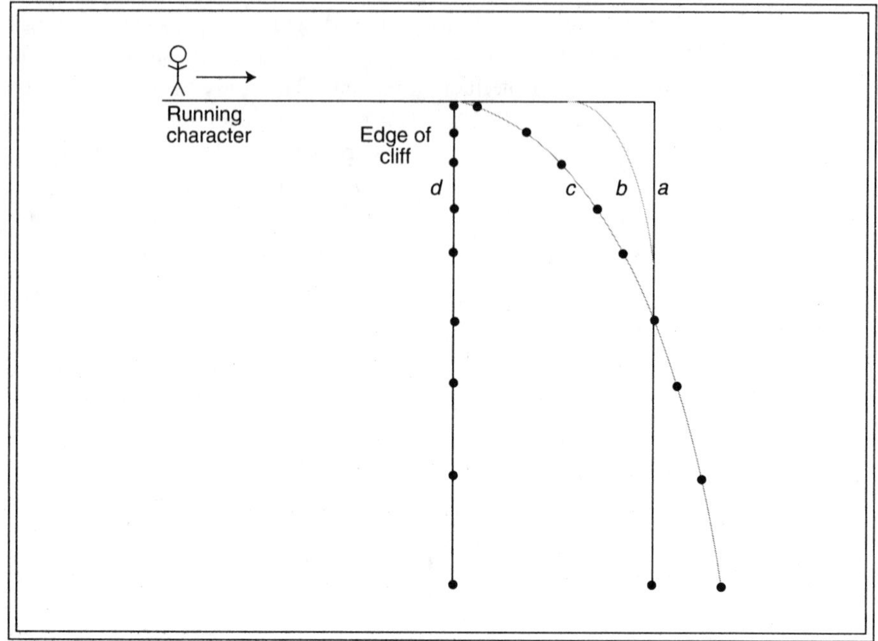

Adapted from McCloskey (1983)

a. It will go on for some horizontal distance and then fall straight down.
b. It will go on for some horizontal distance and then gradually arc downward.
c. It will immediately arc downward, maintaining a constant forward speed and an accelerating downward speed.
d. It will fall straight down as soon as it leaves the edge of the cliff.

Does your answer correspond to any of these four alternatives?

When high school and college students were asked to make predictions in a similar task, 5% opted for the first answer (these may have been fans of the "Road Runner"), 35% opted for the second, 28% selected the third, and 32% chose the fourth (McCloskey, 1983).

The correct answer is c. The object will continue to move at the same rate horizontally, since no force has changed its horizontal movement, and will move downward at an accelerating rate, since gravity is acting on it. This answer is based on the modern Newtonian conception of motion—an object will stay in motion unless some force acts upon it.

An alternative conception, similar to the medieval concept that a moving object acquires some internal momentum or "impetus" that keeps it in motion until the momentum is dissipated, is consistent with the first and second answers. This view was expressed by the student who said, "It's something that carries an object along after a force on it has stopped. Let's call it the force of motion. It's something that keeps the body moving" (McCloskey, 1983, p. 125). Thus this student seems to believe that a moving object requires a force to keep it moving. Students also seem to believe that the ball will drop when the momentum is dissipated: "I understand that friction and air resistance adversely affect the speed of the ball, but not how. Whether they absorb some of the force that's in the ball . . . " (McCloskey, 1983, p. 126). As can be seen, students are expressing the medieval impetus theory that a moving object is kept moving by its own internal force and that movement is affected as the internal force dissipates. This view, while intuitively appealing, is inconsistent with the modern Newtonian view that objects do not require any force to continue moving at a constant speed (or to remain at rest). Instead, an external force is required to alter the velocity of a moving (or resting) body.

THE BALL PROBLEM. As another example of students' misconceptions of motion, consider the problem shown in Figure 6–6. In this problem, suppose that you are running forward at a constant speed with a heavy ball in your hand. As you are running, you drop the ball. Where will the ball land? Choose a line in Figure 6–7 corresponding to the path that the ball will take once you drop it.

As in the study involving the cliff, the most popular answer was consistent with the impetus theory—49% of the students predicted that the ball would fall straight down. Six percent thought the ball would move backward as it fell, and only 45% gave the Newtonian answer that the ball would move forward as it fell. In fact, the ball will continue to move forward at the same rate as the runner and will move downward at an accelerating rate. Using a similar task, Kaiser, Proffitt, and McCloskey (1985) found that elementary school children were far more likely to give incorrect answers than adults.

You may be wondering whether training in physics helps to reduce learners' misconceptions of motion. To examine this question, McCloskey (1983) gave a modified version

FIGURE 6–6 Where will the ball fall?

Suppose you are running at a constant speed, holding a heavy ball. If you drop the ball at point X, where will the ball fall? Draw the path of the falling ball.
Point X
(drop ball)

FIGURE 6–7 Three possible paths for a falling ball

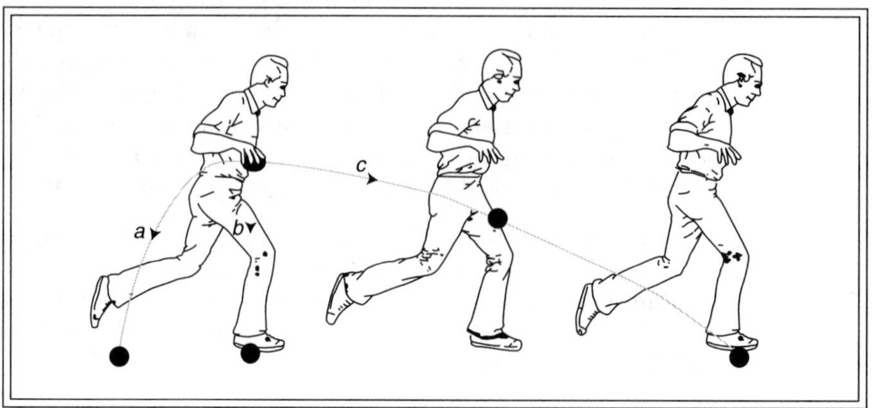

Adapted from McCloskey (1983)

of the ball problem to college students who had taken no physics courses and to college students who had taken at least one physics course. In this study, 80% of the nontrained students thought the ball would drop straight down, whereas only 27% of the physics-trained group opted for this "impetus" view; alternatively, 13% of the nontrained students thought the ball would continue forward after being dropped, compared to 73% of the trained group. Thus, while training in physics shows some positive effect, more than one-quarter of the trained students still held non-Newtonian conceptions of motion. In addition, McCloskey (1983) noted that some ideas are particularly resistant to instruction, such as the belief that impetus acquired when an object is set into motion serves to keep the object in motion. For example, 93% of the students held this belief prior to instruction in physics, and 80% retained it even after instruction.

THE COIN PROBLEM. Clement (1982) provides additional evidence concerning students' preconception that "motion implies a force." For example, a group of college engineering students, most with previous course work in high school physics, was given the coin problem shown in Figure 6–8.

Figure 6–9 shows both the correct answer on the left and the most typical incorrect answer on the right. The overwhelming majority of students (88%) gave incorrect answers based on the idea that if an object is moving upward, some force must be acting on it. A typical student explanation is as follows:

> So there's the force going up and there is the force of gravity pushing it down. And the gravity is less because the coin is still going up until it gets to C. [Draws upward arrow labeled "force of the throw" and shorter downward arrow labeled "gravity" at point B in the figure.] If the dot goes up, the force of the arrow gets less and less because gravity is pulling down on it, pulling down. (Clement, 1982, p. 68)

THE ROCKET PROBLEM. Another problem from Clement's (1982) study is shown in Figure 6–10. Figure 6–11 shows the correct answer, based on Newtonian physics, on the left, and the most common incorrect answer on the right. As in the coin problem, the over-

FIGURE 6–8 The coin problem

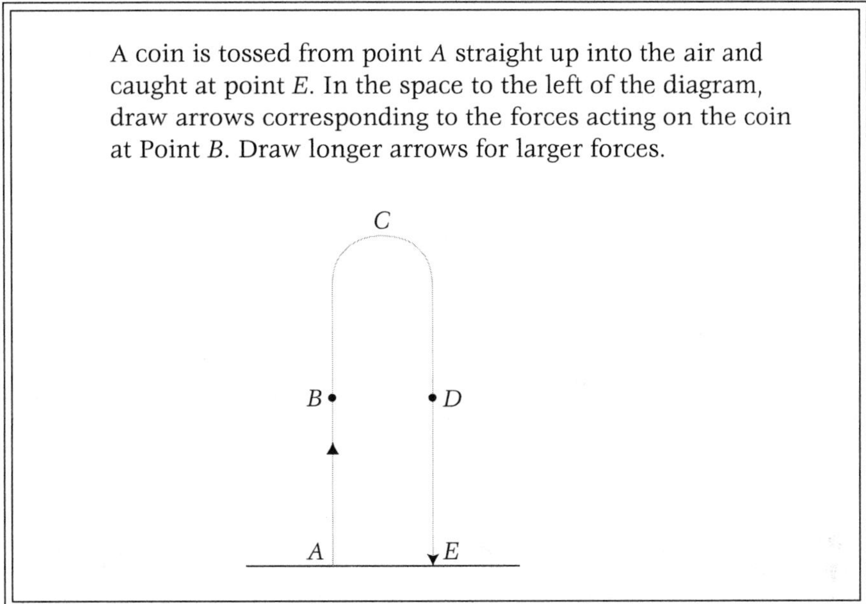

A coin is tossed from point A straight up into the air and caught at point E. In the space to the left of the diagram, draw arrows corresponding to the forces acting on the coin at Point B. Draw longer arrows for larger forces.
C
B
D
A
E

FIGURE 6–9 Two answers to the coin problem

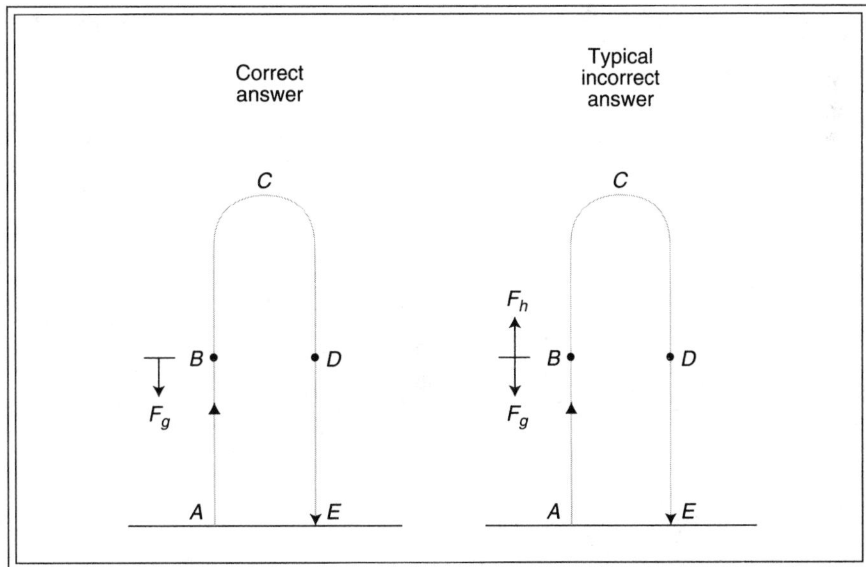

Adapted from Clement (1982)

FIGURE 6–10 What is the path of the rocket?

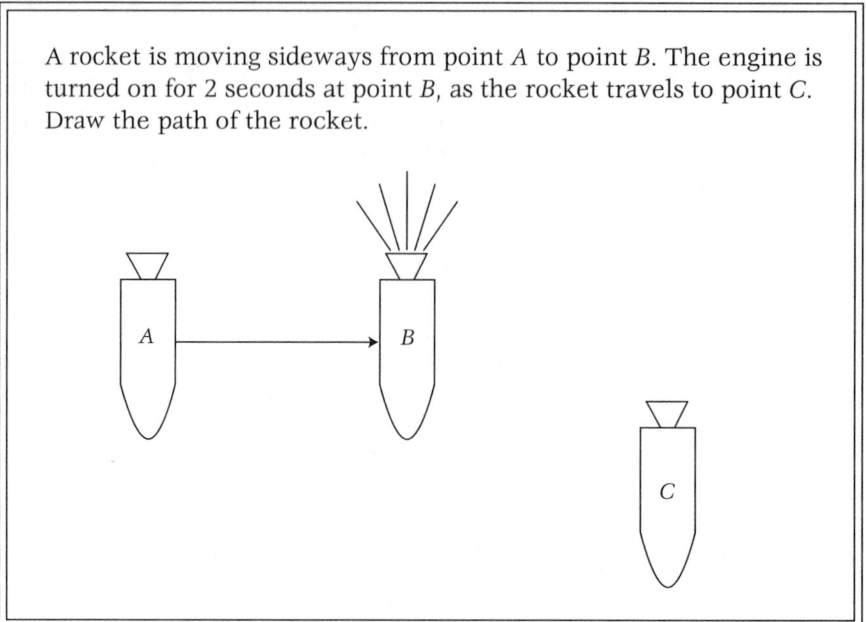

FIGURE 6–11 Two answers to the rocket problem

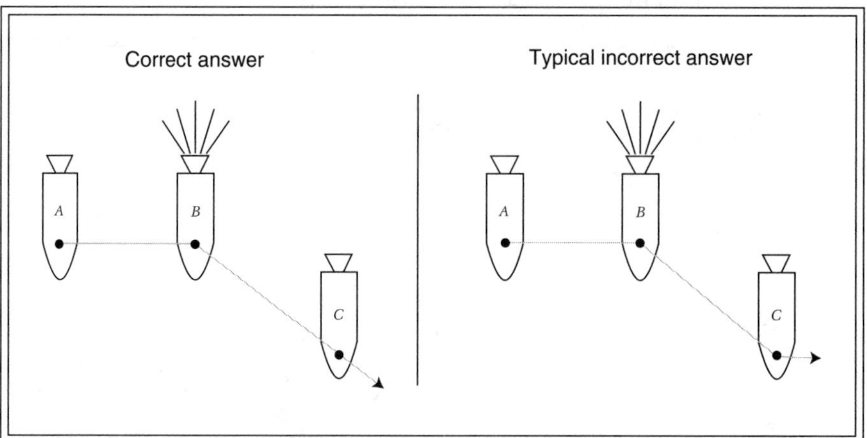

Adapted from Clement (1982)

whelming majority of students opted for incorrect answers. Apparently, students come to college with the preconception that motion implies a force, which can be summarized as follows: If an object is moving, a force is acting upon it; changes in speed or direction occur because the force increases or decreases.

Does a college course in mechanics affect students' conceptions of motion? Table 6–1 shows the percentage of correct answers on the coin and the rocket problems for students before and after a mechanics course. As can be seen, the course tends to double the number of correct responses; however, the error rates are still over 75%. Thus preconceptions built up over a lifetime seem resistant to schooling.

OTHER MISCONCEPTIONS. Similarly, misconceptions have been observed in students' understanding of other scientific concepts, including gravity (Gunstone & White, 1981; Vosniadou, Ioannides, Dimitrakopoulov & Papademetriou, 2001), acceleration (Trowbridge & McDermott, 1981), density (Novick & Nussbaum, 1978, 1981), living versus nonliving (Carey, 1985; Tamir, Gal-Choppin, & Nussinovitz, 1981), chemical equilibrium (Wheeler & Kass, 1978), heat (Carey, 1985; Erickson, 1979; Wiser & Amin, 2001), and the earth as a cosmic body (Nussbaum, 1979; Vosniadou & Brewer, 1992, 1994). For example, Nussbaum (1979) found evidence of a developmental progression in children's conception of the earth as a cosmic body. Fourth-graders viewed the earth as flat, with "down" being toward the "bottom" of the cosmos. Sixth-graders envisioned the earth as round, but "down" still referred to a direction with respect to some cosmic "bottom." Eighth-graders viewed the world as round and tended to see "down" as a direction with respect to the center of the earth. These were the dominant views at each age level, but there was also much variation within each age group.

In reviewing the research on misconceptions of elementary school children (ages 8 to 11), Osborne and Wittrock (1983) found the following examples: "light from a candle goes further at night," "friction only occurs between moving surfaces," "electric current is used up in a light bulb," "a worm is not an animal," "gravity requires the presence of air," "force is a quantity in a moving object in the direction of motion," and "the bubbles in boiling water are bubbles of air." In addition, they reported that as children get older—and presumably learn more school science—some of their misconceptions actually increase before ultimately improving by ages 16 to 18. However, in another review of misconceptions studies, Eylon and Linn (1988) found that adults possess many misconceptions, including

TABLE 6–1

Correct conceptions of motion before and after instruction

	Percentage Correct on Coin Problem	Percentage Correct on Rocket Problem
Before instruction	12%	11%
After instruction	28%	23%

Adapted from Clement (1982)

the ideas that heat and temperature are the same, that heavier objects displace more liquid than lighter objects, and that objects move in the direction they are pushed.

IMPLICATIONS FOR INSTRUCTION: CONFRONTING STUDENTS' MISCONCEPTIONS

The research on students' misconceptions of scientific principles is both frustrating and challenging for science teachers. The results are frustrating because they suggest that students come to the science classroom with many preconceptions that are somewhat resistant to traditional instruction. However, the results are also challenging because they suggest a technique for teaching that is aimed specifically at helping students to revise their scientific intuitions and conceptions.

Consider the following two scenarios. In classroom A, the teacher lectures on the nature of heat flow and gives a demonstration. The teacher pours some water into one beaker and some oil into another, places a thermometer into each beaker, puts the beakers on a hot plate, and turns the hot plate on. Within a few minutes the water is boiling, and the teacher asks a student to read the thermometers on the two beakers. Then, he explains why the oil is hotter than the water. Pleased that the class has learned an important lesson, the teacher dismisses the class.

In classroom B, the teacher suspects that students harbor misconceptions concerning the mechanisms underlying heat flow. She takes two beakers, fills one with water and one with cooking oil, places a thermometer in each, and puts both beakers on a hot plate. She tells the class that she is going to turn on the hot plate until the water boils and asks them to predict how the temperatures will compare when the water reaches a boil. Some students predict that the oil temperature will be lower because "it has not boiled yet." Other students predict that the temperatures will be the same because both beakers have been heated on the hot plate for the same amount of time. Then, students observe what happens by reading the two thermometers when the water is boiling and discover that the oil is hotter than the water. Finally, they must explain why their predictions conflicted with their observations. Both predictions are based on concepts that the teacher would not expect and that would not be exposed through the demonstration method. Although many students recognize that their current theory of heat and temperature is inadequate, few are able to generate an explanation that the teacher would accept. In spite of the students' failures to generate correct predictions, the teacher is pleased. She has exposed a major misconception. That is enough for today, and tomorrow she will help students build an explanation.

The scenario in classroom A is based on the view of science learning as the addition of facts to one's repertoire, whereas the scenario in classroom B follows from the conceptual-change view of science learning. White and Gunstone (1992) refer to the second scenario as predict-observe-explain (POE) and point out its advantages over the demonstration method used in the first scenario. In the predict-observe-explain method, students predict what will happen, observe what happens, and explain why their observations conflict with their predictions. As Clement (1982) and Posner et al. (1982) point out, it is not appropriate to assume that the student's mind is a blank slate. Instead, instructional techniques should take a student's beliefs into account. Much of science instruction involves helping students to change their preconceptions of science. For example, Minstrell (cited in McCloskey, 1983) developed a technique for directly challenging students' misconceptions of motion. Students are presented with problems, such as the ones in the Figures 6–1, 6–4, 6–6, 6–8, and 6–10, and are asked to verbalize their conceptions. The students' conceptions can then be compared to Newtonian conceptions, and the differences can be explicitly pointed out. Minstrell has been successful in changing students' intuitive physics from the medieval impetus view to the modern Newtonian view.

When students' conceptions of real-world physical events conflict with the conceptions underlying school science, students have several options. A common strategy used by students is to learn one set of rules for school science and another for the real world (West & Pines, 1985). In contrast, some students may discard their preexisting conceptions and replace them with concepts that are consistent with current scientific theories.

To induce this second kind of learning, Champagne, Gunstone, and Klopfer (1985) developed an instructional program called *ideational confrontation.* Students are first asked to make predictions about a common physical situation, such as the motion of an empty versus a loaded sled going downhill. Next they develop theoretical explanations to support their predictions. Then the instructor demonstrates the physical situation and provides a scientific explanation. In the ensuing discussions, students must reconcile their predictions with the actual results and must replace their ineffective conceptions with new ones. It is clear from the work of Champagne et al. (1985) that instructional procedures like ideational confrontation require a great deal of time and planning, but there is some evidence that the procedure can be effective. Science instruction needs to make use of techniques that will help students discard misconceptions and replace them with correct conceptions of science.

This approach to teaching science is consistent with the general prescription proposed by Ausubel (1968) in his classic book *Educational Psychology:*

> If I had to reduce all of educational psychology to just one principle, I would say this: The most important single factor influencing learning is what the learner already knows. Ascertain this and teach him accordingly. (p. vi)

In science education, this means that the teacher must begin by helping students to recognize the anomalies between what their theories predict and what really happens.

How does conceptual conflict work in a classroom? Let's visit some fifth- and sixth-grade classrooms where students are learning about the principles of mechanics, such as motion and force. They are asked to make predictions and test them by conducting experiments. They must present scientific explanations and compare them with the explanations offered by other children. They work in small groups and present their work to the entire class for debate. This is the environment created by Vosniadou, Ioannides, Dimitrakopoulou, and Papademetriou (2001) for an eight-lesson unit on mechanics given to students in Greece.

To create cognitive conflict, students were asked to pull a heavy table in the classroom, which they could not move. A common explanation is that there is no force being exerted on the table because it is not moving (i.e., consistent with the impetus view that motion implies force). However, students were taught how use a dynamometer to measure the force being exerted on an object. To their great surprise the dynamometer measurements showed that a force was being exerted on the table when students tried to pull it even though the table did not move. This conflicting information—that an object can be nonmoving and still have a force exerted on it—formed the basis for classroom discussion.

In another attempt to create cognitive conflict, students were asked to predict how much force would be needed to move an object over a surface. A common prediction was that the force must be greater than the weight of the object. However, when they used a dynamometer they found that the force required to make the object move was considerably less than the weight of the object. Through discussion, the students were able to confront their intuitive idea that weight is a property of objects (rather than an interaction between the earth and the object), and to develop the idea that the motion of the object is related to the smoothness of the surface (leading to the concept of frictional force).

Does conceptual-change instruction help students learn? Students who received this kind of conceptual-change instruction showed greater pretest-to-posttest gains on giving conceptually correct answers to physics problems than did students who were exposed to the prescribed science curriculum (Vosniadou et al., 2001).

Cognitive conflict does not always require conducting experiments. Chi (2000) showed that students can experience cognitive conflict when they read a science text. For example, suppose we ask some high school biology students to read a textbook passage about the human circulatory system. As you know, students do not enter this task as blank slates waiting to be filled by the information in the passage. Instead, they bring their own preconceptions about how the circulatory system works, such as the single-loop model shown in the left side of Figure 6–12. According to this model—which is the most common naive mental model of the circulatory system—the arteries carry blood from the heart to the body (where oxygen is deposited and is waste collected) and veins carry blood from the body to the heart (where it is cleaned and reoxygenated). In contrast, the text describes a double-loop model as shown in the right side of Figure 6–12, which includes four separate chambers in the heart as well as a separate loop to and from the lungs.

According to Chi (2000), conceptual change is initiated when students recognize a conflict between their flawed mental model and the model described in the text: "a violation is defined as a conflict between a text sentence and a belief that is embedded in a flawed mental model" (p. 200). For example, students might recognize that the following text sen-

FIGURE 6–12 The single-loop model and the double-loop model of the human circulatory system

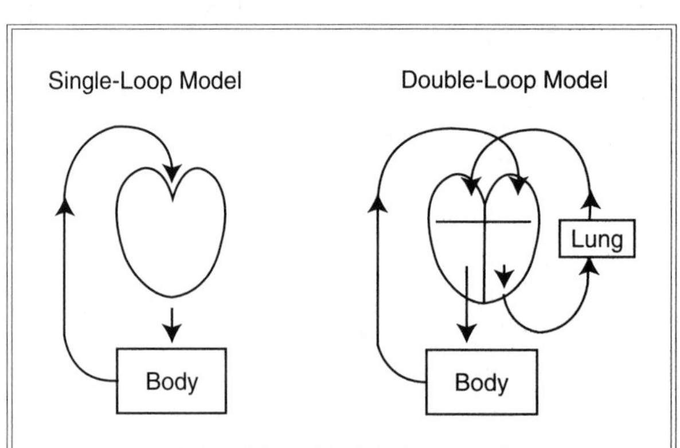

Adapted from Chi (2000)

tence conflicts with their single-loop model: "The right side pumps blood to the lungs and the left side pumps blood to the other parts of the body." When students recognize a violation—that is, a conflict between their model and the text's model—they initiate a process of what Chi (2000) calls *self-repair*: "Self-repair occurs primarily when a mental model conflicts with a text model" (p. 204). In some cases, students misinterpret a violation to be consistent with their model, but sometimes recognition of violation triggers the construction of a new model.

How can we initiate the process of self-repair, which results in the learner recognizing the need to replace the single-loop model? Let's simply ask the learner to explain the text aloud as he or she reads it—a task that Chi calls *self-explanation*. Chi (2000) reports that students who are prompted to explain the text as they read learned much more from the text than did students who were not required to give explanations while reading. Importantly, in detailed analyses of conceptual change in individual students, Chi found that recognition of violations between the student's mental model and the text's model eventually lead to changes in students' models from the single-loop to the double-loop model.

Overall, these studies confirm Limon's (2001) assertion that "cognitive conflict seems to be the starting point in the process of conceptual change" (p. 373). Limon also notes that conceptual change is more likely to occur when the conflict is meaningful to the learner so that the learner wants to have a mental model that will allow him or her to make sense of the situation.

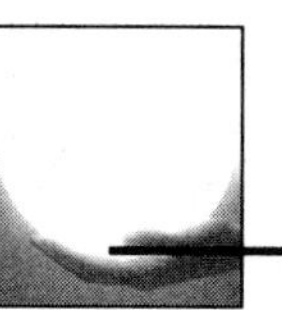

INITIATING CONCEPTUAL CHANGE: CONSTRUCTING A NEW CONCEPTION

THEORY: LEARNING AS ASSIMILATION VERSUS ACCOMMODATION

The traditional and cognitive change approaches to science education offer two fundamentally different views of how students learn—by assimilation versus by accommodation. According to the traditional view, students learn by assimilation; that is, they fit new information into their existing knowledge. For example, if a student learns that water boils at 212 degrees, she can connect this fact to her existing conception that heat causes temperature change. This connection results in a modest form of conceptual change—the existing concepts remain the same, but new information is connected to them. The assimilation view is incomplete because it cannot account for radical forms of conceptual change, such as replacing the impetus theory with the Newtonian theory of motion.

In contrast, conceptual-change theory posits that learning can sometimes involve accommodation rather than assimilation. In accommodative learning, the student "must replace or reorganize his central concepts" because the student's "current concepts are inadequate to allow him to grasp some new phenomenon successfully" (Posner et al., 1982, p. 212). In short, the learner must build a new conception that can accommodate the newly presented information. For example, if a student believes that "equal heat produces equal temperature," she will have to replace that concept when she learns that the same amount of heat results in lower temperature when it is applied to a beaker of water than when it is applied to a beaker of oil.

Unfortunately, simply recognizing an anomaly does not guarantee that a student will find an adequate new conception. Posner et al. (1982, p. 214) posit three characteristics of a new conception in accommodative learning. The new conception must be:

Intelligible: The learner must grasp how the new conception works.
Plausible: The learner must see how the new conception is consistent with other knowledge and explains the available data.
Fruitful: The learner must be able to extend the conception to new areas of inquiry.

In short, the new model must make sense to the learner and be useful in solving old and new problems.

Analogies are a major vehicle for lending meaning to a new conception, so they are instrumental in initiating the process of conceptual change. An analogy occurs when a learner can construct a mapping between the parts and relations of a model (which can be called a *base*) and the corresponding parts and relations in a natural system (which can be called a *target*). Gentner (1983, 1989) proposed a structure-mapping theory in which the objects, attributes, and relations of a base system are matched to the corresponding objects, attributes, and relations of a target system.

For example, consider the electrical circuit shown at the left of Figure 6–13, which consists of a battery, wires, and a resistor. To understand how this system works, a learner could view an electrical circuit as a hydraulic system (or a water-flow system), as shown at the right of Figure 6–13. As you can see, the battery is analogous to a pump, the wire is analogous to a pipe, the resistor is analogous to a constriction in the pipe, and electron flow is analogous to water flow. A relational principle such as "current increases with voltage" is analogous to saying "water flow increases with water pressure"; similarly, the relational principle "current decreases with resistance" is analogous to saying "water flow decreases with pipe narrowness." Some of the mappings between the water-flow system

FIGURE 6–13 Using a water-flow model to understand an electrical circuit

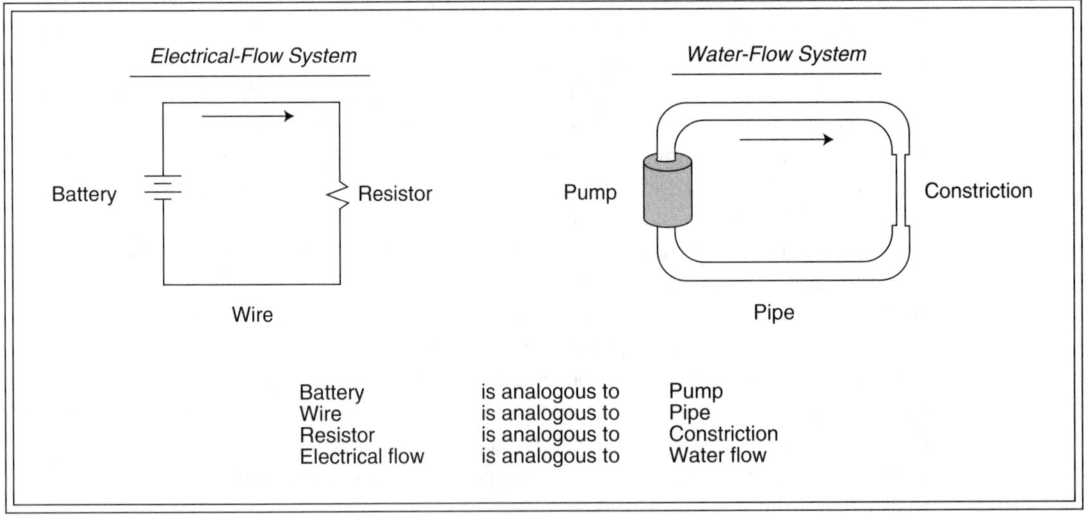

and the electrical-flow system are summarized in Figure 6–13. To use an analogical model effectively, a learner must focus on aspects of the model that are relevant and ignore those that are irrelevant. For example, the learner must ignore the characteristics of water, which would, of course, prove to be disastrous if literally applied to an electrical circuit. Gentner and Gentner (1983) and White (1993) found that students often report using a water-flow analogy to solve problems involving electrical circuits or to understand the formal description in Ohm's law: *current = voltage/resistance*. If a student determines that current is like water flow, voltage is like water pressure, and resistance is like a constriction in a pipe, then the learner can use the water-flow analogy to understand the mechanism explaining Ohm's law.

In this section, I explore research and practice in how analogical models can be used to promote conceptual change.

RESEARCH ON EFFECTIVE ANALOGICAL MODELS

What makes a good analogical model? To help answer this question, please read the pump passage in Figure 6–14 and then try to answer the following question: Suppose you push down and pull up on the pump handle several times but no air comes out. What could be wrong? If you experience difficulty in solving this problem, refer to the pump model shown in Figure 6–15. In the pump model, the pump has been simplified so the learner can see that the valves work like one-way doors and the piston in the cylinder works like a syringe. This graphic example may help the learner to build connections between actions stated in the passage, such as "the inlet valve closes," and a mental model of the system, such as a mental image of a one-way door in the pump being forced closed.

If you are like the students in the studies by Mayer and Gallini (1990), you found that the pump model helped you understand how pumps work. Mayer and Gallini (1990) found that students who looked at a model like the one in Figure 6–15 while reading a passage about how pumps work generated nearly twice as many creative solutions to problems as students who read the passage without seeing the model. In a review of 19 studies, Mayer (1989, 1993b) found that when a pictorial model was added to textbook passages

FIGURE 6–14

A verbal explanation of how a bicycle tire pump works

Bicycle tire pumps vary in the number and location of the valves they have and in the way air enters the cylinder. Some simple bicycle tire pumps have the inlet valve on the piston and the outlet valve at the closed end of the cylinder. A bicycle tire pump has a piston that moves up and down. Air enters the pump near the point where the connecting rod passes through the cylinder. *As the rod is pulled out, air passes through the piston and fills the areas between the piston and the outlet valve. As the rod is pushed in, the inlet valve closes and the piston forces air through the outlet valve.**

**Key information is in italics (which have been added).*

From World Book Encyclopedia *(1990)*

FIGURE 6–15 Coordinating verbal and visual explanations of how a bicycle tire pump works

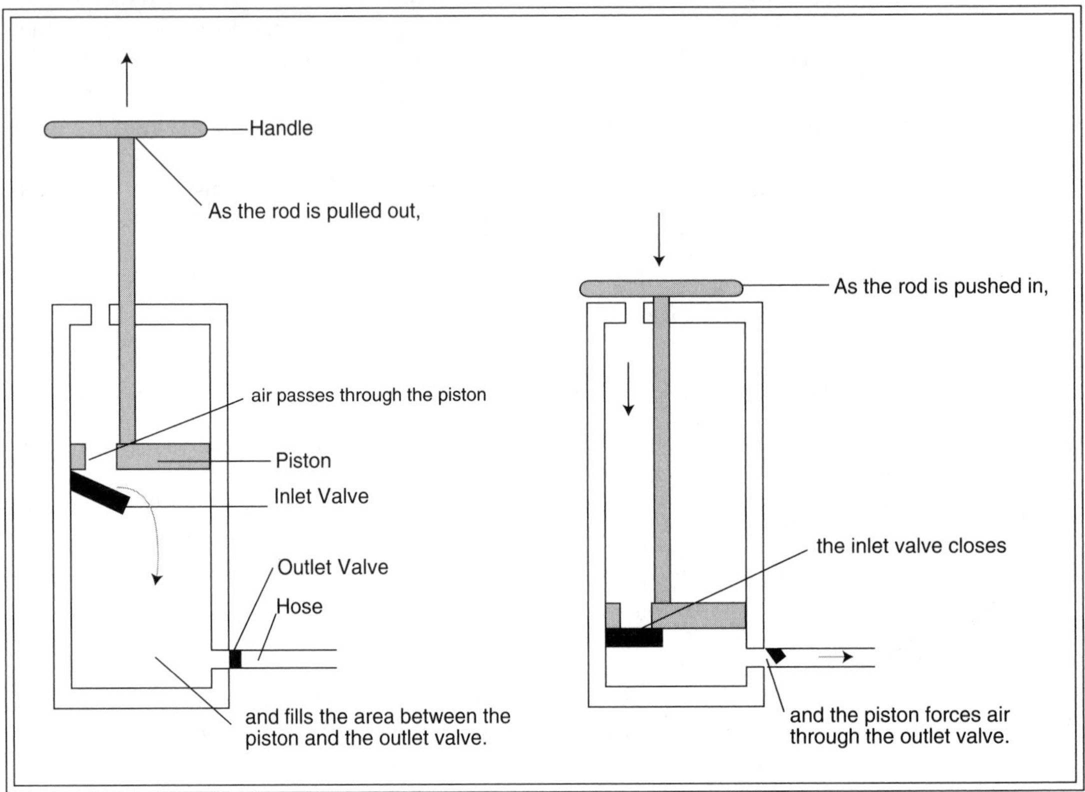

Adapted from Mayer and Gallini (1990)

on how various systems worked, subsequent problem-solving performance was improved by an average of more than 60%.

Although visual models can be effective aids in promoting conceptual change, they are rarely used. In an analysis of science textbooks, Mayer (1993b) found that although almost 50% of the space was devoted to illustrations, less than 10% presented analogical models. Similarly, in his survey of 43 science textbooks, Glynn (1991) reported that "elaborate analogies . . . were relatively rare" (p. 228). Glynn, Yeany, and Britton (1991) point out that

> the present science textbooks and methods of instruction do not yet take into account recent discoveries in the psychology of how students learn science. Discoveries about the constructive nature of students' learning, about students' mental models, and about students' misconceptions have important implications for teachers. (p. 5)

In summary, science educators are being asked to accept a new conception of "learning science as a process of construction and reconstruction of personal theories and models" (Glynn et al., 1991, p. 16).

IMPLICATIONS FOR INSTRUCTION: PROMOTING CONCEPTUAL CHANGE

The implications of research on analogical models in science are straightforward: "Science teachers should view instruction as a process of helping students acquire progressively more sophisticated theories of science phenomena" (Glynn et al., 1991, p. 16). How can teachers put this advise into practice? For example, given that students enter the science classroom with serious misconceptions about motion, how can teachers foster conceptual change? What kinds of experiences can foster conceptual change in sixth-graders? How can we reduce or eliminate students' misconceptions? Is it possible to design instruction that will help students to perform better than untrained students on a test of physics concepts?

In an effort to answer these questions, White (1993; White & Frederiksen, 1998) designed a computer-based microworld called "ThinkerTools," which is intended to help students acquire the concepts of motion and force. Consistent with the conceptual-change theory proposed by Posner and his colleagues (1982), White gives students experience in making predictions about motion that fail and in developing progressively more sophisticated mental models of how the physical world works. Rather than beginning with a formal statement of the laws of motion, such as $F = ma$, instruction is based on qualitative reasoning about how a microworld works.

Students learn to solve problems in a progression of increasingly sophisticated microworlds. The instructional cycle for each microworld in ThinkerTools consists of four phases—motivation, model evolution, formalization, and transfer. In the motivation phase, the teacher asks students to make predictions about real-world physics problems such as the following:

> Imagine that we have a ball resting on a frictionless surface and we blow on the ball. Then, as the ball is moving along, we give it a blow, the same size as the first, in the opposite direction. What will be the effect of this second blow on the motion of the ball? (White, 1993, p. 10)

The teacher tabulates the students' answers and their reasons. For example, some of the most common answers are that the second blow will (1) make the ball turn around and move in the direction of second blow; (2) make the ball slow down; and (3) make the ball stop. This exercise is designed to motivate students to find out who is right and why.

In the model evolution phase of ThinkerTools, groups of two or more students solve problems presented on a computer screen, as shown in Figure 6–16. In the problem in Figure 6–16, the students' job is to make the dot (specified as a large gray circle) hit the target (specified as a large *X*) at a speed of four units. If the students succeed, the dot returns to its starting position in preparation for a new problem; if the students fail, the dot crashes into a wall and explodes. There is no gravity or friction to consider, and the students can affect the movement of the dot by using a joystick. Whenever the students pull the joystick in one of the four directions—right, left, up, or down—and pushes the firing button, the dot receives one unit of push in the direction indicated by the joystick. On the screen, a flaming arrow next to the dot indicates the direction of the push, and a swooshing sound indicates that the dot has received a push. Motion is represented by (1) the dot's movement; (2) small dots, called wakes, that are produced on screen at regular time intervals to indicate the history of the dot's movement; and (3) a sort of speedometer, called a

FIGURE 6–16 A computer-based game for learning physics

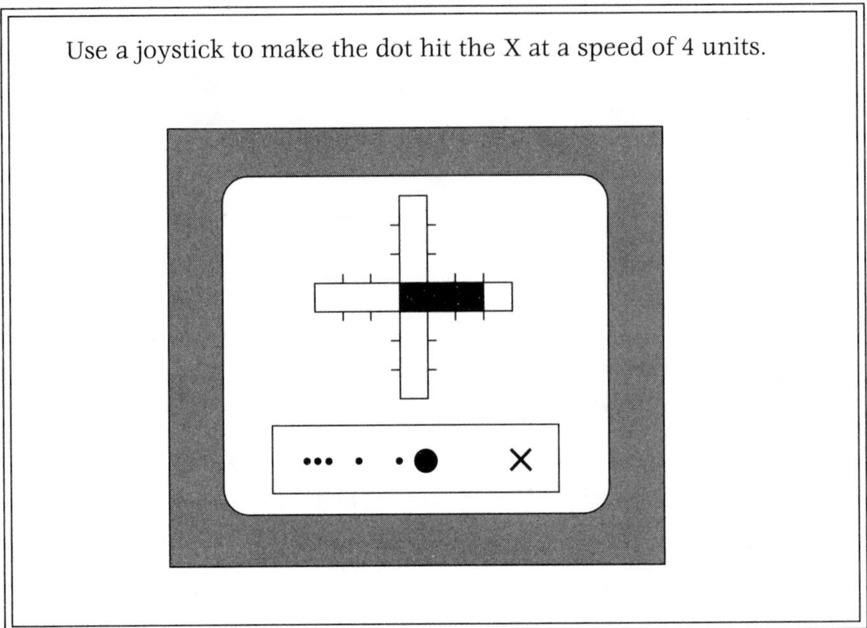

Use a joystick to make the dot hit the X at a speed of 4 units.
X

Adapted from White (1993)

datacross, that shows the speed of the dot in each of the four directions. In another exercise, the students' job is to move the dot along an L-shaped path using the joystick.

In the formalization phase of ThinkerTools, small groups of students work at a computer to determine the validity of each of a set of laws, such as the following:

1. If a dot is moving to the right and you apply an impulse to the right, the dot will speed up. [Correct but not general.]
2. Whenever you apply an impulse to the dot, it changes speed. [Correct but not precise.]
3. If you keep giving the dot impulses in the direction that it is moving, it keeps speeding up. If you keep giving it impulses in the direction opposite to that in which it is moving, it slows down, stops, and goes the other way. [Correct, but neither precise nor general.]
4. You can think of the effect of an impulse as adding to or subtracting from the speed of the dot. If applied in the same direction that the dot is moving, it adds a unit of speed; in the opposite direction, it subtracts. [Correct for the one-dimensional microworld shown in Figure 6–16; this law is useful because it allows precise predictions for any sequence of impulses.]
5. Whenever you give the dot an impulse to the left, it slows down. [Not correct when the dot is moving left or stopped.]

6. Whenever you give the dot an impulse, it speeds up. [Not correct when the impulse is applied in the direction opposite the dot's motion.]
7. Unless you keep applying impulses to the dot, it will slow down. [Not correct because there is no friction in the microworld.] (White, 1993, p. 13)

Then, the teacher leads a class discussion of whether each law is correct or incorrect, and which of the correct laws is the most useful in generating precise solutions to a variety of problems. Rule 4 is typically selected as the most useful rule because it is correct, precise, and general.

In the transfer phase of ThinkerTools, students are asked to explain how the rule they selected as the most useful relates to a real-world problem such as the one given during the motivation phase. For example, if rule 4 is selected as the most useful rule, students can show how it predicts that the second blow will cause the ball to stop. In addition, they can experiment with real objects or with the microworld. For example, by adding friction to the microworld, they can find that the second blow makes the ball turn around and change direction—a prediction that many students made initially. Thus, they can see that the rules they have developed apply to a frictionless world but not to a world with friction.

After working in a one-dimensional microworld, students move to a two-dimensional world in which the dot can move up and down as well as right and left. Then, the student moves to a microworld in which continuous forces can be created by holding down the button on the joystick to release an impulse every 3/4 of a second. Finally, the students learn about a microworld that involves gravity and that focuses on problems concerning the trajectories of dots.

Does experience with ThinkerTools foster conceptual change in science students? To examine this question, White (1993) gave a test of physics concepts to a group of sixth-graders who had received the ThinkerTools curriculum every school day for 45 minutes over a two-month period (trained group) and to an equivalent group of sixth-graders who had no physics experience (control group). Figure 6–17 shows some of the items on the test, in which students are asked to make predictions about the paths and velocities of moving objects. If the students entered the physics classroom with misconceptions about motion, then we would expect the control group to perform poorly on the test. If experience in the ThinkerTools microworld helps students to change incorrect conceptions into correct ones, then we would expect the trained group to perform well on the test. Consistent with these predictions, the control students gave correct answers to 44% of the problems, whereas trained students gave correct answers to 66%. In summary, these results demonstrate that a carefully planned set of experiences can foster conceptual change in students.

Importantly, students learned more deeply with ThinkerTools when they were encouraged to engage in inquiry activities such as predicting a physics principle, generating a prediction, running an experiment, and explaining the results (White & Frederiksen, 1998). In addition, improvements were strongest for the less knowledgeable students, leading White and Frederiksen (1998) to call for "making science accessible to all students" (p. 3).

FIGURE 6–17 Sample questions from a test of physics concepts

Suppose that we are trying to get an ice hockey puck to travel along the track shown below. At the beginning of the track, somebody hits the puck in the direction shown. (*Note*: Each hit of the puck has the same intensity.) In which direction—*A*, *B*, or *C*—will somebody need to hit the puck so that it makes the first turn?

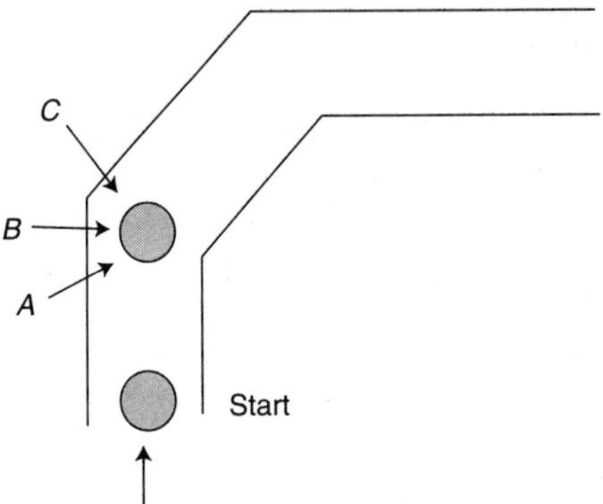

Imagine that you kick a ball sideways off a cliff. Which path will the ball take as it falls to the ground?

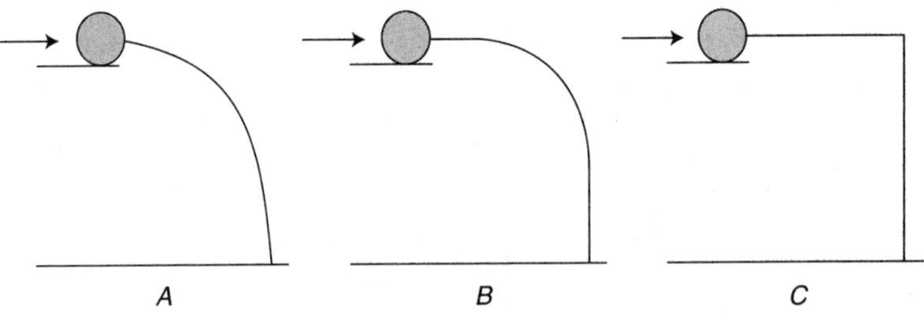

Suppose that two identical boats are trying to cross two identical rivers. The only difference is that one river has a current flowing and the other does not. Both boats have the same motors and leave at the same time. Which boat gets to the other side first?

1. The one crossing the river without a current flowing.
2. The one crossing the river with a current flowing.
3. Both boats get to the other side at the same time.

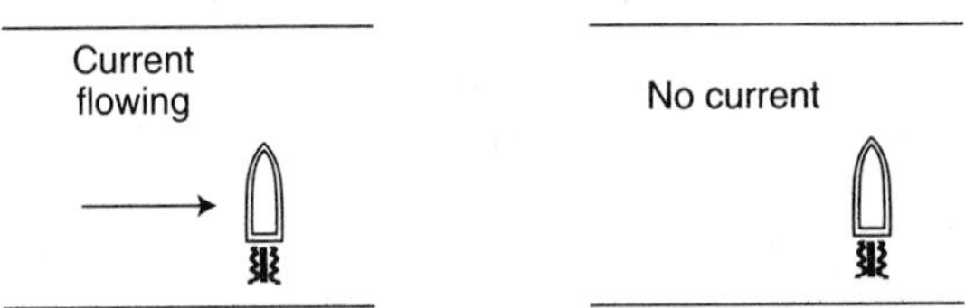

Adapted from White (1993)

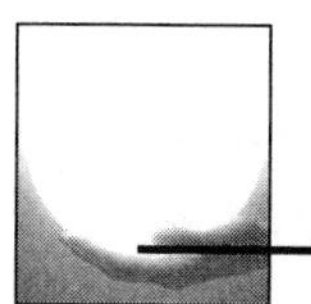

DEVELOPING SCIENTIFIC REASONING: USING A NEW CONCEPTION

THEORY: SCIENTIFIC REASONING AS HYPOTHESIS TESTING VERSUS HYPOTHESIS CREATION

The previous two sections showed how conceptual change depends on anomalies and analogies, respectively. The next step in the process of conceptual change is application—being able to use one's knowledge to reason scientifically through experiments. This section compares two views of scientific reasoning.

According to the traditional approach, scientific reasoning is a process of hypothesis testing in which a learner systematically tests each possible hypothesis. Systematic hypothesis testing is at the heart of Piaget's (1972; Inhelder & Piaget, 1958) formal operational thought and represents a well-recognized form of scientific reasoning. Formal operational thought, expected to occur during adolescence, is the highest level of cognitive development. It involves the ability to think in terms of abstractions, symbols, probabilities, and proportions, and to consider many variables or dimensions at the same time. Each of these skills is a crucial component in scientific tasks such as understanding the principles of motion in physics.

Conceptual-change theory suggests a second kind of scientific reasoning: hypothesis creation. What happens in situations where systematic hypothesis testing fails? When your pool of hypotheses is exhausted, you need a new way of looking at the problem that will allow you to generate new hypotheses. Hypothesis creation occurs when a learner rejects all hypotheses derived from one conception of the problem, and now must generate a new hypothesis based on a new conception of the problem. According to conceptual-change theory, an account of scientific reasoning that ignores hypothesis creation is incomplete.

RESEARCH ON STUDENTS' SCIENTIFIC THINKING

HYPOTHESIS TESTING Most science textbooks and instructional programs assume that high school and college students are capable of scientific thinking. However, there is some startling evidence that some students may enter the science classroom without the prerequisite skills required for scientific thought. For example, many researchers have measured the proportion of college students consistently using formal thought for scientific tasks to be as low as 25% to 50% (Cohen, Hillman, & Agne, 1978; Griffiths, 1976; Kolodiy, 1975; Lawson & Snitgen, 1982; McKinnon & Renner, 1971).

In a major study, Karplus and his colleagues (Karplus, Karplus, Formisano, & Paulsen, 1979) developed two tasks to measure secondary school students' ability to engage in formal thinking—the proportional reasoning task and the control-of-variables task. These tasks were administered to 3,300 secondary school students (generally 13 to 15 years old) in seven industrialized countries: Denmark, Sweden, Italy, United States, Austria, Germany, and Great Britain. Figure 6–18 shows an example of a proportional reasoning task, called the paper clip problem. Students are shown sheets of paper containing two

FIGURE 6–18 A proportional reasoning task: The paper clip problem

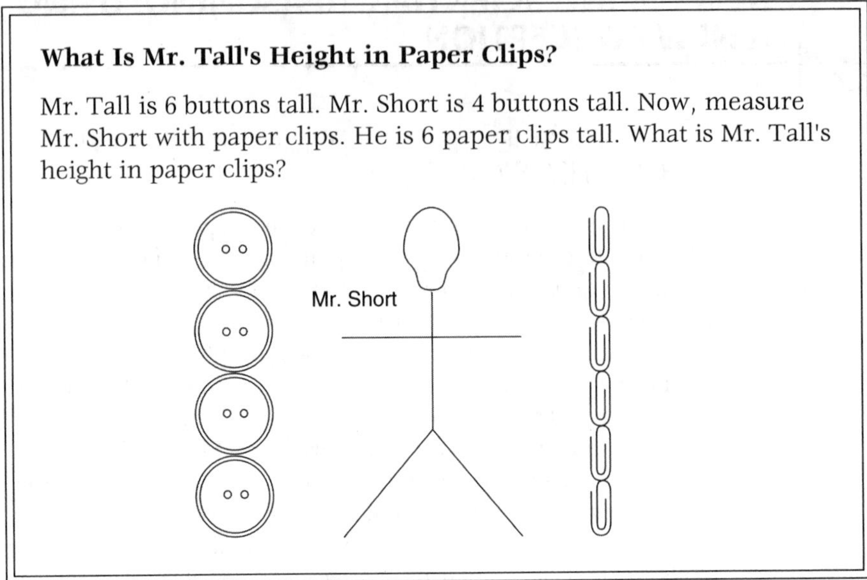

What Is Mr. Tall's Height in Paper Clips?
Mr. Tall is 6 buttons tall. Mr. Short is 4 buttons tall. Now, measure Mr. Short with paper clips. He is 6 paper clips tall. What is Mr. Tall's height in paper clips?
Mr. Short

Adapted from Karplus et al. (1979)

stick figures, Mr. Tall and Mr. Short. When the heights of these two characters are measured using rows of large round buttons, it is found that Mr. Tall is six buttons tall and Mr. Short is four buttons tall. Then the students are asked to measure the height of Mr. Short using standard paper clips (the answer is 6), and to figure out the height of Mr. Tall in paper clips as well. In addition, students are asked to explain how they figured out the height of Mr. Tall.

Student answers can be classified as follows:

Intuitive: This approach either does not fully use the available data or uses the data in an illogical way. Examples of students' intuitive explanations include, "The way I got that Mr. Tall is 12 paper clips is I just doubled 6 buttons," and "I added 6 and 4 together."

Additive: This approach uses a single difference between Mr. Tall and Mr. Short (such as their height difference in buttons) uncoordinated with other differences, and solves the problem by adding this difference to some number. For example, one student said, "If Mr. Tall is 6 buttons and Mr. Short is 4 buttons, that is a difference of 2. Now Mr. Short is 6 paper clips tall, so I took the 2 and added it to 6 and got 8."

Transitional: This approach partially uses proportional reasoning, but fails to generate a completely correct procedure. For example, one student said, "I divided 4 into 6; 4 is how many buttons Mr. Short is and 6 is the amount of paper clips, and I got 1 1/2. Then I added 6, the amount of buttons of Mr. Tall, to 1 1/2 and got 7 1/2."

Ratio: This is the correct procedure for answering the paper clip problem, and involves deriving a proportion or ratio, and using the proportion to generate the answer. For example, one student said, "I got this by putting their height in buttons into a fraction (4/6) and by putting their height in paper clips into a fraction (6/*x*) and solved it. The result is 9." Another example is, "1 button = 1 1/2 paper clips; 1 1/2 × 6 = 9."

The results of the study are not encouraging. Figure 6–19 shows the percentage of U.S. students using each of the four strategies (based on two proportional reasoning tasks). As can be seen, few students use the ratio procedure, with the most commonly used method being the intuitive strategy.

The same general pattern of results was obtained in each of the seven countries that Karplus et al. (1979) studied.

Another problem used by Karplus et al. (1979) is the control-of-variables task. In this problem, the student is shown a track with a target ball in it, as shown in Figure 6–20. The student is told that if she rolls another ball down the track, it will collide with the target and make it move some distance. The student has the option of using a heavy metal ball or a light glass ball (both of equal size), and of placing it either high, medium, or low in the

FIGURE 6–19 Performance of U.S. students on a proportional reasoning task

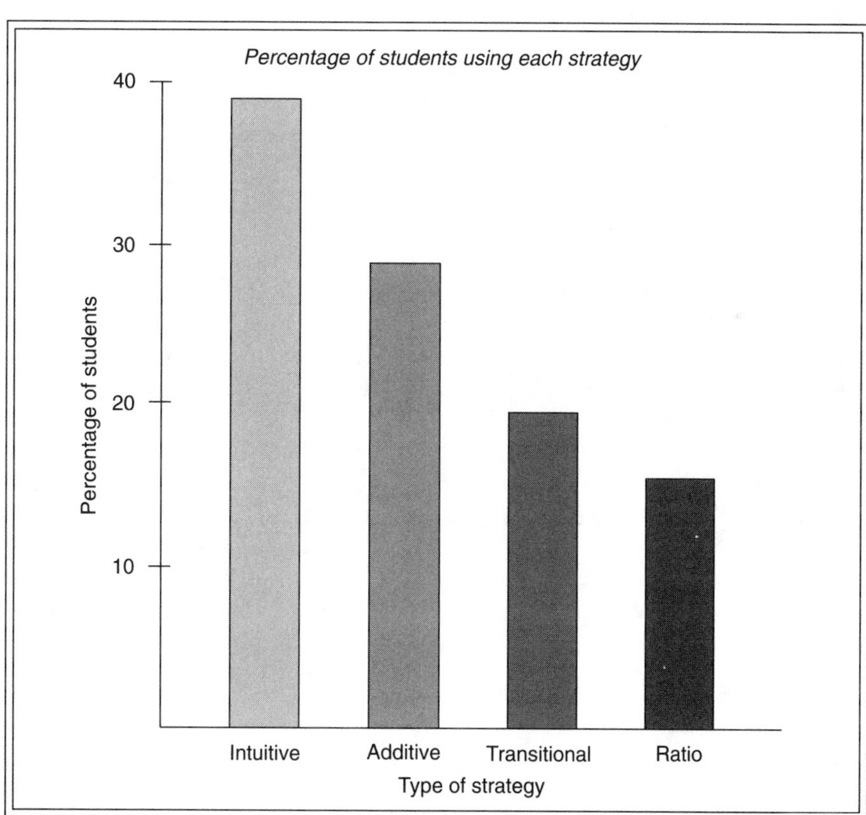

Adapted from Karplus et al. (1979)

FIGURE 6–20 A control-of-variables task: The track problem

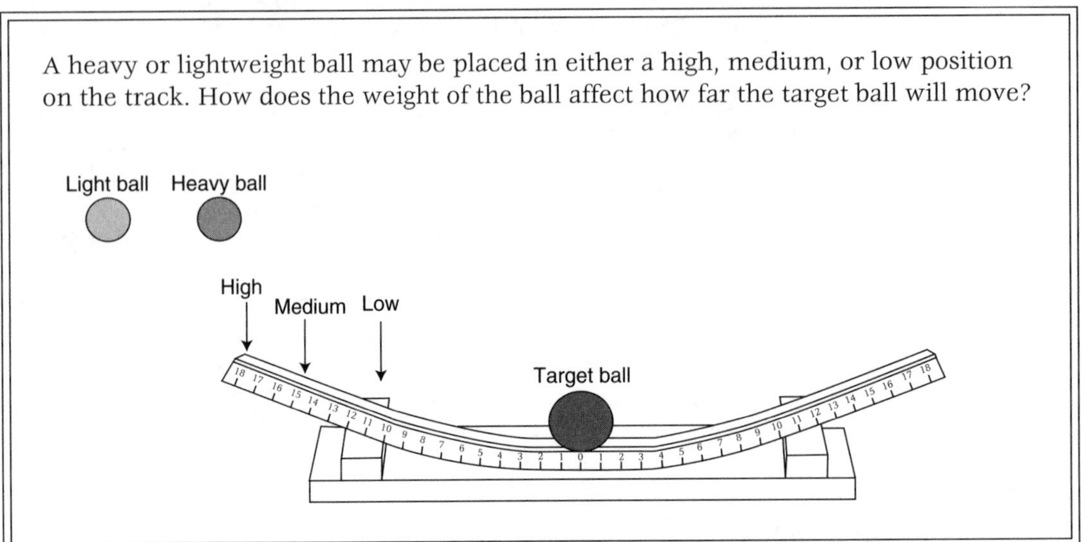
A heavy or lightweight ball may be placed in either a high, medium, or low position on the track. How does the weight of the ball affect how far the target ball will move?
Light ball
Heavy ball
High
Medium
Low
Target ball

Adapted from Karplus et al. (1979)

track. They are then asked a series of questions to determine whether they understand how to control variables during experimentation, such as:

> Suppose you want to know how much difference the weight of the ball makes in how far the target goes. You are going to use two balls on the target. Where would you start the heavy ball? Where would you start the light ball? Please explain your answers carefully. (p. 101)

Karplus et al. (1979) discovered that students gave three types of answers to this question:

Intuitive: This approach allows for any starting position. For example, one student said, "I would start the heavy sphere at medium to see if, even though the sphere is heavy, it will make a difference. I started the light one at high so it would pick up speed and knock the ball far."

Transitional: This approach calls for starting the balls at the same position, but does not provide a complete rationale. For example, a student explained, "Start them at the same place and give them the same speed, then measure how far the target goes up the other side."

Control: This approach calls for starting the balls at the same place and stating that equality of conditions is crucial. For example, one student reasoned, "The main reason of this experiment is the weight difference, so you would have to keep all other factors the same."

Figure 6–21 shows the percentage of U.S. students who used each approach to a control-of-variables problem. The results of this study, like those of the proportional reasoning study, are not encouraging. Again, similar patterns were obtained in each of the industrialized countries studied.

FIGURE 6–21 Performance of U.S. students on a control-of-variables task

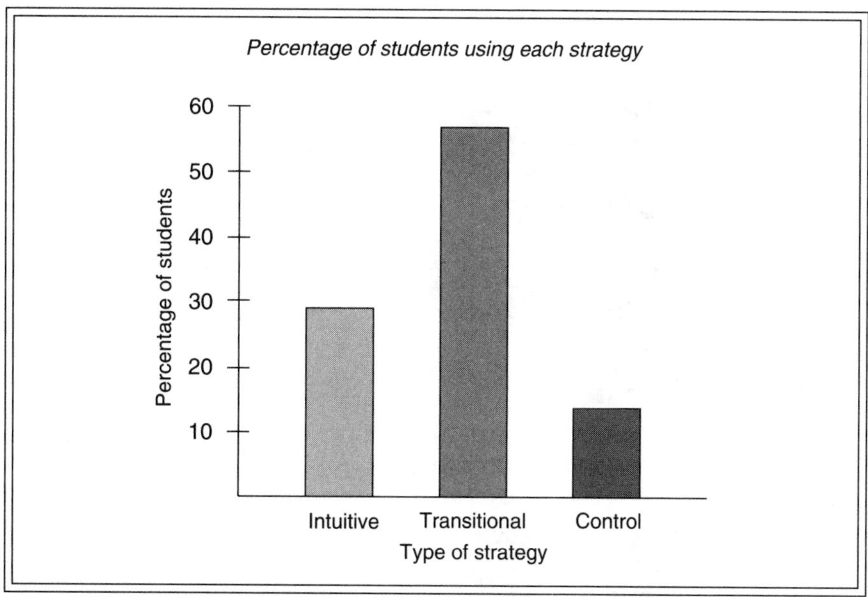

Adapted from Karplus et al. (1979)

These results, based on a large sample of students, clearly corroborate the findings of other researchers that the development of formal thought cannot be assumed to be complete in adolescents. Overall, Karplus et al. (1979) found 251 students (or about 7% of their sample) who consistently used a ratio strategy on the paper clip task and a control strategy on the track task; in contrast, they identified 422 students (or about 14%) who consistently used intuitive reasoning on all clip-task questions and all track-task questions. Based on their total sample of 3,300 students, Karplus et al. (1979) found that about 37% of eighth-graders do not use formal operational thinking in either the proportional reasoning or control-of-variable task, and that another 36% fail to use formal operational thinking on both types of tasks. Thus the majority of eighth-graders do not consistently show evidence of formal operational reasoning.

Klahr (2000) found similar evidence that students have difficulty with two important aspects of scientific reasoning—generating theories and interpreting data. Elementary school students in grades three through six were taught how to control a programmable toy vehicle called Big Trak, using a keypad such as shown in Figure 6–22. For example, to make the vehicle turn right 15 minutes (i.e., 90 degrees), move forward 5 steps, and fire its gun 3 times, you would press CLR (to clear all previous commands), the right arrow, the number 15, the up arrow, the number 5, the fire button, the number 3, and the GO button (to run the program). Then, students were asked to figure out what the RPT button does. They could program the Big Trak as many times as they wanted. The correct answer is that RPT *n* means repeat the last *n* steps, but only 2 out of 22 students discovered this rule.

FIGURE 6–22 The keyboard for programming Big Trak: What does RPT do?

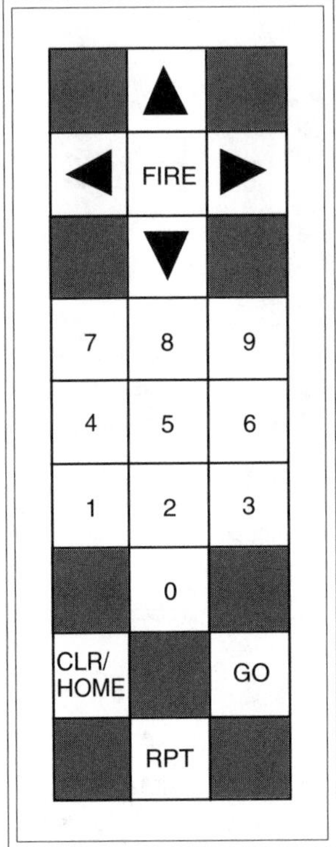

From Klahr (2000)

When this task was given to elementary school children, they demonstrated difficulty in considering possible theories. They tended to focus on one kind of theory—counter theories in which RPT *n* means to repeat something (e.g., the entire program, the last step, the next step) *n* times; almost none of the children ever considered selector theories in which RPT *n* means one repeat of something (e.g., the last *n* steps, the first *n* steps, the *n*th step). In addition, when students ran an experiment and found that the results conflicted with their predictions, they did not change from a counter theory to a selector theory. Instead, they either ignored the results or tested a different version of the counter theory. Klahr (2000, p. 119) concludes that students need to learn "domain-general skills" for how to generate theories and how to interpret relevant data.

HYPOTHESIS CREATION. How do people make scientific discoveries? For example, suppose that you wanted to discover how the genes in the simple bacterium *E. coli* control the production of glucose, which is needed for the bacterium to live. When lactose is present, the *E. coli* secretes enzymes, called beta-gal, that convert the lactose into glucose. The top panel of Figure 6–23 shows some of the genes that may be involved in glucose production: the beta-genes produce beta-gal, which converts lactose into glucose, whereas the I-gene, P-gene, and/or O-gene may be involved in controlling the beta genes.

Let's try an experiment that is simulated on a computer screen. Suppose you allow 100 micrograms of lactose, represented as a large white square, to enter the *E. coli*. As soon as the lactose is under the beta genes, they produce 50 micrograms of beta-gal, represented as small black rectangles. The beta-gal (small black rectangles) breaks the lactose (large white rectangle) into glucose, which is represented as white triangles. This reaction takes about 12 seconds and is summarized in the bottom three panels of Figure 6–23.

Suppose that you can conduct experiments by manipulating three variables and seeing the results simulated on the screen. First, you select one of six amounts of lactose to be input—0, 100, 200, 300, 400, or 500 micrograms. Second, you select one of four types of mutations—normal *E. coli*, I-gene mutation, P-gene mutation, or O-gene mutation. In this experiment, only one gene can be mutated on a chromosome. If a gene is mutated, it does not work. Third, you select one of two chromosome structures—haploid, which contains one set of genes, and diploid, which contains two sets of genes so a gene can be mutated on one chromosome but not the other, and vice versa. If the I-gene, P-gene, or O-gene controls the beta genes by chemical signal, then the beta-genes will produce beta-gal as long as one of the two chromosomes contains the needed genes. If the I-gene, P-gene, or O-gene controls the beta-genes by physical contact, then beta-gal will be produced only when the activator gene is on the same chromosome as the enzyme-producing genes. For each experiment, you learn how much beta-gal was produced. The goal is to determine what controls how much beta-gal is produced.

What is your initial hypothesis? If you are like the subjects in a study conducted by Dunbar (1993), you might begin by hypothesizing that one of the genes (such as the P-gene) activates the production of beta-gal. Based on the first study, in which 100 units of lactose were input and 50 units beta-gal were output, you may have the idea that when a certain amount of lactose is input, the beta-genes in normal *E. coli* will produce half that amount of beta-gal. To test your hypothesis, you introduce 200 micrograms of lactose into a haploid with a P-gene mutation. If the P-gene activates the production of beta-gal, then no beta-gal should be produced. However, when you conduct the experiment you find that 100 micrograms of beta-gal were produced, the same amount as you would expect for normal *E. coli*.

Undaunted, you may now try a new hypothesis—namely, that the I-gene activates beta-gal production. However, when 200 micrograms of lactose are put into a haploid with a mutated I-gene, 876 micrograms of beta-gal are produced. Clearly, the hypothesis is not supported. Similarly, to test the hypothesis that the O-gene activates the beta-genes, you put 200 micrograms of lactose into a haploid with a mutated O-gene. In contrast to your prediction, 527 micrograms of beta-gal are produced. These results are summarized in Table 6–2. Overall, normal *E. coli* and *E. coli* with P-gene mutations produce an amount of beta-gal that is half the amount of lactose added; *E-coli* with a mutated I-gene produces 876 units of beta-gal, regardless of how much lactose is added; and *E-coli* with a mutated O-gene produces 527 micrograms of beta-gal, regardless of how much lactose is added.

Dunbar (1993) found that all 20 of the subjects in his experiment began with the hypothesis that one of the genes—either I, O, or P—detected the presence of lactose and activated the beta-genes to produce of beta-gal. However, these hypothesis generated predictions that conflicted with the results—in no case did a mutated gene result in zero production of beta-gal. After an hour of experimentation, most of the subjects concluded that

FIGURE 6–23 How do genes in E. coli control production of glucose?

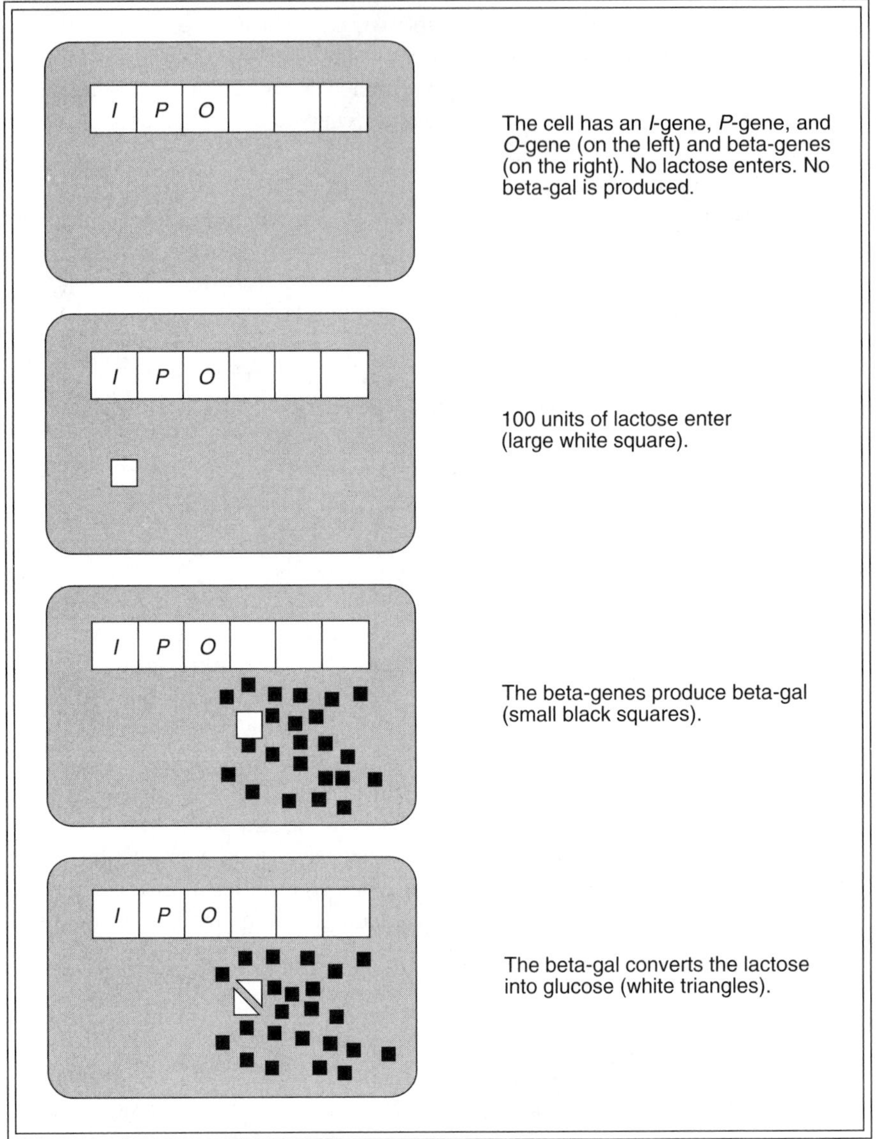

I
P
O
The cell has an *I*-gene, *P*-gene, and *O*-gene (on the left) and beta-genes (on the right). No lactose enters. No beta-gal is produced.
I
P
O
100 units of lactose enter (large white square).
I
P
O
The beta-genes produce beta-gal (small black squares).
I
P
O
The beta-gal converts the lactose into glucose (white triangles).

Adapted from Dunbar (1993)

TABLE 6–2

Results of experiments with *E. coli*

Cell Type	Mutated Genes	Amount of Lactose Input	Amount of Beta-Gal Output
Haploid	None	100	50
Haploid	P	200	100
Haploid	I	200	876
Haploid	O	200	527

Adapted from Dunbar (1993)

all three genes worked in combination as activators, a conclusion that is inconsistent with the data but consistent with their initial view that the genes are activators.

In contrast, seven subjects constructed a radically different hypothesis that involved inhibition, and of these, four subjects actually discovered the correct hypothesis—that the I- and O-genes worked together as inhibitors as follows: When no lactose is present, the I-gene sends an inhibitor that binds to the O-gene, blocking the production of beta-gal by the beta-genes. When lactose is introduced, the inhibitor (which is produced by the I-gene) binds with the lactose and not the O-gene. Thus, the beta-genes are no longer inhibited, so they produce beta-gal. After the beta-gal converts all of the lactose to glucose, the *E. coli* returns to the inhibited state until more lactose is added. A Nobel Prize was awarded to Jacques Monod and Francois Jacob in 1965 for the discovery of this mechanism.

Why did some students retain their initial activation theory of how genes control enzyme production, whereas other people were able to invent a new theory based on inhibition? Both groups conducted about the same number of experiments, but they differed in their goals. The activation theory people focused on trying to find a situation in which no beta-gal was produced, that is, on finding a situation that confirmed their hypothesis. The inhibition theory people focused on trying to discover why *E. coli* with mutated I-genes or O-genes produced such large outputs of beta-gal, that is, on finding an explanation for an anomaly. Sample comments that subjects made as they solved the problem are given in Figure 6–24. These results are consistent with the findings from other research on scientific reasoning in which unsuccessful problem solvers displayed *confirmation bias*—a strategy of trying to find evidence to support one's theory (Klahr & Dunbar, 1988; Klayman & Ha, 1987). Chinn and Brewer (1993) identified strategies that science students use to discount anomalous data and therefore avoid conceptual change.

IMPLICATIONS FOR INSTRUCTION: TEACHING SCIENTIFIC REASONING

In essence the science educator is confronted with two different conceptions of scientific inquiry: scientific reasoning as the systematic testing of hypotheses and scientific reasoning as the creation of hypotheses. Although Piagetian research on formal operations

FIGURE 6–24 Two approaches to scientific discovery

AN ACTIVATION-THEORY STUDENT SEEKS TO CONFIRM A HYPOTHESIS

"Right now, my objective is to find a way such that nothing is produced. That's my objective. Um. Ok. So, so far I've tried the combinations of *O* absent. I've tried the combination of *I* absent. *O* absent, *I* absent. Uh . . . *I* present, *O* present, *P* present, it gives me 200. If I take away the *P*, it gives me 876. No, if I take away *I*, it gives me a much much greater amount. . . . Question: How to . . . make nothing appear? Have I tried all the combinations?"

AN INHIBITION-THEORY STUDENT SEEKS TO EXPLAIN A DISCREPANCY

"As long as there's lactose present there's beta; you can break it down into glucose. In this case [points to the result for the *I*-gene mutant] they seem to be unregulated. They produce this much [points to an output of 876]. Why do they produce 876?"

From Dunbar (1993)

emphasized the generality of hypothesis testing strategies (Inhelder & Piaget, 1958), more recent research on conceptual change pointed to the domain specificity of scientific discovery (Carey, 1986; West & Pines, 1985). For example, Kuhn, Amsel, and O'Loughlin (1988) note:

> The lack of generality of formal operational strategies across a range of content . . . has left science educators wondering whether it is reasonable to suppose that they reflect developmental stages in scientific thinking, appropriate as the focus of attention of educators wishing to design curricula to develop scientific thinking skills. (p. 232)

According to the systematic testing view, students need training in how to systematically test their hypotheses, including training in how to control for extraneous variables. In short, they must overcome unsystematic or illogical hypothesis testing. According to the conceptual-change view, students need to learn to seize on discrepancies or anomalies as interesting facts to be explained, and to seek alternative theories that can better account for the data. In other words, they need to overcome the tendency to seek data that confirm their theory and to ignore discrepant data.

TEACHING HYPOTHESIS TESTING. An important educational question that emerges from this research is whether scientific thinking can be taught. To address this question, Lawson and Snitgen (1982) used an inquiry-based approach to a college course entitled "Biological Science for the Elementary Teacher." Students were given problems, asked to generate experiments, carry them out, and to compare their results with other students. For example, students were asked to determine the energy source(s) for growing plants. This required systematically varying variables such as watering, lighting, and soil composition, and noting their effects on various seed parts.

Concepts relevant to the control of variables were introduced during the discussion and applied in subsequent experiments. A similar procedure was used to introduce examples of proportional reasoning.

Students were given pretests and posttests. Figure 6–25 shows that there were substantial pretest-to-posttest gains in performance on tests of proportional reasoning and control-of-variables—both of which were explicitly taught as part of the inquiry-based course; however, scores on tests of conservation of weight and volume were not affected by instruction and were not explicitly part of the instruction. These results are promising because they suggest that scientific reasoning can be taught through a carefully planned inquiry-based approach to science, and are consistent with previous experiments that successfully increased scientific thinking (i.e., formal thinking) in science students (Lawson & Wollman, 1976; McKinnon & Renner, 1971; Wollman & Lawson, 1978). However, the findings must be viewed critically in light of the fact that no control group received noninquiry training.

Hands-on experience is sometimes viewed as a guaranteed means of fostering creativity in students; similarly, the quality of a school's science program is often measured by the amount of laboratory experience given to students. Yet the research presented in this section implies that hands-on laboratory work can be unproductive, especially when students do not approach problems scientifically. It is not lab activity per se that induces science learning; instead, students must be encouraged to think scientifically about situations, to control variables, to test hypotheses, and so on. Thus, even though lab experience is an important component in school science programs, it must be administered in a way that fosters scientific thinking rather than blind activity.

FIGURE 6–25 Changes in scientific thinking following training

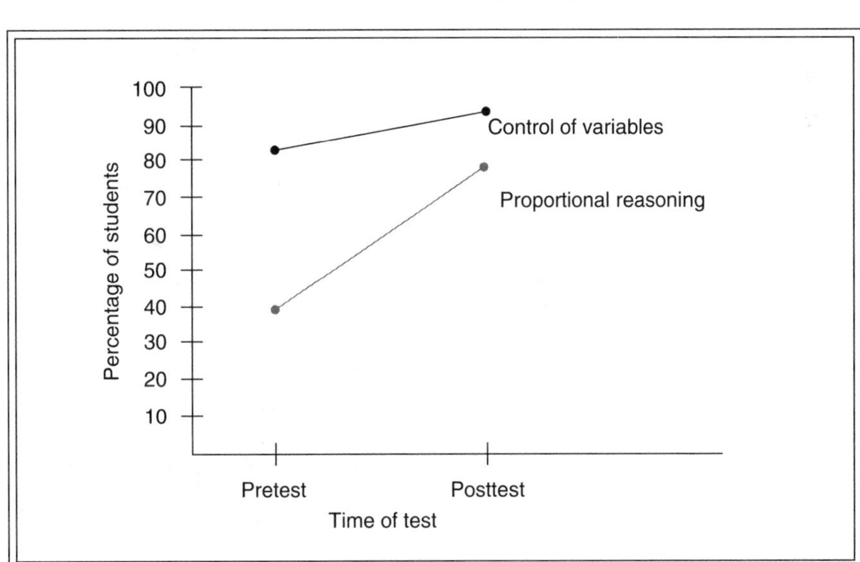

Adapted from Lawson and Snitgen (1982)

TEACHING HYPOTHESIS CREATION. Scientific thinking requires a sensitivity to evidence that refute one's theory. However, Kuhn et al. (1988) found that students often misunderstood the distinction between theory and data. For example, students ranging in age from eight years old to adult were asked to determine which features of tennis balls—such as size, texture, or color—affected the quality of a player's serve. When asked to state whether a certain piece of evidence supported or refuted their theory, students of all ages had difficulty. When asked to suggest evidence that would refute their theory, many were unable to do so. These results are consistent with the idea that many students view data only as evidence that could support rather than refute a theory.

Can students learn to change their view of scientific experimentation? Carey, Evans, Honda, Jay, and Unger (1989) developed a three-week science unit for seventh-graders that focused on students' beliefs about formulating and testing hypotheses. As part of the unit, students made and tested hypotheses about why bread dough rises. They began with the question, "What makes bread rise?" The teacher mixed yeast, flour, sugar, salt, and warm water in a flask with a corked top. Soon the mixture began to bubble and the cork flew off. The next question was "Why do yeast, flour, sugar, salt, and warm water produce a gas?" The students conducted experiments using various combinations of ingredients, but their goal seemed to be to reproduce the bubbling phenomenon. They worked unsystematically and failed to determine which ingredients are needed to produce bubbles. When the teacher asked the students to draw conclusions from their experiments, they were unable to do so. Next the teacher helped the class design well-controlled experiments that revealed that the bubbling is caused by only yeast, sugar, and water. The teacher continued the lesson by emphasizing that the goal of experimentation is to determine why these ingredients produce bubbling. The act of constructing an explanation required the students to consider theories such as the bubbles are caused by a chemical reaction involving the three ingredients or the bubbles are caused by the process of the yeast eating the sugar and producing gas as a result of the metabolism. Here the class learned to seek evidence that could refute or support each theory. Experiments were designed and conducted, and the students had to determine how the results related to the possible explanations. Throughout the lesson, the students were learning that the goal of experimentation is to explain why something happened rather than to produce a certain result.

Carey et al. (1989) assessed the effectiveness of their lesson by interviewing students before and after instruction. Students were asked about the purpose of science, experiments, hypotheses, research ideas, and results. Figure 6–26 lists several levels of answers for the various questions in the interview. For example, a low-level answer concerning experimentation is that "an experiment is when you try something new"—that is, an activity that is not guided by a question or idea. A high-level answer is that "an experiment is when scientists test to see if they need to change their idea." Figure 6–27 summarizes the pretest to posttest gains for each topic. Overall, scores improved substantially, showing that the instructional program was successful in changing students' scientific thinking. Success in teaching of scientific thinking skills has been reported by a growing number of researchers (Eylon & Linn, 1988; Halpern, 1992). These results encourage a revision of science education curricula to emphasize the nature of scientific reasoning as a creative process.

FIGURE 6–26

A survey about scientific thinking

The goals of science are:

__________ (1) to discover new things, e.g., "to find a cure for cancer"

__________ (2) to find out how things work, e.g., "to find out how animals get oxygen"

__________ (3) to explain why things are the way they are, e.g., "to explain why the dinosaurs became extinct"

An experiment is:

__________ (0) when you try something new

__________ (1) when scientists try to find out about the thing they're experimenting on

__________ (2) when scientists test to see if their idea is right

__________ (3) when scientists test to see if they need to change their idea

Scientists do their work by:

__________ (0) doing experiments on whatever they feel like

__________ (1) gathering new information, e.g., "putting things under microscopes to see how they behave"

__________ (2) gathering information for a purpose, e.g., "walking through a forest, finding something new, and trying to learn more about it"

__________ (3) creating ideas and testing them, e.g., "probably thinking up an idea, and then building an experiment out of the idea"

An unexpected result shows:

__________ (1) that something needs to be changed to make the experiment come out right

__________ (2) that either the experiment or the scientist's idea must be changed

__________ (3) that the scientist's idea must be changed to fit with the new result

Note: To determine overall score, add the number of points on each item

Adapted from Carey et al. (1989)

FIGURE 6–27 Pretest and posttest scores of students given a lesson on scientific thinking

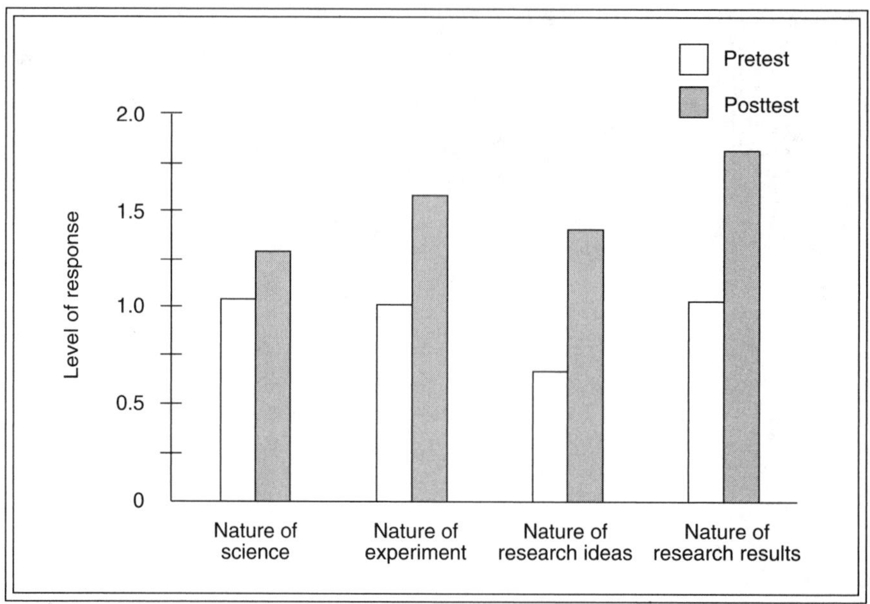

Adapted from Carey et al. (1989)

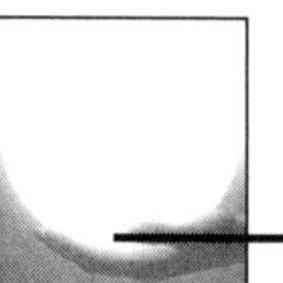

BUILDING SCIENTIFIC EXPERTISE: LEARNING TO BUILD AND USE SCIENTIFIC KNOWLEDGE

THEORY: QUANTITATIVE VERSUS QUALITATIVE DIFFERENCES

The foregoing sections show that science learning involves recognizing one's misconceptions, building new conceptions, and using the new conceptions in scientific reasoning. Another approach to the study of science learning involves comparing novices, such as students in a beginning science course, to experts, such as established scientists. The main question addressed in this approach is, What do experts know that novices do not?

Experts and novices may differ *quantitatively*—in terms of how much they know—as well as *qualitatively*—in terms of what they know. According to a traditional view of cognitive growth, experts simply know more about a domain than novices. For example, an experienced physicist knows more facts and formulas about the physical world than a first-year physics student. In contrast, according to the cognitive-change view, in addition to possessing more facts, an expert's knowledge is qualitatively different from a novice's knowledge. For example, an experienced physicist is not only faster in solving problems but goes about solving problems in a way that differs from a first-year physics student.

These two contrasting views present important implications for instruction. If becoming an expert is mainly a process of acquiring more and more information, then instruction should emphasize the acquisition of facts and formulas. Instead, if the development of expertise involves a progressive restructuring of knowledge, then instruction must help students not only to acquire facts but also to reorganize their knowledge in useful ways. In short, if experts look at problems differently than novices do, then instruction should encourage novices to think like experts. Research comparing expert and novice physicists provides convincing evidence that the expert-novice shift involves a qualitative change rather than solely a quantitative one (Carey, 1986).

RESEARCH COMPARING NOVICE AND EXPERT PHYSICISTS

Let's begin with a typical problem similar to those found in first-year physics courses (Larkin, McDermott, Simon, & Simon, 1980a, 1980b)—the car problem in Figure 6–28. This problem comes from a domain in physics called *kinematics.* Kinematics involves the study of motion, and the kinematics chapter in a physics textbook generally contains about a dozen formulas expressing relations among variables such as time, distance, average velocity, initial velocity, terminal velocity, and acceleration. Some potentially useful formulas for the car problem are listed in Figure 6–28.

If you have had an introductory physics course and are willing to engage in some serious thinking, you may be able to solve this problem. However, if you are an experienced physicist who has spent many years studying and using physics, you can probably solve this problem almost immediately without much effort. For example, Larkin et al. (1980a, 1980b) found that first-year physics students took four times longer than physics professors to solve problems like this one. This difference in performance prompts the question of what an expert knows about physics that a novice does not.

FIGURE 6–28 The car problem

A car traveling 25 meters per second is brought to rest at a constant rate in 20 seconds by applying the brake. How far did it move after the brake was applied?

Here are some useful equations:

1. distance = average speed × time
2. final speed = initial speed + (acceleration × time)
3. average speed = (initial speed + final speed)/2
4. distance = (initial speed × time) + 1/2(acceleration) × time^2
5. final speed^2 – initial speed^2 = 2(acceleration × distance)

Adapted from Larkin, McDermott, Simon, and Simon (1980b)

Mayer (1992) has identified four types of knowledge involved in physics expertise:

Factual knowledge: Basic knowledge of physics, including physical laws such as *force = mass × acceleration.*

Semantic knowledge: Knowledge of the concepts that underlie the variables in physical laws, such as knowing what force, mass, and acceleration mean.

Schematic knowledge: Knowledge of problem types, such as knowing whether a given problem involves conservation of momentum.

Strategic knowledge: Knowledge of how to generate and monitor plans for solving a problem, such as working backward from the goal to the givens.

In this section, we examine how expert physicists differ from novice physicists in terms of factual knowledge, semantic knowledge, schematic knowledge, and strategic knowledge. These differences are summarized in Table 6–3.

EXPERT/NOVICE DIFFERENCES IN FACTUAL KNOWLEDGE. Why do experts solve the car problem so much more quickly than novices? One possibility is that experts' factual knowledge is stored more accessibly than novices'. Suppose, for example, that novices store factual knowledge in small or separate units, such as individual formulas:

Formula 1: distance = average speed × time
Formula 3: average speed = (initial speed + final speed)/2

whereas experts store such factual knowledge in large or interconnected units such as combined formulas:

Formulas 1–3: distance = [(initial speed + final speed)/2] × time

Experts can thus work more quickly than novices on problems requiring the use of many equations because they do not have to retrieve as many pieces of information. If experts look for a formula involving distance, they can find what they need by retrieving one large formula, whereas novices would first retrieve formula 1 and then need to search for a formula involving average speed (i.e., formula 3).

TABLE 6–3

Expert versus novice differences in physics

Type of Knowledge	Novices	Experts
Factual knowledge	Possess small functional units of knowledge	Possess large functional units of knowledge
Semantic knowledge	Build naive representations	Build physics-based representations
Schematic knowledge	Categorize based on surface similarities	Categorize based on structural similarities
Strategic knowledge	Work backward from unknown to givens	Work forward from givens to unknown

Adapted from Mayer (1992)

In order to examine this hypothesis about expert/novice differences, Larkin (1979) presented kinematics problems like the car problem to first-year physics students (novices) and physics professors (experts). The subjects were asked to "think aloud" by describing what was going on inside their heads as they solved the problem. An analysis of their *thinking-aloud protocols*—the transcripts of what they said as they worked—revealed that experts and novices both generated several formulas but at different rates. Novices produced formulas individually, at a random rate, suggesting that the formulas are stored separately in memory. In contrast, experts produced formulas in clusters, generating some in a rapid burst, followed by a delay and then another burst of multiple formulas. This pattern suggests that experts store their factual knowledge in large units consisting of two or more formulas.

These results are summarized in the top row of Table 6–3. Novices store their factual knowledge of physics as individual equations that are separate from one another (i.e., small units) whereas experts possess interconnected solution equations that can be accessed as a whole (i.e., large units). Thus, while novices have to proceed step-by-step and do a lot of checking, experts are able to solve the problem all at once using a more integrated procedure.

EXPERT/NOVICE DIFFERENCES IN SEMANTIC KNOWLEDGE. A second kind of knowledge needed to solve the car problem is semantic knowledge, that is, knowledge of concepts underlying the problem situation. Physicists need to know not only the formulas but also what the terms in the formulas mean and how they relate to descriptions in physics problems. For example, consider the three-cart problem in Figure 6–29. What do you see when you look over this problem?

FIGURE 6–29 The three-cart problem

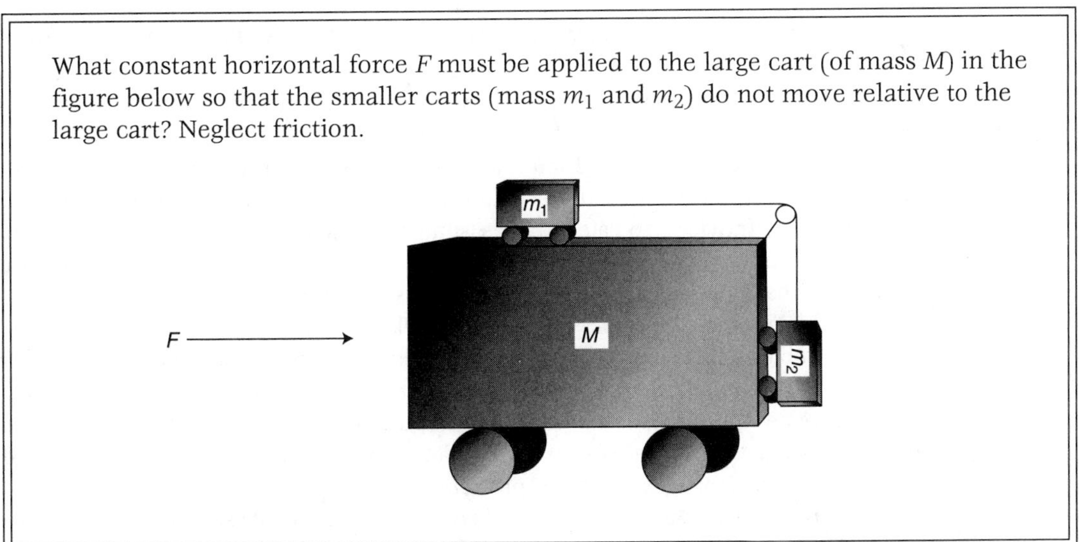

What constant horizontal force F must be applied to the large cart (of mass M) in the figure below so that the smaller carts (mass m_1 and m_2) do not move relative to the large cart? Neglect friction.
m_1
F
M
m_2

Adapted from Larkin (1983)

If you are like the novices in a study by Larkin (1983), you see the most obvious surface entities: a large cart, two small carts, some ropes, and a pulley. This view is not much help in determining which formulas to use to solve the problem because it does not allow you to make a connection between the surface features of the problem and the underlying physics principles. For example, here's how a typical first-year physics student got stuck in trying to solve the three-cart problem (Larkin, 1983, p. 81):

> Well, I'm right now trying to reason why it isn't going to move. . . . Once I visualize it, I can probably get started. But I don't see how it is going to work.

Based on students' thinking-aloud protocols, Larkin (1983) concluded that novices build naive representations of the problem that are not semantically related to physics concepts.

In contrast, if you are like the experts in Larkin's (1983) study, you may be able to see the physics concepts, such as forces, underlying the problem. For example, a typical expert saw beyond the surface features of the problem (Larkin, 1983):

> Well, with a uniformly accelerating frame of reference, all right? So that there is a pseudo-force on m_1 to the left that is just equivalent, just necessary to balance out the weight of m_2. (p. 81)

According to Larkin's analysis of thinking-aloud protocols, experts tend to build physics-based representations. Instead of seeing ropes and carts, they see an object at rest on an accelerating frame of reference, and they see two forces acting on the small cart—on the left is a pseudoforce caused by the motion of the large cart acting to the left and on the right is a tension force caused by the connection to the pulley.

The second row of Table 6–3 summarizes the conclusion that the novice's representation of the problem is based on surface features, whereas the expert's representation is based on underlying physics conceptions. The expert is better able than the novice to access the appropriate formulas by virtue of being able to view the problem in terms of its underlying physics variables.

EXPERT/NOVICE DIFFERENCES IN SCHEMATIC KNOWLEDGE. A third kind of knowledge needed to solve physics problems is schematic knowledge, that is knowledge of problem types. For example, suppose that you are given several physics problems, such as those in Figure 6–30, and asked to sort them into groups.

Did you put problems 1 and 2 into the same category, and problem 3 into a different category? That's what happened when Chi, Feltovich, and Glaser (1981) asked eight undergraduates (novices) to categorize 24 similar problems like those found in Figure 6–30. According to Chi et al. (1981), the novices sorted the problems based on surface similarities, that is, on the physical characteristics of the objects. For example, novices placed problems involving blocks on an inclined plane (such as problems 1 and 2) in one category, problems involving springs (such as problem 3) in another category, problems involving pulleys in another, and so on. When the novices were asked to justify putting problems 1 and 2 in the same category, they emphasized the similarities in their physical features, saying, "These deal with blocks on an inclined plane," or "blocks on inclined planes with angles," or "inclined plane problems."

In contrast, when Chi et al. (1981) asked eight advanced physics graduate students (experts) to sort the problems, they placed problems 2 and 3 into one category and problem 1 into a different one. If you did the same, you are thinking like an expert. According

FIGURE 6–30 Which two problems belong in the same category?

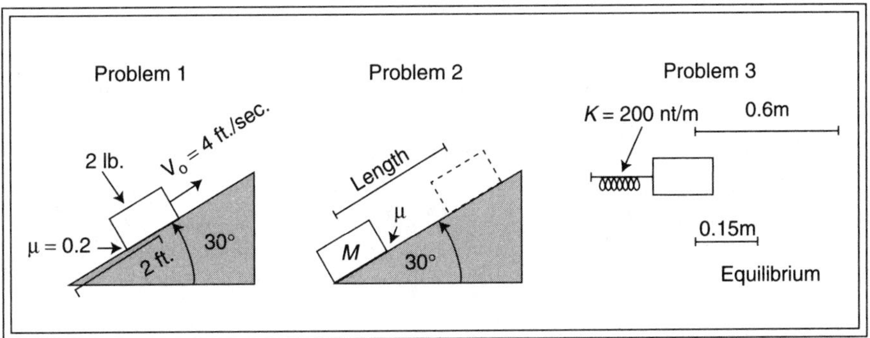

Adapted from Chi, Feltovich, and Glaser (1981)

to Chi et al. (1981), experts categorize the problems based on structural similarities, that is, on the physics principle required to solve them. For example, problems 2 and 3, although involving different objects, both are based on the law of conservation of energy, so experts put them together. When asked to explain why they placed problems 2 and 3 in the same category, experts gave answers such as, "conservation of energy," or "work-energy theorem," or "These can be done from energy considerations; either you should know the principle of conservation of energy or work is lost somewhere."

In summary, experts and novices seem to possess different categories for problems. As shown in the third row of Table 6–3, novices base their categories on surface similarities, whereas experts base theirs on structural similarities.

EXPERT/NOVICE DIFFERENCES IN STRATEGIC KNOWLEDGE. A fourth difference between experts and novices concerns their solution strategies. For example, suppose I were to ask you to describe what you are thinking as you solve the car problem shown in Figure 6–28. When Larkin et al. (1980a, 1980b) asked first-year physics students (novices) to do this, they tended to work backward from the goal to the given. When dealing with the car problem, a novice begins by asking, "What am I trying to find?" and determines that the main unknown is the distance the car travels. Then, the novice decides to use Formula 1 because it is the best-known formula involving distance. The next step is to look for the values of average speed and time in the problem. The novice finds average time—20 seconds—but not average speed. Again, the novice asks, "What am I trying to find?" and decides that it is average speed. She remembers a formula involving average speed—namely, formula 3—and then searches for the values of initial speed and final speed. She finds initial speed (25 meters per second) but becomes confused, not realizing that the final speed must be 0 meters per second. Having failed to solve formula 3, the novice looks for another formula involving distance and finds formula 4. Trying to solve for distance in formula 4, she sees that the problem contains values for initial speed (25 meters per second) and time (20 seconds) but not for acceleration. Her next goal is to find an equation involving acceleration, so she selects formula 2. This time she also finds values for initial speed, final speed, and time, and therefore is able to compute a value for acceleration using formula 2. She now can plug this value into formula 4 and derive a value for distance. Thus, the novice works backward, beginning with what she is trying to find and moving toward the givens. In the process she uses formulas 1, 3, 4, 2, and 4, in that order.

In contrast, when Larkin et al. (1980a, 1980b) asked experienced physicists to solve this problem, they tended to work forward from the givens to the unknown. For example, an expert begins by using formula 3, which calls for adding initial speed (25 meters per second) to final speed (0 meters per second), and dividing the sum by 2 to determine average speed (12.5 meters per second). Then, the expert plugs the newly calculated value of average speed (12.5 meters per second) and the value of time (20 seconds) from the problem into formula 1, yielding a value for distance: $12.5 \times 20 = 250$ meters. Thus, the expert solves the problem by working forward, that is, by systematically combining the given values to produce a calculated value of the unknown.

As a way of further testing these observations, Larkin et al. (1980a, 1980b) produced a computer program that simulates the problem-solving performance of experts and novices. The expert program works forward and uses large functional units, while the novice program works backward and uses small functional units. The main output of the program is a listing of the order in which formulas were used. The output of the expert program is fairly consistent with that of human experts, and the output of the novice program is fairly consistent with that of the human novices. Thus there is some reason to believe that the simulations correctly describe expert/novice differences.

Why do experts work forward whereas novices work backward? The choice of strategy may be influenced by the way that the subjects store their factual knowledge. If experts store knowledge in large units, as previously described, then they can simply plug values into a large solution formula. However, if novices store knowledge in small units, as previously described, they must figure out how to put the equations together, a process that lends itself to working from the unknown back to the goal. This difference in expert versus novice strategies is summarized in the fourth row of Table 6–3. However, subsequent research in other domains, such as medical expertise, reveals that even experts may work backward when they are given an unfamiliar problem (Groen & Patel, 1988). For first-year physics problems, experts work forward more often than novices because problems that are unfamiliar for novices, and therefore require a backward-moving strategy, are often familiar for experts, and therefore permit a forward-moving strategy.

IMPLICATIONS FOR INSTRUCTION: FOSTERING SCIENTIFIC EXPERTISE

Research on expertise raises the practical question of how a teacher could help a student move from novice to expert status. Shavelson (1972, 1974) provided an interesting analysis of changes in the way that students structure their knowledge of physics following instruction. In one study, high school students in the trained group read lessons about Newtonian physics over the course of five days, while control students did not receive physics instruction. Students were given pretests and posttests measuring achievement and knowledge structure.

The achievement test measured retention of material from the lesson, using a standard multiple-choice format. As expected, the control group did not show a significant pretest to posttest gain (30% to 32%), but the trained group did show a significant pretest to posttest gain (33% to 54%).

The knowledge structure test listed 14 key concepts. For each key concept, the subjects were given one minute to write down all the words they could think of. The 14 key concepts are momentum, inertia, power, mass, time, work, weight, acceleration, force, distance, velocity, impulse, speed, and energy. Based on the word association responses given for the knowledge structure test, Shavelson was able to determine how strongly each of the 14 key words was related to each of the other words. For example, if a subject listed many of the same words for force and mass, then a relatedness index would indicate that these two concepts were highly related. As expected, the pretest results indicated that subjects entered the study with preexisting conceptions of Newtonian mechanics terms; clusters of terms were related by the students, although not in the way that Newtonian physics prescribes. The knowledge structure test was given after each of the five lessons. As Figure 6–31 shows, the relatedness

FIGURE 6–31 Changes in knowledge structure following physics instruction

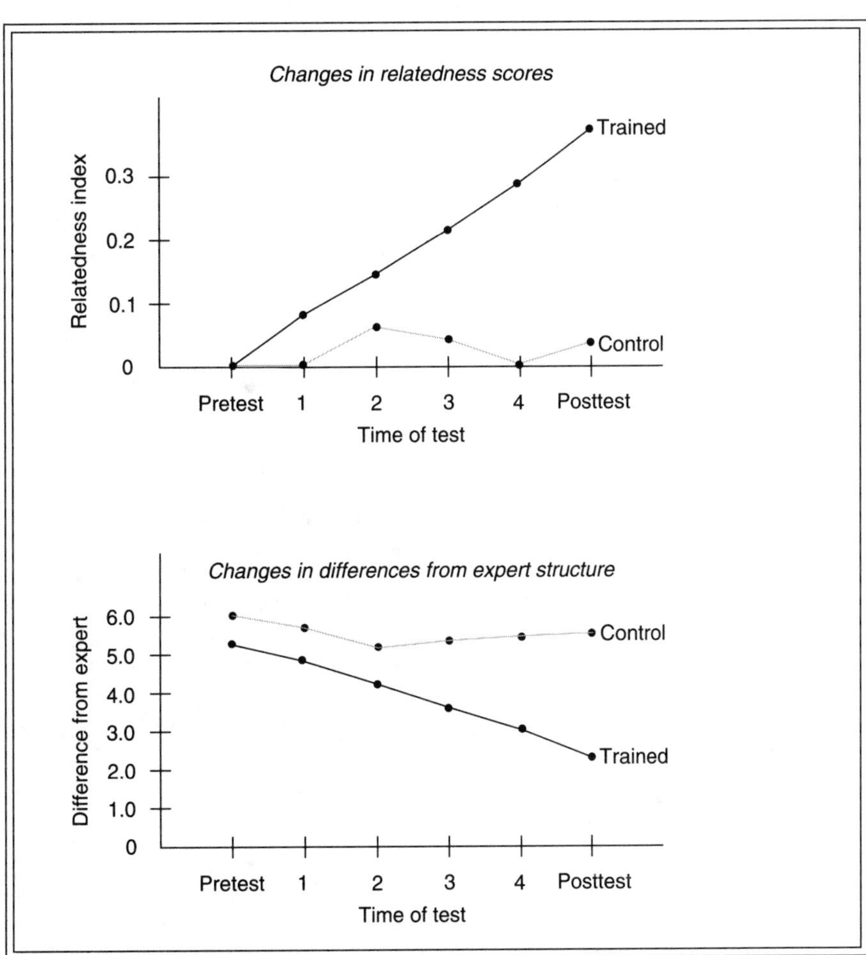

Adapted from Shavelson (1972)

index increased each day for the trained group but remained low throughout the study for the control group. In addition, Shavelson derived the expert word-association responses based on the actual relations expressed in physics equations. Figure 6–31 demonstrates that the difference between the expert knowledge structure and that of the trained group decreased with each day of instruction; in contrast, the control group showed no change. These results are consistent with the idea that training in physics not only enhances general achievement but also influences the way in which knowledge is organized in memory. With training, the students are less likely to organize key concepts based on their underlying meanings and more likely to relate them based on the rules of physics.

What are the instructional implications of this line of research? Simon (1980) suggested that science training should include two basic goals: to provide a rich knowledge base (e.g., lots of experience with the major formulas in kinematics), and to develop general problem-solving strategies relevant to the science (e.g., how to recognize problem types and work forward). Simon (1980) argued that there is no substitute for experience, and Hayes (1985) estimated that to become an expert in a field requires approximately 10 years of study. In addition, to achieve expertise one must have extensive experience with worked-out examples done by experts (Simon, 1980).

A major controversy in science education concerns the relative merits of teaching the fruits of scientific research (science facts) versus teaching how to do science (scientific thinking). The research on expertise suggests that facts and hands-on experience alone are not sufficient. Students need both a certain amount of basic factual knowledge as well as training in problem-solving skills that can applied to this knowledge. Unfortunately, many science textbooks contain large numbers of relatively isolated facts about the physical world. Student memorization of a large number of such facts should not be the main goal of science instruction. Instead, the goal must be to help students understand the physical and natural events in the world. This goal requires well-organized knowledge as well as practice in scientific problem solving.

CHAPTER SUMMARY

The traditional view of science learning involves adding more and more information to one's memory. According to the cognitive-change view, however, learning occurs when one's knowledge is radically restructured; that is, when one's current conception (or mental model) is replaced with a new one. Conceptual change involves three steps: (1) recognizing an anomaly, (2) constructing a new model, and (3) using a new model.

This chapter examines four aspects of conceptual change in science learning. First, learners enter the science classroom with many preexisting misconceptions or incomplete conceptions that conflict with the teacher's conceptions. Conceptual-change theory emphasizes that the goal of science is explanation rather than solely description of the natural universe. Students often develop naive conceptions of physics, based on the idea that "motion implies force." For example, this explanation leads them to predict that when a rolling object falls off a cliff it will go straight down. Instruction is needed to help learners recognize when their conceptions are inadequate to explain the available data and need to be discarded. A technique for helping students recognize anomalies is the predict-observe-explain method in which students predict the outcome of a simple experiment, observe that the outcome conflicts with their prediction, and then try to explain the discrepancy.

Second, learners must replace their misconceptions with new conceptions; that is, they must find a new mental model that explains the data better than their previous one. According to conceptual-change theory, science learning depends on accommodation rather than solely assimilation. Accommodative learning occurs when a learner builds a new analogy between the scientific system (called the target) and a more familiar model (called the base), such as viewing an electrical circuit as a hydraulic system. Science instruction should help students build a progression of increasingly more powerful explanations of various natural phenomenon. For example, the microworld ThinkerTools helps students to explore the laws of motion and, thereby, to replace their naive conceptions with Newtonian conceptions of motion.

Third, students need to develop scientific thinking skills, such as how to use their conceptions to solve problems. Conceptual-change theory emphasizes scientific discovery in addition to more routine thinking involving the systematic testing of hypotheses. In particular, students must learn to search for new models that will explain phenomenon rather than for evidence that will support their current theory. Piagetian-inspired research on formal operations shows that students often enter the science classroom without the skills needed for systematic scientific reasoning, including how to control variables and how to think in terms of proportions and probabilities. In addition, research on scientific discovery reveals that students often see their goal as trying to create a certain phenomenon rather than to explain the mechanism that produces the phenomenon; in short, students seek to provide evidence that supports their current theory rather than evidence that refutes it and supports a competing theory. There is encouraging evidence that both kinds of scientific reasoning can be taught. Clearly students can learn techniques that improve their performance on control-of-variables tasks and that help them view scientific reasoning as a search for a new explanation of data.

Finally, students need to acquire the knowledge needed to change from novices to experts. Consistent with conceptual-change theory, the learner who enters as a novice is qualitatively different from the expert. If we take a snapshot of the novice's knowledge structure before instruction and the expert's knowledge structure after extensive experience, we find four major differences: (1) novices organize factual knowledge in small units, whereas experts build large units; (2) novices possess semantic knowledge that encourages them to build naive representations of problems, whereas experts build physics-based representations; (3) novices have schematic knowledge in which problems are categorized based on surface similarities, whereas experts focus on structural similarities; and (4) novices' strategic knowledge is based on working backward, whereas experts work forward. Thus the acquisition of scientific knowledge includes not only adding information to memory but also reorganizing knowledge in coherent and useful ways.

In conclusion, a major conceptual change in science education involves viewing science learning as a process of making conceptual changes in students' knowledge rather than as a process of adding information to students' memories.

SUGGESTED READINGS

Carey, S. (1985). *Conceptual change in childhood.* Cambridge: MIT Press. (Argues for the conceptual-change view of learning and development, using examples from children's conceptions of biology.)

Gabel, D. L. (Ed.). (1994). *Handbook of research on science teaching and learning.* New York: Macmillan. (Reviews many of the central issues in science education.)

Limon, M., & Mason, L. (Eds.). (2002). *Reframing the process of conceptual change.* Dordrecht, The Netherlands: Kluwer. (Contains integrative summaries by leading researchers in conceptual change.)

Section II
Instruction

The second section of this book examines instruction that is intended to promote meaningful learning through giving productive feedback, making the learning situation more concrete or familiar, explaining how to solve example problems, guiding the learner's cognitive processing during learning, teaching appropriate learning strategies, teaching appropriate problem-solving strategies, creating opportunities to work in social groups, and motivating students to work hard. Chapter 7 explores the role of feedback in classroom management, response learning, concept learning, and skill learning. Chapter 8 reviews methods of instruction that rely on making the situation more concrete, allowing the learner to actively manipulate objects, and requiring learners to figure out a rule or principle on their own. Chapter 9 looks at instructional methods that explain examples or cases. Chapter 10 examines instructional techniques for improving the understandability of prose such as adding test questions, providing headings and outlines, and beginning with a familiar analogy. Chapter 11 focuses on the teaching of learning strategies, such as how to memorize lists, how to outline paragraphs, and how to summarize paragraphs. Chapter 12 examines the teaching of problem-solving strategies including several popular school-based programs. Chapter 13 reviews instructional methods based on learning in social groups including reciprocal teaching, cooperative learning, and participatory modeling. Chapter 14 explores instructional methods aimed at motivating students to try hard, including motivation based on the students' interest in an academic task, motivation based on the students' beliefs about their ability to perform an academic task, and motivation based on the students' assessment of why they failed or succeeded on an academic task. The goal of each instructional method is to enable transfer in which students are able to use what they have learned in new situations.

CHAPTER 7 Teaching by Giving Productive Feedback

CHAPTER OUTLINE

A Response Learning Task

The Law of Effect

How Do Classroom Management Techniques Affect Classroom Behavior?

How Do Rewards Affect Classroom Activities?

How Does Feedback Affect Response Learning?

How Does Feedback Affect Concept Learning?

How Does Feedback Affect Skill Learning?

Chapter Summary

When a learner is practicing a cognitive skill, a teacher can provide feedback to help promote meaningful learning. This chapter focuses on the educational implications of Thorndike's famous law of effect, the idea that learning occurs when a learner does something and receives feedback. Since the early part of the twentieth century, and even continuing on today, classroom instruction has probably been more strongly influenced by the law of effect than by any other idea in the psychology of learning. To help you better understand this principle and its relation to instruction, this chapter investigates how the law of effect can be related to classroom management. Then we explore the role of feedback in response learning, concept learning, and skill learning. For each topic, the chapter contrasts a behaviorist versus cognitive view of the learner and the learning process. Providing feedback is a long-standing method of instruction that dates back to the start of educational psychology. The premise of this chapter is that all forms of feedback are not equally useful in promoting meaningful learning: Meaningful learning can be promoted when feedback is presented as information intended to guide the learner's construction of knowledge and instill intrinsic motivation, but meaningful learning is not promoted when feedback is presented as reinforcement intended to automatically increase or decrease a response.

A RESPONSE LEARNING TASK

Let's try a simple learning task. You will need about 10 pennies (numbered 1 through 10) and a small square of paper (e.g., about 3 inches by 3 inches). Place the paper flat on the floor about 3 feet away from you. Then sit down with the pennies near you. With your eyes closed, toss each penny toward the square, trying to get the penny as close to the square as possible. After you have tossed 10 pennies, take a ruler and measure how many inches each penny landed away from the square. (If a penny landed on the square, its score is 0.) Now fill in the left portion of Figure 7–1. Place a dot indicating how far away the first penny landed from the target, how far the second penny landed, and so on for all 10 pennies. This is your *baseline* performance (i.e., your performance before any training).

Now, let's see whether you can teach yourself to be more accurate. Collect the 10 pennies and sit down where you sat before. With your eyes closed, toss a penny toward the square. Then open your eyes and measure how far off you were. Close your eyes and toss the next penny; then open your eyes and measure how far off you were. Repeat this procedure for 20 tosses. Now fill in the middle portion of Figure 7–1. Place a dot indicating how far away the first penny landed, and so on for all 20 pennies. This is your *training* performance (i.e., your performance during the training period).

Finally, repeat the procedure you used for the baseline. Sit down and, with your eyes closed, toss each of the 10 pennies. Then measure how far off each one was and fill in

FIGURE 7–1 Fill in your performance on a simple motor learning task

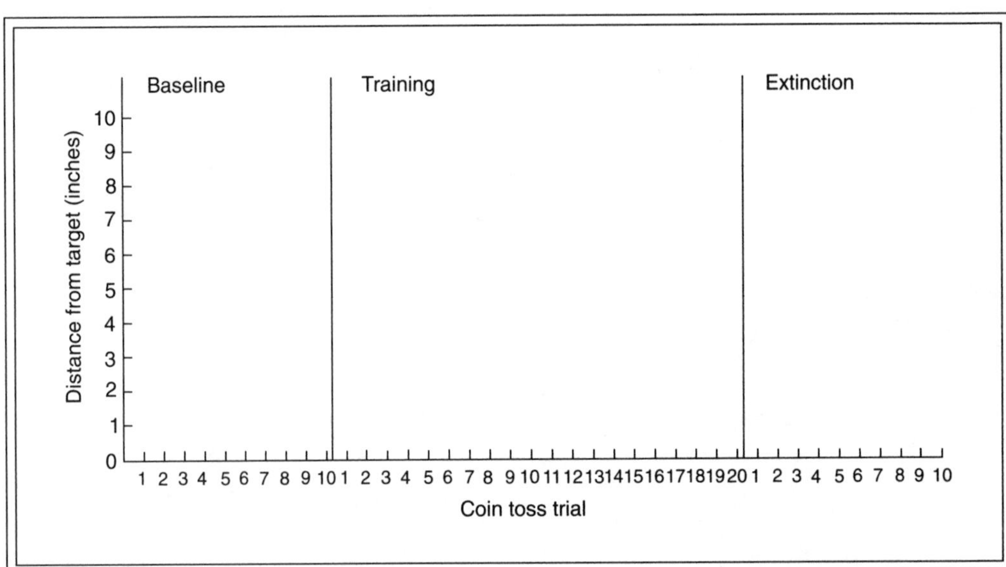

the results on the right-hand portion of Figure 7–1. This is your *extinction* performance (i.e., your performance after training, when feedback is no longer given for each response).

Are you more accurate in tossing pennies during the training period than during the baseline period? If so, we might be tempted to say that you are learning! Why does your performance increase during the training phase? One possible answer is that you had more practice. However, if you conducted the baseline part of the task for many tosses, you might find no improvement in your performance. Practice—by itself—might not be enough to enable learning. Thus, a second explanation is that during the training period you had practice with feedback. The feedback tells you how far away each penny landed from the target. Thus, knowing the effects of your behavior seems to be a potent force in helping you to change your behavior.

Does your accuracy decrease during the extinction period? If so, we can say that feedback is needed for you to maintain your performance. If you are able to maintain a high level of accuracy even during the extinction period, we can say that you have learned to provide intrinsic feedback. That is, you have learned to be able to tell whether your performance is accurate without external feedback.

How does feedback affect learning? This chapter explores two views of feedback—feedback as reinforcement and feedback as information. According to the *reinforcement view,* which is based on behaviorist approaches to learning, feedback serves to strengthen or weaken responses or, more specifically, the association between a stimulus and a response. In short, rewards make the association to a response stronger, whereas punishments make the association weaker. The process of response strengthening or weakening is automatic, not requiring any cognitive interpretation by the learner. In contrast, the *information view,* which is based on cognitive approaches to learning, holds that feedback is information that the learner interprets in order to make sense of a learning episode. Learning depends not on the feedback but rather on the learner's interpretation of the meaning of the feedback. If you are interested in promoting meaningful learning, feedback is useful to the extent that it provides information that guides the learner's construction of knowledge.

In this chapter, you will learn how feedback can be used to promote meaningful learning in each of three kinds of learning situations: response learning, concept learning, and skill learning. *Response learning* refers to the acquisition of a new response, such as tossing a coin so that it lands on a target. In response learning, the outcome of learning is a change in a single aspect of the learner's behavior. Academic examples of response learning include learning to say "six" when you are presented with a flash card that states "3 + 3," learning to raise your hand before you speak in class, or learning to turn a handle on a water fountain to get a drink. *Concept learning* refers to the acquisition of a new classification rule based on experience with instances, such as learning to add "s" to a noun to signify plural. In concept learning, the outcome is being able to classify stimuli, such as sorting cards with the letter "a" into one pile and the letter "b" into another pile or to tell whether a given animal is a dinosaur. *Skill learning* refers to the acquisition of a new procedure—or set of steps—for doing some task. In skill learning, the outcome of learning is being able to compute answers for two-column multiplication problems such as $35 \times 67 =$ ____.

THE LAW OF EFFECT

THORNDIKE'S THEORY

To get a better understanding of response learning, let's consider an early study performed by E. L. Thorndike (1898, 1911). Figure 7–2 shows a puzzle box used by Thorndike. As you can see, the puzzle box is a cage containing a door that can be opened from inside the cage. A hungry cat was placed inside the puzzle box with a dish of food outside. In a typical experiment, the cat had to learn to unlatch the door by pulling a string. The first time the cat was put into the puzzle box, the cat engaged in many behaviors, including scratching the bars, meowing, and pouncing on the floor. Eventually, the cat accidentally pawed at the string; this action opened the door and allowed the cat to escape and eat the food in the dish. On subsequent trials, the cat tended to spend less time engaging in irrelevant behaviors such as pouncing and meowing and tended to require less time before pulling the string. After many trials, the cat would immediately pull the string upon being placed

FIGURE 7–2 A puzzle box

"When put into the box the cat would show evident signs of discomfort and of impulse to escape from confinement. It tries to squeeze through any opening; it claws and bites at the wire; it thrusts its paws out through any opening and claws at everything it reaches. . . . It does not pay very much attention to the food outside but seems simply to strive instinctively to escape from confinement. . . . The cat that is clawing all over the box in her impulsive struggle will probably claw the string or loop or button so as to open the door. And gradually all the other unsuccessful impulses will be stamped out and the particular impulse leading to the successful act will be stamped in by the resulting pleasure, until, after many trials, the cat will, when put in the box, immediately claw the button or loop in a definite way."

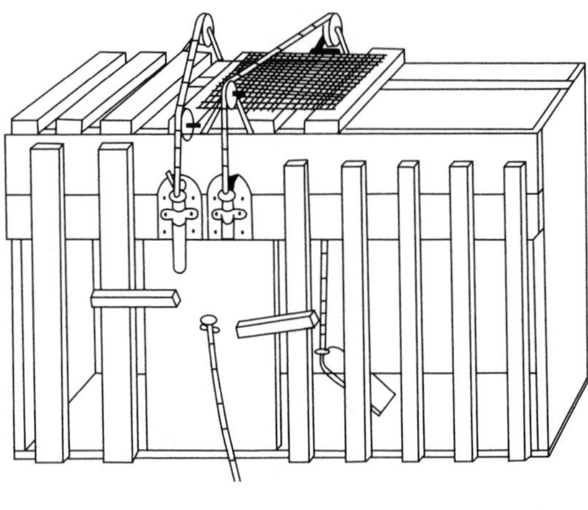

From Thorndike (1898, p. 13)

FIGURE 7–3 Time spent in the puzzle box on each trial.

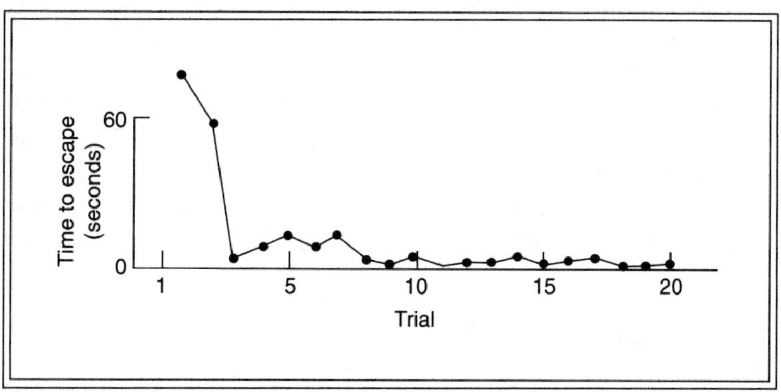

Adapted from Thorndike (1898)

into the puzzle box. Figure 7–3 shows the time (in seconds) the cat spent in the puzzle box before pulling the string for each of 20 trials. As you can see, the cat required a minute or more on the first two trials but required just a few seconds by the 20th trial.

The change in the cat's performance suggests that the cat learned something. According to Thorndike, the cat learned to form a strong association between the stimulus—being in the puzzle box—and a response of pulling the string. At the start of the experiment, the cat had many responses associated with the stimulus, including pouncing, meowing, and scratching. However, each time the cat engaged in one of these behaviors, the result was not positive; thus, according to Thorndike, the association between the stimulus (i.e., being in the puzzle box) and the response (e.g., meowing) was weakened. Similarly, each time the cat pulled the string, the result was positive; thus, according to Thorndike, the association between the stimulus (i.e., being in the puzzle box) and the response (i.e., pulling the string) was strengthened. At first, the response of pulling the string was very weakly associated with the stimulus of being in the box, but by the end of the experiment, the association was strong. At first, several irrelevant behaviors were strongly associated with being in the box, but by the end of the experiment, those associations were weaker. Thus, according to Thorndike, learning to make an appropriate response involves strengthening the relevant association and weakening the other associations. The principle underlying this learning is called the *law of effect,* because learning depends on the effect of each response. The law of effect is the idea that if a behavior is followed by a pleasing state of affairs, it is more likely to occur again in the future under the same circumstances, and if a behavior is followed by a displeasing state of affairs, it is less likely to be given again in the future. Here is how Thorndike (1911) summarized the law of effect:

> Of several responses made to the same situation, those which are accompanied or closely followed by satisfaction . . . will, other things being equal, be more firmly connected to the situation, so that, when it recurs, they will be more likely to recur; those which are accompanied or closely followed by discomfort . . . will, other things being equal, have their connections with the situation weakened, so that when it recurs, they will be less likely to occur. The greater the satisfaction or discomfort, the greater the strengthening or weakening of the bond. (p. 244)

The law of effect is widely recognized as one of the consistent pillars of the psychology of learning, and no principle of learning has had a greater impact on education than the law of effect. However, as you will see, in spite of the demonstrated effectiveness of practice with feedback, the preponderance of research evidence shows that something is terribly wrong with Thorndike's explanation of how learning happens. Throughout this chapter, you should be seeking to answer the question, Is feedback (such as rewards and punishments) a form of reinforcement that automatically strengthens or weakens responses (as Thorndike posited), or is feedback a form of information that the learner consciously interprets to make sense of the learning episode (as cognitive theory posits)?

SKINNER'S THEORY

Skinner (1938, 1953, 1957, 1968, 1969) conducted extensive research that served to improve on Thorndike's methodology and modify his theories. For example, with respect to methodology, Skinner developed devices that have been called *Skinner boxes*. Figure 7–4 shows a Skinner box for a white laboratory rat. The Skinner box consists of a metal cage, a metal grid floor, a bar that can be pressed down, and a food tray that is connected to a machine that delivers food pellets. First, let's put a white lab rat into the Skinner box. The rat will engage in many behaviors but will rarely press the bar. Thus, the baseline rate of bar pressing is very low, as shown in the left portion of Figure 7–5. Now let's adjust the food pellet machine so that it delivers a food pellet to the food tray each time that the bar is pressed. At first, the rat—like Thorndike's cat—engages in many irrelevant activities. Eventually, the rat—like Thorndike's cat—will accidentally produce the desired behavior. As soon as the rat presses the bar, a food pellet appears in the tray and the rat presumably will eat the pellet. Over the course of this learning session, the rate of bar pressing will increase dramatically, as shown in the right-hand side of Figure 7–5. The Skinner box is an

FIGURE 7–4 A Skinner box

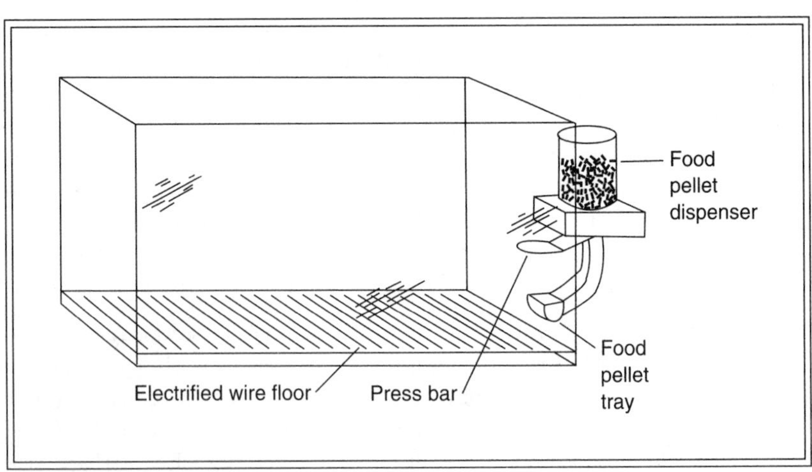

Courtesy of Ralph Gerbrands Co., Arlington, MA

FIGURE 7–5 Rate of bar pressing for each 10-minute time block in the Skinner box

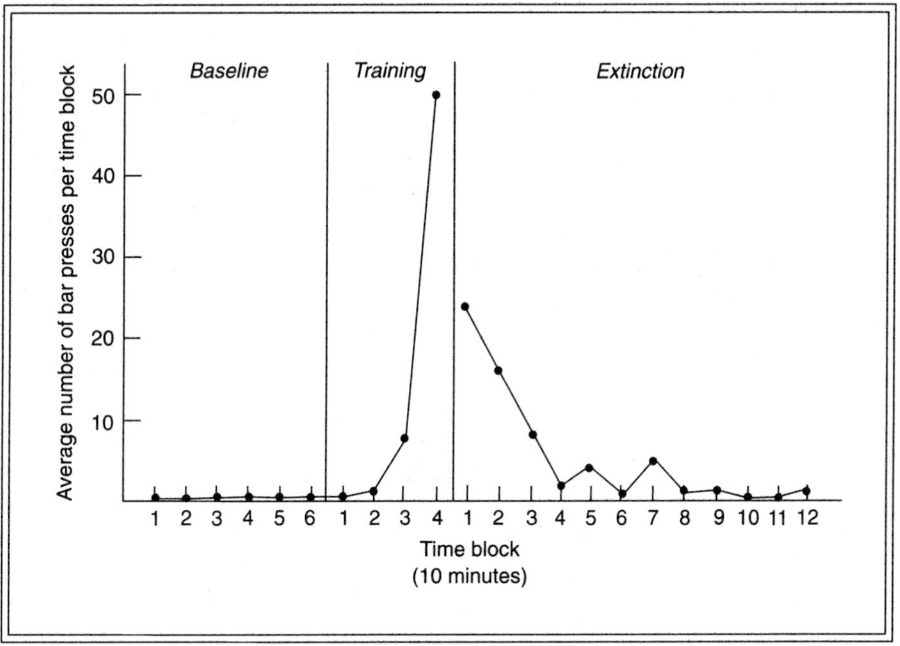

Modified from Skinner (1938)

improvement over Thorndike's puzzle box because the animal does not have to be placed back into the box after each successful response.

To describe the learning process, Skinner developed *reinforcement theory*. The main idea in reinforcement theory is that reinforcers can control behavior. A reinforcer is any stimulus that, when contingent on a response, serves to increase the rate of responding. This definition has two components:

1. *Contingency.* The occurrence of the reinforcer depends on (e.g., follows immediately upon) the occurrence of the learner's response.
2. *Rate of responding.* The reinforcer serves to increase the learner's rate of responding.

The food pellet fits the definition of a reinforcer because (1) the food pellet is delivered immediately after the bar is pressed (i.e., the delivery of the food pellet is contingent on the learner's pressing the bar), and (2) the rate of bar pressing increases when bar pressing is reinforced.

IS REWARD MORE EFFECTIVE THAN PUNISHMENT? A reinforcer may be positive or negative. A positive reinforcer is anything that, when presented contingent on a response, tends to increase the probability or rate of that response. A negative reinforcer is anything that, when taken away contingent on a response, tends to increase the probability or rate of that response. Presenting a food pellet to a hungry rat is an example of a positive reinforcer, whereas stopping an electrical shock is an example of a negative reinforcer. Thus, a response can be reinforced by either presenting a reward or taking away a punishment.

In contrast, two kinds of stimuli may serve to decrease the rate or frequency of responding: (1) presenting an aversive stimulus contingent on a response, and (2) taking away a rewarding stimulus contingent on a response. You can consider these to be forms of punishment. For example, the rat might decrease its rate of bar pressing if a shock follows each bar press or if pressing a bar causes a machine to stop supplying food pellets for 60 seconds.

Although the original law of effect as presented in the preceding section gave equal status to reward and punishment, this version did not survive Thorndike's lifetime. Toward the end of his scientific career, after hundreds of studies, Thorndike (1932) felt compelled to revise the law of effect by downplaying the role of punishment in changing behavior:

> In the early statements of the Law of Effect, the influence of satisfying consequences of a connection in the way of strengthening it was paralleled by the influence of annoying consequences in the way of weakening it. . . . I now consider that there is no such complete and exact parallelism. In particular, the strengthening of a connection by satisfying consequences seems in view of our experiments . . . to be more universal, inevitable, and direct than the weakening of a connection by annoying consequences. (p. 276)

Skinner's later application of reinforcement theory to instruction was also based on the power of rewarding appropriate behavior through positive reinforcement rather than punishing incorrect behavior. Thus, the remainder of this chapter focuses mainly on the uses of reward in school-related tasks and how feedback affects meaningful learning.

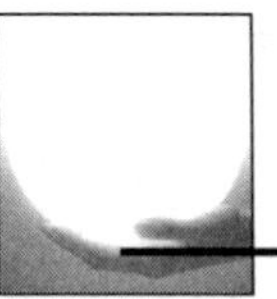

HOW DO CLASSROOM MANAGEMENT TECHNIQUES AFFECT CLASSROOM BEHAVIOR?

CLASSROOM MANAGEMENT

As you may have noticed, the law of effect (or reinforcement theory) suggests many classroom applications, including classroom management—techniques for maintaining a productive learning environment in the classroom. In any classroom, students will exhibit some behaviors that are disruptive and some behaviors that are productive for learning. One goal of a classroom management program is to decrease the frequency of disruptive behaviors and increase the frequency of productive behaviors. As you can see, this situation seems similar to that of Thorndike's puzzle box or the Skinner box because we have some target behavior that we want to increase or decrease. Thus, a major question is whether the principles of reinforcement developed from animal research can be applied successfully to humans. In this section, we explore two examples of how the law of effect can be applied to the task of classroom management—contingency contracting and token economies—after briefly exploring the predictions of behaviorist and cognitive theories.

BEHAVIORIST VERSUS COGNITIVE THEORIES OF CLASSROOM MANAGEMENT

According to a behaviorist view, classroom management techniques automatically change classroom behaviors: Behaviors that are are punished will gradually decrease, and behaviors that are rewarded will gradually increase. According to cognitive theories, classroom management techniques serve as information that the learner interprets and uses for building useful mental representations of the situation. Punishments serve to reduce a behavior when a learner understands the cause-and-effect chain leading to negative consequences (i.e., "if I do this, the result will be that") and wants to avoid a negative consequence. Rewards serve to increase a behavior when a learner understands the cause-and-effect chain leading to positive consequences (i.e., "if I do this, the result will be that") and wants the positive consequence.

RESEARCH ON CLASSROOM MANAGEMENT

CONTINGENCY CONTRACTING *Contingency contracting* is one application of reinforcement techniques to a classroom situation. In contingency contracting, the student and teacher make a sort of contract that specifies which student activities will lead to which rewards or punishments. For example, Sulzbacher and Houser (1968) conducted a study involving children in a special education class. The first step was to define the behavior to be changed; in this study, the teacher attempted to decrease the frequency of children making a disruptive gesture referred to as the "naughty finger." The next step was to determine a contingent event that might serve to decrease the rate of responding; in this study, the teacher used a loss of 1 minute of recess time from a 10-minute recess. As you can see, this contingency seems to involve both punishment and reward; for each inappropriate behavior, a rewarding stimulus (1 minute of recess) is taken away, but for appropriate behavior, no time will be lost from recess. This procedure is called *response cost* because inappropriate behavior costs the student in terms of diminishing a reward. Another frequently used contingency is called *time out*—for each case of inappropriate behavior the child is moved to a quiet place for a short time. These techniques seem to be more useful than traditional types of punishment, such as verbal disapproval or threats. The third step in classroom management is to establish a clear procedure for administering the program, with clearly articulated rules.

For nine days, the teacher simply kept track of the frequency of occurrences of the "naughty finger." This is the baseline period, and as you can see in Figure 7–6, the rate of responding for the class was about 15 occurrences per day. At the beginning of the 10th day, the teacher began the training period by making the following announcement:

> From now on there will be a special ten-minute recess at the end of the day. However, if I see the naughty finger or hear about it I will flip down one of these cards, and you will have one minute less of recess whenever this happens. Remember, every time I flip down one of these cards, all of you lose a minute from your recess. (Sulzbacher & Houser, 1968, p. 88)

As you can see in Figure 7–6, the number of occurrences of the "naughty finger" fell to fewer than five per day. After 18 days of training, the teacher told the class that the recess policy no longer was in effect. As you can see in the right portion of Figure 7–6, during the first nine days of this extinction period, the rate of responding increased. By the ninth day, the rate was back up to where it had been before training!

Two aspects of Figure 7–6 merit special attention. First, note that the rate of responding fell dramatically on day 10. This fall cannot be attributed to the training, because training had just begun; instead, the students seem to be able to adjust their performance based on

FIGURE 7–6 Number of disruptive behaviors per day in a special education classroom

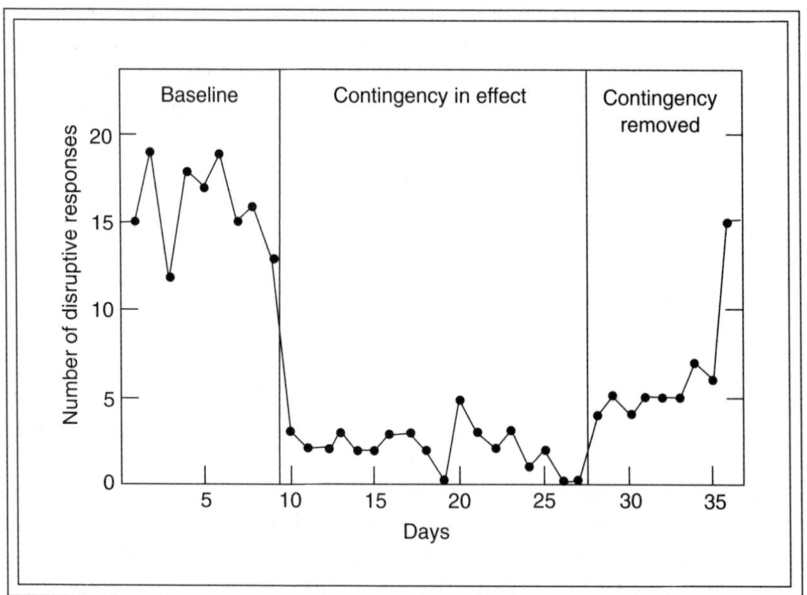

From Sulzbacher and Houser (1968)

the verbal instructions of the teacher. According to a behaviorist interpretation of the law of effect, the change in behavior should be gradual and should occur only after the punishments are administered. According to the cognitive interpretation of the law of effect, students use the information presented to build a mental model of the situation, which allows them to change their behavior. As you can see, the results are most consistent with the cognitive rather than the behaviorist interpretation. Second, note that the suppression of the disruptive behavior is short-lived. Once the contingencies are removed, the disruptive behavior seems to return to its former strength. Thus, punishment was not very effective in permanently changing behavior.

TOKEN ECONOMIES Token economies are another application of reinforcement theory to a classroom situation. In a token economy, students are given tokens (e.g., check marks by their names on a blackboard) for appropriate behaviors, and these tokens can be traded in for prizes or privileges. Alternatively, tokens can be given for inappropriate behaviors, and these tokens are later exchanged for various levels of punishment. The first step is to describe clearly the behavior to be changed. For example, suppose a teacher wishes to reduce the amount of disruptive behavior in a classroom. For purposes of our example, let's define disruptive behavior as any one of the following behaviors: (1) motor behaviors (e.g., walking around the room), (2) aggressive behaviors (e.g., hitting or kicking another person), (3) disturbing someone else's property (e.g., grabbing another person's book or tearing another person's paper), (4) making noise (e.g., stamping feet or clapping hands), (5) verbalizations (e.g., blurting out answers or talking out of turn), (6) turning around (e.g., looking to the rear of the class when the teacher is in front of the class), or (7) inappropriate tasks (e.g., drawing a picture during a spelling lesson) (O'Leary, Becker, Evans, & Saudargas, 1969). The second step is to find a contingent stimulus that will serve as an effective reinforcer for the children who produce these behaviors. Weil and Murphy (1982) suggested three categories of rewards for classroom management:

1. ***Social rewards*** (e.g., smiles, praise, or hugs)
2. ***Material rewards*** (e.g., stickers, stars, and awards)
3. ***Tokens*** (e.g., tickets, passes, or check marks on a chart) that can be redeemed for valued prizes or privileges

For our example, let's rely on tokens. In our classroom token economy, a child receives from 1 to 10 points after each 30-minute lesson for each of four lessons on each afternoon. The points (or tokens) are placed in a small booklet on each child's desk. On redemption days, the child can trade in points for prizes, such as 25 points for a level 1 prize, 35 points for a level 2 prize, and so on. The third step is to implement the program clearly and consistently. The rules are made clear to the student. For example, the teacher could write the following rules on the blackboard:

> We sit in our seats; we raise our hands to talk; we do not talk out of turn; we keep our desks clear; we face the front of the room; we work very hard; we do not talk in the hall; we do not run; and we do not disturb reading groups. (O'Leary et al., 1969, p. 5)

The teacher reviews the rules regularly. In addition, the teacher puts the token system into effect during short structured afternoon activities, such as spelling or science lessons in which the entire class participates. As part of the token economy, the teacher praises appropriate behaviors and ignores inappropriate behaviors. Threats such as "If you're not quiet by the time I count to three . . . " and commands such as "Sit in your seat" have been eliminated.

The example just outlined is similar to a token economy program for second-graders that was carefully studied by O'Leary et al. (1969). In a classroom of 21 students, the teacher identified seven students who tended to frequently produce disruptive behaviors such as those previously described. As part of the study, observers noted whether each of the seven children was engaged in appropriate or disruptive behavior during various 20-second periods throughout the school day. Figure 7–7 shows the percentage of time that the seven children were engaged in disruptive behaviors at different points in the study. First, there was a baseline period during which no changes were made in the classroom. The children were disruptive on more than half of the observations made. A few days later, the teacher introduced the classroom rules and wrote them on the board. This step did not result in any major change in disruptive behavior. A few days later, the classroom afternoon structure was changed into easily identifiable 30-minute lessons. Structure had no major impact either. A few days later, the teacher began a policy of praising appropriate behavior and ignoring disruptive behavior during the afternoon. The result was a modest increase in disruptive behavior. Finally, a few days later, the teacher began the token economy system of presenting points to each child after each of four 30-minute lessons each afternoon. As you can see in Figure 7–7, the token economy procedure resulted in a dramatic reduction of disruptive behavior. Then the token system was stopped. Disruptive behavior returned almost to its original baseline level. However, when the token economy was reestablished, disruptive behavior fell again. Finally, during a follow-up period, the

FIGURE 7–7 Percentage of disruptive behaviors per day during the afternoon in a second-grade classroom

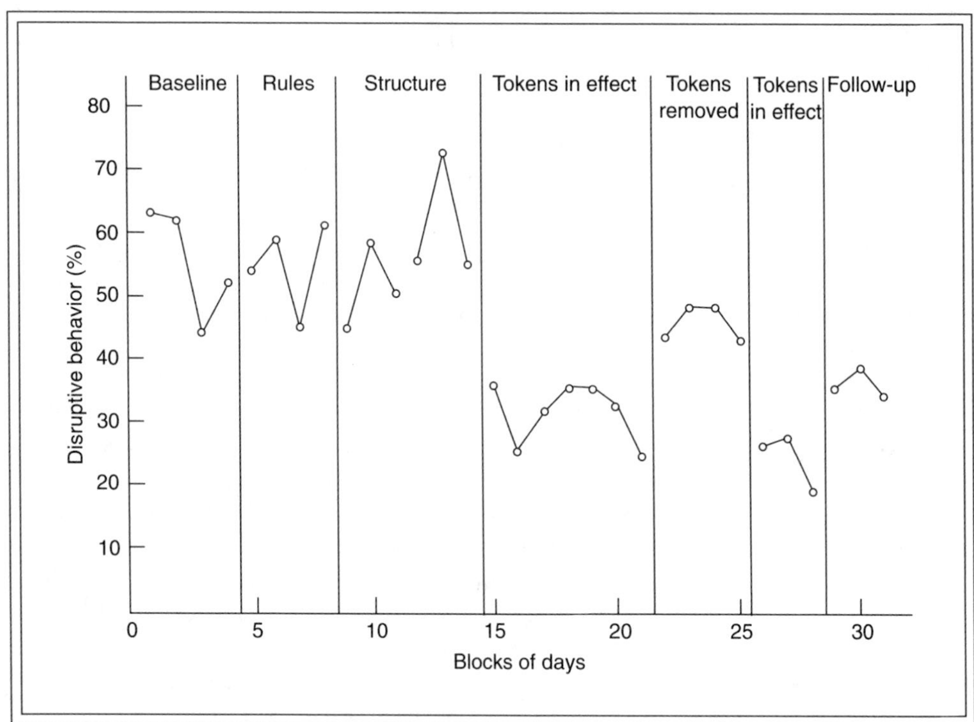

From O'Leary et al. (1969)

teacher stopped giving tokens but continued using rules, structured lessons, and praise. In addition, the teacher gave stars for good behavior—with each day beginning with a clean wall chart for each child's stars. The final panel of Figure 7–7 shows that disruptive behavior increased but was still maintained at well below the baseline level. These results support the cognitive theory because behavior changed immediately.

The preceding discussion is based only on performance during the afternoon (i.e., the time when the token economy was in effect). During the morning, no token economy was ever in effect. Did the reduction in disruptive behavior during the afternoon transfer to the morning? Figure 7–8 summarizes the percentage of disruptive behavior during the morning for each phase of the study. As you can see, the token economy procedure did not cause a large change in disruptive behavior during the morning even though there was a large change in disruptive behavior during the afternoon. Apparently, the children were able to discriminate between conditions under which appropriate behavior resulted in rewards (i.e., afternoon) and conditions during which appropriate behavior did not result in rewards (i.e., mornings).

In a subsequent study involving six disruptive ninth-graders, Main and Munro (1977) were able to replicate many of the results of the O'Leary et al. study. As in the O'Leary

FIGURE 7–8 Percentage of disruptive behaviors per day during mornings in a second-grade classroom

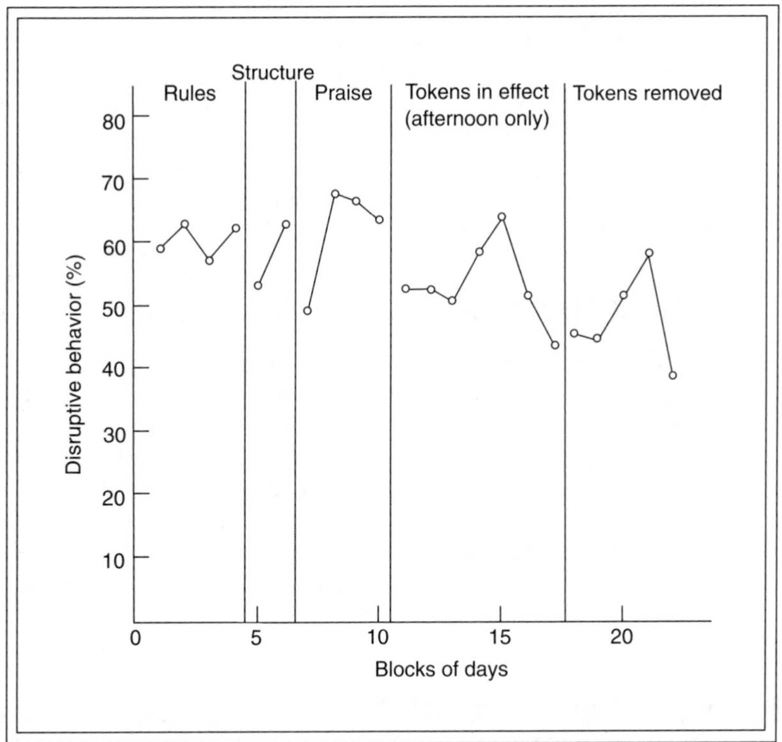

From O'Leary et al. (1969)

study, providing structured lessons and praising appropriate behavior while ignoring inappropriate behavior had only a slight effect on reducing disruptive behavior. Use of tokens greatly reduced disruptive behaviors; withdrawal of tokens produced an increase in disruptive behavior. During a final follow-up period, the token system was reestablished but tokens were gradually thinned out, leaving a contract system and teacher praise. This follow-up procedure was successful in maintaining a relatively low level of disruption.

Overall, there are many success stories involving the use of rewards and punishments to influence how children behave in classrooms (Schloss & Smith, 1998). However, it is useful to examine how and when such procedures work. From the examples reviewed in this section, we can begin to see the characteristics of a successful classroom token economy. First, the systems have clearly stated rules and structure. Students know what is expected of them and what will happen if they behave in certain ways. Second, the systems tend to use reward rather than punishment. For example, Bandura and Walters (1963) found that when a model (e.g., a teacher) uses punishment on a child, the child is more likely to use aggression as a way of controlling others. Madsen, Becker, and Thomas (1968) found that verbal punishments (e.g., saying "Stop that!") tend to increase disruptive behaviors.

Similarly, ignoring disruptive behavior does not help to reduce it. However, a time-out—such as having to sit for 3 minutes watching a sand timer—was effective in reducing disruptions in a physical education class (White & Bailey, 1990). Third, the systems are administered in a way that always allows for fairly rapid recognition of appropriate behavior. Students receive feedback within a few minutes of their behavior, and prior inappropriate behavior cannot cancel out rewards for current appropriate behavior. In the first example, feedback was given to the entire class; in the second example, feedback was given to each student separately. Overall, classroom management techniques require that the students understand why they are being rewarded or punished, so more is involved than simply dispensing rewards and punishments.

IMPLICATIONS OF RESEARCH ON CLASSROOM MANAGEMENT

The limitations of classroom management systems are also clear from the preceding examples. It is difficult to establish a program that works (i.e., a program that eventually can end the constant use of material rewards). Students may come to rely heavily on external rewards as a guide to how they should behave; instead, a goal of many classroom management systems is to help children develop intrinsic or self-motivated methods of behavior control. When the goal is to promote transfer—that is, to encourage productive changes in behavior that will last—classroom management techniques should be seen as information that is used by the learner to understand how the classroom community works.

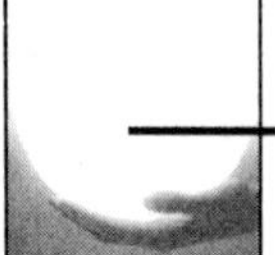

HOW DO REWARDS AFFECT CLASSROOM ACTIVITIES?

HIDDEN COSTS OF REWARD FOR CLASSROOM ACTIVITIES

Suppose a teacher wants to encourage students to engage in certain learning activities such as reading books or drawing pictures? A straightforward approach based on the law of effect would be to offer rewards for participating in the targeted activities. If a teacher wants a student to read, she can give the student a gold star for each book the student reads. If a teacher wants a student to draw a picture, the teacher can offer a certificate for completing an art project. What's wrong with such a straightforward application of the law of effect? I explore some hidden costs of reward when using contingency contracting and token economies to promote classroom activities that are already valued by the students.

BEHAVIORIST VERSUS COGNITIVE THEORIES OF REWARD

There are many how-to books for classroom management. However, to effectively use the techniques discussed in these books, it is important to understand the theory of how reinforcers (e.g., tokens) affect behavior. In this chapter, we explore two kinds of theories of reinforcement—behaviorist theories and cognitive theories. Behaviorist theories are based on Thorndike's and Skinner's interpretations of the law of effect, namely, the idea that a reinforcer (such as a token) serves to stamp in (reinforce) a response (such as appropriate behavior) and its link with a stimulus (such as the classroom environment). The strength of the stimulus-response association is automatically increased each time the response is reinforced; the process does not require active awareness or interpretation by the learner. In contrast, cognitive theories are based on an alternative interpretation of the law of effect, namely, the idea that the learner actively thinks about and interprets the feedback and its relation to the learner's response. Thus, feedback in cognitive theory serves as information that the learner uses in building a plan for responding.

RESEARCH ON HIDDEN COSTS OF REWARD

HIDDEN COSTS OF CONTINGENCY CONTRACTING Let's examine what these two theories predict in a simple reward situation. Suppose we observe a preschool to see how children spend their free time. We find that many of the children spend a large portion of their free time in a drawing activity—using colored marking pens and large sheets of drawing paper. Let's take those children who like to spend free time drawing and assign them to one of three groups. In the expected reward condition, we will make a contingency contract with each child: The child agrees to produce some drawings in exchange for an extrinsic reward (i.e., a certificate with a gold seal and ribbon). In the unexpected reward condition, no contract is made, but the child is given the same reward (i.e., a certificate) after drawing some pictures. However, the child does not know in advance that a reward will be given for drawing. Finally, in the no reward condition, the child does not receive a reward (i.e., certificate) for engaging in the drawing activity.

To see how rewards affect behavior, let's examine how our preschoolers spend their free time after the rewards are given. Let's come back to the preschool a week or two later and observe the percentage of free time spent in drawing. What do the behaviorist and cognitive theories predict? The behaviorist theory would predict that children in the expected reward condition and the unexpected reward condition should spend more free time drawing because they were rewarded for drawing. In contrast, the cognitive theory predicts that the expected reward condition children will spend less time drawing than children in the other two groups. One cognitive theory—called *overjustification* (Lepper & Greene, 1978)—states that the children are interpreting or justifying their own behavior and extrinsic rewards. If a child engages in a behavior, that behavior must be justified by the child. Thus, children who draw without expecting to receive a reward (no reward and unexpected reward conditions) can justify their behavior by saying they draw because they like to draw; in contrast, children who draw with the expectation of receiving a certificate (expected reward condition) can justify drawing by saying they draw because they get something for it. When rewards are no longer given, the justification for engaging in the drawing behavior is reduced for these children.

In a classic study, Lepper, Greene, and Nisbett (1973) carried out the procedure just described. Figure 7–9 summarizes the percentage of free time spent in the drawing activity for children who had experienced the three treatment conditions. As you can see, the results conflict with the behaviorist theory, which states that the two rewarded groups should behave similarly—but is consistent with the cognitive theory, which states that children in the expected reward condition (or expected award condition) should spend less time drawing than children in the other groups. Apparently, when children are rewarded for engaging in a behavior that is already interesting to them, the effect can be to

FIGURE 7–9 Some hidden costs of reward for preschoolers

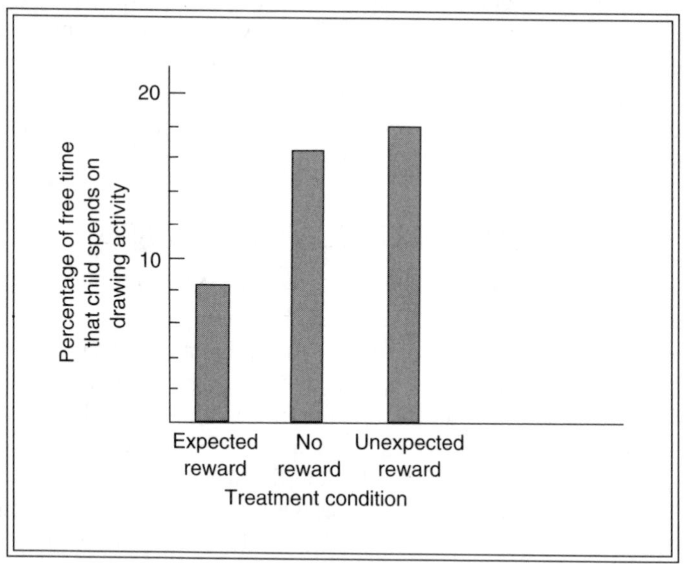

Adapted from Lepper, Greene, and Nisbett (1973)

diminish their intrinsic motivation for engaging in that behavior. Lepper and Greene (1975) refer to this process as "turning play into work."

HIDDEN COSTS OF TOKEN ECONOMIES This research shows that there can be some "hidden costs of reward" (Lepper & Greene, 1978). Based on their findings, Lepper et al. (1973) recommend caution in using token economies, especially when rewards are given out for behaviors that are already intrinsically satisfying to children:

> It has already been recommended by some thoughtful proponents of token economies that their use be limited to circumstances in which less powerful techniques have been tried and found inadequate—in other words, only when they are necessary. . . . The present study provides some empirical evidence of an undesirable consequence of the unnecessary use of extrinsic rewards, supporting the case for the exercise of discretion in their application. (p. 136)

Greene, Sternberg, and Lepper (1976) obtained similar results in a classroom token economy. Fourth- and fifth-graders were given rewards for spending time on certain math activities (such as creating geometric designs), some of which were already interesting to the students. Once the reward phase of the study ended, students could spend their math time as they wished. Students tended to spend less time with the previously rewarded activities than did a control group that received no rewards. In most cases, students who had been rewarded for engaging in certain math activities spent less than half as much time on those activities during the withdrawal phase as they had during the baseline phase. Again, the hidden cost of reward can be a drop in students' intrinsic motivation for rewarded activities. Similar results have been obtained by Ross (1975), Lepper and Greene (1975), and Deci (1971).

In a recent review of research, Cameron and Pierce (1994) found evidence that was consistent with the results of Lepper, et al. (1973): Across 50 comparisons, students who received expected rewards averaged lower intrinsic motivation than nonrewarded students—as indicated by spending less of their subsequent free time on the rewarded task. Cameron and Pierce (1994) conclude: "Expected tangible rewards produce a decrease in intrinsic motivation as measured by free time on task when they are given to individuals simply for engaging in the task" (p. 394). In another large-scale review of research, Deci, Koestner, and Ryan (1999) found that "tangible rewards . . . typically decrease intrinsic motivation for interesting activities" (pp. 658–659).

These analyses should not be taken to mean that reward always hurts intrinsic motivation. For example, in their review, Cameron and Pierce provide consistent evidence that giving rewards does not decrease intrinsic motivation in a wide variety of situations, including when the reward is not expected or when rewards are offered for successful performance rather than participation. Sometimes, offering rewards for high task performance can even increase intrinsic motivation (Eisenberg, Pierce, & Cameron, 1999). Instead of asking whether rewards increase or decrease intrinsic motivation, researchers are now seeking to understand the conditions under which rewards can affect intrinsic motivation (Eisenberg et al. 1999; Lepper, Keavney, & Drake, 1996; Pintrich & Schunk, 1996).

What does this research on rewards tell us about teaching for meaningful learning? An important way to promote teaching for meaningful learning is to instill a sense of intrinsic motivation that propels the learner when confronted with new academic tasks. Research on reward shows us that there are serious limitations in the classic view of rewards as ways of strengthening specific behaviors. Instead, this line of research shows that rewards (and punishments) constitute information that is interpreted by the learner. These interpretations affect the nature of what is learned and therefore the potential for transfer.

For example, when a child receives an expected rewarded for doing something he or she already likes to do, the child's interpretation of the reward may be, "I really do not like doing this after all." The result can be a decrease in motivation to perform the task and hence an impediment to transfer. As another example, when a child receives an unexpected reward for doing something he or she likes to do, the child may interpret the reward to mean "I really like doing this, and I get recognized for it." The result can be an increase in intrinsic motivation, or at least no decrease, and hence no negative consequences for transfer. Finally, when a child is rewarded for achieving a challenging goal, the child may interpret the reward as "I was able to do something that was hard, and the teacher thinks I'm good at it." The result can be an increase in intrinsic motivation, which leads to the potential for transfer. In short, rewards don't affect learning, but the learner's interpretation of rewards does. Similarly, getting a wrong answer should be interpreted not as a failure but rather as a challenge to try harder. When the instructional goal is to promote transfer, special consideration must be given to helping the learner interpret rewards (and punishments) in ways that increase rather than decrease intrinsic motivation.

IMPLICATIONS OF RESEARCH ON THE HIDDEN COSTS OF REWARD

The instructional prescription "use positive reinforcement" is one that needs to be applied in light of research on the hidden costs of rewards. Indiscriminate use of rewards to reinforce all desired behaviors can backfire. Students should not be rewarded for doing things that they already enjoy doing. For example, if a student enjoys reading novels and spontaneously does so, it would not always be appropriate to enter into a contingency contract in which the student receives prizes for reading and reporting on a certain number of books. Similarly, in many cases where rewards are used, the ultimate goal should be to encourage the student to develop intrinsic motivation. Motivation is explored in Chapter 14.

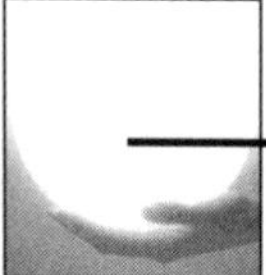

HOW DOES FEEDBACK AFFECT RESPONSE LEARNING?

RESPONSE LEARNING IN THE CLASSROOM

Another major instructional application of Thorndike's work has been an emphasis on drill-and-practice with feedback. For example, consider the following dialogue:

TEACHER: "How do you spell *behavior*?"
STUDENT: "B-e-h-a-v-e-r."
TEACHER: "No, you have the first two syllables correct, but the last syllable is misspelled."
STUDENT: "B-e-h-a-v-i-o-r."
TEACHER: "Right."

In this case, the teacher presents a question (i.e., a stimulus) and the student spells a word (i.e., a response). If the response is correct, the teacher says "right," and if the response is wrong, the teacher says no and gives a hint.

BEHAVIORIST VERSUS COGNITIVE THEORIES OF RESPONSE LEARNING

Let's examine two contrasting interpretations of how feedback affects response learning. First, according to a reinforcement interpretation, feedback serves to reinforce (or strengthen) the association between the response and the stimulus. In the spelling example, the reinforcer is "right," and this serves to strengthen the student's tendency to emit the correct spelling for *behavior*. Feedback automatically stamps in the correct response without the learner's having to actively be aware that learning is taking place. Second, according to a cognitive interpretation, feedback serves as information to the learner. The learner can interpret this information and use it as a key in generating responses. In the spelling example, the feedback concerning the location of the error is helpful information that the learner can use in generating a better response. Feedback is actively interpreted by the learner so that its effect depends on how the learner thinks about it. In summary, the controversy concerning how feedback affects learning centers on the question, Does feedback serve as a reinforcer that automatically stamps in a response, or does feedback serve as information that is interpreted by the learner?

RESEARCH ON RESPONSE LEARNING

PRACTICE WITH AND WITHOUT FEEDBACK Early work by Thorndike (1931) clearly demonstrated that feedback improved response learning in humans. In one study, subjects were seated at a desk with a pencil and a large pad of paper. The subjects were asked to close their eyes and draw a line 4 inches long and to continue trying to draw 4-inch lines, keeping their eyes closed throughout. They were asked to perform this task day after day until 3,000 lines had been drawn. The results of this tedious study were clear: Repetition of the response 3,000 times caused no learning. The performance of the subjects at the end of the study was no better than the performance at the start of the study. However, in another experiment, Thorndike gave feedback after each line drawing: "right" if the line was within 1/8 inch of the target length and "wrong" if it was not. Under these conditions, subjects' performance did improve. After approximately 4,000 trials, performance increased from 13% correct to 25% correct. Based on research studies like these, Thorndike concluded that practice alone would not promote learning but practice with feedback would. His argument was so compelling that it served to change school practices; instead of forcing students to practice without feedback, schools began to make use of praise and reward as techniques for increasing learning. Feedback was viewed as a way of reinforcing correct responses.

QUALITY OF FEEDBACK Subsequent research suggests that feedback may serve as information rather than reinforcement. If feedback serves mainly as a reinforcer, then the important aspect of feedback is to tell the learner whether the response was correct. If feedback serves mainly as information that is actively interpreted by the learner, then detailed feedback should be more effective than simple "right-wrong" feedback. An early study by Trowbridge and Cason (1932; reported in Adams, 1976) helped to test these predictions. Students were blindfolded and asked to draw one hundred 3-inch lines. Some students were told "right" for each line within 1/8 inch of the target and "wrong" for all other lines ("right-wrong" feedback group); some students were told how many eighths of an inch too long or too short each line was ("how much" feedback group); some students received no feedback (no feedback group). As you can see in Figure 7–10, the no-feedback group showed no improvement, thus confirming Thorndike's observation that practice alone does not enhance learning. Moreover, the "right-wrong" group showed some improvement, ending up with an average error of about 1/2 inch. This result is also consistent with Thorndike's research showing that "right-wrong" feedback aided learning. However, the main new result in Figure 7–10 is that the "how much" feedback group showed dramatic improvement from the start, ending up with an average error of less than 1/8 inch. Thus, the group given detailed feedback learned more rapidly and more completely than the group given only "right-wrong" feedback. This study suggests that learners can use the information in feedback to help revise their plans for how to generate lines. It is interesting to note that the most useful information came on errors; in other words, subjects in the "how much" group seem to have been able to learn from their mistakes. This result conflicts with reinforcement theory's assertion that learning occurs mainly when a correct response is reinforced. In summary, these results are most consistent with the feedback-as-information view rather than the feedback-as-reinforcement view of response learning.

DURATION OF FEEDBACK Subsequent research also provides additional support for the feedback-as-information view. For example, let's consider what would happen if you provided feedback for part of the time and then stopped giving feedback. If feedback served mainly as reinforcement, then once the feedback is taken away we can expect extinction (i.e., performance will deteriorate). If feedback serves as information that the

FIGURE 7–10 Motor skill learning with varying amounts of feedback

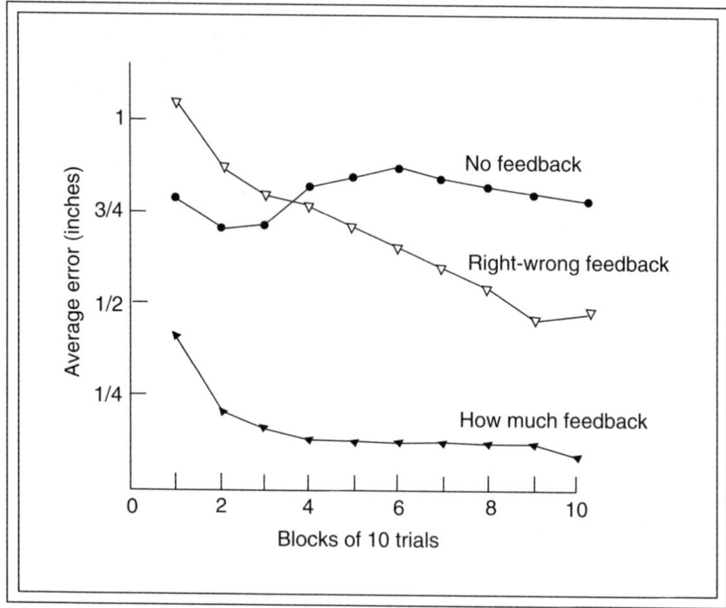

Adapted from Trowbridge and Cason (1932)

learner uses for building an internal plan or procedure, then once a correct plan is learned, feedback is no longer needed. To test these conflicting predictions, Newell (1974; described in Adams, 1976) gave subjects 75 tries at moving a lever 9.5 inches. Some subjects received feedback after each try (all feedback group); some subjects received feedback after the first 52 tries but not the last 23 tries (52-trial feedback group); some subjects received feedback on the first 17 tries but not on the last 58 tries (17-trial feedback group); some subjects received feedback after just the first 2 tries (2-trial feedback group). As you can see in Figure 7–11, the group given feedback on all 75 tries and the group given feedback on 52 tries both performed about the same. Apparently, after 52 tries the subjects had acquired an internal procedure for how to generate internal feedback concerning the appropriate response so that external feedback was no longer needed. However, when feedback was taken away early in the learning (e.g., after 2 or 17 tries), performance deteriorated, as would be expected under extinction. Apparently, subjects had not yet developed a way of generating internal feedback, so they were lost once external feedback was taken away. These results suggest that "what is learned" as a result of feedback is not always just the stamping in (reinforcement) of a response; rather, under some conditions, learners can build a cognitive plan that allows them to generate internal feedback.

Finally, growing evidence indicates that practice with feedback causes qualitative differences in what is learned (Anderson, 1993; Singley & Anderson, 1989). For example, a child's computational skill goes through several stages rather than simply a series of strengthening associations. As responses become automatized through practice with feed-

FIGURE 7–11 Effects of withdrawal of feedback early versus late in motor skill learning

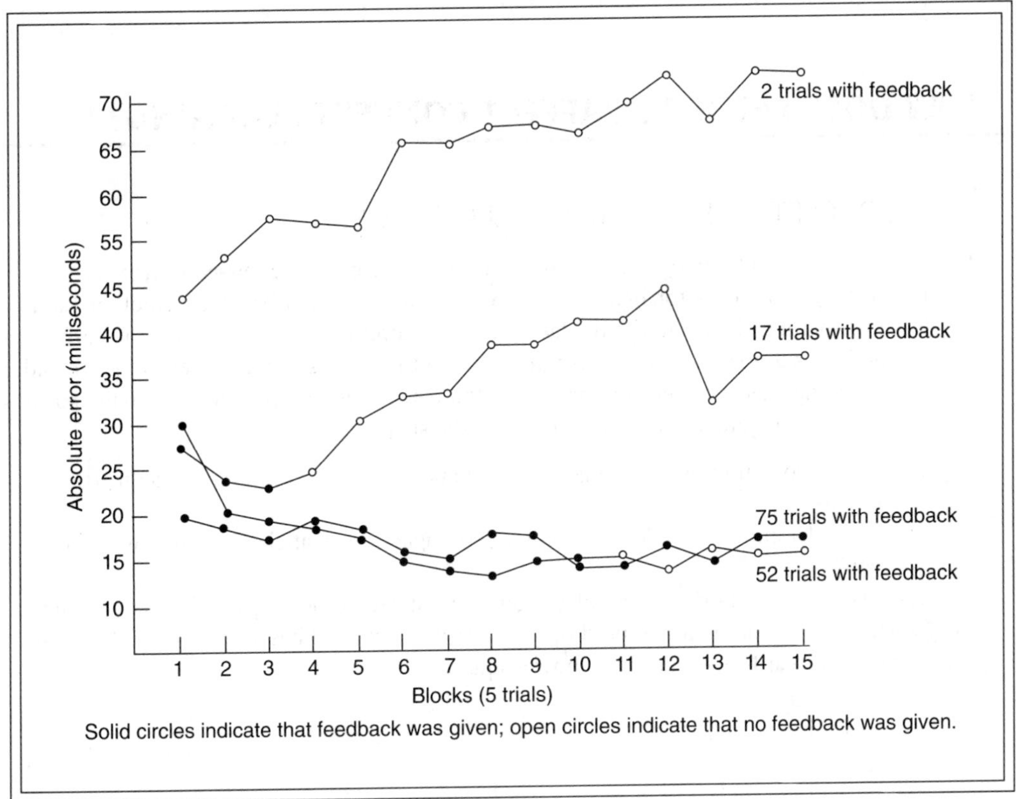

Adapted from Newell (1974)

back, the learner is able to use those automatized procedures in more complicated tasks. In summary, although feedback can be used to enhance response learning, the effective use of feedback must be based on an understanding of how the learner interprets the information in feedback.

IMPLICATIONS OF RESEARCH ON RESPONSE LEARNING

The research presented in this section highlights the crucial role that feedback plays in response learning. However, the research indicates that feedback does not simply stamp in (or reinforce) the response. Instead, students think about the feedback and use the feedback as information to help them interpret their learning. Thus, high-quality feedback is most useful (i.e., learners need to be told specifically about what they are doing that is correct or incorrect rather than just be told "right" or "wrong"). Furthermore, eventually, students may learn to give themselves feedback on a well-practiced task. Thus, teacher-provided feedback should be withdrawn only when the learner has reached a level of automatic internal feedback, an event that may take many trials of practice but that should be the ultimate goal of instruction for response learning.

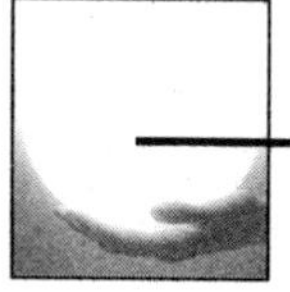

HOW DOES FEEDBACK AFFECT CONCEPT LEARNING?

CONCEPT LEARNING IN THE CLASSROOM

So far in this chapter you have seen how the law of effect can be related to response learning, such as simple motor behavior or appropriate classroom behavior. Another kind of learning that may be related to the law of effect is concept learning. In concept learning, a person learns to make the same response to an entire set of stimuli. For example, consider the following classroom episode in which the teacher holds up cards portraying various geometric shapes and asks students to name the shape.

TEACHER: Do you know what a geometric shape is? Can you name some geometric shapes?

STUDENT: Ummm . . . circle . . . square . . . triangle . . . rectangle . . . Is that what you mean?

TEACHER: Yes, that's right. Let's play a game about geometric shapes. It's called, Name That Shape. I am going to hold up some cards. Each card has a shape on it. For example, some cards, like this one, show a square:

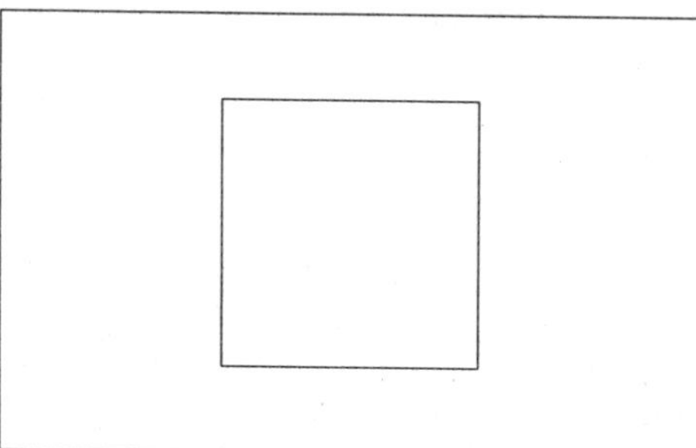

Other cards, like this one, show a circle:

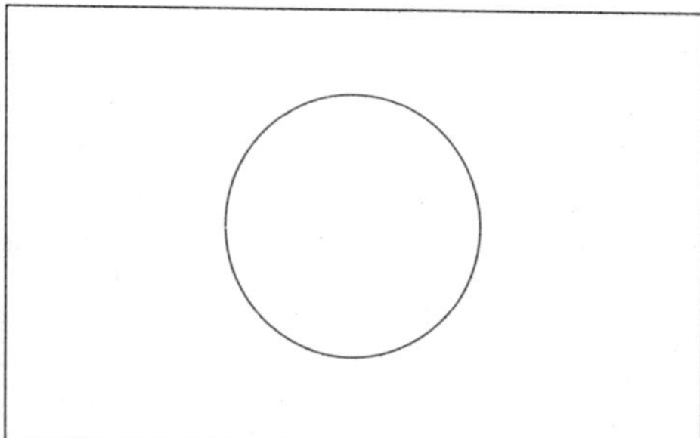

Other cards will show other shapes like rectangles, triangles, and so on. Your job is to tell me the name of the shape. Now, let's begin. What is this? [A small square.]

STUDENT: I don't know.
TEACHER: It's a square. Now, what is this? [A medium square.]
STUDENT: Square.
TEACHER: Right, it's a square. Very good. Now, what is this? [A medium rectangle.]
STUDENT: Square.
TEACHER: Sorry, that's not right. It's a rectangle.

In this example of a concept learning task, the teacher presents a series of instances one at a time. For each instance, the student must tell which category it belongs to and then the teacher gives feedback, namely, the correct category. In this example, the student seems to classify all four-sided shapes as squares. Thus, the student has acquired a concept of square that is a bit too broad, because it includes rectangles, parallelograms, and so on.

BEHAVIORIST VERSUS COGNITIVE THEORIES OF CONCEPT LEARNING

Concept learning, like response learning, has been studied intensively (Mayer, 1992). In most concept learning tasks, like the preceding one, students begin by making many errors, but with practice and feedback, they eventually learn to categorize instances without error. In fact, after practice with feedback, students are even able to correctly categorize instances they have not yet seen. For example, in the Name That Shape game, students eventually learn to correctly name a certain circle or square even though they have not previously seen the particular circle or square before. That's what makes it concept learning.

What is the learning process that accounts for concept learning? As in the previous section on response learning, the two fundamental kinds of theories are behaviorist and cognitive. A behaviorist theory of concept learning extends Thorndike's and Skinner's interpretations of the law of effect to the learning of concepts. For each instance that is presented, the learner strengthens the association between each feature of that instance and the correct response. For example, for the first instance in the foregoing episode, the learner associates the response "square" with each of the stimulus features "has four sides," "each side is equal," "sides all at right angles," "black ink," "small size," and so on. At the end of the first instance, after the student has been told it's a "square," the following are some of the S-R associations that exist in the learner (with the number of times a stimulus has been associated with a response indicated in parentheses):

STIMULUS	*STRENGTH OF ASSOCIATION*	*RESPONSE*
Has four sides	—(1)—	Square
Each side is equal	—(1)—	Square
Sides all at right angles	—(1)—	Square
Black ink	—(1)—	Square
Small size	—(1)—	Square

The second instance has several stimulus features that are associated (albeit weakly) with the "square," so the student has a weak tendency to answer "square." After receiving feedback on the second instance, the learner associates the response "square" with the stimulus features "has four sides," "each side is equal," "sides all at right angles," "black ink," and "medium size." At the end of this second instance, the following are some of the S-R associations that are accumulating in the learner:

STIMULUS	*STRENGTH OF ASSOCIATION*	*RESPONSE*
Has four sides	—(2)—	Square
Each side is equal	—(2)—	Square
Sides all at right angles	—(2)—	Square
Black ink	—(2)—	Square
Small size	—(1)—	Square
Medium size	—(1)—	Square

The third instance has some features that are associated with "square," so the student says "square." However, after receiving feedback, the learner associates each feature of the third instance with "rectangle," yielding the following accumulated associations:

STIMULUS	*STRENGTH OF ASSOCIATION*	*RESPONSE*
Has four sides	—(2)—	Square
Has four sides	—(1)—	Rectangle
Each side is equal	—(2)—	Square
Only opposite sides equal	—(1)—	Rectangle
Sides at right angles	—(2)—	Square
Sides at right angles	—(1)—	Rectangle
Black ink	—(2)—	Square
Black ink	—(1)—	Rectangle
Small size	—(1)—	Square
Medium size	—(1)—	Square
Medium size	—(1)—	Rectangle

As you can see, each time the student sees an instance and gets feedback, new S-R connections are established or old ones are strengthened. Concept learning is a process of building connections based on feedback.

In contrast, the cognitive theory rejects the idea that the learner is being passively conditioned by the feedback. Instead, the learner is actively testing a hypothesis. For example, after the first instance, the learner may select the hypothesis: If it has four sides, it's a square. The learner keeps the hypothesis if it generates the correct answer and selects a new one if it generates an incorrect answer. On the third trial, the hypothesis produces an incorrect answer, for example, so the learner may generate a new hypothesis, such as, if it is small, it is a square. In the strictest version of this cognitive (or hypothesis testing) theory, the learner has no memory for past errors when selecting a new hypothesis.

As you can see, the two theories offer different interpretations of how feedback promotes concept learning. The behaviorist theory sees the learner as passive; the cognitive theory sees the learner as actively forming hypotheses. The behaviorist theory sees learning as a gradual process of building associations; the cognitive theory sees learning as "all-or-none" (i.e., the student either has the correct hypothesis or not). The behaviorist theory sees learning occurring when feedback is given; the cognitive theory sees learning occurring only after the learner makes an error (i.e., the learner changes hypotheses only after making an error).

RESEARCH ON CONCEPT LEARNING

CHANGING THE RULE PRIOR TO SOLUTION Which theory best accounts for the fact that people learn concepts when they are given feedback? Suppose that you are in a concept learning situation involving stimuli that are complicated drawings and responses that are either "yes" or "no." The teacher presents a stimulus, you give a response, and the teacher tells you the correct answer. Further, let's suppose that partway through the concept learning task, but before you have completely learned the concept, the teacher reverses the rule for classifying the drawings as "yes" or "no." Let's say that you make an error on the 20th trial, and we reverse the rule for the rest of the task. Instead of saying "yes" for white and "no" for black, as in trials 1–20, the teacher now says "yes" for black and "no" for white. The teacher does not tell you that the rule has changed, of course.

What do the behaviorist and cognitive theories predict about our rule reversal task? According to the behaviorist theory, reversing the rule should have a devastating effect on learning—the learner will have to unlearn all the associations that have been building up over the first 20 trials and then form associations in the opposite direction. Thus, learners who have the rule reversed before they have finished learning a concept should require many more trials to learn than learners who have had the same rule throughout. According to the cognitive theory, reversing the rule should have no effect on the rate of learning. If a learner has made an error (e.g., on the 20th trial), that means that the learner has not yet selected the correct hypothesis. After making an error, the learner will simply put the failed hypothesis back in the pool of hypotheses, "stir" the pool of hypotheses, reach in, and take out a hypothesis again. Thus, each time the learner makes an error, the learner essentially starts over again fresh—changing the rule has no effect, because the learner has learned nothing yet!

Bower and Trabasso (1963) conducted a series of experiments like the one already described. As predicted by the cognitive theory, reversing the rule prior to solution did not slow down learning: Learners required about the same amount of time and number of stimuli to learn when the same rule was used throughout as when the rule was reversed after an error during the learning phase. Apparently, the learners in Bower and Trabasso's study did not gradually build up stimulus-response associations but rather seemed to actively form and test hypotheses.

DEVELOPMENTAL DIFFERENCES IN CONCEPT LEARNING The Kendlers (Kendler & Kendler, 1962, 1975) also investigated two conflicting theories of concept learning. Figure 7–12 summarizes the experimental method used. The subject was presented with a pair of stimuli consisting of a combination of large black, large white, small black, or small white shapes and was asked to point to the correct one. First, the subject learned one concept, such as to always point to the large object for each pair of objects that was presented. After the subject could choose the correct object without error on a long string of trials, the rule was changed without telling the subject. For some subjects the rule was changed to a *reversal shift* (also called intradimensional shift); this involved reversing

FIGURE 7–12 The reversal shift task

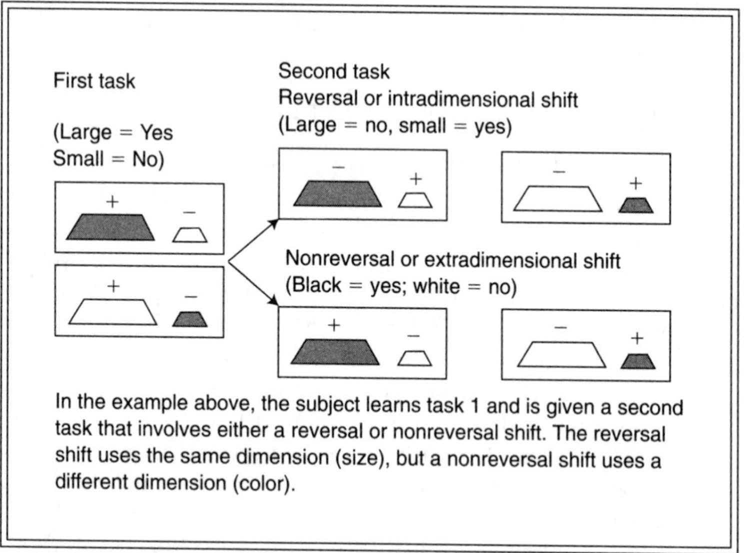
First task
(Large = Yes
Small = No)
Second task
Reversal or intradimensional shift
(Large = no, small = yes)
Nonreversal or extradimensional shift
(Black = yes; white = no)
In the example above, the subject learns task 1 and is given a second task that involves either a reversal or nonreversal shift. The reversal shift uses the same dimension (size), but a nonreversal shift uses a different dimension (color).

Adapted from Kendler and Kendler (1962)

the rule such as changing from "point to large" to "point to small." For other subjects, the rule was changed to a *nonreversal shift* (also called extradimensional shift); this involved basing the rule on a different dimension such as size instead of color. For example, the rule could be changed from "point to large" to "point to black."

Which would be more difficult to learn, a reversal or nonreversal shift? According to single association theory (like the behaviorist theories previously described), a reversal shift should be harder because the subject must unlearn four old S-R associations and replace them with four opposite ones. For example, large black was "yes" and now is "no"; large white was "yes" and now is "no"; small black was "no" and now is "yes"; small white was "no" and now is "yes." In contrast, only two new associations need to be learned for the nonreversal shift—large black remains "yes" and small white remains "no" in both parts of the study. According to a mediational theory (like our cognitive theories), during the first part of the task the student learns to pay attention to the relevant dimension (e.g., size is the relevant dimension in the first part of our example), and the student learns to assign the correct values on that dimension (e.g., large size is "yes" and small size is "no"). A reversal shift involves changing only one aspect of the rule—the dimension is still size, but the values are changed. In contrast, for a nonreversal shift, two things are changed—both the dimension and the values. Thus, in searching for a new hypothesis, the reversal shift should be easier than the nonreversal shift.

As you can see, the two theories make opposite predictions. The Kendlers found that laboratory animals tended to have more trouble with reversal than nonreversal shifts, suggesting that they learned in a way best described by a behaviorist interpretation.

Preschoolers also tended to find the reversal shift more difficult than the nonreversal shift, but older children and adults found the nonreversal shift to be more difficult than the reversal shift. As the age of the children increased, the tendency for nonreversals to become more difficult than reversals increased. These findings suggest that as children get older their concept learning process changes away from a behaviorist style and toward a more cognitive approach.

IMPLICATIONS OF RESEARCH ON CONCEPT LEARNING

The behaviorist and cognitive views of concept learning suggest quite different strategies for teaching concepts to students. The behaviorist approach, as promoted in Skinner's (1968) view of programmed instruction, requires asking easy questions so that students can give correct answers that will be rewarded. Learning occurs, according to this view, when the student gives a correct response and is rewarded for that response. In contrast, the cognitive approach requires that the student be free to make errors—because it is only after making an error that a student forms a new hypothesis.

The foregoing research suggests that preschool children have a tendency to learn concepts in a way suggested by behaviorist theories. Concept learning at this age should be based on eliciting correct responses that can be rewarded. However, throughout elementary school and beyond, there is an increasing tendency to learn concepts by actively forming hypotheses. Concept learning at these ages should be based on allowing the child to construct hypotheses and test them and, especially, to see how a hypothesis can be falsified. In fact, hypothesis testing strategies can be productively taught to elementary school children (Olton & Crutchfield, 1969). Strategy instruction is discussed in Chapter 12.

Suppose we want to teach students how to recognize dinosaurs. If you view learning as the strengtening and weakening of associations, you would want the learner to say "yes" for stegasaurus, "yes" for brachiosaurus, and "yes" for triceratops, and you would want the learner to say "no" for snake, "no" for frog, and "no" for elephant. In short, students would learn many separate S-R connections, as shown in the top of Figure 7–13. To promote this learning, you would base your teaching on the law of effect by rewarding students for the correct response.

In contrast, if you view learning as the building of a general rule—that is, as hypothesis testing—you want the learner to figure out that dinosaurs are large, extinct reptiles. This learning outcome is shown in the bottom of Figure 7–13. Using this rule, students can classify stegasaurus, brachiosaurus, and triceratops as members of the dinosaur category and snake, frog, and elephant as nonmembers. To promote this learning, you would base your teaching on helping students see errors in their rules.

What are the implications of research on concept learning for teaching for meaningful learning? When students focus on building S-R connections, transfer is limited, so students are able to answer questions mainly about the items that were presented to them. However, when students focus on building general classification rules, the potential for transfer is enhanced, so students are able to answer questions about new instances they have never seen before. In short, it is easier to transfer when you have learned a general rule than when you have learned a collection of specific S-R connections, so teaching for transfer in concept learning involves helping students build useful classification rules. For

FIGURE 7–13 Two approaches to concept learning

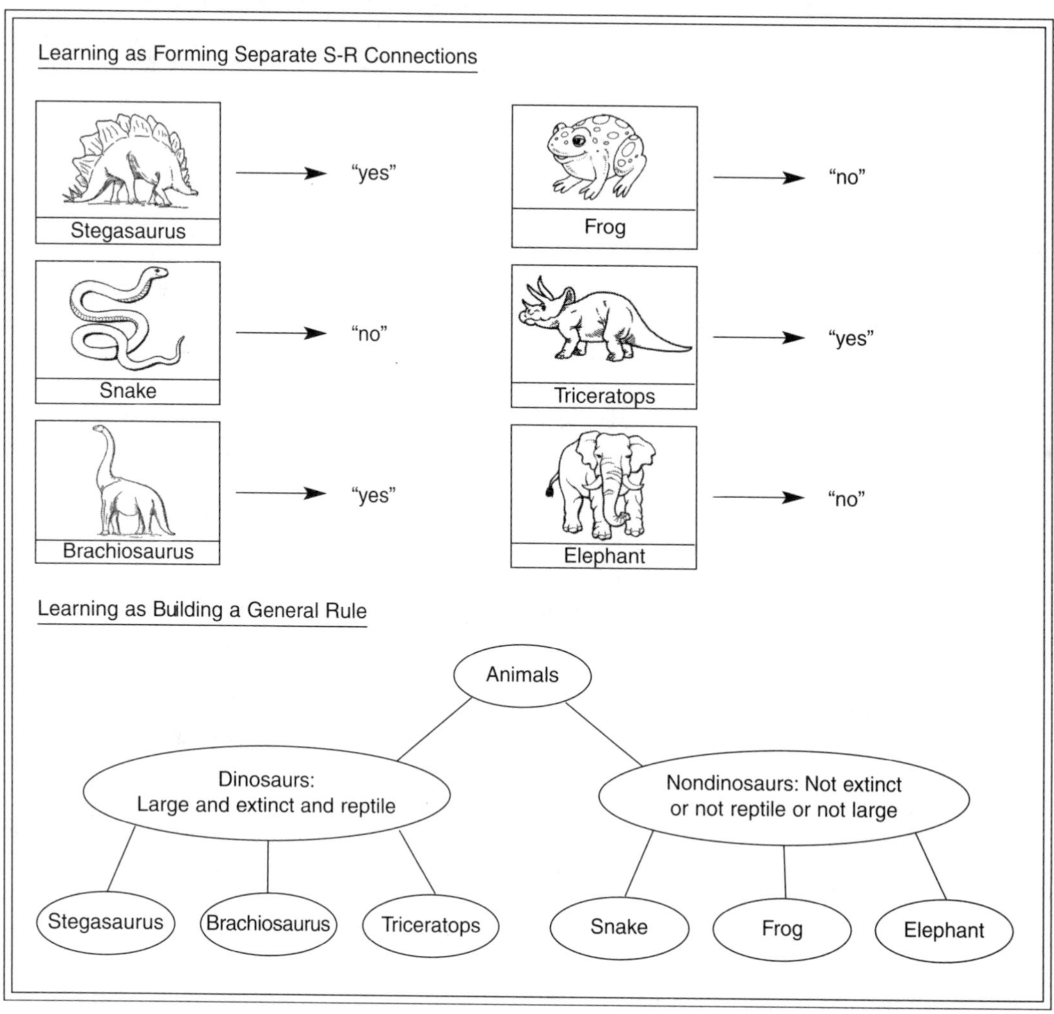

example, Ross (2000) showed that children benefit from practice in articulating the classification rule for deciding whether a particular instance belongs to a category. Novak (1998) argued that the active process of concept formation is facilitated by asking students to draw and justify graphic representations—which he calls "concept maps"—consisting of nodes (with instance names) and links connecting them (with labels).

In summary, feedback is effective in teaching concepts. However, research on concept learning shows that for most school-age students, feedback influences learning because it provides information relevant to the learner's active search for hypotheses rather than because it stamps in a particular response. Chapter 9 explores how to help students form more complex concepts based on learning from examples.

HOW DOES FEEDBACK AFFECT SKILL LEARNING?

SKILL LEARNING IN THE CLASSROOM

Skill learning involves learning how to do something, so learning how to use a word processor is an example of skill learning. Suppose you are sitting at a computer that is running a word processor. On the screen you see a page of text, but you also have a printout of the page with some corrections that need to be made, as shown in Figure 7–14. Write a brief summary of what you would do for each correction, but write it as a set of rules that you could explain to someone else. Which of the following best corresponds to how you explained the first correction?

_____ to carry out the first correction, press the up arrow key 17 times and press the back arrow key 65 times and then press the keys n-o-t-space-o-n-l-y-space-w-i-l-l-space-t-h-e-space-u-n-i-t-space-n-o-d-e-s-space-i-n-space-t-h-e-s-e-space-t-r-a-c-e-s

_____ to carry out the first correction, move the cursor to the first space in the first line and type in "not only will the unit nodes in these traces"

_____ when you want to insert text, move the cursor to where the text should be inserted and type in the inserted text

Which of the following best corresponds to how you explained the last correction?

_____ to carry out the last correction, press the down arrow key one time, press the right arrow key 51 times, press the delete key 11 times, press the keys t-a-r-g-e-t

_____ to carry out the last correction, move the cursor to select the word "illustrates" press delete, then type "target"

_____ when you want to replace text, highlight the text to be replaced and type in the new text

If you focus on specific behaviors, then you probably checked the first answer (or even the second answer) for each of these questions, but if you focus on more general principles of word processing, you probably checked the third answer.

BEHAVIORIST VERSUS COGNITIVE THEORIES OF SKILL LEARNING

The role of feedback in skill learning can be analyzed from a behaviorist or cognitive point of view. According to the behaviorist view, learning involves adding specific responses to one's repertoire, and feedback is needed to help learners add appropriate responses. This view is consistent with the theory of specific transfer in which transfer occurs only when two tasks share many common behaviors. According to the cognitive view, learning involves making sense of the learning situation, so feedback is needed to help learners build broad rules or procedures. This view is consistent with the theory of specific transfer of general principles in which transfer occurs when a principle or strategy learned in one situation can be applied to a new situation.

FIGURE 7–14 A word-processing task

not only will the unit nodes in these traces
accrue strength with days of practice, but also
the element nodes will accrue strength. As will
be seen, this power function prediction
corresponds to the data about practice. A set of
experiments was conducted to test the prediction
about a power-law increase in *the* strength with
extensive practice. In one experiment subjects
studied subject-verb-object sentences of the form
(Thee lawyer hated the doctor). After studying
these sentences they were transferred to a
~~furthermore, the thought prevents the stud~~y
sentence recognition paradigm in which they had to
discriminate these sentences from foil ~~by the mind~~
sentences made of the same words as the *target* ~~illustrates~~
sentence but in new combinations. There were 25 days of
tests and hence practice. Each day subjects were tested
on each sentence 12 times (in one group) or 24
times in the other group. There was no difference

From Singley and Anderson (1989)

RESEARCH ON SKILL LEARNING

Suppose we find a group of people who know how to type but who have never used a word processor. (It was easier to find such people in the 1980s than it would be today.) After explaining the commands for the word processor, we give our students 3 hours of practice per day for four days on word-processing tasks such as the one in Figure 7–14. Some students use the same word processor every day (Group AAAA); others use one kind of word processor on the first two days, but on the last two days they use a different kind of word processor that has different commands than the first one (Group BBAA).

When Singley and Anderson (1985, 1989) conducted this study, they essentially were looking for transfer: If skill learning involves acquiring specific behaviors, Group AAAA should outperform Group BBAA on days 3 and 4. The rationale is that quite different sequences of key presses are needed for the same tasks in the two different word processors. If skill learning involves building general strategies, both groups should perform about the same on days 3 and 4. The rationale is that both groups received practice in the same kinds of solution strategies, with only the specific commands being different.

Figure 7–15 shows the average time (in seconds) to carry out a correction for the two groups on each of the four days of learning. As you can see, Group AAAA showed a pattern

FIGURE 7–15 Average time to make a correction across four days for two groups

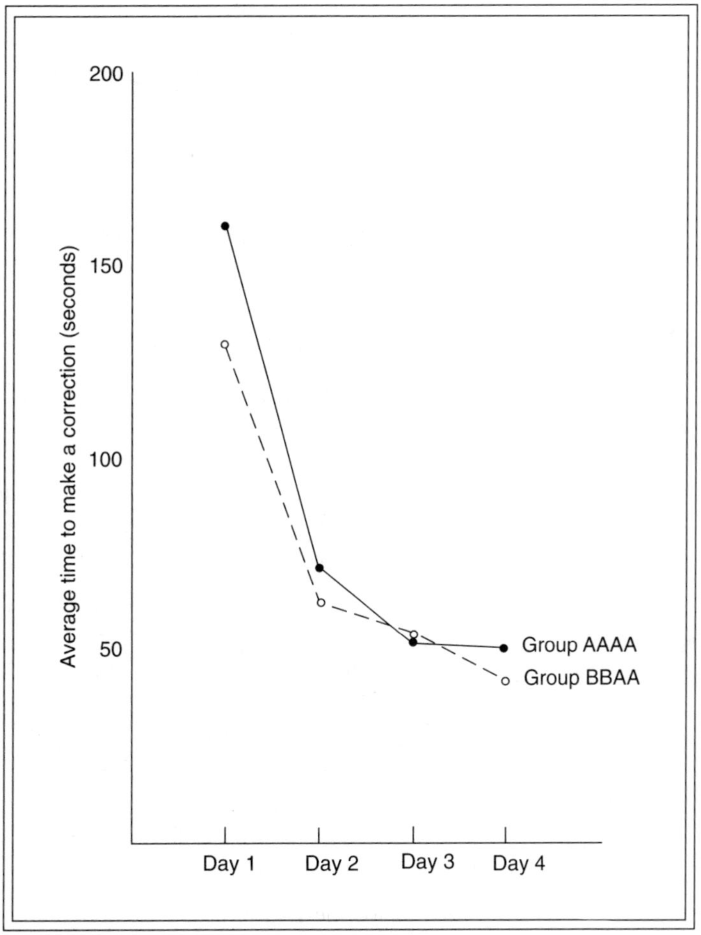

Average time to make a correction (seconds)
200
150
100
50
Day 1
Day 2
Day 3
Day 4
Group AAAA
Group BBAA

Adapted from Singley and Anderson (1989)

of skill learning in which the time needed to carry out a correction decreased across the four days. Importantly, Group BBAA showed the same pattern of skill learning even though students had to switch word processors. In short, Group BBAA showed a high level of transfer from one word processor to another.

Why was there high positive transfer? According to Anderson (1993), both groups learned general strategies or rules rather than solely specific behaviors. Similar to the theory of specific transfer of general principles described in Chapter 1, transfer is facilitated when learners focus on general strategies rather than specific behaviors. What the word processors had in common was not specific keystrokes (such as which keystrokes to press) but rather general rules (such as how to insert text or how to replace text). Singley and Anderson (1989) conclude that "the very high level of positive transfer observed between [word processors] that shared few commands reinforces the position that superficial identical elements of the type that Thorndike advocated are inadequate" and "provides further support for an abstract representation of elements" (p. 112). According to this view, the key to transfer of cognitive skills rests in representing them as general rules rather than as specific behaviors.

IMPLICATIONS OF RESEARCH ON SKILL LEARNING

Building on earlier research on motor skill learning, Anderson and his colleagues (Anderson, 1993) offer a three-stage theory of cognitive skill learning.

Cognitive stage. The learner works from instructions and represents the steps in the skill as verbal statements—which can be called *declarative knowledge*. For example, in learning to drive using a manual transmission, you might tell yourself, "Second is directly below first" (Anderson, 2000, p. 310).

Associative stage. The learner begins to be able to carry out a procedure more easily without needing to verbalize each step. The new skill is changed from *declarative knowledge* (i.e., factual statements) into *procedural knowledge* (i.e., a sort of mental program). For example, at this stage of learning to use a manual transmission, you might be able to shift gears without having to verbalize what you are doing.

Autonomous stage. The learner is able to carry out the skill rapidly and errorlessly without paying attention to it. The learner may even be unable to verbally describe the skill, such as not being able to tell someone how to tie his or her shoes.

What is learned that can be transferred from one skill to another? At first, in the cognitive stage, the learner acquires factual statements such as: "The backwards arrow key is in the lower right corner of keyboard." Next, in the associative stage, the unit becomes a collection of productions (Anderson, 1993), that is, IF-THEN pairs, such as "If you want to move the cursor one space back, press the backwards arrow key." Through practice, learners consolidate knowledge by collapsing several specific procedures into a single one. For example, the actions in erasing a letter may become one production: "If you want to erase a letter, move the cursor to the right of the letter and press the delete key." Finally, in the autonomous stage, the learner may create more generalizable productions by combining specific productions into a more general one. For example, the many specific procedures for replacing various texts can be generalized into a general production: "If you want to replace text, highlight the to-be-replaced text with the cursor and type in the new text." As you can see, skill learning involves building units of knowledge that are increasingly more transferable—beginning with specific verbal statements that change to specific procedures that change to more general procedures. Thus, the key to transfer of skill learning is to help students build general procedures. Anderson and his colleagues (Anderson, 2000) developed computer tutoring systems for skills ranging from writing geometry proofs to writing computer programs. In each case, teaching for transfer is accomplished by giving students practice in solving problems and providing feedback aimed at helping them build generalized solution procedures.

CHAPTER SUMMARY

This chapter began with a look at Thorndike's famous law of effect, the idea that feedback following a response serves to determine the likelihood that the response will be made again. Then it examined situations that seem related to the law of effect: classroom management, response learning, concept learning, and skill learning.

In each case, we compared two contrasting views of the learner. The behaviorist view is that the learner is passively being conditioned by the feedback; that is, feedback serves as reinforcement that automatically stamps in (or stamps out) responses. This view is most consistent with the theory of specific transfer described in Chapter 1, because what is learned is a specific stimulus-response (S-R) association. In contrast, the cognitive view is that the learner is actively interpreting the feedback that is given; that is, feedback serves as information that the learner uses in building a learning outcome. This view is most consistent with the theory of specific transfer of general principles described in Chapter 1, because what is learned is a general attitude, rule, or procedure.

For classroom management, we found that token economies and contingency contracting can serve to increase desired behaviors and decrease undesired behaviors. However, the mechanism underlying the behavior change seems to be best described by a cognitive theory (i.e., by assuming that the learner attempts to interpret or justify the rewards or punishments that are given). An aspect of teaching for meaningful learning involves helping the learner to achieve an interpretation that fosters intrinsic motivation rather than dependence on external rewards.

For response learning, practice with feedback tended to enable improvements in performance, whereas practice alone did not affect performance. Again, however, the mechanism underlying the behavior change seems best described by a cognitive theory (i.e., by assuming that the learner uses feedback as information). Teaching for meaningful learning involves helping the learner build a mental program for producing appropriate behaviors (including self-feedback) rather than learning specific behaviors themselves.

For concept learning, practice with feedback again served to improve performance. Again, a cognitive theory (i.e., hypothesis testing) seemed to be the best explanation of the behavior change. Teaching for meaningful learning involves helping the learner discover a general rule rather than solely strengthening specific associations.

For skill learning, practice with feedback resulted in improved performance, and again, a cognitive theory (i.e., that learners build increasingly general rules) was the best explanation of the behavior change. Teaching for meaningful learning involves helping the learner compile general procedures rather than a chain of specific behaviors.

In summary, we are left with a sort of irony. The basic findings of Thorndike and Skinner and other behaviorist-oriented researchers seem to be fairly well established—the appropriate use of feedback (or reinforcers) given after the learner's responses can serve to change behavior. However, the processes of response learning, concept learning, and skill learning do not seem to fit the theoretical description given by the behaviorists. Instead, as we have seen in this chapter, the learner appears to be actively involved in trying to interpret the feedback that is given. Any effective use of feedback or reinforcement techniques requires an understanding of the active cognitive processing by the learner. In essence, we leave with a modified view of the law of effect: It is not the feedback that changes behavior, but rather the learner's interpretation and understanding of that feedback. When the goal of teaching is to promote transfer, teachers should make sure that learners interpret feedback in productive ways. Students engage in meaningful learning when they build intrinsic motivation that supports a self-monitored change in behavior, general rules that support concept learning, and general procedures that support skilled performance. In short, teaching for meaningful learning occurs when learners use feedback to make sense out of a learning episode rather than to acquire a collection of specific responses.

SUGGESTED READINGS

Cameron, J., & Pierce, W. D. (1994). Reinforcement, reward, and intrinsic motivation: A meta-analysis. *Review of Educational Research*, 64, 363–423. (Reviews research on the hidden costs of reward.)

Deci, E. L., Koestner, R., & Ryan, R. M. (1999). A meta-analytic review of experiments examining the effects of extrinsic rewards on intrinsic motivation. *Psychological Bulletin*, 125, 625–668. (Reviews research on the hidden costs of rewards.)

Singley, M. K., & Anderson, J. R. (1989). *The transfer of cognitive skill*. Cambridge, MA: Harvard University Press. (Describes the process of skill learning.)

Thorndike, E. L. (1913). *Educational psychology*. New York: Columbia University Press.(Presents Thorndike's famous "law of effect.")

Teaching by Providing Concreteness, Activity, and Familiarity

CHAPTER OUTLINE

The Parallelogram Problem

Concrete Methods

Discovery Methods

Inductive Methods

Chapter Summary

This chapter investigates three instructional methods aimed at producing meaningful learning through guided exploration—concrete methods that make the learning task more concrete, discovery methods that make the learning task more active, and inductive methods that make the learning task more familiar. In each case, the learner explores a problem or task and is given various forms of guidance—including concrete materials (concrete methods), hints (discovery methods), and links to prior experience (inductive methods). For each technique, the chapter provides an example, explains the underlying theoretical concepts, describes some representative classic research, suggests some implications for instruction, and provides current applications using computers.

THE PARALLELOGRAM PROBLEM

Consider the parallelogram in Figure 8–1. How would you teach children to solve problems like the parallelogram problem in this figure? Let's assume that the children have already learned how to find the area of a rectangle but have not yet learned about the area of a parallelogram.

The Gestalt psychologist Wertheimer (1959) contrasts two distinct methods of instruction for this material. The first method is to teach the child to find the height and the base and to plug them into the formula Area = height × base. In the parallelogram problem in Figure 8–1, the child must find that the height is 5, the base is 11, so the area is 5 × 11, or 55. Wertheimer calls this approach the "rote method" because the child learns to mechanically apply a formula. The rote method is summarized in the top of Figure 8–2.

The second method suggested by Wertheimer is to allow the child to have *structural insight* (i.e., to see how a parallelogram can be changed into a rectangle by moving the triangle on one end to the other end). Once the child sees how to restructure the parts of a parallelogram into a rectangle, the child can go ahead using a previously learned method for finding the area of a rectangle. Wertheimer calls this approach the *meaningful method* because the learner understands how the parts of a parallelogram fit together. The middle of Figure 8–2 summarizes the meaningful method.

Why should we be concerned whether a child learns by rote or by understanding? Isn't it enough to teach the child how to use the formula effectively so that the child can get the right answer on parallelogram problems? Wertheimer's answer to these questions is that *understanding* is important for some instructional objectives but not for others. For example, according to Wertheimer, both methods of instruction lead to good performance on standard problems like those given as examples during instruction. Thus, if the goal of instruction is efficient application of a rule on standard problems, the meaningful method of instruction is not needed. However, what happens when you present children with unusual problems such as shown in the bottom of Figure 8–2? According to Wertheimer, the children who learned by understanding are able to solve transfer problems, whereas the children who learned by rote say, "We haven't had that yet." Thus, the payoff for mean-

FIGURE 8–1 Find the area of a parallelogram

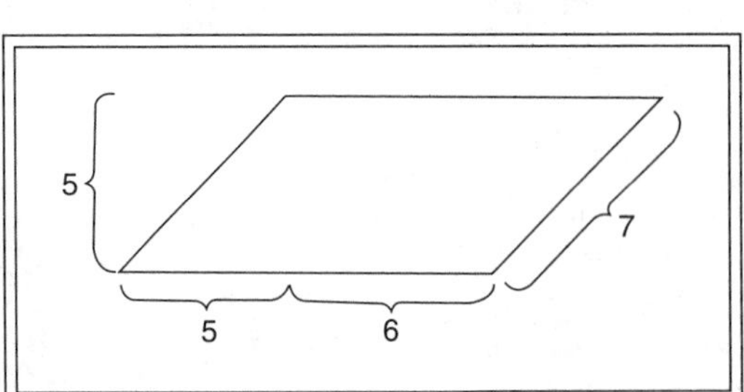

FIGURE 8–2 Rote and meaningful methods of instruction for the parallelogram problem

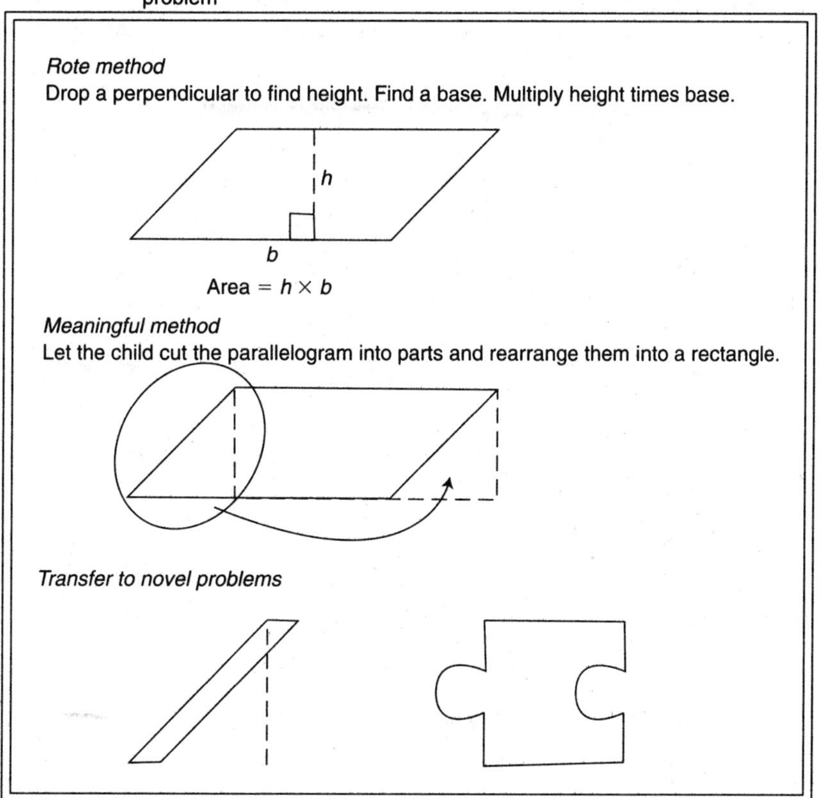

ingful methods of instruction is not in exact retention of the taught material but rather in creative transfer to new situations. If the goal of instruction is that the child be able to creatively apply learning in new situations, then meaningful methods of instruction are important.

Rote method
Drop a perpendicular to find height. Find a base. Multiply height times base.
h
b
Area = h × b
Meaningful method
Let the child cut the parallelogram into parts and rearrange them into a rectangle.
Transfer to novel problems

Wertheimer and other Gestalt psychologists (Katona, 1940; Kohler, 1925) distinguished between learning by rote and learning by understanding. Even though their work provides many interesting examples of the distinction, the cognitive theory underlying the distinction was not well spelled out. In this chapter, therefore, we investigate several well-known attempts to provide meaningful methods of instruction: concrete methods, discovery methods, and inductive methods. Each represents a form of guided exploration in which a learner is asked to solve a problem and is given some support along the way—including relating the problem to concrete objects (concrete methods), giving hints to keep the learner on track (discovery-oriented methods), and relating the task to something the learner already knows (inductive methods).

CONCRETE METHODS

EXAMPLE OF A CONCRETE METHOD

One way to make an idea more meaningful is to make it more concrete. For example, in the parallelogram problem, the teacher may make the concept of area more concrete by using 1 × 1 inch squares. Figure 8–3 shows how using 1 × 1 squares can give a concrete way of representing area. These materials are called *concrete manipulatives,* because the student can physically move and rearrange them.

THEORY: MAPPING CONCEPTS TO CONCRETE MODELS

Why does a concrete representation of the material to be learned influence learning? One explanation comes from Bruner's (1964) theory of cognitive development. According to Bruner, children develop modes of representing information in the following order:

Enactive mode—using actions to represent information, such as tying a shoe.
Iconic mode—using visualization to represent information, such as thinking of a friend's face.

FIGURE 8–3 How many unit squares are needed to cover the parallelogram?

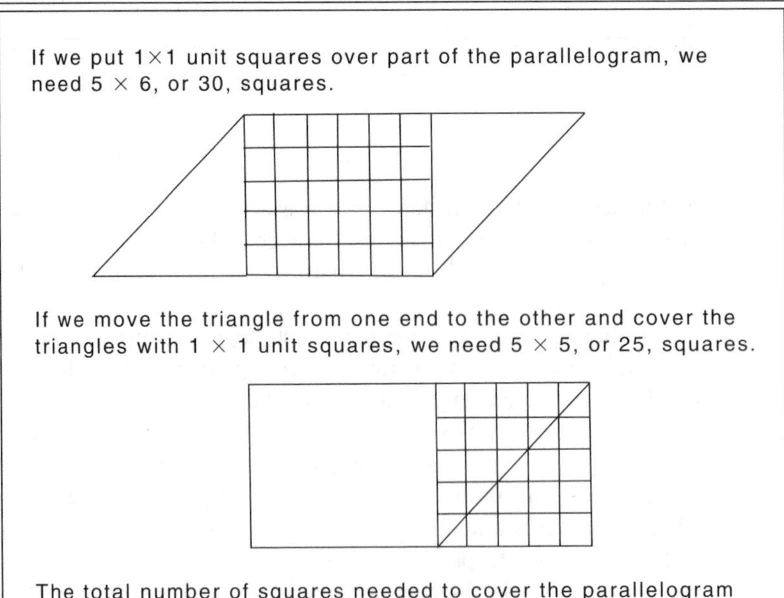

If we put 1×1 unit squares over part of the parallelogram, we need 5 × 6, or 30, squares.
If we move the triangle from one end to the other and cover the triangles with 1 × 1 unit squares, we need 5 × 5, or 25, squares.
The total number of squares needed to cover the parallelogram is 11 × 5, or 55.

Symbolic mode—using language or other symbols to represent information, such as knowing that the area of a circle equals pi times the square of the radius.

In learning a new skill, such as arithmetic, several modes of representation may be involved, as shown in Figure 8–4. The enactive mode involves the physical actions of counting aloud with fingers; the iconic mode involves visualizing bundles of sticks that can be grouped by 10s; the symbolic mode involves numerals.

The development of understanding must progress through the same stages as representation in intellectual development: understanding first by doing, then by visualizing, and eventually by symbolic representation. Bruner and Kenney (1966) state this idea as follows: "We would suggest that learning mathematics may be viewed as a microcosm of intellectual development. It begins with instrumental activity, a kind of definition of things by doing." Eventually, mathematical operations "become represented . . . in the form of . . . images," and finally, "with the help of symbolic notation, the learner comes to grasp the formal or abstract properties of the things he is dealing with" (p. 436). According to this view, understanding progresses from the level of active manipulation of objects and images and eventually leads to symbolic representation. Therefore, instruction that begins with formal symbolic representations without first allowing the learner to develop an enactive or iconic representation will lead to rote learning. Concrete manipulatives may be useful in connecting one mode of representation to another.

RESEARCH AND DEVELOPMENT: CONCRETE MANIPULATIVES IN MATHEMATICS

BUNDLES OF STICKS Brownell (1935) was one of the first to demonstrate the important pedagogic role of concrete analogies in school learning. For example, Brownell

FIGURE 8–4 Three ways of representing a problem

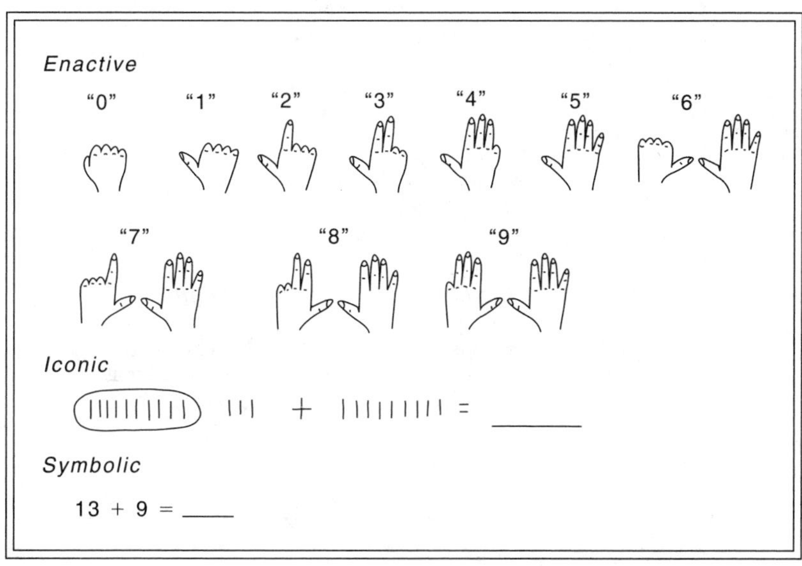

suggested using manipulatives such as bundles of little sticks to concretize the subtraction algorithm. Suppose you wanted to teach children to subtract two-digit numbers such as 65 − 28 = _____. One method of instruction would be to drill the student on the subtraction procedure as shown in the top of Figure 8–5. An alternative, which Brownell called the *meaningful method,* is to show how the problem can be represented as bundles of sticks, as shown in the bottom of Figure 8–5. In this system, place value can be represented by tying sticks together into bundles of 10 each.

In a careful research study, Brownell and Moser (1949) taught two groups of third-graders, one by the standard method and the other by the meaningful method. On subsequent tests, both groups of children were able to solve two-digit subtraction problems like those given during instruction; however, the children who learned with the concrete analogy performed better than the standard group in learning to solve different kinds of problems. Apparently, the advantage of meaningful learning comes when the child is asked to transfer to new situations.

According to Brownell (1935), a student needs to relate each piece of information together within a meaningful framework: "One needs a fund of meanings, not a myriad of automatic responses" (p. 10). Brownell noted that drill is appropriate only after "ideas and processes already understood are to be practiced to increase efficiency" (p. 19).

Let's suppose that concrete manipulatives such as bundles of sticks can help children to understand the concepts of number, place value, sets, and operations on sets. Is it better to

FIGURE 8–5 How to make arithmetic more concrete

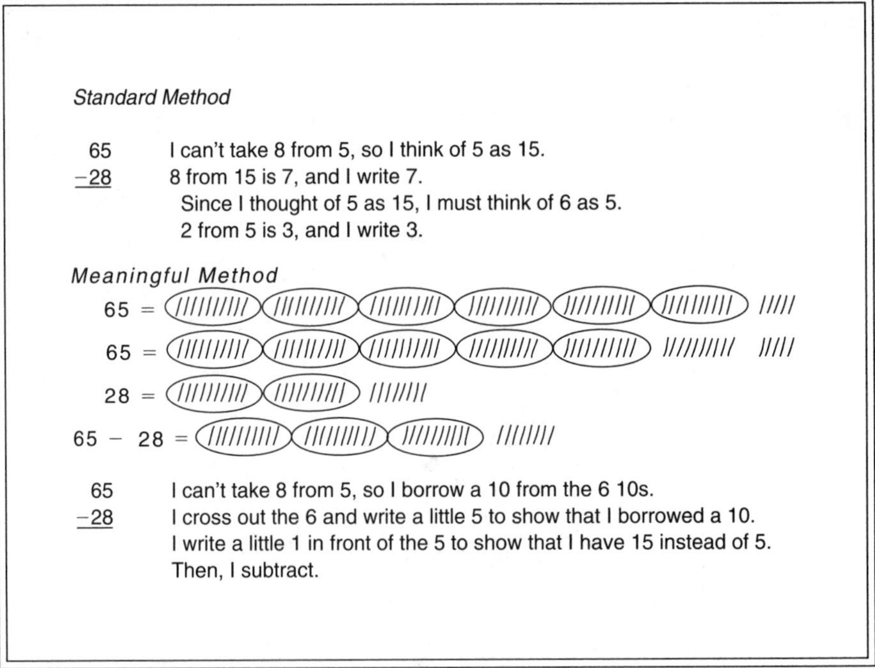

Adapted from Brownell and Moser (1949)

avoid teaching computational procedures until students first understand the concepts, or is it better to present the computational procedures first and then show how they relate to concrete manipulatives? As Resnick and Ford (1981) pointed out, "This is the sort of question that research has not yet answered" (p. 110).

More recently, English (1997) has shown how concrete manipulatives—such as using bars and blocks to represent a two-digit number—rely on a form of analogical reasoning. For example, 43 can be represented as four 10-unit bars and 3 single-unit blocks. In thinking by analogy, when you are presented with an unfamiliar problem such as 43 − 27 = _____ (target problem), you can think of a familiar representation of the problem such as representing 43 as a collection of bars and blocks from which 27 must be taken (base problem). Then you can think through your answer using the base problem—that is, taking away two 10-unit bars, opening one 10-unit bar into 10 single-unit blocks and taking away 7, and then counting the remaining as one 10-unit bar and 6 one-unit blocks. Then you can convert your answer from the base problem into the form of the target problem, 43 − 27 = 16. Yet, like earlier work on concrete manipulatives, English (1997) notes: "Research on analogical reasoning in mathematical problem solving by elementary school children is in its infancy" (p. 199).

MONTESSORI MATERIALS Montessori (1964) developed concrete materials that can be used to teach the structure underlying arithmetic. For example, Figure 8–6 shows some Montessori materials that can be used to teach the concept of place value. These materials allow the child to progress from representing numbers as beads (with units, tens, and hundreds) to expanded notation using the colored labels, to standard notation using superimposed labels. To teach computational algorithms, the Montessori materials include wooden

FIGURE 8–6 Some Montessori materials for numbers

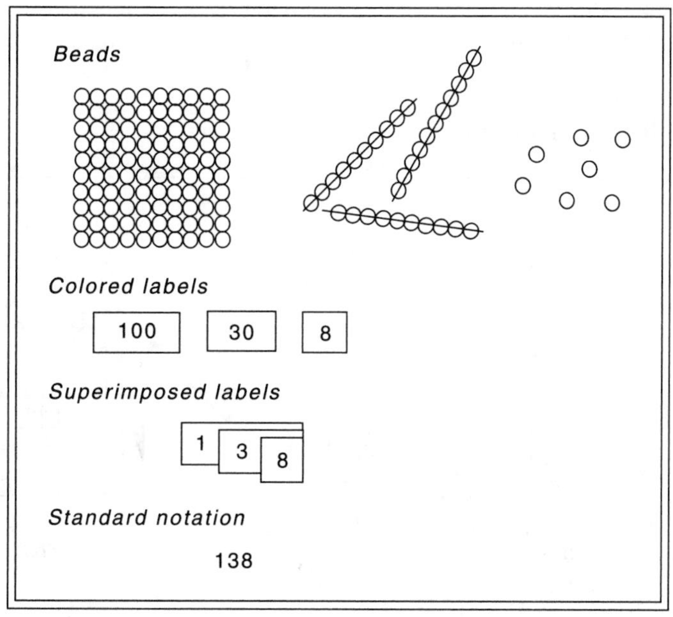

squares with 1 printed in green, 10 printed in blue, or 100 printed in red. A problem can be translated from standard notation into colored squares, such as shown in Figure 8–5. Then a child can learn the procedure of carrying as trading in 10 green unit-squares for one blue 10-square, or trading 10 blue 10-squares for one red 100-square. Once the child is proficient at such exchanges, the symbolic notation for carrying can be introduced. For example, the 1 written at the top of the 10s column in the standard algorithm corresponds to exchanging 10 units for one 10 in colored squares.

DIENES BLOCKS Another set of concrete materials was developed by Dienes (1960, 1967). For example, place value and computation can be represented using multibase arithmetic blocks (MAB), also known as Dienes blocks, such as shown in Figure 8–7. The blocks come in units that are about 1 cubic centimeter; units can be snapped together into lines of 10, called longs; longs can be attached to form 10 × 10 squares, called flats; flats can be piled together to form 10 × 10 × 10 cubes, called blocks.

Bruner and Kenney (1966) showed how materials adapted from Dienes blocks can be used to teach the underlying structure of factoring quadratic equations. Figure 8–8 shows that materials consisted of units (i.e., 1 by 1 blocks), longs (i.e., blocks that are 1 by X), and flats (i.e., blocks that are X by X). To make a square that is (X + 1) by (X + 1), you need one flat, two longs, and a unit. To make a square that is (X + 2) by (X + 2) you need one flat, four longs, and four units. To make a square that is (X + 3) by (X + 3) you need one flat, six longs, and nine units, and so on. Once the child can represent squares using blocks such as the (X + 1) square, the formal notation can be given such as $(X + 1)^2 = X^2 + 2X + 1$. Bruner and Kenney suggest that instruction should begin by giving children a chance to actively manipulate actual objects and eventually progress towards the symbolic representation of the problem.

Based on his observations of children, Bruner (1960) argued for the importance of teaching the underlying structure of mathematics and science to children: "Grasping the structure of a subject is understanding it in a way that permits many other things to be related to it meaningfully. To learn structure, in short, is to learn how things are related. . . . The teaching

FIGURE 8–7 Dienes blocks for numbers

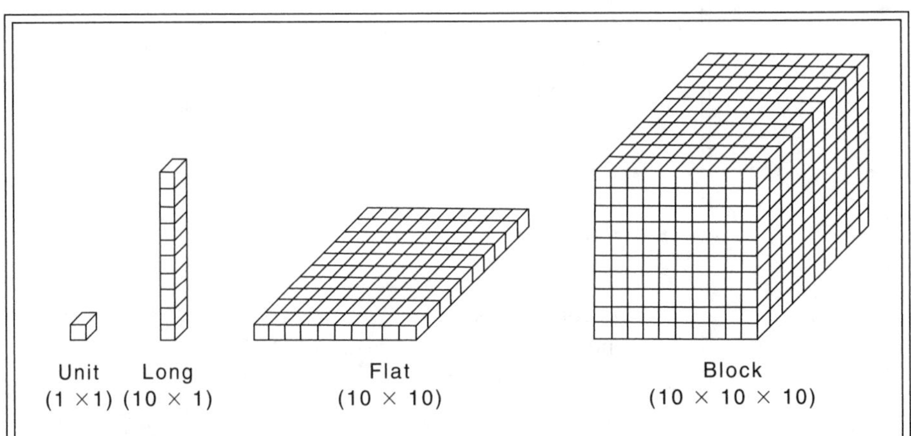

FIGURE 8–8 Using modified Dienes blocks to teach quadratic factoring

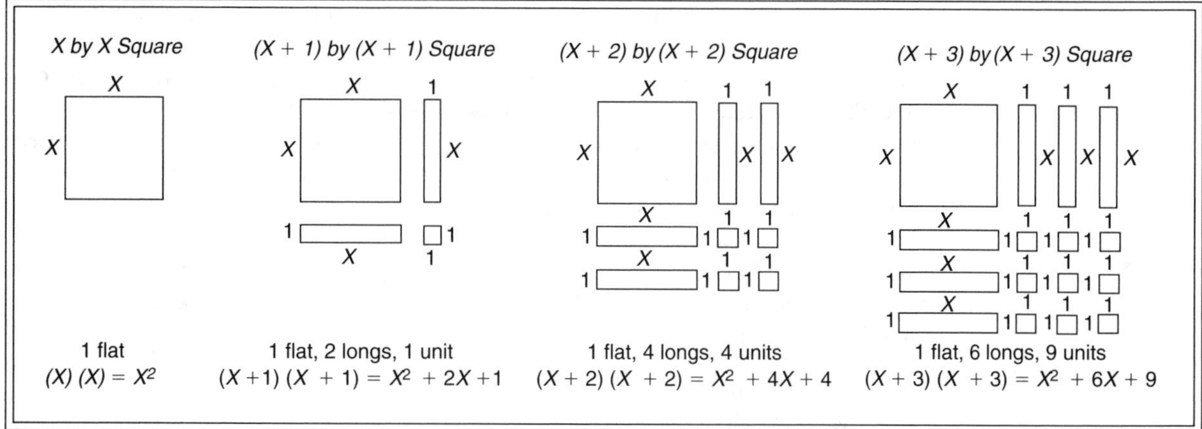

Adapted from Bruner and Kenney (1966)

and learning of structure, rather than simply the mastery of facts and techniques, is at the center of the classic problem of transfer" (pp. 3–11). For example, the child who learns through manipulating beads or blocks that 7 + 3 is the same as 6 + 4 or 2 + 8 has learned something about how arithmetic facts are related to one another.

IMPLICATIONS OF CONCRETE METHODS

So far we have sampled some of the commonly used manipulatives in mathematics instruction. Other manipulatives include attribute blocks, Cuisenaire rods, and geoboards. These materials are used in an attempt to present the underlying structures of mathematics in a simple and concrete way to children.

During the 1960s, mathematics curricula were reformed to emphasize this structure-oriented approach and to deemphasize drill-and-practice. However, in a review of manipulatives in mathematics instruction, Resnick and Ford (1981) pointed out that there has been very little research to identify the psychologically important structures that underlie mathematics: "The structure-oriented methods and materials have not been adequately validated by research, and we know little from school practice about the effects of the curriculum reforms upon the quality of children's mathematical learning" (p. 126). In another review of concrete manipulative, Hiebert and Carpenter (1992) concluded: "Despite the intuitive appeal of using materials, investigations of the effectiveness of concrete materials in classrooms have yielded mixed results" (p. 70). According to these authors, the effectiveness of concrete materials can be enhanced when students have opportunities to reflect on the underlying principles, perhaps through discussions with peers. In sum, concrete methods must take into account the way that the learner tries to make sense of the manipulatives; once a learner understands a concept, drill-and-practice may be needed to ensure increased efficiency.

COMPUTER APPLICATIONS: COMPUTER SIMULATIONS IN SCIENCE

More recently, advances in educational computing technology have made it possible to allow students to interact with computer simulations of real-world objects and events. These computer simulations—called *microworlds*—allow learners to interact with and think about concrete representations of otherwise abstract ideas. Educational computer simulations are not magical toys that guarantee meaningful learning, but when used wisely, they offer a way of bringing the power of concrete manipulatives to a whole new level.

In the top-left frame of Figure 8–9, you see a number line running from −9 to +9 with a bunny sitting on the space for 0. Suppose you wanted to have the bunny enact the procedure for the problem, 4 − −5 = ___, which you can read as "4 minus negative 5." Write down the steps you would ask the bunny to carry out. If you are like most successful problem solvers, your list would consist of the following steps:

1. The bunny moves to 4.
2. The bunny faces left.
3. The bunny jumps backwards 5 steps.
4. The bunny lands on 9, which is the answer.

In this example, the symbolic number sentence, 4 − −5 = 9, can be translated into a concrete situation involving a bunny moving along a number line. This concrete representation allows you to make a conceptual distinction between a minus sign (in which case the bunny faces left) and a negative number such as −5 (in which case the bunny jumps backwards five steps).

Does practice in relating symbols to concrete situations help students understand how to add and subtract signed numbers? Moreno and Mayer (1999) tested this issue with high-achieving sixth-grade students who had no previous experience with adding and subtracting signed numbers. All students received practice on 64 problems spaced across four different sessions. For each problem presented on a computer screen (such as 4 − −5 = ___), the control group typed in an answer and then the correct answer appeared on the screen. For each problem presented on the computer screen, the experimental group used a joystick to move the bunny along the number line and typed in an answer based on the where the bunny ended up; then the computer presented an annotated animation of the bunny correctly moving along the number line, ending with the final answer (such as shown in Figure 8–9). Thus, both groups solved the same problems, but the experimental group also worked on relating the problem to a concrete context of a bunny moving along a number line. In this study involving high-achieving students, the experimental group showed large pretest-to-posttest gains in correctly solving problems (i.e., up 25%), whereas the control group did not (i.e., up 6%).

What was learned by students in the control and experimental groups? Some students—particularly those in the control group—may tend to form specific S-R associations, such as memorizing that when the question is "4 − −5 = ___" the answer is "9." This kind of very specific learning would not lead to much transfer on a posttest. In contrast, other students—particularly those in the experimental group—may have created more general principles for understanding the problems. Many students enter the learning situation with what can be called a *negative-bias bug:* a misconception in which students fail to recognize that the "−" symbol sometimes is a minus sign and sometimes is a negative

FIGURE 8–9 Selected frames from the bunny simulation

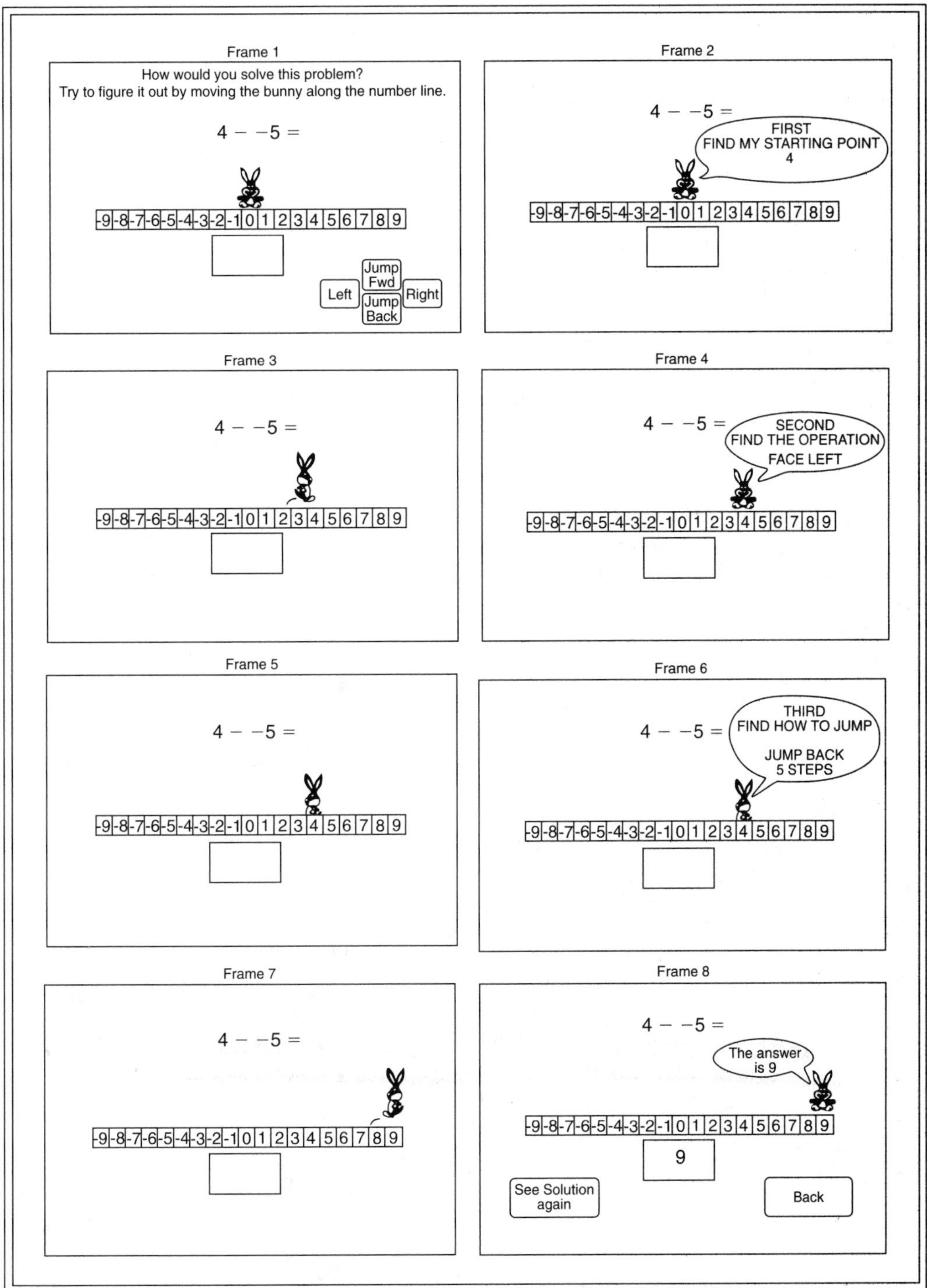

From Moreno and Mayer (1999)

sign. Whenever a problem contains two "−" symbols, the students interpret this to mean that they should find the absolute difference between the numbers and then either place a negative sign in front or not (e.g., $-3 - 1 = 2$ or -2; $7 - -2 = 5$ or -5; $-8 + -1 = 7$ or -7). If learning is more general, students may learn to make a distinction between the minus sign (which means to subtract) and the negative sign (which means that the number is negative), thus eliminating the negative-bias bug and increasing the potential for transfer. In Moreno and Mayer's (1999) study, the control group displayed the negative bias bug 15% of the time on the pretest and 15% of the time on the posttest, suggesting little progress in building a general distinction between minus and negative. The experimental group displayed the negative-bias bug 23% of the time on the pretest and 9% of the time on the posttest, demonstrating a large improvement in building a general principle. Apparently, building a general principle (such as the distinction between minus signs and negative signs) is a major accomplishment that may be an important key to transfer. Somewhat similar results were obtained by Schwartz, Nathan, and Resnick (1996) in which students learned to represent adding and subtracting signed numbers as the building and comparing of trains of various lengths along a number line.

Let's now move from arithmetic to algebra. Consider the following problem:

> A huge ant is terrorizing San Francisco. It travels east toward Detroit, which is twenty four hundred miles away, at four hundred miles per hour. The Army learns of this one hour later and sends a helicopter west from Detroit at six hundred miles per hour to intercept the ant. If the ant left at 2 p.m., what time will the helicopter and ant collide (ignoring any time changes)? (Nathan, Kintsch, & Young, 1992, p. 349)

If you are like most of the college students in Nathan, Kintsch, and Young's study, you had some difficulty with this problem. Overall, less than half the students correctly solved problems like this one on a pretest.

To help students improve, you could provide a review of algebra and exposure to three time-rate-distance word problems like the ant problem. However, students who received this kind of instruction (control group) showed little pretest-to-posttest gain in correctly solving other word problems (i.e., up 6%). In contrast, you could help students learn how to relate the problem to a concrete situation by letting them use a computer program (called ANIMATE) designed to allow learners to animate the problem. For example, for the ant problem, students could select an image of an ant from a menu and place it on the left side of the screen and select an image of a helicopter and place it on the right side of the screen. Then, they could create a system of distance-rate-time equations and fill in the relevant numbers (such as typing in rate as 400 for the ant and rate as 600 for the helicopter). They could run the animation at any time and revise it based on what they saw. As you can see, solving problems with the ANIMATE program helps students understand the connection between words in the problem and a concrete visual representation. Students who received practice in using the ANIMATE program to work on three time-rate-distance problems (experimental group) showed large pretest-to-posttest gains in correctly solving other word problems (i.e., up more than 300%).

What is learned by the control and experimental groups? According to Nathan, Kintsch, and Young, students in the experimental group are more likely than students in the control group to learn general strategies for how to represent word problems—a skill they refer to as being able to build a situation model of the problem. Consistent with this analysis, they

found that errors in representing the problem decreased only slightly from the pretest to the posttest for the control group (i.e., down 10%), whereas such errors dropped greatly for the experimental group (i.e., down 69%). When it comes to meaningful learning, it appears that being able to build situation models using pictures of objects is a general skill that can enable transfer.

My goal is not to review the volumes of research on computer-based tutoring but rather to examine a few exemplary research studies on the use of computerized concrete manipulatives. As you can see, there is encouraging evidence that concretizing an abstract concept or procedure can help students understand and learn in ways that promote transfer. Further, computer-based visualizations seem to work because they help students build general principles or strategies that apply across situations—such as recognizing the difference between minus and negative or being able to construct situation models. In a pioneering set of studies, White and Frederiksen (1998; White, 1984, 1993) found similar positive effects on understanding when high school students learn and discuss physics principles within the context of a visually concrete computer game.

In computer-based microworlds, the student is able to relate general principles to more familiar objects by manipulating simulated objects on the computer screen. The research results are promising because they show that *concrete manipulatives* can be moved productively to the computer screen. The number of commercially available educational computer simulations is increasing, and research such as highlighted in this section suggests that some simulations may be useful. However, not all computer games are useful instructional tools. What makes a "good" game? The foregoing examples suggest that good games are based on appropriate design principles, are presented at a level that is appropriate for students, and focus on teaching generalizable skills that are fundamental parts of the academic program. Clearly, encouraging students to interact with, think about, and talk about concrete representations of otherwise abstract ideas provides a potentially useful path to meaningful learning.

DISCOVERY METHODS

EXAMPLE OF DISCOVERY METHODS

Let's return to the parallelogram problem shown in Figure 8–1. What else can be done to make the rule for finding area more understandable? One suggestion is to encourage the learner to try to solve problems actively before being presented with the rule to be learned. For example, you could give the student a paper parallelogram and a scissors and ask the learner to cut up the paper and rearrange it as a rectangle. In this case, we want the learner to cut the triangle from one end and place it on the other end (as shown in the middle frame of Figure 8–2). Then, the rule can be given.

THEORY: THE JOY OF DISCOVERY

Bruner (1961) helped to instigate modern interest in discovery learning in his famous essay "The Act of Discovery." Bruner's paper distinguished between two modes of instruction: expository mode, in which the teacher controls what is presented and the student listens, and hypothetical mode, in which the student has some control over the pace and content of instruction and may take on an "as if" attitude. The hypothetical mode allows the learner to discover new rules and ideas rather than simply memorize rules and ideas that the teacher presents. According to Bruner, the discovery of rules results in better learning—because the learner has organized the material in a useful way—and results in the student's becoming a better learner and problem solver in general because the student gets practice in processing information.

RESEARCH AND DEVELOPMENT: DISCOVERY OF RULES

Although Bruner is an eloquent proponent of the discovery method and although his suggestions were implemented in some curricular projects (Davis, 1973), you might wonder whether or not there is any empirical evidence that discovery enhances learning. During the 1960s a flurry of research was concerned with the question of how much guidance a teacher should provide (Shulman & Keisler, 1966). Although the researchers often used terms in different ways, we can define three basic levels of guidance in instruction:

1. ***Pure discovery.*** The student receives representative problems to solve with minimal teacher guidance.
2. ***Guided discovery.*** The student receives problems to solve, but the teacher provides hints and directions about how to solve the problem to keep the student on track.
3. ***Expository.*** The final answer or rule is presented to the student.

Let's look at how these methods can be used to help students learn how to solve logical reasoning problems and mathematical reasoning problems.

LOGICAL REASONING An early study by Craig (1956) was the forerunner of more recent method-of-instruction studies. Students were given training in "finding the word that doesn't belong" in sets of five words. For example, given

CYCLE SELDOM SAWDUST SAUSAGE CELLAR

the appropriate answer is to mark CYCLE, since it does not share the same initial sound (i.e., "sigh") as any of the other words. Items were organized in sets of four, all having the same relational rule (e.g., initial sound), and each training booklet contained several such types of rules.

Two instructional methods were used: A guided discovery group was told the relation (e.g., "look for initial sound") at the beginning of each set of four items but was not told the answer per se; the other group, which could be called "pure discovery," was not given any hints. Results indicated that the group given some guidance learned more efficiently, retained more, and transferred just as well as the pure discovery group. This study calls into doubt the emphasis on extreme classroom freedom and independence; some learners simply may not be able to discover the appropriate concepts and rules without some direction from the teacher.

Kittel (1957) reported a study using material similar to Craig's but that involved all three levels of guidance—pure discovery, guided discovery, and expository. The training, like Craig's involved giving the learner a set of five words, such as

GONE START GO STOP COME

and asking the learner to mark the word that doesn't belong. In this example, the relational principle is "form two pairs of opposites"; hence, the correct answer is "GONE." In the training booklets, each set of three items had the same principle, and there were 15 such principles in all.

Some subjects were not given any direction (pure discovery); some subjects were told the principle (e.g., "form two pairs of opposites") for each set of problems but were not given the answer (guided discovery); some subjects were told both the principle and the correct answer for each problem (expository). Figure 8–10 summarizes some of the major results of the study. As the figure shows, the pure discovery group performed worse than the other two groups on immediate retention, suggesting that pure discovery resulted in less initial learning. On tests of transfer and long-term retention, the guided discovery group outperformed both the pure discovery group and the expository group. Apparently, the pure discovery group did not discover many of the principles during learning; in addition, while the guided discovery and expository groups seem to have learned equal amounts during initial learning, the extra processing and thinking during learning led the guided discovery group to retain the information and transfer the information better than the expository group.

MATHEMATICAL REASONING The foregoing results suggest that a major drawback of pure discovery methods is that some students may fail to discover the underlying principle. To overcome this problem, Gagné and Brown (1961) conducted a study in which students learned to solve series sums and derive formulas using three different instructional methods. For example, students learned how to compute the sum of "1,3,5,7,9 . . ." and to

FIGURE 8–10 How much guidance should be given during learning?

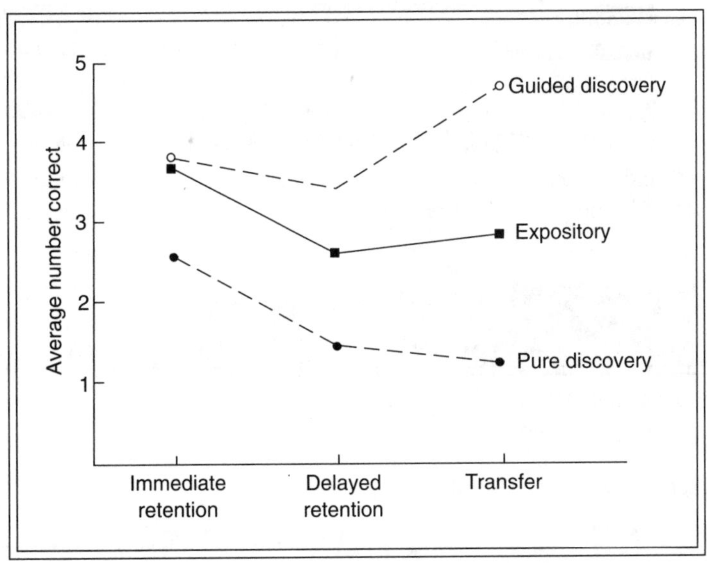

Adapted from Kittel (1957)

write a formula for the series. In the pure discovery method students were given problems to solve; however, if they were unable to solve the problem, hints were provided until the correct principle was found. Thus, the pure discovery method was modified to make it more like guided discovery (i.e., to ensure that the student actually learned). In the guided discovery method, problems were given along with a systematic succession of questions to aid the student, thus, providing more guidance concerning how to solve the problem. The expository group was given problems along with the solution formula already worked out. All students had to continue working until they were able to master four separate series; thus, all students were forced to learn equal amounts.

Table 8–1 shows the amount of time and number of errors in learning under the three methods of instruction and the amount of time and number of errors on a subsequent transfer test for the three treatment groups. As the table shows, the guided discovery group took the longest amount of time to learn but performed best on the transfer test. The pure discovery group also performed well on transfer, presumably because of the procedure of ensuring that initial learning actually occurred.

IMPLICATIONS OF DISCOVERY METHODS

Our review of research on discovery identifies the following patterns:

1. Pure discovery methods often require excessive amounts of learning time, result in low levels of initial learning, and result in inferior performance on transfer and long-term retention. However, when the principle to be learned is obvious or when a strict criterion of initial learning is enforced, pure discovery subjects are likely to behave like guided discovery subjects. Apparently, pure discovery encourages learners to get cognitively involved (Anastasiow, Sibley, Leonhardt, & Borish, 1970) but fails to ensure that they will come into contact with the rule or principle to be learned.
2. Guided discovery may require more or less time than expository instruction, depending on the task, but tends to result in better long-term retention and transfer than expository instruction. Apparently, guided discovery both encourages learners to search actively for how to apply rules and makes sure that the learner comes into contact with the rule to be learned.
3. Expository instruction may sometimes result in less learning time than other methods and generally results in equivalent levels of initial learning as compared to

TABLE 8–1

Effects of discovery methods on learning and transfer

	Pure Discovery	Guided Discovery	Expository
Learning time (errors)	28(6)	46(17)	41(9)
Transfer time (errors)	20(2)	17(1)	27(6)

Adapted from Gagné and Brown (1961)

> guided discovery. However, if the goal of instruction is long-term retention and transfer, expository methods seem inferior to guided discovery. Apparently, expository instruction does not encourage the learner to actively think about the rule but does ensure that the rule is learned.

When the goal of instruction is long-term retention and transfer of learned principles, the teacher needs to use enough guidance so that the student finds the to-be-learned principle but not so much guidance that the student is discouraged from working actively on understanding how the principle can be applied. The learner's level of prior knowledge is likely to play an important role because students with low prior knowledge may need more guidance, whereas students with high prior knowledge may need less guidance.

COMPUTER APPLICATIONS: DISCOVERY IN COMPUTER PROGRAMMING

Although research in the 1960s tended to argue against the usefulness of pure discovery, the introduction of computers into schools during the 1980s brought renewed calls for discovery learning. For example, Papert (1980), in his influential book *Mindstorms*, argues eloquently for two important aspects of computing instruction: (1) hands-on discovery in which students are allowed to "learn without being taught" (i.e., students receive unstructured, hands-on computer experience that is not tied to any curricular demands), and (2) LOGO environment, in which students work in a powerful and responsive computer environment that is supposedly provided by the programming language LOGO.

To understand the LOGO environment, let's focus briefly on *turtle graphics*, generally the first aspect of LOGO to be learned by elementary school children. You begin with a "turtle," represented as a triangular cursor on a computer screen, as shown in Figure 8–11. You can turn the turtle by issuing commands such as RIGHT _____ or LEFT _____, where each command is followed by a number that indicates how many degrees the turtle will turn. For example, RIGHT 90 means turn the turtle 90 degrees clockwise from its current position and LEFT 90 means turn the turtle 90 degrees counterclockwise from its current position. You can move the turtle by issuing commands such as FORWARD _____ or BACK _____, where each command is followed by a number indicating how many steps the turtle will take. Examples of these four commands are given in Figure 8–11.

Suppose you want to draw a square. What commands would you type into the keyboard? One way to correctly solve this problem would be to type

```
FORWARD 100
RIGHT 90
FORWARD 100
RIGHT 90
FORWARD 100
RIGHT 90
FORWARD 100
RIGHT 90
```

FIGURE 8–11 Some LOGO commands

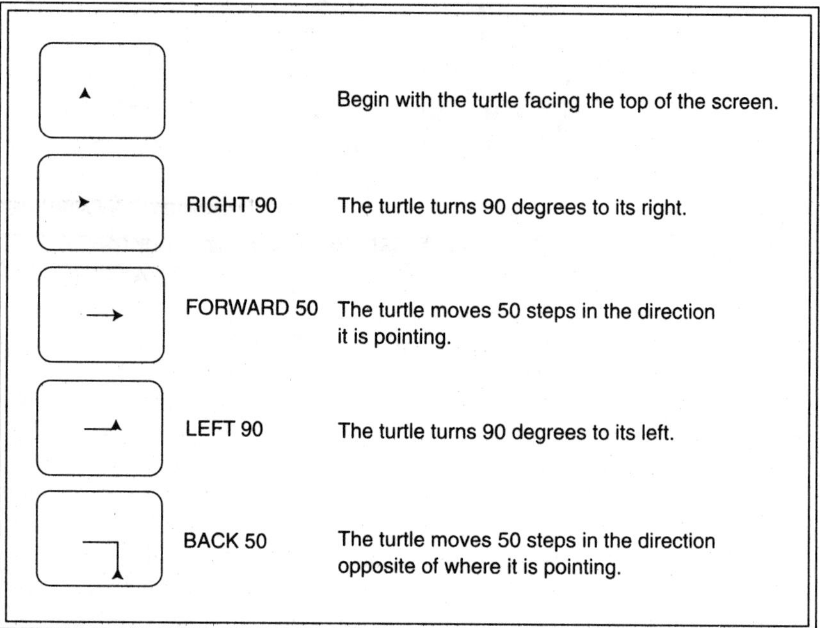

Begin with the turtle facing the top of the screen.
RIGHT 90
The turtle turns 90 degrees to its right.
FORWARD 50
The turtle moves 50 steps in the direction it is pointing.
LEFT 90
The turtle turns 90 degrees to its left.
BACK 50
The turtle moves 50 steps in the direction opposite of where it is pointing.

However, the following commands (using abbreviations) were produced by a child who was trying to draw a square (Papert, 1980):

FD 100
RT 100
FD 100
ERASE I (This undoes the previous command.)
RT 10
LT 10
LT 10
FD 100
RT 100
LT 10
RT100
LT 10
FD 100
RT 40
FD 100
RT 90
FD 100

As you can see, the child had a difficult time turning the turtle at right angles, presumably because the child did not know that 90 degrees is a right angle. However, once you have developed a program to draw a square you can name and save the program, such as by naming it SQUARE. Then you can "call" this program at any time within another program simply by typing SQUARE as a command. For example, if you wanted to draw a house (i.e., a square with a triangle on top), you could use the SQUARE command within your program, since drawing a square is a component in drawing a house. Then you could name that new program HOUSE and use it within a larger program, and so on.

According to Papert, as children explore LOGO, they develop "powerful ideas" concerning how to solve problems procedurally—including how to modularize a program and call each subprogram when needed. What evidence is there to support Papert's demand for unrestricted, hands-on experience in a LOGO environment and his claim that learning LOGO will transfer to other problem-solving domains? Regrettably, the evidence that is available does not support the use of pure discovery as an effective instructional method. Real children in real classrooms generally have difficulty learning even the fundamentals of LOGO programming (Dalbey & Linn, 1985; Kurland & Pea, 1985; Mayer, 1988; Pea & Kurland, 1984; Perkins, 1985). For example, Kurland & Pea (1985) tested seven children, ages 11 to 12, who averaged more than 50 hours of hands-on LOGO programming learning under discovery conditions. Children were given programs and asked to predict the output. The children had little trouble with short, simple programs that involved only commands to move or turn the turtle. However, on transfer problems that involved using fundamental programming concepts, students performed poorly. Through in-depth interviews, Kurland & Pea found that the children had developed incorrect conceptions of how programs operated. Furthermore, even though "none of these sources of confusion will be intractable to instruction," pure-discovery students faced an "absence of instruction" (Kurland & Pea, 1985, p. 242). Apparently, hands-on experience does not guarantee productive learning of LOGO, and these results suggest that "discovery needs to be mediated within an instructional context" (p. 242).

Similar difficulties have been observed in students learning BASIC, another "beginner's language" (Bayman & Mayer, 1983; Linn, 1985; Mayer, 1985). For example, in one study (Bayman & Mayer, 1983; Mayer, 1985), low-ability college students learned BASIC either through hands-on experience only or through hands-on experience supplemented with direct instruction in the basic programming concepts, such as how data are stored in memory. Students who learned with only hands-on experience exhibited many misconceptions of fundamental programming concepts, such as not knowing how data are stored in memory, not understanding where incoming data come from, and not understanding how the computer determines which command it will follow next. In contrast, as expected, students who were given direct instruction in how these concepts related to each command displayed many fewer misconceptions. On programming tests involving transfer, such as writing or interpreting complex programs, the group given added direct instruction performed better than the hands-on only group. Although hands-on experience was not effective for low-ability students, complementary studies found that hands-on experience was effective for high-ability students. Presumably, the high-ability students came to the learning situation with appropriate knowledge they could use to interpret their programming experiences. These results show that hands-on experience does not always lead to meaningful learning of programming concepts, especially when students lack appropriate prerequisite knowledge.

In summary, there is very little evidence to support eloquent calls for pure discovery as the way of teaching programming to children (Mayer, 1988). Based on the present research, the most productive approach appears to be a mix of teacher-based instruction and student-based exploration. However, students need to be tested frequently to determine whether they are acquiring useful programming concepts. If they are not, direct instruction is warranted.

Guided discovery is helpful because it helps students reflect on their learning so they are more likely to build general principles and strategies that enable transfer. What are some general principles in LOGO? Two useful design principles are modularity—breaking a procedure into parts—and reusability—using the same subprocedure more than once. Regrettably, many students who learn LOGO through hands-on exploration fail to develop basic design principles such as modularity and reusability (Fay & Mayer, 1994).

Suppose you wish to provide some guidance to students as they learn to program in LOGO. The first step could be to introduce them to the concepts of modularity and reusability before describing any programming command. For example, Figure 8–12 presents the concept of modularity in concrete, familiar terms without any computer commands. As you can see, a large task (drawing a house) is broken down into distinct subtasks (drawing a roof, frame, and door). To help them apply design principles to LOGO, students can be given some programs to write along with hints, such as shown in the house assignment in the top of Figure 8–13. After they finish their program, they receive feedback that shows step by step how to apply modularity and reusability to the house program, as shown in the bottom of Figure 8–13. The feedback is intended to foster reflection on how the design principles can be used in writing LOGO programs.

Fay and Mayer (1994) taught LOGO programming to computer-naive college students using a discovery or guided discovery method. Some students learned by being given a manual about LOGO commands and then engaging in hands-on writing of programs for programming assignments over four 1-hour sessions (discovery group). They were allowed to run their programs on computers and revise them if they did not work. Others received the same experience along with a bit more guidance about design principles, including receiving general pretraining on the design principles, hints on the program assignments to promote use of design principles, and feedback about how the programs related to design principles (guided discovery).

Does focused guidance affect learning? In writing programs during the learning phase of the experiment, the guided discovery group created modules and reused them often, whereas the discovery group rarely did. This evidence shows that the guided discovery students were better able to develop an understanding of general design principles. On a posttest involving new LOGO programming problems, the guided discovery group achieved a higher percentage correct than did the discovery group. This evidence indicates that learning the design principles helped students transfer their learning of LOGO to new problems. However, the groups did not differ on posttests that were not directly related to the design principles of modularity and reusability, such as tests of spatial reasoning. Taken together, the results are consistent with the theory of specific transfer of general principles. It appears that transfer was enhanced by guiding students in their learning of design principles that are directly related to writing LOGO programs. When students rely solely on free exploration—without any guidance—they learn to write LOGO programs, but the programs are inelegant and transfer to new programming is limited. In a more recent study, Lehrer, Lee, and Jeong (1999) found that LOGO learning was greatly enhanced when students were encouraged to reflect on program design by taking the role of program designer for peer audiences.

FIGURE 8–12 Excerpt from design instruction

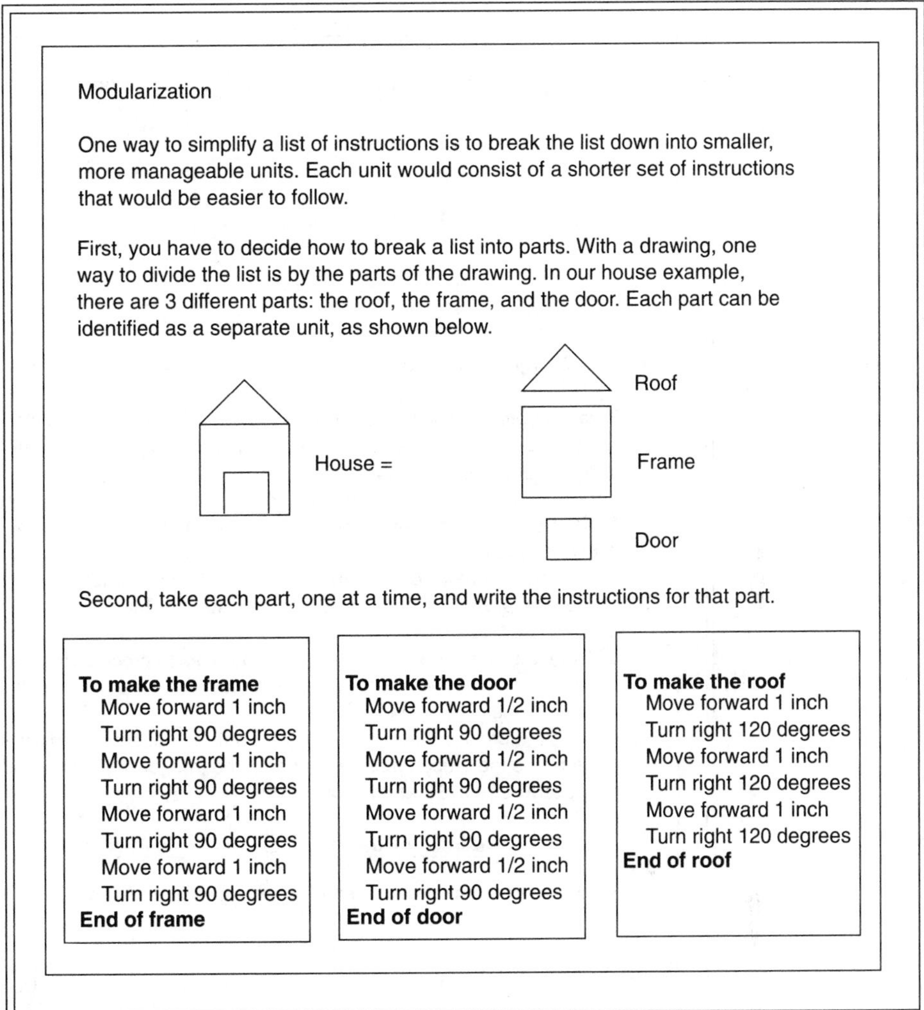

Modularization

One way to simplify a list of instructions is to break the list down into smaller, more manageable units. Each unit would consist of a shorter set of instructions that would be easier to follow.

First, you have to decide how to break a list into parts. With a drawing, one way to divide the list is by the parts of the drawing. In our house example, there are 3 different parts: the roof, the frame, and the door. Each part can be identified as a separate unit, as shown below.

Second, take each part, one at a time, and write the instructions for that part.

To make the frame
Move forward 1 inch
Turn right 90 degrees
Move forward 1 inch
Turn right 90 degrees
Move forward 1 inch
Turn right 90 degrees
Move forward 1 inch
Turn right 90 degrees
End of frame

To make the door
Move forward 1/2 inch
Turn right 90 degrees
Move forward 1/2 inch
Turn right 90 degrees
Move forward 1/2 inch
Turn right 90 degrees
Move forward 1/2 inch
Turn right 90 degrees
End of door

To make the roof
Move forward 1 inch
Turn right 120 degrees
Move forward 1 inch
Turn right 120 degrees
Move forward 1 inch
Turn right 120 degrees
End of roof

From Fay and Mayer (1994)

In another LOGO study, Lee and Thompson (1997) provided 16 hours of instruction in LOGO based on a discovery or guided discovery method. In each session, all students received an introduction to new programming commands and sets of LOGO programming problems for in-class student activity. Guided discovery students received a worksheet that guided them through the processes of decomposing, planning, executing, identifying errors, and debugging errors, and classroom discussion was tied to reflecting on these steps. Discovery students received a less structured worksheet, and classroom discussion was free ranging. Posttest results revealed the guided discovery students outperformed the

FIGURE 8–13 House problem with cues and feedback

Assignment 1: Write a program, named HOUSE, that will draw the house below.

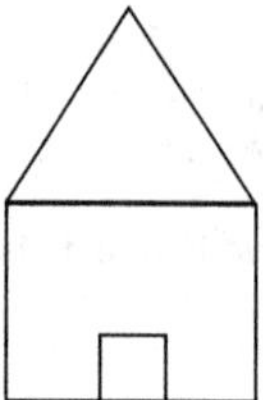

How to Design Your Program

1. Break the program down into smaller parts. (MODULARIZATION)
2. Check to see if there are some parts that are the same. If there are, one procedure may be used for both parts. (REUSABILITY)
3. Check each part to see if there are sequences of actions that are repeated. The repeated sequences will be written using the REPEAT command. (REUSABILITY)
4. Write a procedure for each of the parts, one at a time. (MODULARIZATION)
5. a) Run the procedures, one at a time, and edit any mistakes. (MODULARIZATION)
   b) Note the location of the turtle at the end of each procedure. If necessary, write the commands that will move the turtle to the proper location for it to draw the next procedure.
6. Arrange the order of the procedures and write a procedure named HOUSE that includes the procedures for the parts and the "joining" commands. Run the procedure HOUSE and fix any errors.

Example of How to Design and Write Assignment 1

1. Break the program down into smaller parts (MODULARIZATION)

Roof Frame Door

2. Check to see if some parts are the same. (REUSABILITY)
   Frame & Door are both squares. Can make one procedure and use a variable input to change the length of the sides.
3. Check each part for repeated sequences of actions (REUSABILITY)

   Door and frame are squares. A square repeats the sequence "move forward, turn right 4" times. Can use REPEAT command.

   Roof is an equilateral triangle. It repeats the sequence "move forward, turn right" 3 times. Can use REPEAT command.
4. Write a procedure for each part, one at a time (MODULARIZATION)

```
TO SQUARE:SIDE
  REPEAT 4[FD:SIDE RT 90]
END
```

This is the procedure to make the frame and the door. SIDE is the length of the sides.

FIGURE 8–13 (cont.)

```
TO TRIANGLE:SIDE
   REPEAT 3[FD:SIDE RT 120]
END
```

This is the procedure to make the roof. SIDE is the length of the sides.

5. a) Run the procedures, one at a time, and edit mistakes (MODULARIZATION)

SQUARE 80

SQUARE 20

TRIANGLE 80

Each procedure started and ended with the turtle facing the top of the screen.

b) Write commands to move the turtle from its position at the end of one procedure to the correct position for it to start drawing next procedure.

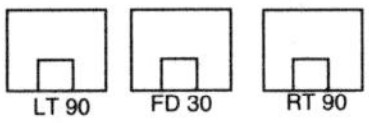

LT 90 FD 30 RT 90

To move the turtle from end position of the door to correct position to start the frame you need the commands: LT 90 FD 30 RT 90

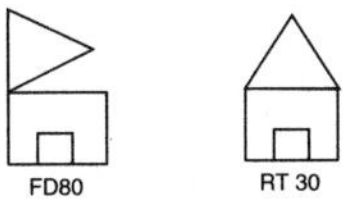

FD80 RT 30

To move the turtle from the end position of the frame to the correct position to start the roof you need: FD 80 RT 30

<u>Example of Program HOUSE</u>

```
TO HOUSE
   SQUARE 20
   LT 90 FD 30 RT 90
   SQUARE 80
   FD 80 RT 30
   TRIANGLE 80
END
```

Other Procedures

SQUARE:SIDE

```
TO SQUARE:SIDE
   REPEAT 4[FD:SIDE RT 90]
END
```

TRIANGLE:SIDE

```
TO TRIANGLE:SIDE
   REPEAT 3[FD:SIDE RT 120]
END
```

If you followed the steps for designing a program, your program should be similar to this one. If it isn't, review the steps and compare what you did at each step with the example shown on the previous page.

From Fay and Mayer (1994)

discovery students on almost every aspect of LOGO programming, including being able to generate and debug programs.

Overall, research on teaching computer programming serves as a case example of the benefits of guided discovery methods over pure discovery methods. Hands-on exploration can result in deep learning or shallow learning, depending on the degree to which students learn general principles and strategies. Pure discovery methods often fail to support transfer because students fail to gain the insights they need; in contrast, appropriate levels of guidance can promote transfer to the extent they enable students to build generalizable principles and strategies. The pattern of results, first popularized in the 1960s, once again has been replicated in the domain of teaching and learning computer programming.

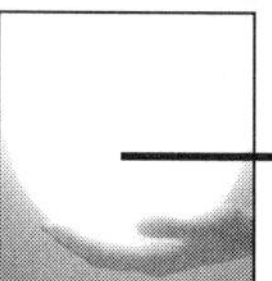

INDUCTIVE METHODS

EXAMPLE OF INDUCTIVE METHODS

Another issue concerning how to teach students to solve parallelogram area problems—such as in Figure 8–1—concerns when to present the formula or rule. We could begin by stating the rule, area = height × base, and then ask students to solve problems. This is a deductive method, because the rule is given first. Alternatively, we could begin by asking students to solve problems and only after the students have built up some good intuitions, then present the formula. With the inductive method, the rule is given only after the learner has induced the underlying framework for the rule.

THEORY: ASSIMILATION TO EXISTING KNOWLEDGE

Ausubel (1968) and Mayer (1999) have suggested that meaningful learning involves actively connecting new material with existing knowledge. Thus, learners must be challenged into thinking about how new principles or laws relate to other ideas in the learners' memory. In inductive methods of instruction, learners are exposed to long periods of mental searching before they can verbalize the rule, or what Hendrix (1947, 1961) called "nonverbalized awareness." This period of mental searching helps to activate more of the learner's prior knowledge and enables the learner to actively encode the strategy or concept to be learned into a wider or more meaningful context. In contrast, deductive methods of instruction do not encourage this search and predispose the learner toward encoding an isolated series of mechanical steps.

RESEARCH AND DEVELOPMENT: INDUCTION OF MATHEMATICAL PRINCIPLES

As early as 1913, Winch presented evidence demonstrating the superiority of deductive methods over inductive methods for short-term retention performance and the superiority of inductive methods for certain types of transfer performance. In a literature review covering the subsequent half century, Hermann (1969) concluded that there still was qualified support for the claim.

COMPUTATIONAL PRINCIPLES In a well-controlled classroom study, Worthen (1968) used two methods to teach children such concepts as notation, addition, and multiplication of integers, the distributive principle of multiplication over addition, and exponential multiplication and division. One group was given inductive instruction: Examples were presented for the children to solve, followed by verbalization of the required principle or concept. Another group was given deductive instruction: Verbalization of the required concept or principle was followed by examples for the children to solve. Significant effects as a result of instructional method were found in measures of learning ease (inductive inferior to deductive), long-term retention (inductive superior to deductive), and transfer (inductive superior to deductive), with no differences in subject attitude.

As a part of a larger study, Roughhead and Scandura (1968) used inductive and deductive methods to teach children about series summation. In a deductive method, the rule was given and applied to several problems; then the subjects were asked to solve similar problems that were based on the same rule. In the inductive method, subjects were asked to solve some problems; then the rule was given and applied to similar problems. The deductive group learned faster than the inductive group; however, in a transfer task, the inductive group learned to solve the new problems faster than the deductive group. These results are summarized in Figure 8–14.

STATISTICAL PRINCIPLES Another study (Mayer & Greeno, 1972) varied the sequencing in a programmed text for the concept of binomial probability (i.e., the probability of obtaining *R* successes in *N* trials). An inductive booklet began by presenting underlying concepts such as "trial," "success," and "probability of success" and gradually put the parts together into a formula by the end of the booklet. A deductive booklet began by presenting the computational formula in symbolic notation and then gradually showed

FIGURE 8–14 Effects of deductive and inductive methods on learning and transfer

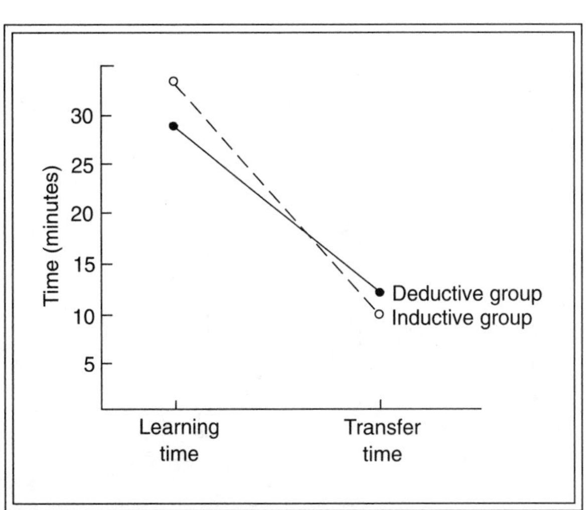

Adapted from Roughhead and Scandura (1968)

how the component variables figured in using the formula. Although both booklets presented the same basic information and same computational examples, the inductive booklet was sequenced to move from example to rule, and the deductive booklet was sequenced to move from rule to example. Figure 8–15 summarizes the groups' performance on a subsequent test that included problems just like those given in the booklet (Type F), problems that were slightly modified from those given in the booklet (Type T), problems that were unanswerable (Type U), and questions about when and how to use the formula (Type Q). Emphasis on the formula (i.e., deductive training) resulted in better performance on problems like those that the student was trained to solve, but emphasis on underlying concepts resulted in better performance on recognizing when the formula did not apply and on creative question answering. The Mayer and Greeno study suggests that deductive methods are better for simple retention of a basic rule while inductive methods are better for situations in which the rule must be transferred to new situations.

IMPLICATIONS OF INDUCTIVE METHODS

Research on sequencing of instruction suggests that deductive methods lead to superior performance in cases of one single rule to learn or a limited number of problems to be solved. Explicit instruction and practice in applying a specific rule is most effective when the goal of instruction is limited to behaviors that are similar or identical to those being taught. In contrast, the foregoing research demonstrates that inductive methods of instruction are useful when the goal of instruction is the ability to learn how to form rules (rather than learning of a specific rule) or how to transfer to new situations. By being encouraged

FIGURE 8–15 Effects of inductive and deductive methods on problem solving

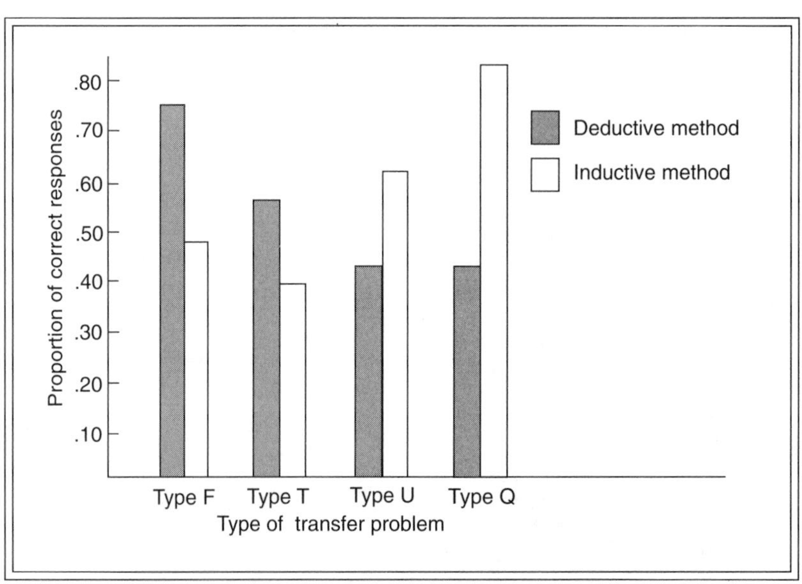

Adapted from Mayer and Greeno (1972)

to think actively about how to solve problems during instruction, the learner develops problem-solving strategies that can be applied in many situations.

COMPUTER APPLICATIONS: LEARNING FROM SIMULATED EXPERIENCES

In the inductive approach, teachers begin with the learner's concrete experiences and carefully relate those experiences to abstract principles. In the deductive approach, teachers present a to-be-learned principle for students to memorize and apply. As you could see in the previous sections, classic laboratory research shows that students are better able to transfer when they learn by an inductive rather than a deductive approach. Do inductive approaches also promote learning of academic material in classrooms?

An example of a popular inductive approach is the predict-observe-explain (POE) method for teaching scientific principles (White & Gunstone, 1992). In the POE method, a teacher presents a familiar concrete situation and asks the student to predict what will happen and justify that prediction (predict phase), the student observes what happens (observe phase), and the student explains any differences between the predicted and the observed result (explain phase).

For example, suppose I asked you which would be a better way to keep a can of soda cold for a picnic—rapping it in aluminum foil or wrapping it in wool? Not only must you choose an answer, you must also explain why you gave that answer. This is the predict phase. Then you conduct an experiment—such as watching a computer simulation of heat transfer through the wrapping over time. This is the observe phase. Then you engage in a discussion with peers and the teacher about the observations you just made. This is the explain phase.

What would happen to eighth-grade students who took a semester-long science course based on this kind of inductive teaching approach? To help answer this question, Linn and Hsi (2000) report on a project in which students learn general science principles by carefully examining familiar situations involving heat and temperature, thermal equilibrium, and insulation and conduction. These situations include figuring out whether a metal desk feels cooler than a wooden desk, whether soup stays warmer in a small cup or a large bowl, whether it's better to use a wooden spoon or a metal spoon to stir a pot of boiling noodles, whether it's a good idea to leave a car window slightly open when it will sit in the sun all day, or how to keep some pizzas warm for 30 minutes. The instructional method is inductive to the extent that it begins with the learner's familiar experience—such as experience with warm food getting cold—and carefully moves toward building abstract principles, such as a theory of heat transfer.

Linn and Hsi report that the instruction also relies on technology—such as computers to make visible changes in temperature in objects over time—and on peers, such as group discussions involving what happens in the concrete situations. For example, a useful computer simulation called "Heat Bars" allows the student to select bars of materials such as aluminum, glass, or plastic; place one end of each bar next to a heat source for a selected amount of time; and then watch the heat flow across the bar over time. In this way the student can see, for example, that heat flow is slower for some materials than for others. Using a program called Electronic Laboratory Notebook, students are able to make predictions, run experiments, collect data, and generate principles that are shared with others.

FIGURE 8–16 A transfer problem for the Design-A-Plant game

Design a plant to live in an environment that has low sunlight.

Circle the type of root (1 or more):

Branching

Nonbranching

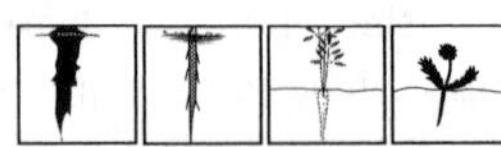

Deep, Thick | Deep, Thin | Shallow, Thick | Shallow Thin | Deep, Thick | Deep, Thin | Shallow, Thick | Shallow, Thin

Circle the type of stem (1 or more):

Short

Long

Thick Bark | Thin Bark | Thick No Bark | Thin No Bark | Thick Bark | Thin Bark | Thick No Bark | Thin No Bark

Circle the type of leaf (1 or more):

Thin

Thick

Small, Thick skin | Small, Thin skin | Large, Thick skin | Large Thin skin | Small, Thick skin | Small, Thin skin | Large, Thick skin | Large, Thin skin

Why do you think that the plant you designed will survive in this environment?

From Moreno, Mayer, Spires, and Lester (2001)

Over many years of refining their instructional program called Computers as Learning Partners (CLP), a multidisciplinary research team produced a series of eight versions—each one intended as an improvement over the previous one. Before taking the course, almost all students were unable to provide scientifically valid answers to questions about temperature and heat, whereas afterwards they showed a large improvement. Most important, with each new revision, the percentage of successful students increased. When tested in high school, students who had taken the CLP course showed better performance on science tests involving high-level thinking than did comparable non-CLP students. Linn and Hsi's (2000) report shows that an inductive approach that builds on students' familiar experiences can be a useful way to teach for transfer, but the road to crafting a useful curriculum requires a long-term, multidisciplinary effort.

In a smaller-scale study, Moreno, Mayer, and Lester (2000) developed an educational computer game aimed at teaching principles of environmental science through concrete experience as simulated on a computer screen. In the program, students meet Herman the Bug, who takes them on a space trip to a new planet that has certain environmental conditions—such as low rainfall and heavy winds. The student's job is to design a plant that will survive on the planet by selecting appropriate roots, stems, and leaves. For example, in a rainy environment, is it better to have roots that are thick or thin, deep or shallow, branched or nonbranched? Along the way, Herman provides explanations for why the student's choice leads to the plant's death or survival. The program, called Design-A-Plant, is based on an inductive method to the extent that it begins with simulated, familiar experience and builds on that experience to help students understand general principles.

Does the Design-A-Plant experience help students learn generalizable principles about plant growth? To test this question, Moreno et al. (2000) asked students to solve new problems presented in paper-and-pencil form. For some problems, students were given new environmental conditions (not encountered during instruction) and asked to select appropriate roots, stem, and leaves and to write a justification; for other problems, they were shown a picture of a plant with certain roots, stem, and leaves and asked to describe an environment in which it would survive and give an explanation for their response. Figure 8–16 shows an example of a transfer problem. Students who learned with the Design-A-Plant game generated more correct solutions on the transfer test than did students who received the identical information presented in traditional textbook format. The improvement on this problem-solving transfer test was 24% for college students and 48% for high-school students over their peers who learned from traditional deductive-based text (Moreno et al. 2000; Moreno et al. 2001). Clearly, an inductive approach of building on the simulated experience of learners can promote meaningful learning.

CHAPTER SUMMARY

This chapter has explored three representative techniques for providing meaningful methods of instruction—concrete materials, discovery activities, and inductive sequencing. In each case, there is some laboratory-based evidence and classroom-based evidence that meaningful methods of instruction encourage the learner to become more cognitively involved in the learning task, and thus the outcome of learning allows for better problem-solving transfer. Designing classroom programs aimed at promoting transfer may involve aspects of all three techniques—providing concrete materials, opportunities for active problem solving, and links to familiar experiences. For example, Brenner et al. (1997) developed an effective middle-school pre-algebra unit that used concrete manipulatives to represent functional relations (concrete method), related algebraic problems to familiar situations involving pizzas (inductive method), and required active discussion of problem-solving strategies (discovery method).

The major curriculum development efforts of the 1960s attempted to incorporate aspects of meaningful methods of instruction. Since that time, there has been a reaction against developments such as the "new math." In an effort to reestablish the traditional emphasis on "getting the right answer," the pendulum seems to have swung "back to basics" in the 1970s and 1980s. Since then, the pendulum continues to swing, sometimes in ways that lose the positive features of both "meaningful" and "basic" approaches.

If you are concerned with teaching for meaningful learning, you might want to ask, "Will meaningful methods ever again become an acceptable part of school learning?" This chapter provided current computer applications that may help the pendulum swing in the direction of guided exploration. During the 1970s, teaching machines, including classroom computers, were best adapted for drill and practice on basic skills. However, as computers become more powerful, they enable meaningful methods of instruction (e.g., computerized visualization systems, LOGO environments, and computer simulation games) aimed at teaching transferable problem-solving skills. Whether these advances will rekindle a more lasting and productive interest in meaningful learning remains to be seen. What is new, however, is the growing realization that promoting student exploration is not enough; student exploration must be supplemented with guidance that promotes reflection and helps students to find generalizable rules and principles that can live on in new situations. Crafting such lessons involves the skillful use of many techniques, including those based on concreteness, activity, and familiarity.

SUGGESTED READINGS

Bruner, J. S. (1968). *Toward a theory of instruction.* New York: Norton. (A classic call for meaningful methods of instruction.)

Linn, M. C., & Hsi, S. (2000). *Computers, teachers, peers: Science learning partners.* Mahwah, NJ: Erlbaum. (A description of a project aimed at helping students learn science with understanding.)

Mayer, R. E. (1988). *Learning and teaching computer programming.* Hillsdale, NJ: Erlbaum. (A collection of papers concerning instructional methods for teaching computer programming.)

Wertheimer, M. (1959). *Productive thinking.* New York: Harper and Row. (A classic call for learning by understanding.)

CHAPTER 9 Teaching by Explaining Examples

CHAPTER OUTLINE

Introduction

Worked-Out Examples

Case-Based Learning

Chapter Summary

This chapter is based on the idea that deep learning occurs when you are to able focus on a realistic problem and reflect on successful ways of solving it. In particular, it explores two instructional approaches to learning by example: providing worked-out examples and engaging learners in simulated cases. Example-based and case-based learning represent two promising attempts to promote learning for transfer.

INTRODUCTION

How can we help people learn in ways so they can transfer what they have learned to new situations? An intriguing answer is to help them organize what they learned into a collection of examples—which can be called *base problems.* When they are confronted with a new problem—which can be called a *target problem*—their task is to find a base problem in their existing knowledge that is similar to the target problem and that can be used to successfully guide its solution. The similarity between a target and a base problem should be based on *structural features*—the relations among the elements in the problem—rather than *surface features*—the actual elements themselves.

Consider the three statistics problems in Figure 9–1. Please circle two problems that are similar and put an X through the one that does not belong with the other two. If you based your decision on surface features you probably circled problems 1 and 3, because they both deal with the effects of experience on typing speed, and you put an X through problem 2, because it has an entirely different cover story. If you based your decision on structural features, you probably circled problems 1 and 2, because both describe a comparison between two means—a situation that is appropriate for a *t*-test statistic. You probably put an X through problem 3, because it describes a different situation—correlation between two variables. In short, when you search for a similar problem based on structural features,

FIGURE 9–1

Which problem does not belong with the others?

PROBLEM 1

A personnel expert wishes to determine whether experienced typists are able to type faster than inexperienced typists. Twenty experienced typists (i.e., with 5 or more years of experience) and 20 inexperienced typists (i.e., with less than 5 years of experience) are given a typing test. Each typist's average number of words typed per minute is recorded.

PROBLEM 2

A college dean claims that good readers earn better grades than poor readers. The grade point averages (GPAs) are recorded for 50 first-year students who scored high on a reading comprehension test and for 50 first-year students who scored low on a reading comprehension test.

PROBLEM 3

A personnel expert wishes to determine whether typing experience goes with faster typing speeds. Forty typists are asked to report how many years they have worked as typists and are given a typing test to determine their average number of words typed per minute.

Adapted from Quilici and Mayer (1996)

you need to abstract out the underlying principle or solution method in the problem. Quilici and Mayer (1996) found that students required guidance to learn how to categorize statistics word problems like those in Figure 9–1 on the basis of structure rather than surface features.

This chapter explores a form of meaningful learning that does not necessarily require explicit social interaction but does involve modeling—learning by example. In learning by example, students are exposed to problems, their solutions, and explanations of their solutions. The example problems serve as the basis for figuring out how to solve new problems.

Learning from examples is based on a theory of analogical problem solving in which you solve a target problem by using a base problem that you already know about. As summarized in Figure 9–2, there are three cognitive processes in analogical problem solving: (1) *recognizing,* in which you recognize a base problem that is similar to a target problem you want to solve; (2) *abstracting,* in which you abstract a solution method or principle from the base problem; and (3) *mapping,* in which you apply the solution method to the target problem. For example, if you were trying to solve problem 1 in Figure 9–1, you might recognize that you know how to solve a similar problem (i.e., problem 2). Using problem 2, you might abstract the general solution principle of comparing the mean score of one group against the mean score of the other group using a *t*-test. Finally, you might apply that principle back to problem 1, yielding a test comparing two means in that problem.

WORKED-OUT EXAMPLES

Perhaps the most basic form of learning from examples is to provide students with exposure to worked-out examples (or worked examples). A worked-out example consists of three parts: (1) a problem, (2) a solution, and (3) a commentary. The first part of a

FIGURE 9–2 Three processes in analogical thinking

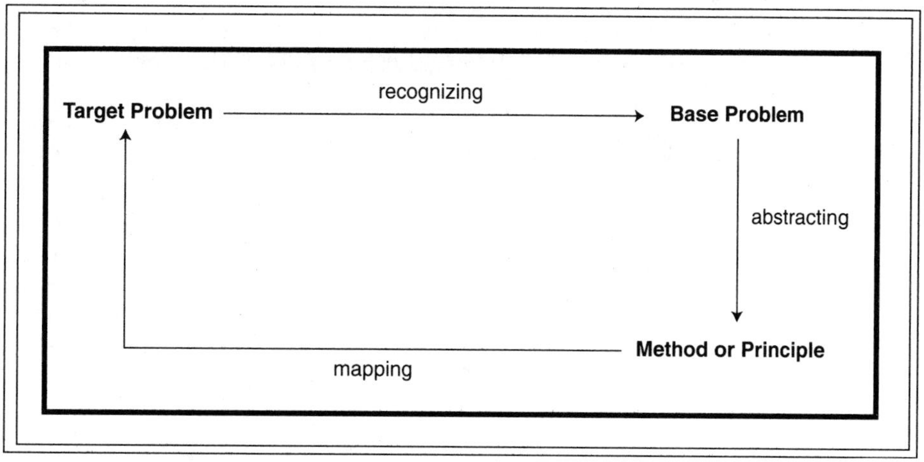

Adapted from Quilici and Mayer (1996)

worked-out example is a statement of the problem, such as "Solve for a: $a + b - g = c$." The second part of a worked-out example is a step-by-step description of the solution, such as: "$a + b = c + g$, $a = c + g - b$." The description may be presented in a variety of representations, including symbols (as in this example), words, or pictures; and in a variety of levels of detail ranging from simply presenting the final answer to painstakingly describing each small step. The third part of a worked-out example is a commentary, which explains why various steps were taken and describes the rationale for each step. For example, next to the solution steps the following comments could be printed: "First, add g to both sides. Then, subtract b from both sides." The commentary may take the form of a transcript or video of someone modeling his or her thought process as he or she solves the problem, or it may be much more cursory. The commentary may include words, pictures, or symbols, or any combination of these.

WORKED-OUT EXAMPLES CAN LEAD TO FASTER LEARNING AND BETTER TRANSFER

Suppose we want junior high school students to learn how to solve simple equations in which they must isolate one variable on the left side of the equation and have all other variables on the right side. In short, we want them to be able to solve for a in the following three problems:

1. Solve for a: $a - k = t$
2. Solve for a: $a + c - n = s$
3. Solve for a: $b + c - f = g + a - v$

One way to teach this is to give students practice in solving equations such as the eight problems listed on the left side of Figure 9–3. Students continue on each problem until they get the right answer. This is a straightforward example of learning by doing, because students learn by actively generating answers to problems until they get them right. The right side of Figure 9–3 shows another way of helping students learn how to solve equations. Problems are presented as pairs, with the first member of the pair presented as a worked-out example and the second member of the pair presented for the student to solve using the same method as in the worked-out example. This is a straightforward example of learning from examples, because students see the solution method for various types of problems.

Which method results in faster learning? When Cooper and Sweller (1987) conducted this study with junior high school students in Australia, they found that students who learned by doing (e.g., the left side of Figure 9–3) took twice as much time to learn as students who learned from worked-out examples (e.g., the right side of Figure 9–3). As you can see in the left column of Figure 9–4, the learning-by-doing group took an average of 495 seconds, as compared to 215 seconds for the learning-from-examples group. These results may reflect the fact that students who learned by doing had eight problems to solve whereas students who learned from examples had only four problems to solve—and even had guidance on those through seeing the preceding worked-out example.

Clearly, if your goal is faster learning, it appears that learning from examples is more efficient than learning by doing. However, learning by doing may challenge students to learn more deeply so that when they are given new problems they will outperform students who learned from examples. Thus, performance on the transfer problems is the key

FIGURE 9–3

Two ways of learning to solve equations: Learning by doing and learning from examples

Learning by Doing	*Learning from Examples*
Solve each equation for *a*.	Use each worked-out example to help you solve the next equation for *a*.
$a + b = c$	$a + b = c$ $a = c - b$
$a + h = u$	$a + h = u$
$a - b = c$	$a - b = c$ $a = c + b$
$a - v = f$	$a - v = f$
$a + b - g = c$	$a + b - g = c$ $a + b = c + g$ $a = c + g - b$
$a + e - v = s$	$a + e - v = s$
$a - b + g = c$	$a - b + g = c$ $a + g = c + b$ $a = c + b - g$
$a - r + y = k$	$a - r + y = k$

Adapted from Cooper and Sweller (1987)

FIGURE 9–4

Average time (in seconds) to learn and to solve transfer problems for two instructional groups

		Transfer Test		
Group	*Learning*	*Problem 1*	*Problem 2*	*Problem 3*
Learning from examples	215	14	25	157
Learning by doing	495	15	27	300

Adapted from Cooper and Sweller (1987)

to determining the effectiveness of the two instructional methods. The right three columns in Figure 9–4 show the average time to solve each of the three test problems listed at the beginning of this subsection: problems 1 and 2 are near-transfer problems because they are the same form as problems that were presented during the learning portion of the study, whereas problem 3 is a far-transfer problem because it has a different form than any of the problems presented during learning. As you can see, the groups did not differ much in the time it took them to solve near-transfer problems (i.e., problems 1 and 2) even though the learning-from-example group spent much less time during the learning phase than the learning-by-doing group. Even more startling, the learning-from-example group required approximately half as much time to solve the far-transfer problem (problem 3) as the learning-by-doing group.

These results call into question the idea that learning by doing always leads to deeper learning. Cooper and Sweller's (1987) results show that students learn faster and are better able to transfer what they have learned when they are shown how to solve a problem and then given a similar problem to try on their own. How can you account for the advantage of learning from examples? In a recent review, Sweller (1999) argues that students in both groups engage in schema acquisition in which they learn the solution procedure for each of several kinds of equation-solving problems. For example, for the problem $a - b = c$, the student learns that when the problem is of the form "target variable minus first variable equals second variable," the solution is to add the first variable to both sides of the equation, yielding "target variable equals second variable plus first variable." When the procedure is so well learned that it can be applied without any mental effort, it is said to be *automated.* Sweller (1999) proposes that students who learn by doing must put so much effort into discovering the solution procedure that they do not get as much of a chance to automate it; in contrast, students who learn from examples are shown the procedure and then practice applying it, yielding a higher level of automation.

What happens on the near- and far-transfer tests for students who have high and low levels of schema automation? The answer is based on cognitive load theory—the idea that people have only a limited amount of cognitive capacity for solving problems in their working memories. Because the near-transfer problems are fairly easy, they do not create a heavy cognitive load; thus, even if the solution procedures are not automated, students in both groups have sufficient capacity to apply them. The far-transfer problem is more complex because it requires using combinations of procedures different from those explicitly presented in the original learning problems. This complexity places a heavy load on working memory. If the schemas are not automated, cognitive capacity must be used to correctly apply the procedures, which may interfere with the cognitive processing required to devise a workable solution plan. Thus, students with automated schemas have a greater advantage on the far-transfer problems. Sweller (1999) concludes that the "differential performance by the two groups on the transfer problem can be explained by differential automation" (p. 80).

WORKED-OUT EXAMPLES CAN LEAD TO REDUCED COGNITIVE LOAD DURING LEARNING AND TRANSFER

If worked-out examples help students to automate their schemas for solving various types of problems, the students should experience less cognitive load during learning and on the transfer test. How can we tell how much cognitive effort a student is using? One way is to ask students to rate their level of mental effort on a 9-point scale from "very, very low mental effort" (as 1 on the scale) to "very, very high mental effort" (as 9 on the scale).

This procedure was used by Paas and van Merrienboer (1994), who taught Dutch high school students from a technical school to solve geometry problems using a conventional approach and a worked-out example approach. In both cases, students received computer-based training on six problems during the instructional phase of the study. Students in the conventional group were given a problem, such as shown at the top of Figure 9–5, and asked to generate a solution. If students were unable to solve the problem after attempting it, they were shown the worked-out solution. Students in the worked-out example group were given a problem and its worked-out solution such as shown in the middle of Figure 9–5. Students were instructed to study the worked-out example. In both treatments, students saw a total of six problems. Then, as a test, all students solved six transfer problems such as shown at the bottom of Figure 9–5.

How does worked-out example training affect learning? As you can see in the first column of Figure 9–6, students who received conventional instruction took more than twice as much time to learn as students who learned from worked-out examples. Importantly, students who received conventional instruction also reported a higher level of cognitive load than did students who received worked-out examples (as shown in the second column). This pattern is consistent with the idea that students in the conventional group were less able to automate the solutions than were students in the worked-out example group.

How does worked-out example training affect transfer? It might not be surprising that the conventional training took longer and required more mental effort than the worked-out example training. After all, students in the conventional group had to try to solve six geometry problems (followed by studying worked-out examples), whereas students in the worked-out example group only had to study six worked-out examples. If you are interested in teaching for meaningful learning, your major focus in this study concerns what happens when students are asked to solve transfer problems. As you can see in the third column of Figure 9–6, the worked-out example group solved more than twice as many transfer problems as did the conventional group, in spite of requiring less than half as much training time. Consistent with cognitive load theory, the worked-out example group reported less mental effort on the transfer problems than did the conventional group (as shown in the fourth column). Apparently, the worked-out example group was able to automate some of the solution procedures, which allowed them to devote more attention to devising useful solution plans on the transfer problems.

WHAT CAN BE DONE TO MAKE WORKED-OUT EXAMPLES MORE EFFECTIVE?

Sometimes students have difficulty solving a transfer problem even though they have just studied a worked-out example involving the same solution method. For example, consider the car problem at the top of Figure 9–7. Suppose you have just studied the short worked-out example given in the middle of Figure 9–7. Do you think this would help you solve the test problem? If you are like most students in a study by Reed, Dempster, and Ettinger (1985), the short worked-out example is not much help. The top of Figure 9–8 shows the

FIGURE 9–5 Two ways of learning to solve geometry problems: learning by doing and learning from examples

Learning by Doing

Given:
P1 (15, 60)
P2 (−50, 20)

Calculate the length of line P1−P2

Length of line P1−P2 = ☐

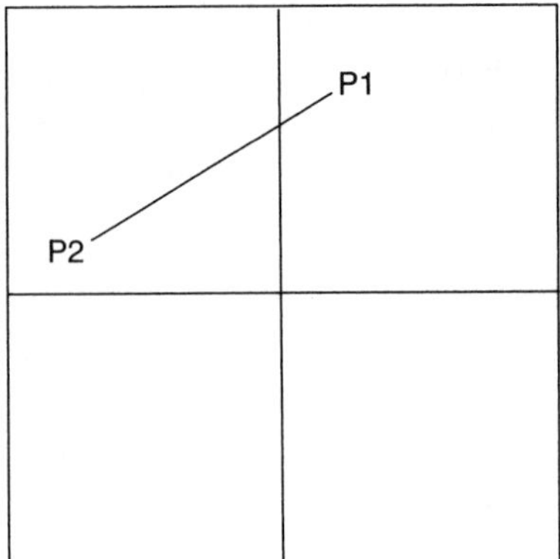

Learning From Examples

Given:
P1(15, 60)
P2(−50, 20)
Calculate length of line P1−P2

SOLUTION

1. Design right-angled triangle *abc* by drawing lines from P1 and P2 parallel to the *X*- and *Y*-axis

2. Length of side a = P1(y) − P2(y) = 40
   Length of side b = P1(x) + P2(x) = 65

3. By using Pythagorean theory, the length of line P1−P2 (= c) can be calculated:
   $c^2 = a^2 + b^2 \longrightarrow c = \sqrt{5825} = 76.3$

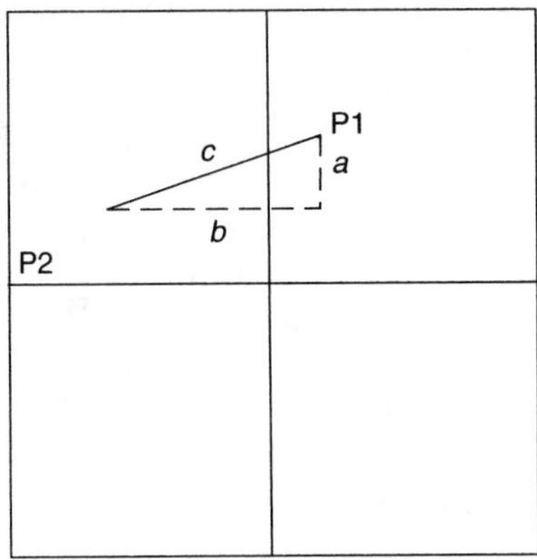

A Transfer Problem

Given:
- P1 (−15, 40)
- P2 (*X*,15)
- P3 (*X*,15)
- P4 (25, 30)
- Angle μ = 125°
- Angle τ = 110°

Calculate distance P2−P3

Distance P2−P3 = ☐

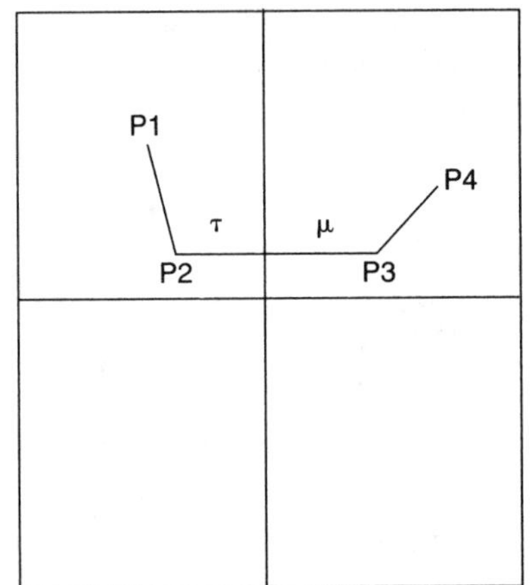

Adapted from Paas and van Merrienoer (1994)

FIGURE 9–6

Performance on learning and transfer for two instructional groups

Group	*Learning*		*Transfer Test*	
	Time (in Seconds)	*Effort Rating*	*Percent Correct*	*Effort Rating*
Learning by Doing	1406	4.50	28%	6.10
Learning from Examples	625	3.30	62%	5.20

Adapted from Paas and van Merrienboer (1994)

percent correct on a test problem for students who previously studied an equivalent worked-out example and for students who previously studied an unrelated worked-out example (i.e., a solution for a problem that is not like the car problem shown at the top of Figure 9–7). As you can see, students perform poorly under both conditions.

Why did experience with a worked-out example fail to transfer to the solution of an equivalent problem? One obstacle may be that the worked-out example was not useful in helping the student abstract the solution method. To overcome this obstacle, we could elaborate on the example in ways to help the student understand the solution method. An elaborated worked-out example is given at the bottom of Figure 9–7. Another obstacle is that the student may not know when or how to apply the solution method from the worked-out example. To help overcome this obstacle, we could allow the student to refer to the elaborated worked-out example while solving the transfer problem—a situation that was not allowed for the short worked-out example.

The bottom of Figure 9–8 shows that students who received the elaborated version of the worked-out example (and were allowed to refer to it) were much more likely to solve the transfer problem than were students who received an unrelated worked-out example. Apparently, sometimes students need special training aimed at helping them (a) abstract out the solution method from a worked-out example, and (b) determine when that solution method might be useful in subsequent problems. Subsequent research has shown that transfer is improved when the worked-out examples are elaborated in ways that meet these criteria (Reed, 1999).

CAN STUDENTS LEARN TO MAKE BETTER USE OF WORKED-OUT EXAMPLES?

It is clear from Reed's (1999; Reed, Dempster, & Ettinger, 1985) research that students often fail to adequately take advantage of worked-out examples. However, there is encouraging evidence that successful problem solvers have developed skills that allow them to learn and use worked-out examples more effectively. For example, Chi, Bassok, Lewis, Reimann, and Glaser (1989) asked students to read a physics chapter that contained worked-out examples, such as computing the mass of a weight that was suspended by two strings. This worked-out example consisted of two diagrams and 19 steps, such as "F_a, F_b,

FIGURE 9–7

A transfer problem and two kinds of worked-out examples

TRANSFER PROBLEM

A car travels south at the rate of 30 miles per hour (mph). Two hours later, a second car leaves to overtake the first car, using the same route and going 45 mph. In how many hours will the second car overtake the first car?

A SHORT WORKED-OUT EXAMPLE

Problem: A car traveling at a speed of 30 miles per hour (mph) left a certain place at 10:00 A.M. At 11:30 A.M., another car departed from the same place at 40 mph and traveled the same route. In how many hours will the second car overtake the first car?

Answer: The problem is a distance-rate-time problem in which

$$\text{distance} = \text{rate} \times \text{time}$$

Because both cars travel the same distance, the distance of the first car (D1) equals the distance of the second car (D2). Therefore, D1 = D2 or R1 × T1 = R2 × T2, where R1 = 30 mph, R2 = 40 mph, and T1 = T2 + 3/2 hr. Substituting gives the following:

$$30 \times (T2 + 3/2) = 40 \times T2$$
$$30T2 + 45 = 40 \times T2$$
$$T2 = 4.5 \text{ hr}$$

AN ELABORATED WORKED-OUT EXAMPLE

Problem: A car traveling at a speed of 30 miles per hour (mph) left a certain place at 10:00 A.M. At 11:30 A.M. another car departed from the same place at 40 mph and traveled the same route. In how many hours will the second car overtake the first car?

Answer: The problem is a distance-rate-time problem in which

$$\text{distance} = \text{rate} \times \text{time}$$

We begin by constructing a table to represent the distance, rate, and time for each of the two cars. We want to know how long the second car travels before it overtakes the first car. We let t represent the number that we want to find and enter it into the table. The first car then travels $t + 3/2$ hours because it left $1\frac{1}{2}$ hours earlier. The rates are 30 mph for the first car and 40 mph for the second car. Notice that the first car must travel at a slower rate if the second car overtakes it. We can now represent the distance each car travels by multiplying the rate and the time for each car. These values are shown in the following table.

Car	*Distance (miles)*	*Rate (mph)*	*Time (hr)*
First	$30(t + 3/2)$	30	$t + 3/2$
Second	$40 \times t$	40	t

Because both cars have traveled the same distance when the second car overtakes the first, we set the two distances equal to each other:

$$30(t + 3/2) = 40t$$

Solving for t yields the following:

$$30t + 45 = 40t$$
$$45 = 10t$$
$$t = 4.5 \text{ hr}$$

Adapted from Reed, Dempster, and Ettinger (1985)

FIGURE 9–8

Percent correct on transfer test after studying four types of worked-out examples

	Unrelated worked-out example	*Equivalent worked-out example*
Short version	18%	25%
Elaborated version	17%	69%

Adapted from Reed, Dempster, and Ettinger (1985)

and F_c are all forces acting on the body" and "From the figure we see that $F_{ax} = -F_a \cos 30 = -0.866F_a$" (Chi et al., 1989, p. 150). The students were asked to talk aloud, describing their learning process as they read the chapter. Then they took a test consisting of problems like those they had just read about and were allowed to refer back to the chapter. Based on their test performance, students were classified as good or poor problem solvers.

Good and poor problem solvers differed in the way they studied the example problems. Good problem solvers tended to continually explain the solution steps to themselves—a process that Chi and her colleagues call giving *self-explanations.* In contrast, poor problem solvers generated few self-explanations as they studied the example problems. The top of Figure 9–9 shows the mean number of each of three kinds of statements that good and poor students made as they read worked-out examples in the chapter. First, good problem solvers generated five times as many explanation statements—that is, statements that provide a rule or cause, such as "The force of the negative Y will be equal to the force of the positive Y, and they'll all equal out"—as did poor problem solvers (Chi et al., 1989, p. 159). Second, good problem solvers generated three times as many monitoring statements—that is, statements in which students reflect on the state of their own comprehension, such as "I'm trying to think where Forces F_b and F_a are going to get the thing"—as did poor problem solvers (Chi et al., 1989, p. 159). Third, good problem solvers generated twice as many other kinds of statements—that is, statements in which students paraphrase or elaborate, such as "Okay, so three forces are on two strings, and from the string going down to the object"—as did poor problem solvers (Chi et al., 1989, p. 163). Overall, good problem solvers generated an average of 142 lines of protocol while studying the example problems, whereas poor problem solvers generated an average of 21 lines.

Good and poor problem solvers also differed in the way that they referred back to the example problems while they solved test problems. Good problem solvers referred back to example problems mainly when they wanted to focus on a specific solution method, whereas poor problem solvers referred back to example problems with a more general goal of just trying to get some sort of hint. The bottom portion of Figure 9–9 shows the mean number of times per problem that good and poor problem solvers referred back to an example problem for each of three purposes. First, poor problem solvers were more likely than good problem solvers to reread verbatim one or more lines from an example problem. Second, poor problem solvers were more likely than good problem solvers to copy an

FIGURE 9–9

Differences in how good and poor problem solvers study and use worked-out examples

AVERAGE NUMBER OF STATEMENTS MADE WHILE STUDYING WORKED-OUT EXAMPLES

Type of Statement	*Type of Problem Solver*	
	Good	*Poor*
Explanation	15	3
Monitoring	20	7
Other	16	7

AVERAGE NUMBER OF USES OF WORKED-OUT EXAMPLES WHILE SOLVING A TEST PROBLEM

Type of Use	*Type of Problem Solver*	
	Good	*Poor*
Reread	0.6	4.2
Copy	1.1	2.2
Check	1.0	0.3

Adapted from Chi, Bassok, Lewis, Reimann, and Glaser (1989)

equation, label, or diagram from a problem. Third, good problem solvers were more likely than poor problem solvers to check an example problem for a specific result or method in the context of solving a problem. Chi et al. conclude that good problem solvers have specific goals when they refer back to the examples, such as looking for a method to find the value of a particular force. In contrast, poor problem solvers—who initially spend less time studying the example problems—have general goals that require them to reread large portions of the entire problem.

In summary, this research shows that it may not be enough to simply put worked-out examples in textbooks or classroom lectures. Students also need to study the examples so they will be able to use them later as aids in problem solving. By engaging in an active process of explaining the examples to themselves, students can abstract out the underlying solution method in a way that makes sense to them and thereby increase the chances for transfer. Chi (1996) has shown how tutors can encourage this process of self-explanation by asking appropriate questions. As Chi and Bassok (1989) pointed out: "We view examples as an essential instrument from which to learn. . . . When students fail to generalize from examples, perhaps we should attribute the failures not to the characteristics of the examples, but rather to the disposition of the learner. . . . We view self-explanation as a mode of studying that can mediate learning" (p. 265). In short, students are more likely to learn from examples when they engage in a process of self-explanation while studying the examples.

CASE-BASED LEARNING

A somewhat more complex form of learning from examples is case-based learning. In case-based learning the learner is presented with a realistic problem scenario—that is, a *case*—that can be studied retrospectively by examining how the problem was solved or, interactively, by trying to solve the problem. The problems in case-based learning are more realistic and more complex than the problems used in worked-out examples. Some forms of case-based learning can also be called *problem-based learning* or *theme-based learning*.

What is a case? A case is a description of a realistic problem scenario that is relevant to a particular profession or field of study. For aviation crash investigators, a case may be a description of a plane crash, including all documentation. For medical professionals, a case may be a written medical history of a particular patient, along with all test results. For legal professionals, a case may be the transcript of a trial, along with all evidentiary exhibits. For business professionals, a case may be the written description of how a corporation was reorganized to increase efficiency. For teaching professionals, a case may be a video showing various teachers trying to teach a lesson on a particular topic. For chess players, a case may be the transcript (i.e., list of moves) of a championship game. The description can be presented in a variety of forms, including on paper (as text and graphics), as video, or even as a live enactment. As you might expect, case-based learning is used in a variety of professional training programs, including medicine (Barrows & Tamblyn, 1980), business (Gijselaers, Tempelaar, & Keizer, 1993), and education (Lundeberg, Levin, & Harrington, 1999).

Cases are used in two major ways to promote meaningful learning—*retrospective case-based learning,* in which a learner looks back over the history of a problem and attempts to resolve it, and *interactive case-based learning,* in which a learner attempts to solve a problem and receives realistic feedback and commentary. In retrospective case-based learning, the cases may include detailed descriptions of one or more attempts to solve the problems and their consequences, as well as advice and commentary on decisions and choices that were made. Retrospective case-based learning involves discussion and analysis of previous cases. In interactive case-based learning, the cases may include feedback on what happens in response to each decision or choice the learner makes, as well as the opportunity for the learner to seek advice and commentary at various choice points in the problem. Interactive case-based learning can take the form of computer-based simulations of realistic problems or role-playing within live enactments of realistic problems.

How does case-based learning work? Case-based learning is intended to promote analogical problem solving. Practicing on a variety of cases helps learners build a collection of *base problems* (or *source problems*) in their long-term memories. When confronted with a new problem (which can be called a *target problem*), the learner is reminded of a relevant base problem (i.e., recognition) that can be used to generate a solution plan (i.e., abstraction), which is then applied back to the target problem (i.e., mapping). For example, suppose a teacher has observed many videos showing successful and unsuccessful ways of responding to a disruptive student. When confronted with a disruptive student in her classroom, the teacher is reminded of one of the successful cases, abstracts the general strategy used in that case, and applies it in her current situation.

Research on expertise shows that experienced problem solvers in fields such as chess, physics, medicine, and computer programming know a large number of specific examples that they use to make analogical inferences during problem solving (Mayer, 1992b). The goal of case-based learning is to help compensate for the lack of this kind of knowledge in novices so they can still engage in analogical reasoning. Kolodner (1997) notes that "reasoners naturally use their own experiences for such reasoning" but "novices . . . might not have previously had the most relevant experiences." In case-based learning, "their own experiences are augmented, in effect, by those of others to enable them to reason beyond what they could based only on what they already know" (p. 57).

RETROSPECTIVE CASE-BASED LEARNING

Suppose you want to help a beginning teacher learn how to design effective mathematics lessons for fifth grade. Which of the following would be the most effective way to help the beginning teacher learn useful skills in a way that promotes transfer? (a) Ask her to read a book on how to teach math in elementary school and test her on the contents. (b) Ask her to reflect on how to teach math to fifth-graders and write an essay on her conclusions. (c) Ask her to visit the classrooms of successful fifth-grade math teachers and analyze what she sees. (d) Ask her to analyze a collection of videos of successful fifth-grade math teachers and analyze what she sees.

The first answer—reading a book—can provide some useful information, but the teacher may have difficulty in transferring her academic book learning to the real world of her classroom. The second answer—reflecting on one's philosophy of teaching—is a useful exercise for promoting transfer but may fail if students fail to discover useful content to be transferred. The next two answers are case-based approaches designed to provide useful information about how to teach and promote transfer of that information through analogical reasoning. Because in some situations it may be impractical or inefficient to visit various classrooms, teacher educators have increasingly become interested in the fourth answer—the use of *videocases* (Lampert & Ball, 1998; Richardson & Kile, 1999).

How can videocases be used to promote learning? Lampert and Ball (1998) produced a computer-based hypermedia program consisting of videoclips of teachers as they taught mathematics in an elementary school classroom, interviews with students and parents, teachers' planning documents, and students' written work. Preservice teachers were asked to use the computer-based program to answer questions such as, "What did Deborah (the teacher on the tape) do if the student gave the wrong answer?" Interestingly, most preservice teachers did not focus on teaching of mathematics content and often failed to back up their general observations with specific evidence. Based on these results, Lampert and Ball decided to include more structured tasks and guidance in how to use the videocases.

In a similar study, Levin (1999) found that the quality of group discussions about videocases was the key to cognitive changes in preservice teachers. Based on preliminary evidence she concluded that "the discussion of a case is a valuable pedagogical tool for case-based teaching" but "we need . . . careful studies that continue to test the . . . claims made about the case method" (p. 157).

Does learning from videocases work? The answer is not yet available. Richardson and Kile (1999) note: "Unfortunately, there is very little research on outcomes of the use of videocases. In fact, there is little solid empirical work on case use in education. The literature about the use of cases in teacher education is primarily analytic, speculative, and at times, promotional" (p. 124). In a review of research on learning from videocases in education, Richardson and Kile conclude that "comparative case studies of the use of videocases and other methods of teacher education would be useful" (p. 136). Similarly, Levin (1999) notes that "there are still many unanswered questions and untested claims about case-based pedagogy" (p. 141).

INTERACTIVE CASE-BASED LEARNING

Suppose you have been hired to teach new account executives at Ameritech Publishing how to sell Yellow Pages advertising. Which of the following options would you choose?

(a) Present a seminar—complete with overhead slides—on the basic principles of selling Yellow Pages advertising.
(b) Host a panel discussion in which experienced account executives give pointers on how to sell Yellow Pages advertising.
(c) Have an experienced account executive go around with newly hired account executives for a few weeks, providing comments and critiques as the new account executive strives to sell advertising.
(d) Create a computerized simulation of various selling scenarios along with opportunities to see relevant video comments from experienced salespeople.

The first option provides useful information, but it may not be in a form that people can use in the context of their jobs; that is, people may not be able to recall the most relevant principle when they are confronted with a choice in the field. The second option provides a collection of useful "war stories," but the new account executives may not index (or link) them in ways that allow for later retrieval; that is, they may not be able to recall a relevant story when they are confronted with a choice in the field. The third option could provide new account executives with useful information that is indexed (or linked) to relevant real-world situations, but the training might turn out to be somewhat expensive and impractical. It requires a major investment of the time of experienced employees and assumes that they will always offer the most appropriate comments. The fourth option provides an interesting way to help novices develop a rich set of cases that are indexed for future reference.

Burke (1998) described a computer-based simulation intended to teach new account executives at Ameritech Publishing how to sell Yellow Pages advertising. The learner sits at a computer terminal and participates in realistic work situations that are presented on the screen in the form of videoclips and on-screen text. The learner participates by clicking on buttons or typing in what he or she wants to say. For example, consider the following dialog between the student and the virtual customer as the deal is closed:

STUDENT: So we're going to go ahead with the 1/4-page ad with color?
CUSTOMER: OK.
STUDENT: Just sign right here.
CUSTOMER: [signs]
STUDENT: I think the color is really going to attract people to your ad.
CUSTOMER: I sure like the way it looks.

STUDENT: Ask your customers what they think. I'll bet you'll find it's an attention getter. Thanks for your time.

CUSTOMER: See you next year.

STUDENT: See you. [leaves]

Although this seems like a successful transaction, the computer program is reminded of a story from an expert about the risks of staying around after the sale is closed. The program asks the student if he would like to get a "story showing the risks of your approach." When the student responds positively, the program says: "You kept talking after the sale was closed. Nothing bad happened, but here's a story in which doing that led to problems." Then a videoclip appears in which an experienced salesperson describes a personal story about a time he "talked [himself] out of a sale" (Burke, 1998, pp. 178–79). The transcript of his story is shown in Figure 9–10.

In this scenario, the student is likely to remember the story, to abstract its theme as what can happen from talking too much after the sale is closed, and to recall the story in the future when he may feel inclined to talk too much after a sale is closed. According to Schank (1997), this kind of case-based learning is effective because people are most eager to learn after they have made a mistake; the story comes "just in time," so it is more likely to be memorable and to be indexed properly as a story about talking too much after the sale is closed. A lecture format in which students must memorize rules such as "Don't continue talking after the sale is closed" is less likely to produce learning that will transfer to problem solving in the field because the rules are not tightly connected with situations. In conclusion, the computer-based simulations help learners amass a collection of stories (with clear morals); when confronted with a problem in the field, learners are reminded of a relevant story, the moral of which can help guide the learner's behavior. In short, case-based simulations are intended to promote analogical reasoning.

FIGURE 9–10

An expert's story on "How I Talked Myself Out of a Sale"

I was in the South Bend/Mishawaka area. This was my first or second year. I was calling on a swimming pool contractor. He had a quarter page in South Bend. I was proposing a quarter page in another directory. It was sitting on his kitchen table. And the guy was hesitating; he didn't know . . . So after a few more attempts, he says to me, "OK, I'll go with the other quarter page." He bought it. I pushed the order in front of him. He signed it. It's done. As I'm putting my stuff together, I made a comment that cost me the quarter page. I said, as I'm packing up, "I'm sure that you're going to get a lot of phone calls from that new ad." He looked at me and he said, "You know, I don't need any more phone calls. I'll tell you what, let's not do that this year, maybe next." I talked myself out of a quarter page. I've never done it since. I walked out. There was nothing I could say. I had it and I lost it. All I had to say was, "Thank you very much Joe. See you next year." But I didn't. I had to tell him about the calls, which I'd already done twenty times. . . .

From Burke (1998, pp. 178–179)

Does the Yellow Pages simulation work? Regrettably, Burke offers no scientifically valid evidence concerning the program's effectiveness. In a broader review of case-based training projects ranging from computer simulations for training business consultants at Andersen Consulting to role-playing enactments for training technology consultants at Diamond Technology Partners, Schank (1997) offers no specific evidence but alludes to "various formal and informal surveys" (p. 163). Although Schank claims that "there is compelling empirical evidence that the training is effective" (p. 163), researchers need to provide specific documentation. Clearly, there is a need to determine whether case-based simulations work, under which conditions they work, and how they work.

As you can see, case-based learning depends on analogical reasoning: When confronted with a new problem or dilemma (target problem), you try to solve it by using a problem or dilemma you already know (base problem). Although research on learning from cases is just beginning, it appears that several factors are particularly important in designing effective case-based instruction. First, learners need to build a repertoire of cases in their memories—that is, they need to build a storehouse of base problems. This can be accomplished by exposing learners to a variety of cases. Second, the cases need to be *indexed* so that the learner can find the appropriate case when it is needed—that is, the cases need to be indexed in a way that promotes the process of recognition, can be accomplished by presenting a relevant case at a time when the learner has just made a mistake in a simulation. Third, the cases need to be *annotated* so that the solution method or principle is clear to learners—that is, the cases need to be annotated in a way that promotes the process of abstraction. This can be accomplished by adding commentary or discussion. Fourth, the relevant features in the cases need to be labeled so that the learner can relate them back to a target problem—that is, the cases need to be *labeled* in a way that promotes the process of mapping. This can also be accomplished through commentary and discussion. In short, learners need more than exposure to cases; they need to interact with cases in ways that will subsequently promote effective analogical transfer.

CHAPTER SUMMARY

This chapter explored instructional methods aimed at promoting analogical transfer, or being able to solve a new problem by remembering how to solve an old problem. In particular, it explored the use of worked-out examples and the use of cases. Substantial research support exists for the appropriate use of worked-out examples as a way of promoting transfer, including evidence that students can learn more from studying worked-out examples than from actually solving the same problems. One explanation is that when students learn by solving problems they must devote so much cognitive capacity to the details of managing the solution that they are less able to pay attention to the general solution principle being used. In contrast, with worked-out examples, learners can understand and store a collection of base problems in ways that make them more accessible when solving new problems.

The use of worked-out examples can be critiqued in a number of ways. First, a shortcoming of worked-out examples is that they are fairly narrow in their applicability. For instance, knowing an example for a particular way of solving an algebra equation (such as subtracting the same variable from both sides) applies only to other algebra equation problems that require the same solution method. Second, and even more serious, the emphasis on worked-out examples reduces the need for students to ever engage in creative problem solving. When students see a new problem, instead of having to create a solution, they simply need to match it to a worked-out example; in this way, a novel problem requiring creative problem solving is turned into a routine exercise requiring much less mental effort. Although some may see this aspect as a shortcoming, others may see it as an achievement that helps beginners think more like experts.

Case-based learning holds great potential, but there is a need for scientifically sound research that examines the conditions under which it works. We reviewed several exciting developments in the use of videocases in teacher education and the use of case-based simulations in business training. In spite of the popularity of case-based methods in professional education, including exciting advances in the development of computer-based multimedia and simulations, their effectiveness needs to be investigated. In short, research on case-based instructional programs has not kept pace with development. In particular, it would be useful to know how to help learners store cases in flexible ways so that they can retrieve and use relevant cases when they are confronted with related problems in the field.

SUGGESTED READINGS

Lundeberg, M. A., Levin, B. B., & Harrington, H. L. (Eds.). (1999). *Who learns what from cases and how?* Mahwah, NJ: Erlbaum. (Reviews research on case-based learning.)

Reed, S. K. (1999). *Word problems.* Mahwah, NJ: Erlbaum. (Reviews research on learning from examples.)

Schank, R. (1997). *Virtual learning.* New York: McGraw-Hill. (Describes computer simulations that use case-based learning.)

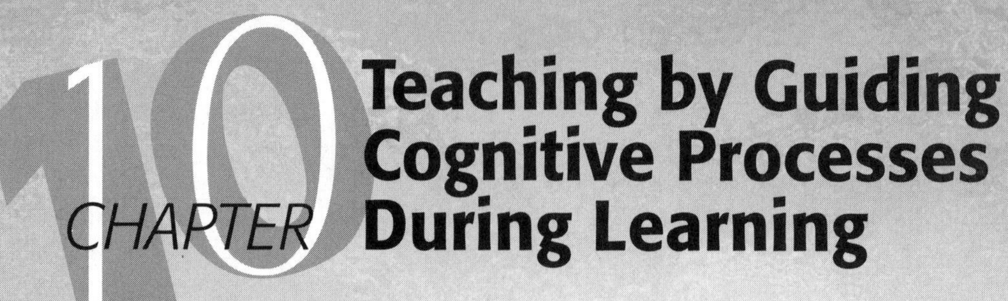

CHAPTER 10 Teaching by Guiding Cognitive Processes During Learning

CHAPTER OUTLINE

How to Improve a Textbook Lesson

Cognitive Theory of Instruction

Adjunct Questions

Signaling

Advance Organizers

Chapter Summary

This chapter explores ways of helping students learn deeply from prose and is particularly concerned with instructional techniques that can make prose more understandable. For example, some instructional techniques for promoting meaningful learning from prose include adjunct questions, signaling, and advance organizers. This chapter considers how each of these techniques affects the student's cognitive processing during learning and the cognitive outcome of learning.

HOW TO IMPROVE A TEXTBOOK LESSON

Sometimes a person can read a new lesson in a textbook and then use the information creatively to solve problems. At other times, a person can read the same information, retaining much of it without being able to solve problems. For example, Figure 10–1 shows a lesson about radar that you might find in a school textbook. Please read the lesson just once, but read carefully. When you are finished, try to answer the questions in Figure 10–2. Be sure to go in order, starting with question 1 and working down. Notice that Figure 10–2 contains recall, problem-solving, and verbatim recognition questions.

FIGURE 10–1

The radar passage

Radar means the detection and location of remote objects by reflection of radio waves. The phenomenon of acoustic echoes is familiar: sound waves reflected from a building or cliff are received back at the observer after a lapse of a short interval. The effect is similar to you shouting in a canyon and seconds later hearing a nearly exact replication of your voice. Radar uses exactly the same principle except that the waves are radio waves, not sound waves. These travel very much faster than sound waves, 186,000 miles per second, and can cover much longer distances. Thus, radar involves simply measuring the time between transmission of the waves and their subsequent return or echo and then converting that to a distance measure.

To send out the radio waves a radio transmitter is connected to a directional antenna that sends out a stream of short pulses of radio waves. This radio pulse that is first transmitted looks like the effect of tossing a pebble into a quiet lake. It creates concentric circles of small waves that continue to grow outward. Usually both a transmitter and a receiver are employed separately but it is possible to use only one antenna in which pulse transmission is momentarily suppressed in order to receive echo pulses. One thing to remember, though, is that radar waves travel in fundamentally straight lines and that the curvature of the earth eventually interferes with long-range transmission. When you think about the reception of the returning pulses or echoes you should remember that any object in the path of the transmitted beam reflects some of the energy back to the radio receiver. The problem then becomes transmitting the pulses picked up by the receiver to a display mechanism for visual readout. One mechanism in large use is the cathode-ray tube, a familiar item in airport control towers, which looks somewhat like a television screen.

It is easiest to understand how radar is displayed if you begin with one of the earliest models used during the 1930s. These types of displays were able to focus the broad radar pulse into a single beam of light that proceeded from the left of screen to the right. When no object impedes the traveling radar pulse it continues its travel until lost from the screen on the right. When there is an object present the pulse would strike it and begin to travel back to the receiver. When the object is struck by the radar pulse, it creates a bright spot on the face of the screen and the distance of

FIGURE 10–1

(cont.)

the object can be measured by the length of the trace coming from the object back to the receiver. With this model, however, you are only able to measure the distance of an object and not its absolute location, since the beam of light on the screen actually represents the entire width of the broader radar pulse.

Models employed today use two simple techniques that make location of objects much easier. First, the transmitter now operates much like the searchlight used in airports. It emits a single beam of radar pulses that make continuous circular sweeps around the area under surveillance. Secondly, the display screen is adjusted so that its center corresponds to the point where the radar pulses begin. The radar pulse seen on the screen operates like the second hand of a clock, which continually moves. When an object is present, it leaves a bright spot on the face of the screen. An additional feature is that the face of the screen actually shows a maplike picture of the area around the radar giving distance and, of course, location. Thus, it is easy now to determine the location of objects by noting their location on the screen's map.

Adapted from Clarke (1977)

If you are like most people, you had a hard time in trying to understand the radar lesson. For example, in a study (Mayer, 1983b), college students who had listened to the radar lesson recalled less than 20% of the information and scored below 30% on problem solving. However, students did seem to learn some specific pieces of information. For example, they scored at about 80% correct on verbatim recognition, and they recalled about 50% of the specific facts, such as the speed at which radar travels. Thus, if you are like most people who read this passage, you were able to remember some specific factual details, but you had trouble using the information to solve problems. In short, you did not learn in a way that promoted transfer.

The goal of this chapter is to explore some techniques for increasing the understandability of textbooks. What can we do to increase the learner's understanding in learning from prose? In particular, this chapter focuses on three techniques: adjunct questions, signaling the organization of prose, and concrete advance organizers. After presenting a brief cognitive analysis of prose learning, this chapter examines some examples, theories, research, and implications for each of these techniques.

COGNITIVE THEORY OF INSTRUCTION

WHAT IS STRUCTURE BUILDING?

This chapter is based on the idea that meaningful learning from prose—such as textbooks, lectures, or even computer-based presentations—occurs when the learner builds a coherent

FIGURE 10–2

A test for the radar passage

RECALL TEST

1. Write down all you can remember about the radar passage.

PROBLEM-SOLVING TEST

2. It was pointed out that the curvature of the earth limits the effectiveness of radar beyond a certain distance. One way around this limitation, of course, is to set up radar detection centers at various places on earth such that all areas are covered. Can you think of another way of doing this?
3. If an object remained at a constant distance from the receiver but its location changed with each measurement, what form would the object's movement take? Explain and/or diagram.

VERBATIM RECOGNITION TEST

Each of the following questions contains two statements, one of which is taken verbatim from the passage you just read and another that has slight changes. Read each pair of statements carefully and then check the one statement that you think came directly (word for word) from the passage.

4. ______ It is easiest to understand how radar is displayed if you begin with one of the earliest models used during the 1930s.
   ______ It is easiest to understand how radar is displayed if you begin with one of the earliest models used during the 1940s.
5. ______ The phenomenon of acoustic echoes is familiar: sound waves reflected from a building or cliff return to the observer after a lapse of a short interval.
   ______ The phenomenon of acoustic echoes is familiar: sound waves reflected from a building or a cliff are received back at the observer after a short interval.
6. ______ When an object is present, it leaves a bright spot on the face of the screen.
   ______ When an object is present, it leaves a lighted area on the face of the screen.

cognitive structure. For example, in a review of research on text comprehension, Gernsbacher (1990) concluded that "the goal of comprehension is to build a coherent mental representation or structure of the information being comprehended" (p. 1). In short, the learner seeks to build a coherent cognitive structure that makes sense, by being internally consistent (i.e., coherent internal connections) and consistent with existing knowledge (i.e., coherent external connections). This section explores what a coherent cognitive structure is and how to help learners build one.

WHAT IS A COHERENT COGNITIVE STRUCTURE?

In their efforts to help answer this question, researchers have offered several ways of characterizing the nature of cognitive structure, including rhetorical structures and mental models. Rhetorical structures are common ways of organizing verbally presented information. They also can be called text structures (Cook & Mayer, 1988), rhetorical patterns (Chambliss & Calfee, 1998), top-level structure (Meyer, 1975), and macrostructure (Kintsch, 1998). They are important in meaningful learning because learners who wish to understand a lesson seek to impose some structure on it. Chambliss and Calfee (1998) summarized the educational significance of these structures: "Good writers employ a handful of structural patterns for organizing ideas and composing texts. Good readers know these patterns well and use them to comprehend a passage by making order out of it" (p. 29).

The following are some common rhetorical structures found in expository writing, that is, writing that is intended to inform or explain:

Generalization presents a main idea and supporting evidence, such as stating that pumps have been around for a long time and then giving the dates for the invention of different kinds of pumps.

Enumeration presents a list of facts, such as listing the major uses of pumps.

Sequence describes a logically connected series of events or steps in a process, such as describing the steps in how a bicycle tire pump works.

Classification breaks material into classes or categories, such as distinguishing the types and subtypes of pumps.

Comparison/contrast shows the characteristics of two or more things along several dimensions, such as describing the differences among centrifugal, sliding vane, lift, and tire pumps in terms of size, typical uses, and origin.

These five rhetorical structures can be represented respectively as a network, a list, a flowchart, a hierarchy, and a matrix, as shown in Figure 10–3. A major task of learners is to appropriately impose a rhetorical structure on incoming prose.

FIGURE 10–3 Five rhetorical structures

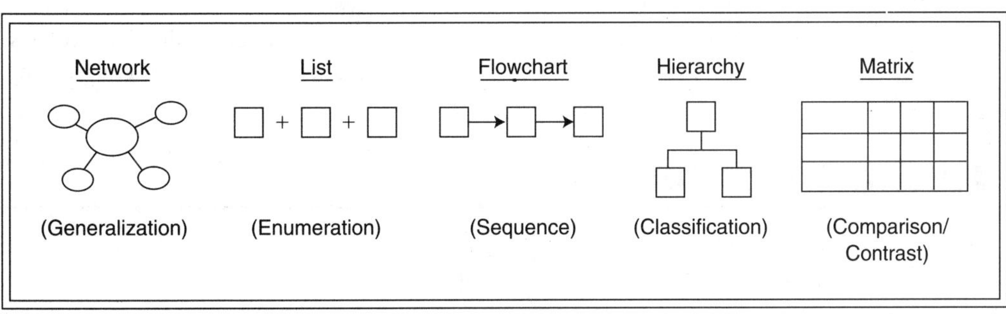

Adapted from Cook and Mayer (1988); Chamblis and Calfee (1988)

Let's focus on sequence structures in which the reader's task is to mentally construct a mental model of the operation of some system such as how a pump works. A mental model is a mental representation of the key parts of a system as well as the cause-and-effect relations among state changes in these parts. A mental model includes (a) component models—the location and potential states of each major part in the system, such as knowing that a pump includes a handle that can be up or down, a piston that can be up or down, an inlet valve that can be open or closed, an outlet valve that can be open or closed, a cylinder that can have high or low air pressure, and so on; and (b) a causal model—the cause-and-effect chain of how a change in the state of one part can affect a state change in another part, such as knowing that as the handle is pushed down the piston moves down, which in turn causes the inlet valve to close, which causes the air pressure in the cylinder to get higher, which causes the outlet valve to open, and so on. When the to-be-learned material is an explanation of how something works, the learner's job is to build a mental model.

HOW TO GUIDE STRUCTURE BUILDING DURING LEARNING

Chapter 1 presented a cognitive theory of instruction in which meaningful learning depends on the learner's carrying out three cognitive processes: selecting, organizing, and integrating. The goal of this chapter is to examine how to design text-based instruction so that it provides guidance to the reader about how to select relevant material, how to organize the material into a structure, and how to integrate the structure with previous knowledge. For example, in reading a passage about radar, the learner needs to be able to (1) focus on the main steps and elements in the process, such as transmission (a pulse travels away from the source), reflection (a pulse strikes a remote object), reception (a pulse returns to the source), measurement (the time is measured), and conversion (the time is converted into distance); (2) organize the steps into a cause-and-effect chain, such as putting these steps into a causal order; and (3) integrate the process with prior knowledge, such as knowing that if you throw a ball it can bounce off an object and return to you.

In this chapter we examine adjunct questions as a way to guide the process of selecting, signaling as a way to guide organizing, and advance organizers as a way to guide integrating. Adjunct questions are printed questions that are inserted into a text and are intended to draw attention to important material; signaling consists of outlines, headings, and signal words such as "first . . . second . . . third" intended to clarify the conceptual organization of the material; and advance organizers are text, illustrations, or both presented before a text and are intended to prime relevant prior knowledge so that the learner is able to connect the text material with appropriate prior knowledge. However, a careful analysis shows that some of these devices may guide more than one of the cognitive processes involved in meaningful learning.

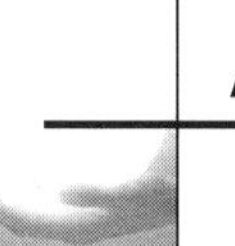

ADJUNCT QUESTIONS

EXAMPLE OF ADJUNCT QUESTIONS

The radar passage in Figure 10–1 can be altered by inserting questions into the text. Figure 10–4 suggests some of the kinds of questions that could be inserted after each paragraph.

FIGURE 10–4

Adjunct questions for the radar passage

Radar travels at a rate of ______.
Radar means the detection and location of remote objects by ______.
Radar uses ______ waves.
Radar travels in ______ lines.
The earliest display models were used in ______.
Modern display screens operate like ______.

THEORY: ADJUNCT QUESTIONS GUIDE THE PROCESS OF SELECTING

Adjunct questions may serve several functions, including both *forward* and *backwards* effects. The forward effect refers to the idea that questions inform the reader concerning what to pay attention to in subsequent portions of the text. For example, if you see that all of the questions deal with specific factual statements you will be more likely to focus on this type of information in subsequent sections of the passage. The backwards effect refers to the idea that questions require that the reader go back and review portions of the passage that have already been read. Thus, the questions serve to repeat specific portions of the text, allowing more exposure to the material. Thus, the forward effect refers to selective attention to the type of information mentioned in the questions, whereas the backwards effect refers to the amount of attention being paid to the specific information mentioned in the questions. Presumably, adjunct questions can be used to direct and magnify the reader's attention. In addition, questions about the structure of the passage (e.g., "What is the main idea?") may enhance building of internal connections, whereas questions about applying information to a familiar situation (e.g., "Can you give an example?") may enhance building of external connections.

RESEARCH ON ADJUNCT QUESTIONS

Modern research on adjunct questions began with studies by Rothkopf and his colleagues (Rothkopf, 1966; Rothkopf & Bisbicos, 1967). For example, in a typical study, students were asked to read a passage entitled, "The Sea Around Us," either with or without adjunct questions. Performance on subsequent retention tests was much higher for students who had read passages with adjunct questions. Since this pioneering work, subsequent research has focused on two main issues: where to place questions and what types of questions to use.

PLACEMENT OF QUESTIONS First, let's consider the placement of questions. In Rothkopf's (1966) study, some students received the questions after the text (postquestion group), some students received the questions before the text (prequestion group), and some received no questions at all (read-only group). Figure 10–5 shows the performance on tests for incidental (i.e., previously unquestioned material) and intentional (i.e., previously questioned material) learning. As you can see, performance on intentional learning is enhanced for both prequestion and postquestion groups, but performance on incidental learning is enhanced mainly for the postquestion group.

FIGURE 10–5 Intentional and incidental learning for three adjunct question groups

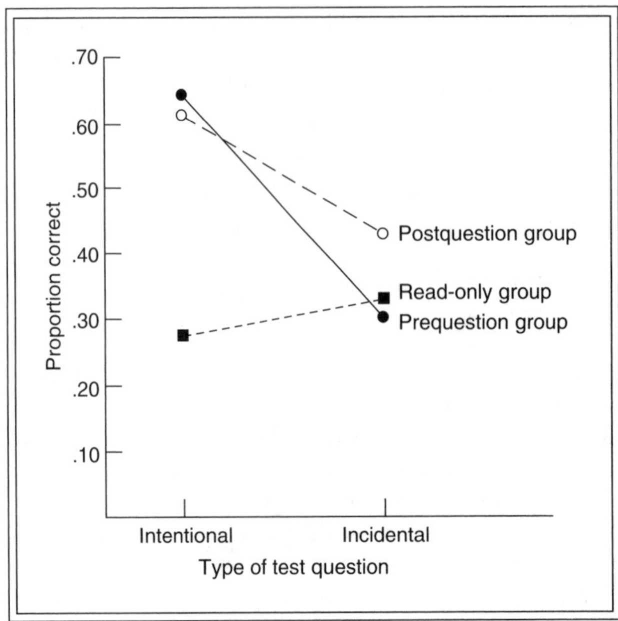

Adapted from Rothkopf (1966)

In another study, Boker (1974) asked students to read a 250-word lesson on historical geology. The lesson was divided into 10 sections, and two factual multiple-choice questions were placed either before each section (prequestion group), after each section (postquestion group), or not at all (read-only group). Subjects then took a 40-item posttest that included the 20 adjunct questions (intentional learning) plus 20 similar questions covering other factual information from the lesson (incidental learning). The test was given both immediately after reading the passage (immediate test) and one week later (delayed test). The students were allowed to read at their own rates, but they were not allowed to go back to previous sections of the text, and they were not allowed to look at the text when they were given adjunct questions to answer. Figure 10–6 summarizes the results. The prequestion and postquestion groups both performed better than the read-only group on intentional learning, presumably because they had paid more attention to this information in the passage. However, the postquestion group performed better than the read-only group on incidental learning, while the prequestion group performed worse. This pattern suggests that the prequestions may have served to focus the readers' attention on information that was relevant to the questions. The same pattern was obtained on the immediate and delayed tests.

In a review of 35 adjunct question studies, Anderson and Biddle (1975) found that even though both prequestions and postquestions generally enhance performance on tests of intentional learning, prequestions can often have the effect of inhibiting performance on

FIGURE 10–6 Performance on immediate and delayed test for three adjunct question groups

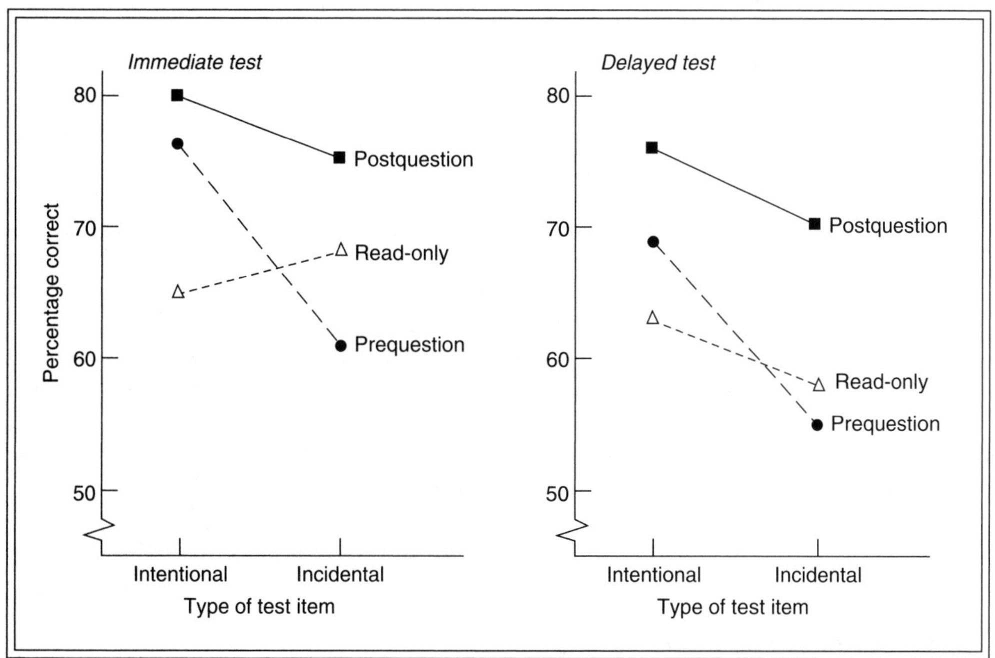

Adapted from Boker (1974)

new test items. Apparently, questions can serve as cues to readers concerning what to pay attention to.

TYPES OF QUESTIONS A second major research issue concerns the type of questions to ask. For example, Rickards and DiVesta (1974) asked college students to read an 800-word passage about a fictitious African nation "Mala." One group of subjects had rote questions printed after every two paragraphs, such as "How many inches of rain fall per year in southern Mala?" Another group had meaningful questions printed after every two paragraphs, such as, "Why can it be said that southern Mala is a desert?" A control group was given irrelevant questions after every two paragraphs. On a recall test, the meaningful question group recalled about 35 pieces of information, compared to about 21 pieces of information for the rote question group and 15 for the control group. Rickards and DiVesta suggest that the meaningful questions encouraged learners to organize the material into an outline structure rather than memorize a list of facts.

Although these studies suggest that meaningful questions lead to broader learning than rote questions, another important issue is whether this result is due to forward or backwards processing. To investigate the effects of question type on forward processing, McConkie, Rayner, and Wilson (1973) asked students to read a series of six 500-word passages on topics such as set theory, the biosphere, and the Reconstruction Era. After each of the first five passages, subjects received one type of question—such as number questions

("In New York City, _____% of all tetanus cases occurred with addicts.") or structure questions ("Which point did the author make after saying that the slaves who had acquired some education and skills under slavery became leaders?"). After the sixth passage, all students received all types of questions. Performance on the test after passage 6 indicated that students tended to perform best on the type of question they had received on previous passages; however, in some cases, performance was enhanced for other question types as well.

In a similar study, Mayer (1975b) asked students to read six passages on mathematical probability theory, with one type of question printed after each passage. Some students were asked to compute numerical values (calculation group), some were asked to recite formal definitions of terms (definition group), some were asked to state principles in terms of concrete models (principle group), and some received no questions on the first six passages (control group). After the seventh and eighth passages, all students received all three types of questions. Figure 10–7 summarizes the results. Students tended to perform best on the type of problem they expected, but the principle group performed well on all types. Apparently, the principle questions encouraged learners to engage in the process of integrating old and new knowledge, even on passages 7 and 8.

Even young children can benefit from answering adjunct questions. For example, consider the factual paragraph about the skunk at the top of Figure 10–8. This paragraph con-

FIGURE 10–7 Percentage correct for four groups on three types of test items

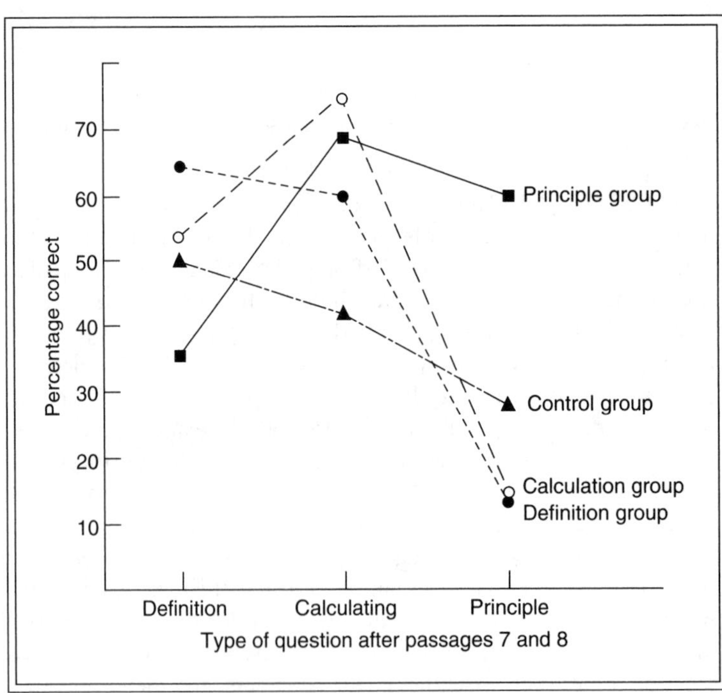

Adapted from Mayer (1975)

FIGURE 10–8

Facts about the western spotted skunk

BASE PARAGRAPH

The western spotted skunk lives in a hole in the ground. The skunk's hole is usually found on a sandy piece of farmland near crops. Often the skunk lives alone, but families of skunks sometimes stay together. The skunk mostly eats corn. It sleeps just about anytime except between three o'clock in the morning and sunrise. The biggest danger to the skunk is the great horned owl.

PARAGRAPH WITH ELABORATION PROVIDED

The western spotted skunk lives in a hole in the ground in order to protect itself and its family. The skunk's hole is usually found on a sandy piece of farmland near crops where it is easy to dig a hole to live in and eat what the farmer grows. Often the skunk lives alone, but families of skunks sometimes stay together until the young skunks are old enough and strong enough to look after themselves. The skunk mostly eats corn that is found in the farmer's field around its home. It sleeps just about anytime except between three o'clock in the morning and sunrise when it can look for food without being seen by other animals that might eat it. The biggest danger to the skunk is the great horned owl, whose night vision is so good that it can see skunks when they are out in the dark.

PARAGRAPH WITH ELABORATIVE QUESTIONS

The western spotted skunk lives in a hole in the ground. Why would that animal do that? The skunk's hole is usually found on a sandy piece of farmland near crops. Why would that animal have that? Often the skunk lives alone, but families of skunks sometimes stay together. Why would that animal do that? The skunk mostly eats corn. Why would that animal do that? It sleeps just about anytime except between three o'clock in the morning and sunrise. Why would that animal do that? The biggest danger to the skunk is the great horned owl. Why would that animal have that?

Note: Underlining denotes material that is added to the base paragraph. No underlining was given to students.

Adapted from Wood, Pressley, & Winne (1990)

tains six facts about the western spotted skunk, but the paragraph may not be very meaningful to students. To help students understand the facts, we could add an explanation for each fact, as indicated in the middle paragraph in Figure 10–8. Finally, we could prompt students to generate their own explanation for each fact by inserting a why question after each sentence, as indicated in the bottom paragraph in Figure 10–8. The inclusion of why questions represents a form of *elaborative interrogation* (Wood, Pressley, & Winne, 1990), and encourages students to mentally elaborate on the presented material.

To test the value of adjunct questions aimed at elaborative interrogation, Wood et al. (1990) asked students to listen to nine paragraphs without any adjuncts (control group), with elaborations provided (elaborations-provided group), or with why questions (elaborative interrogation group). The results are promising: Students in the elaborative interrogation group recalled 21% more of the facts than the control group, but the elaborations-provided group performed at the same level as the control group. Importantly, students in the elaborative interrogation group recalled 86% of the facts for which they had generated correct answers and 14% of the facts for which they had generated incorrect answers. Apparently, the act of successfully answering questions helped students learn the facts in ways that improved their ability to recall them.

Do questions promote meaningful learning? The answer seems to depend on the way that questions are used. In a review of questions used for probing elementary school textbooks, Allington and Weber (1993) pointed out that "the vast majority of questions . . . are single answer questions" (p. 50). In short, "most of the questions posed by teachers are known-answer questions" (p. 63). Such questions may focus students' attention on specific facts but do little to guide the way that readers organize and integrate the material. However, research presented in Chapter 11 shows that training students in how to ask and answer questions during learning can promote understanding that leads to transfer.

IMPLICATIONS OF RESEARCH ON ADJUNCT QUESTIONS

The foregoing section shows that adjunct questions can serve many functions, including helping the learner to pay more attention to the material, focusing the learner's attention on certain types of information, and, when used skillfully, guiding how learners organize and integrate the material. The placement and type of questions are crucial in determining how the learner will process the information. If the goal of instruction is memorization of specific information, rote questions (both before and after a passage) may be useful. Explicit behavioral objectives (e.g., "In this lesson you will learn how to define adjunct question.") may serve the same function as prequestions (i.e., directing the learner's attention). If the goal of instruction is the ability to apply information in new situations, meaningful questions should be used (especially after a portion of a passage or lecture). Thus, inserting meaningful questions (e.g., "Why do prequestions have a different effect than postquestions?") is a way of promoting transfer.

SIGNALING

EXAMPLE OF SIGNALING

Let's return to the radar passage in Figure 10–1. What else can be done to enhance the learner's understanding of this passage? Some researchers suggest that we could make the structure of the passage more obvious to the reader. For example, we could outline the passage and place headings in the passage that correspond to the major subdivisions in the passage. Figure 10–9 gives an example of how we could revise the radar passage by using signals to the reader concerning the structure of the passage. Notice that the headings show the reader the major topics.

FIGURE 10–9

A signaled version of the radar passage

DEFINITION

Radar involves five basic steps. Once you understand these five steps, you will have a basic knowledge of how radar works. The five steps are

1. Transmission—A radio pulse is sent out.
2. Reflection—The pulse strikes and bounces off a remote object.
3. Reception—The reflected pulse returns to the source.
4. Measurement—The amount of time between transmission and reception is measured.
5. Conversion—This information can be translated into a measure of distance if we assume the pulse travels at a constant speed.

Thus, radar involves the detection and location of remote objects by reflection of radio waves.

ECHO EXAMPLE

To see how these five steps of radar relate to one another, let's consider an example. The example is a familiar phenomenon, an acoustic echo.

1. First, you shout in a canyon. This is like transmission of a pulse.
2. Second, the sound waves are reflected from a cliff. This is like reflection of a pulse off a remote object.
3. Third, a nearly exact replication of your voice is received back at the observer. This is like reception of a radar pulse.
4. Fourth, a short lapse occurs between shouting and hearing an echo. This corresponds to measurement of time.
5. Fifth, you notice that the farther away a cliff is, the longer it takes to receive back an echo. This corresponds to conversion of time to a measure of distance of remote objects.

The same principle is used in radar except that the waves involved are radio waves, not sound waves. These travel very much faster than sound waves, 186,000 miles per second, and can cover much longer distances.

DEVICES

Let's consider the actual devices that are used for the five steps of radar.

Transmission. To send out the radio waves, a radio transmitter is connected to a directional antenna that sends out a stream of short pulses of radio waves. As an example of how the antenna sends out radio waves, think of tossing a pebble into a quiet lake. The pebble creates concentric circles of small waves that continue to grow outward.

Reflection. Any object in the path of the transmitted beam reflects some of the energy back to the radio receiver.

Reception. Usually a transmitter and a receiver are employed separately, but it is possible to use only one antenna. In this case, pulse transmission is momentarily

FIGURE 10–9

(cont.)

suppressed in order to receive echo pulses. One thing to remember about the reception of returning pulses or echoes is that radar waves travel in fundamentally straight lines and that the curvature of the earth eventually interferes with long-range transmission.

Measurement and conversion. The problem then becomes transmitting the pulses picked up by the receiver to a display for visual readout. One mechanism in large use is the cathode-ray tube, a familiar item in airport control towers, which looks somewhat like a television screen.

EARLY DISPLAY SYSTEM

The earliest display system, used during the 1930s, dealt with the five steps of radar as follows:

To represent transmission, the display system focused the broad radar pulse into a single beam of light, which proceeded from left of the screen to right. When no object impedes the traveling radar pulse, it continues to travel until lost from the screen on the right.

To represent reflection, a bright spot is created on the face of the screen when an object is struck. Thus, when an object is present, the pulse would strike it and begin to travel back to the receiver.

To represent reception, there is a trace on the screen coming from the object back to the receiver.

To represent measurement and conversion, the distance of the object can be measured by the length of the trace. With this system, however, you are only able to measure the distance to the object, not its absolute location.

MODERN DISPLAY SYSTEMS

Display models employed today use different techniques for representing the five steps of radar and thus make location of objects much easier.

For transmission, the transmitter emits a single beam of radar pulses that make continuous circular sweeps around the area under surveillance. Thus, an example is to think of the transmitter as being like the searchlight used at airports. In addition, the display screen is adjusted so that its center corresponds to the point where the radar pulse begins. As an example, the radar pulse seen on the screen operates like the second hand of a clock, which continually moves.

For reflection, when an object is present it leaves a bright spot on the face of the screen.

For reception, there is a trace coming back from the bright spot to the center of the screen.

For measurement and conversion, the face of the screen actually shows a maplike picture of the area around the radar, giving distance and, of course, location. Thus, it is easy now to determine the location of objects by noting their location on the screen's map.

THEORY: SIGNALING FOSTERS THE PROCESS OF ORGANIZING

Signaling techniques refer to the placement of noncontent words in a passage that serve to emphasize the conceptual structure or organization of the passage. In a pioneering analysis of signaling devices, Meyer (1975, p. 77–80) suggested four types of signals:

1. *Cues about relations among topics*—such as "first," "second," "third," or "the problem is . . ." and "the solution is . . ."
2. *Abstracted statements of key information that is to follow*—such as "the main ideas to be discussed in this paper are . . ."
3. *Summary statements,* which are like abstracts except that they occur at the end of a passage—such as "the main ideas in this paper were . . ."
4. *Pointer words,* which indicate the author's perspective or emphasize important information—such as "more important" or "regrettably."

In an updated analysis of signaling, Lorch (1989) identified a half-dozen signaling devices that can be organized into three broad classes: (1) *relevance indicators* (such as "Let me stress that . . .") and *typographical cues* (such as underlining, setting in boldface, coloring, centering) are ways to highlight key ideas; (2) *enumeration devices* (such as numbering items in a list) and *function indicators* (such as "thus" and "in summary") are ways to specify the relations among ideas in a sentence or section; and (3) *repetition* (including some preview and summary statements) and *titles, headings,* and *subheadings* are ways to show the overall organization of the material.

Signals do not provide any substantive information, but they do make the structure of the passage clearer. For example, Lorch (1989) defined signals as "writing devices that emphasize aspects of the text's content or structure without adding to the content of the text" (p. 209). Thus, signals provide a conceptual framework for the reader to use in selecting relevant information (i.e., the selecting process) and in organizing the information into a coherent representation (i.e., the organizing process).

RESEARCH ON SIGNALING

To investigate the role of signaling on learning from expository prose, Meyer (1975) asked subjects to read and later to recall passages about breeder reactors, schizophrenia, or parakeets. Signaled passages included all the previously mentioned signals, whereas the nonsignaled passages were created by deleting many of the signal words. Results indicated that signals tended to increase the number of idea units recalled, but the effect was small and not statistically significant. However, in a review of subsequent research on signaling, Lorch (1989) concluded that "virtually all types of signals produce better memory for information they cue in a text" (p. 209).

Although signals do not always have a large overall effect on learning, Meyer (1981) argued that signals should produce a strong effect under certain conditions. Thus, the main question addressed in this section is, Under what conditions does signaling influence meaningful learning?

SIGNALS ARE MORE EFFECTIVE FOR LESS SKILLED READERS First, signaling should be most effective for learners who do not normally use what Meyer (1981) calls "the structure strategy"—readers who do not normally follow the general outline of the passage.

For example, Meyer asked older and younger adults to read either signaled or nonsignaled passages and then take a 20-item short-answer comprehension test. The results indicated that signaling improved recall more strongly for older adults—who presumably do not normally use the structure strategy—than for younger adults. In addition, Figure 10–10 shows the average number of idea units recalled by good, average, poor, and underachieving readers who learned from either signaled or nonsignaled text (Meyer, Brandt, & Bluth, 1980). Signaling did not help the good readers but did have a strong positive effect for less able readers—who presumably are less likely to structure the material spontaneously. However, when students were tested several days later on a delayed recall test, the effects of signaling were no longer evident, suggesting that signaling may affect only the ease of initial encoding.

SIGNALS HELP LEARNERS BUILD A MENTAL OUTLINE OF THE TEXT Second, signaling is most useful when learners would not otherwise be able to construct a mental outline of the text. For example, Lorch, Lorch, and Inman (1993) asked students to read a 2,400-word passage on energy problems and their solutions. The signaled version included overviews, headings, and summaries, whereas the nonsignaled version did not. The signaled group recalled 80% of the key topics in the outline, compared to 48% for the nonsignaled group; importantly, the signaled group was far more likely than the nonsignaled group to recall the topics in the order they were presented. Thus, signals helped students to pay attention to the key topics and to organize them into a coherent outline structure. Lorch et al. (1993) conclude that "signals can aid readers in constructing a complete and coherent representation of a text's topic structure" (p. 288).

FIGURE 10–10 Effects of signaling on recall

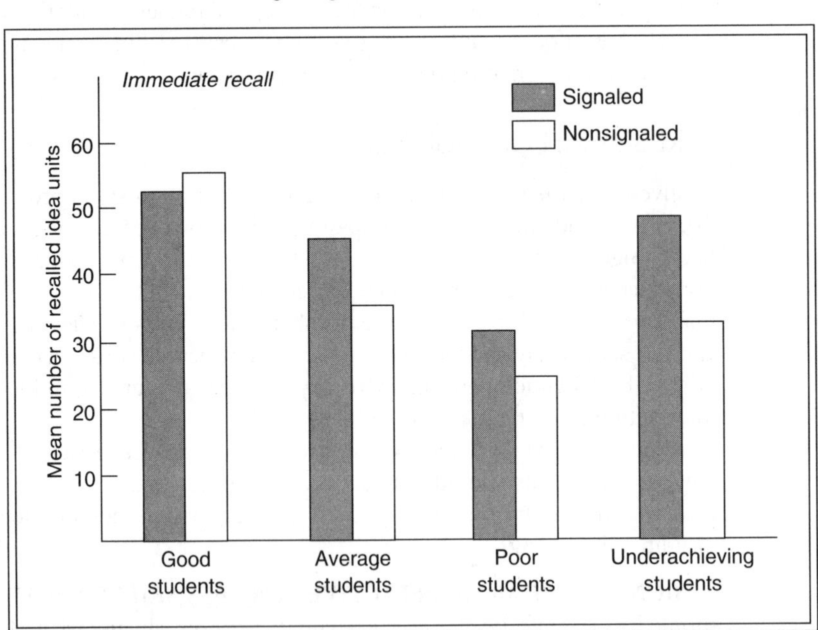

Adapted from Meyer, Brandt and Bluth (1980)

In a follow-up study, Lorch and Lorch (1995) found that giving students cues on the test to remind them of the topical organization helped students who had read signaled texts more than students who had read nonsignaled texts. They concluded that students use different learning strategies for processing signaled and nonsignaled texts: When the text is signaled, students strive to organize it based on a hierarchical structure, but when the text is not signaled, they are more likely to organize it as a random list of facts.

SIGNALS PROMOTE SELECTIVE RETENTION AND TRANSFER Third, signaling is more likely to enhance retention of the conceptually relevant information than lower-level details and is more likely to improve creative problem solving than verbatim retention of specific facts. This prediction follows from the idea that signaling helps the reader to reorganize the material into a coherent structure rather than a list of specific propositions. For example, Meyer and Rice (1981) reported that signaling increased recall of logical relations from 49% (without signals) to 59% (with signals) but improved overall recall by only four percentage points. Similarly, Meyer (1981) reported that signaling helped older adults recall more conceptual information (increasing recall of major conceptual ideas from 47% to 67%) but not more details (9% with signals versus 14% without signals).

In another study, Loman and Mayer (1983) asked students to read a passage about red tides either with or without signals. Three types of signals were used: preview sentences to emphasize the structure of the passage, underlined headings to identify each of the major conceptual parts of the passage, and logical connective phrases, such as "because of this," to clarify the cause-and-effect chain within each part. Figure 10–11 gives the nonsignaled and signaled versions of the red tides passage. Subjects were asked to recall the passage and take both a verbatim recognition test and a problem-solving test with questions such as "How can you prevent red tides?" Figure 10–12 shows that the signaled subjects recalled about 50% more conceptual information than the nonsignaled subjects but both groups recalled about the same amount of nonconceptual information. Thus, the evidence shows that signals can direct a reader's attention towards conceptual information. In addition, the signaled subjects generated about 50% more good answers to problem-solving questions than the nonsignaled subjects, but the groups did not differ on verbatim recognition. More recently, Mautone and Mayer (2001) found that adding signals to a text or narration on how airplanes achieve lift substantially increased students' problem-solving transfer performance. Apparently, signals encouraged learners to organize the material around conceptual information, which is useful for promoting transfer to creative problem solving.

REWRITING TEXT TO SIGNAL COHERENCE Fourth, signals are most effective when the text is poorly written. If you are trying to build a coherent structure from text, a major cognitive challenge is to find coherence among ideas in the text. Regrettably, many textbooks do not provide help much with this challenge (Britton, Gulgoz, & Glynn, 1993; Chambliss & Calfee, 1998). For example, the top of Figure 10–13 shows a portion of an original passage about the Vietnam War used in basic training by the U.S. Air Force. Let's consider the first two elements: (1) "Air War in the North, 1965" and (2) "By the fall of 1964, Americans in both Saigon and Washington had begun to focus on Hanoi as the source of the continuing problem in the South." If you are trying to establish coherence

FIGURE 10–11

Nonsignaled and signaled versions of the red tides passage

NONSIGNALED VERSION

"The Mystery of the Red Tides"

What makes the sea turn red and causes thousands of fish to die? As far back as anyone could remember the blame was placed on the "red tides."

In 1947, scientists finally traced the condition called the red tides to a microscopic sea organism called the dinoflagellate.

The dinoflagellate is so tiny that 6000 of these organisms may be contained in a single drop of water. It stands on the border between plant and animal in its classification. It manufactures its own food, as plants do. But it moves freely and eats other organisms, as animals do.

Dinoflagellates are normally only one of the many kinds of organisms found in plankton. Plankton is the name given to all very small forms of sea life. However, when the air and water are calm and warm, dinoflagellates multiply or "bloom" with amazing speed. The surface of the water appears to be covered with a red carpet.

The "blooming" dinoflagellates give off a poisonous secretion. Many fish die. Their bodies are washed up on the beach. Beaches are not fit for use. Fish that are not killed may become poisonous to animals or people who eat them. Commercial fishing comes to a halt.

As dinoflagellates exhaust the food and oxygen in an area, they die. After a time, the sea returns to normal. But when conditions are right, the red tide blooms again.

At least nine times in this century, the west coast of Florida has been plagued by the red tide. In 1957, the Arabian Sea was affected. At different times, the coasts of western Australia and Peru have suffered from this invasion from the sea.

SIGNALED VERSION

"The Mystery of the Red Tides"

What makes the sea turn red and causes thousands of fish to die? As far back as anyone could remember the blame was placed on the "red tides."

In 1947, scientists finally traced the condition called the red tides to a microscopic sea organism called the dinoflagellate.

The purpose of this lesson is to explain the life cycle of dinoflagellates. The dinoflagellate is so tiny that 6000 of these organisms may be contained in single drop of water. It stands on the border between plant and animal in its classification. It manufactures its own food, as plants do. But it moves freely and eats other organisms, as animals do.

There are three main phases in the life cycle of dinoflagellates: dinoflagellates bloom, dinoflagellates secrete poison, and dinoflagellates die.

1. *Dinoflagellates bloom.* Dinoflagellates are normally only one of many kinds of organisms found in plankton. Plankton is the name given to all very small forms of sea life. However, when the air and water are calm and warm, this

FIGURE 10–11 (cont.)

causes the dinoflagellates to multiply or "bloom" with amazing speed. Because of this, the surface of the water appears to be covered with a red carpet.

2. *Dinoflagellates secrete poison.* The "blooming" dinoflagellates give off a poisonous secretion that causes many fish to die. Their bodies are washed up on the beach. As a result, beaches are not fit for use. Fish that are not killed may become poisonous to animals or people who eat them. Because of this, commercial fishing comes to a halt.
3. *Dinoflagellates die.* As dinoflagellates exhaust the food and oxygen in an area, the result is that they die. After a time, the sea returns to normal. But when conditions are right, the red tide blooms again.

At least nine times in this century, the west coast of Florida has been plagued by the red tide. In 1957, the Arabian Sea was affected. At different times, the coasts of western Australia and Peru have suffered this invasion from the sea.

From Liddie (1977)

FIGURE 10–12 Effects of signaling on "what is learned"

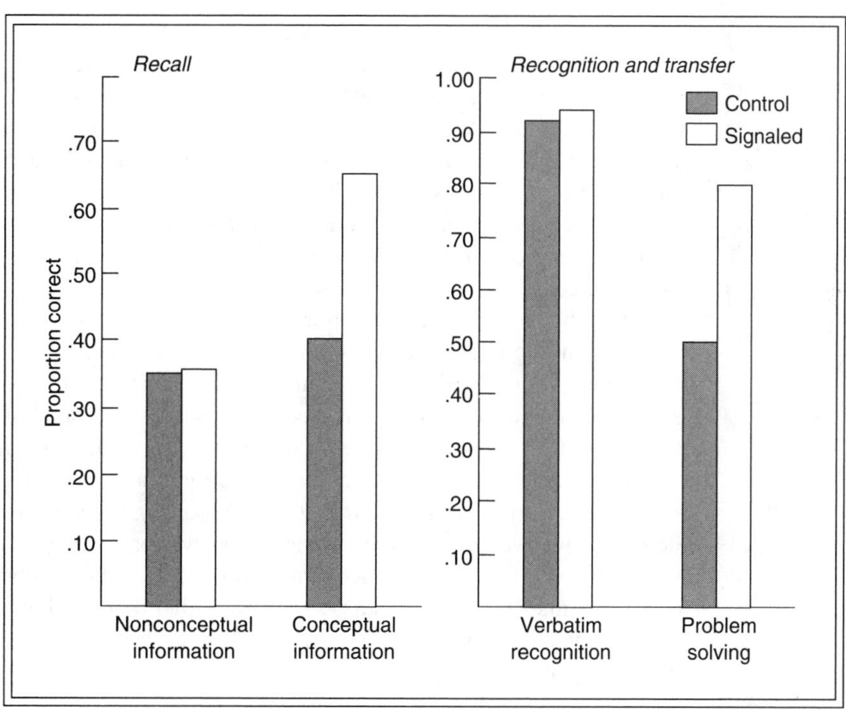

Adapted from Loman and Mayer (1983)

FIGURE 10–13

Excerpts from original and revised text

ORIGINAL VERSION

Air War in the North, 1965

By the fall of 1964, Americans in both Saigon and Washington had begun to focus on Hanoi as the source of the continuing problem in the South. As frustration mounted over the inability of the ARVN to defeat the enemy in the field, pressure to strike directly at North Vietnam began to build. Although there was near unanimity among American officials over the aerial extension of the war into North Vietnam, serious differences arose over both the objective and the methods to be used.

Most members of the Johnson administration believed bombing attacks would accomplish several things. They would demonstrate clearly and forcefully the United States' resolve to halt communist aggression and to support a free Vietnam. At the same time, they would provide a boost for the sagging morale of the South Vietnamese. They would also make Hanoi pay an increasingly high price for supporting the Vietcong. Particularly among civilian advocates, the motivation for such a campaign was psychological rather than military, the primary objective not being Hanoi's capability but its willingness to support the war. "In a very real sense," explained Maxwell Taylor, "the objective of our campaign is to change the will of the enemy leadership."

REVISED VERSION

The 1965 Air War in North Vietnam

By the beginning of 1965, American officials in both South Vietnam and the U.S. had begun to focus on North Vietnam as the source of the continuing war in South Vietnam. The South Vietnamese army was losing the ground war against North Vietnam, and this caused frustrations among the American officials. The frustrations led to pressure to bomb North Vietnam. The idea of bombing North Vietnam found support among nearly all the American officials. However, the civilian and military officials had serious differences over both the objective and the methods of the bombing attacks.

Most of both civilian and military members of the Johnson administration believed bombing attacks would accomplish several things. The bombing attacks would demonstrate clearly and forcefully the United States' resolve to halt communist aggression and to support a free South Vietnam. At the same time, the bombing attacks would provide a boost for the South Vietnamese morale which was sagging because they were losing the war. The bombing attacks would also make North Vietnam pay an increasingly high price for supporting the war. Among the civilian officials, the motivation for the bombing attacks was psychological rather than military. For the civilian officials, the primary objective of the bombing was to break North Vietnam's willingness to support the war rather than its ability. Maxwell Taylor explained the civilian view: "The objective of our air campaign is to change the will of the enemy leadership."

From Britton and Gulgoz (1991)

between these two elements (i.e., the title and the first sentence), a common strategy is to look for the repetition of the same word. However, after a careful search, you find that the title and first sentence do not share any content words, so they lack any obvious coherence links.

The lack of coherence links means that you must work hard to create coherence by inferring missing information. For example, you can use your general knowledge that events in one year (e.g., 1964) can cause events in the following year (e.g., 1965). In reading "By the fall of 1964" in the second element, you must make the inference "causing events in 1965." In addition, you can use your specific knowledge that "North" in the title refers to "North Vietnam" and that "Hanoi" in the text refers to the "capital of North Vietnam." In reading "North" in the first element, you must infer "North Vietnam," and in reading "Saigon" in the second element, you must infer "capital of South Vietnam." Further, when you read "continuing problem in the South" you must infer that the problem is "the war in South Vietnam."

Let's suppose you want to rewrite the passage so that it guides the reader's search for coherence. Building on theories of reading comprehension, Britton and Gulgoz (1991) rewrote the passage based on three major principles:

(1) "Make the learner's job easier by rewriting the sentence so it repeats, from the previous sentence, the linking word to which it should be linked" (p. 331). For example, readers may not realize that "the continuing problem in the South" (in the first sentence) refers to the same thing as "the inability of the ARVN to defeat the enemy in the field" (in the second sentence). These sentences were rewritten so that they had the word *war* in common: The revised first sentence contained "the continuing war in South Vietnam," and the revised second sentence contained "the South Vietnamese army was losing the ground war against North Vietnam." Overall, the text was rewritten so that the same term was always used to refer to the same concept in the text. For example, each of 12 different terms for air attacks (e.g., "bombing operations" and "air raids") became "air attacks," each of 15 different terms for North Vietnam (e.g., "Hanoi" and "North") became "North Vietnam," each of 6 different terms for South Vietnam (e.g., "Saigon" and "South") became "South Vietnam," each of 23 different terms for American officials (e.g., "Americans" and "Washington") became "American officials."

(2) "Make the learner's job easier by arranging the parts of each sentence so the learner first encounters the old part . . . and next encounters the new part . . ." (p. 331). For example, the second sentence starts with a new idea ("As frustration mounted") and then presents an old idea that was contained in the previous sentence ("over the inability of the ARVN to defeat the enemy . . ."). To put the old part before the new, the clause should read: "The inability of the ARVN to defeat the enemy in the field caused frustration." When we also incorporate principle 1, the revised sentence becomes "The South Vietnamese army was losing the ground war against North Vietnam, and this caused frustrations."

(3) "Make the learner's job easier by making explicit any implicit references" (p. 332). For example, the word *frustrations* implies that someone is frustrated, but the second sentence does not explicitly state who is frustrated; to change that implicit

reference to an explicit one, the second sentence acquires the following ending: "among the American officials." A portion of the revised version is shown at the bottom of Figure 10–13.

Does adding coherence cues affect learning? On a free recall test, students given the revised version produced 59 facts from the text, whereas students given the original version produced 35 facts—indicating a 68% improvement for revising the passage. On a comprehension test requiring inference, students given the revised version correctly answered 46%, whereas students given the original version correctly answered 37%—indicating a 24% improvement for revising the passage. The inference score is particularly important because it represents a measure of transfer and hence an indication that providing explicit cues for how to build coherence is one way to teach for transfer. In a review of 18 studies like this one, Britton et al. (1993) concluded that "many textbooks are poorly written" (p. 36) and "rewriting existing textbooks can result in improved learning" (p. 1). In sum, the key to improving text understanding is not to simply add signals but rather to add signals that guide the reader's process of structure building.

Can writers learn to revise textbooks based on principles for guiding the reader's cognitive processing? Britton (1996) reports that students who were trained on Britton and Gulgoz's principles correctly changed 57% of the problems in one textbook passage and 79% of the problems in another. Apparently, progress has been made in designing textbooks that teach for transfer, but more refinement is needed.

IMPLICATIONS OF RESEARCH ON SIGNALING

Signaling the conceptual structure of a passage can be accomplished by using outlines, headings, organizing sentences, and logical connectives. Such techniques will be most effective for students who do not normally pay attention to the outline structure of a passage, for passages that are poorly written, and when the goal of instruction is retention of the major conceptual information for creative problem solving. Apparently, signals can influence the processes of selecting and organizing incoming material.

ADVANCE ORGANIZERS

EXAMPLE OF ADVANCE ORGANIZER

What else can be done to improve the reader's understanding of the radar lesson in Figure 10–1? Some researchers suggest presenting a concrete model of the principles to be learned. For example, the main conceptual information in the passage concerns the idea of a radar pulse: A pulse is transmitted, it bounces off a remote object, it travels back to a receiver, and the time and angle of the pulse can be converted to measures of distance and location. These ideas are presented in the passage, but most readers fail to remember them. Figure 10–14 presents a diagram that clearly summarizes the principles of radar as

FIGURE 10–14 An advance organizer for the radar passage

There are five steps in radar.

1. Transmission: A pulse travels from an antenna.

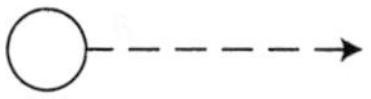

2. Reflection: The pulse bounces off a remote object.

3. Reception: The pulse returns to the receiver.

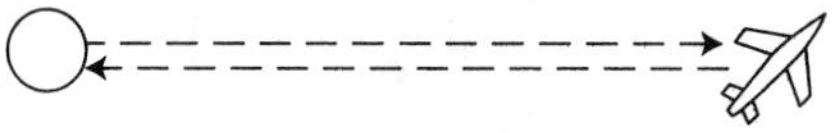

4. Measurement: The difference between the time out and the time back tells the total time traveled.

Out Back

5. Conversion: The time can be converted to a measure of distance, since the pulse travels at a constant speed.

_________ seconds = _________ miles

From Mayer (1983b)

described in the passage. The diagram does not add any information not already in the passage, but it does provide a familiar way to organize the passage. If you had seen this diagram for 60 seconds before you read the radar lesson, do you think you would have understood the passage better?

In a study (Mayer, 1983b), students who were given this diagram for 60 seconds before they listened to the passage performed quite differently on tests than subjects who received the same lesson but without the diagram. For example, the diagram students recalled 50% more information overall than the no-diagram group; in particular, recall was enhanced for conceptual information in the lesson. In addition, problem-solving scores for the diagram group were twice as high as for the no-diagram group. Apparently, the diagram helped learners to reorganize the lesson around the major points of the passage rather than trying to memorize the passage as presented. Not surprisingly, the diagram students actually performed worse than the no-diagram group on tests of verbatim recognition, presumably because the diagram helped learners to put the information into their own words. These results are summarized in Figure 10–15.

FIGURE 10–15 Effects of advance organizer on retention and transfer

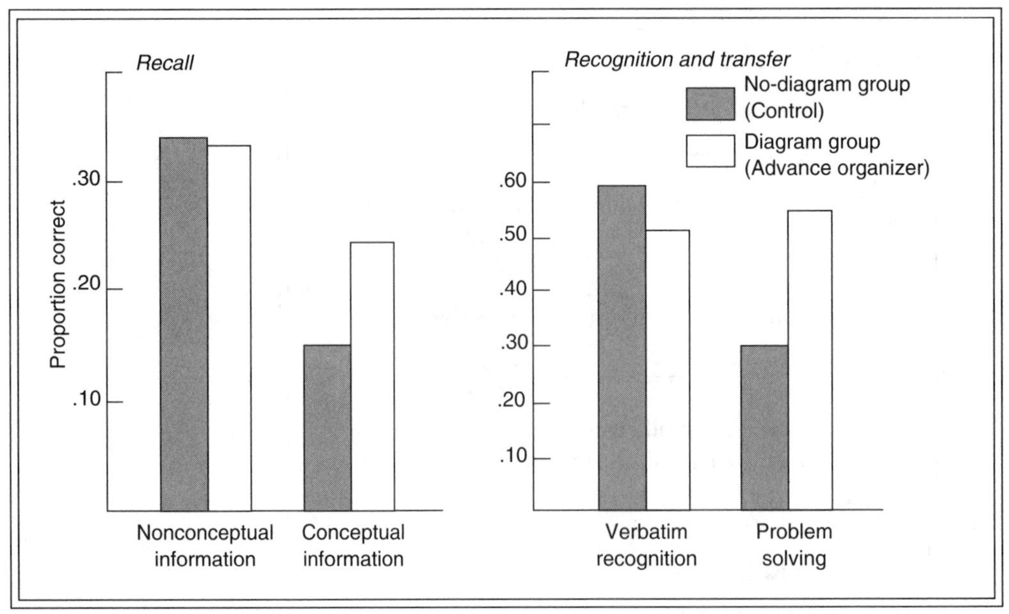

Adapted from Mayer (1983b)

THEORY: ADVANCE ORGANIZERS FOSTER THE PROCESS OF INTEGRATING

An advance organizer is information that is presented prior to learning and that can be used by the learner to organize and interpret new incoming information. According to Ausubel (1968) the function of the organizer is "to provide ideational scaffolding for the stable incorporation and retention of more detailed and differentiated material that follows" (p. 148). In short, the advance organizer activates or provides organized prior knowledge that can be used to assimilate the incoming information. Both Mayer (1979) and Derry (1984) offer similar theories in which advance organizers help learners connect the presented material with what they already know. Advance organizers may influence cognitive processing in several ways, such as by providing prerequisite knowledge or helping learners make connections between incoming information and prior knowledge (i.e., the process of *integrating*). Advance organizers that serve to make appropriate prerequisite knowledge available to the learner by providing new information are called *expository organizers;* advance organizers that serve to build external connections with existing knowledge that is relevant to the new information by reminding the learner about prior knowledge are called *comparative organizers.*

EXPOSITORY ORGANIZERS FOR PREREQUISITE KNOWLEDGE Let's look at an example of an expository organizer, that is, an advance organizer that provides new information to be used to assimilate the passage. Ausubel (1960) asked college students to read a 2,500-word passage about metallurgy after reading either a 500-word expository organizer that presented the underlying concepts or a 500-word historical passage. The advance organizer group performed better on a subsequent test of retention, presumably because the learners were able to tie the information to knowledge structures presented in the organizer.

COMPARATIVE ORGANIZERS FOR EXTERNAL CONNECTIONS Now let's look at an example of a comparative advance organizer, that is, an advance organizer that primes the learner's existing knowledge. Ausubel and Youssef (1963) asked college students to read a 2,500-word passage on Buddhism after reading either a comparative advance organizer that pointed to the relation between Buddhism and Christianity or a nonorganizing historical introduction. Retention for the target passage was higher for the advance organizer group, presumably because of the learners' being encouraged to understand new concepts (Buddhism) in terms of existing knowledge about Christianity.

RESEARCH ON ADVANCE ORGANIZERS

Ausubel (1960, 1968) was the first to study systematically the role of advance organizers in meaningful learning from prose. Over the course of a long series of studies such as those just summarized, Ausubel obtained consistent but small advantages in retention due to advance organizers. Ausubel's work stimulated a great deal of research on advance organizers since the 1960s (Corkill, 1992; Mayer, 1979), although some reviews (e.g., Barnes & Clawson, 1975) pointed out that many advance organizer studies fail to yield significant results. Thus, there is not a single answer to the question, Do advance organizers facilitate learning? Instead, it may be more fruitful to determine the conditions under which advance organizers are most likely to influence learning. Thus, the remainder of this section focuses on the question. Under what conditions do advance organizers foster learning?

ADVANCE ORGANIZERS ARE MORE EFFECTIVE WHEN LEARNERS LACK PRIOR KNOWLEDGE First, advance organizers should be most effective in situations where the learner either does not possess or would not normally use appropriate prerequisite knowledge for organizing incoming information. Advance organizers should be most effective for students who lack prior knowledge but not as effective for those who possess prior knowledge. For example, West and Fensham (1976) asked high school students to learn about the principle of equilibrium after presentation of an advance organizer or a control introduction. In addition, all subjects were pretested to determine their background knowledge in the area. Results indicated a pattern of knowledge-by-treatment interaction (KTI) in which advance organizers significantly increased learning for subjects who scored low in background knowledge but not for those who scored high. When remedial pretraining was provided to students who scored low in prerequisite knowledge, the effects of advance organizers were eliminated. Similar results have been reported in other studies that measure the amount of background knowledge or domain-specific ability (Mayer, 1979).

ADVANCE ORGANIZERS PROMOTE TRANSFER Second, the effects of advance organizers should be most visible for tests that involve creative problem solving or transfer to new situations, because the advance organizer allows the learner to organize the material into a familiar structure. For example, in the radar study (Mayer, 1983b) cited earlier, the advance organizer group performed better on creative problem solving but worse on verbatim retention than a control group. Advance organizers could hinder verbatim retention because learners reorganize the material and put it into their own words. The dependent measures used in some advance organizer studies may be more like verbatim retention than creative problem solving; hence, we would not expect to find a strong positive effect for advance organizers in those studies. In a series of studies that measured creative problem solving, Mayer (1979) found consistently strong transfer effects due to advance organizers.

CONCRETE MODELS AS ADVANCE ORGANIZERS Third, advance organizers must be correctly designed to be effective. Ausubel (1968) called for using abstract advance organizers that are "presented at a higher level of abstraction, generality, and inclusiveness" (p. 148). However, Mayer (1987a) suggested that concrete advance organizers may be more effective in serving to provide appropriate prerequisite knowledge. Similarily, in a recent review, Corkill (1992) concluded that "it appears that a concrete example works better than an abstract one" (p. 59). For example, Royer and Cable (1975, 1976) asked subjects to read an abstract passage on the flow of heat through metals or the conduction of electricity after reading a passage that presented either relevant physical analogies or only relevant abstract principles. In their study, a concrete analogy for electricity involved the following: Impurities in the conducting wire are like having bulky objects such as a pack of cigarettes in a row of toppling dominoes, because an obstacle interrupts the orderly transfer of energy. Results showed that preexposure to the concrete analogies significantly facilitated learning and memory for the second passage.

As another example of a concrete analogy, let's consider the way in which most textbooks present the concept of Ohm's law. In an analysis of science textbooks White and Mayer (1980) found that most textbooks include a brief biography of Ohm, a formal statement of the law such as $R = V/I$, a statement of the law in words, definitions of key terms, computational examples of how to derive numerical values, and practical facts about metals. One book provided an analogy of a boy pushing a cart up a steep road: The angle of the slope is analogous to resistance; the boy's push is analogous to voltage; and the actual speed up the hill is analogous to intensity. Mayer (1983b) used another concrete model of an electrical circuit: The amount of congestion in the wire is analogous to resistance; the number of electrons pumped out of the battery per time unit is analogous to voltage; the actual number of electrons passing any point per time unit is analogous to intensity. When students were presented with diagrams for this model prior to reading a passage on Ohm's law, their retention of information was enhanced, especially their retention of conceptual information from the passage (Mayer, 1983b).

Similarly, Mayer (1975a, 1976, 1979) asked nonprogrammers to read a 10-page manual on BASIC-like computer programming. A concrete model of the computer such as is shown in Figure 10–16 was presented for 3 minutes either before or after reading the passage. The concrete model represented memory as an erasable scoreboard, input as a ticket window, output as a note message pad, and executive control as a shopping list with pointer arrow. Students who received the model prior to reading the manual performed

FIGURE 10–16

An advance organizer for a manual on BASIC computer programming

For purposes of this manual, let's assume that the computer consists of four main parts:

1. *Memory scoreboard.* There are several scoreboard boxes, each with a name such as A1, A2, A3 and so on. A number can be written in each box; when a new number is put in, the old number must be erased.
2. *Input window.* Data numbers waiting to be processed form a queue for the input window. The numbers are processed one at a time in the "in" part of the window; after processing, the data number is moved to the "out" part of the window.
3. *Program list and pointer arrow.* The computer has a list of things to do. It begins with the first thing on the list. When that is done, it moves to the next thing on the list, and so on.
4. *Output pad.* Messages from the computer to you are written on an output pad, with one message written per line on the pad.

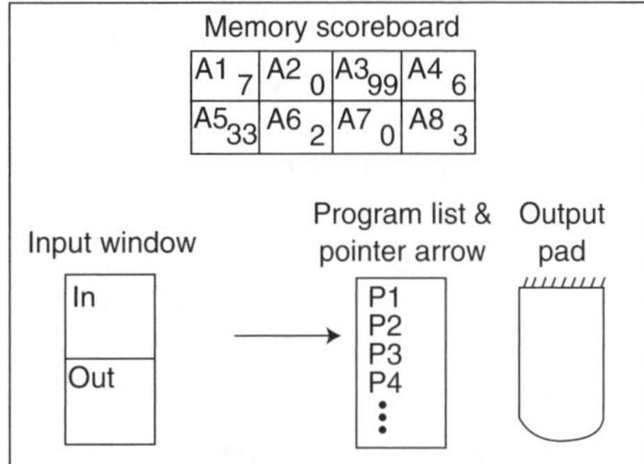

Adapted from Mayer (1975b)

much better on recall of conceptual information and on creative problem solving (e.g., generating complicated programs), while students who received the model after reading the manual performed better on recall of grammatical details and on solving problems just like those given in the manual. The same pattern was obtained when students were given actual physical models that could be manipulated or pictorial diagrams that could not be manipulated. Apparently, the concrete model served to help the learner understand and organize the information during learning.

ILLUSTRATIONS AS CONCRETE MODELS IN TEXT Because some effective advance organizers include simple illustrations, a reasonable extension is to consider the role of illustrations in text. For example, please read the text in Figure 10–17. This text can be called *explanative text* because it explains how a cause-and-effect system works. What are some illustrations that could be used to guide the reader's cognitive processing? Based

FIGURE 10–17

Excerpt from pumps passage

Bicycle tire pumps vary in the number and location of the valves they have and in the way air enters the cylinder. Some simple bicycle tire pumps have the inlet valve on the piston and the outlet valve at the closed end of the cylinder. A bicycle tire pump has a piston that moves up and down. Air enters the pump near the point where the connecting rod passes through the cylinder. *As the rod is pulled out, air passes through the piston and fills the area between the piston and the outlet valve. As the rod is pushed in, the inlet valve closes and the piston forces air through the outlet valve.**

**Key information is in italics (not italicized in original text).*

From World Book Encyclopedia (1991)

on an analysis by Levin (1989; Levin & Mayer, 1993), let's look at four possible kinds of illustrations we could use to supplement the text on how pumps work:

Decorative illustrations are intended to entertain the reader, such as showing a picture of a child riding a bicycle.

Representational illustrations portray a single element, such as showing a picture of a bicycle tire pump.

Organizational illustrations depict the relations among the elements, such as showing a line drawing of a tire pump with each component labeled.

Explanative illustrations explain how a system works, such as frames showing the state of the pump when the handle is up and when the handle is down.

Which kinds of illustrations are most likely to promote deep learning that leads to transfer? Because decorative and representational illustrations do not provide much guidance for how to build a coherent mental representation, they are not likely to promote transfer. However, organizational and explanative illustrations have potential to guide readers as they build coherent structures based on their prior knowledge and thus have potential to promote transfer.

Illustrations are often used in text but rarely in ways designed to promote deep learning. For example, Mayer (1993) found that 55% of the space in a sample of science textbooks was devoted to graphics, but 85% of the illustrations were decorative or representational. The remaining 15% were organizational or explanative and thus seemed to be designed to promote deep learning.

You might be tempted to ask, "Do illustrations improve learning?" However, that question is too broad, like asking whether words improve learning. Indeed, some illustrations promote learning and some do not. Thus, a more reasonable question is, How do illustrations guide a reader's cognitive processing during learning? One important role for illustrations is to help learners integrate the presented information with their existing knowledge so that they build a coherent mental model of the to-be-learned system.

What makes a good illustration? To help answer that question, Mayer and Gallini (1990) asked inexperienced students to read a passage explaining how pumps work, such as excerpted in Figure 10–17. If students build a mental model of how pumps work, they should be able to produce a step-by-step explanation when asked to do so (which we call a recall test), and they should be able to write useful answers to problem-solving transfer questions such as, What could be done to make a pump more reliable, that is, to make sure it would not fail? (which we call a transfer test). In spite of the fact that the text included an explanation, students who read the text performed poorly on both conceptual recall and problem-solving transfer.

What happens when we add combined organizational and explanative illustrations such as shown in Figure 10–18? The illustrations do not add any new words and only provide a concrete visualization of the explanation in the text. Yet students who read a text with these illustrations (text-with-illustrations group) performed approximately four times better than the text-only students on conceptual recall. Because the text was long and contained much extraneous information, the words repeated in the illustrations could have served as cues to focus on the conceptually relevant material. More important, the text-with-illustrations group produced about 69% more correct solutions on problem-solving transfer than did the text-only group. These results are summarized in Figure 10–19. Although explanative illustrations promoted increased transfer performance,

FIGURE 10–18 Captioned illustration for pumps passage

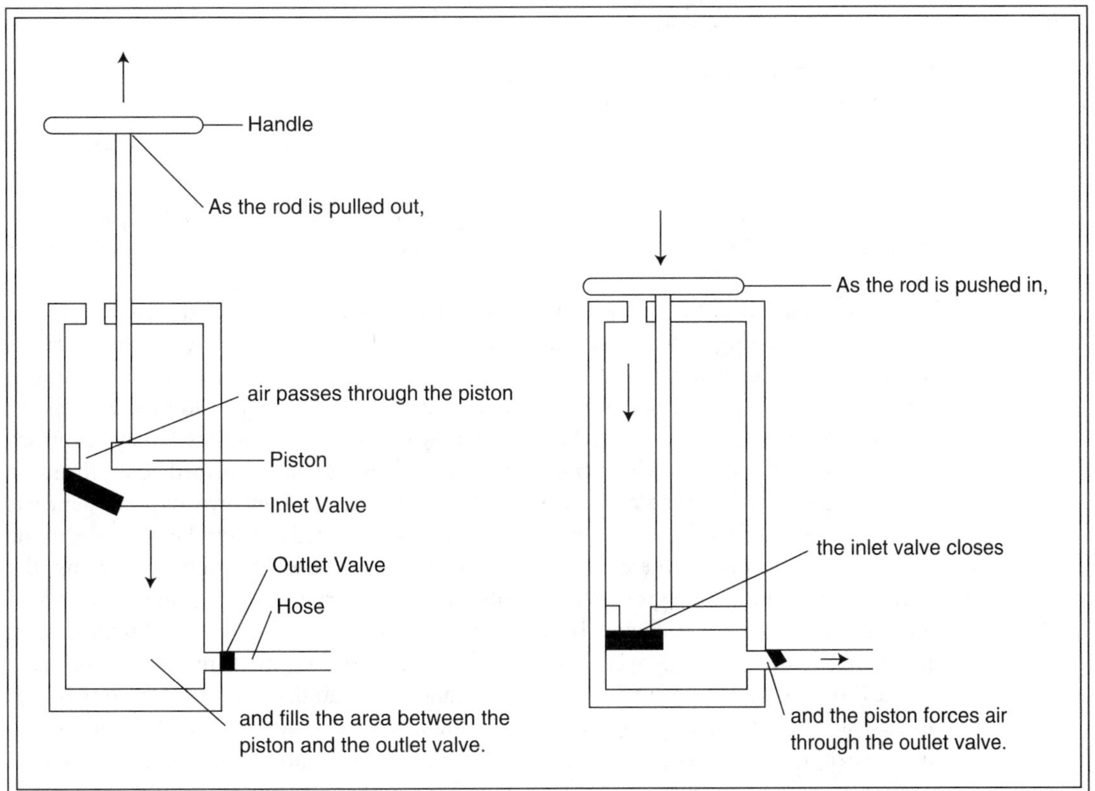

Adapted from Mayer and Gallini (1990)

FIGURE 10–19 Adding illustrations to text improves learning

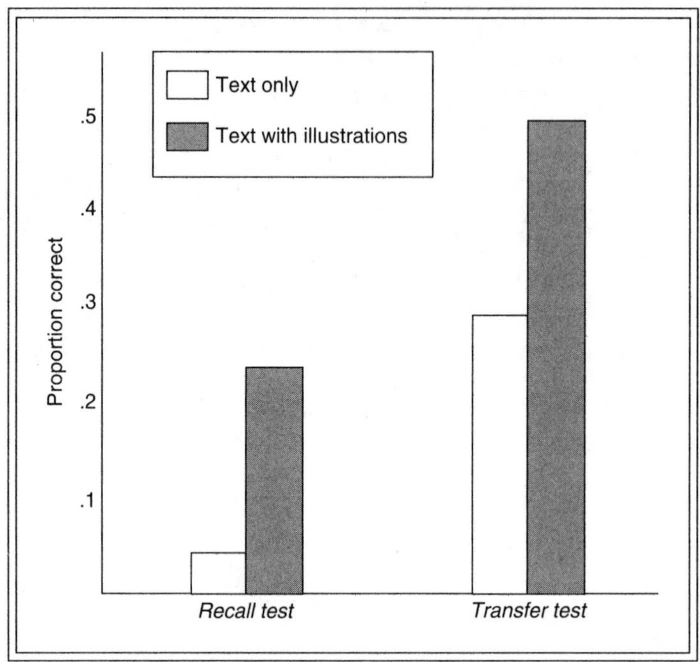

Adapted from Mayer and Gallini (1990)

other types of illustrations did not. Apparently, the key to meaningful learning about how some system works is to use multiframe illustrations showing the various states of the system.

In an extension of this work, Mayer and Anderson (1991) produced a short narrated animation explaining how a bicycle tire pump works. Figure 10–20 shows selected frames along with the concurrent narration. Students received the narrated animation (narration-with-animation group) or the narration alone (narration-only group) and then were asked to write an explanation (recall test) and solve new problems (transfer test). As you can see in Figure 10–21, students who received the narrated animation performed about the same as students who received narration alone on the recall test; the high level of performance is attributable to the fact that the narration was short and focused only on the key steps in the explanation. However, if the animation promoted deeper, more transferable learning, the narration-with-animation group should outperform the narration-only group on the transfer test. As you can see in Figure 10–21, adding animation resulted in a 100% increase in problem-solving transfer. Mayer (2001b) and Sweller (1999) provide reviews of dozens of studies confirming the positive effects of illustrations and animations on promoting meaningful learning. Another important line of research shows that adding graphic organizers to text—such as a matrix—can improve both retention and transfer performance (Kiewra, Kauffman, Robinson, DuBois, & Staley, 1999; Robinson & Kiewra, 1995).

FIGURE 10–20 Selected frames and sound track from a multimedia presentation

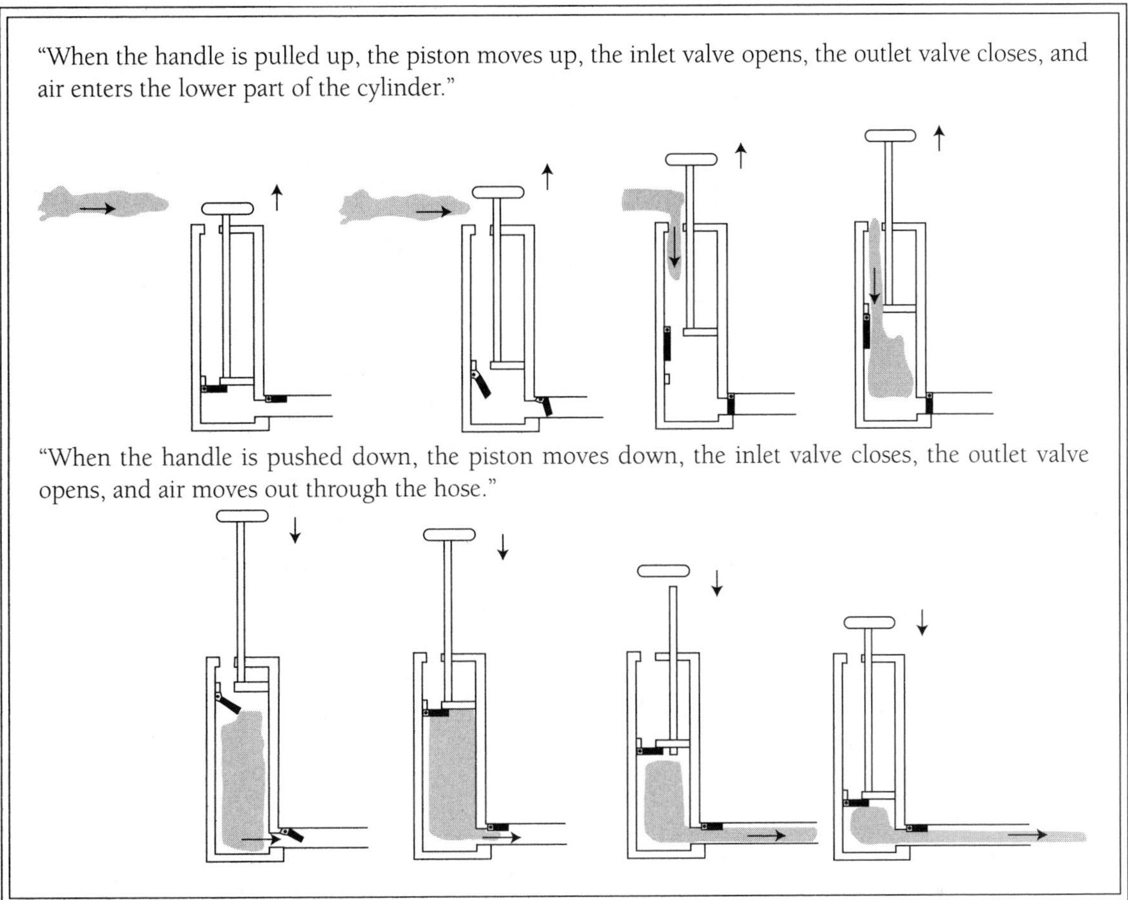

"When the handle is pulled up, the piston moves up, the inlet valve opens, the outlet valve closes, and air enters the lower part of the cylinder."
"When the handle is pushed down, the piston moves down, the inlet valve closes, the outlet valve opens, and air moves out through the hose."

From Mayer and Anderson (1991)

IMPLICATIONS OF RESEARCH ON ADVANCE ORGANIZERS

These results allow us to propose the conditions under which advance organizers should be used. First, they should be used when students lack the prerequisite knowledge that is necessary for understanding the material to be learned. If no prerequisite knowledge is needed, or if students are likely to already possess and use such knowledge, advance organizers are not needed. Second, advance organizers should be used when the goal of instruction is transfer of learning to new problems. If the goal is verbatim retention of specific information or performance on problems like those given in instruction, advance organizers are not needed. Third, advance organizers should be easy for the student to acquire and use and should present an integrated model of the material to be learned. Concrete analogies—even presented as captioned illustrations—seem to be particularly useful in meeting these criteria.

FIGURE 10–21 Adding animation to narration improves learning

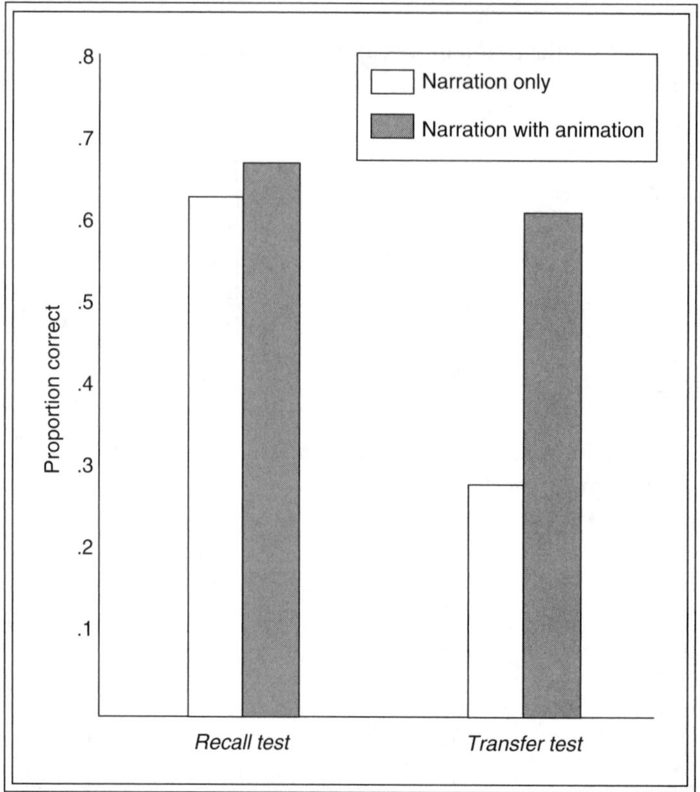

Adapted from Mayer and Anderson (1991)

CHAPTER SUMMARY

This chapter examined three techniques for improving the understandability of a textbook lesson (or even a lecture or multimedia presentation). The goal is to figure out how to design prose presentations so that learners can transfer what they learn to solving new problems. In particular, this chapter provided some examples of how instructional methods influence the learner's meaningful processing of information. If the goal is to direct the reader's attention (i.e., selecting), prequestions and signals should be used. If the goal is to encourage building of internal connections (i.e., organizing), signaling and certain types of postquestions should be used. If the goal is to encourage building of external connections (i.e., integrating), advance organizers and certain types of postquestions should be used. In short, the use of any text device should be guided by an understanding of which cognitive processes it is most likely to affect.

SUGGESTED READINGS

Chambliss, M. J., & Calfee, R. C. (1998). *Textbooks for learning.* Oxford, England: Blackwell. (Proposes theory-based principles for textbook design.)

Corkill, A. J. (1992). Advance organizers: Facilitators of recall. *Educational Psychology Review, 4,* 33–68. (Reviews research on advance organizers.)

Lorch, R. F. (1989). Text-signaling devices and their effects on reading and memory processes. *Educational Psychology Review, 1,* 209–234. (Reviews research on signaling.)

CHAPTER 11 Teaching by Fostering Learning Strategies

CHAPTER OUTLINE

How to Turn a Passive Learning Task Into an Active Learning Task

Mnemonic Strategies

Structure Strategies

Generative Strategies

Chapter Summary

The process of meaningful learning depends both on the material that is presented (i.e., the teaching side of the process) and on the way that the material is processed by the learner (i.e., the learning side of the process). Thus two ways of fostering the process of meaningful learning are improving the way that material is presented (i.e., instructional methods) and improving the way that students process information (i.e., learning and thinking strategies). Previous chapters focused on instructional methods as the key to promoting student learning. This chapter takes a more direct approach by exploring whether students can learn to be more effective learners. In short, we seek to help learners build learning strategies that allow them to learn in ways that promote transfer. In this chapter, you will learn about three types of learning strategies—mnemonic strategies for memorizing material, structure strategies for helping students to organize material, and generative strategies for helping students integrate new material with their existing knowledge.

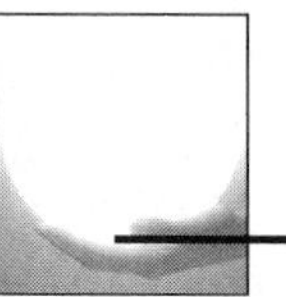

HOW TO TURN A PASSIVE LEARNING TASK INTO AN ACTIVE LEARNING TASK

Reading a textbook lesson or listening to a lecture seems to be a passive task. Yet successful students turn this seemingly passive task into an active one in which they try to make sense of the presented material. For example, please read the lightning passage in Figure 11–1, using any strategies that will help you learn it. In an attempt to take an active approach, you might read every word aloud or even copy the entire passage into a notebook. What's wrong with either of these approaches? In spite of your being prompted to be behaviorally active (i.e., talking or writing), you are not being cognitively active (i.e., you are not trying to make sense of the material). Learning strategies are intended to help learners become cognitively active learners.

A learning strategy refers to cognitive processing performed by a learner at the time of learning that is intended to improve learning. This definition has three main parts: (1) a learning strategy involves intentional cognitive processing by the learner; (2) a learning strategy occurs at the time of learning; and (3) a learning strategy is intended to improve learning. This definition is broad enough to include techniques ranging from strategies for memorizing facts in a lesson, to strategies for outlining a lesson, to strategies for summarizing a lesson.

Learning strategies may focus mainly on helping you recall specific facts, on helping you organize the material into a coherent structure, or on helping you to integrate the material with your prior knowledge and experience. If you focus on learning strategies for memorizing, you might choose a few key ideas and try to commit them to memory. For example, to remember that negative charges fall to the bottom of the cloud and positive charges rise to the top, you might imagine the cloud as a wrestling ring in which a big, muscular figure with a plus sign on his chest is stepping on a defeated wrestler with a minus sign on his chest. In this way, you can remember that the pluses are above the minuses in the cloud.

If you focus on learning strategies for organizing, you might create a flowchart showing the main steps in lightning formation, such as "cool, moist air moves over warm surface" followed by "air becomes heated and rises" followed by "air forms a cloud," and so on. In this way, you select relevant information and organize it into a structure (i.e., a cause-and-effect chain).

If you focus on learning strategies for integrating, you might ask yourself why questions, such as "Why do negative charges in the cloud move toward the ground?" In trying to answer, you might recall that negatives and positives attract, so the negative charges in the cloud are attracted to the positive charges on the earth's surface. In this way you actively relate the presented material to your existing knowledge.

What does a skilled learner know about how to process passages or lectures that a less-skilled learner does not know? A less-skilled learner might view a passage or lecture as a list of unrelated facts in which the goal is to carefully study every word. A more-skilled learner may view a passage or a lecture as an organized body of knowledge that makes sense. Such a reader knows how to select relevant material, how to organize the material into a coherent structure, and how to integrate the material with existing knowledge. These kinds of cognitive processes are primed by *learning strategies*. Learning strategies may be crucial for a student's success in school. Although some students acquire these skills without explicit training, other students do not master even the most basic learning

FIGURE 11–1

A passage about lightning

Lightning can be defined as the discharge of electricity resulting from the difference in electrical charges between the cloud and the ground.

When the surface of the earth is warm, moist air near the earth's surface becomes heated and rises rapidly, producing an updraft. As the air in these updrafts cools, water vapor condenses into water droplets and forms a cloud. The cloud's top extends above the freezing level. At this altitude, the air temperature is well below freezing, so the upper portion of the cloud is composed of tiny ice crystals.

Eventually, the water droplets and ice crystals in the cloud become too large to be suspended by updrafts. As raindrops and ice crystals fall through the cloud, they drag some of the air from in the cloud downward, producing downdrafts. The rising and falling air currents within the cloud may cause hailstones to form. When downdrafts strike the ground, they spread out in all directions, producing gusts of cool wind people feel just before the start of the rain.

Within the cloud, the moving air causes electrical charges to build, although scientists do not fully understand how it occurs. Most believe that the charge results from the collision of the cloud's light, rising water droplets and tiny pieces of ice against hail and other heavier, falling particles. The negatively charged particles fall to the bottom of the cloud, and most of the positively charged particles rise to the top.

The first stroke of a cloud-to-ground lightning flash is started by a stepped leader. Many scientists believe that it is triggered by a spark between the areas of positive and negative charges within the cloud. A stepped leader moves downward in a series of steps, each of which is about 50 yards long, and lasts for about 1 millionth of a second. It pauses between steps for about 50 millionths of a second. As the stepped leader nears the ground, positively charged upward-moving leaders travel up from such objects as trees and buildings, to meet the negative charges. Usually, the upward moving leader from the tallest object is the first to meet the stepped leader and complete a path between the cloud and earth. The two leaders meet generally about 165 feet above the ground. Negatively charged particles then rush from the cloud to the ground along the path created by the leaders. It is not very bright and usually has many branches.

As the stepped leader nears the ground, it induces an opposite charge, so positively charged particles from the ground rush upward along the same path. This upward motion of the current is the return stroke and it reaches the cloud in about 70 microseconds. The return stroke produces the bright light that people notice in a flash of lightning, but the current moves so quickly that its upward motion cannot be perceived. The lightning flash usually consists of an electrical potential of hundreds of millions of volts. The air along the lightning channel is heated briefly to a very high temperature. Such intense heating causes the air to expand explosively, producing a sound wave we call thunder.

strategies. In spite of this problem, until quite recently, not much emphasis was placed on teaching students how to learn. This chapter deals with the teaching of learning strategies.

A growing number of psychologists and educators argue for the importance of teaching students how to learn (i.e., of including learning strategies as part of the curriculum). For example, Norman (1980) observed:

> It is strange that we expect students to learn yet seldom teach them anything about learning . . . We sometimes require students to remember a considerable body of material, yet seldom teach them the art of memory. It is time that we make up for this lack, time that we developed the applied disciplines of learning . . . and memory. We need to develop the general principles of how to learn, how to remember . . . and then develop applied courses, and then establish the place of these methods in an academic curriculum. (p. 97)

Norman referred to an emerging discipline of cognitive engineering—the development of ways to control our own cognitive processes.

Can students be taught to be more efficient processors of information? Are there learning strategies that can be taught to students that will improve their understanding of material such as in Figure 11–1? If you had investigated these questions a few decades ago, you would have found that teachers rarely taught learning skills in elementary classrooms (Durkin, 1979). Today, however, "we now have a large number of studies that demonstrate that cognitive strategies can successfully improve instruction in a number of domains as reflected by improved student scores" (Pressley & Woloshyn, 1995, p. iv). In short, the teaching of cognitive strategies represents "the most important instructional advance of the past 15 years" (p. iii).

The issue of learning strategies is explored in this chapter. In particular, this chapter investigates three techniques for improving verbal learning: (1) mnemonic strategies for increasing memory of relevant material, (2) structure strategies for organizing material, and (3) generative strategies for integrating new material with existing knowledge.

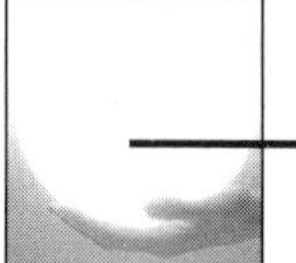

MNEMONIC STRATEGIES

WHAT ARE MNEMONIC STRATEGIES?

To learn the lightning explanation in Figure 11–1, you need to remember certain basic facts about key terms, such as "*stepped leader* is the negative charge that moves from the cloud to the ground" and "*freezing level* is the level that the top of the cloud is above." Part of school learning involves memorizing facts. Facts are simple verbal propositions that link one element with another. For example, students may be asked to memorize the states and their capitals, such as "the capital of California is Sacramento," or mathematical definitions, such as "a square is a polygon that has four equal sides and four equal angles." Some facts can be viewed as paired associates in which the first element in a pair (such as "the capital of California") is associated with the second element in a pair (i.e., "Sacramento").

Mnemonic strategies are techniques that help students memorize material such as facts. Memorization means that you are able to remember and use the material without conscious mental effort. For example, when I ask, "What is the capital of California," you can say,

"Sacramento" without effort. How do mnemonic strategies promote transfer? On the surface, it might seem contradictory to say that memorization is a good way to promote transfer. However, mnemonic strategies promote transfer in two ways. First, when you have memorized basic facts, it takes minimal mental effort to use them in higher-order thinking. For example, if you already know the definitions of many words, it is easier to comprehend the theme of a passage than if you have to try to make sense of each new word. Second, when the to-be-learned material seems senseless, mnemonic strategies offer a means of creating some degree of meaningfulness, usually by embedding the material in a more concrete context.

THEORY: HOW DO MNEMONIC STRATEGIES WORK?

Mnemonic strategies involve time-tested activities that help the learner to remember material. In a historical review of mnemonics, Yates (1966) noted that Simonides developed an imagery-based mnemonic system 2,500 years ago. Since that time, most practitioners of mnemonics have attempted to develop useful techniques rather than to provide a theory of human memory. In contrast, Paivio (1971) argued that mnemonic strategies may work for a number of reasons:

Dual coding. Many memory strategies involve using imagery as well as verbal representations. This approach provides two distinct codings of the same material; hence, there are more ways to find the information in memory.

Organization. Many memory strategies provide a coherent context or organization into which new information can be fit. The organization serves to hold the information together rather than as many separate bits.

Association. Many memory strategies involve forming strong associations between elements. Stronger associations allow for superior remembering.

As you can see, mnemonic methods prompt the learner to become more cognitively active by forming images or making mental connections, although a precise theory is still forthcoming. Thus, the present section presents a typical mnemonic strategy—the keyword method—aimed at getting facts firmly into memory.

RESEARCH: DO MNEMONIC STRATEGIES WORK?

KEYWORD METHOD The modern impetus for educational applications of mnemonic techniques comes from research on the keyword method for teaching foreign language vocabulary by Atkinson and Raugh (Atkinson, 1975; Atkinson & Raugh, 1975; Raugh & Atkinson, 1975). For example, in memorizing Spanish-to-English vocabulary such as "carta" means (postal) "letter," the keyword method involves two stages:

1. *Acoustic link.* You change the foreign language word into an easily pronounced English keyword that sounds like part of the foreign word. For example, you could convert "carta" into "cart."
2. *Imagery link.* You form an interacting image to combine the keyword and the corresponding English word. For example, you could imagine a large postal letter in a shopping cart, such as shown in Figure 11–2. It is not necessary that the image be unusual or bizarre.

FIGURE 11–2 An image that links the keyword "cart" with "letter"

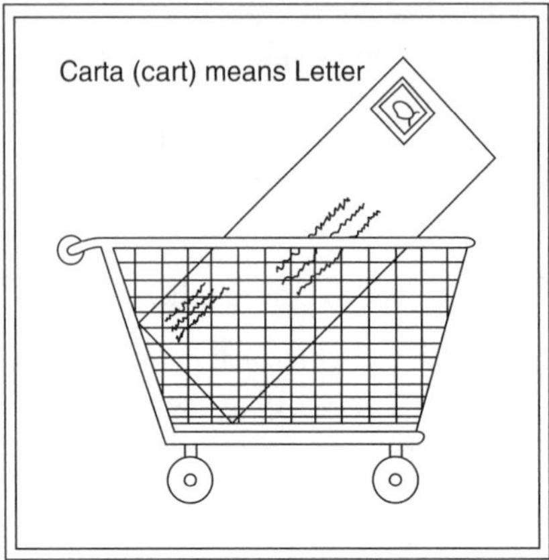

From Pressley and Levin (1978)

In a typical experiment, Raugh and Atkinson (1975) asked college students to learn 60 Spanish-to-English vocabulary pairs in 15 minutes. Examples (with keywords in parentheses) include charco (charcoal)/puddle, gusano (goose)/worm, nabo (knob)/turnip, and trigo (tree)/wheat. Experimental students were given pretraining in use of the keyword method. During learning, the keywords were provided but the subjects had to generate their own images. Control students were given the same 60 vocabulary pairs, including keywords, for the same amount of time as the experimental group. These students were instructed to rehearse the pairs so they could perform well on the test. On a subsequent test, the experimenter read the Spanish words and asked the students to write the corresponding English word. The experimental group scored 88% correct on this test, compared to 28% for the control group. In another study involving Russian vocabulary, students who used the keyword method recalled 72%, compared to 46% for the control group (Atkinson & Raugh, 1975).

Based on these results, it appears that the keyword method is far more effective than other methods, such as rehearsal and recitation. In teaching college students, Raugh and Atkinson (1975) suggested that the keyword method works best when the instructor provides the keyword (i.e., a short English word that sounds like part of the foreign language word) and when the learner is allowed to form his/her own image. However, Pressley and his colleagues (Pressley, 1977; Pressley & Dennis-Rounds, 1980; Pressley & Levin, 1978) found that younger children experience difficulty in spontaneously generating useful images even when they are trained to do so. Pressley and Dennis-Rounds found evidence that children as old as 12 do not spontaneously use the keyword method even after they received training in how to use it. Thus, Levin (1981) and Pressley (1977) suggest that when the students are children, the keyword method should be adapted to provide both keywords and pictures.

As an example, consider how the keyword method could be adapted to help elementary school children learn English vocabulary. In a typical study (Levin, McCormick, Miller,

Berry, & Pressley, 1982), fourth graders learned the definitions of 12 verbs, such as *celebrate, gesture, glisten, harvest, hesitate, intend, introduce, object, orbit, persuade, relate,* and *resolve.* Students in the experimental group learned a keyword for each vocabulary word; the keyword was a familiar word that sounded like a salient part of the vocabulary word, such as the keyword "purse" for the vocabulary word *persuade.* Then the experimental students were given pictures that showed the keyword interacting with the definition of the vocabulary word, such as a woman being persuaded to buy a purse; at the bottom of the picture was the vocabulary word's formal definition. The top panel of Figure 11–3 provides an example picture. The control students were given training in recognizing the words and were given sentences such as, "The woman's friend was trying to persuade her to buy a pocketbook." They also were given the formal definition for each word in the same words as in the experimental group. Control students were given the same amount of time to learn the definitions and were told to use their own best method. On a subsequent test, the keyword students recalled 83% of the definitions, compared to 55% for the control students.

These results suggest that recall is aided by giving children explicit pictures that connect the keyword and its definition. However, Levin et al. (1982) also found that pictures that do not explicitly connect the vocabulary word to the keyword, such as in the bottom panel of Figure 11–3, do not improve learning. Similarly, in another study (Levin et al., 1982), subjects who learned vocabulary with pictures that gave both the keyword and the vocabulary word (e.g., top panel of Figure 11–4) recalled almost twice as many definitions as subjects who learned with pictures that failed to give the keyword (e.g., bottom panel of Figure 11–4). These results suggest that pictures or keywords alone are not enough to enhance memory in elementary school children; successful keyword techniques in children seem to require pictures showing both the keyword and the vocabulary word.

In another series of experiments, Pressley, Levin, and McCormick (1980) used a modified version of the keyword method to teach Spanish-to-English vocabulary to second- and fifth-graders. All subjects learned the keyword for each Spanish word, but unlike previous studies, no pictures were used for the experimental group. Instead, the experimental group was instructed as follows: "The Spanish word ______ sounds like ______ (keyword) and means ______. Make up a sentence in your head about a ______ (keyword) and a ______ (translation) doing something together in order to remember the meaning of ______ (Spanish word).“ The control group was told, ”The Spanish word ______ means ______. Try hard to remember that the Spanish word ______ means ______." Although all subjects learned the same keyword and spent the same time learning, the experimental group remembered more than twice as many Spanish-to-English vocabulary items as the control group—72% correct versus 27% correct, respectively.

Does using the keyword method to memorize vocabulary words affect higher-level learning as well? To examine this question, Jones, Levin, Levin, and Beitzel (2000) taught some elementary school students how to apply the keyword method to learning the definitions of 16 unfamiliar words that were subsequently used in a story. For example, for the definition "carlin—old woman," students might recode "carlin" as "car" and generate an imageful sentence such as "The old woman was driving a car." Other students were instructed to use a more conventional strategy of forming a sentence using the word, such as "The carlin had great difficulty climbing the stairs." As a retention test, students were asked to write the definitions for all of the words they could remember. As a transfer test, students were asked to read a story containing the words and then to answer comprehension questions that did not

FIGURE 11–3 Keyword pictures for learning the definition of persuade

From Levin, McCormick, Miller, Berry, and Pressley (1982)

FIGURE 11–4 Keyword pictures for learning the definition of surplus

From Levin, McCormick, Miller, Berry, and Pressley (1982)

directly involve any of the vocabulary words. Consistent with previous research (Levin, Levin, Glasman, & Norwall, 1992), students who received instruction in how to use the keyword method correctly remembered 91% of the word definitions, compared to 51% for students who were taught to use the conventional strategy. Importantly, students who were taught how to use the keyword method generated correct answers on 68% of the comprehension items that were unrelated to the vocabulary words, compared to 51% for the students who were taught to use the conventional strategy. These results show that memorizing the meaning of vocabulary words helps promote understanding of a passage that uses the words—even those parts of the passage that do not involve the vocabulary words. In short, it appears that students who successfully use the keyword method are also more likely to show evidence of understanding, as measured by transfer tests. In a recent review, Pressley and Woloshyn (1995) concluded, "We are optimistic that the keyword method will prove to be a potent strategy that can be taught quickly and efficiently" (p. 67).

The keyword method is just one example of a successful mnemonic strategy for memorizing facts. There are many other mnemonic strategies that have educational potential for helping students learn facts or lists (Paivio, 1971; Pressley & Woloshyn, 1995).

IMPLICATIONS OF MNEMONIC STRATEGIES

Suppose that students are required to learn foreign language vocabulary or definitions of English words as part of the regular instructional program. Some students will have no difficulty with this task and do not need special training in mnemonic strategies. However, some students will have great difficulty, and for them, training in mnemonics holds some promise. For example, this section showed that learning of paired associates can be improved through explicit instruction in the keyword method. Mnemonic strategies may positively affect transfer because they allow the learner speedy access to relevant knowledge that is needed on transfer tests.

The work of Pressley and Levin showed that mnemonic strategies need to be adapted to the needs of the student. For example, in learning the keyword method, some students may not be able to form their own images and may need teacher-provided images. These students can benefit from practice in using teacher-imposed images to remember paired associates. Others may be able to form images on their own but may need to be told to do so by the teacher. These students can benefit from practice in forming useful images for paired associates. Finally, for students who are proficient at using the keyword method but unsure about when to use it, practice is needed in recognizing appropriate learning tasks.

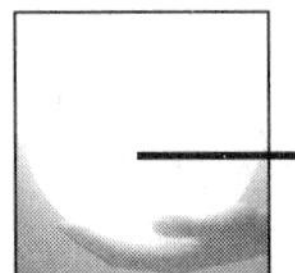

STRUCTURE STRATEGIES

WHAT ARE STRUCTURE STRATEGIES?

Let's return to the lightning passage in Figure 11–1. Suppose we want to help the reader to mentally organize this information. We might ask the reader to create an outline or a flowchart showing the steps in the cause-and-effect chain. Structure strategies such as writing an outline or drawing a graphic enable the learner to impose organization on the material. This section explores the idea that students can learn strategies for how to organize verbal material. In particular, it focuses on mapping and outlining methods.

THEORY: HOW DO STRUCTURE STRATEGIES WORK?

Structure strategies prompt active learning by encouraging learners to mentally select relevant pieces of information and relate them to one another within a structure. In a previous chapter, we referred to this process as building internal connections. However, students may need training in how to identify key ideas and connect them into a coherent organization.

Graesser (1981) distinguished between narrative prose, such as stories, and expository prose, such as explanations of events or objects. This distinction is important because ample evidence indicates that students are better able to organize and remember narrative passages than expository passages that are equally complex (Graesser, Hauft-Smith, Cohen, & Pyles, 1980). Apparently, people have had a great deal of experience with stories and therefore have developed expectations about how events and states in stories can be organized.

In contrast, most people lack extensive experience in reading expository prose and therefore are less likely to possess strategies for organizing it. Meyer, Brandt, and Bluth (1980) argued that readers may use a default strategy of organizing expository prose as a list of facts. One implication of this lack of experience is that students could profit from explicit training concerning expository prose structures. Successful training would help students to build internal connections among the central ideas in a passage. The outcome of such learning would be manifested in increased memory for the central ideas in a passage (rather than details) and in superior performance of problem-solving tests involving inference.

RESEARCH: DO STRUCTURE STRATEGIES WORK?

Learning to outline textbook material or lecture material is widely recognized in the folk wisdom of our culture as an important study skill. What evidence exists that structure strategies such as outlining techniques improve learning? This section explores two effective techniques for teaching students how to structure text material: mapping (in which students create graphic outlines) and outlining (in which students create written outlines).

MAPPING METHODS Suppose that you were asked to read a passage about wounds from a nursing textbook. To help you organize the material you could try to construct an outline. To do this, you must first identify and summarize each of the ideas in the text (i.e., what you will write on each line of the outline) and then you must determine how they are related to one another (i.e., which ideas are subordinate to which other ideas).

Dansereau and his colleagues (Chmielewski & Dansereau, 1998; Dansereau, 1978; Dansereau et al., 1979; Dansereau & Newbern, 1997; Holley, Dansereau, McDonald, Garland, & Collins, 1979) have developed a technique called *knowledge mapping* in which the student identifies ideas and relations among them. In a typical outline, the only kind of relation is subordination (i.e., one idea is subordinate to another). To help the student

FIGURE 11–5

Six types of links for expository prose

Hierarchy Structures

Part (of) Link hand ↑ p ↓ finger	The content in a lower node is part of the object, process, idea, or concept contained in a higher node.	*Keywords* is part of is a segment of is a portion of
Type (of)/Example (of) Link school ↑ t ↓ private	The content in a lower node is a member or example of the class or category of processes, ideas, concepts, or objects contained in a higher node.	*Keywords* is a type of is in the category is an example of is a kind of

Chain Structures

Leads to Link practice ↑ l ↓ perfection	The object, process, idea, or concept in one node leads to or results in the object, process, idea, or concept in another node.	*Keywords* leads to results in causes is a tool of produces

Cluster Structures

Analogy Link College ↓ a ↓ factory	The object, idea, process, or concept in one node is analogous to, similar to, corresponds to, or is like the object, idea, process, or concept in another node.	*Keywords* is similar to is analogous to is like corresponds to
Characteristic Link sky ↓ c ↓ blue	The object, idea, process, or concept in one node is a trait, aspect, quality, feature, attribute, detail, or characteristic of the object, idea, process, or concept in another node.	*Keywords* has is characterized by feature is property is trait is aspect is attribute is
Evidence Link broken arm ↓ e ↓ X-ray	The object, idea, process, or concept in one node provides evidence, facts, data, support, proof, documentation, confirmation for the object, idea, process, or concept in another node.	*Keywords* indicates illustrated by demonstrated by supports documents is proof of confirms

From Holley et al. (1979)

better understand the relationships among ideas in a passage, Dansereau and his colleagues identified several kinds of links. As summarized in Figure 11–5, the relation between one idea and another can be any of the following: part of, type of, leads to, analogous to, characteristic of, or evidence for.

Figure 11–6 shows how the linking analysis can be used to build a knowledge map for a passage on wounds from a nursing textbook. As you can see, the discussion of wounds can be broken into two major parts: "types of wounds" and "process of wound healing." The types of wounds include "open," "closed," "accidental," and "intentional"; types of "open

FIGURE 11–6 A network of a chapter from a nursing textbook

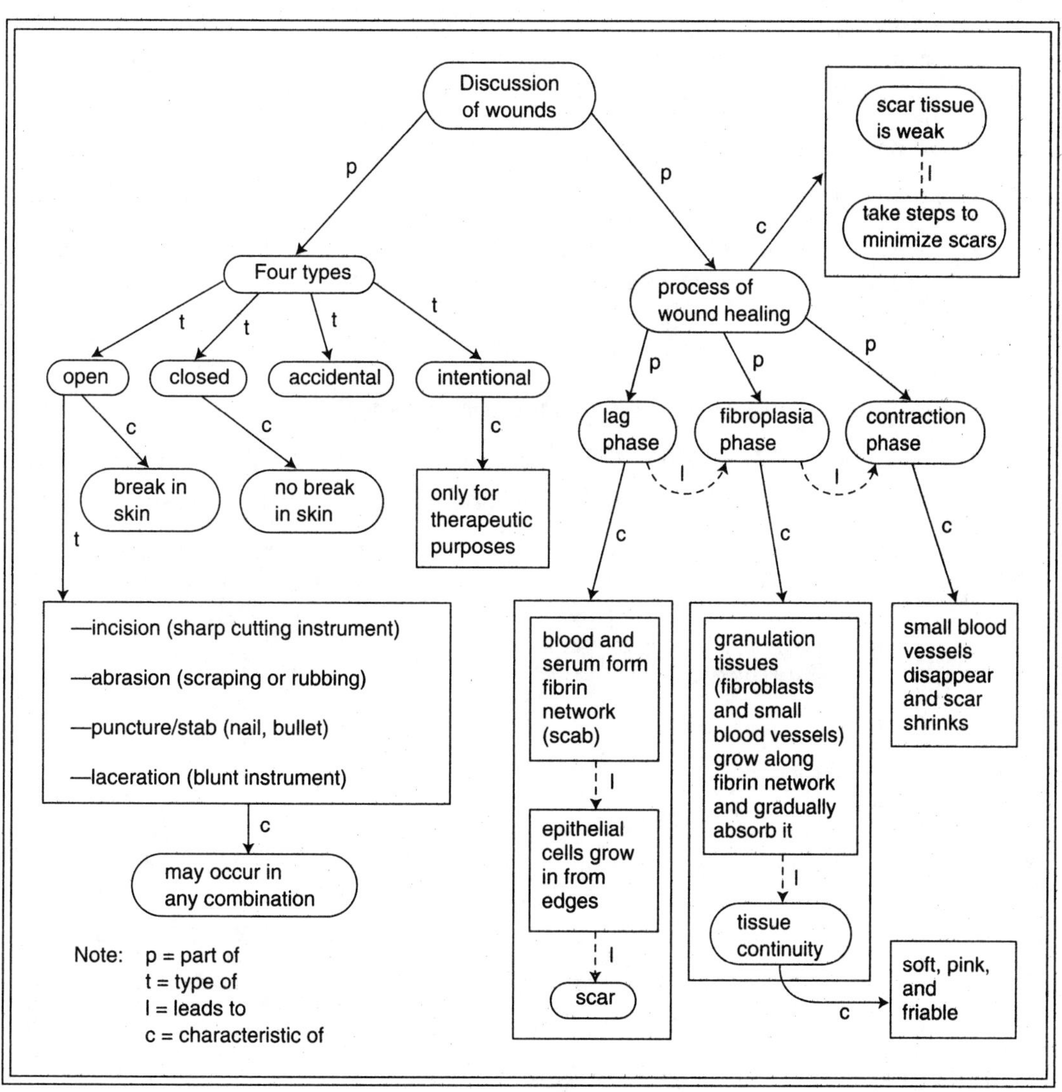

From Holley et al. (1979)

wounds" include "incision," "abrasion," "puncture," "laceration"; a characteristic of "open wounds" is that there is a "break in the skin"; and so on. Knowledge mapping involves breaking a passage into parts (i.e., ideas) and then identifying the linking relations among the parts. The result is a graphic representation of the passage, that is, a knowledge map.

Does mapping training affect student learning? To test the effectiveness of mapping training, Dansereau and his colleagues (Holley, Dansereau, et al., (1979) trained college students to recognize types of links (such as in Figure 11–5), to apply the knowledge mapping procedure to sentences, to apply the mapping procedure to passages, and, finally, to apply the mapping procedure to their own textbooks. Training required approximately five and one-half hours spread over four sessions. Mapping-trained students and control students who received no training were then asked to study a 3,000-word passage from a geology textbook. On subsequent tests, including multiple-choice, fill-in, short-answer, and essay, the mapping-trained subjects performed much better than the control subjects in remembering the main ideas but not in remembering the details. In addition, the positive effects of mapping training seemed to be particularly strong for students with low grade point averages but not for students with high grade point averages. Apparently, high-GPA students have already developed their own techniques for organizing prose material. These results are summarized in Figure 11–7.

In another study (Dansereau et al., 1979), students who took a learning strategy class that met for 12 two-hour sessions were compared to a control group. All students were

FIGURE 11–7 Proportion correct on posttests for networking and control groups

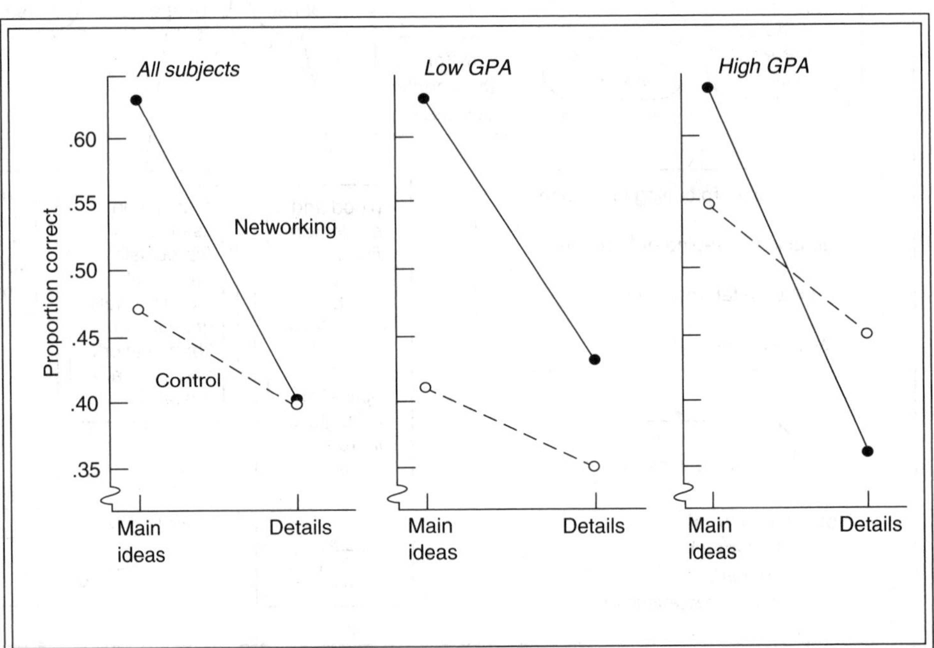

Adapted from Holley et al. (1979)

given a pretest and posttest in which they read a 3,000-word textbook passage and answered multiple-choice and short-essay questions. Students who had received training in knowledge mapping showed an improvement from a score of 47 on the pretest to a score of 57 on the posttest, whereas the control subjects averaged a score of 47 on both the pretest and the posttest. Other types of strategy training, such as paraphrasing and forming mental images, were not as successful as training in knowledge mapping. Apparently, students can be trained to organize information as they study, and this training is useful for long textbook passages.

More recently, Chmielewski and Dansereau (1998) asked students to study a passage about cocaine for 6 minutes and a passage about the nervous system for 6 minutes. For both passages, the students were not allowed to write any notes, and five days later, the students were asked to write down all they could recall from the two passages. In previous sessions, some students had received 3 hours of knowledge mapping training (mapping group), whereas other students (control group) had not. Figure 11–8 shows the amount

FIGURE 11–8 Mapping-trained students recall more from text than control students

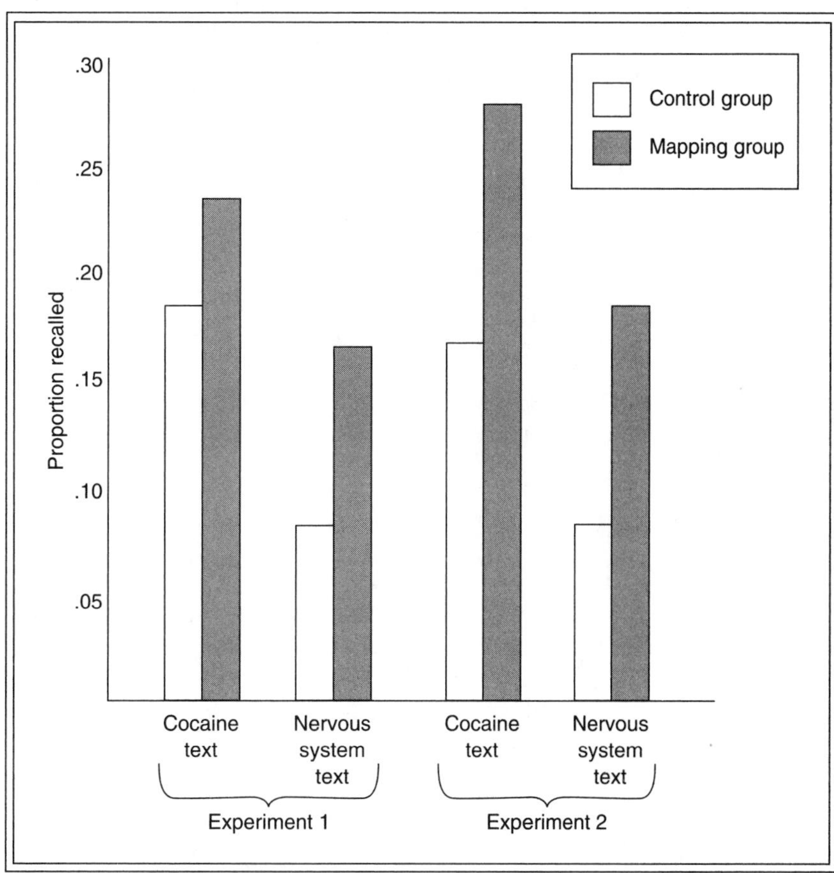

Adapted from Chmielewski and Dansereau (1998)

recalled for each passage across two different experiments. On the recall tests, students in the mapping group recalled an average of 60% more of the important ideas than did students in the control group. The results represent an important form of transfer, because students in the mapping group were not actually allowed to draw any knowledge maps for the two passages they studied. Chmielewski and Dansereau conclude that "training participants on the construction and use of knowledge maps positively transfers to text processing when a mapping strategy is not explicitly used" (p. 412).

As you can see, knowledge mapping involves using what Holley and Dansereau (1984) call a *spatial learning strategy.* Another popular spatial learning strategy is *concept mapping* (Novak, 1998) in which students produce maps consisting of nodes (i.e., concepts) and links (i.e., labeled lines between nodes). Unlike in knowledge mapping, the links in concept mapping do not necessarily have to correspond to preestablished types. For example, Figure 11–9 shows a concept map produced by a six-year-old student after about 30 minutes of instruction on concept mapping (Novak & Gowin, 1984). In reviewing several decades of research on concept mapping, Novak (1998) noted that "learners needed to construct their own maps and learn this method of organizing their own knowledge" (p. 31). Concept mapping training has not been subjected to the same level of rigorous empirical study as knowledge mapping training, and therefore some additional research is warranted to pinpoint its place in classrooms.

OUTLINING METHODS Consider the supertanker passage in Figure 11–10. If you were supposed to read this passage as part of a course assignment, you might try to outline it. However, Meyer and her colleagues (Meyer, 1975, 1981; Meyer, Brandt, & Bluth, 1980) found that certain basic outline forms, called *top-level structures,* correspond to most expos-

FIGURE 11–9 A concept map

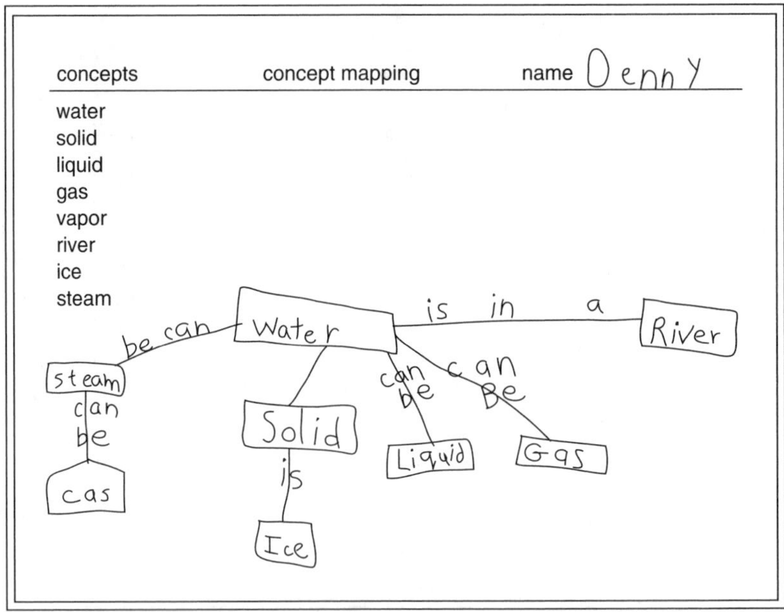

From Novak and Gowin (1984), p. 177

FIGURE 11–10

The supertanker passage

A PROBLEM OF VITAL CONCERN IS THE PREVENTION OF OIL SPILLS FROM SUPERTANKERS. A typical supertanker carries a half-million tons of oil and is the size of five football fields. A wrecked supertanker spills oil in the ocean; this oil kills animals, birds, and microscopic plant life. *For example, when a tanker* crashed *off the coast of England, more than 200,000 dead seabirds* washed *ashore.* Oil spills also kill microscopic plant life *which provide food for sea life and produce 70 percent of the world's oxygen supply.* Most wrecks RESULT FROM THE LACK of power and steering equipment to handle [emergencies] . . ., *such as storms. Supertankers have only one boiler to provide power and one propeller to drive the ship.*

THE SOLUTION TO THE PROBLEM IS NOT TO IMMEDIATELY HALT THE USE OF TANKERS ON THE OCEAN since about 80 percent of the world's oil supply is carried by supertankers. INSTEAD, THE SOLUTION LIES IN THE TRAINING OF OFFICERS OF SUPERTANKERS, BETTER BUILDING OF TANKERS, AND INSTALLING GROUND CONTROL STATIONS TO GUIDE TANKERS NEAR SHORE. First, OFFICERS OF SUPERTANKERS MUST GET top TRAINING in how to run and maneuver their ships. Second, tankers should be BUILT with several propellers *for extra control* and backup boilers *for emergency power.* Third, GROUND CONTROL STATIONS SHOULD BE INSTALLED at places where supertankers come close to shore. These stations would act like airplane control towers, guiding *tankers along busy shipping lanes and through dangerous channels.*

Note: Capitalized = message; lowercase = major details; italics = minor details; underlined = signaling. Regular font was used in actual passage.

From Meyer, Brandt, and Bluth (1980)

itory passages such as the supertanker passage. Five top-level structures are summarized in Figure 11–11: covariance, comparison, collection, description, and response.

An important educational hypothesis is that if a student knows about these kinds of structures, the student will have an easier time outlining the passage. Which structure corresponds to the supertanker passage? According to Meyer, the supertanker passage is based on a response structure because it states a problem and a solution. Figure 11–12 shows how the supertanker passage can be broken down with response as its top-level structure as well as other structures in the lower parts of the passage.

Skill at identifying the top-level structure of a passage is a characteristic of good readers. In a classic study, Meyer et al. (1980) asked ninth-graders to read several passages, including the supertanker passage, and then take immediate and delayed recall tests. Figure 11–13 shows that most good readers (as measured by a standard reading achievement test) recalled the top-level structure of the passage while most poor readers did not. In other words, good readers were likely to organize their recall protocol for the supertanker passage around the problem/solution format, while most poor readers tended to organize recall as a list of facts. In addition, Figure 11–13 shows that students who used the same top-level structure as the author also tended to recall more information from the passage.

FIGURE 11–11

Five top-level structures

Top-Level Structure	*Definition*	*Example*
Covariance	Causal relationship between antecedent and consequence	"Lack of power and steering in supertankers" leads to "oil spills."
Comparison	Similarities and differences between two or more topics	"Ground control stations for supertankers" are analogous to "control towers for aircraft."
Collection	Several objects or events or ideas belong to the same group or can be sequenced in time or space	"Three ways to improve super-tanker safety" are "training officers," "building safer ships," and "installing group control systems."
Description	General statement along with supporting detail, attribute, explanation, or setting	"Oil spills kill wildlife" is exem-plified by "200,000 seabirds died."
Response	Question and answer, problem and solution, or remark and reply	"A problem is that supertankers spill oil" and "a solution is to improve their safety."

Adapted From Meyer (1975, 1981)

Cook and Mayer (1988) trained students to identify five prose structures that are found in science textbooks: generalization, enumeration, sequence, classification, and compare/contrast. Examples and definitions are given in Figure 11–14. As you can see, Cook and Mayer's prose structures are somewhat different from those suggested by Meyer, although some structures are quite similar. One reason for the differences may be that Meyer's structures are based on general expository prose while Cook and Mayer's structures are based on passages found in chemistry, biology, and physics textbooks.

As a first step, Cook and Mayer (1988) conducted a study to determine whether students could be taught to recognize the five structures summarized in Figure 11–14. Some college students (structure training group) were given a booklet that described and exemplified the five structures, while other subjects (control group) received no training. Then all subjects were given worksheets containing 20 science passages (i.e., four passages for each of the five structure types); subjects were asked to sort the passages into five groups based on the structure of the material (rather than content). Results indicated that the structure training group correctly sorted 79% of the passages, compared to 61% correctly sorted passages for the control group. The next step in Cook and Mayer's project was to provide an extensive training program to junior college students who were taking a chemistry course. The training involved an initial session in which students learned to recognize three types of prose structures—generalization, enumeration, and sequence. Subsequent

FIGURE 11–12 A structural analysis of the supertanker passage

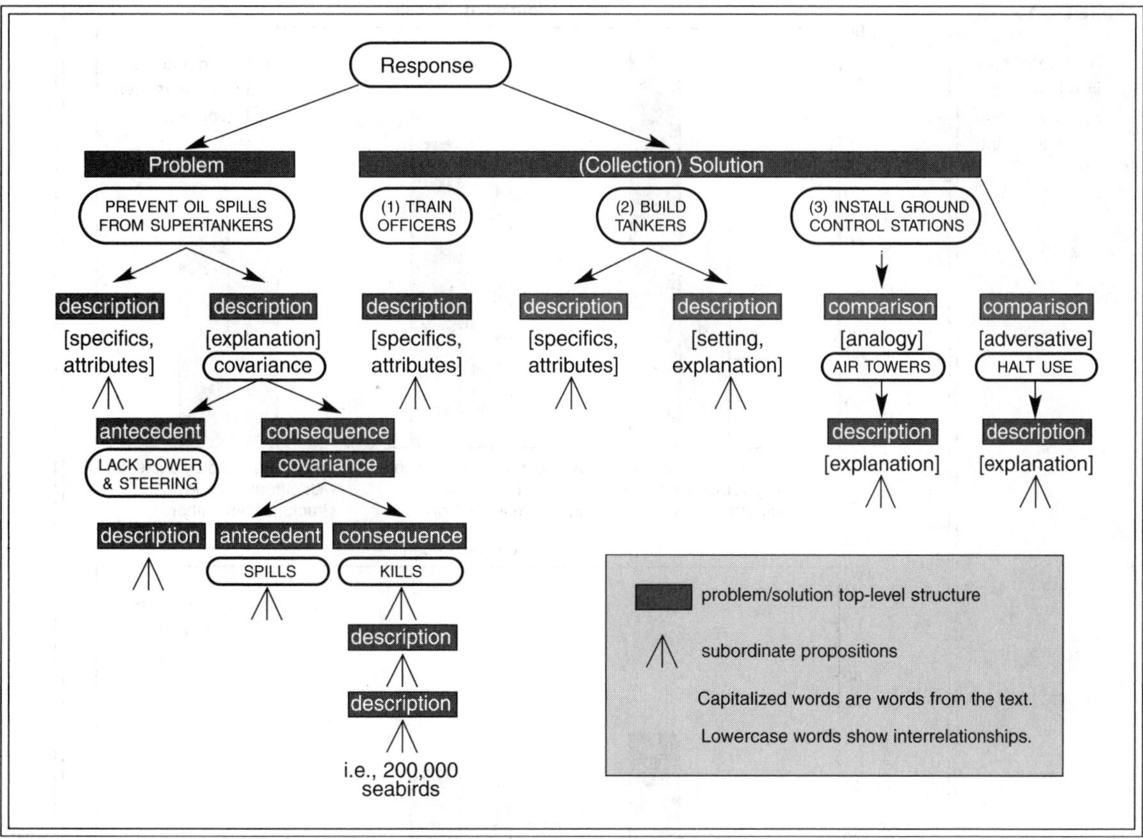

From Meyer, Brandt, and Bluth (1980)

training involved asking the student to fill out worksheets such as shown in Figure 11–15; the student filled out three worksheets for each of the three structures based on nine sections from the students' chemistry textbook. The instructor provided feedback after each worksheet. In contrast, students from another section of the course received no training and served as a control group.

To assess the effectiveness of the training, Cook and Mayer gave a pretest and posttest to all students. Each test consisted of reading three passages (i.e., generalization, enumeration, and sequence passages on science material other than chemistry). After reading, students were asked to recall each passage and to answer questions about verbatim details (retention questions) and about applying the information to solve a problem (problem-solving questions). Figure 11–16 summarizes the results. As you can see, the structure trained group showed an increase in recall of high-level information but not low-level information, as compared to the control group. Similarly, the structure trained group showed an increase in problem-solving transfer but not in retention of facts, as compared to the control group.

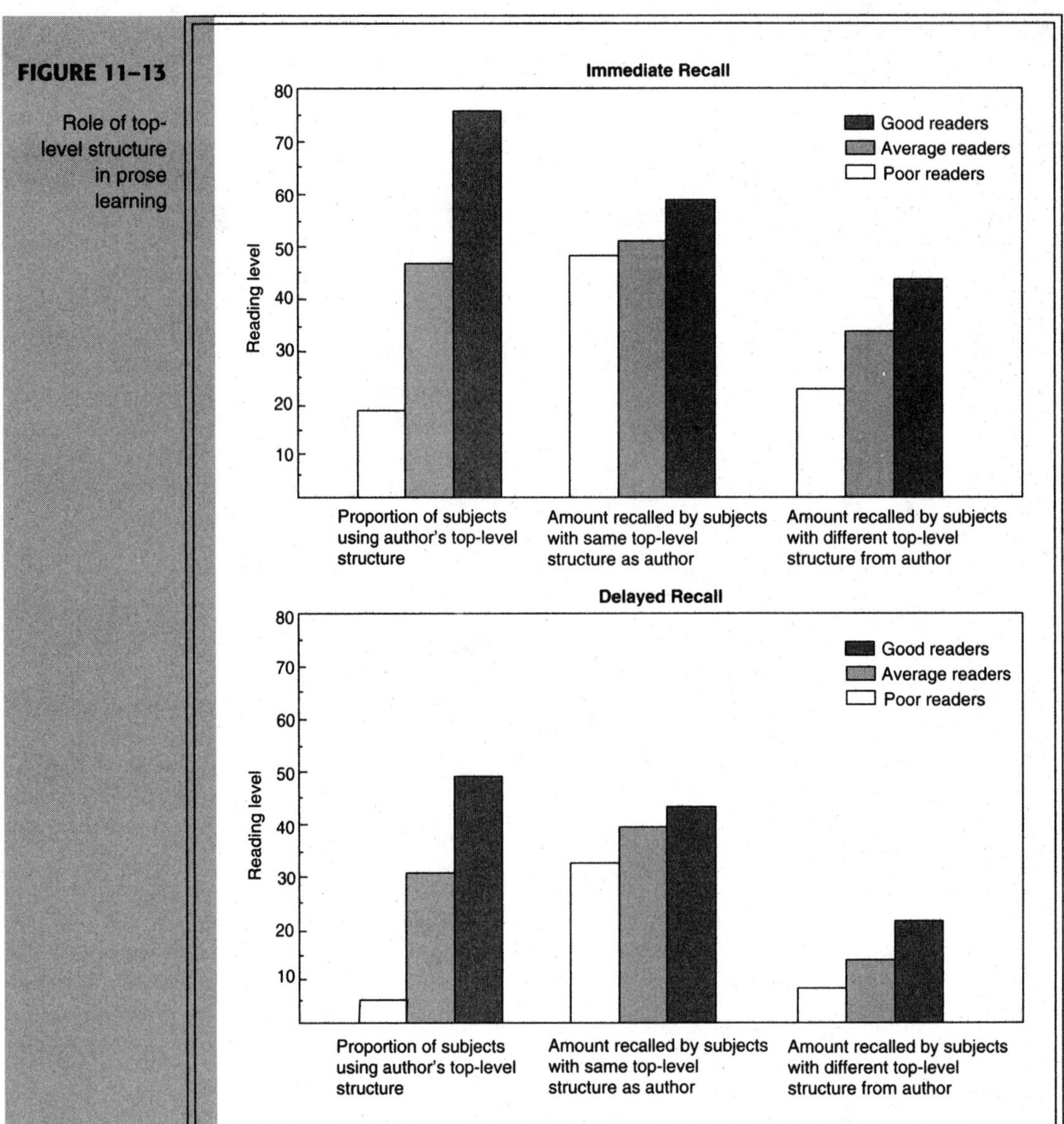

FIGURE 11–13

Role of top-level structure in prose learning

Apparently, students can transfer their training in general prose structures to the outlining of new passages, resulting in a more coherent mental organization of the material.

Another way to encourage learners to organize material is to provide a structure for them to use during learning. For example, Kiewra et al. (1991) asked students to view a 19-minute videotaped lecture on creativity. Some students were told to take notes by writing on blank sheets of paper (conventional group), and some were told to take notes by filling in cells of a 5 × 9 matrix with the names of five types of creativity printed along the rows and the names of the nine dimensions printed along the columns (matrix group). If the matrix provides cues for how to organize and integrate notes, the matrix group should outperform the conventional group on remembering (retention test) and using the material (transfer test). Figure 11–17 confirms this prediction, with the matrix group remembering 30% more on the retention test and generating 18% more correct answers on the transfer test than the conventional group. These results show that not all notetaking activities are equally productive. When notetaking activity is structured, students appear to learn more deeply.

IMPLICATIONS OF STRUCTURE STRATEGIES

Suppose that students are asked to read a chapter in their science textbook. Some students will read the material and be able to correctly answer questions about the main concepts in the chapter. These students are able to figure out what is important and what is not important. If asked, they would be able to provide an outline of the passage similar to the author's. These students do not need training in structure strategies.

In contrast, other students will read the material, perhaps even carefully read each word, and still not be able to correctly answer questions about the main ideas in the passage. These students are not aware of the way that sections of science books are organized, such as generalization or sequence or classification, and they could not produce a coherent outline of the material. These students seem to be excellent candidates for training in structure strategies.

The research presented in this section shows that students can be taught to use effective strategies for organizing expository material. Two central features of successful training systems are (1) emphasis on specific types of structures commonly found in expository prose, and (2) extensive practice in recognizing and applying these structures when actually reading textbooks.

The initial step in structure training is to give students clear definitions and examples of the major prose structures that they are likely to find in the textbook. This section described two different structure training systems—knowledge mapping and outlining—and both systems began by giving the students clear definitions and examples of a small set of structures. Because different subject matter domains rely on different types of structures (e.g., biology emphasizes classification, while chemistry emphasizes sequence), the teacher may choose a few basic structures that are most commonly used in the class's textbook. Students then need practice in recognizing which paragraphs in the textbook correspond to which structures.

The second major step is to help students outline their textbook based on the underlying prose structure. For example, once a student recognizes that a paragraph is generalization, the student should be able to list the main assertion followed by supporting evidence. Feedback from the teacher (or other models) is useful so that the student can compare his or her outline to the teacher's.

Structure strategies are likely to be most useful for less-skilled readers—since skilled readers presumably possess organizing skills—and for unfamiliar expository material—since students have more experience with the structure of stories.

FIGURE 11–14

Five prose structures for science text

Generalization	*Example*
1. Passage always has a main idea. 2. Most of the other sentences in the passage try to provide evidence for the main idea by either clarifying or extending. a. Explain the main idea by using examples or illustrations. These tend to *clarify* the main idea. b. Explain the main idea in more detail; extend the main idea. 3. Things to look for: definitions, principles, laws. 4. Reading objectives: Understand the main idea; be able to explain it in your own words, using the supporting evidence.	Irritability is defined as an organism's capacity to respond to conditions outside itself. An organism responds to a stimulus from the environment. The stimulus may be light, temperature, water, sound, the presence of a chemical substance, or a threat to life. The organism's response is the way it reacts to a stimulus. For example, a plant may have a growth response. This happens when a root pushes toward water or a stem grows unevenly and bends toward light.
Enumeration	*Example*
1. List facts one after the other. 2. There are two general kinds of enumeration passages: a. Specified—actually lists the facts by numbering them. b. Unspecified—lists facts in paragraph form, with each fact stated in one or more sentences. 3. It is difficult to produce a single statement that summarizes the information accurately. 4. Reading objectives: Note the general topic; more important, though, is the retention of each subtopic or the individual facts.	There are four general properties of solids: 1. Tenacity is a measure of a solid's resistance to being pulled apart. 2. Hardness is a measure of a substance's ability to scratch another substance. 3. Malleability refers to a solid's ability to be hammered or rolled into thin sheets. 4. Ductility is the ability to be drawn out in the form of wires.
Sequence	*Example*
1. Describes a continuous and connected series of events or the steps in a process. 2. Examples of sequences include changes as the result of growth, a biological process, steps in an experiment, or the evolution of some event. 3. Signal words: "The first step in," "stages," "and then." 4. Reading objectives: a. Be able to describe each step in the sequence.	Hearing can be described in five separate stages. First, sound waves are captured by the external portion of the ear. The outer ear's function is to focus or concentrate these sound waves. During the second stage, the sound waves travel down the auditory canal (a tube embedded in the bones of the skull) and strike the tympanic membrane or eardrum. The third stage occurs when the vibrations of the eardrum begin a series of similar vibrations in several

FIGURE 11–14

(cont.)

b. Be able to tell the differences between each stage or step.

small bones. These vibrations are then transmitted to the inner ear (called the cochlea) during the fourth stage. At this point, the vibrations are turned into neural impulses that are sent to the brain. The fifth and final stage of the hearing process represents the brain's interpretation of the sound patterns.

Classification	*Example*
1. Groups or segregates material into classes or categories. 2. Develops a classification system to be used in the future to classify items. 3. Signal words: "can be classified," "are grouped," "there are two types of" 4. Reading objectives: a. Know and be able to list class or grouping factors. b. Understand how the classes differ. c. Be able to classify new information.	Experimental variables can be grouped into one of two categories: either a manipulated variable or a controlled variable. A variable that can be acted on directly is called a manipulated variable. The flow of steam into a room is an example of a manipulated variable, because it can be controlled directly. In contrast, a variable that can't be acted on directly called a controlled variable. The temperature of a room is an example of a controlled variable because it must be achieved through manipulating another variable. In this case, it must be achieved through manipulating the flow of steam.

Compare/Contrast	*Example*
1. Primary objective is to examine the relationship between two or more things. 2. Compare means to analyze both the similarities and differences while contrast focuses only on the differences. 3. Signal words include "in contrast to," "the difference between," etc. 4. Reading objectives: be able to discuss similarities/differences between things.	There are two different hypotheses for the origin of the earth: the nebular hypothesis and the comet-produced hypothesis. The nebular hypothesis maintains that our planet began in an aggregation of interstellar gas and dust. This theory is gaining more and more acceptance. In contrast, the comet-produced hypothesis states that the earth began as a piece of the sun that was ripped out by a comet. The first hypothesis assumes the earth began as small elements that combined into larger ones. The latter hypothesis asserts the earth was essentially already formed when it began taking on its present-day characteristics.

From Cook and Mayer (1988)

FIGURE 11–15

Worksheets for generalization, enumeration, and sequence passages

Generalization

Step 1: Identify the generalization (main idea).

List and define key words in the generalization.

Word Definition

Restate the generalization in your own words.

Step 2: What kind of support is there for the generalization? Does it use examples, illustrations? Does it extend or clarify the generalization?

Supporting Evidence Relation to Generalization

Enumeration

Step 1: What is the general topic?

Step 2: Identify the subtopics.
A.
B.
C.
D.

Step 3: Organize and list the details within each subtopic. (Do one subtopic at a time, use your own words.)
A.
B.
C.
D.

Sequence

Step 1: Identify the topic of the passage.

Step 2: Take each step, name it, and then outline the details within each.
Step 1
Step 2
Step 3
Step 4

Step 3: Discuss (briefly) what is different from one step to the next.
Step 1 to 2
Step 2 to 3
Step 3 to 4

From Cook and Mayer (1988)

FIGURE 11–16 Pretest-to-posttest changes for trained and control groups

Group	Recall: Low Level	Recall: High Level	Retention of Facts	Problem Solving
Trained	−4%	11%	14%	24%
Control	3%	0%	1%	−3%

Adapted from Cook and Mayer (1988)

FIGURE 11–17 Students learn more deeply when they take notes using a matrix

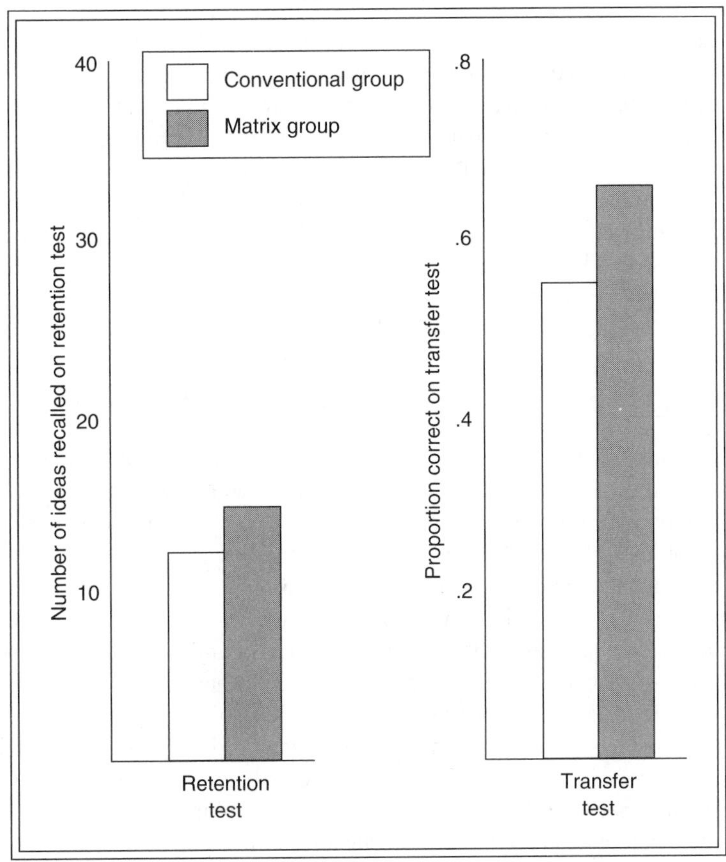

Adapted from Kiewra et al. (1991)

GENERATIVE STRATEGIES

WHAT ARE GENERATIVE STRATEGIES?

The preceding sections explored ways to help the learner to remember specific facts and organize material into a structure. Another aspect of active learning is integrating the material with existing knowledge. Generative strategies are learning strategies aimed at helping the learner to integrate presented information with existing knowledge and experience. For example, in reading the lightning passage (Figure 11–1), we could teach a student to take summary notes or to generate and answer questions.

THEORY: HOW DO GENERATIVE STRATEGIES WORK?

Rothkopf (1970) coined the term *mathemagenic activity* to refer to any activity of the learner that gives birth to knowledge. For example, taking notes, underlining, answering questions, or repeating aloud all are mathemagenic activities. In taking a cognitive perspective, you can ask, "How can such activities promote meaningful learning?" Based on the model of meaningful learning presented in this book, these activities are intended to promote meaningful learning partly because the learner is encouraged to integrate incoming material with existing knowledge. In particular, Wittrock (1974, 1990) argued that learning is a generative process in which the learner must actively generate the relations among ideas—activities that I have called building internal and external connections. Some learning activities such as notetaking may help some students to engage in generative processing.

RESEARCH: DO GENERATIVE STRATEGIES WORK?

Consider the following scenario: You enter a lecture hall where the professor is giving a lecture on the formation of lightning. You sit down and glance at the notes of the student sitting on your right. She has written a series of verbatim phrases from the instructor such as "cool, moist air" on one line, "forms a cloud" on the next line, "reaches freezing level" on the next line, and so on. To her, notetaking seems to involve selecting relevant facts to write down. You look to the student on your left. She has written a sort of outline consisting of five major steps labeled 1 through 5, and under each she has listed some component processes labeled by letters such as a, b, c. To her, notetaking seems to mean organizing relevant facts into a structure. Finally, you look over the shoulder of the student in front of you. She has written a summary in her own words describing how lightning forms, and in the margin she has written some comments based on her own knowledge (such as "positive and negative charges attract"). To her, notetaking seems to mean trying to elaborate on the material and relate it to what she already knows.

This section focuses mainly on aspects of notetaking reflected in the third student—using notetaking as a way to integrate the presented information with past experience. Generative strategies are intended to promote deep understanding by prompting the learner to put the material into his or her own words, distill its main message, and relate it with other knowledge. Two important generative strategies are summarizing and questioning.

SUMMARIZING METHODS Under some conditions, notetaking may help the learner to build external connections (i.e., to relate the information presented to existing knowledge). The learner may be encouraged to explain an idea in his/her own words or to relate information to a familiar concrete model. For example, Mayer (1980) asked college students to read a manual on computer programming with one programming command described on each page. For some students, after each page they were asked to explain the command in their own words and relate it to a concrete familiar situation (elaboration group). Other students read each page without elaborating (non-elaboration group). Students in the elaboration group tended to recall more conceptual information from the booklet and to perform better on problem-solving tests that involved applying commands to new tasks than did the non-elaboration group. However, the non-elaboration group performed just as well as the elaboration group on recall of details from the manual and on solving problems just like those given in the manual. Apparently, elaborative notetaking encouraged readers to relate the presented information to what they already knew, resulting in meaningful learning.

In a similar series of studies, Peper and Mayer (1978) asked college and high school students to view a 15-minute videotaped lecture on computer programming or statistics. Some students were asked to take notes during the lecture, while others were not allowed to take notes. Following the lesson, students were given problem-solving tests that included problems like those given during the lecture (near transfer) and problems that required creative use of the information in new situations (far transfer).

Figure 11–18 shows that for low-ability subjects, the notetaking group excelled on far transfer, whereas the non-notetaking group excelled on near transfer. For high-ability subjects, notetaking increased performance by a modest amount on both types of questions. If notetaking served mainly to focus the learner's attention, we would expect superior performance on problems like those given in the lesson; if notetaking served mainly to elicit integrative processing (i.e., building external connections), we would expect better performance on tests of creative transfer. Thus, the increase in far transfer performance is most consistent with the idea that notetaking in this study resulted in building external connections.

In addition, subsequent recall tests revealed that notetakers excelled mainly on recall of conceptual information but not on recall of specific details and that notetakers produced more "intrusions" about information that was not in the booklet. If notetaking served mainly to focus attention on the main facts in the lesson, we would expect better recall of specific facts. If notetaking helped the learner to construct coherent external connections, we would expect better recall of the basic conceptual principles in the passage. These results are consistent with the idea that when appropriate dependent measures—such as far transfer or recall of concepts—are used, evidence for integrative processing emerges.

It should be pointed out that some more restricted forms of notetaking may not elicit the building of external connections. For example, Mayer and Cook (1981) asked students to listen to a passage about how radar works. Some were asked to repeat each phrase verbatim during pauses in the presentation. Verbatim shadowing of the passage resulted in poorer recall for the conceptual principles and in poorer performance on creative problem solving than in a control group that simply listened to the passage. Thus, verbatim copying seems unlikely to lead to the building of external connections even though the learner is being forced to be behaviorally active.

Other ways of encouraging students to construct external connections (as well as internal connections) in a passage include summary notetaking. In a summary notetaking

FIGURE 11–18 Effects of notetaking on creative problem solving

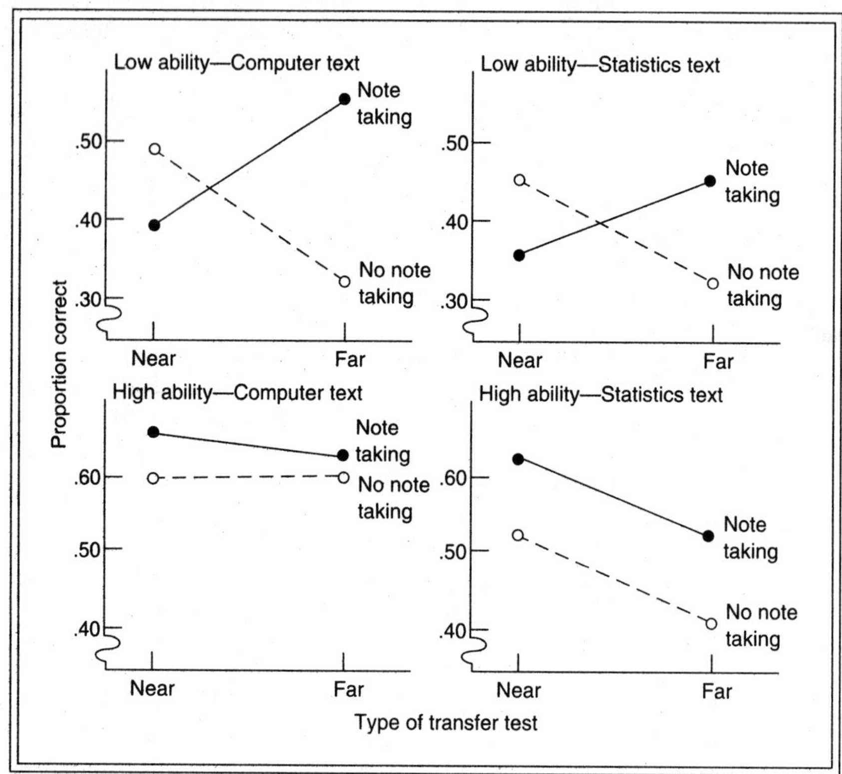

Adapted from Peper and Mayer (1978)

study, Doctorow, Wittrock, and Marks (1978) asked elementary school students to read a passage and then recall the passage. Some students were asked to generate a summary sentence that expressed the main idea for each paragraph (summary group); some students were given a two-word heading for each paragraph that summarized the main idea (heading group); some students received both treatments (summary and heading group); and some subjects read the passage without headings or summary notetaking.

Figure 11–19 summarizes the results on a subsequent retention test for good readers who were given an 1,125-word passage for 20 minutes and for poor readers who were given a 372-word passage for 8 minutes. As the figure shows, for both good and poor readers, the summary group retained more than 50% more information than did the control group, and this advantage was enhanced when headings were provided for each paragraph. Wittrock (1974) argued that subjects who write summaries engage in *generative learning*—generating connections among ideas in the passage rather than memorizing specific words.

Suppose students are asked to take notes in any way that would help them as they read a philosophy text. As a result, some students write verbatim words and phrases (verbatim notes group), whereas other students summarize the main ideas in their own words (summary notes group). Which form of notetaking is more effective? If summary notes require

FIGURE 11–19 Effects of summary notetaking and headings on prose comprehension

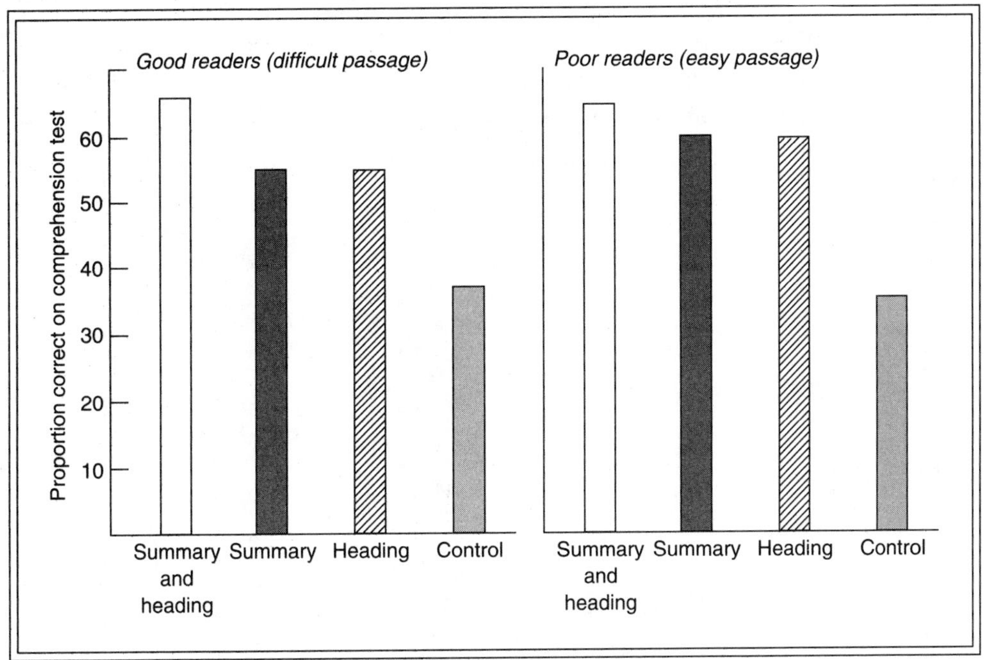

Adapted from Doctorow, Wittrock, and Marks (1978)

deeper processing by the learner (including organizing and integrating the material), you would expect the summary notes group to outperform the verbatim notes group on being able to use the presented information to answer essay questions. This is exactly what happened in a recent study by Slotte and Lonka (1999). For example, Figure 11–20 shows the essay test scores on defining key concepts, comparing and contrasting several different ideas, and evaluating the author's views on a given topic. As you can see, for each type of essay question, students who opted to take summary notes outperformed students who opted to take verbatim notes. These results are consistent with the observation that notetaking activities are not all equally useful ways to promote transfer. It appears that notetaking is more likely to promote transfer when learners generate summaries in their own words rather than copy verbatim words and phrases.

What can be done to help students reflect on their notes and organize them into coherent summaries? To study this issue, King (1992) presented students with a 20- to 30-minute social science lecture on a topic such as "civil liberties" and asked them to take notes. The students were involved in a remedial study skills course and had been selected because of their relatively low verbal ability scores. During a subsequent study period, some students (notetaking-with-review) were told to prepare for a test by reviewing their notes, whereas other students (notetaking-with-summarizing) were told to prepare for a test by using their notes and recollections to write a summary of the main points from the lecture. Students in the notetaking-with-summarizing group were taught how to write a summary by writing a sentence stating the main point and then writing sentences linking the main point of each subtopic back with

FIGURE 11–20 Students who take summary notes produce better answers to transfer questions than students who take verbatim notes

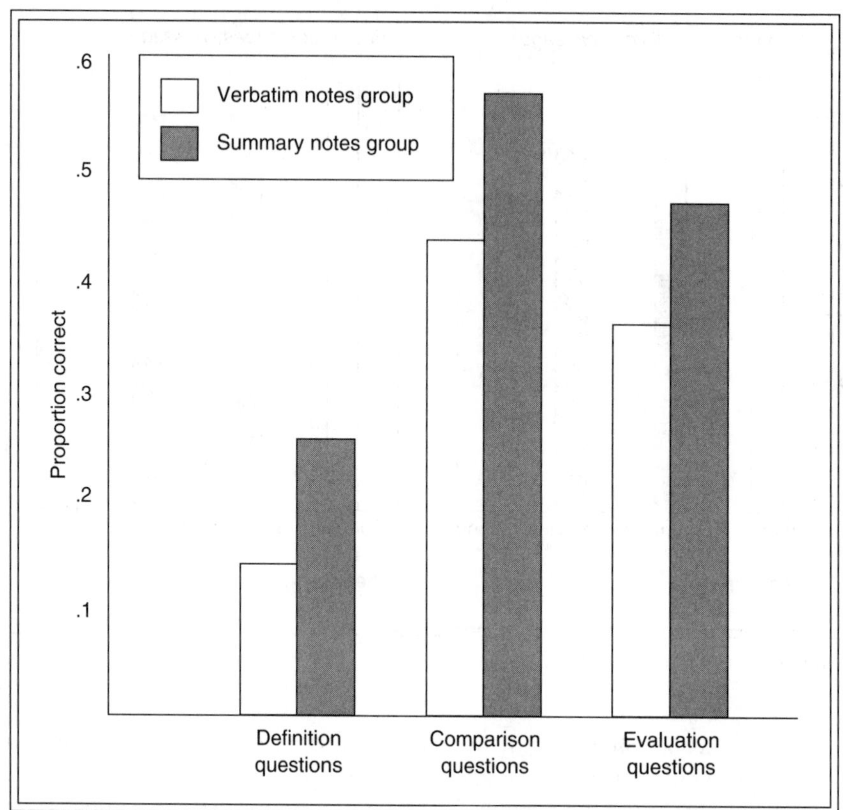

Adapted from Slotte and Lonka (1999)

the main topic. In addition, they were told to write using their own words. These activities appear designed to help students select relevant ideas (by choosing the points to be summarized), organize them into a coherent structure (by linking the subtopics to the main topic), and integrate them with prior knowledge (by writing in one's own words). Students who were taught to summarize their notes actually took more complete notes than those who were not, perhaps in anticipation of the summarization activity. Specifically, the notetaking-with-summarizing group had 29% more of the important ideas in their notes than did the notetaking-with-review group. What happened after the groups reviewed or summarized their notes? On a comprehension test for the lecture, the notetaking-with-summarizing group scored 25% higher than the notetaking-with-review group. These results show that students can learn how to be active notetakers in ways that are more likely to promote deep learning.

In a recent review of programs aimed at teaching students how to write summaries, Pressley and Woloshyn (1995) concluded that "summarization training is a powerful intervention" (p. 62).

QUESTIONING METHODS Listening to a lecture or reading a textbook chapter may appear to be a passive activity. How can we turn it into an active learning experience in which the learner tries to make sense of the material? One approach is to teach students how to generate and answer appropriate questions as they learn.

A first step is to examine what successful learners do as they read a textbook. Chi, Bassok, Lewis, Reimann, and Glaser (1989) compared how successful and less successful students read a physics lesson that included worked-out problems. Students were asked to talk aloud as they read. For example, they might say, "Ummm, this would make sense because they're connected by a string that doesn't stretch" or "If the string's going to be stretched, the earth's going to be moved, and the surface of the incline is going to be depressed." In these comments, you can see that the students are trying to explain the worked-out problems to themselves, creating what Chi et al. call *self-explanations.* In creating self-explanations, students turn the seemingly passive task of reading a textbook lesson into an active task of sense making. Importantly, students who were successful in solving physics problems generated five times as many self-explanations while reading as did the less successful students. These results suggest that successful learners are more likely to know how to engage in active cognitive processing during learning—that is, they ask themselves questions and answer them.

If successful problem solvers are more likely to engage in self-explanations while learning, what would happen if we encourage inexperienced students to engage in generating self-explanations? To examine this question, Chi, de Leeuw, Chiu, and LaVancher (1994) asked eighth-graders who had never taken a biology course to read a 101-sentence passage on the human circulatory system. Some students were told to explain what each sentence means after reading it (self-explanation group), whereas others were told to repeat each sentence after reading it (control group). Students in the self-explanation group showed a much greater improvement on transfer questions than did the control group. These transfer questions required making inferences that went beyond simple retention of the facts, such as "Why doesn't the pulmonary vein have a valve in it?" Subsequent interviews revealed that 57% of the self-explanation group developed an accurate mental model of how the human circulatory system works, compared to 22% for the control group. Developing an accurate mental model is an indication of meaningful learning and is useful for solving problem-solving transfer problems. Apparently, students learned more deeply when they were required to engage in explaining text as they read.

The self-explanation results encourage the idea that low-achieving students might benefit from training in how to generate and answer appropriate questions as they read a textbook or listen to a lecture. In an exemplary study, King (1992) taught self-questioning skills to college students who had been diagnosed as having learning difficulties. First, the students were given a list of 13 general questions, as listed in Figure 11–21. King (1992) designed the questions to "guide students in processing the lecture content by . . . analyzing the ideas and concepts in the lecture, determining how those ideas relate to each other, and relating new information to their own prior knowledge or experience" (p. 309). The instructor modeled (a) how to use the general questions to generate specific questions relevant to a specific lecture and (b) how to answer the specific questions based on the lecture content. Next, the students worked individually to generate questions and answers. The

FIGURE 11–21

A questioning strategy

QUESTIONS	*COGNITIVE PROCESSES THE QUESTIONS ARE INTENDED TO INDUCE IN LEARNERS*
Explain why. . . .	analysis of processes and concepts—explicit or implicit in the lecture
(Explain how. . . .)	translating terms into different vocabulary
What is the main idea of . . . ?	identification of central idea explicit or implicit in the lecture
How would you use . . . to . . .?	application of information in another context—perhaps relating to prior knowledge or experience
What is a new example of . . . ?	generation of novel examples of a concept or procedure—perhaps involving relating to prior knowledge or experience
What do you think would happen if . . . ?	retrieval of background knowledge and integration with lecture material to make predictions
What is the difference between . . . and . . . ?	analysis of two concepts—comparison and contrast of concepts
How are . . . and . . . similar?	analysis of two concepts—comparison and contrast of concepts
What conclusions can you draw about . . . ?	drawing conclusions based on the content presented
How does . . . affect . . . ?	analysis of relationships among ideas
What are the strengths and weaknesses of . . . ?	analysis and integration of concepts
What is the best . . . and why?	evaluation of ideas based upon criteria and evidence
How is . . . related to . . . that we studied earlier?	activation of prior knowledge and integration with new information

From King (1992)

students shared their questions and answers with the class and received constructive feedback. Finally, they practiced by taking notes on a short lecture and then generating questions and answers based on their notes.

Does training in self-questioning affect learning from a lecture? To test this question, King (1992) asked students to take notes on a 20- to 30-minute lecture on a social science topic such as "civil liberties" and then review the notes (notetaking with review) or engage in self-questioning (notetaking with questioning). The lecture notes of the notetaking-with-questioning group contained 33% more of the important ideas than did the lecture notes of the notetaking-with-review group, suggesting that the questioning training helped students focus on the important material. In addition, the notetaking-with-questioning group generated 13% more correct answers on a comprehension test (involving transfer) than did the notetaking-with-review group, suggesting that questioning helped students learn more deeply.

If your goal is teaching for transfer, the process of generating and answering thought-provoking questions can help learners reflect on the presented material. For example, King, Staffieri, and Adelgais (1998) taught middle school students how to ask a series of thought-provoking questions based on science lessons. The questioning pattern begins with a knowledge-review question, such as "How does the muscular system work, Kyle?" and follows up with probing questions, such as "Can you tell me more?", and hint questions, such as "Why are muscles important?" Students worked in pairs taking turns as question asker and question answerer. Figure 11–22 gives a portion of a transcript involving Kyle (who serves as the question asker) and Jon (who serves as the question answerer).

Students who participated in generating and answering questions about science lessons (questioning group) performed about as well as other students (no-questioning group) on remembering the factual material—the scores were 66% correct versus 63% correct, respectively. However, on tests of problem-solving transfer in which students had to make inferences, the questioning group scored 68% higher than the no-questioning group—the scores were 57% versus 34%, respectively. Overall, this research shows how questioning strategies can be used to promote deep understanding that leads to transfer. In this case, questions prime more than simply selecting relevant information; it appears that skillfully used questions can guide the process of organizing and integrating knowledge.

IMPLICATIONS OF GENERATIVE STRATEGIES

Suppose that a class is listening to a lecture on American history. Does listening mean that learning must be a passive process in which the students simply take the teacher's words and put them into their memories? This section showed that learning—even learning from lecture—can be an active process. The student can control the learning process by using generative techniques such as summarizing and questioning.

When the goal of instruction is verbatim retention of specific facts, verbatim copying (or underlining in textbooks) guides the learner's attention. When the goal of instruction is retention of important material and transfer, students need to engage generative activities aimed at building connections among ideas.

The active cognitive processing elicited by generative activities such as summarizing and questioning presumably can be taught. Some students spontaneously take a generative stance and do not need training in generative strategies. Other students engage in generative activities only when told to do so. These students need practice in generative activities such as summarizing and questioning and in seeing that these activities can improve their test performance. Finally, some students do not know what it means to be an active learner. These students may benefit from direct instruction and practice in generative activities and in comparing their summaries or questions to those of the teacher or other students.

In summary, an activity such as notetaking is not necessarily a mindless chore with no benefit to the learner. On the contrary, in learning to productively take notes, a student can

FIGURE 11–22

Using questions to guide learning

Jon:	How does the muscular system work, Kyle?	knowledge-review question
Kyle:	Well . . . it retracts and contracts when you move.	comprehension statement
Jon:	Can you tell me more?	probing question
Kyle:	Um . . . well . . .	
Jon:	Um, why are muscles important, Kyle?	hint question
Kyle:	They are important because if we didn't have them we couldn't move around.	comprehension statement
Jon:	But . . . how do muscles work? Explain it more.	probing question
	Can you give an example?	probing question
Kyle:	Um, muscles have tendons. Some muscles are called skeletal muscles. They are in the muscles that—like—in your arms—that have tendons that hold your muscles to your bones—to make them move and go back and forth. So you can walk and stuff.	comprehension statement
Jon:	Good. Alright!	feedback (accuracy and praise)
	How are the skeletal muscles and the cardiac muscles the same?	thinking question
Kyle:	Uhh—the cardiac and the smooth muscles?	
Jon:	The cardiac and the skeletal.	
Kyle:	Well, they're both a muscle. And they're both pretty strong. And they hold things. I don't really think they have much in common.	knowledge construction (integration, similarities)
Jon:	Okay. Why don't you think they have much in common?	probing question
Kyle:	Because the smooth muscle is—I mean the skeletal muscle is voluntary and—the cardiac muscle is involuntary. Okay, I'll ask now.	knowledge construction (integration, differences)

From King, Staffieri, and Adelgais (1998)

learn how to control his or her cognitive processes, including guiding attention, finding organization in what is presented, and relating what is presented to what the student already knows.

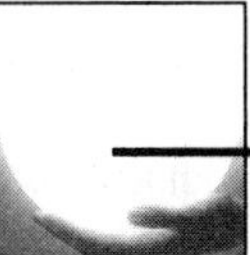

CHAPTER SUMMARY

This chapter explored three types of learning strategies—mnemonic strategies aimed at increasing the amount of information learned, structure strategies aimed at helping students build internal connections, and generative strategies aimed at helping students build external connections. The building of internal and external connections allows for meaningful learning that enables the student to transfer what was learned to new situations.

Several mnemonic strategies repeatedly have been shown to be successful, including the keyword method, which we explored in this chapter. However, developmental differences are evident in students' ability to learn and spontaneously use mnemonic strategies.

Structure strategies such as mapping and outlining can also successfully help students to mentally organize presented material. This kind of training seems to have its strongest effects on transfer performance. Chapter 10 provides some additional examples of research on the role of text adjuncts designed to help learners see the organization of the material.

Generative strategies, including summarizing and questioning, are aimed at building external connections and show their strongest effects on tests of transfer. Chapter 10 provides some additional examples of research on the role of text adjuncts designed to help learners integrate new material with their prior knowledge.

The theme of this chapter is that teaching of learning strategies is an appropriate instructional activity, although in practice little time is devoted to teaching students how to learn (Weinstein & Mayer, 1985). Teaching students how to remember information, how to determine what is important, or how to figure out the theme of a passage may be just as important for the student's academic success as teaching specific facts and concepts. This chapter showed how learning strategies can be taught effectively within regular subject matter contexts (i.e., using textbook material that is part of the regular program). In the course of teaching science or history, for example, the teacher can also help the student learn how to effectively read, process, and remember the material in a textbook.

The appropriateness of strategy training also depends on the teacher's goals. When the goal is to help students memorize paired associates as in foreign language vocabulary, mnemonic strategies are warranted. When the goal is to teach students how to figure out what is important and what is not important in a passage, structure strategies are called for. When the goal is to determine the theme of the passage, generative strategies can be taught. The appropriateness of any strategy training also depends partly on the learner (e.g., whether the learner would normally use the strategy). Before strategy training is carried out, each student should be tested to determine whether he or she knows how to use a particular strategy. If a student is already proficient in using a strategy, training is not needed for that student.

SUGGESTED READINGS

Pressley, M., & McCormick, C. B. (1995). *Cognition, teaching, and assessment.* New York: HarperCollins. (Reviews research on teaching of learning strategies.)

Pressley, M., & Woloshyn, V. (1995). *Cognitive strategy instruction.* Cambridge, MA: Brookline Books. (Reviews research on teaching of learning strategies.)

CHAPTER 12

Teaching by Fostering Problem-Solving Strategies

CHAPTER OUTLINE

Can Problem-Solving Skills Be Taught?

What Makes an Effective Problem-Solving Program?

Productive Thinking Program

Instrumental Enrichment

Project Intelligence

The Case for Improving Problem-Solving Skills Instruction

Chapter Summary

This chapter examines whether students can be taught strategies that help them become more effective problem solvers. I begin by establishing four criteria for effective problem-solving programs. Then, I examine three school-based projects aimed at boosting students' problem-solving skills. The research encourages continuing work on identifying the teachable aspects of problem-solving transfer.

CAN PROBLEM-SOLVING SKILLS BE TAUGHT?

An important goal of most educational institutions is the improvement of the human mind. But what exactly does it mean to improve someone's mind? One interpretation is that students should become more effective problem solvers: We want students, when faced with a new problem, to be able to figure out an appropriate solution. For example, after studying basic arithmetic, a fourth-grade student is asked the following (Davis & Maher, 1997, p. 106):

> How many different pizzas can be made if every pizza has cheese, but to this you can add whichever of the following toppings you wish and in any combination you wish:
>
> green peppers
> sausage
> mushrooms
> pepperoni

If you have not yet learned the formula for computing the number of combinations, this problem requires creative problem solving.

As another example, after studying a science lesson on heat and temperature, an eighth-grade student is given the following problem (adapted from Linn & Hsi, 2000, p. 143):

> Which container would be best for keeping soup hot—a large bowl or a small bowl?

Answering this question requires creatively using what you know about the concept of heat flow and the insulating properties of various materials.

As a final example, after studying international diplomacy involving social, political, and economic issues, high school students were asked to grapple with the following problem:

> In 1492, there was a proposal that all Jews be expelled from Spain. The two monarchs, Ferdinand and Isabella, who sent Columbus on his voyage, were very strong Catholics. Spain was very divided at the time. There were different ethnic groups, different political groups, and different religions in the country. As a way of unifying the country, it was proposed that Spain tell all the Jews they had four months to either convert to Catholicism or leave Spain for good. There was a Jewish man named Abrabanel who was an advisor to the King and Queen. He was supposed to advise them on what to do about this proposal to expel the Jews from Spain. Imagine that you are Abrabanel. Think about what you would have done if you had been asked for advice. (Torney-Punta, 1994, p. 111)

In solving this problem, students must use what they know about religious minorities as well as the social, political, and economic climate of the period.

Being able to solve problems such as these can be taken as an indication of an educated mind. In solving these problems the student needs more than simply remembering an answer; the student needs to create a novel solution. The educational goal of improving students' minds prompts the question of whether problem-solving skills can be taught. This chapter explores the question, Is it possible to teach our students to become better problem solvers? Most of the chapters in this book examine ways of teaching that promote transfer, but this chapter takes a more direct approach by asking how we can teach problem-solving skills.

In this chapter, I establish four criteria for teaching problem-solving strategies and then examine how well each of three school-based programs meets the criteria. In addition, this chapter explores the question of how thinking-strategies training should be incorporated into the curriculum.

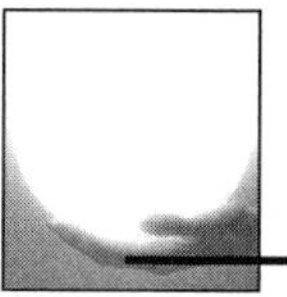

WHAT MAKES AN EFFECTIVE PROBLEM-SOLVING PROGRAM?

Consider the following scenario. The president of your country has announced a national goal of ensuring that all children who enter school as kindergartners are intellectually ready to learn. Your country stands ready to spend billions of dollars over the ensuing years to increase the intellectual ability of needy preschoolers. Suppose you are appointed to a government board charged with designing an educational program to improve children's intellectual ability. What would you do?

As you probably suspect, this scenario is not made up. In 1965, the United States initiated a national program called Head Start, which sought to improve the intellectual functioning of preschool children living in poverty. For the next 35 years, Head Start became "the most important social and educational experiment of the second half of the twentieth century" (Zigler & Muenchow, 1992, p. 2). One of the founding goals of Head Start was to "improve the child's mental processes" (p. 20), and increases in intelligence test scores became the main objective for demonstrating success. Today, Head Start remains an important national commitment, but one that could benefit from research and theory in meaningful learning (Caruso, Taylor, & Detterman, 1982; Zigler & Muenchow, 1992). Throughout its history and continuing into the twenty-first century, the goal remains the same: "All children in America will start school ready to learn" (Zigler & Muenchow, 1992, p. 211). If you were in charge, what would you do "to improve intellectual functioning" (Caruso et al., 1982, p. 51)?

First you might wonder whether intellectual functioning (as measured by IQ tests) can actually be improved. Some promising news comes from Flynn (1998), who has been tracking IQ scores in 20 industrialized countries around the world. Flynn's major finding, called the *Flynn effect*, is that "IQ scores have been rising for most of the 20th century in every country for which pertinent data are available" (Martinez, 2000, p. 90). For example, from 1918 to 1995, the average IQ score in the United States increased by 25 points—almost two standard deviations. Flynn concludes that "somewhere out there environmental variables of enormous potency are creating IQ differences" (p. 53). Martinez provides additional data showing that educational experience can have a marked effect on people's IQ scores, and he therefore sees education as a means of cultivating human intelligence.

If you wished to design an instructional program aimed specifically at improving students' intellectual ability, you would need to make some decisions about what to teach, where to teach, how to teach, and when to teach. These four issues are summarized in Figure 12–1. To help you in your decision process, let's begin with some commonsense

FIGURE 12–1

Four issues for thinking skills programs

Issue	Alternatives
1. What to teach	Thinking as a single intellectual ability versus thinking as a collection of smaller component skills.
2. Where to teach	In general, domain-independent courses or within existing, specific subject areas.
3. How to teach	Focus on product through rewarding correct answers versus focus on processes that the student learns to model.
4. When to teach	After basic skills are mastered versus before.

Adapted from Mayer (1997)

principles for how to teach students to be better problem solvers (Mayer, 1997, p. 480). Please rate your degree of agreement with each statement by circling a number from 1 (strongly disagree) to 7 (strongly agree).

1. The ability to solve problems depends on improving the human mind. The mind is like a mental muscle that needs to be strengthened.
   (disagree) 1 2 3 4 5 6 7 (agree)
2. Like any other academic subject, problem-solving courses should be required for all students. The general skills students learn in a problem-solving course will be useful in their problem solving in other academic subjects ranging from language arts to mathematics to science to history.
   (disagree) 1 2 3 4 5 6 7 (agree)
3. Like the training of any skill, the best way to learn how to be a better problem solver is through regular mental exercises. Students need practice in giving the right answer to exercise problems.
   (disagree) 1 2 3 4 5 6 7 (agree)
4. Students cannot learn about higher-order thinking skills until they have mastered lower-level basic skills. For example, students cannot learn how to design compositions until they know how to spell and punctuate, and they cannot solve complex math word problems until they have mastered basic arithmetic procedures.
   (disagree) 1 2 3 4 5 6 7 (agree)

These principles seem to square with conventional wisdom and provide a prescription for how to improve students' intellectual ability. Regrettably, though, they conflict with relevant research and theory (Mayer, 1997), so let's review each one in more detail.

WHAT TO TEACH: ONE ABILITY VERSUS MANY COGNITIVE SKILLS

LOOKING FOR INTELLIGENCE AS ONE OR MANY As reflected in the first item in my survey, the first major issue concerns whether humans possess one single intellectual ability (single intelligence theory) or many smaller skills that together account for a person's intellectual ability (cognitive skills theory). One of the earliest battles between these two views can be seen in early conceptions of intelligence testing proposed by Galton and by Binet. In trying to measure intellectual ability, Galton (1883) and Binet (1911/1962) had to consider whether intelligence was a single ability or a collection of smaller skills.

For example, suppose you wish to measure human intellectual ability and you believe that problem solving depends on a single ability—such as how fast your brain worked or how sensitive your mind was to small differences. To measure speed of mental functioning you could test people on reaction time tasks, such as pressing a button as soon as a light appeared. To measure sensitivity, you could ask people to hold two weights and decide which was heavier. Galton (1883) was the first to propose that intellectual functioning depended on a single mental ability (which he called the *human faculty*) and to devise clever ways to measure it. Yet subsequent research showed that his tests failed to correlate with any practical measures of intellectual ability such as school grades (Sternberg, 1990).

In contrast, suppose that you are asked to devise a test that would predict school success so that students with potential learning problems could be given special assistance. If you see intellectual ability as reflected in possessing a collection of smaller, component skills, the test should focus on many small skills. In response to just such a call from the French Ministry of Education, Binet (1911/1962) was the first to propose that intellectual ability—at least the ability to learn—depended on possessing many smaller skills and to show how such skills can be measured. For example, based on his studies of individual differences among French school students, Binet offered one of the first arguments for the cognitive skills theory:

> [I]ntelligence is not a simple indivisible function with a particular essence of its own . . . but, it is formed by the combination of all the minor functions . . . all of which have proved to be plastic and subject to increase. With practice, enthusiasm, and especially with method, one can succeed in increasing one's attention, memory, and judgment, and in becoming literally more intelligent than before; and this process will go on until one reaches one's limit. (p. 150)

Binet even devised a series of exercises that he called *mental orthopedics:* "In the same way that physical orthopedics straightens a crooked spine, mental orthopedics strengthens, cultivates, and fortifies attention, memory, perception, judgment, and will" (p. 150). Unlike Galton's tests, Binet's tests did correlate—although not perfectly—with school success.

If you accept Binet's assertions that intellectual performance is based on small intellectual skills that can be identified and taught, the next task becomes one of trying to better describe these skills. In his theory of multiple intelligences, for example, Gardner (1983, 1999) proposed a collection of intellectual skills, including linguistic intelligence, musical intelligence, logical-mathematical intelligence, spatial intelligence, bodily-kinesthetic intelligence, and personal intelligence. Suppose we wish to dig deeper and ask, "Can intellectual performance within any of these domains be analyzed into component processes?" Mayer (1992) has shown that there are two major kinds of cognitive processing:

1. *Representational processes*—for building a coherent and useful internal representation of the problem.
2. *Solution processes*—for creating, carrying out, and monitoring a plan.

The specific representational and solution processes may depend on the specific intellectual task.

Using a cognitive approach, problem-solving courses can teach strategies for representation of problems and searching for solutions. Some suggestions for representational strategies are to relate the problem to a previous problem, restate the problem in other words, and draw a picture or diagram. Some suggestions for searching include working from the goal to the givens, breaking the problem into subgoals, and only making moves that solve a particular subproblem.

POLYA'S TEACHING OF PROBLEM SOLVING Polya's (1945, 1965) program for teaching problem solving has influenced the development of many more recent programs. For example, Polya's (1965) observations of high school mathematics students led him to emphasize techniques for representing and planning problem solutions:

> I wish to call heuristics . . . the study of the means and methods of problem solving. . . . I am trying, by all means at my disposal, to entice the reader to do problems and to think about the means and methods he uses in doing them. . . . What is presented here are not merely solutions but case histories of solutions. Such a case history describes the sequence of essential steps by which the solution has been eventually discovered, and tries to disclose the motives and attitudes prompting these steps. The aim . . . is to suggest some general advice or pattern which may guide the reader in similar situations. (p. 8)

In short, Polya argued that students should be asked to solve problems and to observe others solve problems, with the emphasis on the process of problem solving rather than on the final answer. Some of the heuristics suggested by Polya are to find a related problem that you can solve, break the problem down into smaller parts, and draw a picture of the problem.

In his classic little book *How to Solve It,* Polya (1945) offered the following four-step general procedure for solving problems, especially mathematics problems.

1. *Understand the problem.* The problem solver must see what is given, what is unknown, and what operations are allowed. In short, the problem solver must represent the problem.
2. *Devise a plan.* The problem solver must determine a general course of attack, such as restating the problem so that it is more like a familiar problem.
3. *Carry out the plan.* The problem solver must carry out the computations and other needed operations.
4. *Look back.* The problem solver looks over the processes he/she went through, trying to see how this experience can be helpful in solving other problems.

Figure 12–2 provides an example of how these four steps can be applied to the problem of finding the volume of the frustrum of a right pyramid.

Although Polya's ideas have been highly influential, especially among some mathematics educators, you might wonder whether there is any evidence that problem-solving heuristics (or skills) can be taught. To help answer that question, Schoenfeld (1979) taught heuristics for mathematical problem solving to college students. The trained group was given a five-problem pretest, training on how to solve 20 example problems, and then a five-problem posttest. The trained group was given a list and description of heuristics, such as partially shown in Figure 12–3. Then, in each session all the problems were solvable by the same heuristic, and subjects were explicitly told which heuristic to apply to the problems. The control group received the same pretest, the same 20 example problems,

FIGURE 12–2

Polya's four steps in problem solving

PROBLEM

Find the volume of the frustrum of a right pyramid with a square base, given the altitude of the frustrum, the length of a side of its upper base, and the length of a side of its lower base.

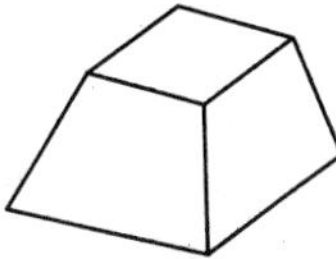

STEP 1: Understand the Problem.

What Is Given?
The altitude, the length of the upper base, the length of the lower base.

What Is Unknown?
The volume of the frustrum.

a
a = upper base
b = lower base
h = height
h
b

STEP 2: Devise a Plan.

Is There a Related Problem?
The volume of a right pyramid can be obtained as follows:

$$\text{Volume} = \frac{(\text{base})^2 \times (\text{height})}{3}$$

Can You Restate the Unknown?
Find the volume of the large pyramid minus the volume of the small pyramid.

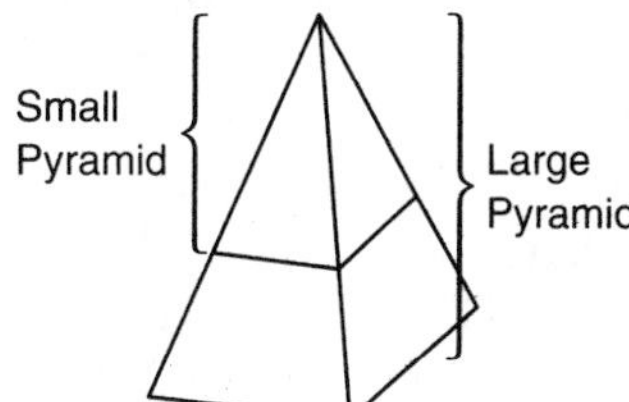

STEP 3: Carry Out the Plan.

Calculate volume of large pyramid.
Calculate volume of small pyramid.
Subtract the second from the first.

STEP 4: Look Back.

This technique can be applied to other problems, such as, "Find the area of a donut, given the radius to the inside and outside."

Adapted from Polya (1968).

FIGURE 12–3

Five problem-solving strategies taught by Schoenfeld

1. Draw a diagram if at all possible.
2. If there is an integer parameter, look for an inductive argument.
3. Consider arguing by *contrapositive* or *contradiction*.
   Contrapositive: Instead of proving the statement "If *X* is true, then *Y* is true," you can prove the equivalent statement "If *Y* is false, then *X* must be false."
   Contradiction: Assume, for the sake of argument, that the statement you would like to prove is false. Using this assumption, go on to prove either that one of the given conditions in the problem is false, that something you know to be true is false, or that what you wish to prove is true. If you can do any of these, you have proved what you want.
4. Consider a similar problem with fewer variables.
5. Try to establish subgoals.

Adapted from Schoenfeld (1979)

and the same posttest as the trained group. However, the control group was not given a list of heuristics, and the problems in each session were not all solvable by the same heuristic.

The results showed that the trained group increased from an average score of 20% correct on the pretest to 65% on the posttest, whereas the control group averaged 25% correct on both tests. Although the sample size was small in this study, the results suggest that it is possible to identify teachable aspects of problem solving—in this case, some Polya-like heuristics within the domain of mathematics.

CRITERION 1: TEACH COMPONENT SKILLS With respect to the issue of what to teach, I interpret the current research base to favor teaching of component skills rather than teaching of a single monolithic ability. For example, problem solving can be broken down into individual representational or solution strategies that can be taught. Training in problem solving involves teaching students the component processes in problem solving. The particular list of problem-solving strategies (or skills) tends to vary depending on the subject matter of the problems to be solved. The implications for the design of a problem-solving program are that the content of the course should be definable skills for representing and solving problems, including skills for planning and monitoring one's plans. Subsequent sections of this chapter explore some of the specific content of problem-solving programs.

WHERE SHOULD PROBLEM-SOLVING STRATEGIES BE TAUGHT?

LOOKING FOR INTELLIGENCE AS SPECIFIC OR GENERAL As reflected in the second item in my survey, the second issue concerns whether problem-solving strategies are general or specific. The instructional implication concerns whether problem solving should be taught as a separate general course or within specific subject areas. Thus, once we have pinpointed important cognitive skills—such as how to represent a problem or how to devise a solution plan—should we teach these as general or specific skills? Should we expect students to learn general problem-solving strategies that can be applied to a wide variety of tasks, or should we expect students to perform well mainly on applying specific strategies to problems like those given in training? For example, suppose that your goal is to teach students a planning strategy such as how to break a problem into parts. Should you teach this as a general skill in a separate lesson on general problem solving, or should you teach how to break down a math problem into parts (during mathematics instruction), how to break a composition into its parts (during language instruction), how to analyze a historical problem (during history instruction), and so on?

Early research on intelligence testing addressed the issue of whether intellectual ability is general or specific. Consider the following situation: You give a large battery of cognitive tests to a large group of people. If intelligence is general, tests measuring the same skill—such as memory or learning—should correlate with one another; that is, people who score high on one memory test should tend to score high on other memory tests, people who score high on one learning test should score high on other learning tests, and so on. Spearman (1927) found some evidence that all the tests correlated with one another, so he took this as evidence for general aspects of intelligence (which he called g-factors). He also found that certain clusters of tests correlated particularly well, so he took this as evidence for specific aspects of intelligence (which he called s-factors). Later, Thurstone (1938) repeated this kind of study using more sophisticated statistical analyses. This time, he found evidence for only seven primary mental abilities. For example, tests of mathematical thinking measured something different from tests of verbal thinking. These results suggest that intellectual ability may be domain specific—that is, cognitive skills that are useful in one subject area (such as being able to plan an essay) may not have much in common with cognitive skills used in an unrelated subject area (such as being able to plan a solution to a math word problem).

WHAT EXPERTS KNOW What does it take to be an expert in some field—general mental ability or specific cognitive skills? This question was addressed in a classic study by de Groot (1965) in which he compared the cognitive functioning of chess experts and novices. If chess expertise is a general skill, you can expect experts to perform better than novices on all kinds of memory tests. In contrast, de Groot found that experts and novices performed at similar levels on standard memory tests; however, experts outperformed novices on remembering the position of chess pieces on the board of an actual game. In short, experts performed well on domain-specific tests of memory—remembering chess positions from real games—but not on domain-general tests of memory, such as remembering a list of words. In fact, novices and experts even performed the same on remembering the position of chess pieces that had been placed randomly on the board (Chase & Simon, 1973). Apparently, experts developed skill in how to mentally group pieces into meaningful clusters, effectively increasing their memory for chess pieces. These results suggest that expertise is highly domain specific; that is, the cognitive skills needed for cognition in one domain (such as chess) are not related to other domains. Thorndike's research on the problems with general transfer, discussed in Chapter 1, tells a similar story.

CRITERION 2: TEACH WITHIN SPECIFIC DOMAINS Overall, the question of where to teach is still somewhat controversial, but I interpret the research base to favor embedding instruction within specific domains. Research on intelligence testing, on expertise, and on cross-discipline transfer all suggest that it is best to have students learn on problem-solving tasks that are similar to the tasks they will be expected to perform later. There is no convincing evidence that learning to solve problems in one subject area—such as solving logic problems—has a strong effect on solving problems in another subject area—such as writing persuasive essays (Mayer, 1992).

HOW SHOULD PROBLEM-SOLVING SKILLS BE TAUGHT?

PROCESS VERSUS PRODUCT The third question in the survey you took at the beginning of this chapter concerns the issue of how to teach—by focusing on giving students practice in producing the right answer or in helping students understand the process of successful problem solving. Once a set of problem-solving skills has been identified, the next issue concerns how to teach these skills to students. "We should be teaching students how to think; instead we are primarily teaching them what to think." So asserts Lochhead (1979, p. 1) in the introduction to the book he wrote with John Clement, *Cognitive Process Instruction*. What Lochhead and others are saying is that teachers are emphasizing *product* (i.e., getting the right answer) instead of *process* (i.e., how to go about solving problems).

BLOOM AND BRODER'S TEACHING OF PROBLEM SOLVING In one of the first experimental research studies on teaching problem solving, Bloom and Broder (1950) carried out a program to improve the problem-solving performance of college students at the University of Chicago. The university required that students pass a series of comprehensive examinations in subject matter areas. As you might expect, some students (called "model students") performed quite well on the exams. In contrast, other students (called "remedial students") who were just as motivated, studied just as hard, and scored just as high in scholastic aptitude as the model students were unable to pass the exams. Although the model and remedial students seemed equivalent in ability, knowledge, and motivation, the remedial students apparently lacked skills necessary to answer the questions. Thus, Bloom and Broder sought to develop a training program to help the remedial students think like the model students for exam questions.

In determining what to teach, Bloom and Broder distinguished between

Product of problem solving—whether the student produced the correct answer, and
Process of problem solving—the thought process that a person engages in.

Figure 12–4 shows an economics exam problem and the answers given by three students. As you can see, although the students generated the same final answer, their descriptions of how they generated the answer are quite different. Bloom and Broder decided that the training program for remedial students should focus on the teaching of useful problem-solving strategies rather than on reinforcing students for emitting correct answers.

In determining how to teach, Bloom and Broder decided to let remedial students compare their solution strategies with those used by the model students. Using a *thinking aloud* procedure, remedial students were asked to describe their thought process for a problem, and model students were asked to describe their thought process for the same problem. Then the remedial students were asked to find the differences between how they solved the problem and how the model students solved the problem. For example, Figure 12–5 shows a list of differences that remedial students found between their strategies and those of model students. This model-based training is similar in some ways to the cognitive apprenticeship approach explored in Chapter 13.

FIGURE 12–4

How three students solved the inflation problem

PROBLEM

Some economists feel that there is danger of an extreme inflationary boom after the war. It is the opinion of such economists that the government should control the boom in order to prevent a depression such as the one following the stock-market crash of 1929.

Determine whether each of the following specific suggestion would be *consistent* with the policy of controlling the boom or is directly *inconsistent* with the policy.

26. Lower the reserve that banks are required to hold against deposits.
27. Reduce taxes considerably.
28. Encourage the federal reserve banks to buy securities in the open market.

MARY'S ANSWER

Mary W. (Score 2): (Read the statements and the directions.)

(Read item 26.) "Look down to see what I'm supposed to do.

(Reread the statements and the directions.) "Not quite sure what I'm doing." (Reread the statements and the directions for the third time.)

(Reread item 26.) "Not sure of this, so on to second one.

(Read item 27.) "Say inconsistent, because if there is inflationary boom, if people make more money, taxes have to keep up with it to take away the money so they can't spend it.

(Read item 28.) "Trying to figure out what bearing that had exactly.

(Reread item 26.) "I'm a time waster, say 26 would be consistent—no, that I know, banks have reserve—idea is to get people to deposit as much as possible—not answer 28.

(Reread item 28.) "Say inconsistent, I feel it is."

Diagnosis: unsystematic, jumps around, uses "feeling" rather than "reasoning," not confident.

JAMES'S ANSWER

James S. (Score 2): (Read the statements.) "In other words, the OPA and such.

(Read the directions.) "Take for granted they're going to control the boom.

(Read item 26. Reread item 26.) "That would be inconsistent.

(Read item 27.) "That would be inconsistent, because you can't have too great a boom as long as you have taxes, at least in my interpretation of boom—although if taxes go up, prices go up—no, I'll stick to my answer.

(Read item 28.) "Consistent—however, I think I need more subject-matter background to tell how I thought it out—more of a guess—don't think inconsistent, so put consistent."

Diagnosis: translates problem into something more familiar (OPA), lacks subject-matter knowledge, guesses.

(continued)

FIGURE 12–4 (cont.)

DORA'S ANSWER

Dora Z. (Score 2): (Read the statement and the directions—emphasizing the key words.)

(Read item 26.) "Lower the reserve, raise the amount of money in circulation—if you raise the money in circulation—inconsistent. By raising the money in circulation you don't control a boom.

(Read item 27.) "Also inconsistent for the same reason.

(Read item 28.) "Open market—think what the open market is. This would take money out of circulation, therefore would be consistent."

Diagnosis: focused on key ideas, reduced three items to a single problem, attempted to determine how money supply is affected by each item, attacks problem on basis of single rule or principle, higher-order problem solving.

Adapted from Bloom and Broder (1950)

In a typical experiment, remedial students were given 10 to 12 training sessions in which they compared their solution strategies to those of models. Students who were trained tended to score about .5 to .7 grade points higher on the exam and expressed more self-confidence than students of equivalent ability and background who were not given training. Thus, Bloom and Broder were able to influence problem-solving performance in subject areas by focusing on process rather than product and by giving students practice in comparing their strategies to those of models.

CRITERION 3: FOCUS ON THE PROBLEM-SOLVING PROCESS In summary, research suggests that the method for teaching problem solving should focus on *process* rather than *product* and that students need practice in relating their own problem-solving processes to those of models. This modeling technique has become the basis for many of the problem-solving programs discussed in subsequent sections of this chapter.

WHEN SHOULD PROBLEM-SOLVING STRATEGIES BE TAUGHT?

The last question in the survey you completed at the start of the chapter concerns the issue of when to teach high-order thinking skills—after lower-level skills have been mastered (prior automatization theory) or while lower-level skills are being mastered (constraint removal theory). According to the prior automatization view, lower-level skills should be memorized so well that they do not require any mental effort. For example, students should be able to sight-read words without hesitation before they learn reading comprehension skills. In this way, they can devote all their cognitive resources to learning the higher-order skills and not be distracted by having to think about how to use lower-level skills.

FIGURE 12–5

Students' lists of differences between model student and self

Jean's List

1. I didn't think it necessary to formulate the general rule.
   Generalization too broad.
   Verbalization reversed actually.
2. Lack of understanding of given terms.
   Define and illustrate as alternatives.
   I looked for "true" and "false"—others looked for "best." Didn't interpret directions properly.
   I looked for answer—didn't have an answer before I looked. Higher degree of inaccuracy. (I get this OK with syllogisms.)
3. He associated and brought in intermediary events with dates. I did the same with the second part, but didn't know country.
4. He employed an illustration for proof.
   Should set up criteria for an answer: if not enough, set up illustrations and examples.
5. Didn't get essential terms of what I was looking for before I began reading alternatives.
   Jumped to conclusion without carrying illustrative reasoning through.
   Did read terms thoroughly but didn't keep them in mind; reversed them.
6. Didn't define terms of statements. Got it right through outside example.
7. Should pull out main words. Got it right, though.
8. Didn't establish relations between terms. Got it right, though.
   Careless about selecting right alternative.
   Keeping directions in mind. I think in terms of "true" and "false" instead of "scientific study," etc.

Ralph's List

1. Find rule or formula that applies to problem under consideration.
2. Apply rule and formulate answer, then check with offered answers.
3. Progress into problem by formula that has been generalized through application.
4. Rules should deal with specific problem.
5. Try to read directions clearly the first time.
6. Do not answer by guessing or supposition.
7. Think before the formulation of answer.
8. Direct thought in stream which has been pointed in the direction of the problem at hand.
9. Emphasis on the major ideas in the problem, not all ideas.
10. Box off ideas into main question in the problem.
11. Reason from known knowledge or examples.
12. In graphs, formulate a specific picture.

Adapted from Bloom and Broder (1950)

What's wrong with the prior automatization view? It means that much of school—and certainly much of elementary school—must be devoted to senseless memorizing. Students are likely to get the idea that school is not a very interesting place. In contrast, the constraint removal view holds that students can engage in higher-order skills even before they have fully mastered lower skills. However, the teacher must scaffold the task by removing the need to perform some of the lower-level skills. For example, if the goal is to teach reading comprehension—which is a higher-order thinking skill—but students cannot sight-read words very well, the teacher can read the passage to the students.

APPRENTICESHIP Chapter 13 examines the role of cognitive apprenticeship, in which beginners are allowed to work with experienced practitioners on authentic tasks. Tharp and Gallimore (1988) referred to this arrangement as *assisted performance* because students are allowed to perform challenging tasks but receive help on portions that they cannot yet perform. Similarly, Lave and Wenger (1991) showed how apprenticeship works in a wide variety of cultures—ranging from midwives in Mexico to tailors in Liberia to meat cutters in the United States. In each case, beginners work on high-level tasks but are given help on portions of the task that they have not yet mastered. These appear to be successful case studies of how people can learn higher-order skills before they have completely mastered all lower-level skills.

CRITERION 4: TEACH HIGHER-ORDER SKILLS EARLY RATHER THAN LATE In summary, there is increasing evidence to support the call for teaching of higher-order thinking skills to students who may not have yet mastered all relevant basic skills.

IMPLICATIONS FOR TEACHING PROBLEM SOLVING

This brief historical overview helps to provide some tentative answers to our four questions. First, once you choose the kinds of problems that the students need to be able to solve, the intellectual performance required for these problems should be broken into smaller skills that can be taught instead of teaching problem solving as a monolithic ability. Second, it seems to make the most sense to teach specific problem-solving skills within specific contexts; it may also be possible to teach what appear to be general domain-free strategies, but not much evidence exists that these will transfer beyond the contexts they are taught in. Third, students should learn problem solving by focusing on process rather than product and should have models to which they can refer—that is, examples of how successful problem solvers go about solving problems. Fourth, students can learn higher-order skills even though they may not have fully mastered lower-level skills.

The next section explores three widely used problem-solving courses that have been well received in school settings. Each is an independent problem-solving course rather than an attempt to integrate problem solving within subject matter domains. For each program, this section presents the underlying theory, briefly describes the program, and evaluates the changes in students' thinking. The three programs are the Productive Thinking Program, Instrumental Enrichment, and Project Intelligence.

PRODUCTIVE THINKING PROGRAM

BACKGROUND

During the 1960s, several large-scale curriculum development efforts were carried out, including projects that emphasized teaching students in elementary and secondary schools how to think. One of the best known and most thoroughly studied curriculum development projects for teaching thinking skills is the Productive Thinking Program (Covington, Crutchfield, & Davies, 1966; Covington, Crutchfield, Davies, & Olton, 1974), which seeks to teach general problem-solving skills to fifth- and sixth-grade students. The Productive Thinking Program involves a series of printed workbooks that provide practice in solving detective stories. Students are introduced to the process of problem solving and are invited to emulate the problem-solving strategies of models.

DESCRIPTION

The program consists of 15 cartoonlike booklets, each about 30 pages in length. Each booklet presents a detective story involving two children, Jim and Lila, as well as Jim's Uncle John and Mr. Search. The story presents clues and asks the reader to answer questions aimed at "restating the problem in his own words," "formulating his own questions," and "generating ideas to explain the mystery" (Covington & Crutchfield, 1965, p. 3). After the reader has generated some ideas, Jim and Lila give theirs. Thus, Jim and Lila serve as "models to be emulated" (p. 3). Like all realistic models, they make some mistakes at first, but with the help of comments from the adults in the booklet, they eventually figure out the mystery.

Figure 12–6 gives a few pages from one of the first lessons in the program, "The Riverboat Robbery." As you read the lesson, you are given some information and asked to generate some responses. Then you get feedback by seeing what Jim and Lila do and how Uncle John critiques their strategies. (If you read the entire booklet carefully, you will discover that the culprit is Mr. Larkin, the bank manager.) Each lesson is designed to teach some of the strategies listed in Figure 12–7 (on p. 417); for example, "The Riverboat Robbery" attempts to teach strategies 4, 5, 6, 9, 11, and 15.

EVALUATION

More than a dozen studies have evaluated the effectiveness of the Productive Thinking Program (Mansfield, Busse, & Krepelka, 1978), so "the effects of Productive Thinking have been particularly well researched" (Adams, 1989, p. 38). For example, Olton and Crutchfield (1969) gave training in the Productive Thinking Program to 25 fifth-graders, while an equal number of fifth-graders received no training. Figure 12–8 (on p. 418) gives examples of pretests given before training, posttests given immediately after training, and delayed posttests given 6 months after training. Figure 12–9 (on p. 419) shows that the trained group and control group scored at about the same level on the pretest, but the trained group outperformed the control group on the immediate and delayed posttest.

In interpreting these results you should note that the test problems were similar to the types of problems given in the booklets and that factors other than training, such as higher motivation by the trained subjects, may account for differences among the groups. In a review of a dozen evaluation studies, Mansfield et al. (1978) concluded that the effects of the Productive Thinking Program are smaller in well-controlled studies and seem limited to problems like those given in the lessons. Concerning the issue of transfer of problem-solving strategies to new problems, Mansfield et al. (1978) concluded that "it is unclear whether the effects of training are sufficiently generalizable to be useful in real-life problem

FIGURE 12–6

Excerpts from "The Riverboat Robbery"

The TV Announcer:

"Following the robbery, things moved quickly. The captain of the boat called the Elmtown police. When the boat docked in Elmtown, the police were already on guard there. No one was allowed on or off the boat except the police and our reporter and TV cameraman."

"Here is the police chief on the boat, telling our reporter what has happened so far:"

FIGURE 12–6

(cont.)

1

What persons besides Louie might be the thief?

Before Lila tells her idea, what thoughts do you have about other possible suspects? Use your reply notebook to write down all the ideas you can think of.

There are several people besides Louie who might have stolen the money. You may have thought of the steward who called Mr. Burk to the phone, or perhaps you even considered the riverboat captain.

Lila has another possible suspect in mind.

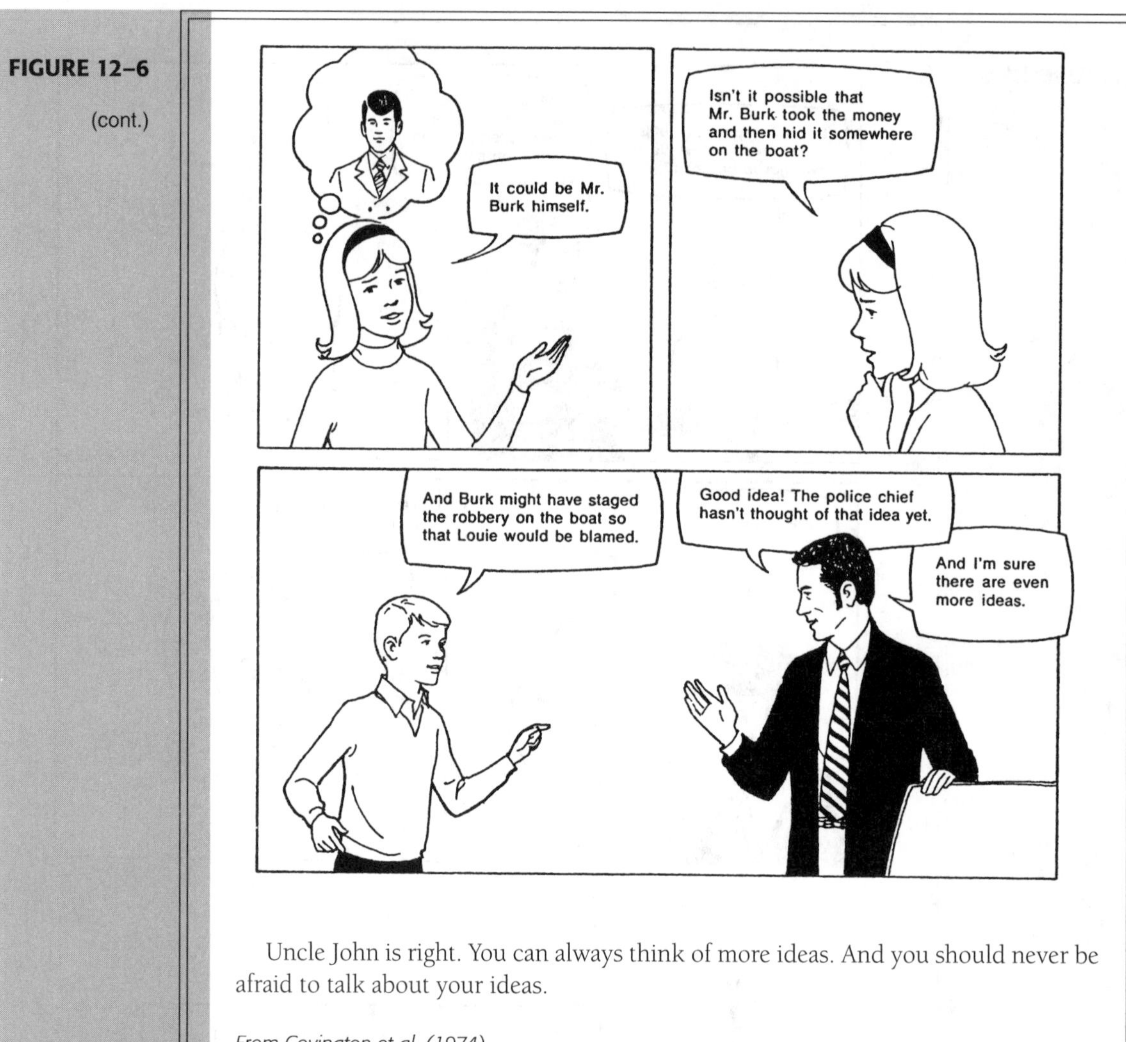

FIGURE 12–6 (cont.)

Uncle John is right. You can always think of more ideas. And you should never be afraid to talk about your ideas.

From Covington et al. (1974)

solving situations" (p. 522). Nickerson (1999) also noted "the limitation of the gains to problems similar to those encountered in the program material" (p. 402). Apparently, it is possible to teach students to perform well on a certain class of problem, but no strong evidence exists that such training transfers to other domains.

Overall, the Productive Thinking Program is consistent with the criteria for a successful thinking skills program: It teaches a limited number of component skills (as listed in Figure 12–7), its effects are strongest for the specific domain used during instruction, the instructional method relies heavily on modeling of cognitive processing, and it seeks to

FIGURE 12–7

Some problem-solving skills taught in the Productive Thinking Program

1. Take time to reflect on a problem before you begin to work. Decide exactly what the problem is that you are trying to solve.
2. Get all the facts of the problem clearly in mind.
3. Work on the problem in a planful way.
4. Keep an open mind. Don't jump to conclusions about the answer to a problem.
5. Think of many new ideas for solving a problem. Don't stop with just a few.
6. Try to think of unusual ideas.
7. As a way of getting ideas, pick out all the important objects and persons in the problem and think carefully about each one.
8. Think of several general possibilities for a solution and then figure out many particular ideas for each possibility.
9. As you search for ideas, let your mind freely explore things around you. Almost anything can suggest ideas for a solution.
10. Always check each idea with the facts to decide how likely the idea is.
11. If you get stuck on a problem, keep trying. Don't be discouraged.
12. When you run out of ideas, try looking at the problem in a new and different way.
13. Go back and review all the facts of the problem to make sure you have not missed something important.
14. Start with an unlikely idea. Just suppose that it is possible and figure out how it could be.
15. Be on the lookout for odd or puzzling facts in a problem. Explaining them can lead you to new ideas for solution.
16. When there are several puzzling things in a problem, try to explain them with a single idea that will connect them all together.

Adapted from Covington et al. (1974)

attain high-order skills even though learners may not have yet mastered all lower-level skills.

INSTRUMENTAL ENRICHMENT

BACKGROUND

Suppose a boy develops in an environment that does not offer much human contact or much opportunity to learn. After many years of living this way, the boy is brought to school, where he performs poorly on intellectual tasks and is labeled mentally retarded.

FIGURE 12–8

Some pretests and posttests given to study the effectivness of the Productive Thinking Program

Pretests	
Controlling the weather	Student thinks of various consequences of man's future ability to change the weather.
Project for a village	Student puts himself in the shoes of a Peace Corps volunteer who must first acquaint himself with the customs and mores of a tribal village. Then, without offending such customs, he must figure out ways the inhabitants can earn money for their village needs.
Immediate Posttests	
Transplanting organs	Student thinks of various consequences of man's future medical ability to transplant bodily organs from one person to another.
"Black House" problem	Student attempts to solve a puzzling mystery problem in which he must make an insightful reorganization of the elements of the problem.
Delayed Posttests	
The missing jewel problem	Student attempts to solve a puzzling mystery problem in which she must make an insightful reorganization of the elements of the problem.
The nameless tomb	Student works on a hypothetical problem in archeology in which she must discover which of 10 possible suspects is buried in a nameless ancient tomb.

You might be somewhat skeptical of this labeling and ask questions such as, "Does the boy have potential for a higher level of intellectual functioning than he is currently performing? What types of natural experiences would lead to the boy's reaching or not reaching his highest potential? If the boy missed many of the natural experiences needed for intellectual development, can instruction help him reach a higher level of intellectual functioning?"

These kinds of questions were addressed by Feuerstein (1979, 1980; Feuerstein, Jensen, Hoffman, & Rand, 1985), based on his work with special education adolescents in Israeli schools. First, if a student performs poorly on academic tasks, Feuerstein prefers to label that child a "retarded performer." Feuerstein found that it is useful to make a distinction between a child's manifested low level of functioning (i.e., retarded performance) and the child's actual potential for intellectual performance. He even developed a test called the *learning potential assessment device* (LPAD) to evaluate how much improvement he could expect for each retarded performer. Instead of being a static mental ability test, the LPAD presents the student with learning tasks and measures the amount of teacher intervention needed to help the student accomplish the tasks.

FIGURE 12–9 Effects of training in productive thinking on creativity

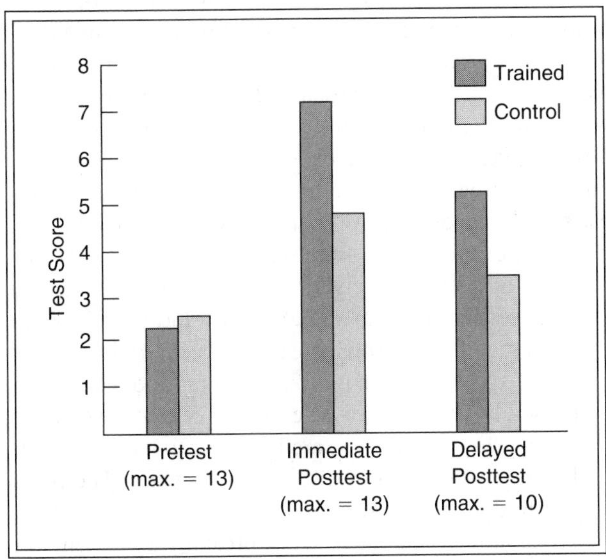

Adapted from Olton and Crutchfield (1969)

Second, Feuerstein noticed that students who have trouble learning in school often come from homes in which parents do not explain, discuss, or interpret events (including their culture) to their children. Feuerstein notes that such children are *mediationally deprived;* that is, the normal events in their lives do not seem to have any meaning or purpose, because no one provides any interpretation of them. Mediationally deprived students have trouble responding to new problems or new learning tasks. According to Feuerstein, these children have been denied exposure to what he calls *mediated learning experiences* (MLE). For example, in playing with a typewriter, a child can learn about cause and effect. A parent might say, "When you press the A key, it makes this metal strike the ink and print a letter A on the paper." As another example, a family trip to the beach can be the basis for learning to plan. A parent might say, "Bring your bucket and shovel in case you want to build sand castles." As another example (Feuerstein, 1980, p. 21), a parent can ask a child to go to the store: "Please buy three bottles of milk so that we will have some left over for tomorrow when the shops are closed." This example demonstrates the role of planning much more than the statement "Please buy three bottles of milk." In these examples of MLEs the parent helps interpret events so that the child can see the meaning or purpose or intentionality in the surrounding world.

Third, Feuerstein developed a program called *instrumental enrichment* (IE) that is intended to provide low-functioning students with the kinds of mediated learning experiences that children normally receive. To compensate for the inadequate MLEs of his students, he provides them with a series of problems—each one different—that serve as the basis for discussion and interpretation with an adult. Feuerstein's Instrumental Enrichment Program is recognized as "possibly the most widely used program for intellectual-skills training in the world" (Sternberg, 1991, p. x).

DESCRIPTION

Feuerstein's instructional enrichment (IE) program consists of a series of paper-and-pencil exercises for low-functioning adolescents. The program is intended to be administered as an adjunct to regular academic instruction; for example, IE could occur for 3 to 5 hours per week over a 2-year period, for a total of 200 to 300 hours. The tasks are organized into 15 instruments, with each instrument focusing on one or more cognitive skills.

Figure 12–10 gives an example exercise from the "Organization of Dots," the first instrument in the IE program. The student's job is to connect the dots so that they form the same shapes as in the model (i.e., two squares and a triangle). Each dot can be used only once, and each shape must be the same size as in the model. However, the drawn shapes can overlap and be in different orientations than the model shapes are. For each exercise, the teacher introduces the problem and allows for individual work on the problem. Then the class discusses methods for solving each problem and the teacher summarizes them. Thus, students get exposed to many novel problems and learn to compare their approach to the methods used by others. Because each problem is novel, the students cannot memorize answers. Exercises such as these are intended to teach students how to generate and evaluate problem representations and solution strategies. The problems are organized so that they increase in difficulty. According to Feuerstein, the Organization of Dots problems teach students the following cognitive skills: breaking a problem into parts, representing a problem, and thinking hypothetically. Other instruments focus on spatial orientation, temporal relations, family relations, numerical progressions, analytic perception, transitive relations, and syllogisms.

EVALUATION

Does the IE program help students to become better able to deal with new problems (i.e., to become better thinkers)? Feuerstein and his colleagues (1980; Feuerstein, 1979) report an evaluation study comparing adolescent special education students who received IE over a 2-year period with students who received the normal enrichment procedures. Both groups performed at the same level on pretests of cognitive skill, but after 2 years, the IE group scored higher on tests involving spatial and mathematical reasoning (i.e., tests of spatial relations, figure grouping, number, and addition). Follow-up studies on the same

FIGURE 12–10 Example exercises from the organization of dots

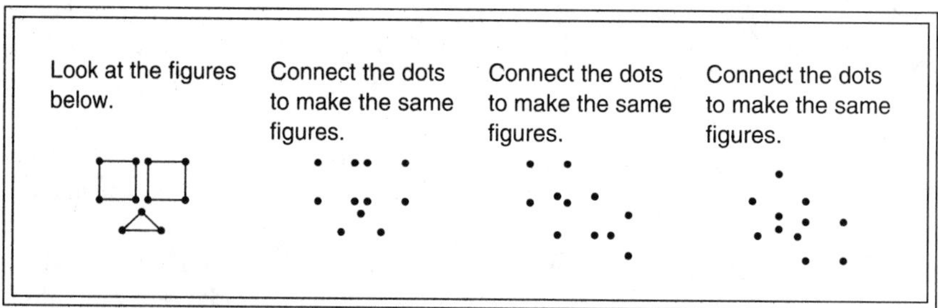

Adapted from Feuerstein (1980)

students 2 years later found the IE group still scored higher than the control group on tests of nonverbal intelligence.

Blagg (1991) conducted "arguably the most thorough and carefully planned evaluation of an intellectual-skills training program that has been done" (Sternberg, 1991, p. x). Low-achieving 14-year-old students from four schools in England received 2 to 2.5 hours of IE training per week, for an average of 112 hours over the course of the training. Overall, the IE training did not produce significant increases in general intelligence, reading skills, or mathematics skills, but teachers indicated that students became more active contributors to class discussions, more likely to defend their opinions on the basis of logical evidence, more able to describe different strategies for solving problems, and more likely to spontaneously read and follow instructions carefully. Even these positive changes, however, did not generalize to other subject areas; that is, they were not observed by other teachers. In a review of Blagg's study, Haywood (1992) pointed to flaws in the way that teachers were trained and supervised. Similarly, Kozulin and Presseisen (1995) provided evidence that "the amount of IE instruction, the quality of the mediation provided by the IE teacher, and the presence of special bridging exercises to content areas of curriculum constitute the decisive factors of success in IE implementation" (p. 73).

Feuerstein's program seems consistent with the four criteria for a successful program described in the preceding section. First, the program content focuses on a set of small cognitive tasks, mainly specific strategies for representing problems and planning solutions. Second, although the program appears to teach general problem-solving skills independent of subject matter area, the skills that are taught actually are quite specific and similar to tasks on nonverbal intelligence tests. Bransford, Arbitman-Smith, Stein, and Vye (1985) point out that "there is an emphasis on training students to solve certain types of problems so that they will be able to solve similar problems on their own within each instrument" (p. 201). However, Feuerstein does not assume that learning one instrument—that is, one kind of problem—will help a student learn another instrument that requires different cognitive skills. Instead, the IE program seems to be providing students with many specific subskills that, taken together, are useful for performance on tests of nonverbal intelligence. Third, the method involves lots of practice in modeling of the processes used by successful problem solvers. Fourth, the program does not wait until the learner has mastered all basic skills before attempting to teach higher-order skills.

PROJECT INTELLIGENCE

BACKGROUND

Consider the following scenario: The country you live in has decided to make a national commitment to improving the intellectual performance of its citizens. The nation's president has appointed you as the first Minister of State for the Development of Human Intelligence. What can you do to improve the people's problem-solving skills?

Although this may seem like an artificial problem, it was a real problem for Dr. Luis Alberta Machado, who was appointed in the 1980s to head the new Ministry for the

Development of Human Intelligence in the country of Venezuela, the first such ministry in the world. Minister Machado (1981) summarized the rationale for his ministry as follows:

> In the same way that investment of resources and political strategy are planned so should the different nations by means of a common effort, plan the attainment of a higher degree of intelligence in the least time possible by all mankind. . . . When the necessary means are organized to systematically improve the intelligence of all people, mankind will have taken the most important step towards progress. (pp. 3–4)

Similarly, Dominguez (1985) noted that "in Venezuela we are attempting to put these ideas about the modifiability of human intelligence to work in the service of mankind" (p. 531).

As part of his assignment, Dr. Machado enlisted a group from Harvard University, Bolt Beranek and Newman (a research and development company in Cambridge, Massachusetts), and the Venezuelan Ministry of Education to develop a one-year course in thinking skills for seventh-grade students in Venezuela. A primary goal of the course was "to raise the intelligence of participating Venezuelan seventh graders" (Martinez, 2000, p. 157), and the project was named "Project Intelligence." Importantly, the thinking skills course—named Odyssey—was to receive a rigorous, scientifically valid evaluation, a feature that is sometimes lacking in curriculum development efforts.

DESCRIPTION

Odyssey consists of one hundred 45-minute lessons, presented across six lesson series (or books)—*Foundations of Reasoning, Understanding Language, Verbal Learning, Problem Solving, Decision Making,* and *Inventive Thinking* (Adams, 1986, 1989). Within each lesson series, the lessons are arranged into units that share a similar theme—such as six lessons on classifying items based on their characteristics ("observation and classification"), five lessons on recognizing patterns in orderings ("ordering"), and four lessons on solving analogy problems ("analogies").

To ensure consistent classroom implementation, each lesson followed the same format based on suggested scripts, although "the scripts were not intended to be followed literally in class" (Nickerson, 1994, p. 857). For example, Figure 12–11 shows a problem and proposed teaching script for a lesson on sequences and change contained in the first book, *Foundations of Reasoning.* The lesson begins by the teacher leading a discussion on how to solve some sample problems. Then students are given an opportunity to solve some problems on their own. Finally, students are asked to explain their solutions to others. This lesson is intended to teach some fairly specific target skills, such as identifying which dimensions to pay attention to, distinguishing among various types of changes, and recognizing the next item in a sequence on the basis of previous changes in a given dimension. Adams (1989) noted that "the thrust of the course was to be conveyed through direct instruction modeled on the Socratic Inquiry Method . . . and capitalizing on structured discovery" (p. 70).

EVALUATION

Does a year's worth of Odyssey help students become better thinkers? In a well-controlled evaluation study (Herrnstein, Nickerson, Sanchez, & Swets, 1986; Nickerson, 1994), 463

FIGURE 12–11 An Odyssey lesson

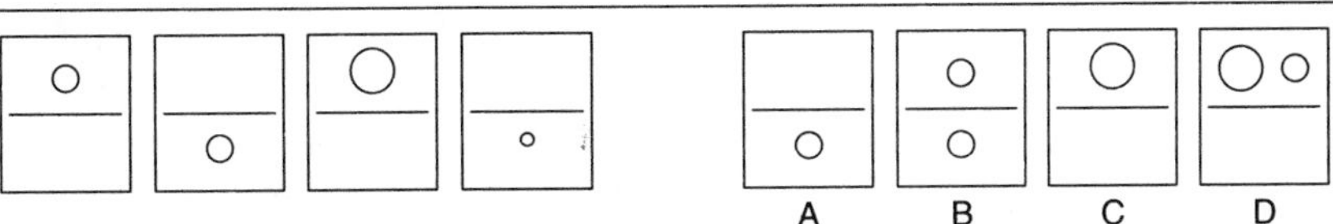

O [TEACHER]: Observe the first figure of row one. What does the first box in row one contain?
• [STUDENT]: A line with a circle above it.

O: Look at the second box. What does it contain?
•: The same line with a circle beneath it.

O: What change has taken place?
•: The position of the circle has changed from above the line to below the line.

O: Observe the third figure. How has it changed from the second?
•: The circle returned to the upper part, and it has become larger.

O: Look at the fourth figure. What has happened now?
•: The circle is again below the line, and it has become smaller.

O: Along how many dimensions have we observed changes? What are they?
•: Two. The circle has changed positions with respect to the line, from above to below, from below to above, and from above to below. The circle changed size in the third and fourth figures.

O: Yes. One of these changes occurred in all four of the figures, and one in only two. Which is the change that all of these figures share?
•: The change in the position of the circle.

O: Yes. And would you call the changes in the position of the circle alternating or progressive?
•: Alternating.

O: Yes. The circle moves from above to below to above, repeatedly, so it is an alternating sequence.

Adapted from Adams (1986)

seventh-grade students from six schools in Venezuela received 45-minute training sessions for four days per week over the course of an academic year (covering 56 lessons), whereas a matched control group did not receive any special training in thinking skills. Students in both groups were tested on a battery of cognitive tests before and after the course. Although both groups improved, the trained group improved more than twice as much as the control group on cognitive skills that were specifically targeted in the program, indicating the course was successful in teaching targeted thinking skills. Interestingly, the trained group also improved more than the control group on several intelligence tests, although the differences were much smaller (with the trained group showing improvements ranging from 21% to 68% more than the control group). Nickerson points out, "It was not feasible to obtain data in subsequent years" (p. 859), so it is not possible to know whether the effects of the program were long lasting. Overall, "Project Intelligence enhanced the magnitude of students' intelligent behavior and transferability to new and authentic tasks, at least in the short term" (Grotzer & Perkins, 2000, p. 496).

Project Intelligence, and its courseware "Odyssey," is offered as an exemplary success story in the teaching of thinking (Adams, 1989; Grotzer & Perkins, 2000; Martinez, 2000; Nickerson, 1994; Perkins & Grotzer, 1997). In short, it has earned its place among "an increasing number of studies [that] provide evidence that targeted attempts to teach people to think better can be worthwhile" (Perkins & Grotzer, 1997, p. 1126). As you can see, the course is consistent with the criteria for successful thinking skills programs: It targets a collection of component skills, the skills are taught within the specific context that students are expected to use them, teachers and students model and discuss the process of problem solving, and the higher-order skills are taught before all lower-level skills are mastered.

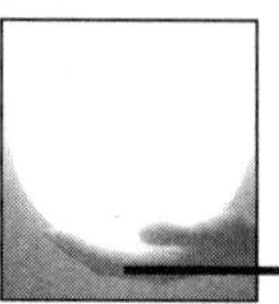

THE CASE FOR IMPROVING PROBLEM-SOLVING SKILLS INSTRUCTION

In the previous sections, you learned about three popular problem-solving courses that have been used in schools. Of course, many other problem-solving courses (Chance, 1986; Chipman, Segal, & Glaser 1985; Grotzer & Perkins, 2000; Martinez, 2000; Nickerson, Perkins, & Smith, 1985; Perkins & Grotzer, 1997; Segal, Chipman, & Glaser, 1985) are available, but these three courses are among the most carefully evaluated. How do the programs we have reviewed rate on the four criteria for an effective problem-solving program? Consistent with the criteria, each program focuses on a set of specific problem-solving skills, contextualizes the skills within tasks like those the learner is expected to perform, gives students practice in the process of problem solving (including modeling of good procedures), and teaches higher-order skills before students have mastered lower-level skills.

What is the place of general thinking skills courses? Given the importance of the issue, you might be surprised that there has not been more research on the cognitive consequences of thinking skills courses. Perhaps it is easier to develop and market thinking-skills courses than to determine whether they promote appropriate cognitive changes in learners. There is some reason for optimism, however, because each of the three courses we examined appear to be supported, at least under some circumstances, by solid evaluation results. Yet we are faced, in some respects, with a paradox. Although these problem-solving courses appear to deal with general thinking ability, they actually focus on a series of individual skills that help performance mainly on specific tasks like those used in the program. It follows that a more fruitful approach to the teaching of problem solving would be to identify target tasks required for success in school and then teach the cognitive processing skills required to succeed on those tasks. Embedding problem-solving instruction within specific courses makes good sense, given the domain-specificity of problem solving (Mayer, 1999), and is the approach taken in a new generation of successful programs. Thus, I presented these three classic programs only as examples to be examined rather than as a sort of endorsement. Instead, the future of problem-solving instruction seems to rest with subject-matter-specific programs, such as teaching students how to comprehend text through reciprocal teaching (Brown & Palinscar, 1989; Palinscar & Brown, 1984) as described in Chapter 13 or teaching students how to create and evaluate solution plans for complex mathematics problems presented via video (Bransford et al., 1996).

The new generation of thinking skills instruction is based on four guiding principles:

1. *Focus on a few well-defined skills.* Nebulous skills such as "improving intelligence" or "teaching thinking" must be recast as well-defined target skills such as "being able to identify an unclear sentence." For example, in the reciprocal teaching program, students learn four well-defined comprehension strategies: questioning, in which a student creates an appropriate question answered by the passage; clarifying, in which a student identifies a potentially confusing part of the passage; summarizing, in which a student produces a summary for a passage; and predicting, in which a student suggests what will occur next in the passage. Rather than try to improve students' "verbal comprehension skills" as a monolithic ability, the program seeks to teach a focused collection of effective strategies.
2. *Contextualize the skills within authentic tasks.* General skills such as "planning" must be recast within a specific context such as "planning an outline for writing an essay." For example, in the reciprocal teaching program, students work on authentic tasks, such as trying to make sense of actual text found in a classroom book. Rather than work on contrived exercises, students work on a real academic task.
3. *Personalize the skills through social interaction and language-based discussion of the process of problem solving.* Practice on getting the right answer must be recast as including discussion of the problem-solving process. For example, in the reciprocal teaching program, students work in discussion groups, taking turns playing the role of the teacher. They hear the teacher model how she or he goes about using a strategy. They get to try to describe their own cognitive processes and receive critiques from others. Rather than work alone at their seats, students engage in a community of learners working together to learn.
4. *Accelerate the skills so that students learn them along with lower-level skills.* The order of learning must be recast so that the focus is on learning to use both low- and high-order skills. For example, in the reciprocal teaching program, students learn high-order skills such as how to summarize at the same time they learn lower-order skills such as how to produce grammatically correct sentences. Rather than have to completely master sight-reading skills before learning comprehension skills, students are able to learn both kinds of skills together.

Where will the new generation of thinking skills instruction take us? Instead of relying solely on general problem-solving courses, every subject matter will incorporate teaching of relevant cognitive skills. Mayer (1999) shows how school subjects such as reading, writing, mathematics, and science can be analyzed into component cognitive processes that students can learn. Rather than seek to improve scores on intelligence tests, the goal is to help students develop cognitive skills they need to excel on real academic tasks ranging from comprehending a passage to writing an essay to solving a mathematical business problem to testing a scientific theory.

Let's return for a moment to the thorny problem of Project Head Start—perhaps, the world's boldest experiment in improving human cognition. Overall, research shows that students who receive experience in Head Start score higher on intelligence tests than matched control students immediately after instruction, but the IQ advantage fades away after one or two years (Martinez, 2000; Zigler & Muenchow, 1992). In short, the program appears to be successful in promoting cognitive change, but the cognitive effects are not long-lived. How can this be explained? First, the content of Head Start programs is sometimes not well-defined. Research on teaching thinking shows that the most successful programs begin with a small collection of well-defined skills. Second, the instructional methods used in Head Start may not be consistent with the project goals. Research on teaching thinking skills shows the advantages of helping students discuss the process of problem solving. Third, the assessment of Head Start programs is closely tied to IQ gains, but research on teaching thinking skills shows that improvements occur mainly in the specific domains that were taught. Finally, Head Start represents a fairly short-term experience involving only a small part of the child's life. Yet the teaching of appropriate cognitive skills requires a broad, long-term commitment. The most important lesson of Project Head Start is that the teaching of cognitive skills—including problem-solving strategies—requires an effective and continuing instructional program.

CHAPTER SUMMARY

This chapter investigated techniques for teaching students how to think. Four important issues for designing instruction in thinking skills are (1) what to teach (i.e., is problem solving a single ability or many component skills?), (2) where to teach (i.e., should problem solving be a separate course or be integrated into specific subjects?), (3) how to teach (i.e., should students practice giving the right answers for problems or discuss the process of solving problems?), and (4) when to teach (i.e., should students master lower-order skills before learning higher-order skills?). Historically, schools began by teaching thinking as if it were a single ability; however, systematic research seems to show that problem-solving training is most effective when the material to be taught consists of a collection of well-defined component skills. Historically, schools have taught thinking skills independent of subject matter domains in hopes that such skills would transfer to many situations; however, systematic research shows that students tend to learn specific skills that can be applied mainly in the same kinds of contexts as the examples used during instruction. Historically, schools began with attempts to teach thinking skills through drill-and-practice in applying rules; however, systematic research suggests that students also profit from generating and analyzing worked-out examples and comparing their own solution processes to those of experts. Historically, schools began by insisting that basic skills be mastered before high-order skills were taught; however, systematic research shows that high-order skills can be learned along with lower-level ones.

This chapter reviewed three popular problem-solving courses—the Productive Thinking Program, Instrumental Enrichment, and Project Intelligence. All share a focus on individual skills (rather than general ability), being more effective on tests of specific transfer (rather than general transfer), teaching the process of problem solving (rather than focusing on product), and teaching higher-order skills before lower-level skills are mastered (rather than after).

The new generation of thinking skills instruction builds on these principles, and is exemplified by reciprocal teaching of comprehension strategies as described in Chapter 13.

SUGGESTED READINGS

Adams, M. J. (1989). Thinking skills curricula: Their promise and progress. *Educational Psychologist, 24*, 24–77. (Describes problem-solving courses.)

Halpern, D. F. (Ed.). (1992). *Enhancing thinking skills in the sciences and mathematics.* Hillsdale, NJ: Erlbaum. (Describes research on teaching of thinking skills.)

Martinez, M. E. (2000). *Education as the cultivation of intelligence.* Mahwah, NJ: Erlbaum. (Calls for the teaching of thinking skills.)

Perkins, D. N., & Grotzer, T. A. (1997). Teaching intelligence. *American Psychologist, 52*, 1125–1133. (Describes problem-solving courses.)

Teaching by Creating Cognitive Apprenticeship in Classrooms

CHAPTER OUTLINE

Introduction

Learning In and Out of School

Traditional and Cognitive Apprenticeship

Reciprocal Teaching

Cooperative Learning

Participatory Modeling

Chapter Summary

Throughout human history people have learned through various forms of apprenticeship in which they participated on authentic tasks under the supervision of more-experienced mentors. This chapter explores the idea that academic learning can be seen as a sort of cognitive apprenticeship in which students and teachers work together to master authentic academic tasks. In particular, the chapter lays out the case for cognitive apprenticeship and then examines three ways of implementing cognitive apprenticeship in classrooms: reciprocal teaching, cooperative learning, and participatory modeling. Within each approach, I search for how the social context of learning can promote deep understanding in learners.

INTRODUCTION

Imagine that you are in a mathematics classroom. The teacher writes the following problem on the chalkboard:

$$\frac{3}{4} \times \frac{2}{3} =$$

She asks, "Who can tell me how to find three-fourths times two-thirds?" She calls on Sarah, who walks to the board and completes the problem as follows:

$$\frac{3}{4} \times \frac{2}{3} = \frac{6}{12} = \frac{1}{2}$$

As she writes, Sarah says: "Three times two is six; four times three is twelve. Six twelfths is one half." This episode is summarized on the left side of Figure 13–1.

Now let's leave the world of school mathematics and enter Sarah's kitchen. She is on a diet that allows her to have only a certain number of portions of various food categories each day. Sarah is ready for a snack consisting of cottage cheese. In her diet program, a portion of cottage cheese is 2/3 cup. However, because she has already done some snacking today, her diet plan allows her to have only 3/4 of her portion of cottage cheese. Thus, she needs to figure out how to get three fourths of two thirds of a cup of cottage cheese.

FIGURE 13–1 How do you get 3/4 of 2/3 cup of cottage cheese?

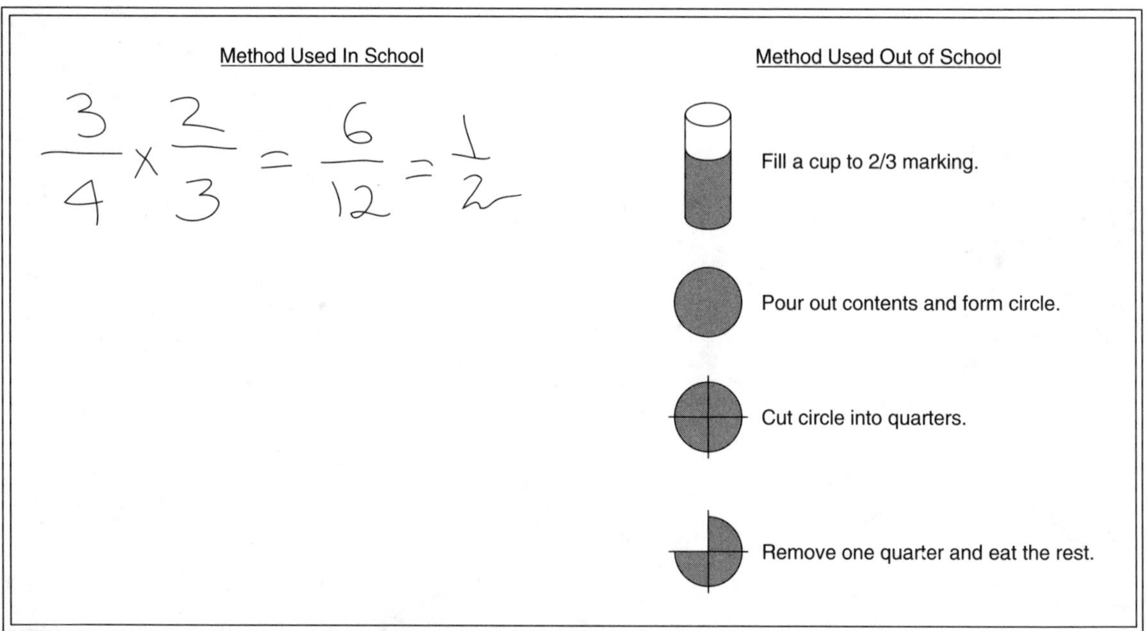

Sarah goes to the refrigerator, takes out a container of cottage cheese, pours it into a measuring cup until it reaches the 2/3-cup level. She then empties the contents of the measuring cup onto a cutting board, shapes it into a circle, and with a knife cuts it into quarters. She removes one quarter, placing it back in the container of cottage cheese, and then puts the rest in a bowl to eat. This episode is summarized on the right side of Figure 13–1.

These two episodes represent how people solve problems in school and outside of school. In the school-based example, the problem solver engages in what can be called *symbol manipulation*—she applies the school-taught algorithm of multiplying the numerators, multiplying the denominators, and reducing the resulting fraction. In the real-world example, the problem solver uses a more intuitive procedure that is unlikely to have been taught in school.

According to research by Lave (1988) and Nunes, Schliemann, and Carraher (1993), people are likely to use formal mathematical procedures for problems encountered in school and informal mathematical procedures for equivalent problems encountered outside of school. For example, Lave reports that when the cottage cheese problem was encountered by a Weight Watchers dieter in his kitchen, he used the procedure described on the right side of Figure 13–1 and "at no time did the Weight Watchers dieter check his procedure against a paper and pencil algorithm" (p. 165) such as shown on the left side of Figure 13–1.

These examples help to distinguish two views of the generality of learning. According to the classic view of learning, students abstract a general procedure from instruction and apply it across a wide variety of problems. Such a view would predict that people would use a school-taught procedure to solve the cottage cheese problem. In contrast, the situated view of learning is that students acquire a specific procedure based on the context in which it was encountered and are able to use it mainly within that context. The cottage cheese example supports a theory of *situated learning*—the idea that learning is shaped by and depends on the situation in which it takes place, including the social and cultural context of learning. An important challenge for educators is to create the kinds of social contexts that foster meaningful learning—that is, being able to use what is learned to solve new problems in new situations.

An interest in the social context of learning has encouraged many educators to examine the classic work of the Russian psychologist Lev Vygotsky (1978; Wertsch, 1985), who developed one of the first theories of learning in social context. For example, consider a situation in which an elementary school class is discussing the story "Freddie Finds a Frog" (Tharp & Gallimore, 1988). In the story, Freddie shows his newly found frog to Mr. Mays. Mr. Mays suggests that he might like to take Freddie's frog fishing. This grisly proposal upsets Freddie. The teacher notices that none of children understand the double meaning of Mr. Mays's proposal to take the frog fishing or why it upset Freddie. In the dialogue that follows, the teacher assists the children in making sense out of Mr. Mays's joke (Tharp & Gallimore, 1988, p. 19):

TEACHER: What did Mr. Mays say he would do with the frog?
LON: He would take . . .
MELE: . . . water, um fishing.
TEACHER: Do frogs like to go fishing? [The children give several opinions—Frogs don't like water, don't like flies, don't like fish.]

BILL: They use for da bait.

TEACHER: If you use it for bait, what do you have to do to the frog? [The children give several opinions, including one explanation of disgust.]

ALICE: Put it on a hook.

This instructional episode demonstrates two important aspects of Vygotsky's theory—that learning occurs in a social context and that learning occurs within a child's zone of proximal development. Vygotsky's (1978) theory emphasizes the role of social collaboration in the development of new skills: "Human learning presupposes a specific social nature and a process by which children grow into the intellectual life of those around them" (p. 88). Vygotsky proclaims the essential role of social collaboration in learning: "Learning awakens a variety of internal developmental processes that are able to operate only when the child is interacting with people in his environment and in cooperation with his peers" (p. 90).

The social context of learning is reflected in the way that the students and teacher jointly try to make sense of the story; by discussing the story, under the guidance of the teacher, the students participate in a sort of collective sense making. In the process, they are learning reading comprehension strategies that will serve them in the future. Vygotsky (1978) refers to this process as *internalization*—"internal reconstruction of an external operation" (p. 56). In this case, each student learns strategies for how to make sense of text passages based on working on this task with a more skilled reader.

The zone of proximal development (ZPD) refers to the difference between the child's current level of performance and the level of performance that the child could attain with expert guidance. Vygotsky (1978) defines the ZPD as "the distance between the actual developmental level as determined by individual problem solving and the level of potential development as determined through problem solving under adult guidance in collaboration with more capable peers" (p. 86).

For example, the children reading "Freddie Finds a Frog" do not perform well in understanding the double meaning of Mr. Mays's joke, but with assistance from the teacher, they are able to do so. Thus, comprehension of the double meaning of a joke is within the children's zone of proximal development. According to Vygotsky (quoted in Wertsch & Stone, 1985), instruction is effective "when it proceeds ahead of development" so that it "awakens and rouses to life those functions which are in a stage of maturing, which lie in the zone of proximal development." In this example, the teacher focuses on helping children move from their current level to their potential level of reading comprehension performance.

The role of teacher, according to this Vygotskian view, is that of someone who provides assistance to students who are engaged in a cognitive task. Tharp and Gallimore (1988) propose a redefinition of teaching: "Teaching must be redefined as assisted performance. Teaching consists in assisting performance. Teaching occurs when performance is achieved with assistance" (p. 21). Importantly, Tharp and Gallimore (1988) note that assistance should be gauged to the student's needs: "Teaching consists in assisting performance through the zone of proximal development. Teaching can be said to occur when assistance is offered at points in the zone of proximal development at which performance requires assistance" (p. 31). Similarly, students may be seen as apprentices—learning to perform intellectually like the expert members of their societies.

Although Vygotsky's theory offers many provocative implications for education, it is wise to ask whether his claims can be substantiated. Because he worked in Russia in the years following the Russian Revolution through his death in 1934, and because he aimed to develop a Marxist theory of human intellectual functioning, Vygotsky's standards of scientific research differed from those prevailing in much of the rest of Europe and the Americas. Cole and Scribner (1978) offer the following methodological critique:

> Vygotsky's references . . . to experiments conducted in his laboratory sometimes leave readers with a sense of unease. He presents almost no raw data and summaries are quite general. Where are the statistical tests that record whether or not observations reflect real effects? . . . Those steeped in the methodology of experimental psychology as practiced in most American laboratories may . . . consider [Vygotsky's research] to be little more than interesting demonstrations or pilot studies. (p. 11).

Regrettably, selected portions of classroom transcripts, such as the instructional sequence involving "Freddie Finds a Frog," also fail to yield the kind of convincing evidence that many scientists would require. Yet in spite of the scientific shortcomings of Vygotsky's theory, his ideas are simply too intriguing to ignore.

Modern research on apprenticeship, in the tradition of Vygotsky, offers some potential benefits and costs to educational psychology. On the positive side, broadening our conceptions of acceptable educational practices and educational research frees us from what Lave (1988) calls "the claustrophobic view of cognition from inside the laboratory and school" (p. 1). Research in which learners are observed in natural situations can provide important information that traditional experimental methods cannot. On the negative side, ethnographic studies of how people behave in natural settings may be difficult to interpret because different observers may see different things in viewing the same situation. Sternberg (1990) observed that it has "often been difficult to draw conclusions from the research. . . . One can read into the research almost whatever one wishes" (p. 16). A complete theory of learning and instruction is likely to depend on both experimental and observational data.

What is the role of apprenticeship in promoting meaningful learning? Rather than building educational practice solely on the pronouncements of experts—however interesting the ideas might be—the approach I take in this book is to search for methods of teaching for meaningful learning that are based on scientific research. Extreme views, such as the idea that all learning can take place only in a social context, are probably not testable in scientific research and ultimately are probably not very productive stances. Instead, let's focus on the intriguing idea that some educational practices can be improved by making better use of the social context of learning.

This chapter examines the idea that meaningful learning can take place in an apprenticeship context and samples the research literature testing this idea. In particular, it explores the distinction between formal and informal learning, focuses on apprenticeship as the major instructional technique used in informal learning situations, and examines three versions of cognitive apprenticeship applied to classroom learning: reciprocal teaching, cooperative learning, and participatory modeling.

LEARNING IN AND OUT OF SCHOOL

Suppose we took the brightest students from a community, treated them to the best schooling available, and returned these star pupils to serve their community. Sometimes learning in schools does not match the needs of students out of school. For example, when the Indians of the Five Nations were invited in 1744 by the commissioners from Virginia to send boys to the College of William and Mary, they politely refused on the following grounds:

> Several of our young people were formerly brought up at the colleges of the northern provinces; they were instructed in all your sciences; but when they came back to us . . . [they were] ignorant of every means of living in the woods . . . neither fit for hunters, warriors, or counselors; they were totally good for nothing. (Drake, 1934, as cited in Rogoff, 1990, p. 42)

This example points to the importance of considering the cultural context of schooling.

As a more modern example, consider the plight of successful school students in rural Zambia who experience a kind of "alienation between the process of schooling and the mainstream of local culture" (Serpell, 1993, p. 138). One local official observed: "Here in the village we have our traditional wisdom, and it's the wisdom of life here in the village. In school there is another kind of wisdom, the wisdom of the nation" (p. 136). Success in the village requires learning the traditional cultural values as well as skills needed for local agriculture and health care. In contrast, "the form in which the Western educational tradition has been institutionalized in Zambia's system of primary schooling is often dysfunctional in its consequences for the young people who enroll in it as well as for the rural communities it purports to serve" (p. 246). According to Serpell, Zambian schools are based on a Western conception of development so that successful students become part of a "culture that came from outside—a culture which is tied to—the white-man's way of life" (p. 137). Educated students are expected to move out of the rural villages to the city, where they lose a sense of membership in their original communities. "Sending me to school, I have to be a bwana [colonial master]," says one of Serpell's most successful subjects, adding, "You have to be a muzungu [someone with the cultural values of Europeans]" (p. 185).

Echoes of the same dilemma can be heard in the complaints of students in Western cultures: "Why do I have to learn this?" says a student in a math class. "I know I'll never use it in real life." Is there any truth to this common complaint about the irrelevance of schooling? To help answer this question, let's examine the relation between learning in and out of school.

Suppose that a student is given the problem 750 ÷ 5 = _____ as part of an exercise in a math classroom. Based on her schooling in arithmetic, she might produce an answer using the procedure shown in the left side of Figure 13–2. She begins by putting the problem in the proper format, then carries out each step in the division procedure. We would all probably be pleased because the student has mastered an important mathematical skill that will serve her well in the future. We could say that she has demonstrated competence in *school mathematics*—the formal procedures taught in mathematics classrooms.

FIGURE 13–2 School and street mathematics

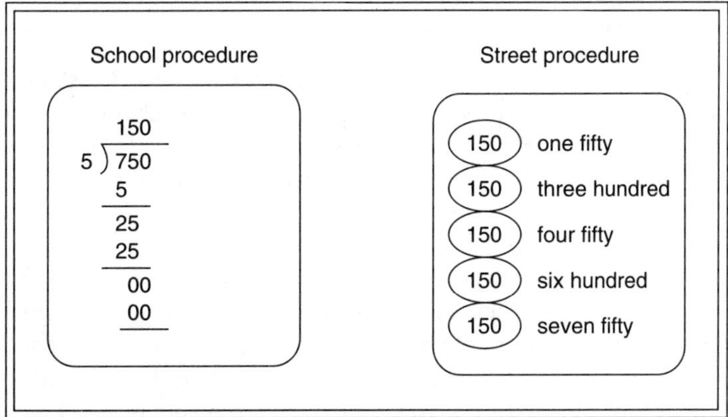

In contrast, consider the procedure used by an uneducated oyster fisher who has just learned that oysters are selling at 5 for 750:

> I don't know these things; I didn't go to school. I know about oysters because we fish; the price of oysters we have to know. If they're selling 5 oysters at 750, then they're selling each one at 150. (Nunes, Schliemann, & Carraher, 1993, p. 15)

Although her lack of formal education would make it difficult for her to solve the problem 750 ÷ 5 = _____, she was readily able to compute the answer when the problem occurred within the context of her job as an oyster fisher. Like many people around the world, she successfully uses mathematical techniques that she did not learn in school (as summarized in the right side of Figure 13–2). This is an example of *street mathematics*—the informal procedures that people use in the context of everyday life.

What are the similarities and differences between formal and informal mathematics? What happens when school mathematics and street mathematics exist within the same person? Do people use school-taught procedures when confronted with a problem in school and non-school-taught procedures when confronted with an analogous problem outside of school? These kinds of questions were addressed in a research program by Nunes et al. (1993).

One study examined the mathematical competence of five children, ages 9 to 15, who worked as street vendors in the Brazilian city of Recife. Most had received some schooling, including classroom instruction in basic arithmetic and word problems, and all were experienced street vendors. First, an informal test was administered to assess each child's competence in street mathematics. The experimenter visited the child's stand at a street corner or an open market and asked to purchase a certain number of some item. For example, in the following transcript, the experimenter (referred to as "customer") asks to buy 10 coconuts that cost 35 each:

CUSTOMER: How much is one coconut?
M: Thirty-five.
CUSTOMER: I'd like ten. How much is that?

M: [Pause] Three will be one hundred and five; with three more, that will be two hundred and ten. [Pause] I need four more. That is . . . [Pause] three hundred and fifteen . . . I think it is three hundred and fifty.

As you can see, the child correctly computes that 10 times 35 is 350. However, the child doesn't use the procedure taught in Brazilian schools of simply placing a zero to the right of any number that is being multiplied by 10. Instead, the child converts multiplication into repeated addition by threes—105 + 105 + 105 + 35. Another example of street vendor performance on the informal test is shown in the top of Figure 13–3.

In the same study, children were given a formal test designed to test each child's competence in school mathematics. Each child received paper and pencil, and then the experimenter dictated a series of arithmetic problems and word problems using the same arithmetic operations as in the informal test. For example, an arithmetic problem based on the coconut problem is "105 + 105," and a word problem is "Mary bought 10 bananas; each banana cost 35; how much did she pay altogether?" An example of street vendor performance on formal problems is shown in the bottom of Figure 13–3.

Figure 13–4 shows the overall percentage correct on equivalent arithmetic problems that occur in verbal form in everyday life (on the informal test) and in school-like form as word problems and symbol problems. As you can see, the street vendors were nearly errorless in computing answers to arithmetic problems in the street but performed much more poorly when equivalent problems were presented in school-like form. In short, children who are "capable of solving a computational problem in the natural situation" often "fail to solve the same problem when it is taken out of context" (Nunes et al., 1993, p. 23).

FIGURE 13–3

How young street vendors perform on informal and formal tests of mathematics

Performance by MD, a 9-year-old street vendor, on two problems.

MD performed errorlessly on all informal test items but correctly solved only 10% of the computation problems presented on the formal test.

Informal test

Customer: OK, I'll take three coconuts [at a price of 40 each]. How much is that?

Child: [Without gestures, calculates out loud] Forty, eighty, one twenty.

Formal test

Child solves the item

$$\begin{array}{r} 40 \\ \underline{\times\ 30} \end{array}$$

and obtains 70 as the answer.

She then explains the procedure: "Lower the zero; four and three is seven."

Adapted from Nunes, Schliemann, and Carraher (1993)

FIGURE 13–4 Percent correct on informal and formal tests by young street vendors

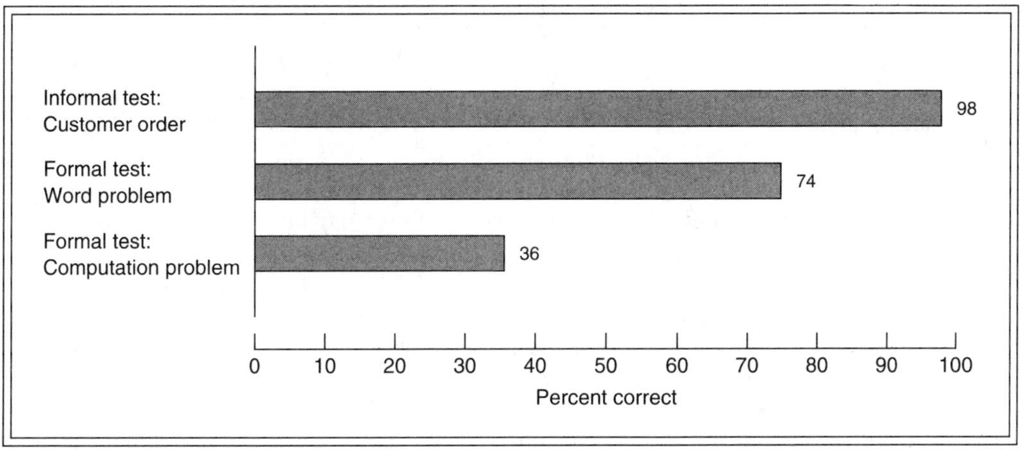

Adapted from Nunes, Schliemann, and Carraher (1993)

What can we conclude from studies of Brazilian street vendors? These results demonstrate that "daily problem solving may be accomplished by routines different from those taught in schools" (Nunes et al., 1993, p. 26). In spite of the fact that the children in this study had received formal instruction in arithmetic computational procedures, they invented their own procedures to solve computational problems in the context of their roles as street vendors. Although they had difficulty in correctly applying school-taught procedures in a formal school-like context, they were highly successful in applying their own invented procedures in an informal everyday context. These findings "raise doubts about the pedagogical practice of teaching children how to solve mathematical operations simply with numbers" (p. 25) and point to the role of cultural context in learning. In short, there is some support for students' claims that they do not use school-taught math outside of school.

This line of research has important implications for teaching that is intended to promote transfer. The major finding is that students often fail to transfer what they learned in school to problems outside of the school setting and often fail to transfer what they learned outside of school to solving problems in school. Thus, these findings indicate a need to teach in ways that promote transfer—that is, ways that help students be able to use what they learned in school when they are confronted with problems outside of school.

TRADITIONAL AND COGNITIVE APPRENTICESHIP

Research on formal and informal learning raises important questions about the nature of schooling. Why is it that people can learn so well in the context of their everyday lives but often fail to learn within the context of schools? How can schools be changed to incorporate the positive features of natural learning outside of schools? Or as Serpell (1993) asks,

"Given that education can and does take place informally in the context of everyday life, why was it felt at a certain point in history that a more explicit, deliberately instructive set of activities should be introduced in the form of schooling?" (p. 82).

Let's compare how people learn new skills, such as arithmetic, in school and outside of school. In schools, cognitive skills are taught as general and abstract procedures that are separate from everyday life; for example, since arithmetic is taught as symbol manipulation, students learn general procedures for how to carry out arithmetic operations on numerical symbols. In everyday environments, cognitive skills are learned as concrete and specific procedures that fit in the context of everyday life; for example, in computing prices, street vendors invent repeated addition as a way of carrying out multiplication.

Advocates for incorporating apprenticeship techniques into schools base their arguments on evidence that apprenticeship is a successful method of instruction that emerged in societies around the world over the course of human history (Lave & Wenger, 1991; Rogoff, 1990). In a recent review, Lave and Wenger (1991) describe apprenticeship programs ranging from Yucatec Mayan midwives in Mexico to Vai and Gola tailors in Liberia. Without tests or classrooms or lectures, a Mayan girl in Mexico eventually learns how be a midwife responsible for overseeing childbirth in her community, and a Vai worker in Liberia learns how to be a tailor who can produce ready-to-wear garments.

For example, Jordan (1989, as cited in Lave & Wenger, 1991, pp. 68–69) describes the apprenticeship of Yucatec midwives:

> Apprenticeship happens as a way of, and in the course of, daily life. It may not be recognized as a teaching effort at all. A Mayan girl who eventually becomes a midwife most likely has a mother or grandmother who is a midwife, since midwifery is handed down in family lines. . . . Girls in such families, without being identified as apprentice midwives, absorb the essence of midwifery practice as well as specific knowledge about many procedures, simply in the process of growing up. They know what the life of a midwife is like (for example, that she needs to go out at all hours of the day or night), what kinds of stories the women and men who come to consult her tell, what kinds of herbs and other remedies need to be collected, and the like. As young children they might be sitting quietly in a corner as their mother administers a prenatal massage; they would hear stories of difficult cases, of miraculous outcomes, and the like. As they grow older, they may be passing messages, running errands, getting needed supplies. A young girl might be present as her mother stops for a postpartum visit after the daily shopping trip to the market. Eventually, after she has had a child herself, she might come along to a birth, perhaps because her ailing grandmother needs someone to walk with, and thus find herself doing for the woman in labor what other women had done for her when she gave birth; that is, she may take a turn . . . at supporting the laboring woman. . . . Eventually, she may even administer prenatal massages to selected clients. At some point she may decide that she actually wants to do this kind of work. She then pays more attention, but only rarely does she ask questions. As time goes on, the apprentice takes over more and more of the work load, starting with the routine and tedious parts, and ending with what is in Yucatan the culturally most significant, the birth of the placenta. (pp. 932–934)

In this form of apprenticeship, work and learning are inseparable. Thus, there is no need to provide formal training that is distinct from the real world.

Lave and Wenger (1991) also summarize a study of an apprenticeship program for tailors in Liberia:

> Apprenticeship, averaging five years, involved a sustained, rich structure of opportunities to observe masters, journeymen, and other apprentices at work, to observe frequently the full process of producing garments, and of course, the finished products. . . . Apprentices first learn to make hats and drawers, informal and intimate garments for children. They move on to more external, formal garments, ending with the Higher Heights suit. . . . Learning processes do not merely reproduce the sequence of production processes. In fact, production steps are reversed, as apprentices begin by learning the finishing stages of producing a garment, go on to learn to sew it, and only later learn to cut it out. . . . The learning of each operation is subdivided into phases I have dubbed "way in" and "practice." Way in refers to the period of observation and attempts to construct a first approximation of the garment. . . . [In] the practice phase apprentices reproduce a production segment from beginning to end. (pp. 71–72)

In these examples, people learn not by being instructed but by participating in what Lave and Wenger call "a community of practice"—a group of people working on the same tasks. Whether the apprenticeship is implicit as with Yucatec midwives or more explicit as with Vai and Gola tailors, the apprentice must be accepted as what Lave and Wenger call *a legitimate peripheral participant*—someone who is allowed to be a member of a community of practice under the guidance of those who are more knowledgeable. For example, Lave and Wenger (1991) observe that "children are, after all, quintessentially legitimate peripheral participants in adult social worlds" (p. 32). Finally, apprentices engage in what Lave and Wenger call *situated learning activity*—working on real tasks within a community of practice. In short, observational studies of apprenticeship in various cultures suggest a broader conception of how people learn, including the idea that people can learn as participants on real tasks within a social context.

Although studies of successful apprenticeship programs encourage a broader view of acceptable educational practice, they do not provide a ready-made blueprint for how to reform schooling. How can the techniques of naturally occurring apprenticeship in informal learning situations be applied to the formal learning situations found in schools? The first step is a change in the way that students, teachers, and classes are viewed. By infusing apprenticeship principles into schools, the students become cognitive apprentices within the classroom, teachers (and highly able students) become master learners within the classroom, and classes are transformed into the communities of practice working together to master academic tasks.

Collins, Brown, and Newman (1989) point to the proven role of apprenticeship as an instructional vehicle:

> Only in the last century, and only in industrialized nations, has formal schooling emerged as a widespread method of educating the young. Before schools appeared, apprenticeship was the most common means of learning and was used to transmit the knowledge required for expert practice in fields from painting and sculpturing to medicine and law. (p. 453)

The goal of cognitive apprenticeship is to help students learn the cognitive "processes that experts use to handle complex tasks" (p. 457) through guided experience on intellectual tasks. In spite of its apparent effectiveness in informal learning situations, "apprenticeship as a form for producing knowledgeably skilled persons has been overlooked" (Lave & Wenger, 1991, p. 62) in modern schooling.

Although cognitive and traditional apprenticeship both rely on guided practice as an effective instructional method, cognitive apprenticeship differs from traditional apprenticeship in several ways. First, cognitive apprenticeship takes place within a formal instructional setting—a school, a training program, a computer simulation—whereas traditional apprenticeship occurs within the context of everyday life or work. Second, cognitive apprenticeship emphasizes learning cognitive skills, whereas traditional apprenticeship seems to emphasize physical practical skills.

Three core methods in cognitive apprenticeship are modeling, coaching, and scaffolding (Collins et al., 1989). *Modeling* occurs when a teacher describes her or his cognitive processing in the course of carrying out a task. For example, in modeling of reading comprehension strategies, a teacher might read "aloud in one voice while verbalizing her thought process (e.g., making and testing hypotheses about what the text means, . . . what she thinks will happen next, and so on) in another voice" (p. 481).

Coaching occurs when a teacher offers hints, comments, and critiques to a student who is carrying out a task. For example, in coaching for reading comprehension strategies, a teacher might "choose texts with interesting difficulties, might remind the student that a summary needs to integrate the whole text into a sentence or two, might suggest how to start constructing a summary, might evaluate the summary a student produces . . . or ask another student to evaluate it" (Collins et al., 1989, p. 482).

Scaffolding is needed when a student is working on a task but is not yet able to successfully manage each part without some kind of support. Scaffolding refers to the teacher's performing those parts of a task that a student is not able to accomplish unaided. The teacher must be able to diagnose when a student needs support and know when to gradually remove support. For example, in teaching of reading comprehension strategies, a teacher may provide support to a student who fails to correctly summarize a text by modeling how she or he would summarize it.

The techniques of modeling, coaching, and scaffolding can be found in the three examples of cognitive apprenticeship described in each of the following three sections of this chapter: reciprocal teaching, cooperative learning, and participatory modeling.

RECIPROCAL TEACHING

One way of learning as an apprentice within a group of learners is through *reciprocal teaching*—an instructional technique in which students and teacher take turns leading a dialogue about strategies for how to study some material (Brown & Palinscar, 1989; Palinscar & Brown, 1984). Reciprocal teaching takes place in learning groups consisting of a teacher and one or more students. The goal of each instructional episode is for the group to study a text passage using a variety of reading comprehension strategies. Teacher and students take turns as discussion leaders, although the teacher provides comments, feedback, and hints as needed.

Suppose, for example, that the goal of a unit in a seventh-grade English course is to help students improve their reading comprehension skills. In particular, suppose that we want students to learn to use four widely acclaimed reading comprehension strategies—*questioning,* in which a student generates an appropriate question for a passage; *clarifying,* in which a student detects and corrects any potential comprehension difficulties, such as definitions of unfamiliar words; *summarizing,* in which a student produces a concise summary for a passage; and *predicting,* in which a student suggests what will occur in subsequent text. In typical classroom practice, the teacher may model each of these strategies for students (i.e., modeling method) or may describe each strategy and ask students to apply them in workbook exercises (i.e., direct instruction method). In contrast, in reciprocal teaching, the students get a chance to teach these strategies to the group. In short, the teacher and student reciprocate—the one who was instructed takes the role of teacher, and the one who instructed takes the role of student.

In reciprocal teaching, we begin with a teacher and a group of students who jointly are trying to make sense out of a paragraph, such as the text about crows in Figure 13–5. The participants engage in a structured discussion in which the discussion leader models the cognitive strategies of questioning, clarifying, summarizing, and predicting. At first, the teacher leads the discussion by generating a question about the text, summarizing the gist of the text, clarifying any comprehension problems, and making predictions about subsequent text. When disagreements arise, all participants reread the text and discuss options until consensus is reached. So far, this procedure is much like the strategy training programs discussed in Chapters 11 and 12. However, in reciprocal teaching, the teacher eventually turns over the job of discussion leader to the students, such as Chantel (identified as S1) in Figure 13–5. When a student leads the discussion, the teacher periodically provides guidance on exercising cognitive strategies, such as how to ask appropriate questions or how to generate good summaries. The teacher prompts the student discussion leader, offers critiques, and generally provides support that enables the student to proceed. As the students become more proficient, the teacher reduces the amount of direction and feedback. The teaching dialogue in Figure 13–5 provides an example of reciprocal teaching in action.

Does reciprocal teaching work? To answer this question, Brown and Palinscar (1989) compared four groups of junior high school students who had reading problems. Students in the reciprocal teaching group took turns with the teacher in leading discussions about applying the four reading comprehension strategies; students in the modeling group observed the teacher as she modeled how to apply each of the four comprehension strategies to example paragraphs; students in the explicit teaching group listened to the teacher's description of each strategy and completed paper-and-pencil exercises; and students in the control group received no information about the four strategies. All students received 12 sessions of group instruction along with regular tests of reading comprehension. Figure 13–6 shows the average scores of each group on a pretest and posttest of reading comprehension. As you can see, all groups begin at a level between 40% and 50% correct; however, the reciprocal teaching group shows the largest gain. In a similar study, the reciprocal teaching students showed a 20-month pretest-to-posttest gain on a standardized test of reading comprehension, whereas the control group showed a 1-month gain (Palinscar & Brown, 1984). In addition, Brown and Palinscar (1989) report that the improvements of the reciprocal teaching group are still strong when students are tested 2 or 6 months later.

Why does reciprocal teaching work? The procedure combines several powerful techniques involving the what, where, and who of learning. First, what is learned are cognitive strategies for reading comprehension rather than specific facts and procedures. That is, the

FIGURE 13–5

An example of reciprocal teaching

Text from which students are working:

Crows have another gift. They are great mimics. They can learn to talk and imitate animal sounds. Some have been known to learn 100 words, and even whole phrases. They can imitate the squawk of a chicken, the whine of a dog, or the meow of a cat.

Games have a certain fascination to crows. In a game of hide-and-seek, a crow hides in the hollow of a tree and then sounds a distress caw. The others rush to the spot, look around, then flap away. This may be done over and over, after which the young crow pops out of its hiding place and caws gleefully. Far from being annoyed at this, the flock bursts into loud cawing themselves. They seem to like the trick that has been played on them.

T: Chantel, you're our teacher, right? Why don't you summarize first? Remember, just tell me the most important parts.

S1: Crows have a hundred words they can learn by imitation. They can imitate chickens, the whine of a dog, and cats.

T: Okay. We can shorten that summary a bit.

S2: You could say they can imitate other animals.

T: Oh! Good one! There's a list there, Chantel, did you notice that? It says they can imitate the squawk of a chicken, the whine of a dog or the meow of a cat; and you could call that "animal sounds." Can you ask us a question?

S1: Ain't no questions in here.

S3: The words that need to be clarified are "mimics."

S4: That means imitate, right?

T: Right. How did you figure that out, Shirley?

S4: The paragraph.

T: Show us how somebody could figure out what "mimic" means.

S5: They are great mimics. They can learn to talk and imitate animal sounds.

T: Yes, so the next sentence tells you what it means. Very good, anything else need to be clarified?

All: No.

T: What about that question we need to ask? (pause)
What is the second paragraph about, Chantel?

S1: The games they play.

S3: They do things like people do.

S4: What kinds of games do crows play?

S3: Hide and seek. Over and over again.

T: You know what, Larry? That was a real good comparison. One excellent question could be, "How are crows like people?"

S4: They play hide and seek.

T: Good. Any other questions there?

S2: How come the crows don't get annoyed?

S5: What does annoyed mean?

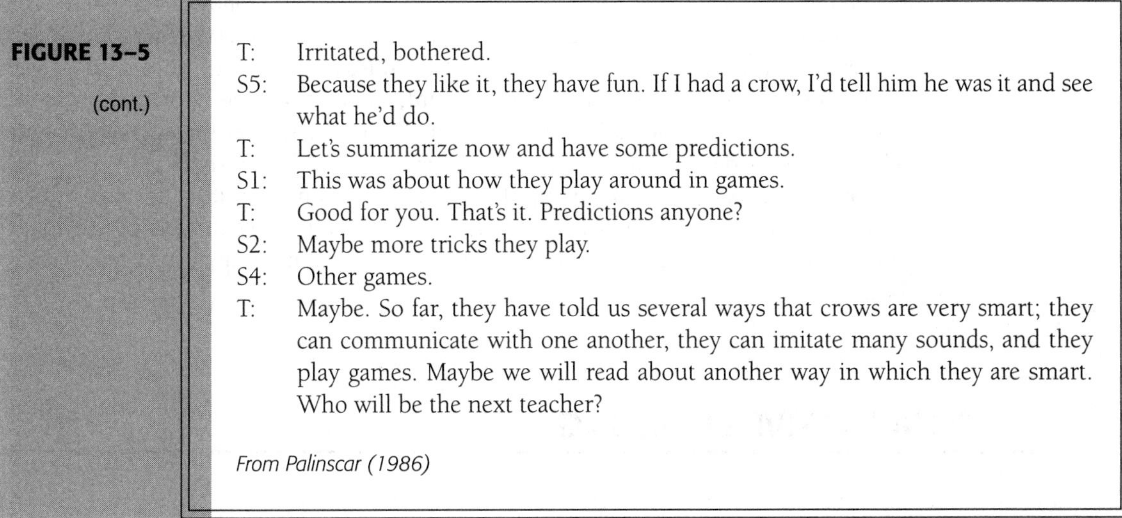

FIGURE 13–5

(cont.)

T: Irritated, bothered.

S5: Because they like it, they have fun. If I had a crow, I'd tell him he was it and see what he'd do.

T: Let's summarize now and have some predictions.

S1: This was about how they play around in games.

T: Good for you. That's it. Predictions anyone?

S2: Maybe more tricks they play.

S4: Other games.

T: Maybe. So far, they have told us several ways that crows are very smart; they can communicate with one another, they can imitate many sounds, and they play games. Maybe we will read about another way in which they are smart. Who will be the next teacher?

From Palinscar (1986)

FIGURE 13–6 Pretest-to-posttest gains in reading comprehension for four groups

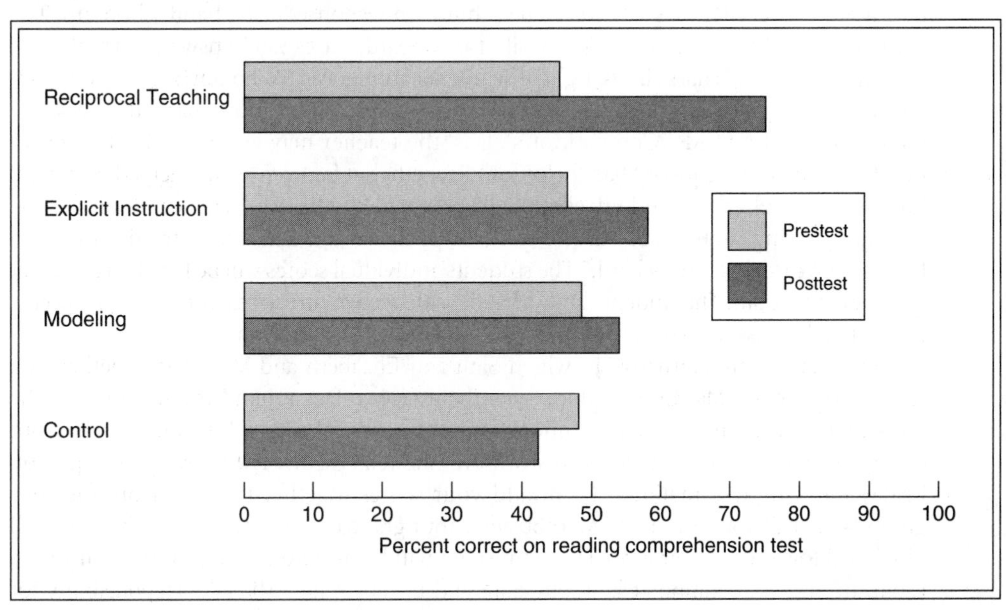

Adapted from Palinscar and Brown (1984)

instruction focuses on how to learn rather than what to learn. Second, learning of the cognitive strategies occurs within real reading comprehension tasks rather than having each strategy taught in isolation. The goal is not to learn isolated strategies per se but to learn them in order to understand the passages. Third, students learn as apprentices within a cooperative group that is working together on a task. The teacher serves as a critic and helper who provides feedback and basic information as needed. In short, the teacher provides *expert scaffolding* within a group that is jointly working on a task. The most distinguishing aspect of reciprocal teaching is that the student assumes the role of the teacher and learns by teaching. In short, the student learns to assume an important role within a social context.

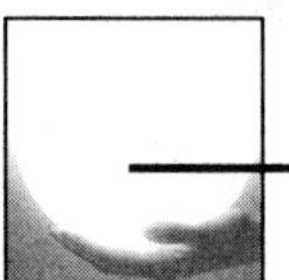

COOPERATIVE LEARNING

Consider two classrooms scenes—one based on competition and one based on cooperation. In one classroom, the teacher, Ms. Competition, writes a math problem, $3\frac{1}{4} - 1\frac{3}{4} = \_\_\_\_$, on the board and calls on Sam to give an answer. Sam writes $2\frac{1}{4}$ on the board as the answer. "That's not right," the teacher says. "Who can help him?" In response, many hands shoot up. The teacher calls on Elizabeth, who calmly walks to the board, erases Sam's answer, and replaces it with the answer $1\frac{2}{4}$. "That's almost right," the teacher announces. "Who can help her finish it?" Of the many wildly waving hands, the teacher chooses Mia, who reduces Elizabeth's answer to its final form, $1\frac{1}{2}$. In Ms. Competition's class, the teacher may euphemistically refer to Elizabeth's "help" for Sam or Mia's "help" for Elizabeth, but far from feeling helped, Sam feels humiliated by Elizabeth and Elizabeth feels betrayed by Mia. The teacher concludes the episode by saying, "You will have a quiz worth 50 points on addition and subtraction of mixed fractions on Friday, so study hard." The students' individual scores will be listed on a sheet at the rear of the room. The students know that they are graded on the basis of how many points they get in the class, with the top 20% of the class getting As, and so on.

Now imagine an alternative in which Sam and Elizabeth and Mia work together as a team. The teacher, Ms. Cooperation, seats them face-to-face around the same table. She gives them sheets that explain addition and subtraction of mixed fractions, worked-out examples, and practice problems to work on. She tells them, "I will give you a quiz on Friday covering this material. I will add your scores together to get a score for your group—let's call your group the Mathbusters. Your grade in math depends on how well all of you do together as a group." The team score will be listed on a sheet at the rear of the room. In Ms. Cooperation's classroom, Sam and Elizabeth and Mia take responsibility for each other's learning and help each other to master the material.

Should the atmosphere of competition that currently prevails in most classrooms be replaced with a cooperative environment? The rationale for cooperative learning environments is that working together on tasks is required in many real-world situations (Slavin, 1982).

> Cooperation is one of the most important human activities. Elephants have survived because of their size; cheetahs because of their speed; humans because of their ability to cooperate for

the good of the group. In modern life, people who can organize as a group to accomplish a common end are likely to be successful . . . in virtually any endeavor. (p. 5)

In spite of the central role of cooperative activities out of schools, cooperation is not generally emphasized in schools. In fact, as Slavin notes, in many classrooms, students may be punished for cheating if they help one another. In classrooms where students are in competition with one another for grades, students are unlikely to encourage each other's academic success.

This comparison of competitive and cooperative classroom environments gives rise to a second way in which apprenticeship principles can be applied to formal education, namely, what Slavin (1983a, 1983b, 1990) calls *cooperative learning*. In cooperative learning, small groups of up to six students who differ in ability work together as a group on an academic task. Rather than competing against each other, members of the group work together and are evaluated as a team. For example, instead of each student trying to outscore his or her peers on a test, in cooperative learning the goal is to improve the combined scores of all members of the group. Thus, if the average score of a group shows improvement on a test, the entire group receives a reward. In summary, in cooperative learning, "students spend much of their class time working in small, heterogeneous groups, in which they are expected to help one another learn" (Slavin, 1983b, p. 431).

Although cooperative learning can be implemented in many different ways, let's examine one of the most well-known versions developed by Slavin and his colleagues (Slavin, 1982, 1983a, 1983b, 1990)—Student Teams Achievement Divisions (STAD). In STAD, students in a classroom are arranged into groups of four to six members, with group names such as Math Monsters, Five Alive, and Fantastic Four. Each group consists of the same balance of high- and low-performing students, boys and girls, and members of racial and ethnic groups as is represented overall in the class. For each instructional lesson, the teacher introduces the material to the whole class through lecture and discussion. Then the students break into their groups to study together until all group members are able to solve problems presented on worksheets. When the team is confident that all members understand the material, each member takes a quiz on the material—but without any help from other team members.

The teacher scores the quizzes in an unusual way. Instead of simply recording the score for each student, the teacher computes the improvement score for each student and adds them all together to get a team improvement score. The teacher determines a base score for each student by taking five less than the student's past quiz average. To compute an improvement score on a quiz, the teacher gives the student one point for each point that the student's quiz score exceeds his or her base score—up to a maximum of 10 points. A perfect quiz score earns 10 improvement points regardless of the student's base score, and no improvement score can be less than 0. For example, if Jose's base score is 21 and his quiz score is 23, his improvement score is 2; if Mary's base score is 18 and her quiz score is 30, her improvement score is 10; and if Pat's base score is 18 and her quiz score is 17, her improvement score is 0. According to Slavin (1982), the "improvement score system gives every student a good chance to contribute maximum points to the team" (p. 9).

The team improvement scores are used as the basis for rewarding students. The class publishes a weekly newsletter that lists the teams ranked in order of team improvement scores as well as the names of individual students who show large improvement or errorless performance. An example of a newsletter is shown in Figure 13–7.

FIGURE 13–7 A newsletter from a cooperative learning classroom

MOUNTAIN VIEW ELEMENTARY SCHOOL

Issue No. 5
March 21, 1995

CALCULATORS OUTFIGURE CLASS

The Calculators (Charlene, Alfredo, Laura, and Carl) calculated their way into first place this week, with big 10-point scores by Charlene, Alfredo, and Carl, and a near-perfect team score of 38! Their score jumped them from sixth to third in cumulative rank. Way to go Calcs! The Fantastic Four (Frank, Otis, Ursula, and Rebecca) also did a fantastic job, with Ursula and Rebecca turning in 10-pointers, but the Tigers (Cissy, Lindsay, Arthur, and Willy) clawed their way from last place last week to a tie with the red-hot Four, who were second the first week and first last week. The Fantastic Four stayed in first place in cumulative rank. The Tigers were helped out by 10-point scores from Lindsay and Arthur. The Math Monsters (Gary, Helen, Octavia, Ulysses, and Luis) held on to fourth place this week, but thanks to their big first-place score in the first week they're still in second place in overall rank. Helen and Luis got each 10 points to help the M.M.'s. Just behind the Math Monsters were the Five Alive (Carlos, Irene, Nancy, Charles, and Oliver), with 10-point scores by Carlos and Charles, and then in order the Little Professors, Fractions, and Brains. Susan turned in 10 points for the L.P.'s, as did Linda for the Brains.

This Week's Rank		This Week's Score	Overall Score	Overall Rank
1st - Calculators		38	81	3
2nd - Fantastic Four	Tie	35	89	1
3rd - Tigers	Tie	35	73	6
4th - Math Monsters		40/32	85	2
5th - Five Alive		37/30	74	5
6th - Little Professors		26	70	8
7th - Fractions		23	78	4
8th - Brains		22	71	7

TEN-POINT SCORERS

Charlene	(Calculators)	Helen	(Math Monsters)
Alfredo	(Calculators)	Luis	(Math Monsters)
Carl	(Calculators)	Carlos	(Five Alive)
Ursula	(Fantastic Four)	Charles	(Five Alive)
Rebecca	(Fantastic Four)	Susan	(Little Professors)
Lindsay	(Tigers)	Linda	(Brains)
Arthur	(Tigers)		

Modified from Slavin (1982)

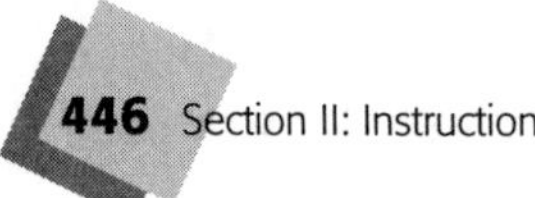

Are cooperative learning methods effective in improving student achievement? To help answer this question, Slavin and Karweit (1984) conducted a yearlong study in ninth-grade mathematics classrooms from an inner-city school. The majority of students were African American, and the average achievement level in mathematics was very low. Some classrooms were selected to use cooperative learning techniques, namely, the STAD procedure described previously. Other classrooms were selected to use a mastery technique that emphasized individual learning. In these classrooms, for each lesson, the teacher instructed the whole class, asked the students to work on individual worksheets, and gave a quiz on the material. If a student scored lower than 80% on the quiz, the student received corrective instruction and then took a final quiz. If a student scored 80% or higher on the quiz, the student received enrichment activities to work on until all students had taken the final quiz.

Students took a mathematics achievement test at the beginning and the end of the academic year. Figure 13–8 shows that the students in classrooms that emphasized cooperative learning improved substantially more than students assigned to classrooms that emphasized individual learning. The amount of change is approximately twice as much for the cooperative learning group as for the individual learning group.

In a review of 323 studies involving cooperative instructional methods, Johnson and Johnson (1990) determined that students averaged higher levels of achievement in cooperative learning situations than in competitive or individualistic ones. Based on these results, Johnson and Johnson concluded that "students at the 50th percentile in a cooperative learning situation will perform at the 75th percentile of students learning in a competitive situation and at the 77th percentile of students learning in an individualistic situation" (p. 24). The superiority of cooperative learning methods has been reported across many subject areas, types of learning materials, and ability levels of learners (Johnson & Johnson, 1985, 1990).

Why does cooperative learning affect student achievement? Slavin (1983b) argues that cooperative learning situations consist of two important ingredients—*cooperative incentive structure* and *cooperative task structure*. Cooperative incentive structure refers to a situa-

FIGURE 13–8 Pretest-to-posttest gains in mathematics achievement for cooperative and individual learning classrooms

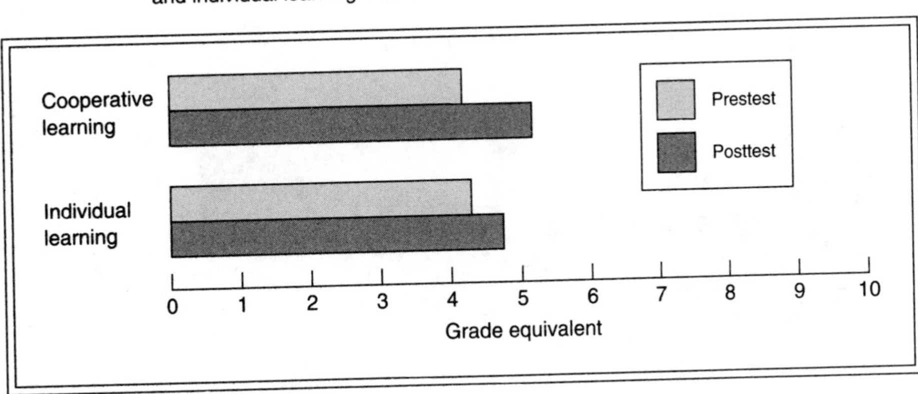

Adapted from Slavin and Karweit (1984)

tion in which rewards depend on group performance. A cooperative incentive structure occurs "when the students are individually assessed and the group members' scores are summed to form group scores" that are "recognized in class newsletters, or qualify the groups for certificates, grades or other rewards" (p. 432). Thus, a cooperative incentive structure involves *group rewards* (i.e., rewards depend on how the group does as a whole) based on *individual accountability* (i.e., each member must make a major contribution to the group).

A cooperative task structure occurs when a heterogeneous group works together on a common task. It refers to a situation "in which two or more individuals are allowed, encouraged, or required to work together on some task, coordinating their efforts to complete the task" (Slavin, 1983b, p. 431). For example, a cooperative task structure occurs when a group of students works together to learn some material in preparation for a test. Cooperative task structure requires that the group, in addition to having a group task, be heterogeneous with respect to ability, gender, and ethnic composition. In short, an important aspect of cooperative task structure is that learning take place in a *social context* consisting of a *heterogeneous group*.

Not all group learning is equally effective. Slavin (1983b) contrasts three scenarios for group learning: group study with group reward for individual learning, group study with group reward for group product, and group study with individual reward. These forms of group learning are summarized in Figure 13–9. In the first scenario, students work in groups to improve their understanding of material and are evaluated as a group, as exemplified in the STAD technique described previously. In this case, the students engage in group study, which fulfills the requirement for a cooperative task structure, and are individually accountable for contributing to the overall success of the group, which fulfills the requirement for a cooperative incentive structure.

In a research review, Slavin (1983b) found that student achievement in classrooms involving this form of cooperative learning was superior to achievement in traditional classroom environments in 89% of the studies surveyed and produced no effect in the

FIGURE 13–9 Effectiveness of three types of group learning

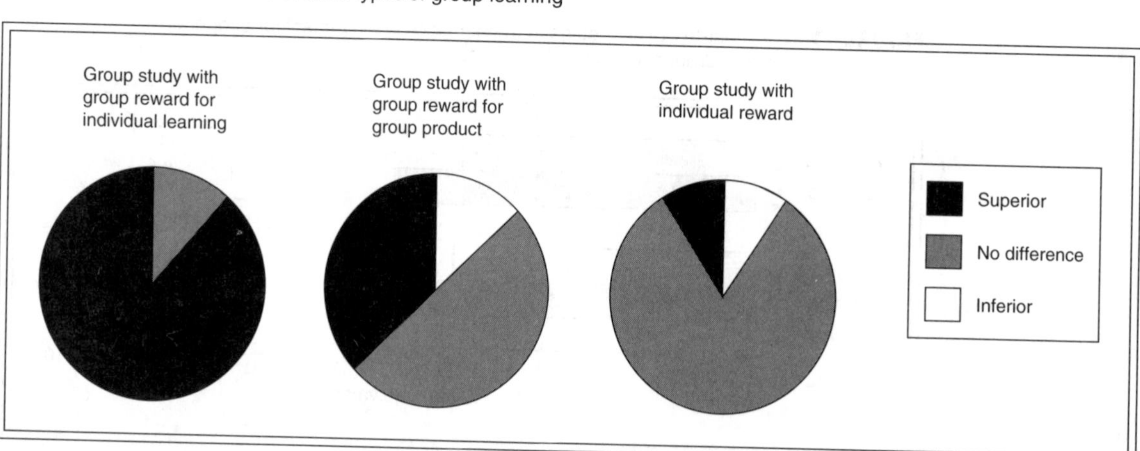

Based on Slavin (1983b)

remaining 11%. These results are illustrated in the lefthand pie chart in Figure 13–9. Slavin concluded that "cooperative learning methods that use group rewards and individual accountability consistently increase student achievement more than control methods in many academic subjects in elementary and secondary classrooms" (p. 443).

A seemingly related version of group learning is for students to work together on a common project, such as producing an entry for a science fair. In this case, students work as a group, but each student may not be individually accountable for contributing to the group. For example, one or two students may do all of the work while the others do not participate much in the project.

In a review, Slavin (1983b) compared cooperative learning methods consisting of group study with group reward for group product versus traditional methods. As illustrated in the middle pie chart in Figure 13–9, most of the studies (62%) failed to find any evidence that cooperative learning improved achievement more than other methods. Slavin concluded that "group study methods that provide group rewards based on the quality of a group product have not been found to improve student achievement" (p. 441). According to Slavin's analysis, an essential aspect of an effective cooperative learning method is that it fosters individual accountability; that is, each individual is essential for the success of the group. Individual accountability is likely to be lacking in cooperative learning situations involving a group product.

The third approach to group learning is for students to work in groups but to be evaluated as individuals. An example is a study group that holds group study sessions in preparation for a test in a traditional classroom. Although this situation involves cooperative task structure, it lacks cooperative incentive structure because the students may compete against each other as individuals for grades. In reviewing studies comparing this form of group learning with traditional methods, Slavin (1983b) found no evidence for its effectiveness. The righthand pie chart in Figure 13–9 shows that 80% of the studies revealed no differences in achievement between cooperative learning and traditional classroom environments, with the remaining studies evenly split between the cooperative and traditional methods being most effective. Slavin concluded:

> The opportunity for students to study together makes little or no contribution to the effects of cooperative learning on achievement. Providing an opportunity for group study without providing further structure in the form of individual assessment and group reward has not been found . . . to increase student achievement more than having students work individually. (p. 439)

It would be incorrect to conclude from this review of research on cooperative learning that learning in small groups is more effective than learning individually. Slavin (1983b) correctly warns that "there is no evidence as of yet that group study per se makes any difference in student achievement" (pp. 440–441). Based on their review of the vast research literature on cooperative learning, Johnson and Johnson (1990) issue a similar warning: "Simply placing students in groups and telling them to work together does not in itself promote higher achievement" (p. 34). Instead, cooperative learning methods have been found to be effective when students are rewarded based on group performance (i.e., cooperative incentive structure) and when each student must participate fully within a group on an academic task (i.e., cooperative task structure).

PARTICIPATORY MODELING

A third way of incorporating apprenticeship into classrooms is *participatory modeling*—in which an expert and a novice each participate in modeling the process for accomplishing some cognitive task. For example, Chapter 12 included a description of Bloom and Broder's (1950) techniques for teaching thinking strategies to college students. In Bloom and Broder's study, an expert described out loud what was going on in his mind as he solved an exam problem; a novice did the same thing and compared his thinking process to that of the expert.

Let's consider two examples of how students accomplish a writing assignment. Suppose that a teacher asks the students in her class to write an essay on an interesting job or occupation. As soon as Mark is given the topic, he begins writing. "An interesting job is being a police officer," he writes. Then he remembers the following information that he adds to his essay: "Police officers ride in fast cars with sirens and catch speeders on the freeway. Once my dad was stopped for speeding." Then, it occurs to him that the job can be dangerous, so he adds: "Sometimes criminals attack police officers so they always have to be ready for action. I saw a wounded officer on TV." Finally, he runs out of ideas, so he concludes by writing: "I would really like to be a police officer one day."

Mark displays the characteristics of a novice writer. When given a topic to write about, novices write the first idea that occurs to them, then the next idea, and so on until they cannot think of any more ideas—a strategy that Bereiter and Scardamalia (1987) call *knowledge telling*.

In contrast, Sheening writes an outline before he begins and revises the outline during the writing process. His outline begins as "1. Introduction—vets love animals. 2. What vets do. 3. How vets help animals. 4. How vets help people. 5. How vets help society." He collects his thoughts and organizes them about each of these topics, and he establishes a theme for his paper—being a veterinarian is one way of expressing your love of animals.

Sheening's writing process reflects many of the characteristics of expert writing. When expert writers are given a topic to write on, they use what Bereiter and Scardamalia (1987) call a *knowledge transforming* strategy, in which they plan what they are going to write and revise what they have written. The processes used for good writers are described in more detail in Hayes and Flower's (1980; Hayes, 1996) analysis of the cognitive processes in writing, discussed in Chapter 4.

How can teachers help students change from the linear writing processes of novices to the reflective writing processes of experts? To accomplish this goal, Scardamalia, Bereiter, and Steinbach (1984) developed an instructional procedure based on modeling of reflective processes in writing. Sixth-grade students participated in a 15-week unit on reflective writing (experimental group) or were given typical classroom instruction (control group).

In the experimental group, the instructor frequently modeled her thinking processes for the group, and the students also frequently modeled their thinking processes for each other. For example, when faced with a writing assignment, the teacher stood in front of the group and produced a thinking-aloud description of how she thought of ideas and organized them, how she decided on the goal of the essay, how she figured out ways to elaborate and improve on what she had, and so on. Later, students were asked to do the same while standing in front of the group.

Whenever the writer got stuck, he or she selected a card from a deck—each card contained a hint about how to generate a new idea (e.g., "An important distinction is . . . or "The history of this is . . ."), how to improve ideas (e.g., "To put it more simply . . ." or "I could give the reader a clear picture by . . ."), how to elaborate (e.g., "An example of this is . . . or "My own experience with this is . . . "), how to set goals (e.g., "My purpose is . . . " or "A goal I think I could write to . . . "), or how to organize ideas (e.g., "If I want to start off with my strongest idea . . . " or "I can tie this together by . . . "). Students learned to determine which category of cue card they needed, select a card from that category, respond to it, and continue their thinking-aloud monologue. The teacher led group discussions following thinking-aloud monologues in which students could critique the processes that had been modeled. In addition, the teacher provided direct instruction on how to write reflectively, using the strategies of expert writers. After experience with these "public demonstrations of planning" (Scardamalia et al., 1984, p. 179), students worked individually on planning essays at their seats. They used the deck of cue cards but gave their thinking-aloud monologue silently to themselves.

As you can see, this procedure is like reciprocal teaching in that teachers and students take turns in modeling a set of cognitive strategies. At first, the teacher models how to plan an essay using prompts from a deck of cue cards, and later students take their turns at planning essays using the cue cards. In addition, as in reciprocal teaching, the students and teachers both provide criticisms and comments on each other's modeling performances.

Does experience in observing, producing, and critiquing thinking-aloud descriptions of expert writing processes have an effect on students' writing processes and products? To provide some information about writing processes, selected students in both groups were tape-recorded as they engaged in thinking-aloud monologues before and after the 15-week instructional unit. Raters tallied the number of reflective statements—that is, statements involving planning and organizing ideas—in each monologue, without knowing whether the monologue occurred before or after instruction or whether the monologue was produced by an experimental or a control student. Figure 13–10 shows that the average number of reflective comments increased from pretest to posttest for

FIGURE 13–10 Pretest-to-posttest changes in the number of reflective statements made while preparing to write an essay

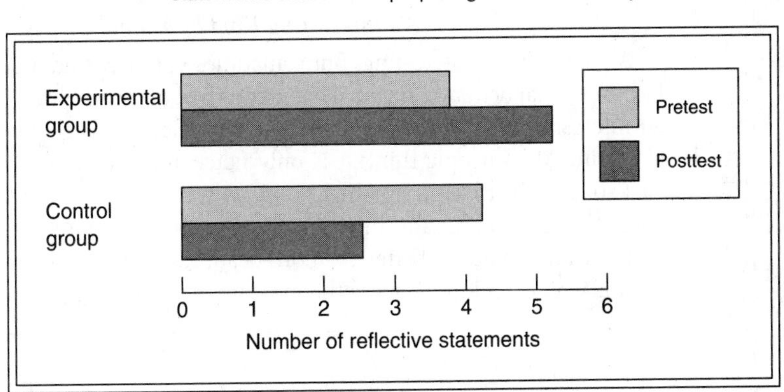

Adapted from Scardamalia, Bereiter, and Steinbach (1984)

experimental students and decreased for control students. This finding indicates that the training was effective in helping students to think more like experts as they planned an essay.

To provide some preliminary data on writing products, students in both groups were asked to write essays before (pretest) and after (posttest) the 15-week instructional unit. Figure 13–11 shows essays written on the pretest and posttest by a student in the experimental group. Raters were given the pretest and posttest essay of each student without any indication of which essay had been written first and which group the writer had been in. For each of several important rating dimensions, the rater's job was to rate how much better one essay was than the other. The average ratings on several key dimensions for the groups are shown in Figure 13–12. If the rater preferred the posttest essay, the difference score is shown as positive in Figure 13–12; if the rater preferred the pretest essay, the difference score is shown as negative in Figure 13–12. Overall, the experimental group showed a greater pretest-to-posttest gain than the control group. This finding is consistent with the idea that the modeling procedures used during instruction had a positive effect in helping students produce more expertlike essays.

As in the teaching of expert writing strategies, Collins and Smith (1982) have proposed three stages for cognitive modeling of expert reading comprehension strategies: stage 1, in

FIGURE 13–11

Examples of essays written before and after reciprocal modeling of writing strategies

(Pretest)
Jobs or Occupation

An interesting job or occupation is being an airline stewardess. I think airline stewardesses have an interesting job because they get to travel all over the world and meet new people. I know because my friend is an airline stewardess and travels a lot. I would like to be an airline stewardess when I grow up.

(Posttest)
An Interesting Kind of Animal

All animals are interesting, but sometimes you may find a person that may like an animal better than you. That proves that all people are different. I think an interesting animal is a tiger because of its fierce and gentle sides makes it exquisite. Most people think it is only fierce and only hurts people but that isn't so. The tiger has so much grace in his walk it almost looks as if he puts a lot of thought into it, and his fur coat is so unique I think it's one of a kind, and nothing could be better or more beautiful than that striped coat to me. That is why I think the tiger is the most interesting animal.

From Scardamalia, Bereiter, and Steinbach (1984)

FIGURE 13–12

Major pretest-to-posttest changes in ratings of essay quality for experimental and control groups

Rating Dimension	Experimental	Control
1. Questioning, speculating, or raising uncertainties	+.67	−.02
2. Suggesting personal involvement or interest in topic	+.59	−.36
3. Attempting to communicate why topic is interesting	+.54	−.36
4. Writing in essay rather than encyclopedia style	+.52	−.34
5. Using content to convey point of essay	+.43	−.11
6. Using attention-getting expressions in opening or closing	+.41	+.12
7. Stating theme or purpose	+.26	−.37

Adapted from Scardamalia, Bereiter, and Steinbach (1984)

which the teacher models the strategy; stage 2, in which the student learns to model the strategy with ongoing support from the teacher; and stage 3, in which the student learns to apply the strategy without ongoing teacher support. For example, in the case of learning reading comprehension strategies, the stages are as follows:

> The first stage will consist of the teacher modeling comprehension, and commenting on his or her monitoring and hypotheses, while reading aloud to a student. The next stage will consist of encouraging students to practice these techniques themselves while reading aloud. The third and final stage will be to have students use these skills while reading silently. (Collins & Smith, 1982, p.182)

The three stages represent a gradual shifting of responsibility from the teacher to the student.

Not all forms of cognitive modeling may be equally effective. For example, in observational modeling (or teacher-only modeling), the teacher models the desired strategy but the students do not. In participatory modeling (or reciprocal modeling), the teacher and student each get opportunities to model and critique the strategy. Scardamalia, Bereiter, and Steinbach's (1984) method for teaching reflective writing strategies is based on participatory rather than observational modeling, as is Bloom and Broder's (1950) successful training of problem-solving strategies as described in Chapter 12.

In a review of research on cognitive strategy instruction, Pressley and Woloshyn (1995) argue that modeling is most effective when both teacher and student participate and interact. They advocate an instructional sequence in which "teachers describe and model strategies initially, and then allow a great deal of student practice in order for students to master those strategies" (p. 10). In contrast, they argue against using a procedure in which the teacher explains a strategy and then assigns unsupervised practice. Although research continues in pursuit of effective ways to use modeling in classrooms, many scholars favor participatory over observational modeling (Collins et al., 1989; Pressley & Woloshyn, 1995).

CHAPTER SUMMARY

"Let's break into small groups and discuss this." These words can be a call to engage in "real learning" or an invitation to waste precious school time. Not all forms of group learning are equally effective, and there is no evidence that learning in groups per se is better than learning individually. This chapter explored the rationale for learning in groups and examined three versions of the cognitive apprenticeship approach.

The Russian psychologist Lev Vygotsky argued that learning always occurs within a social context. Teacher and peer assistance are needed to help students move through their *zones of proximal development*—that is, from their current level of development to their potential level of development under the guidance of more capable peers and teachers. Although aspects of Vygotsky's theory are not based on scientific evidence, the implications for cognitive apprenticeship in the classroom warrant closer examination.

Research shows that students often fail to use school-taught procedures outside of school. For example, young street vendors were able to solve arithmetic problems within the context of their everyday tasks using procedures they invented themselves but were often unable to solve equivalent problems presented as a school-like test.

Many useful skills such as how to become a midwife or a tailor are taught in apprenticeship systems without the need for formal schools, books, and tests. Cognitive apprenticeship involves applying apprenticeship techniques to formal schooling. Three features of cognitive apprenticeship programs are modeling (such as when a teacher describes her cognitive processes in carrying out an academic task), coaching (such as when a teacher offers suggestions or criticisms to a student who is carrying out an academic task), and scaffolding (such as when a teacher supports a student on parts of a task that the student is not yet able to accomplish unaided). Reciprocal teaching, cooperative learning, and participatory modeling are three versions of cognitive apprenticeship.

In reciprocal teaching, the teacher and students take turns in teaching how to perform an academic task, such as how to apply effective reading comprehension strategies. Brown and Palinscar (1989) found that students who learn reading strategies by reciprocal teaching show larger gains in reading comprehension performance than students who learn by more traditional methods.

In cooperative learning, small groups of students study together and are rewarded as a group for each person's performance on the studied task. Slavin (1990) found that students who learn mathematics as part of a cooperative team show larger gains in academic performance than students who learn individually.

In participatory modeling, experts and novices each participate in modeling the cognitive processes required to perform the same academic task, such as how to write an informative essay. Bereiter and Scardamalia (1987) found that students who engaged in this form of modeling learned to write better essays than students who learned by more conventional methods.

SUGGESTED READINGS

Nunes, T., Schliemann, A. D., & Carraher, D. W. (1993). *Street mathematics and school mathematics.* Cambridge, England: Cambridge University Press. (Describes a program of research on mathematic problem solving in school and real-world situations.)

Slavin, R. E. (1990). *Cooperative learning: Theory, research, and practice.* Upper Saddle River, NJ: Prentice Hall. (Summarizes research on cooperative learning.)

Tharp, R. G., & Gallimore, R. (1988). *Rousing minds to life: Teaching, learning, and schooling in social context.* Cambridge, England: Cambridge University Press. (Explains how cognitive apprenticeship can be applied in classrooms.)

CHAPTER 14

Teaching by Priming Students' Motivation to Learn

CHAPTER OUTLINE

Introduction

Motivation Based on Interest

Motivation Based on Self-Efficacy

Motivation Based on Attributions

Chapter Summary

This chapter examines the straightforward idea that students work harder to understand and learn more deeply when they like what they are learning. In short, this chapter examines how to foster motivation in learners as a means of teaching for meaningful learning. This chapter explores three ways to affect a student's motivation: motivation based on interest, motivation based on self-efficacy, and motivation based on attributions.

INTRODUCTION

A MOTIVATIONAL QUESTIONNAIRE

Let's begin by asking you to evaluate some statements about your life as a student. Below is a list of statements concerning your beliefs, feelings, and expectations about this course. Each statement is accompanied by the numbers 1 through 7—with 1 indicating that the statement definitely is not true of you, 7 indicating that the statement definitely is true of you, and the other numbers representing shades in between. For each statement, please circle a number that best corresponds to your level of agreement (with 1 meaning that you strongly disagree and 7 meaning that you strongly agree).

1	2	3	4	5	6	7	I know that I will be able to learn the material for this class.
1	2	3	4	5	6	7	I'm certain I can understand the ideas taught in this class.
1	2	3	4	5	6	7	I am sure I can do an excellent job on the problems and tasks assigned for this class.
1	2	3	4	5	6	7	I work hard to get a good grade even when I don't like a class.
1	2	3	4	5	6	7	Even when study materials are dull and uninteresting, I keep working until I am finished.
1	2	3	4	5	6	7	I work on practice exercises and answer end-of-chapter questions even when I don't have to.
1	2	3	4	5	6	7	If I perform poorly on a test in this class, it is because I did not try hard enough to learn the material.
1	2	3	4	5	6	7	Doing well in this class depends on how much effort I give.
1	2	3	4	5	6	7	Luck does not have much effect on my grade in this course.

These items are inspired by a 56-item test called the Motivated Strategies for Learning Questionnaire (MSLQ) described by Pintrich and De Groot (1990) and by measures of students' beliefs about learning (Borkowski, Weyhing, & Carr, 1988; Graham, 1984, 1991). The first three items are examples for a scale that measures *interest*—how interested you are in learning about a particular topic. If the sum of your ratings to the first three questions is high, for example greater than 15, you seem to be interested in this course. The next three questions come from a scale intended to measure *self-efficacy*—the degree to which you see yourself as competent to accomplish a particular task. Add up the three ratings you gave to these questions; again, if your score is more than 15, you seem to have high efficacy for learning in this course. The next three questions are designed to measure *effort-based attributions*—the degree to which you attribute your academic successes and failures to effort rather than other causes. Add up the total number of points on the last three questions to see whether or not you score high (e.g., 15 or more) in your beliefs about the importance of effort. Because these questions represent just a small sampling of a much larger questionnaire, we cannot expect them to give an exact account of your interest, self-efficacy, and attributional beliefs. Recent advances in motivational theory and research encourage the idea that academic achievement is related to motivational variables such as interest, self-efficacy, and attributional beliefs.

THE ROOTS OF MOTIVATION

Why do some students, when faced with a challenging assignment, work hard to complete every aspect of the task, whereas other students quit early without devoting much effort. Why do some students persist on tasks while others give up? What motivates students to want to learn? What are the roots of students' motivation to learn? These are the kinds of questions that we explore in this chapter. In particular, we examine three possible answers to questions about what motivates students to work hard:

Motivation is based on interest. Students work hard when they value what they are learning, that is, when what they are learning is important to them.

Motivation is based on self-efficacy. Students work hard when they perceive themselves as capable of doing well, that is, when they have confidence in their capabilities for a learning task.

Motivation is based on attribution. Students work hard when they believe that their efforts will pay off, that is, when they attribute their successes and failures to personal effort.

These three views of motivation are summarized in Figure 14–1. As you can see, each answer assumes that a student's motivation to learn in school is based on how the student interprets the learning situation. In short, motivation and cognition are intertwined; wanting to learn (which could be called *achievement strivings*) is related to one's beliefs about learning. The motivation to learn may depend on how the student thinks about the personal relevance of the material, about his or her own competence, and about whether hard work leads to success.

If you are interested in promoting meaningful learning, you must also be interested in priming the learner's motivation to learn. When students are motivated to learn, they try harder to understand the material and thereby learn more deeply, resulting in better ability to transfer what they have learned to new situations. In particular, I focus on intrinsic rather than extrinsic motivation. When the learner's motivation is intrinsic, it comes from within the learner. This chapter reviews techniques for priming *intrinsic motivation*. When motivation is extrinsic, it is imposed on the learner from the outside, such as through external rewards and punishments. The perils of *extrinsic motivation*, such as the negative effects of reward, were examined in Chapter 7.

FIGURE 14–1

Three views of motivation for learning

Theory	Predictions	Example	Implications
Interest theory	Student interest in a school subject or lesson topic predicts student achievement. Adding seductive details to instruction will not improve student achievement.	I work hard because I value this, it is important to me.	Embed lessons within the context of larger projects that interest students.
Self-efficacy theory	Student confidence predicts learning effort and student achievement.	I work hard because I am good at this, I am capable of doing this.	Ask peers to model appropriate learning along with positive efficacy cues, such as "I can do this."
Attribution theory	Students who attribute success and failure to effort work harder and achieve more than students who attribute them to ability.	I work hard because I know my effort will pay off. If I fail, it's because I didn't try hard enough.	Avoid condescending cues, such as pity and sympathy, when a student fails.

DEFINITION AND BACKGROUND

Before we begin, it is useful to define motivation and briefly review the history of research on motivation. Motivation is an internal state that initiates and maintains goal-directed behavior. This definition has four components:

Motivation is personal. It occurs within the student.
Motivation is directed. It is aimed at accomplishing some goal.
Motivation is activating. It instigates action.
Motivation is energizing. It provides for persistence and intensity.

In short, motivation is an inducement to action. For example, when a student studies until late at night for a week to master material for a test, we would say that the student is motivated.

The history of research on motivation over the past 50 years reflects a shift in the way theorists view the nature of the internal state underlying motivation—from drives to cognitions (Weiner, 1990). Fifty years ago, drive theories dominated the field of motivation. Drive theories maintain that motivation results from a situation in which a biological need is not being met—that is, the motivation to act is an automatic consequence of a discrepancy between the current state and a needed state (Hull, 1943). For example, if a rat is deprived of food for a certain period of time, it will be motivated to speedily learn how to get food. When a need is not being met, a drive increases that automatically instigates behavior; when appropriate action is taken, the drive is reduced to an acceptable level so that the behavior can be terminated. According to Hull (1943), some of the primary biological needs include food, water, air, pain avoidance, optimal temperature, sleep, and activity. This view of motivation as drive reduction was based largely on animal research in contrived laboratory situations and for many educational psychologists did "not provide the needed conceptual tools to explain classroom motivation" (Weiner, 1984, p. 15).

In contrast, cognitive theories of student motivation are based on "observations in classrooms as opposed to . . . the behavior of hungry rats" (Weiner, 1984, p. 16). An early attempt to incorporate student cognition (such as expectations) into drive theory can be seen in Atkinson's (1964) theory of *achievement motivation*—the idea that students have a need to achieve success and to avoid failure. According to Atkinson, students must balance the tendency to approach tasks for which they anticipate success (along with the resultant pride) and to avoid tasks for which they anticipate failure (along with the resultant shame). Achievement behavior (such as working hard to learn difficult material) depends on the level of a student's hope for success and fear of failure. Thus, the need for achievement motivates behavior based on a student's expectations about the likelihood of success or failure and potentially resulting pride or shame. Although expectancy theories such as Atkinson's theory of need for achievement "are fading in their impact" (Weiner, 1992, p. 221), more recent cognitive theories build on the idea that active cognitive processing is involved in motivation.

During the past 25 years, cognitive theories have come to dominate motivational research. This chapter explores three of the most active and relevant cognitive approaches to motivation—interest theory, self-efficacy theory, and attribution theory. Unlike drive theories in which motivation is an automatic consequence of biological needs, cognitive theories of motivation view the learner as a decision maker who bases actions on interpretations of incoming information. Unlike drive theories that are based largely on animal research in laboratory settings, cognitive theories are based on research on humans often in natural settings.

As Weiner (1992) pointed out in a recent review, "for motivational psychologists there have been fundamental shifts in theory and research focus" (p. 860), and the basic metaphor for motivated humans has shifted from a robotic machine to a decision maker. "The grand formal theories . . . have for the most part faded away . . . What remains are varieties of cognitive approaches to motivation" (Weiner, 1990, p. 620). Three important cognitive approaches to motivation are presented in the following three sections of this chapter.

MOTIVATION BASED ON INTEREST

INTEREST VERSUS EFFORT

Maria's teacher assigns a chapter on the human digestive system from a biology book. The material is difficult and, for Maria, boring. Maria particularly dislikes memorizing the many technical terms in the chapter. In spite of her boredom, Maria works hard. Each day she sits diligently in class and fills out worksheets covering the material in the book, and each evening she studies the chapter so that she will pass the test she will have to take.

In contrast, Yukari is working on a project she developed herself out of her personal interest in dieting and nutrition. She is curious about why some people are overweight and others are slim. She wants to know how the human digestive system works so that she can figure out how what one eats affects one's weight. In her search for relevant information, she consults many sources, including a chapter on the human digestive system from a biology book. Like Maria, she reads the chapter about how the human digestive system works, but her learning is motivated by an interest in understanding dieting and nutrition. She seeks out information that is relevant to her project, as if she were on some sort of treasure hunt. In short, Maria learns through effort, whereas Yukari learns through interest.

Who will learn more effectively and more deeply? Which form of learning is better—learning based on effort or on interest? More than 80 years ago, the great educational philosopher John Dewey addressed this issue in his little classic *Interest and Effort in Education* (Dewey, 1913). According to Dewey, the interest-based learning of Yukari is more beneficial than the effort-based learning of Maria. Dewey argues that "the great fallacy of the so-called effort theory is that" it equates "certain external activities" with "the exercise and training of mind" (p. 7). Thus, although Maria engages in learning-like behaviors, such behavior does not guarantee that she is actually learning much.

Dewey (1913) clearly distinguished between two litigants in what he called "the educational lawsuit of interest versus effort" (p. 1). The justification for an effort-based approach to schooling is that "life is full of things not interesting that have to be faced" (p. 3), so teachers should not spoil the student by creating a situation in which "everything is made play, amusement . . . everything is sugar coated for the child" (p. 4). "Life is not merely . . . a continual satisfaction of personal interests," so students need "training in devoting [themselves] to uninteresting work" (pp. 3–4). To do otherwise "eats out the fiber of character" and creates a "spoiled child who does only what he likes" (pp. 4–5).

In contrast, the case for interest is that willing attention is more effective for learning than forced effort. Interest causes students to pay attention and actively learn: "If we can secure interest in a given set of facts or ideas we may be perfectly sure that the pupil will direct his energies toward mastering them" (Dewey, 1913, p. 1). Dewey argues that "it is absurd to suppose that a child gets more intellectual or mental discipline when he goes at a matter unwillingly than when he goes out of the fullness of his heart" (pp. 1–2). The effort-based approach to school results in a "character dull, mechanical, unalert, because the vital juice of spontaneous interest has been squeezed out" (p. 3). The educational implications are clear:

> The debate about effort versus interest has important educational implications: Our whole policy of compulsory education rises or falls with our ability to make school life an interesting and absorbing experience to the child. In one sense there is no such thing as compulsory education. We can have compulsory physical attendance at school; but education comes only through willing attention to and participation in school activities. It follows that the teacher must select these activities with reference to the child's interests, powers, and capabilities. (p. ix)

In short, Dewey emphasizes the need to ensure that the student is cognitively active—rather than only physically active—during learning.

Regrettably, Dewey's essay—while emphasizing the importance of interest in learning—is based on logical arguments rather than psychological theory and empirical research. What is interest, and how does it motivate students to learn? Although researchers have begun to make modest progress since Dewey's day, there is still a lack of agreement on how to answer these questions (Renninger, Hidi, & Krapp, 1992). An important first step involves a distinction between two types of interest—individual interest and situational interest. *Individual interest* is a characteristic of the person and is based on a person's dispositions or preferred activities; *situational interest* is a characteristic of the environment such as the task's interestingness. In both cases, however, interest arises out of the interaction between the person and the situation.

INDIVIDUAL INTEREST

Students learn in a qualitatively better way when they work on material that interests them rather than when the material bores them. The results of interest-based learning are qualitatively better than the results of learning based solely on effort, because interested learners process material more deeply. This is a cornerstone of Dewey's (1913) classic treatise on interest and a working hypothesis in much of the recent research on individual interest. In this section, let's explore two straightforward predictions of Dewey's theory of interest:

School subject hypothesis. Student performance in learning a school subject is related to student interest in the subject.

Lesson topic hypothesis. Student performance in learning a lesson is better when the student is interested rather than uninterested in the topic.

The first way of testing Dewey's theory of interest is to ask whether students tend to perform better in subjects they like than in subjects they do not like. For example, in Figure 14–2, please rate your feelings about mathematics, natural science, social science, foreign language, and so on, with 0 indicating that the subject is very uninteresting to you and 4 indicating that it is very interesting. Then, for each subject write down the grade you

FIGURE 14–2

How much do you like each subject? How well did you perform in each subject?

	Please rate your interest (4 = high, 0 = low)	*Please indicate your grade in the last course you took (A = 4, F = 0)*
Mathematics		
Natural science		
Social science		
Literature		
Foreign language		
Art or music		

received the last time you took a class in that subject. If you received good grades in subjects you rated as interesting and poor grades in subjects you rated as uninteresting, then there is a positive correlation between interest and achievement.

In a review covering 25 years of interest research, Schiefele, Krapp, and Winteler (1992) searched for studies that measured both *interest*—how much a student liked a certain school subject, generally measured via a self-rating of interest—and *achievement*—how well the student performed in a certain school subject, generally measured by grades or an achievement test. In all, Schiefele et al. identified 121 studies from 18 different countries. The results were similar for all subjects that were investigated—mathematics, natural science, social science, foreign language, and literature. There was a moderate but persistent correlation (i.e., approximately $r = .30$) between a student's preference for a school subject and academic achievement in that subject. In other words, on average, the more a student liked a particular academic subject, the better the student performed in that subject.

These results might give pause to anyone who believes that ability is the overwhelmingly most important factor in promoting academic achievement in a given subject. The relation between interest and achievement is roughly as strong as the relation between ability and achievement, so anyone interested in predicting school success in a given subject area would be wise to examine both ability and interest.

Regrettably, these correlational results do not tell us about the causal relation between interest and achievement. We cannot tell whether interest causes achievement, in which students perform well in a subject because they like it; or whether achievement causes interest, in which students like a subject because they perform well in it; or both are caused by a third factor, such as ability in which students like and perform well in subjects they are good at. Future research is needed to untangle these issues.

The second way to test Dewey's theory of interest is to compare how students learn from text about a topic that interests them with how they learn from text about a topic that does not interest them. For example, suppose that you were assigned a passage on the psychology of emotion. Please indicate your expectations by answering the questions in Figure 14–3. According to interest theory, you will read more deeply and thereby learn more from the passage if you rated it as interesting rather than boring and as useful rather than worthless.

To investigate this prediction, Schiefele (1992) asked some college students to read a passage on an unfamiliar topic such as "the psychology of emotion" or "the psychology of communication." Before they read the passage, students rated their potential level of interest of the topic, using a questionnaire such as in Figure 14–3. Based on their ratings, half of the students were classified as "high-interest" and half were classified as "low-interest." After reading the passage, the students answered *surface questions* that required recall of individual facts and *deep questions* that required combining information from the text and applying it in a novel situation. Then students rated how deeply they had processed the text—including ratings about activation ("I was completely caught up in what I was reading") and elaboration ("I paraphrased the text in my own words").

If interest leads to deeper processing of the information, as Dewey claimed, high-interest students should perform better than low-interest learners, especially on deep questions. As predicted, the high-interest group performed much better than the low-interest group on deep questions but not on surface questions. In addition, if high-interest students process the material more deeply than low-interest students, level of interest should be related to

FIGURE 14–3

What are your expectations about a passage on the psychology of emotion?

While reading the text on emotion I expect to feel bored.

☐	☐	☐	☐
not at all	somewhat	quite	completely

While reading the text on emotion I expect to feel interested.

☐	☐	☐	☐
not at all	somewhat	quite	completely

I expect the material in a text on emotion to be worthless.

☐	☐	☐	☐
not at all	somewhat	quite	completely

I expect the material in a text on emotion to be useful.

☐	☐	☐	☐
not at all	somewhat	quite	completely

Based on Schiefele (1992)

amount of activation and elaboration during reading. As predicted, there was a strong, positive correlation (approximately $r = .60$) between interest in the topic and measures of activation and elaboration.

In summary, emerging evidence indicates that individual interest is related to academic learning. Hidi and Baird (1986) distinguished between two views of how individual interest may motivate learning—by producing general arousal that automatically facilitates learning and by instigating a process based on the significance of specific material to the reader:

> Thinking of interest as a general arousal experience is inadequate. This notion leads us to believe that all that is needed is to induce a general state of arousal which will automatically facilitate learning the material at hand. What is lost in this notion is the idea of interest as a process responding to the significance of the information. (p. 191)

In short, individual interest in a subject or topic depends on the specific significance of the material to the learner.

SITUATIONAL INTEREST

In contrast to individual interest, situational interest occurs when a learning situation is somehow made more interesting. Dewey (1913) warned that interest should not be viewed as some sort of flavoring that can be sprinkled on an otherwise boring task: "When things have to be made interesting, it is because interest itself is wanting. Moreover, the phrase is a misnomer. The thing, the object, is no more interesting than it was before" (pp. 11–12). Dewey's admonition provides an important working hypothesis for modern research on situational interest. It leads to a straightforward prediction, which can be called the *seductive details hypothesis*—adding interesting, but relevant, details to an otherwise boring text will not improve learning of the text.

Is there any difference in what students learn from a text that contains or does not contain *seductive details*—that is, highly interesting and vivid material that is not closely related to the important information in the text? If we take a somewhat boring text and spice it up by adding an interesting detail to each paragraph, will students learn more from the text? Consider, for example, the passage about insects in Figure 14–4. First read the passage; then close the book and write down all that you can remember.

If you are like students in a study by Garner, Gillingham, and White (1989), you did well in remembering the three seductive details ("When a Click Beetle is on its back, it flips itself into the air and lands right side up while it makes a clicking noise." "When a fly moves its wings about 200 times in a second, you hear a buzzing sound." and "Insects have to protect themselves from snakes, which eat live animals such as insects, worms, frogs, mice, rats, rabbits, and fish.") but not so well in remembering the three most important pieces of information (i.e., the first sentence in each paragraph). However, if you had read the same passage without the seductive details, how do you think you would have done in learning the important information?

Figure 14–5 shows the average amount of important information recalled by college students and by seventh graders who read the insect passage with and without seductive details (about beetles that flip, flies that buzz, and snakes that eat live animals). As you can see, for both age groups, students who read the insect passage without seductive details actually recalled more important information than students who read the insect passage with seductive details. In related studies, adding seductive details did not improve learning

FIGURE 14–4

A passage about insects

Some insects live alone, and some live in large families. Wasps that live alone are called solitary wasps. A Mud Dauber Wasp is a solitary wasp. Click Beetles live alone. When a Click Beetle is on its back, it flips itself into the air and lands right side up while it makes a clicking noise. Ants live in large families. There are many kinds of ants. Some ants live in trees. Black ants live in the ground.

Some insects are fast runners, and others are fast fliers. Cockroaches are very fast runners. It is hard to catch them. They run and hide. Dragonflies are very fast fliers. Flies are about the fastest flying insects. When a fly moves its wings about 200 times in a second, you hear a buzzing sound.

Some insects protect themselves by looking like other animals, and others protect themselves by looking like plants. Insects have to protect themselves from snakes, which eat live animals such as insects, worms, frogs, mice, rats, rabbits, and fish. Birds do not often eat Viceroy Butterflies because they look so much like Monarch Butterflies. Birds seem to know that Monarch Butterflies taste bad. When a Walking Stick sits very still on a twig, it looks like a twig. It is hard for an enemy to find it.

From Garner, Gillingham, and White (1989)

FIGURE 14–5 Students learn less from text with seductive details

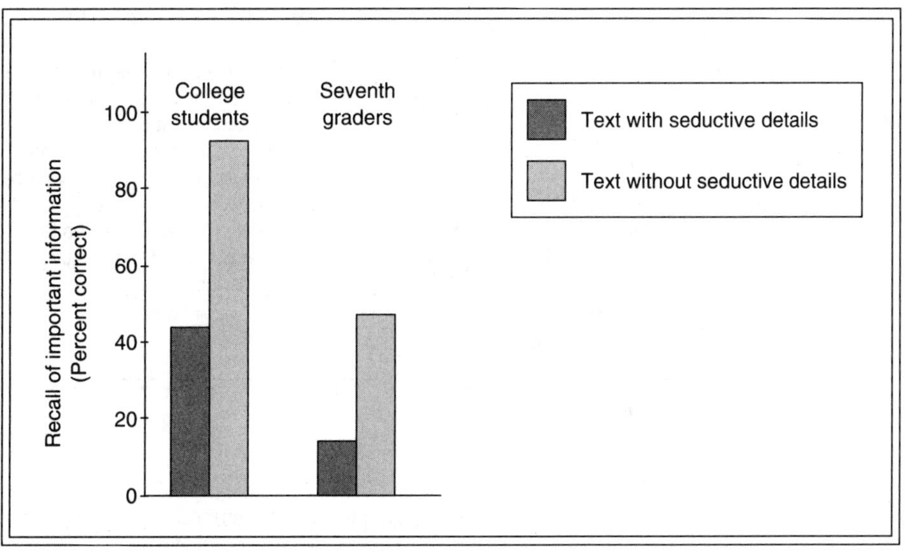

Based on Garner, Gillingham, and White (1989)

of the important information in science text (Hidi & Baird, 1988) or in history text (Duffy et al., 1989), although the details themselves were well recalled. Apparently, seductive details draw the reader's attention away from important information.

In a recent review of research on seductive details, Wade (1992) concluded that "adding seductive details . . . does not facilitate and often has a detrimental effect on learning of important information" (p. 272). According to Wade, the use of seductive details results in "texts that are longer and contain more irrelevant detail" so "students could be reading more but learning less" (p. 274). These results support Dewey's warnings against viewing interest as some sort of spice that can be added to an otherwise boring lesson.

If seductive details disrupt the process of constructing a coherent understanding of the presented material, they should also have a negative impact on transfer performance. To test this idea, Harp and Mayer (1997, 1998) asked students to read an illustrated passage that explained the cause-and-effect steps involved in lightning formation. The passage contained 550 words broken into six paragraphs, along with an illustration for each paragraph. Figure 14–6 shows one of the paragraphs describing how negatively charged particles fall to the bottom of the cloud and positively charged particles rise to the top. It also shows a corresponding illustration depicting the same process of negatively charged particles on the bottom of the cloud and positively charged particles on the top. What is the main point of this paragraph? If you focus on building a cause-and-effect chain, the main step is the separation of charges in the cloud, with negatives going to the bottom and positives going to the top.

Suppose, however, we add seductive details to each paragraph consisting of a sentence and a photograph. For example, after the first sentence of the paragraph we add: "In trying to understand these processes, scientists sometimes create lightning by launching tiny rockets into overhead clouds." To the right of the paragraph we add a photograph of scientists in an open field launching a small rocket into a storm cloud. The seductive details are

FIGURE 14–6 Excerpt from lightning passage

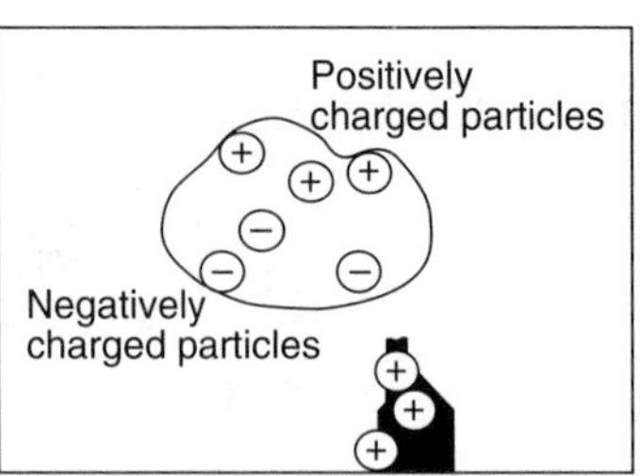

Negatively charged particles fall to bottom of cloud

Within the cloud, the moving air causes electrical charges to build, although scientists do not fully understand how it occurs. Most believe that the charge results from the collision of the cloud's light, rising water droplets and tiny pieces of ice against hail and other heavier, falling particles. The negatively charged particles fall to the bottom of the cloud, and most of the positively charged particles rise to the top.

Adapted from Harp and Mayer (1997)

intended to be interesting and related to the general topic of lightning, but they are irrelevant to the cause-and-effect explanation of how lightning forms.

To assess what students learned, Harp and Mayer asked them to write an explanation of how lightning forms (recall test), and to write answers to problem-solving transfer questions, such as, "Suppose you saw clouds in the sky but no lightning. Why not?" (transfer test). Harp and Mayer counted up the number of steps in the cause-and-effect chain students produced on the recall test, and counted the number of clever answers they gave on the transfer test. Figure 14–7 shows the recall and transfer performance of students who read the passage with or without seductive details. As you can see, adding seductive details severely hurt both recall of the explanation and transfer. In follow-up studies, Harp and Mayer (1998) concluded that seductive details do their damage by encouraging students to impose an inappropriate theme on the passage—such as seeing it as a story about the dangers of lightning rather than as an explanation of how lightning storms form. In this way, seductive-details students are encouraged to integrate the material around inappropriate prior knowledge about the dangers of lightning, select irrelevant material based on this theme, and organize their learning around the theme.

More recently, Mayer, Hieser, and Lonn (2001) asked students to view a multimedia explanation of lighting formation consisting of animation and narration. To spice up the presentation, they added six short video clips with one-sentence narration, such as the same seductive-details sentence as above, along with a 10-second video clip showing scientists setting up rockets in an open field, buttons being pressed on a control box, and small rockets soaring into overhead storm clouds. As with the text-based study, adding seductive details to a multimedia explanation resulted in moderate detriments to recall of the explanation (a decline of 15% on the recall test) and large detriments to the production of clever answers to transfer problems (a decline of 30% on the transfer test). It appears that adding interesting but conceptually irrelevant material to an explanation is not a useful way to teach for transfer.

If adding interesting and vivid details does not facilitate learning, how can educators improve the interest level of text and other instructional materials? To answer this question

FIGURE 14–7 Seductive details hurt recall and transfer

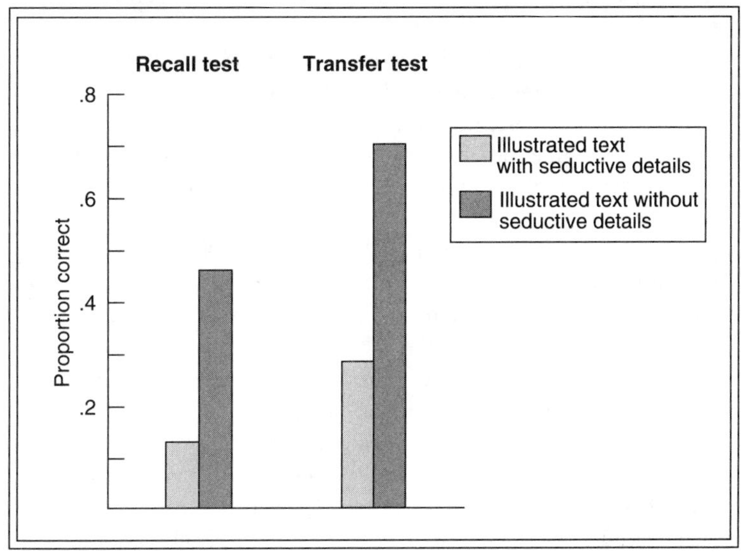

Adapted from Harp and Mayer (1997)

it is useful to distinguish between *emotional interest*—affect that results from overall arousal or excitement—and *cognitive interest*—affect that results from being able to make sense out of text material (Kintsch, 1980; Wade, 1992). Wade (1992) suggests that "rather than focusing on . . . writing techniques that arouse emotional interest, strategies are needed to increase cognitive interest" (p. 274). To create cognitive interest, teachers need to create or select instructional texts that are coherent so that students can easily determine the underlying structure. In summary, structurally coherent text allows students to understand and therefore enjoy learning. Texts that are interesting are texts that students can understand. Techniques for improving text structure are discussed more fully in Chapter 10.

MOTIVATION BASED ON SELF-EFFICACY

"I am confident that I will be able to grasp the main ideas in this chapter." "If I read this section carefully, I will be able to explain what self-efficacy is." "I know that I am capable of scoring an A on a test of the material in this book." If you agree with these statements, you have high self-efficacy for mastering educational psychology; if you mainly disagree with these statements, your self-efficacy could be classified as low.

What is self-efficacy? As you can see from this example, self-efficacy is a kind of personal expectation or judgment concerning one's capability to accomplish some task. Schunk (1991) defines self-efficacy as "an individual's judgments of his or her capabilities to perform given actions" (p. 207), and Bandura (1986) defines it as "people's judgments of their capabilities to organize and execute courses of action required to attain designated types of performance" (p. 391).

Self-efficacy is not the same as self-concept (Marsh & Shavelson, 1985). Self-concept is a general view of one's self across domains; self-efficacy is a specific view of one's capacities in a given domain. Self-concept consists of many dimensions, one of which is self-confidence, which is most like self-efficacy. For example, "I am a smart person" relates to self-concept, whereas "I am confident that I can get an A in my educational psychology course" relates to self-efficacy.

Why is self-efficacy important? A student's self-efficacy may play an important role in the student's academic achievement. Schunk (1991) claims that "there is evidence that self-efficacy predicts . . . academic achievement" (p. 207). According to Bandura (1977), self-efficacy affects the amount of effort and persistence that a person devotes to a task.

Where does self-efficacy come from? Suppose that you are taking a class in how to use a computer-based word processor; since you have never used a word processor before, your self-efficacy for this task is still undeveloped. After a few minutes, you find that you are able to use the program easily, so your self-efficacy increases. You look over to see that other first-time learners like yourself are learning to use the program. Your self-efficacy soars because you assume that "if they can do it, I can do it." Your instructor walks by and says, "You can do this!" Again, your self-efficacy grows. Your initial sense of high anxiety, including high heart rate and nausea, has left, and now you feel more relaxed. This bodily change also signals an increase in self-efficacy. These examples describe four sources of self-efficacy: interpreting one's own performance, interpreting the performance of others, interpreting others' expressions of your capabilities, and interpreting one's physiological state.

Figure 14–8 summarizes a theory of self-efficacy, adapted from Schunk (1989, 1991). In any learning situation, students enter with a sense of efficacy that is based on their aptitudes and past experiences in similar tasks. Students' self-efficacy influences what they do, how hard they try, and how long they persist—that is, what Schunk calls "task engagement

FIGURE 14–8 A model of self-efficacy

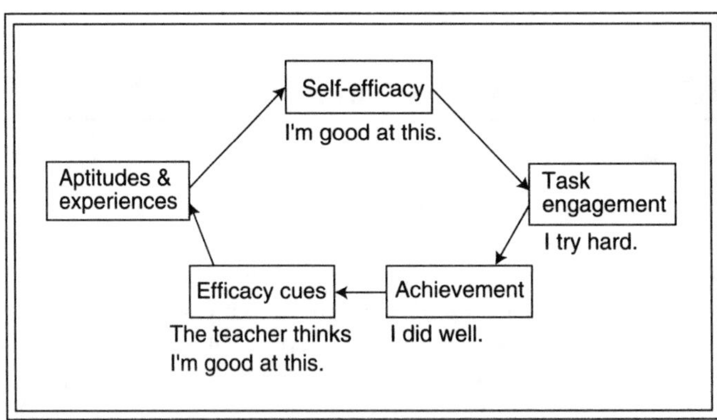

Adapted from Schunk (1989)

variables." Throughout the learning episode, the students seek efficacy cues signaling how well they are capable of doing on the task. They use these efficacy cues to establish their self-efficacy for similar tasks in the future. According to Schunk:

> Students derive cues signaling how well they are learning, which they use to assess efficacy for further learning. Motivation is enhanced when students perceive they are making progress in learning. In turn, as students . . . become more skillful, they maintain a sense of self-efficacy for performing well. (1991, p. 209)

In short, self-efficacy for a given task both influences and is influenced by students' performance on a task. However, self-efficacy is influenced by how students interpret performance feedback rather than the feedback itself; thus, students who have established high levels of self-efficacy over the course of many experiences are unlikely to suffer lowered self-efficacy as the result of negative performance feedback.

Self-efficacy theory predicts that students work harder and longer when they judge themselves as capable than when they judge themselves as unable to perform a task. In this section, we examine two specific predictions: self-efficacy is related to study strategy and to achievement.

The first prediction of self-efficacy theory is that a student's sense of self-efficacy for a given task is related to the way the student goes about learning a task. That is, the more confident students are in their capacity to learn, the more active they will be in the learning process. To test this hypothesis, a first step is to develop a way of measuring the level of students' self-efficacy and the level of students' learning activity. For example, Zimmerman and Martinez-Pons (1990) presented a series of 10 words to elementary and high school students; for each word, students were asked to rate their ability to spell the word on a scale ranging from completely unsure (0) to completely sure (100). The average rating on the 10 words was used as a measure of verbal self-efficacy. To measure learning activity, Zimmerman and Martinez-Pons asked students to respond to eight open-ended questions, such as

> Assume your teacher asks students to write a short paper on a topic such as the history of your community or neighborhood. Your score on this paper will affect your report card grade. In such cases, do you have any particular method to help you plan and write your paper? (p. 53)

A measure of learning activity was computed by tallying the number of times students mentioned self-regulated learning strategies such as setting goals, seeking information, keeping records, seeking peer assistance, reviewing notes, and organizing information. As predicted, students' perceptions of efficacy were correlated with their reported use of active learning strategies ($r = .42$). For example, students who expressed confidence in their spelling ability tended to report using more active learning strategies on a verbal task, whereas students who lacked confidence reported fewer active learning strategies.

In another attempt to test the study strategy hypothesis, Pintrich and De Groot (1990) asked seventh-grade students in science and English classrooms to answer questions about their motivation to learn (such as their self-efficacy) and about their level of activity during learning. For example, to evaluate self-efficacy, they asked students to rate agreement or disagreement on a 7-point scale to statements such as "I expect to do very well in this class" and "I am certain that I will be able to learn the material for this class."

To evaluate degree of active learning, the researchers asked students to rate agreement and disagreement on a 7-point scale to statements such as "When I study for this English class, I put the important ideas in my own words" and "I ask myself questions to make sure I know the material I have been studying." As predicted, Pintrich and De Groot (1990) observed correlations between self-efficacy and use of active learning strategies ($r = .33$ to $r = .44$). Similarly, in a study of arithmetic learning, Schunk (1981) found a positive correlation between self-efficacy and persistence on exercise problems during learning ($r = .30$).

These results are consistent with the idea that self-efficacy is related to deeper and more active processing of information during learning, as suggested by the arrow from "self-efficacy" to "task engagement" in Figure 14–8. However, a more practical issue concerns the relation between self-efficacy and academic achievement and lies at the heart of the second prediction of self-efficacy theory. The theory predicts that self-efficacy is positively related to academic achievement; that is, the more confident a student is in his or her capacity to learn a certain lesson, the greater the probability of success in accomplishing that goal.

To examine this prediction, Schunk and Hanson (1985) asked elementary school children who were having difficulty in arithmetic to judge their capacity to solve 25 different pairs of subtraction problems, such as shown in Figure 14–9. Each pair of problems was presented for 2 seconds, enough time for students to assess problem difficulty but not enough time to actually solve the problems. Students rated their capacity to solve each pair of problems on a 100-point scale ranging from "not sure" (10) to "maybe" (40) to "pretty sure" (70) to "really sure" (100). The average rating for the 25 problems constitutes a measure of self-efficacy. Then students received instruction in how to solve subtraction problems; the number of problems that were correctly completed during instruction provides a

FIGURE 14–9 Can you solve these problems?

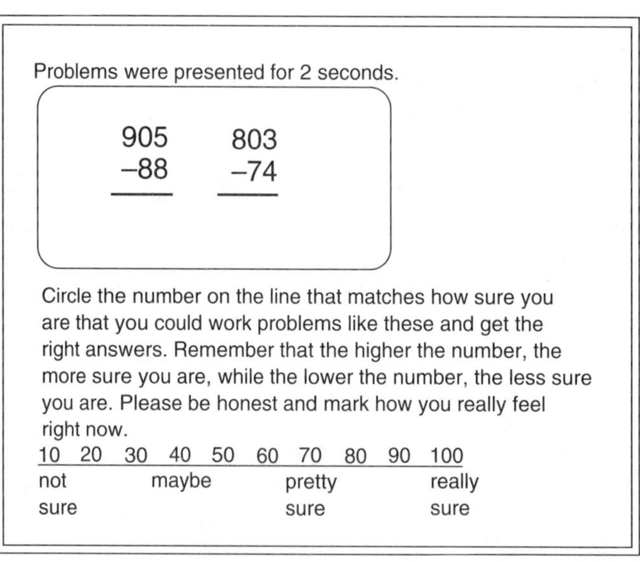

Based on Schunk and Hanson (1985)

measure of ease of learning. Finally, students took a 25-item subtraction test; the number of correct answers on the test constitutes a measure of achievement.

Is self-efficacy related to achievement in subtraction? The answer from Schunk and Hanson's study is clearly yes. The correlation between self-efficacy and achievement was high ($r = .66$). Furthermore, Schunk (1989) reported that similarly high rates were obtained across a series of studies in many domains ($r = .46$ to $r = .90$). Is self-efficacy related to ease of learning? Again, Schunk and Hanson's study produced a strong correlation between self-efficacy and ease of learning ($r = .38$), and Schunk (1989) reported that similarly high correlations were obtained in other studies ($r = .33$ to $.42$). In conclusion, performance during and after learning appears to be related to students' judgments of their capabilities for learning.

Another test of the achievement hypothesis concerns how changes in self-efficacy are related to changes in achievement. According to the theory, when a student's self-efficacy is raised, the student's academic performance also increases. For example, in Schunk and Hanson's (1985) study previously described, students rated their self-efficacy for subtraction, took a subtraction pretest, received instruction, and then again rated their self-efficacy for subtraction and took a subtraction posttest.

Some students received instruction aimed at improving self-efficacy (student-model group). Students in the student model training group viewed two 45-minute videotapes presented on two consecutive days. The tapes portrayed a teacher writing subtraction problems on the board and a student successfully solving them. The student model verbalized aloud the steps in solving the problem and occasionally made positive statements such as "I can do that one" or "I like doing these." The student models in the videotape were selected to be similar to students in the study. When a student model finished a problem, the teacher stated that the solution was correct and then wrote another problem on the board, and so on throughout the videotape. After viewing the videotapes, the students received 40 minutes of workbook-based instruction on each of five consecutive school days. At the beginning of each session, each student was given a workbook containing a sheet explaining how to carry out the needed operations, two worked-out examples, and a series of pages with similar problems to solve. Students were free to consult with a proctor if they needed help. Other students received the same five days of workbook-based instruction but viewed videotapes showing a teacher solving the problems (teacher-model group) or saw no videotapes at all (no model group).

Figure 14–10 summarizes changes in self-efficacy and achievement from before to after instruction. As you can see, the student-model group showed a large change in self-efficacy and in achievement, whereas the changes for the no-model and teacher-model groups were more modest. These results support the idea that modeling "can raise self-efficacy because it implicitly conveys to observers that they are capable of performing the modeled operation" (Schunk & Hanson, 1985, p. 319). Thus, self-efficacy is not based solely on one's prior performance but is also influenced by observing peers. Importantly, the increase in self-efficacy is related to a concurrent increase in academic performance. Schunk and Hanson suggested that "teachers who systematically incorporate peer models into their instruction, at least with children who have skill deficiencies, may help promote children's skills and self-efficacy for acquiring them" (p. 321).

These results provide a consistent picture of how self-efficacy influences academic performance. Students who have confidence in their capabilities engage in deeper processing

FIGURE 14–10 Changes in self-efficacy and achievement for three groups

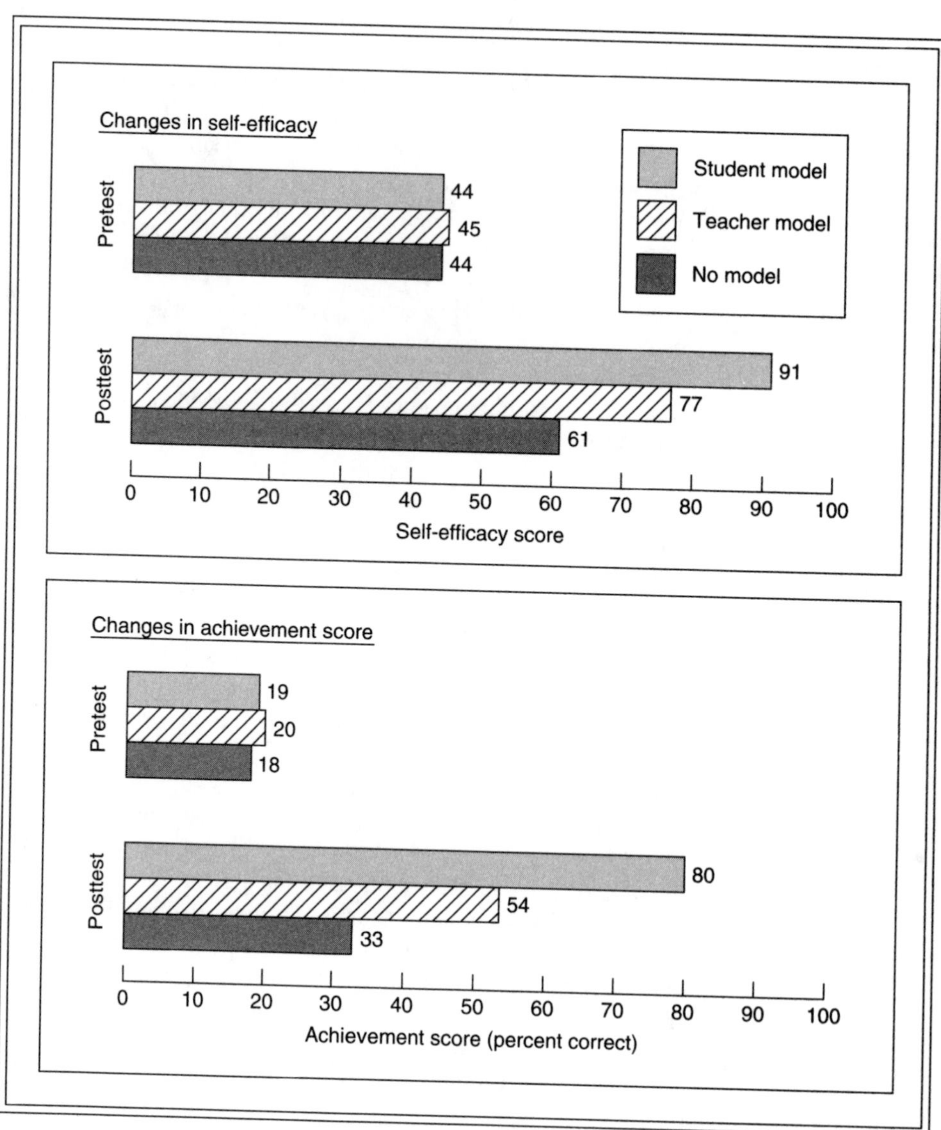

of the material during learning, which in turn results in a better understanding of the material. Thus, when achievement tests emphasize understanding, high self-efficacy students are likely to perform better than low self-efficacy students.

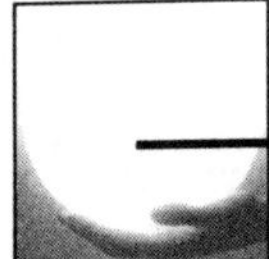

MOTIVATION BASED ON ATTRIBUTIONS

Suppose that you fail a quiz in math class. You search for a reason, a cause, a justification for this outcome. You might, for example, attribute your failure to lack of ability: "I'm not very good in math." Alternatively, you might decide that your performance was caused by lack of effort: "I didn't study enough." Perhaps you might determine that your failure was caused by task difficulty: "That was a really hard quiz." Other possible causes have to do with luck ("I made some unlucky guesses"), mood ("I just had a bad math day"), or hindrance from others ("The guy in front of me was so noisy I couldn't concentrate").

Alternatively, suppose that your history teacher praises you for giving a particularly insightful answer to a question during class discussion. Being an inquisitive person, you seek an explanation for your success. Again, among the possible causes of your success are ability ("I'm really pretty smart in history"), effort ("I guess all my studying is paying off"), ease of task ("That was really a pretty easy question"), luck ("The answer just came to me out of nowhere"), mood ("Everything is going great for me this morning"), or help from others ("The teacher helped by smiling and nodding as I answered").

These stated causes are examples of attribution theory applied to academic learning (Weiner, 1979, 1984, 1985, 1986, 1992). According to attribution theory, students seek to understand the world around them, such as searching for the causes of success and failure on academic tasks. Students may attribute their success or failure to a variety of causes, including ability, effort, task difficulty, and luck. Figure 14–11 shows how each of these causal ascriptions relates to each of three dimensions: *locus* refers to whether the cause is internal or external to the student; *stability* refers to whether the cause is constant or changing over time; and *controllability* refers to whether the cause is or is not influenced by the student. For example, ability is internal, stable, and uncontrollable; effort is internal,

FIGURE 14–11

Why did I fail?

Event	*Attribution*	*Example*	*Locus*	*Stability*	*Controllability*
Failure	Ability	I'm not smart enough	Internal	Stable	Uncontrollable
Failure	Effort	I didn't try hard enough	Internal	Unstable	Controllable
Failure	Task difficulty	This is too hard for me	External	Stable	Uncontrollable
Failure	Luck	I had bad luck	External	Unstable	Uncontrollable

unstable, and controllable; task difficulty is external, stable, and uncontrollable; and luck is external, unstable, and uncontrollable.

According to attribution theory, the causal ascriptions that a student makes are related to academic motivation. First, let's focus on ability and effort. If a student attributes failure to a stable cause such as ability ("I'm not smart enough"), or task difficulty ("This is too hard for me"), the student is likely to give up and to be less persistent when confronted with similar tasks in the future. If a student attributes failure to an unstable cause such as effort ("If I try harder, I can do this") or luck ("If my luck changes, I'll be OK"), the student is likely to persist even in the face of failure. According to Weiner (1992) "achievement-change programs have been developed that attempt to induce individuals to ascribe failure to lack of effort (an unstable cause) rather than to low ability (a stable cause)" (p. 861).

Let's examine two basic predictions of attribution theory for education: *attributional training hypothesis*—students who are trained to attribute academic success or failure to effort are more likely to work hard than students who attribute their performance to ability—and the *attributional feedback hypothesis*—teachers who show sympathy or pity when students fail convey the idea that students lack ability.

To investigate the first hypothesis, consider the following scenario. Josh, a sixth-grader with a learning disability, is given a paragraph to read. He reads each word but does not do well on a reading comprehension test. The teacher suspects that Josh is not actively processing the material, so the teacher provides direct instruction in active reading strategies such as summarization, that is, locating the main idea and its supporting details in a paragraph. However, when given a new paragraph to read, Josh does not use the active reading strategies he just learned, and he continues to perform poorly on reading comprehension tests.

What's going on in this situation? On the cognitive level, Josh seems to lack appropriate reading strategies. This problem can be addressed through strategy training, such as teaching Josh how to summarize paragraphs. On the motivational level, Josh may have developed the belief that he will not be able to answer comprehension questions no matter how hard he studies. This problem can be addressed through attributional training, such as helping Josh to recognize that test performance depends on effort during learning (rather than on his innate ability). In the Josh scenario, strategy training alone did not seem to be helpful, perhaps because Josh also needed attributional training. In short, Josh knew what to do (from strategy training), but he did not believe that doing it would really help him.

According to attribution theory, strategy training is only part of the prescription for changing students' academic performance; in addition, students need to change the way they attribute success and failure. To test this hypothesis, Borkowski, Weyhing, and Carr (1988) asked a group of children with reading disabilities and adolescents from special education classes to take pretests, receive training, and then take posttests. The pretest and posttest included a reading strategy test designed to evaluate the degree to which students could summarize a paragraph and a reading comprehension test that tested how well students could answer questions about a passage they read. The reading strategy test asked students to read and then summarize paragraphs; higher scores indicate better summaries. The reading comprehension test was a standardized test that measured students' ability to read passages and then answer inferential questions; higher scores indicate better reading comprehension.

FIGURE 14–12

Partial script for attribution training

Student receives strategy training in how to identify main topic and supporting examples.

Instructor demonstrates how to summarize a paragraph but selects topic sentence at random.

Class discusses reasons for instructor's mistake and concludes that failure was due to a controllable factor: not using the right strategy.

Instructor says, "I need to try to use the strategy." Instructor uses strategy and succeeds in summarizing the paragraph. Instructor emphasizes that effortful use of strategy resulted in success.

Instructor and students take turns summarizing paragraphs. Instructor continues to attribute errors to lack of effort and success to effortful use of correct strategy.

Based on Borkowski, Weyhing, and Carr (1988)

Some students received strategy and attribution training, as summarized in Figure 14–12, whereas others received only strategy training. For attributional training, students learned an association strategy for remembering pairs of pictures and a clustering strategy for remembering a list of items. During learning, the instructor made intentional errors and then discussed with students the importance of not attributing failure to noncontrollable factors such as ability or task difficulty. The instructor modeled positive self-attributions while learning, such as "I need to try to use the strategy," and a discussion of the causes of success emphasized statements such as "I tried hard, used the strategy, and did well." Then students learned the summarization strategy, along with the modeling of attributions during learning that emphasized "strategy use equals success." In contrast, the strategy-only group learned how to summarize paragraphs by finding main ideas and supporting details but did not receive any attributional training.

Figure 14–13 summarizes the pretest-to-posttest changes for the two groups. As you can see, students who were given attribution and strategy training performed better on summarizing paragraphs than strategy-only students. This finding indicates that effective use of strategies depends partly on students' belief that the effort required to use a strategy actually will have an effect on their performance. In addition, the attribution and strategy group performed better than the strategy-only group on reading comprehension questions involving inference but not on questions involving literal memory for the material. Again, the combined training in attribution and strategy was more effective than strategy training alone in producing active learners who could go beyond the information given—that is, learners who were able to transfer.

Students with learning disabilities are often candidates for cognitive strategy instruction. Borkowski, Weyhing, and Carr (1988) conclude that cognitive strategy training will be more effective if it is combined with motivational training:

> Our data suggest that teaching reading strategies alone, or emphasizing the role of effort in isolation, will not prove sufficient for educating students with learning disabilities.

FIGURE 14–13 Learning to read effectively with and without attribution training

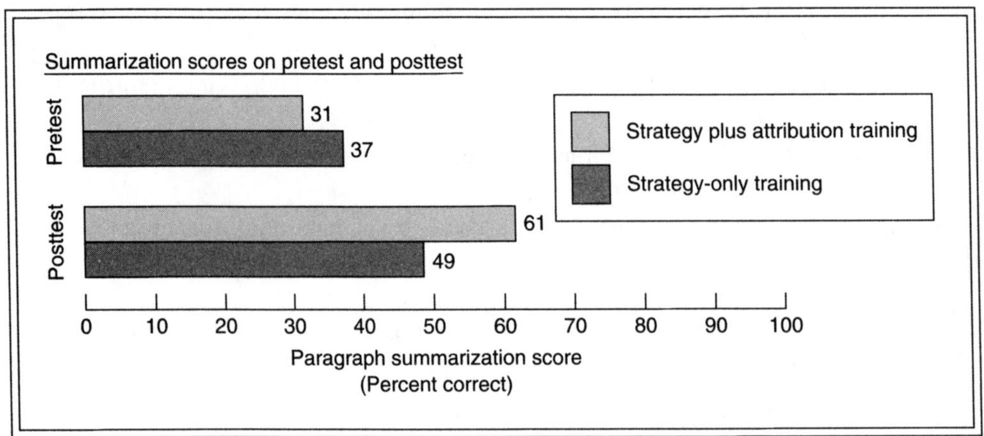

> Attributions linked to specific subject matter should be manipulated systematically in order to enhance the acquisition and generalization of study skills being taught. (p. 52)

In short, students may need to learn about cognitive aids such as effective study skills, and motivational aids such as the belief that academic success depends on actively using effective study aids.

A second important hypothesis based on attribution theory is that students use cues from teachers to make attributions about effort and ability. When a teacher shows a student how to solve a problem, a subtle message is sent: "You were not smart enough to figure it out, so I had to tell you the answer."

Consider the following scenario. Elementary school students are sitting at their desks working on a sheet of 10 arithmetic problems while the teacher circulates around the room. The teacher stops at the desk of one boy, looks casually over his shoulder as he works, and then moves on without comment. She stops at the desk of another boy, looks casually over his shoulder, and says, "Let me give you a hint. Don't forget to carry your tens." The help comes early in the student's work on the problem before it was clear whether the student could solve the problem. A few minutes later, the teacher collects the papers; she informs both the unhelped and the helped boy that they had done well, correctly solving 8 out of the 10 problems.

If you had been a student in the class, how would you rate the unhelped and helped students in terms of ability and effort as shown in Figure 14–14? Place a check mark in the figure that indicates how smart you think each boy is and how much each boy tried.

Graham and Barker (1990) asked elementary school students to view videotapes depicting the situation you just read about and to give ratings as you just did in Figure 14–14. If you are like the 5- to 10-year-old students in Graham and Barker's study, you rated the student who received help from the teacher as less able and less hard working than the student who did not receive help, even though neither student asked for help and

FIGURE 14–14 How smart and how hard-working was each boy?

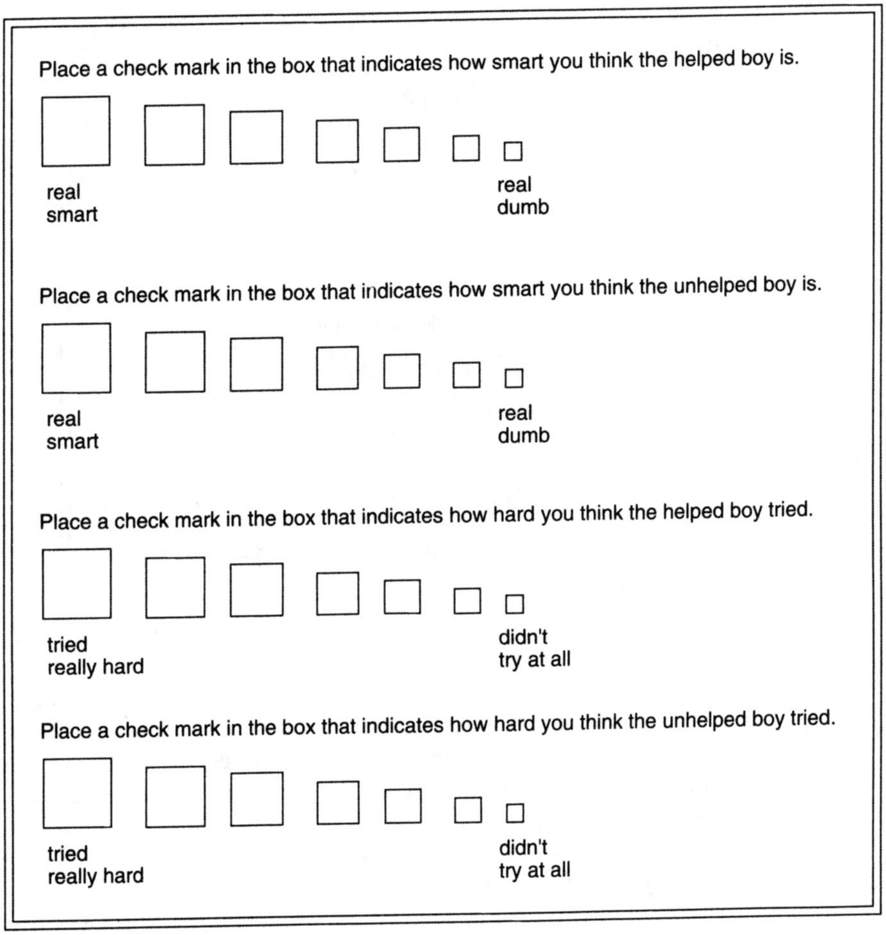

Place a check mark in the box that indicates how smart you think the helped boy is.

☐ ☐ ☐ ☐ ☐ ☐ ☐

real smart — real dumb

Place a check mark in the box that indicates how smart you think the unhelped boy is.

☐ ☐ ☐ ☐ ☐ ☐ ☐

real smart — real dumb

Place a check mark in the box that indicates how hard you think the helped boy tried.

☐ ☐ ☐ ☐ ☐ ☐ ☐

tried really hard — didn't try at all

Place a check mark in the box that indicates how hard you think the unhelped boy tried.

☐ ☐ ☐ ☐ ☐ ☐ ☐

tried really hard — didn't try at all

Based on Graham and Barker (1990)

both correctly solved 8 out of 10 problems. These results are summarized in Figure 14–15.

Consider a related situation in which you, as a sixth-grade student, are given some puzzle problems to solve. You are told that you will have 60 seconds to solve each problem because "one minute is the right amount of time for kids your age" based on a bogus "Table of 6th-Grade Norms." You fail to solve each problem in the time allotted. Whenever you fail to solve a problem within 60 seconds, the experimenter says, "Stop. Your time is up. You didn't get that one right because you didn't solve it in time." Then the experimenter demonstrates the correct solution and says, "I feel sorry for you because you haven't gotten any of these puzzles right so far." She leans forward with hands folded, gazes directly at you, and speaks in a quiet tone. This procedure is repeated for five failed puzzles.

FIGURE 14–15 Student ratings of ability and effort for each boy

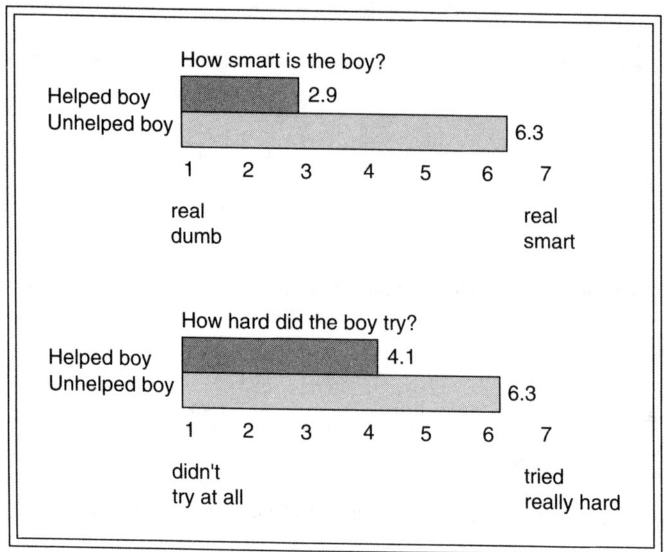

Based on Graham and Barker (1990)

If you are like the children in Graham's (1984) study, you interpret the teacher's sympathetic comments as cues that you lack the ability to solve the problems. When Graham compared sixth-grade students who received sympathy and pity after each failure with those who simply were told they had failed, she found the pitied students were more likely than the unpitied students to rate lack of ability as a cause of their failures.

According to Graham and Barker (1990) and Graham (1984, 1991), help or pity from a well-meaning teacher may be interpreted by the receiving student as a cue that the student lacks the ability to succeed. Figure 14–16 summarizes an attributional model of the process by which teachers' help results in poorer performance:

First, the teacher—who is perceived to have high ability—provides unsolicited help to a student.
Second, the student infers that the teacher gave help because she believes the student lacks ability.
Third, the student perceives himself or herself as having low ability.
Fourth, the student expects his or her lack of ability to result in poor performance on subsequent tasks.
Fifth, the student does not try hard on subsequent tasks.

When a teacher provides unsolicited help to a student, the student may infer that the teacher has a low opinion of his or her ability; when a student thinks that the teacher perceives him or her to have low ability, the student comes to share this belief, which in turn causes the student to expect poor performance on subsequent tasks and therefore to not try hard.

FIGURE 14–16 A student's chain of reasoning about teacher help giving

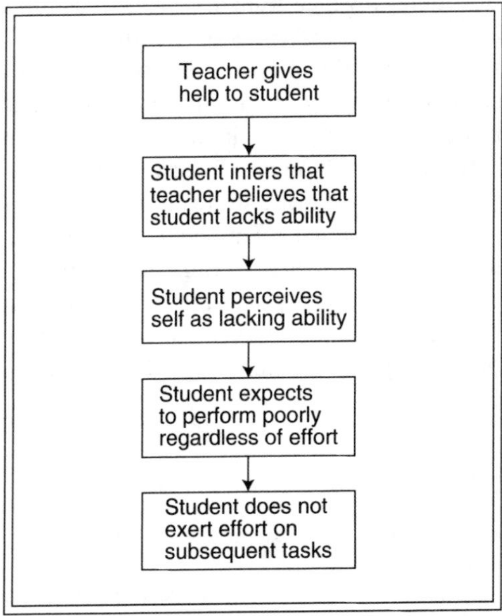

Based on Graham and Barker (1990)

CHAPTER SUMMARY

In this chapter we explored three possible roots of motivation. According to interest theory, students learn best when they can find some personal value in the material. According to self-efficacy theory, students learn best when they are confident in their capabilities to learn the material. According to attribution theory, students learn best when they believe that academic achievement depends on how much effort they devote to learning.

Although these three views of motivation to learn differ, they share features that could eventually become unifying themes. First, these three views of motivation emphasize the domain-specificity of motivation. In contrast to earlier theories that viewed motivation as a general drive (Hull, 1943) or general personality characteristic (Atkinson, 1964), current theories are based on the idea that motivation depends on the student's interaction with the specific material to be learned. Second, these three views of motivation emphasize the connection between motivation and cognition. In contrast to previous theories that viewed motivation to be an automatic drive-reduction system (Hull, 1943), current theories hold that motivation is related to learners' interpretations, memories, beliefs, and self-explanations about the learning situation. Third, these three views are based on research with humans in realistic academic settings rather than on research with hungry rats in contrived situations.

Modern theories of motivation provide useful implications for education. Teachers should create situations that mesh with the interests of the students so that students can see some personal value in learning the material. Teachers should create situations in which students can observe their peers succeeding and also experience success themselves. Teachers should create situations in which students can learn that their academic successes and failures depend on their effort rather than solely on their ability.

This chapter shows how motivational and cognitive processes are both involved in learning, so it is unwise to emphasize one at the expense of the other. Although motivation is widely recognized as a crucial component in education, it has not received as much attention in research or theory as cognition has. For example, Ames and Ames (1984) note that only since the 1960s "has the systematic study of motivational processes in education settings received significant and sustained attention by researchers in psychology and education" (p. xi). Although cognitive theories of learning have come to dominate educational psychology, they "lack an adequate conceptualization of the impact of motivational and emotional factors in learning" (Krapp, Hidi, & Renninger, 1992, p. 4). In short, educational psychologists should continue to examine not only ways of improving student learning but also ways of helping students to want to learn.

SUGGESTED READINGS

Dewey, J. (1913). *Interest and effort in education.* Cambridge, MA: Riverside Press. (A classic little book on the role of interest in learning.)

Renninger, K. A., Hidi S., & Krapp, A. (Eds.). (1992). *The role of interest in learning and development.* Hillsdale, NJ: Erlbaum. (Contains chapters by leading researchers on interest in learning.)

Weiner, B. (1992). Motivation. In M. Alkin (Ed.), *Encyclopedia of educational research* (6th ed) (pp. 860–865). New York: Macmillan. (Reviews research on motivation in school settings.)

REFERENCES

Adams, J. A. (1976). *Learning and memory.* Homewood, IL: Dorsey Press.

Adams, M. J. (1989). Thinking skills curricula: Their promise and progress. *Educational Psychologist, 24,* 24–77.

Adams, M. J. (1990). *Beginning to read.* Cambridge, MA: MIT Press.

Adams, M. J. (Ed.). (1986). *Odyssey: A curriculum for thinking.* Watertown, MA: Charlesbridge Publishing.

Adams, A., Carnine, D. & Gersten, R. (1982). Instructional strategies for studying content area texts in the intermediate grades. *Reading Research Quarterly, 18,* 27–55.

Allington, R. L., & Weber, R. (1993). Questioning questions in teaching and learning from texts. In B. K. Britton, A. Woodward, & M. Binkley (Eds.), *Learning from textbooks: Theory and practice* (pp. 47–68). Hillsdale, NJ: Erlbaum.

Ames, R. E., & Ames, C. (Eds.). (1984). *Research on motivation in education: Vol. 1, Student motivation.* San Diego: Academic Press.

Anastasiow, N. J., Sibley, S. A., Leonhardt, T. M. & Borish, G. D. (1970). A comparison of guided discovery, discovery and didactic teaching of math to kindergarten poverty children. *American Educational Research Journal, 7,* 493–510.

Anderson, J. R. (1993). *Rules of the mind.* Hillsdale, NJ: Erlbaum.

Anderson, J. R. (2000). *Cognitive psychology and its implications* (5th ed.). New York: Worth.

Anderson, J. R. (2000). *Learning and memory* (2nd ed.). New York: Wiley.

Anderson, L. W., Krathwohl, D. R., Airasian, P. W., Cruikshank, K. A., Mayer, R. E., Pintrich, P. R., Raths, J., & Wittrock, M. C. (2001). *A taxonomy for learning, teaching, and assessing.* New York: Longman.

Anderson, R. G., & Biddle, W. B. (1975). On asking people questions about what they are reading. *Psychology of Learning and Motivation, 9,* 90–132.

Anderson, R. G., & Freebody, P. (1981). Vocabulary knowledge. In J. T. Guthrie (Ed.), *Comprehension and teaching: Research reviews.* Newark, DE: International Reading Association.

Applebee, A. N. (1982). Writing and learning in school settings. In M. Nystrant (Ed.), *What writers know.* New York: Academic Press.

Ashcraft, M. H., & Stazyk, E. H. (1981). Mental addition: A test of three verification models. *Memory and Cognition, 9,* 185–196.

Atkinson, J. W. (1964). *An introduction to motivation.* Princeton, NJ: Van Nostrand.

Atkinson, R. C. (1975). Mnemotechnics in second-language learning. *American Psychologist, 30,* 821–828.

Atkinson, R. C., & Raugh, M. R. (1975). An application of the mnemonic keyword method to the acquisition of a Russian vocabulary. *Journal of Experimental Psychology: Human Learning and Memory, 104,* 126–133.

Ausubel, D. P. (1960). The use of advance organizers in the learning and retention of meaningful verbal material. *Journal of Educational Psychology, 51,* 267–272.

Ausubel D. P. (1968). *Educational psychology: A cognitive view.* New York: Holt, Rinehart & Winston.

Ausubel, D. P., & Youssef, M. (1963). The role of discriminability in meaningful parallel learning. *Journal of Educational Psychology, 54,* 331–336.

Baker, L., & Anderson, R. C. (1982). Effects of inconsistent information on text processing: Evidence for comprehension monitoring. *Reading Research Quarterly, 17,* 281–293.

Bandura, A. (1977). Self-efficacy: Toward a unifying theory of behavioral change. *Psychological Review, 84,* 191–215.

Bandura, A. (1986). *Social foundations of thought and action: A social cognitive theory.* Englewood Cliffs, NJ: Prentice-Hall.

Bandura, A., & Walters, R. H. (1963). *Social learning and personality development.* New York: Holt, Rinehart & Winston.

Bangert-Drowns, R. L. (1993). The word processor as an instructional tool: A meta-analysis of word processing in writing instruction. *Review of Educational Research, 63,* 69–93.

Barnes, B. R., & Clawson, E. U. (1975). Do advance organizers facilitate learning? Recommendations for further research based on an analysis of 32 studies. *Review of Educational Research, 45,* 637–659.

Baron, J. (1977). What we might know about orthographic rules. In S. Dornic (Ed.), *Attention and performance VI.* Hillsdale, NJ. Erlbaum.

Baron, J. (1978). The word-superiority effect: Perceptual learning from reading. In W. K. Estes (Ed.), *Handbook of learning and cognitive processes. Vol. 6.* Hillsdale, NJ: Erlbaum.

Barrows, H. S., & Tamblyn, R. (1980). *Problem-based learning: An approach to medical education.* New York: Springer.

Bartlett, E. J. (1982). Learning to revise. Some component processes. In M. Nystrand (Ed.), *What writers know.* New York: Academic Press.

Bartlett, E. J., & Scribner, S. (1981). Text and content: An investigation of referential organization in children's written narratives. In C. H. Frederiksen & J. F. Dominic (Eds.), *Writing. Vol. 2.* Hillsdale, NJ: Erlbaum.

Bartlett, F. C. (1932). *Remembering: A study in experimental and social psychology.* Cambridge, UK: Cambridge University Press.

Bayman, P., & Mayer, R. E. (1983). Diagnosis of beginning programmers, misconceptions of BASIC programming statements. *Communications of the ACM, 26,* 519–521.

Bean, T. W., & Steenwyk, F. L. (1984). The effect of three forms of summarization instruction on sixth graders' summary writing and comprehension. *Journal of Reading Behavior, 16,* 297–306.

Beck, I. L., Perfetti, C. A., & McKeown, M. G. (1982). Effects of long-term vocabulary instruction on lexical access and reading comprehension. *Journal of Educational Psychology, 74,* 506–521.

Beck, I. L., & McKeown, M. G. (1994). Outcomes of history instruction: Paste-up accounts. In M. Carretero & J. F. Voss (Eds.), *Cognitive and instructional processes in history and the social sciences.* Hillsdale, NJ: Erlbaum.

Beck, I. L., McKeown, M. G., Sinatra, G. M., & Loxterman, J. A. (1991). Revising social studies text from a text-processing perspective: Evidence of improved comprehensibility. *Reading Research Quarterly,* 26, 251–276.

Bereiter, C. (1980). Development in writing. In L. W. Gregg, & E. R. Sternberg (Eds.), *Cognitive processes in writing.* Hillsdale, NJ: Erlbaum.

Bereiter, C., & Scardamalia, M. (1987). *The psychology of written composition.* Hillsdale, NJ: Erlbaum.

Berliner, D., & Calfee, R. (Eds.). (1996). *Handbook of educational psychology.* New York: Macmillan.

Binet, A. (1962). The nature and measurement of intelligence. In L. Postman (Ed.), *Psychology in the making: Histories of selected research programs.* New York: Knopf. (Originally published, Paris: Flammarion, 1911.)

Blachman, B. A. (2000). Phonological awareness. In M. L. Kamil, P. B. Mosenthal, P. D. Pearson, & R. Barr (Eds.), *Handbook of reading research,* vol. 3 (pp. 483–502). Mahwah, NJ: Erlbaum.

Blachowicz, C. L. Z., & Fisher, P. (2000). Vocabulary instruction. In M. L. Kamil, P. B. Mosenthal, P. D. Pearson, & R. Barr (Eds.), *Handbook of reading research,* vol. 3 (pp. 503–523). Mahwah, NJ: Erlbaum.

Blagg, N. (1991). *Can we teach intelligence? A comprehensive evaluation of Feuerstein's instrumental enrichment program.* Hillsdale, NJ: Erlbaum.

Bloom, B. S., & Broder, L. J. (1950). *Problem-solving processes of college students.* Chicago: University of Chicago Press.

Bobrow, D. G. (1968). Natural language input for a computer problem solving system. In M. Minsky (Ed.), *Semantic information processing.* Cambridge, MA: MIT Press.

Boker, J. (1974). Immediate and delayed retention effects of interspersing questions in written instructional passages. *Journal of Educational Psychology, 66,* 96–98.

Borkowski, J. G., Weyhing, R. S., & Carr, M. (1988). Effects of attributional retraining on strategy-based reading comprehension in learning-disabled students. *Journal of Educational Psychology, 80,* 46–53.

Bower, G. H., & Trabasso, T. R. (1963). Reversals prior to solution in concept identification. *Journal of Experimental Psychology, 66,* 409–418.

Bradley, L., & Bryant, P. (1978). Difficulties in auditory organization as a possible cause of reading backwardness. *Nature, 271,* 746–747.

Bradley, L., & Bryant, P. (1983). Categorizing sounds and learning to read—a causal connection. *Nature, 301,* 419–421.

Bradley, L., & Bryant, P. (1985). *Rhyme and reason in reading and spelling.* Ann Arbor, MI: University of Michigan Press.

Bradley, L., & Bryant, P. (1991). Phonological skills before and after learning to read. In S. A. Brady & D. P. Shankweiler (Eds.), *Phonological processes in literacy.* Hillsdale, NJ: Erlbaum.

Bransford, J. D., & Johnson, M. K. (1972). Contextual prerequisites for understanding: Some investigations of comprehension and recall. *Journal of Verbal Learning and Verbal Behavior, 11,* 717–726.

Bransford, J. D., Arbitman-Smith, R., Stein, B. S., & Vye, N. J. (1985). Improving thinking and learning skills: An analysis of three approaches. In J. W. Segal, S. F. Chipman, & R. Glaser (Eds.), *Thinking and learning skills: Volume 1, Relating instruction to research.* Hillsdale, NJ: Erlbaum.

Bransford, J. D., Brown, A. L., & Cocking, R. (Eds.). (1999). *How people learn.* Washington, DC: National Academy Press.

Bransford, J. D., Zech, L., Schwartz, D., Barron, B., Vye, N., & The Cognition and Technology Group at Vanderbilt (1996). Fostering mathematical understanding in middle school students: Lessons from research. In R. J. Sternberg & T. Ben-Zeev (Eds.), *The nature of mathematical thinking* (pp. 203–250). Mahwah, NJ: Erlbaum.

Brenner, M. E., Mayer, R. E., Moseley, B., Brar, T., Duran, R., Reed, B. S., & Webb, D. (1997). Learning by understanding: The role of multiple representations in learning algebra. *American Educational Research Journal, 34,* 663–689.

Britton, B. K. (1996). Rewriting: The arts and sciences of improving expository instructional text. In C. M. Levy & S. Ransdell (Eds.), *The science of writing* (pp. 323–346). Mahwah, NJ: Erlbaum.

Britton, B. K., & Gulgoz, S. (1991). Using Kintsch's computational model to improve instructional text: Effects of repairing inference calls on recall and cognitive structures. *Journal of Educational Psychology, 83,* 329–345.

Britton, B. K., Gulgoz, S., & Glynn, S. (1993). Impact of good and poor writing on learners: Research and theory. In B. K. Britton, A. Woodward, & M. Binkley (Eds.),

Learning from textbooks (pp. 1–46). Hillsdale, NJ: Erlbaum.

Brononski, J. (1978). *The common sense of science.* Cambridge, MA: Harvard University Press.

Brown, A. L., & Day, J. D. (1983). Macrorules for summarizing texts: The development of expertise. *Journal of Verbal Learning and Verbal Behavior, 22,* 1–14.

Brown, A. L., Day, J. D., & Jones, R. S. (1983). The development of plans for summarizing texts. *Child Development, 54,* 968–979.

Brown, A. L., & Palinscar, A. S. (1989). Guided, cooperative learning and individual knowledge acquisition. In L. B. Resnick (Ed.), *Knowing, learning, and instruction: Essays in honor of Robert Glaser* (pp. 393–452). Hillsdale, NJ: Erlbaum.

Brown, A. L., & Palinscar, A. S. (1989). Guided, cooperative learning and individual knowledge acquisition. In L. B. Resnick (Ed.), *Knowing, learning, and instruction: Essays in honor of Robert Glaser* (pp. 393–451). Hillsdale, NJ: Erlbaum.

Brown, A. L., & Smiley, S. S. (1977). Rating the importance of structural units of prose passages: A problem of metacognitive development. *Child Development, 48,* 1–8.

Brown, A. L., & Smiley, S. S. (1978). The development of strategies for studying texts. *Child Development, 49,* 1076–1088.

Brown, A. L., Campione, J. C., & Barclay, C. R. (1979). Training self-checking routines for estimating test readiness: Generalization from list learning to prose recall. *Child Development, 50,* 501–512.

Brown, A. L., Campione, J. C., & Day, J. D. (1981). Learning to learn: On training students to learn from texts. *Educational Researcher, 10,* 14–21.

Brown, J. S., & Burton, R. R. (1978). Diagnostic models for procedural bugs in basic mathematical skills. *Cognitive Science, 2,* 155–192.

Brown, J. S., McDonald, J. L., Brown, T. L., & Carr, T. H. (1988). Adapting to processing demands in discourse production: The case of handwriting. *Journal of Experimental Psychology: Human Perception and Performance, 14,* 45–59.

Brownell, W. A. (1935). Psychological considerations in the learning and teaching of arithmetic. In *The teaching of arithmetic: Tenth yearbook of the National Council of Teachers of Mathematics.* New York: Columbia University Press.

Brownell, W. A. and Moser, H. E. (1949). Meaningful vs. mechanical learning: A study on grade 3 subtraction. In *Duke University Research Studies in Education,* No. 8. Durham, NC: Duke University Press.

Bruce, B., Collins, A., Rubin, A., & Gentner, D. (1982). Three perspectives on writing. *Educational Psychologist, 17,* 131–145.

Bruer, J. T. (1993). *Schools for thought.* Cambridge, MA: MIT Press.

Bruner, J. S. (1960). *The process of education.* Cambridge, MA: Harvard University Press.

Bruner, J. S. (1961). The act of discovery. *Harvard Educational Review, 31,* 21–32.

Bruner, J. S. (1964). The course of cognitive growth. *American Psychologist, 19,* 1–15.

Bruner, J. S., & Kenney, H. (1966). *Multiple ordering.* In J. S. Bruner, R. R. Oliver, & P. M. Greenfield (Eds.), *Studies in cognitive growth.* New York: Wiley.

Bryan, W. L., & Harter, N. (1897). Studies in the physiology and psychology of telegraphic language. *Psychological Review, 4,* 27–53.

Burke, R. D. (1998). Representation, storage, and retrieval of tutorial stories in a social simulation. In R. C. Schank (Ed.), *Inside multi-media case based instruction* (pp. 175–284). Mahwah, NJ: Erlbaum.

Bus, A. G., & van IJzendoorn, M. H. (1999). Phonological awareness and early reading: A meta-analysis of experimental studies. *Journal of Educational Psychology, 91,* 403–414.

Caccamise, D. J. (1987). Idea generation in writing. In A. Matsushashi (Ed.), *Writing in real time: Modeling production processes.* Norwood, NJ: Ablex.

Calfee, R., Chapman, R., & Venezky, R. (1972). How a child needs to think to learn to read. In L. W. Gregg (Ed.), *Cognition in learning and memory.* New York: Wiley.

Cameron, J., & Pierce, W. D. (1994). Reinforcement, reward, and intrinsic motivation: A meta-analysis. *Review of Educational Research, 64,* 363–423.

Carey, S. (1985). *Conceptual change in childhood.* Cambridge, MA: MIT Press.

Carey, S. (1986). Cognitive science and science education. *American Psychologist, 41,* 1123–1130.

Carey, S., Evans, R., Honda, M., Jay, E., & Unger, C. (1989). "An experiment is when you try it and see if it works": A study of grade 7 students' understanding of the construction of scientific knowledge. *International Journal of Science Education, 11,* 514–529.

Carpenter, P. A., & Just, M. A. (1981). Cognitive processes in reading: Models based on readers' eye fixations. In A. M. Lesgold & C. A. Perfetti (Eds.), *Interactive processes in reading.* Hillsdale, NJ: Erlbaum.

Carretero, M., & Voss, J. F. (Eds.). (1994). *Cognitive and instructional processes in history and the social sciences.* Hillsdale, NJ: Erlbaum.

Caruso, D. R., Taylor, J. J., & Detterman, D. K. (1982). Intelligence research and intelligent policy. In D. K. Detterman & R. J. Sternberg (Eds.), *How and how much can intelligence be increased* (pp. 45–66). Norwood, NJ: ABLEX.

Carver, R. P. (1971). *Sense and nonsense in speed reading.* Silver Springs, MD: Revrac.

Carver, R. P. (1985). How good are some of the world's best readers? *Reading Research Quarterly, 20,* 389–419.

Case, R., & Okamoto, Y. (1996). The role of central conceptual structures in the development of children's thought. *Monographs of the Society for Research in Child Development, 61(1 & 2),* No. 246.

Catrambone, R. (1995). Aiding subgoal learning: Effects on transfer. *Journal of Educational Psychology, 87,* 5–17.

Cattell, J. M. (1886). The time taken up by cerebral operations. *Mind, 11,* 220–242.

Chall, J. S. (1979). The great debate: Ten years later, with a modest proposal for reading stages. In L. B. Resnick & P. A. Weaver (Eds.), *Theory and practice of early reading.* Hillsdale, NJ: Erlbaum.

Chall, J. S. (1983). *Learning to read: The great debate.* New York: McGraw-Hill.

Chall, J. S., & Squire, J. R. (1991). The publishing industry and textbooks. In R. Barr, M. L. Kamil, P. B. Mosenthal, & P. D. Pearson (Eds.), *Handbook of reading research, Vol. 2* (pp. 120–146). New York: Longman.

Chambliss, M. J., & Calfee, R. C. (1998). *Textbooks for learning.* Oxford, England: Blackwell.

Champagne, A. B., Gunstone, R. F., & Klopfer, L. E. (1985). Effecting changes in cognitive structures among physics students. In H. T. West & A. L. Pines (Eds.), *Cognitive structure and conceptual change.* Orlando, FL: Academic Press.

Champagne, A., Klopfer, L., & Gunstone, R. (1982). Cognitive research and the design of science instruction. *Educational Psychologist, 17,* 31–53.

Chance, P. (1986). *Thinking in the classroom.* New York: Teachers College Press.

Chase, W. G., & Simon, H. A. (1973). Perception in chess. *Cognitive Psychology, 4,* 55–81.

Chi, M. T. H. (1996). Constructing self-explanations and scaffolded explanations in tutoring. *Applied Cognitive Psychology, 10,* 33–49.

Chi, M. T. H. (2000). Self-explaining: The dual processes of generating inference and repairing mental models. In R. Glaser (Ed.), *Advances in instructional psychology: Volume 5, Educational design and cognitive science* (pp. 161–238). Mahwah, NJ: Erlbaum.

Chi, M. T. H., & Bassok, M. (1989). Learning from examples via self-explanations. In L. B. Resnick (Ed.), *Knowing, learning, and instruction* (pp. 251–282). Hillsdale, NJ: Erlbaum.

Chi, M. T. H., De Leeuw, N., Chiu, M-H., & LaVancher, C. (1994). Eliciting self-explanations improves understanding. *Cognitive Science, 18,* 439–477.

Chi, M. T. H., Feltovich, P. J., & Glaser, R. (1981). Categorization and representation of physics problems by experts and novices. *Cognitive Science, 5,* 121–152.

Chinn, C. A. & Brewer, W. F. (1993). The role of anomalous data in knowledge acquisition: A theoretical framework and implications for science instruction. *Review of Educational Research, 63,* 1–49.

Chipman, S. F., Segal, J. W., & Glaser, R. (Eds.), (1985). *Thinking and learning skills, Volume 2.* Hillsdale, NJ: Erlbaum.

Chmielewski, T. L., & Dansereau, D. F. (1998). Enhancing the recall of text: Knowledge mapping training promotes implicit transfer. *Journal of Educational Psychology, 90,* 407–413.

Clarke, A. (1977). *The encyclopedia of how it works.* New York: A&W.

Clement, J. (1982). Students' preconceptions in elementary mechanics. *American Journal of Physics, 50,* 66–71.

Clymer, T. (1963). The utility of phonic generalizations in the primary grades. *Reading Teacher, 16,* 252–258.

Cognition and Technology Group at Vanderbilt (1992). The Jasper series as an example of anchored instruction: Theory, program description, and assessment data. *Educational Psychologist, 27,* 291–315.

Cohen, H., Hillman, D., & Agne, R. (1978). Cognitive level and college physics achievement. *American Journal of Physics, 46,* 1026.

Cole, M., & Scribner, S. (1978). Introduction. In L. S. Vygotsky, *Mind in society: The development of higher psychological processes.* Cambridge, MA: Harvard University Press.

Collins, A., & Smith, E. E. (1982). Teaching the process of reading comprehension. In D. K. Detterman & R. J. Sternberg (Eds.), *How and how much can intelligence be increased* (pp. 173–188). Norwood, NJ: ABLEX.

Collins, A., Brown, J. S., & Newman, S. E. (1989). Cognitive apprenticeship: Teaching the crafts of reading, writing, and mathematics. In L. B. Resnick (Ed.), *Knowing, learning, and instruction: Essays in honor of Robert Glaser* (pp. 453–494). Hillsdale, NJ: Erlbaum.

Cook, L. K. (1982). *The effects of text structure on the comprehension of scientific prose.* Unpublished doctoral dissertation, University of California, Santa Barbara.

Cook, L. K., & Mayer, R. E. (1988). Teaching readers about the structure of scientific text. *Journal of Educational Psychology, 80,* 448–456.

Cooper, G., & Sweller, J. (1987). The effects of schema acquisition and rule automation on mathematical problem-solving transfer. *Journal of Educational Psychology, 79,* 347–362.

Corkill, A. J. (1992). Advance organizers: Facilitators of recall. *Educational Psychology Review, 4,* 33–68.

Covington, M. V., & Crutchfield, R. S. (1965). Facilitation of creative problem solving. *Programmed Instruction, 4,* 3–5, 10.

Covington, M. V., Crutchfield, R. S., & Davies, L. B. (1966). *The productive thinking program.* Berkeley, CA: Brazelton.

Covington, M. V., Crutchfield, R. S., Davies, L. B., & Olton, R. M. (1974). The productive thinking program. Columbus, OH: Merrill.

Craig, R. C. (1956). Directed versus independent discovery of established relations. *Journal of Educational Psychology, 47,* 223–234.

Crowder, R. G. (1982). *The psychology of reading.* New York: Oxford University Press.

Crowder, R. G., & Wagner, R. K. (1992). *The psychology of reading.* New York: Oxford University Press.

Cubberly, E. P. (1920). *The history of education.* Boston: Houghton Mifflin.

Cunningham, A. E. (1990). Explicit vs. implicit instruction in phonemic awareness. *Journal of Experimental Child Psychology, 50,* 429–444.

Dalbey, J., & Linn, M. C. (1985). The demands and requirements of computer programming: A literature review. *Journal of Educational Computing Research, 1,* 253–274.

Dansereau, D. F. (1978). The development of a learning strategies curriculum. In H. F. O'Neill, Jr. (Ed.), *Learning strategies.* New York: Academic Press.

Dansereau, D. F., & Newbern, D. (1997). Using knowledge maps to enhance teaching. In W. E. Campbell & K. A. Smith (Eds.), *New paradigms for college teaching* (pp. 125–147). Edina, NY: Interaction Book Company.

Dansereau, D. F., Collins, K. W., McDonald, B. A., Holley, C. D., Garland, J. C., Diekhoff, G., & Evans, S. H. (1979). Development and evaluation of an effective learning strategy program. *Journal of Educational Psychology, 71,* 64–73.

Davis, G. A. (1973). *Psychology of problem solving: Theory and practice.* New York: Basic Books.

Davis, R. B., & Maher, C. A. (1997). How students think: The role of representations. In L. D. English (Ed.), *Mathematical reasoning* (pp. 93–116). Mahwah, NJ: Erlbaum.

de Groot, A. D. (1965). *Thought and choice in chess.* The Hague, The Netherlands: Mouton.

Deci, E. L. (1971). Effects of externally mediated rewards on intrinsic motivation. *Journal of Personality and Social Psychology, 18,* 105–115.

Deci, E. L., Koestner, R., & Ryan, R. M. (1999). A meta-analytic review of experiments examining the effects of extrinsic rewards on intrinsic motivation. *Psychological Bulletin, 125,* 625–668.

Derry, S. J. (1984). Effects of an organizer on memory for prose. *Journal of Educational Psychology, 76,* 98–107.

Detterman, D. K., & Sternberg, R. J. (1993). *Transfer on trial: Intelligence, cognition, and instruction.* Norwood, NJ: ABLEX.

Dewey, J. (1913). *Interest and effort in education.* Cambridge, MA: Riverside Press.

Dewey, J. (1938). *Experience and education.* New York: Collier.

Dienes, Z. P. (1960). *Building up mathematics.* New York: Hutchinson Educational Ltd.

Dienes, Z. P. (1967). *Fractions: An operational approach.* New York: Herder & Herder.

DiVesta, F. (1989). Applications of cognitive psychology to education. In W. C. Wittrock & F. Farley (Eds.), *The future of educational psychology* (pp. 37–73). Hillsdale, NJ: Erlbaum.

Doctorow, M., Wittrock, M. C., & Marks, C. (1978). Generative processes in reading comprehension. *Journal of Educational Psychology, 70,* 109–118.

Dominguez, J. (1985). *The development of human intelligence: The Venezuelan case.* In J. W. Segal, S. F. Chipman, & R. Glaser (Eds.), *Thinking and learning skills: Volume 1, Relating instruction to research.* Hillsdale, NJ: Erlbaum.

Dossey, J. A., Mullis, I. V. S., Lindquist, M. M., & Chambers, D. L. (1988). *The mathematics report card.* Princeton, NJ: Educational Testing Service.

Dowhower, S. L. (1994). Repeated reading revisited: Research into practice. *Reading & Writing Quarterly, 10,* 343–358.

Duffy, T. M., Higgins, L., Mehlenbacher, B., Cochran, C., Wallace, D., Hill, C., Haugen, D., McCaffrey, M., Burnett, R., Sloane, S., & Smith, S. (1989). Models for the design of instructional text. *Reading Research Quarterly, 24,* 434–457.

Dunbar, K. (1993). Concept discovery in a scientific domain. *Cognitive Science, 17,* 397–434.

Durkin, D. (1979). What classroom observations reveal about reading comprehension. *Reading Research Quarterly, 14,* 481–538.

Ehri, L. C. (1991). Development of the ability to read words. In R. Barr, M. L. Kamil, P. Mosenthal, & P. D. Pearson (Eds.), *Handbook of research on reading, Vol. 2.* White Plains, NY: Longman.

Ehri, L. C., & Robbins, C. (1992). Beginners need some decoding skill to read by analogy. *Reading Research Quarterly, 27,* 13–26.

Ehri, L. C., & Roberts, K. T. (1979). Do beginners learn printed words better in context or in isolation? *Child Development, 50,* 175–685.

Ehri, L. C., Nunes, S. R., Simone, R., Willows, D. M., Schuster, B. V., Yaghoub-Zadeh, Z., & Shanahan, T. (2001). Phonemic awareness instruction helps children learn to read: Evidence from the National Reading Panel's meta-analysis. *Reading Research Quarterly, 36,* 250–287.

Eisenberg, R., Pierce, W. D., & Cameron, J. (1999). Effects of rewards on intrinsic motivation—negative, neutral, and positive: Comment on Deci, Koestner, and Ryan (1999). *Psychological Bulletin, 125,* 677–691.

Elliot-Faust, D. J., & Pressley, M. (1986). How to teach comparison processing to increase children's short- and long-term listening comprehension monitoring. *Journal of Educational Psychology, 78,* 27–33.

Englert, C. S., Raphael, T. E., & Anderson, L. (1989). Exposition: Reading, writing and metacognitive knowledge of learning disabled children. *Learning Disabilities Research, II,* 5–24.

Englert, C. S., Raphael, T. E., Anderson, L. M., Anthony, H. M., & Stevens, D. D. (1991). Making strategies and self-talk visible: Writing instruction in regular and special education classrooms. *American Educational Research Journal, 28,* 337–372.

English, L. D. (1997). *Mathematical reasoning: Analogies, metaphors, and images.* Mahwah, NJ: Erlbaum.

Erickson, G. L. (1979). Children's conception of heat and temperature. *Science Education, 63,* 222–230.

Eylon, B. & Linn, M. C. (1988). Learning and instruction: An examination of four research perspectives in science education. *Review of Educational Research, 58,* 251–301.

Fay, A. L., & Mayer, R. E. (1994). Benefits of teaching design skills before teaching LOGO computer programming: Evidence for syntax-independent learning. *Journal of Educational Computing Research, 11,* 187–210.

Feuerstein, R. (1979). *The dynamic assessment of retarded performers. The learning potential assessment device: Theory, instruments and techniques.* Baltimore: University Park Press.

Feuerstein, R. (1980). *Instrumental enrichment: An intervention program for cognitive modifiability.* Baltimore: University Park Press.

Feuerstein, R., Jensen, M., Hoffman, M. B., & Rand, Y. (1985). *Instructional enrichment, An intervention program for structural cognitive modifiability: Theory and practice.* In J. W. Segal, S. F. Chipman, & R. Glaser (Eds.), *Thinking and learning skills: Volume 1, Relating instruction to research.* Hillsdale, NJ: Erlbaum.

Fitzgerald, J. (1987). Research on revision in writing. *Review of Educational Research, 57,* 481–506.

Fitzgerald, J. & Markman, L. R. (1987). Teaching children about revision in writing. *Cognition and Instruction, 41,* 3–24.

Fitzgerald, J., & Shanahan, T. (2000). Reading and writing relations and their development. *Educational Psychologist, 35,* 39–50.

Fleisher, L. S., Jenkins, J. R., & Pany, D. (1979). Effects on poor readers' comprehension of training in rapid decoding. *Reading Research Quarterly, 15,* 30–48.

Flesch, R. P. (1955). *Why Johnny can't read.* New York: Harper.

Flower, L. (1979). Writer-based prose: A cognitive basis for problems in writing. *College English, 41,* 13–18.

Flower, L., & Hayes, J. R. (1981). Plans that guide the composition process. In C. H. Fredericksen & J. F. Dominic (Eds.), *Writing: Volume 2.* Hillsdale, NJ: Erlbaum.

Flynn, J. R. (1998). IQ gains over time: Toward finding the causes. In U. Neisser (Ed.), *The rising curve: Long-term gains in IQ and related measures* (pp. 25–66). Washington, DC: American Psychological Association.

Frase, L. T. (1982). Introduction to special issue on the psychology of writing. *Educational Psychologist, 17,* 129–130.

Fuson, K. C. (1982). An analysis of the counting-on solution procedure in addition. In T. P. Carpenter, J. M. Moser, & T. A. Romber (Eds.), *Addition and subtraction: A cognitive perspective.* Hillsdale, NJ: Erlbaum.

Fuson, K. C. (1992). Research on whole number addition and subtraction. In D. A. Grouws (Ed.), *Handbook of research on mathematics teaching and learning.* New York: Macmillan.

Gagne, R. M. (1968). Learning hierarchies. *Educational Psychologist, 6,* 1–9.

Gagne, R. M. (1974). *Essentials of learning for instruction.* Hinsdale, IL: Dryden Press.

Gagne, R. M., & Brown, L. T. (1961). Some factors in the programming of conceptual learning. *Journal of Experimental Psychology, 62,* 313–321.

Galton, F. (1883). *Inquiry into human faculty and its development.* London: Macmillan Press.

Gardner, H. (1983). *Frames of mind: The theory of multiple intelligences.* New York: Basic Books.

Gardner, H. (1985). *The mind's new science: A history of the cognitive revolution.* New York: Basic Books.

Gardner, H. (1999). *Intelligence reframed: Multiple intelligences for the 21st century.* New York: Basic Books.

Garner, R., Gillingham, M. G., & White, C. S. (1989). Effects of "seductive details" on macroprocessing and microprocessing in adults and children. *Cognition and Instruction, 6,* 41–57.

Gentner, D. (1983). Structure mapping: A theoretical framework. *Cognitive Science, 7,* 155–170.

Gentner, D. (1989). The mechanisms of analogical learning. In S. Vosniadou & A. Ortony (Eds.), *Similarity and analogical reasoning.* Cambridge, England: Cambridge University Press.

Gentner, D., & Gentner, D. R. (1983). Flowing waters or teeming crowds: Mental models of electricity. In D. Gentner & A. L. Stevens (Eds.), *Mental models.* Hillsdale, NJ: Erlbaum.

Gentner, D., & Stevens, A. L. (Eds.). (1983). *Mental models.* Hillsdale, NJ: Erlbaum.

Gernsbacher, M. A. (1990). *Language comprehension as structure building.* Hillsdale, NJ: Erlbaum.

Gernsbacher, M.A. (Ed.). (1994). *Handbook of psycholinguistics.* San Diego: Academic Press.

Gijselaers, G., Tempelaar, S., & Keizer, S. (Eds.). (1993). *Educational innovation in economics and business administration: The case of problem-based learning.* London: Kluwer.

Glynn, S. M., Britton, B. K., Muth, D., & Dogan, N. (1982). Writing and revising persuasive documents: Cognitive demands. *Journal of Educational Psychology, 74,* 557–567.

Glynn, S. M. (1991). Explaining science concepts: A teaching-with-analogies model. In S. M. Glynn, R. H. Yeany, & B. K. Britton (Eds.). *The psychology of learning science.* Hillsdale, NJ: Erlbaum.

Glynn, S. M., Yeany, R. H., & Britton, B. K. (Eds.). (1991). *The psychology of learning science.* Hillsdale, NJ: Erlbaum.

Goswami, U. (1986). Children's use of analogy in learning to read: A developmental study. *Journal of Experimental Child Psychology, 42,* 73–83.

Goswami, U., & Bryant, P. (1990). *Phonological skills and learning to read.* Hillsdale, NJ: Erlbaum.

Goswami, U., & Bryant, P. (1992). Rhyme, analogy, and children's reading. In P. B. Gough, L. C. Ehri, & R. Treiman (Eds.), *Reading acquisition.* Hillsdale, NJ: Erlbaum.

Gould, J. D. (1978a). How experts dictate. *Journal of Experimental Psychology: Human Perception and Performance, 4,* 648–661.

Gould, J. D. (1978b). An experimental study of writing, dictating, and speaking. In J. Requien (Ed.), *Attention and performance, VII.* Hillsdale, NJ: Erlbaum.

Gould, J. D. (1980). Experiments on composing letters: Some facts, some myths, and some observations. In L. W. Gregg & E. R. Steinberg (Eds.), *Cognitive processes in writing.* Hillsdale, NJ: Erlbaum.

Graesser, A. C. (1981). *Prose comprehension beyond the word.* New York: Springer-Verlag.

Graesser, A. C., Hauft-Smith, K., Cohen, A. D., & Pyles, L. D. (1980). Advanced outlines, familiarity, text genre, and retention of prose. *Journal of Experimental Education, 48,* 209–221.

Graham, S. (1984). Communicating sympathy and anger to black and white children: The cognitive (attributional) consequences of affective cues. *Journal of Personality and Social Psychology, 47,* 40–54.

Graham, S. (1991). A review of attribution theory in achievement contexts. *Educational Psychology Review, 3,* 5–39.

Graham, S., & Barker, G. P. (1990). The down side of help: An attributional-developmental analysis of helping behavior as low-ability cue. *Journal of Educational Psychology, 82,* 7–14.

Greene, D., Sternberg, B., & Lepper, M. R. (1976). Overjustification in a token economy. *Journal of Personality and Social Psychology, 34,* 1219–1234.

Greeno, J. G. (1980). Some examples of cognitive task analysis with instructional implications. In R. E. Snow, P. Frederico, & W. E. Montague (Eds.), *Aptitude, learning, and instruction, Vol. 2.* Hillsdale, NJ: Erlbaum.

Griffin, S., & Case, R. (1996). Evaluating the breadth and depth of training effects when central conceptual structures are taught. In R. Case & Y. Okamoto (Eds.), The role of central structures in the development of children's thought (pp. 83–102). *Monographs of the Society for Research in Child Development, 61,* Serial No. 246, Nos. 1–2.

Griffin, S. A., Case, R., & Siegler, R. S. (1994). Rightstart: Providing the central conceptual prerequisites for first formal learning of arithmetic to students at risk for school failure. In K. McGilly (Ed.), *Classroom lessons: Integrating cognitive theory and classroom practice.* Cambridge, MA: MIT Press.

Griffin, S. A., Case, R., & Capodilupo, S. (1995). Teaching for understanding: The importance of ventral conceptual structures in the elementary school mathematics curriculum. In A. McKeough, J. Lupart, & A. Marini (Eds.), *Teaching for transfer: Fostering generalization in learning.* Hillsdale, NJ: Erlbaum.

Griffiths, D. (1976). Physics teaching: Does it hinder intellectual development? *American Journal of Physics, 44,* 81–85.

Grinder, R. E. (1989). Educational psychology: The master science. In W. C. Wittrock & F. Farley (Eds.), *The future of educational psychology* (pp. 3–18). Hillsdale, NJ: Erlbaum.

Groen, G. J., & Parkman, J. M. (1972). A chronometric analysis of simple addition. *Psychological Review, 97,* 329–343.

Groen, G. J., & Patel, V. L. (1988). The relationship between comprehension and reasoning in medical expertise. In M. T. H. Chi, R. Glaser, & M. J. Farr (Eds.), *The nature of expertise.* Hillsdale, NJ: Erlbaum.

Grotzer, T. A., & Perkins, D. N. (2000). Teaching intelligence: A performance conception. In R. J. Sternberg (Ed.), *Handbook of intelligence* (pp. 492–515). New York: Cambridge University Press.

Grouws, D. A. (Ed.) (1992). *Handbook of research on mathematics teaching and learning.* New York: Macmillan.

Gunstone, R. F., & White, R. T. (1981). Understanding of gravity. *Science Education, 65,* 291–300.

Haberlandt, K. (1984). Components of sentence and word reading times. In D. E. Kieras & M. A. Just (Eds.), *New methods in reading comprehension research.* Hillsdale, NJ: Erlbaum.

Halpern, D. (Ed.) (1992). *Enhancing thinking skills in the sciences and mathematics.* Hillsdale, NJ: Erlbaum.

Halsford, G. S. (1993). *Children's understanding: The development of mental models.* Hillsdale, NJ: Erlbaum.

Hansen, J., & Pearson, P. D. (1983). An instructional study: Improving the inferential comprehension of good and poor fourth-grade readers. *Journal of Educational Psychology, 75,* 821–829.

Hansen, J. (1981). The effects of inference training and practice on young children's comprehension. *Reading Research Quarterly, 16,* 391–417.

Harp, S. F., & Mayer, R. E. (1997). The role of interest in learning from scientific text and illustrations: On the distinction between emotional interest and cognitive interest. *Journal of Educational Psychology, 89,* 82–102.

Harp, S. F., & Mayer, R. E. (1998). How seductive details do their damage: A theory of cognitive interest in science learning. *Journal of Educational Psychology, 90,* 414–434.

Hartley, J. (1984). The role of colleagues and text-editing programs in improving text. *IEEE Transactions on Professional Communication, 27,* 42–44.

Hayes, J. R. (1985). Three problems in teaching general skills. In S. F. Chipman, J. W. Segal, & R. Glaser (Eds.), *Thinking and learning skills: Volume 2, Research and open questions.* Hillsdale, NJ: Erlbaum.

Hayes, J. R. (1996). A new framework for understanding cognition and affect in writing. In C. M. Levy & S. Ransdell (Eds.), *The science of writing* (pp. 1–28). Mahwah, NJ: Erlbaum.

Hayes, J. R., & Flower, L. S. (1980). Identifying the organization of writing processes. In L. W. Gregg & E. R. Steinberg (Eds.), *Cognitive processes in writing.* Hillsdale, NJ: Erlbaum.

Hayes, J. R., & Flower, L. S. (1986). Writing research and the writer. *American Psychologist, 41,* 1106–1113.

Hayes, J. R., Waterman, D. A., & Robinson, C. S. (1977). Identifying relevant aspects of a text problem. *Cognitive Science, 1,* 297–313.

Haywood, C. (1992). Evaluation of IE in England. *Contemporary Psychology, 37,* 206–208.

Hegarty, M., Mayer, R. E. & Monk, C. A. (1995). Comprehension of arithmetic word problems: A comparison of successful and unsuccessful problem solvers. *Journal of Educational Psychology, 87,* 18–32.

Hendrix, G. (1947). A new clue to transfer of training. *Elementary School Journal, 48,* 197–208.

Hendrix, G. (1961). Learning by discovery. *Mathematics Teacher, 54,* 290–299.

Hermann, G. (1969). Learning by discovery: A critical review study. *Journal of Experimental Education, 38,* 58–72.

Herrnstein, R. J., Nickerson, R. S., Sanchez, M., & Swets, J. A. (1986). Teaching thinking skills. *American Psychologist, 41,* 1279–1289.

Hidi, S., & Baird, W. (1986). Interestingness—A neglected variable in discourse processing. *Cognitive Science, 10,* 179–194.

Hidi, S., & Baird, W. (1988). Strategies for increasing text-based interest and students' recall of expository texts. *Reading Research Quarterly, 23,* 465–483.

Hiebert, J., & Carpenter, T. P. (1992). Learning and teaching with understanding. In D. A. Grouws (Ed.), *Handbook of research on mathematics teaching and education* (pp. 65–97). New York: Macmillan.

Hillocks, G. (1984). What works in teaching composition: A meta-analysis of experimental treatment studies. *American Journal of Education, 93,* 133–170.

Hillocks, G. (1986). *Research on written composition.* Urbana, IL: National Council of Teachers of English.

Hinsley, D., Hayes, J. R., & Simon, H. A. (1977). From words to equations. In P. Carpenter & M. Just (Eds.), *Cognitive processes in comprehension.* Hillsdale, NJ: Erlbaum.

Holley, C. D. & Dansereau, D. F. (1984). *The development of spatial learning strategies.* In C. D. Holley & D. F. Dansereau (Eds.), *Spatial learning strategies.* Orlando, FL: Academic Press.

Holley, C. D., Dansereau, D. F., McDonald, B. A., Garland, J. C., & Collins, K. W. (1979). Evaluation of a hierarchical mapping technique as an aid to prose processing. *Contemporary Educational Psychology, 4,* 227–237.

Hudson, T. (1983). Correspondences and numerical differences between disjoint sets. *Child Development, 54,* 84–90.

Huey, E. B. (1908). *The psychology and pedagogy of reading.* New York: Macmillan. (Reprinted by MIT Press in 1968.)

Huey, E. B. (1968). *The psychology and pedagogy of reading.* Cambridge, MA: MIT Press. (Originally published in 1908.)

Hull, C. (1943). *Principles of behavior.* New York: Appleton-Century-Crofts.

Hyona, J. (1994). Processing of topic shifts by adults and children. *Reading Research Quarterly, 29,* 76–90.

Inhelder, B., & Piaget, J. (1958). *The growth of logical thinking from childhood to adolescence.* New York: Basic Books. (A. Parson & S. Milgram, Trans.; original French edition, 1955.)

James, W. (1958). *Talks to teachers.* New York: Norton. (Originally published in 1899.)

Johnson, D. W., & Johnson, R. T. (1985). The internal dynamics of cooperative learning groups. In R. Slavin, S. Sharan, S. Kagan, C. Webb, & R. Schmuck (Eds.), *Learning to cooperate, cooperating to learn* (pp. 103–124). New York: Plenum.

Johnson, D. W., & Johnson, R. T. (1990). Cooperative learning and achievement. In S. Sharan (Ed.), *Cooperative learning: Theory and practice* (pp. 23–37). New York: Praeger.

Johnson, R. E. (1970). Recall of prose as a function of the structural importance of linguistic units. *Journal of Verbal Learning and Verbal Behavior, 9,* 12–20.

Johnston, J. C. (1978). A test of the sophisticated guessing theory of word perception. *Cognitive Psychology, 10,* 123–153.

Johnston, J. C. (1981). Understanding word perception: Clues from studying the word superiority effect. In O. J. L. Tzeng & H. Singer (Eds.), *Perception of Print.* Hillsdale, NJ: Erlbaum.

Johnston, J. C., & McClelland, J. L. (1980). Experimental tests of a hierarchical model of word identification. *Journal of Verbal Learning and Verbal Behavior, 19,* 503–524.

Jones, M. S., Levin, M. E., Levin, J. R., & Beitzel, B. D. (2000). Can vocabulary-learning strategies and pair-learning formats be profitably combined? *Journal of Educational Psychology, 92,* 256–262.

Jordan, B. (1989). Cosmopolitical obstetrics: Some insights from the training of traditional midwives. *Social Science and Medicine, 28,* 925–944.

Judd, C. H. (1908). The relation of special training and general intelligence. *Educational Review, 36,* 28–42.

Juel, C., Griffin, P. L., & Gough, P. B. (1986). Acquisition of literacy: A longitudinal study of children in first and second grade. *Journal of Educational Psychology, 78,* 243–255.

Just, M. A., & Carpenter, P. A. (1978). Inference process during reading: Reflections from eye fixations. In J. W. Senders, D. F. Fisher, & R. A. Monty (Eds.), *Eye movements and the higher psychological functions.* Hillsdale, NJ: Erlbaum.

Just, M. A., & Carpenter, P. A. (1981). A theory of reading: From eye fixations to comprehension. *Psychological Review, 87,* 329–354.

Kaiser, M. K., Proffitt, D. R., & McCloskey, M. (1985). The development of beliefs about falling objects. *Perception and Psychophysics, 38,* 533–539.

Kameenui, E. J., Carnine, D. W., & Freschi, R. (1982). Effects of text construction and instructional procedures for teaching word meanings on comprehension and recall. *Reading Research Quarterly, 17,* 367–388.

Karplus, R., Karplus, E., Formisano, M., & Paulsen, A. (1979). Proportional reasoning and control of variables in seven countries. In J. Lochhead & J. Clement (Eds.), *Cognitive process instruction: Research on teaching thinking skills.* Philadelphia: Franklin Institute Press.

Katona, G. (1940). *Organizing and memorizing.* New York: Columbia University Press.

Kearney, H. (1971). *Science and change.* New York: McGraw-Hill.

Kellogg, R. T. (1987). Effects of topic knowledge on the allocation of processing time and cognitive effort to writing processes. *Memory & Cognition, 15,* 256–266.

Kellogg, R. T. (1988). Attentional overload and writing performance: Effects of rough draft and outline strategies. *Journal of Experimental Psychology: Learning, Memory, and Cognition, 14,* 355–365.

Kellogg, R. T. (1994). *The psychology of writing.* New York: Oxford University Press.

Kellogg, R. T. (2000). Writing. In A. Kazdin (Ed.), *Encyclopedia of Psychology.* Washington, DC: American Psychological Association.

Kellogg, R. T., & Mueller, S. (1993). Performance amplification and process restructuring in computer-based writing. *International Journal of Man-Machine Studies, 39,* 33–49.

Kendler, H. H., & Kendler, T. S. (1962). Vertical and horizontal processes in problem solving. *Psychological Review, 69,* 1–16.

Kendler, H. H., & Kendler, T. S. (1975). From discrimination learning to cognitive development: A neobehavioristic odyssey. In W. K. Estes (Ed.), *Handbook of learning and cognitive processes. Vol. 1.* Hillsdale, NJ: Erlbaum.

Kiefer, K. E., & Smith, C. R. (1983). Textual analysis with computers: Tests of Bell Laboratories' computer software. *Research in the Teaching of English, 17,* 201–214.

Kiewra, K. A., Kauffman, D. F., Robinson, D. H., DuBois, N. F., & Staley, R. K. (1999). Supplementing floundering text with adjunct displays. *Instructional Science, 27,* 373–401.

Kiewra, K., DuBois, N., Christain, D., McShane, A., Meyerhoffer, M., & Roskelley, D. (1991). Note-taking functions and techniques. *Journal of Educational Psychology, 83,* 240–245.

Kilpatrick, J., Swafford, J., & Findell, B. (2001). *Adding it up: Helping children learn mathematics.* Washington, DC: National Academy Press.

King, A. (1992). Comparison of self questioning, summarizing, and notetaking-review as strategies for learning from lectures. *American Educational Research Journal, 29,* 303–323.

King, A. (1997). ASK to THINK-TEL WHY: A model of transactive peer tutoring for scaffolding higher level complex thinking. *Educational Psychologist, 37,* 221–236.

King, A., Staffieri, A., & Adelgais, A. (1998). Mutual peer tutoring: Effects of structuring tutorial interaction to scaffold peer learning. *Journal of Educational Psychology, 90,* 134–152.

Kintsch, W. (1976). Memory for prose. In C. N. Cofer (Ed.), *The structure of human memory.* New York: Freeman.

Kintsch, W. (1980). Learning from text, levels of comprehension, or: Why anyone would read a story anyway. *Poetics, 9,* 87–89.

Kintsch, W. (1998). *Comprehension.* New York: Cambridge University Press.

Kintsch, W., & Greeno, J. G. (1985). Understanding and solving word problems. *Psychological Review, 92,* 109–129.

Kittel, J. E. (1957). An experimental study of the effect of external direction during learning on transfer and retention of principles. *Journal of Educational Psychology, 48,* 391–405.

Klahr, D. (2000). *Exploring science.* Cambridge, MA: MIT Press.

Klahr, D., & Dunbar, K. (1988). Dual space search during scientific reasoning. *Cognitive Science, 12,* 1–48.

Klayman, J., & Ha, Y. W. (1987). Confirmation, disconfirmation and information in hypothesis testing. *Psychological Review, 94,* 211–228.

Kohler, W. (1925). The mentality of apes. New York: Harcourt, Brace, Jovanovich.

Kolers, P. A. (1968). Introduction. In E. B. Huey, *The psychology and pedagogy of reading.* Cambridge, MA: MIT Press.

Kolodiy, G. (1975). The cognitive development of high school and college science students. *Journal of College Science Teaching, 5*(1), 20–22.

Kolodner, J. L. (1997). Educational implications of analogy: A view from case-based reasoning. *American Psychologist, 52,* 57–66.

Koskinen, P. S., & Blum, I. H. (1986). Paired repeated reading: A classroom strategy for developing fluent reading. *Reading Teacher, 40*(1), 70–75.

Kozulin, A., & Presseisen, B. Z. (1995). Mediated learning experience and psychological tools: Vygotsky's and Feuerstein's perspectives in a study of student learning. *Educational Psychologist, 30,* 67–75.

Krapp, A., Hidi, S., & Renninger, K. A. (1992). Interest, learning, and development. In K. A. Renninger, S. Hidi, & A. Krapp (Eds.), *The role of interest in learning and development* (pp. 3–25). Hillsdale, NJ: Erlbaum.

Kreiger, L. E. (1975). Familiarity effects in visual information processing. *Psychological Bulletin, 82,* 949–974.

Kuhn, D., Amsel, E., & O'Loughlin, M. (1988). *The development of scientific thinking skills.* San Diego: Academic Press.

Kurland, D. M., & Pea, R. D. (1985). Children's mental models for recursive Logo programs. *Journal of Educational Computing Research, 2,* 235–244.

LaBerge, D., & Samuels, S. J. (1974). Toward a theory of automatic information processing in reading. *Cognitive Psychology, 6,* 293–323.

Lambert, N., & McCombs, B. L. (Eds.). (1998). *How students learn: Reforming schools through learner-centered education.* Washington, DC: American Psychological Association.

Lambert, N. M., & McCombs, B. L. (Eds.). (1998). *How students learn.* Washington, DC: American Psychological Association.

Lampert, M., & Ball, D. (1998). *Investigating teaching: New pedagogies and new technologies for teacher education.* New York: Teachers College Press.

Lane, H. (1976). *The wild boy of Aveyron.* Cambridge, MA: Harvard University Press.

Larkin, J. H. (1979). Information processing models and science instruction. In J. Lochhead & J. Clement (Eds.), *Cognitive process instruction: Research on teaching thinking skills.* Philadelphia: Franklin Institute Press.

Larkin, J. H. (1983). The role of problem representation in physics. In D. Gentner & A. L. Stevens (Eds.), *Mental models.* Hillsdale, NJ: Erlbaum.

Larkin, J. H., McDermott, J., Simon, D. P., & Simon, H. A. (1980a). Models of competence in solving physics problems. *Cognitive Science, 4,* 317–348.

Larkin, J. H., McDermott, J., Simon, D. P., & Simon, H. A. (1980b). Expert and novice performance in solving physics problems. *Science, 208,* 1335–1342.

Lave, J. (1988). *Cognition in practice.* Cambridge, England: Cambridge University Press.

Lave, J., & Wenger, E. (1991). *Situated learning.* New York: Cambridge University Press.

Lave, J., & Wenger, E. (1991). *Situated learning: Legitimate peripheral participation.* Cambridge, England: Cambridge University Press.

Lawson, A. E., & Snitgen, D. A. (1982). Teaching formal reasoning in a college biology course for preservice teachers. *Journal of Research in Science Teaching, 19,* 233–248.

Lawson, A. E., & Wollman, W. T. (1976). Encouraging the transition from concrete to formal operative functioning: An experiment. *Journal of Research in Science Teaching, 13,* 413–430.

Lawson, A. E. (1983). Predicting science achievement: The role of developmental level, disembedding ability, mental capacity, prior knowledge and beliefs. *Journal of Research in Science Teaching, 20,* 117–129.

Leder, G. C. (1992). Mathematics and gender: Changing perspectives. In D. Grouws (Ed.), *Handbook of research on mathematics teaching and learning* (pp. 597–622). New York: Macmillan.

Lee, M., & Thompson, A. (1997). Guided instruction in LOGO programming and the development of cognitive monitoring strategies among college students. *Journal of Educational Computing Research, 16,* 125–144.

Lehrer, R. (1992). Introduction to special feature on new directions in technology—mediated learning. *Educational Psychologist, 27,* 287–290.

Lehrer, R., Lee, M., & Jeong, A. (1999). Reflective teaching of LOGO. *Journal of the Learning Sciences, 8,* 245–289.

Leinhardt, G., Beck, I. L., & Stainton, C. (Eds.). (1994). *Teaching and learning in history.* Hillsdale, NJ: Erlbaum.

Lepper, M. R., & Greene, D. (1975). Turning play into work: Effects of adult surveillance and extrinsic rewards on children's intrinsic motivation. *Journal of Personality and Social Psychology, 31,* 479–486.

Lepper, M. R., & Greene, D. (1978). *The hidden costs of reward.* Hillsdale, NJ: Erlbaum.

Lepper, M. R., Greene, D., & Nisbett, R. E. (1973). Undermining children's intrinsic interest with external rewards: A test of the overjustification hypothesis. *Journal of Personality and Social Psychology, 28,* 129–137.

Lepper, M. R., Keavney, M., & Drake, M. (1996). Intrinsic motivation and extrinsic reward: A commentary on Cameron and Pierce's meta-analysis. *Review of Educational Research, 66,* 5–32.

Lester, F. K., Garofalo, J., & Kroll, D. L. (1989). Self-confidence, interest, beliefs, and metacognition: Key influences on problem-solving behavior. In D. B. McLeod & V. M. Adams (Eds.), *Affect and mathematical problem solving.* New York: Springer-Verlag.

Levin, B. B. (1999). The role of discussion in case pedagogy: Who learns what and how? In M. A. Lundeberg, B. B. Levin, & H. L. Harrington (Eds.), *Who learns what from cases and how?* (pp. 139–158). Mahwah, NJ: Erlbaum.

Levin, J. R. (1981). The mnemonic '80s: Keywords in the classroom. *Educational Psychologist, 16,* 65–82.

Levin, J. R. (1989). A transfer-appropriate-processing perspective of pictures in prose. In H. Mandl & J. R. Levin (Eds.), *Knowledge acquisition from text and pictures* (pp. 83–100). Amsterdam: Elsevier.

Levin, J. R., & Mayer, R. E. (1993). Understanding illustrations in text. In B. K. Britton, A. Woodward, & M. Binkley (Eds.), *Learning from textbooks: Theory and practice* (pp. 95–113). Hillsdale, NJ: Erlbaum.

Levin, J. R., McCormick, C. B., Miller, G. E., Berry, J. K., & Pressley, M. (1982). Mnemonic versus nonmnemonic vocabulary learning strategies for children. *American Educational Research Journal, 19,* 121–136.

Levin, J. R., Levin, M. E., Glasman, L. D., & Nordwall, M. B. (1992). Mnemonic vocabulary instruction: Additional effectiveness evidence. Contemporary Educational Psychology, 17, 156–174.

Levy, C. M., & Ransdell, S. (Eds.). (1996). *The science of writing.* Mahwah, NJ: Erlbaum.

Lewis, A. B., & Mayer, R. E. (1987). Students' miscomprehension of relational statements in arithmetic word problems. *Journal of Educational Psychology, 79,* 363–371.

Lewis, A. B. (1989). Training students to represent arithmetic word problems. *Journal of Educational Psychology, 81,* 521–531.

Liberman, I. Y., Shankweiler, D., Fischer, F. W., & Carter, B. (1974). Explicit syllable and phoneme segmentation in the young child. *Journal of Experimental Child Psychology, 18,* 201–212.

Liddie, W. (1977). *Reading for concepts.* New York: McGraw-Hill.

Limon, M. (2001). On the cognitive conflict as an instructional strategy for conceptual change: A critical appraisal. *Learning and Instruction, 11,* 357–380.

Limon, M., & Mason, L. (Eds.). (in press). *Reframing the process of conceptual change.* Dordrecht, The Netherlands: Kluwer.

Linn, M. C. (1985). The cognitive consequences of programming instruction in classrooms. *Educational Researcher, 14,* 14–16, 25–29.

Linn, M. C., & Hsi, S. (2000). *Computers, teachers, peers: Science learning partners.* Mahwah, NJ: Erlbaum.

Lipson, M. Y. (1983). The influence of religious affiliation on children's memory for text information. *Reading Research Quarterly, 18,* 448–457.

Lochhead, J. (1979). Introduction to cognitive process instruction. In J. Lochhead & J. Clement (Eds.), *Cognitive Process Instruction.* Philadelphia: Franklin Institute Press.

Loftus, E. F., & Suppes, P. (1972). Structural variables that determine problem-solving difficulty in computer assisted instruction. *Journal of Educational Psychology, 63,* 531–542.

Loman, N. L., & Mayer, R. E. (1983). Signaling techniques that increase the understandability of expository prose. *Journal of Educational Psychology, 75,* 402–412.

Lorch, R. F. (1989). Text-signaling devices and their effects on reading and memory processes. *Educational Psychology Review, 1,* 209–234.

Lorch, R. F., & Lorch, E. P. (1995). Effects of organizational signals on text-processing strategies. *Journal of Educational Psychology, 87,* 537–544.

Lorch, R. F., Lorch, E. P., & Inman, W. E. (1993). Effects of signaling topic structure on text recall. *Journal of Educational Psychology, 85,* 281–290.

Low R. (1989). Detection of missing and irrelevant information within algebraic story problems. *British Journal of Educational Psychology, 59,* 296–305.

Low, R., & Over, R. (1993). Gender differences in solution of algebraic word problems containing irrelevant information. *Journal of Educational Psychology, 85,* 331–339.

Low, R., & Over, R. (1990). Text editing of algebraic word problems. *Australian Journal of Psychology, 42,* 63–73.

Low, R., & Over, R. (1989). Detection of missing and irrelevant information within algebraic story problems. *British Journal of Educational Psychology, 59,* 296–305.

Luchins, A. S., & Luchins, E. H. (1970). *Wertheimer's seminars revisited: Problem solving and thinking* (Volume 1). Albany, NY: State University of New York at Albany.

Lundberg, I., Frost, J., & Peterson, O. (1988). Effects of an extensive program for stimulating phonological awareness in preschool children. *Reading Research Quarterly, 23,* 263–284.

Lundeberg, M. A., Levin, B. B., & Harrington, H. L. (Eds.). (1999). *Who learns what from cases and how?* Mahwah, NJ: Erlbaum.

Ma, L. (1999). *Knowing and teaching elementary mathematics.* Mahwah, NJ: Erlbaum.

Macdonald, N. H., Frase, L. T., Gingrich, P. S., & Keenan, S. A. (1982). The writer's workbench: Computer aids for text analysis. *Educational Psychologist, 17,* 172–179.

Machado, L. A. (1981). The development of intelligence: A political outlook. *Intelligence, 5,* 2–4.

Madsen, C. H., Becker, W. C., & Thomas, D. R. (1968). Rules, praise, and ignoring: Elements of elementary classroom control. *Journal of Applied Behavioral Analysis, 1,* 139–150.

Main, G. C., & Munro, B. C. (1977). A token reinforcement program in a public junior-high school. *Journal of Applied Behavior Analysis, 10,* 93–94.

Mandler, J. M., & Johnson, N. S. (1977). Remembrance of things passed: Story structure and recall. *Cognitive Psychology, 9,* 111–151.

Mansfield, R. S., Busse, T. V., & Krepelka, E. J. (1978). The effectiveness of creativity training. *Review of Educational Research, 48,* 517–536.

Markman, E. (1979). Realizing that you don't understand: Elementary school children's awareness of inconsistencies. *Child Development, 50,* 643–655.

Markman, E. M. (1985). Comprehension monitoring: Developmental and educational issues. In S. F. Chipman, J. W. Segal, & R. Glaser (Eds.), *Thinking and learning skills: Vol. 2, Research and open questions.* Hillsdale, NJ: Erlbaum.

Markman, E. M., & Gorin, L. (1981). Children's ability to adjust their standards for evaluating comprehension. *Journal of Educational Psychology, 73,* 320–325.

Marks, C. B., Doctorow, M. J., & Wittrock, M. C. (1974). Word frequency in reading comprehension. *Journal of Educational Research, 67,* 259–262.

Marr, M. B., & Gormley, K. (1982). Children's recall of familiar and unfamiliar text. *Reading Research Quarterly, 18,* 89–104.

Marsh, H. W., & Shavelson, R. J. (1985). Self-concept: Its multifaceted, hierarchical structure. *Educational Psychologist, 20,* 107–125.

Martinez, M. E. (2000). *Education as the cultivation of intelligence.* Mahwah, NJ: Erlbaum.

Matsuhashi, A. (1982). Explorations in the real-time production of written discourse. In M. Nystrand (Ed.), *What writers know.* New York: Academic Press.

Matsushashi, A. (Ed.). (1987). *Writing in real time: Modeling production processes.* Norwood, NJ: Ablex.

Mattingly, I. G. (1972). Reading, the linguistic process and linguistic awareness. In J. Kavanagh & I. Mattingly (Eds.), *Language by ear and by eye.* Cambridge, MA: MIT Press.

Mautone, P., & Mayer, R. E. (2001). Signaling as a cognitive guide in multimedia learning. *Journal of Educational Psychology, 93,* 377–389.

Mayer, R. E. (1975a). Information processing variables in learning to solve problems. *Review of Educational Research, 45,* 525–541.

Mayer, R. E. (1975b). Different problem solving competencies established in learning computer programming with and without meaningful models. *Journal of Educational Psychology, 67,* 725–734.

Mayer, R. E. (1975c). Forward transfer of different reading strategies evoked by test-like events in mathematics text. *Journal of Educational Psychology, 67,* 165–169.

Mayer, R. E. (1976). Some conditions of meaningful learning for computer programming: Advance organizers and subject control of frame sequencing. *Journal of Educational Psychology, 68,* 143–150.

Mayer, R. E. (1977). Problem-solving performance with task overload: Effects of selfpacing and trait anxiety. *Bulletin of the Psychonomic Society, 9,* 283–286.

Mayer, R. E. (1978). Qualitatively different encoding strategies for linear reasoning: Evidence for single association and distance theories. *Journal of Experimental Psychology: Human Learning and Memory, 4,* 5–18.

Mayer, R. E. (1979). Twenty years of research on advance organizers: Assimilation theory is still the best predictor of results. *Instructional Science, 8,* 133–167.

Mayer, R. E. (1980). Elaboration techniques that increase the meaningfulness of technical text: An experimental test of the learning strategy hypothesis. *Journal of Educational Psychology, 72,* 770–784.

Mayer, R. E. (1981a). *The promise of cognitive psychology.* New York: Freeman.

Mayer, R. E. (1981b). Frequency norms and structural analysis of algebra story problems into families, categories, and templates. *Instructional Science, 10,* 135–175.

Mayer, R. E. (1982a). Learning. In H. E. Mitzel (Ed.), *Encyclopedia of educational research* (5th ed.). Washington, DC: American Educational Research Association.

Mayer, R. E. (1982b). Memory for algebra story problems. *Journal of Educational Psychology, 74,* 199–216.

Mayer, R. E. (1982c). Different problem solving strategies for algebra word and equation problems. *Journal of Experimental Psychology: Learning, Memory, and Cognition, 8,* 448–462.

Mayer, R. E. (1983a). *Thinking, problem solving, cognition.* New York: Freeman.

Mayer, R. E. (1983b). Can you repeat that? Qualitative and quantitative effects of repetition and advance organizers on learning from science prose. *Journal of Educational Psychology, 75,* 40–49.

Mayer, R. E. (1984). Aids to prose comprehension. *Educational Psychologist, 19,* 30–42.

Mayer, R. E. (1985). Learning in complex domains: A cognitive analysis of computer programming. *Psychology of Learning and Motivation, 19,* 89–130.

Mayer, R. E. (1987a). *Educational psychology: A cognitive approach.* Boston: Little, Brown.

Mayer, R. E. (1987b). The elusive search for teachable aspects of problem solving. In J. A. Glover & R. R. Ronning (Eds.), *Historical foundations of educational psychology* (pp. 327–348). New York: Plenum.

Mayer, R. E. (Ed.) (1988). *Teaching and learning computer programming.* Hillsdale, NJ: Erlbaum.

Mayer, R. E. (1989). Models for understanding. *Review of Educational Research, 59,* 43–64.

Mayer, R. E. (1992a). Cognition and instruction: Their historic meeting within educational psychology. *Journal of Educational Psychology, 84,* 405–412.

Mayer, R. E. (1992b). *Thinking, problem solving, cognition* (2nd ed.). New York: Freeman.

Mayer, R. E. (1993a). Education psychology—past and future. *Journal of Educational Psychology, 85,* 351–553.

Mayer, R. E. (1993b). Illustrations that instruct. In R. Glaser (Ed.), *Advances in instructional psychology: Volume 4* (pp. 253–284). Hillsdale, NJ: Erlbaum.

Mayer, R. E. (1996a). Learners as information processors: Legacies and limitations of educational psychology's second metaphor. *Educational Psychologist, 31,* 151–161.

Mayer, R. E. (1996b). Learning strategies for making sense out of expository text: The SOI model for guiding three cognitive processes in knowledge construction. *Educational Psychology Review, 8,* 357–371.

Mayer, R. E. (1997). Incorporating problem solving into secondary school curricula. In G. D. Phye (Ed.), *Handbook of academic learning* (pp. 474–492). San Diego, CA: Academic Press.

Mayer, R. E. (1999). *The promise of educational psychology: Learning in the content areas.* Upper Saddle River, NJ: Merrill/Prentice Hall.

Mayer, R. E. (1999). *The promise of educational psychology: Learning in the content areas.* Upper Saddle River, NJ: Prentice Hall.

Mayer, R. E. (2001a). Changing conceptions of learning: A century of progress in the scientific study of education. In L. Corno (Ed.), *Education across a century: The centennial volume, One hundredth yearbook of the National Society for the Study of Education* (pp. 34–75). Chicago: National Society for the Study of Education.

Mayer, R. E. (2001b). *Multimedia learning.* New York: Cambridge University Press.

Mayer, R. E. (in press). E. L. Thorndike's enduring contributions to educational psychology. In B. Zimmerman & D. Schunk (Eds.), *Educational psychology: A century of contributions.* Mahwah, NJ: Erlbaum.

Mayer, R. E., & Anderson, R. B. (1991). Animations need narrations: An experimental test of a dual-coding hypothesis. *Journal of Educational Psychology, 83,* 484–490.

Mayer, R. E., & Cook, L. K. (1981). Effects of shadowing on prose comprehension and problem solving. *Memory & Cognition, 8,* 101–109.

Mayer, R. E., & Gallini, J. (1990). When is an illustration worth ten thousand words? *Journal of Educational Psychology, 82,* 715–726.

Mayer, R. E. & Greeno, J. G. (1972). Structural differences between learning outcomes produced by different instructional methods. *Journal of Educational Psychology, 63,* 165–173.

Mayer, R. E., & Hegarty, M. (1996). The process of understanding mathematics problems. In R. J. Sternberg & T. Ben-Zeev (Eds.), *The nature of mathematical thinking.* Mahwah, NJ: Erlbaum.

Mayer, R. E., & Wittrock, M. C. (1996). Problem-solving transfer. In D. C. Berliner & R. C. Calfee (Eds.), *Handbook of educational psychology* (pp. 47–62). New York: Macmillan.

Mayer, R. E., Hieser, J., & Lonn, S. (2001). Cognitive constraints on multimedia learning: When presenting more material results in less learning. *Journal of Educational Psychology, 93.*

Mayer, R. E., Larkin, J. H., & Kadane, J. (1984). A cognitive analysis of mathematical problem solving ability. In R. Sternberg (Ed.), *Advances in the psychology of human intelligence* (pp. 231–273). Hillsdale, NJ: Lawrence Erlbaum Associates.

Mayer, R. E., Sims, V., & Tajika, H. (1995). A comparison of how textbooks teach mathematical problem solving in Japan and the United States. *American Educational Research Journal, 32,* 443–460.

Mayer, R. E., Stiehl, C. C., & Greeno, J. G. (1975). Acquisition of understanding and skill in relation to subjects' preparation and meaningfulness of instruction. *Journal of Educational Psychology, 67,* 331–350.

McCloskey, M. (1983). Intuitive physics. *Scientific American, 248*(4), 122–130.

McCloskey, M., Caramazza, A., & Green, B. (1980). Curvilinear motion in the absence of external forces: Naive beliefs about the motion of objects. *Science, 210* (No. 4474), 1139–1141.

McConkie, G. W. (1976). The use of eye-movement data in determining the perceptual span in reading. In R. A. Monty & J. W. Senders (Eds.), *Eye movements and psychological processes.* Hillsdale, NJ: Erlbaum.

McConkie, G. W., & Rayner, K. (1975). The span of the effective stimulus during a fixation in reading. *Perception & Psychophysics, 17,* 578–586.

McConkie, G. W., Rayner, K., & Wilson, S. J. (1973). Experimental manipulation of reading strategies. *Journal of Educational Psychology, 65,* 1–8.

McCutchen, D. (2000). Knowledge, processing, and working memory: Implications for a theory of writing. *Educational Psychologist, 35,* 13–23.

McCutchen, D., Francis, M., & Kerr, S. (1997). Revising for meaning: Effects of knowledge and strategy. *Journal of Educational Psychology, 89,* 667–676.

McKeough, A., Lupart, J., & Marini, A. (1995). *Teaching for transfer: Fostering generalization in learning.* Mahwah, NJ: Erlbaum.

McKeown, M. G., Beck, I. L., Omanson, R. C., & Perfetti, C. A. (1983). The effects of long-term vocabulary instruction on reading comprehension: A replication. *Journal of Reading Behavior, 15,* 3–18.

McKeown, M. G., & Beck, I. L. (1990). The assessment and characterization of young learners' knowledge of a topic in history. *American Educational Research Journal, 27,* 688–726.

McKeown, M. G., Beck, I. L., Sinatra, G. M., & Loxterman, J. A. (1992). The contribution of prior knowledge and coherent text to comprehension. *Reading Research Quarterly, 27,* 79–93.

McKinnon, J. W., & Renner, J. W. (1971). Are colleges concerned with intellectual development? *American Journal of Physics, 39,* 1047–1052.

Meyer, B. J. F. (1975). *The organization of prose and its effects on memory.* Amsterdam: North-Holland.

Meyer, B. J. F. (1977). The structure of prose: Effects on learning and memory and implications for educational practice. In R. C. Anderson, R. J. Spiro, &

W. E. Montague (Eds.), *Schooling and the acquisition of knowledge.* New York: Wiley.

Meyer, B. J. F. (1981). *Basic research on prose comprehension: A critical review.* In D. F. Fisher & C. W. Peters (Eds.), *Comprehension and the competent reader: Inter-spaciality perspectives.* New York: Praeger.

Meyer, B. J. F. (1985). *Prose analysis: Purposes, procedures, and problems.* In B. K. Britton & J. B. Black (Eds.), *Understanding expository prose.* Hillsdale, NJ: Erlbaum.

Meyer, B. J. F., & McConkie, G. W. (1973). What is recalled after hearing a passage? *Journal of Educational Psychology, 65,* 109–117.

Meyer, B. J. F., Brandt, D. H., & Bluth, G. J. (1980). Use of top-level structure in text: Key for reading comprehension of ninth-grade students. *Reading Research Quarterly, 16,* 72–103.

Meyer, B. F. J. & Rice, G. E. (1981). Information recalled from prose by young, middle, and old adults. *Experimental Aging Research, 7,* 253–268.

Myers, M., & Paris, S. B. (1978). Children's metacognitive knowledge about reading. *Journal of Educational Psychology, 70,* 680–690.

Montessori, M. (1964). *Advanced Montessori method.* Cambridge, MA: Bentley.

Moreno, R., & Mayer, R. E. (1999). Multimedia supported metaphors for meaning making in mathematics. *Cognition and Instruction, 17,* 215–248.

Moreno, R., Mayer, R. E., & Lester, J. C. (2000). Life-like pedagogical agents in constructivist learning environments: Cognitive consequences of their interaction. *Proceedings of ED-MEDIA 2000* (pp. 741–746). Charlottesville, VA: AACE Press.

Moreno, R., Mayer, R. E., Spires, H., & Lester, J. C. (2001). The case for social agency in computer-based teaching: Do students learn more deeply when they interact with animated pedagogical agents? *Cognition and Instruction, 19,* 177–214.

Nagy, W. E., & Anderson, R. C. (1984). How many words are there in printed school English? *Reading Research Quarterly, 19,* 304–330.

Nagy, W. E., & Herman, P. A. (1987). Breadth and depth of vocabulary knowledge: Implications for acquisition and instruction. In M. McKeown & M. Curtis (Eds.), *The nature of vocabulary acquisition.* Hillsdale, NJ: Erlbaum.

Nagy, W. E., & Scott, J. A. (2000). Vocabulary processes. In M. L. Kamil, P. B. Mosenthal, P. D. Pearson, & R. Barr (Eds.), *Handbook of reading research,* vol. 3 (pp. 269–284). Mahwah, NJ: Erlbaum.

Nagy, W. E., Herman, P. A., & Anderson, R. C. (1985). Learning words from context. *Reading Research Quarterly, 20,* 233–253.

Nathan, M. J., Kintsch, W., & Young, E. (1992). A theory of algebra-word-problem comprehension and its implications for the design of learning environments. *Cognition and Instruction, 9,* 329–389.

Nation, K., & Hulme, C. (1997). Phonemic segmentation, non-onset-time segmentation, predicts early reading and spelling skills. *Reading Research Quarterly, 32,* 154–167.

National Council of Teachers of Mathematics (1989). *Curriculum standards for teaching mathematics.* Reston, VA: Author.

Nelson, N., & Calfee, R. C. (1998). The reading-writing connection. In N. Nelson & R. C. Calfee (Eds.), *Ninety-seventh yearbook of the National Society for the Study of Education* (Part II, pp. 1–52). Chicago: National Society for the Study of Education.

Nemko, B. (1984). Another look at beginning readers. *Reading Research Quarterly, 19,* 461–467.

Newell, K. M. (1974). Knowledge of results and motor learning. *Journal of Motor Behavior, 6,* 235–244.

Nickerson, R. S. (1994). Project intelligence. In R. J. Sternberg (Ed.), *Encyclopedia of human intelligence: Volume 2* (pp. 857–860). New York: Macmillan.

Nickerson, R. S. (1999). Enhancing creativity. In R. J. Sternberg (Ed.), *Handbook of creativity* (pp. 392–430). New York: Cambridge University Press.

Nickerson, R. S., Perkins, D. N., & Smith, E. E. (1985). *The teaching of thinking.* Hillsdale, NJ: Erlbaum.

Nold, E. W. (1981). Revising. In C. H. Frederiksen & J. F. Dominic (Eds.) *Writing: Vol 2.* Hillsdale, NJ: Erlbaum.

Norman, D. A. (1980). Cognitive engineering and education. In D. T. Tuma & F. Reif (Eds.), *Problem solving and education: Issues in teaching and research.* Hillsdale, NJ: Erlbaum.

Novak, J. D. (1998). *Learning, creating, and using knowledge.* Mahwah, NJ: Erlbaum.

Novak, J. D., & Gowin, D. B. (1984). *Learning how to learn.* New York: Cambridge University Press.

Novick, S., & Nussbaum, J. (1978). Junior high school pupil's understanding of the particle nature of matter: An interview study. *Science Education, 62,* 273–281.

Novick, S., & Nussbaum, J. (1981). Pupil's understanding of the particulate nature of matter: A cross-age study. *Science Education, 65,* 187–196.

Nunes, T., Schliemann, A. D., & Carraher, D. W. (1993). *Street mathematics and school mathematics.* Cambridge, England: Cambridge University Press.

Nunes, T., Schliemann, A. D., & Carraher, D. W. (1993). *Street mathematics and school mathematics.* New York: Cambridge University Press.

Nussbaum, J. (1979). Children's conception of the earth as a cosmic body: A cross-age study. *Science Education, 63,* 83–93.

Nystrand, M. (1982a). Rhetoric's "audience" and linguistic's "speech community": Implications for understanding writing, reading, and text. In M. Nystrand (Ed.), *What writers know.* New York: Academic Press.

Nystrand, M. (1982b). An analysis of errors in written communication. In M. Nystrand (Ed.), *What writers know.* New York: Academic Press.

Nystrand, M. (1986). *The structure of written communication: Studies in reciprocity between writers and readers.* Orlando, FL: Academic Press.

Oakhill, J., & Beard, R. (Eds.). (1999). *Reading development and the teaching of reading: A psychological perspective.* Oxford, UK: Blackwell.

Oakhill, J., & Yuill, N. (1996). Higher order factors in comprehension disability: Processes and remediation. In C. Cesare & J. Oakhill (Eds.), *Reading comprehension difficulties.* Mahwah, NJ: Erlbaum.

O'Leary, K. D., Becker, W. C., Evans, M. B., & Saudargas, R. A. (1969). A token reinforcement program in a public school: A replication and systematic analysis. *Journal of Applied Behavior Analysis, 2,* 3–13.

Olton, R. M., & Crutchfield, R. S. (1969). *Developing the skills of productive thinking.* In P. Mussen, J. Langer, & M. V. Covington (Eds.), *New directions in developmental psychology.* New York: Holt, Rinehart and Winston.

Osborn, J., & Lehr, F. (Eds.). (1998). *Literacy for all: Issues in teaching and learning.* New York: Guilford.

Osborne, R. J., & Wittrock, M. C. (1983). Learning science: A generative process. *Science Education, 67,* 489–908.

Paas, F. G. W. C., & van Merrienboer, J. J. G. (1994). Variability of worked examples and transfer of geometrical problem-solving skills: A cognitive load approach. *Journal of Educational Psychology, 86,* 122–133.

Paige, J. M., & Simon, H. A. (1966). Cognitive processes in solving algebra word problems. In B. Kleinmuntz (Ed.), *Problem solving: Research, method, and theory.* New York: Wiley.

Paivio, A. (1971). *Imagery and verbal processes.* New York: Holt, Rinehart & Winston.

Palinscar, A. S. (1986). Metacognitive strategy instruction. *Exceptional Children, 53,* 118–124.

Palinscar, A. S., & Brown, A. L. (1984). Reciprocal teaching of comprehension-fostering and monitoring activities. *Cognition and Instruction, 1,* 117–175.

Papert, S. (1980). *Mindstorms.* New York: Basic Books.

Paris, S. G., & Lindauer, B. K. (1976). The role of inference on children's comprehension and memory for sentences. *Cognitive Psychology, 8,* 217–227.

Paris, S. G., Lindauer, B. K., & Cox, G. L. (1977). The development of inferential comprehension. *Child Development, 48,* 1728–1733.

Paris, S. G., & Upton, L. R. (1976). Children's memory for inferential relationships in prose. *Child Development, 47,* 660–618.

Parkman, J. M., & Groen, G. J. (1971). Temporal aspects of simple addition and comparison. *Journal of Experimental Psychology, 89,* 333–342.

Pea, R. D., & Kurland, D. M. (1984). On the cognitive effects of learning computer programming. *New Directions in Psychology, 2,* 137–168.

Pearson, P. D., & Gallagher, M. (1983). The instruction of reading comprehension. *Contemporary Educational Psychology, 8,* 317–344.

Pearson, P. D., Hansen, J., & Gordon, C. (1979). The effect of background knowledge on young children's comprehension of explicit and implicit information. *Journal of Reading Behavior, 11,* 201–209.

Pearson, P. D., & Fielding, L. (1991). Comprehension instruction. In R. Barr, M. L. Kamil, P. B. Mosenthal, & P. D. Pearson (Eds.), *Handbook of reading research, Vol 2.* New York: Longman.

Pedersen, E. L. (1989). The effectiveness of WRITER'S WORKBENCH and MACPROOF. *Computer-Assisted Composition Journal, 3,* 92–100.

Pennington, B. F., Groisser, D., & Welsh, M. C. (1993). Contrasting cognitive deficits in attention deficit disorder versus reading disability. *Developmental Psychology, 29,* 511–523.

Peper, R., & Mayer, R. E. (1978). Note taking as a generative activity. *Journal of Educational Psychology, 70,* 514–522.

Perfetti, C. A., & Hogaboam, T. (1975). The relationship between single word decoding and reading comprehension skill. *Journal of Educational Psychology, 67,* 461–469.

Perfetti, C. A., & Lesgold, A. M. (1979). Coding and comprehension in skilled reading and implications for reading instruction. In L. B. Resnick & P. A. Weaver (Eds.), *Theory and practice of early reading.* Hillsdale, NJ: Erlbaum.

Perkins, D. N. (1985). The fingertip effect: How information processing technology shapes thinking. *Educational Researcher, 14,* 11–14.

Perkins, D. N., & Grotzer, T. A. (1997). Teaching intelligence. *American Psychologist, 52,* 1125–1133.

Pflaum, S. W., Walberg, H. J., Karegianes, M. L., & Rasher, S. P. (1980). Reading instruction: A quantitative analysis. *Educational Researcher, 9,* 12–18.

Piaget, J. (1926). *The language and thought of the child.* London: Kegan Paul, Trench, Trubner and Company.

Piaget, J. (1972). Intellectual evolution from adolescent to adulthood. *Human Development, 15,* 1–12.

Pianko, S. (1979). A description of the composing process of college freshman writers. *Research in the Teaching of English, 13,* 5–22.

Pichert, J., & Anderson, R. C. (1977). Taking different perspectives on a story. *Journal of Educational Psychology, 69,* 309–315.

Pintrich, P. R., & De Groot, E. V. (1990). Motivational and self-regulated learning components of classroom academic performance. *Journal of Educational Psychology, 82,* 33–40.

Pintrich, P. R., & Schunk, D. H. (1996). *Motivation in education.* Upper Saddle River, NJ: Merrill/Prentice Hall.

Polya, G. (1945). *How to solve it.* Princeton, NJ: Princeton University Press.

Polya, G. (1965). *Mathematical discovery.* New York: Wiley.

Polya, G. (1968). *Mathematical discovery* (vol. 2). New York: Wiley.

Posner, G. J., Strike, K. A., Hewson, P. W., & Gertzog, W. A. (1982). Accomodation of a scientific conception: Toward a theory of conceptual change. *Science Education, 66,* 211–227.

Pressley, M. (1977). Children's use of the keyword method to learn simple Spanish vocabulary words. *Journal of Educational Psychology, 69,* 465–472.

Pressley, M. (1990). *Cognitive strategy instruction that really improves children's academic performance.* Cambridge, MA: Brookline Books.

Pressley, M. (1998). *Reading instruction that works: The case for balanced teaching.* New York: Guilford.

Pressley, M., & Dennis-Rounds, J. (1980). Transfer of a mnemonic keyword strategy at two age levels. *Journal of Educational Psychology, 72,* 575–582.

Pressley, M., & Levin, J. R. (1978). Developmental constraints associated with children's use of the keyword method of foreign language vocabulary learning. *Journal of Experimental Child Psychology, 26,* 359–372.

Pressley, M., & McCormick, C. B. (1995). *Cognition, teaching, and assessment.* New York: HarperCollins.

Pressley, M., & Woloshyn, V. (1995). *Cognitive strategy instruction.* Cambridge, MA: Brookline Books.

Pressley, M., Levin, J. R., & McCormick, C. B. (1980). Young children's learning of foreign language voccabulary: A sentence variation of the keyword method. *Contemporary Educational Psychology, 5,* 22–29.

Quilici, J. H., & Mayer, R. E. (1996). Role of examples in how students learn to categorize statistics word problems. *Journal of Educational Psychology, 88,* 144–161.

Raugh, M. R., & Atkinson, R. C. (1975). A mnemonic method for learning a second language vocabulary. *Journal of Educational Psychology, 67,* 1–16.

Rayner, K., & Duffy, S. A. (1986). Lexical complexity and fixation times in reading: Effects of word frequency, verb complexity, and lexical ambiguity. *Memory & Cognition, 14,* 191–201.

Rayner, K., & Pollatsek, A. (1989). *The psychology of reading.* Upper Saddle River, NJ: Prentice Hall.

Rayner, K., & Raney, G. E. (1996). Eye movement control in reading and visual search: Effects of word frequency. *Psychonomic Bulletin & Review, 3,* 245–248.

Rayner, K., & Sereno, S. C. (1994). Eye movements of reading: Psycholinguistic studies. In M. A. Gernsbacher (Ed.), *Handbook of psycholinguistics* (pp. 58–81). San Diego: Academic Press.

Rayner, K., Binder, K. S., Ashby, J., & Pollatsek, A. (2001). Eye movement control in reading: Word predictability has little influence on initial landing positions in words. *Vision Research, 41,* 943–954.

Rayner, K., Well, A. D., & Pollatsek, A. (1980). Asymmetry of the effective visual field in reading. *Perception and Psychophysics, 27,* 537–544.

Read, C. (1981). Writing is not the inverse of reading for young children. In C. H. Frederiksen & J. F. Dominic (Eds.), *Writing: Volume 2.* Hillsdale, NJ: Erlbaum.

Reed, S. K. (1987). A structure-mapping model for word problems. *Journal of Experimental Psychology: Learning, Memory, and Cognition, 13,* 124–139.

Reed, S. K. (1999). *Word problems.* Mahwah, NJ: Erlbaum.

Reed, S. K., Dempster, A., & Ettinger, M. (1985). Usefulness of analogous solutions for solving algebra word problems. *Journal of Experimental Psychology: Learning, Memory, and Cognition, 11,* 106–125.

Reicher, G. M. (1969). Perceptual recognition as a function of the meaningfulness of stimulus material. *Journal of Experimental Psychology, 81,* 275–280.

Reichle, E. D., Pollatsek, A., Fisher, D. L., & Rayner, K. (1998). Toward a model of eye movement control in reading. *Psychological Review, 105,* 125–157.

Renninger, K. A., Hidi, S., & Krapp, A. (Eds.). (1992). *The role of interest in learning and development.* Hillsdale, NJ: Erlbaum.

Resnick, L. B. (1982). Syntax and semantics in learning to subtract. In T. Carpenter, J. Moser, & T. Romberg (Eds.), *Addition and subtraction: A cognitive perspective.* Hillsdale, NJ: Erlbaum.

Resnick, L. B. (1987). Learning in school and out. *Educational Researcher, 16*(9), 13–20.

Resnick, L. B. (1989). Introduction. In L. B. Resnick (Ed.), *Knowing, learning, and instruction: Essays in honor of Robert Glaser* (pp. 1–24). Hillsdale, NJ: Erlbaum.

Resnick, L. B., & Ford, W. W. (1981). *The psychology of mathematics for instruction.* Hillsdale, NJ: Erlbaum.

Richardson, V., & Kile, R. S. (1999). Learning from videocases. In M. A. Lundeberg, B. B. Levin, & H. L. Harrington (Eds.), *Who learns what from cases and how?* (pp. 121–136). Mahwah, NJ: Erlbaum.

Richardson, K., Calnan, M., Essen, J., & Lambert, M. (1975). Linguistic maturity of 11-year-olds: Some analysis of the written compositions of children in the National Child Development Study. *Journal of Child Language, 3,* 99–116.

Rickards, J. P., & DiVesta, F. J. (1974). Type and frequency of questions in processing textual material. *Journal of Educational Psychology, 66,* 354–362.

Rieben, L., & Perfetti, C. A. (Eds.). (1991). *Learning to read: Basic research and its implications.* Hillsdale, NJ: Erlbaum.

Riley, M., Greeno, J. G., & Heller, J. (1982). The development of children's problem solving ability in arithmetic. In H. Ginsburg (Ed.), *The development of mathematical thinking.* New York: Academic Press.

Rippa, S. A. (1980). *Education in a free society.* New York: Longman.

Robinson, C. S., & Hayes, J. R. (1978). Making inferences about relevance in understanding problems. In R. Revlin & R. E. Mayer (Eds.), *Human reasoning.* Washington: Winston.

Robinson, D. H., & Kiewra, K. A. (1995). Visual argument: Graphic organizers are superior to outlines in improving learning from text. *Journal of Educational Psychology, 87,* 455–467.

Robinson, F. P. (1941). *Diagnostic and remedial techniques for effective study.* New York: Harper.

Robinson, F. P. (1961). *Effective study.* New York: Harper.

Rogoff, B. (1990). *Apprenticeship in thinking: Cognitive development in a social context.* Oxford, England: Oxford University Press.

Rogoff, B., & Lave, J. (Eds.). (1984). *Everyday cognition: Its development in social context.* Cambridge, MA: Harvard University Press.

Roller, C. M. (1990). The interaction between knowledge and structure variables in the processing of expository prose. *Reading Research Quarterly, 25,* 79–89.

Rosenshine, B. V. (1980). Skill hierarchies in reading comprehension. In R. J. Spiro, B. C. Bruce & W. F. Brewer (Eds.), *Theoretical issues in reading comprehension.* Hillsdale, NJ: Erlbaum.

Ross, B. H. (2000). Concepts: Learning. In A. Kazdin (Ed.), *Encyclopedia of psychology.* Washington, DC: American Psychological Association.

Ross, M. (1975). Salience of reward and intrinsic motivation. *Journal of Personality and Social Psychology, 32,* 245–254.

Rothkopf, E. Z. (1966). Learning from written materials: An exploration of the control of inspection by test-like events. *American Educational Research Journal, 3,* 241–249.

Rothkopf, E. Z. (1970). The concept of mathemagenic activities. *Review of Educational Research, 40,* 325–336.

Rothkopf, E. Z., & Bisbicos, E. (1967). Selective facilitative effects of interspersed questions on learning from written material. *Journal of Educational Psychology, 58,* 56–61.

Roughhead, W. G., & Scandura, J. M. (1968). What is learned in mathematical discovery. *Journal of Educational Psychology, 59,* 283–289.

Royer, J. M., & Cable, G. W. (1975). Facilitated learning in connected discourse. *Journal of Educational Psychology, 67,* 116–123.

Royer, J. M., & Cable, G. W. (1976). Illustrations, analogies, and facilitative transfer in prose learning. *Journal of Educational Psychology, 68,* 205–209.

Rubman, C. N., & Waters, H. S. (2000). A, B seeing: The role of constructive processes in children's comprehension monitoring. *Journal of Educational Psychology, 92,* 503–514.

Rumelhart, D. E. (1975). Notes on a schema for stories. In D. G. Bobrow & A. Collins (Eds.), *Representation and understanding.* New York: Academic Press.

Salomon, G., & Perkins, D. (1989). Rocky roads to transfer: Rethinking mechanisms of a neglected phenomenon. *Educational Psychologist, 24,* 113–142.

Samuels, S. J. (1967). Attentional processes in reading: The effect of pictures in the acquisition of reading responses. *Journal of Educational Psychology, 58,* 337–342.

Samuels, S. J. (1979). The method of repeated readings. *The Reading Teacher, 32,* 403–408.

Sawyer, R. J., Graham, S., & Harris, K. R. (1992). Direct teaching, strategy instruction, and strategy instruction with explicit self-regulation: Effects on the composition skills and self-efficacy of students with learning disabilities. *Journal of Educational Psychology, 84,* 340–352.

Scandura, J. M., Frase, L. T., Gagne, R. M., Stolorow, K. A., Stolorow, L. M., & Groen, G. (1981). Current status and future directions of educational psychology as a discipline. In F. Farley & N. J. Gordon (Eds.), *Psychology and education.* Berkeley, CA: McCutchan.

Scardamalia, M. (1981). How children cope with the cognitive demands of writing. In C. H. Frederiksen & J. F. Dominic (Eds.), *Writing: Vol 2.* Hillsdale, NJ: Erlbaum.

Scardamalia, M., & Bereiter, C. (1985). Fostering the development of self-regulation in children's knowledge processing. In S. F. Chipman, J. W. Segal, & R. Glaser (Eds.), *Thinking and learning skills: Research and open questions* (pp. 563–577). Hillsdale, NJ: Erlbaum.

Scardamalia, M., Bereiter, C., & Goelman, H. (1982). The role of production factors in writing ability. In M. Nystrant (Ed.), *What writers know.* New York: Academic Press.

Scardamalia, M., Bereiter, C., & Steinbach, R. (1984). Teachability of reflective processes in written composition. *Cognitive Science, 8,* 173–190.

Schank, R. (1997). *Virtual learning.* New York: McGraw-Hill.

Schiefele, U. (1992). Topic interest and levels of text comprehension. In K. A. Renninger, S. Hidi, & A. Krapp (Eds.), *The role of interest in learning and development* (pp. 151–182). Hillsdale, NJ: Erlbaum.

Schiefele, U., Krapp, A., & Winteler, A. (1992). In K. A. Renninger, S. Hidi, & A. Krapp (Eds.), *The role of interest in learning and development* (pp. 183–212). Hillsdale, NJ: Erlbaum.

Schloss, P. J., & Smith, M. A. (1998). *Applied behavior analysis in the classroom* (2nd ed.). Boston: Allyn and Bacon.

Schoenfeld, A. H. (1979). Explicit heuristic training as a variable in problem-solving performance. *Journal for Research in Mathematics Education, 10,* 173–187.

Schoenfeld, A. H. (1985). *Mathematical problem solving.* Orlando: Academic Press.

Schoenfeld, A. H. (1988). When good teaching leads to bad results: The disasters of "well-taught" mathematics classes. *Educational Psychologist, 23,* 145–166.

Schoenfeld, A. H. (1991). On mathematics and sense-making: An informal attack on the unfortunate divorce of formal and informal mathematics. In J. F. Voss, D. N. Perkins, & J. W. Segal (Ed.), *Informal reasoning and education* (pp. 311–343). Hillsdale, NJ: Erlbaum.

Schoenfeld, A. H. (1992). Learning to think mathematically: Problem solving, metacognition, and sense making in mathematics. In D. A. Gouws (Ed.), *Handbook of research on mathematics teaching and learning.* New York: Macmillan.

Schunk, D. H. (1981). Modeling and attributional effects on children's achievement: A self-efficacy analysis. *Journal of Educational Psychology, 73,* 93–105.

Schunk, D. H. (1989). Self-efficacy and achievement behaviors. *Educational Psychology Review, 1,* 173–208.

Schunk, D. H. (1990). Introduction to the special section on motivation and efficacy. *Journal of Educational Psychology, 82,* 3–6.

Schunk, D. H. (1991). Self-efficacy and academic motivation. *Educational Psychologist, 26,* 207–231.

Schunk, D. H., & Hanson, A. R. (1985). Peer models: Influences on children's self-efficacy and achievement. *Journal of Educational Psychology, 77,* 313–322.

Schvaneveldt, R., Ackerman, B. P., & Semelar, T. (1977). The effect of semantic context on children's word recognition. *Child Development, 48,* 612–616.

Schwartz, B. B., Nathan, M. J., & Resnick, L. B. (1996). Acquisition of meaning for arithmetic structures with the Planner. In S. Vosniadou, E. De Corte, R. Glaser, & H. Mandl (Eds.), *International perspectives on the design of technology-supported learning environments* (pp. 61–80). Hillsdale, NJ: Erlbaum.

Segal, J. W., Chipman, S. F., & Glaser, R. (Eds.), (1985). *Thinking and learning skills: Volume 1, Relating instruction to research.* Hillsdale, NJ: Erlbaum.

Serpell, R. (1993). *The significance of schooling.* Cambridge, England: Cambridge University Press.

Shavelson, R. J. (1972). Some aspects of the correspondence between content structure and cognitive structure in physics instruction. *Journal of Educational Psychology, 63,* 225–234.

Shavelson, R. J. (1974). Some methods for examining content structure and cognitive structure in instruction. *Educational Psychologist, 11,* 110–122.

Shepherd, D. L. (1978). *Comprehensive high school reading methods.* Columbus, OH: Merrill.

Shulman, L. S., & Keisler, E. R. (1966). *Learning by discovery.* Chicago: Rand McNally.

Shulman, L. S., & Quinlan, K. M. (1996). The comparative psychology of school subjects. In D. Berliner & R. Calfee (Eds.), *Handbook of educational psychology.* New York: Macmillan.

Siegler, R. S. (1987). The perils of averaging data over strategies: An example from children's addition. *Journal of Experimental Psychology: General, 116,* 250–264.

Siegler, R. S., & Jenkins, E. (1989). *How children discover new strategies.* Hillsdale, NJ: Erlbaum.

Silver, E. A. (1981). Recall of mathematical problem information: Solving related problems. *Journal for Research in Mathematics Education, 12,* 54–64.

Silver, E. A., & Kenney, P. A. (2000). *Results from the seventh mathematics assessment of the National Assessment of Educational Progress.* Reston, VA: National Council of Teachers of Mathematics.

Simon, H. A. (1980). Problem solving and education. In D. T. Tuma & F. Reif (Eds.), *Problem solving and education: Issues in teaching and research.* Hillsdale, NJ: Erlbaum.

Singer, H. (1981). Teaching the acquisition phase of reading development: An historical perspective. In O. J. L. Tzeng & H. Singer (Eds.), *Perception of print.* Hillsdale, NJ: Erlbaum.

Singer, M., Revlin, R., & Halldorson, M. (1990). Bridging inferences and enthymemes. In A. C. Graesser & G. H. Bower (Eds.), *Inferences and text comprehension.* San Diego: Academic Press.

Singley, M. K., & Anderson, J. R. (1985). The transfer of text-editing skill. *Journal of Man-Machine Studies, 22,* 403–423.

Singley, M. K., & Anderson, J. R. (1989). *The transfer of cognitive skill.* Cambridge, MA: Harvard University Press.

Skinner, B. F. (1938). *The behavior of organisms: An experimental analysis.* Englewood Cliffs, NJ: Prentice Hall.

Skinner, B. F. (1953). *Science and human behavior.* New York: Macmillan.

Skinner, B. F. (1957). *Verbal behavior.* Englewood Cliffs, NJ: Prentice Hall.

Skinner, B. F. (1968). *The technology of teaching.* Englewood Cliffs, NJ: Prentice Hall.

Skinner, B. F. (1969). *Contingencies of reinforcement: A theoretical analysis.* Englewood Cliffs, NJ: Prentice Hall.

Slavin, R. (1982). *Cooperative learning: Student teams.* Washington, DC: National Education Association.

Slavin, R. (1983a). When does cooperative learning increase student achievement? *Psychological Bulletin, 94,* 429–445.

Slavin, R. (1983b). *Cooperative learning.* New York: Longman.

Slavin, R. (1990). *Cooperative learning: Theory, research, and practice.* Englewood Cliffs, NJ: Prentice Hall.

Slavin, R. E., & Karweit, N. L. (1984). Mastery learning and student teams: A factorial experiment in urban general mathematics classes. *American Educational Research Journal, 21,* 725–736.

Slotte, V., & Lonka, K. (1999). Review and process effects of spontaneous notetaking on text comprehension. *Contemporary Educational Psychology, 24,* 1–20.

Smith, E. E., & Spoehr, K. T. (1974). The perception of printed English: A theoretical perspective. In B. H. Kantowitz (Ed.), *Human information processing: Tutorials in performance and cognition*. Hillsdale, NJ: Erlbaum.

Snow, C., Burns, M., & Griffin, P. (Eds.). (1998). *Preventing reading difficulties in young children*. Washington, DC: National Academy Press.

Solomon, G., & Perkins, D. N. (1989). Rocky roads to transfer: Rethinking mechanisms of a neglected phenomenon. *Educational Psychologist, 18,* 42–50.

Soloway, E., Lochhead, J., & Clement, J. (1982). Does computer programming enhance problem solving ability? Some positive evidence on algebra word problems. In R. J. Seidel, R. E. Anderson, & B. Hunter (Eds.), *Computer Literacy*. New York: Academic Press.

Sovik, N., Arntzen, O., & Samuelstuen, M. (2000). Eye-movement parameters and reading speed: A study of oral and silent reading performances of twelve-year-old children. *Reading & Writing, 13,* 237–255.

Spearman, C. (1927). *The abilities of man*. New York: Macmillan.

Spector, J. E. (1995). Phonemic awareness training: Application of principles of direct instruction. *Reading & Writing Quarterly, 11,* 37–51.

Spoehr, K. T., & Schuberth, R. E. (1981). Processing words in context. In O. J. L. Tzeng & H. Singer (Eds.), *Perception of print*. Hillsdale, NJ: Erlbaum.

Stahl, S. A., & Fairbanks, M. M. (1986). The effects of vocabulary instruction: A model-based meta-analysis. *Review of Educational Research, 56,* 72–110.

Stahl, S. A., McKenna, M. C., & Pagnucco, J. R. (1994). The effects of whole-language instruction: An update and a reappraisal. *Educational Psychologist, 29,* 175–185.

Stallard, C. K. (1974). An analysis of the writing behavior of good student writers. *Research in the Teaching of English, 8,* 206–218.

Stanovich, K. E. (1980). Toward an interactive-compensatory model of individual differences in the development of reading fluency. *Reading Research Quarterly, 16,* 32–65.

Stanovich, K. E. (1986). Mathews effects in reading: Some consequences of individual differences in the acquisition of literacy. *Reading Research Quarterly, 21,* 360–407.

Stanovich, K.E. (1991). Discrepancy definitions of reading disability: Has intelligence led us astray? *Reading Research Quarterly, 26,* 7–29.

Steinberg, E. R. (1980). A garden of opportunities and a thicket of dangers. In L. W. Gregg & E. R. Steinberg (Eds.), *Cognitive processes in writing*. Hillsdale, NJ: Erlbaum.

Sterkel, K. S., Johnson, M. I., & Sjorgren, D. (1986). Textual analysis with composites to improve the writing skills of business communication students. *Journal of Business Communication, 23,* 43–61.

Sternberg, R. J. (1985). *Beyond IQ: A triarchic theory of human intelligence*. Cambridge, England: Cambridge University Press.

Sternberg, R. J. (1990). *Metaphors of mind: Conceptions of the nature of intelligence*. New York: Cambridge University Press.

Sternberg, R. J. (1991). Forward. In N. Blagg, *Can we teach intelligence? A comprehensive evaluation of Feuerstein's instrumental enrichment program* (pp. ix–xiv). Hillsdale, NJ: Erlbaum.

Sternberg, R. J., & Ben-Zeev, T. (Eds.). (1996). *The nature of mathematical thinking*. Mahwah, NJ: Erlbaum.

Stotsky, S. (1990). On planning and writing plans—Or beware of borrowed theories. *College Composition and Communication, 41,* 37–57.

Strike, K. A., & Posner, G. J. (1985). A conceptual change view of learning and understanding. In L. West & L. Pines (Eds.), *Cognitive structure and conceptual change*. San Diego: Academic Press.

Strike, K. A., & Posner, G. J. (1992). A revisionist theory of conceptual change. In R. A. Duschl & R. J. Hamilton (Eds.), *Philosophy of science: Cognitive psychology, and educational theory and practice*. Albany, NY: State University of New York Press.

Sternberg, R. J., & Ben-Zeev, T. (Eds.). (1996). *The nature of mathematical thinking*. Mahwah, NJ: Erlbaum.

Suchman, L. A. (1987). *Plans and situated actions*. Cambridge, England: Cambridge University Press.

Sulzbacher, S. I., & Houser, J. E. (1968). A tactic to eliminate disruptive behaviors in the classroom: Group contingent consequences. *American Journal of Mental Deficiency, 73,* 88–90.

Sweller, J. (1999). *Instructional design in technical areas*. Camberwell, Australia: ACER Press.

Tamir, P., Gal-Choppin, R., & Nussinovitz, R. (1981). How do intermediate and junior high school students conceptualize living and nonliving? *Journal of Research in Science Teaching, 18,* 241–248.

Taylor, B. (1980). Children's memory for expository text after reading. *Reading Research Quarterly, 15,* 399–411.

Taylor, B. M., & Beach, R. W. (1984). The effects of text structure instruction on middle-grade students' comprehension and production of expository text. *Reading Research Quarterly, 19,* 134–146.

Tharp, R. G., & Gallimore, R. (1988). *Rousing minds to life: Teaching, learning, and schooling in social context*. Cambridge, England: Cambridge University Press.

Thorndike, E. L. (1898). Animal intelligence: An experimental study of the associative processes in animals. *Psychological Review,* Monograph Supplement, 2(8).

Thorndike, E. L. (1903). *Educational psychology*. New York: Lemcke and Buechner.

Thorndike, E. L. (1906). *Principles of teaching based on psychology*. New York: Seiler.

Thorndike, E. L. (1911). *Animal intelligence.* New York: Macmillan.

Thorndike, E. L. (1913). *Educational psychology, Volume 2: The psychology of learning.* New York: Teachers College, Columbia University.

Thorndike, E. L. (1913a). *Educational psychology.* New York: Columbia University Press.

Thorndike, E. L. (1922). *The psychology of arithmetic.* New York: Macmillan.

Thorndike, E. L. (1931). *Human learning.* New York: Century.

Thorndike, E. L. (1932). *The fundamentals of learning.* New York: Teachers College Press.

Thorndike, E. L., & Woodworth, R. S. (1901). The influence of improvement in one mental function upon the efficiency of other functions. *Psychological Review, 8,* 247–261.

Thorndyke, P. W. (1977). Cognitive structures in comprehension and memory for narrative discourse. *Cognitive Psychology, 9,* 77–110.

Thurstone, L. L. (1924). The nature of intelligence. New York: Harcourt, Brace.

Thurstone, L. L. (1938). *Primary mental abilities.* Chicago: University of Chicago Press.

Torney-Punta, J, (1994). Dimensions of adolescents' reasoning about political and historical issues: Ontological switches, developmental processes, and situated learning. In M. Carretero & J. F. Voss (Eds.), *Cognitive and instructional processes in history and the social sciences* (pp. 103–122). Hillsdale, NJ: Erlbaum.

Trowbridge, D. E., & McDermott, L. C. (1981). Investigation of student understanding of the concept of acceleration in one dimension. *American Journal of Physics, 49,* 242–253.

Trowbridge, M. H. & Cason, H. (1932). An experimental study of Thorndike's theory of learning. *Journal of General Psychology, 7,* 245–258.

Tulving, E., & Gold, C. (1963). Stimulus information and contextual information as determinants of tachistoscopic recognition of words. *Journal of Experimental Psychology, 66,* 319–327.

Van Haneghan, J., Barron, L., Young, M., Williams, S., Vye, N., & Bransford, J. (1992). The Jasper Series: An experiment with new ways to enhance mathematical thinking. In D. F. Halpern (Ed.), *Enhancing thinking skills in the sciences and mathematics.* Hillsdale, NJ: Erlbaum.

Verschaffel, L., De Corte, E., & Pauwels, A. (1992). Solving compare problems: An eye movement test of Lewis and Mayer's consistency hypothesis. *Journal of Educational Psychology, 84,* 85–94.

Verschaffel, L., Greer, B., & De Corte, E. (2000). *Making sense of word problems.* Lisse, The Netherlands: Swets & Zeitlinger.

Vosniadou, S., & Brewer, W. (1992). Mental models of the earth: A study of conceptual change. *Cognitive Psychology, 34,* 535–558.

Vosniadou, S., & Brewer, W. F. (1994). Mental models of the day/night cycle. *Cognitive Science, 18,* 123–183.

Vosniadou, S., Ioannides, C., Dimitrakopoulou, A., & Papademetriou, E. (2001). Designing learning environments to promote conceptual change in science. *Learning and Instruction, 11,* 381–419.

Vosniadou, S., Pearson, P. D., & Rogers, T. (1988). What causes children's failures to detect inconsistencies in text? Representation versus comparison difficulties. *Journal of Educational Psychology, 80,* 27–39.

Voss, J. F., & Bisanz, G. L. (1985). Knowledge and processing of narrative and expository texts. In B. K. Britton & J. R. Black (Eds.), *Understanding expository text.* Hillsdale, NJ: Erlbaum.

Vygotsky, L. S. (1978). *Mind in society: The development of higher psychological processes.* Cambridge, MA: Harvard University Press.

Wade, S. E. (1992). How interest affects learning from text. In K. A. Renninger, S. Hidi, & A. Krapp (Eds.), *The role of interest in learning and development* (pp. 255–278). Hillsdale, NJ: Erlbaum.

Wagner, R. K., & Torgesen, J. K. (1987). The nature of phonological processing and its causal role in the acquisition of reading skills. *Psychological Bulletin, 101,* 192–212.

Wagner, S., & Kieran, C. (Eds.) (1989). *Research issues in the learning and teaching of algebra.* Reston, VA: National Council of Teachers of Mathematics.

Weaver, C. A., & Kintsch, W. (1991). Expository text. In R. Barr, M. L. Kamil, P. B. Mosenthal, & P. D. Pearson (Eds.), *Handbook of reading research, Vol. 2.* New York: Longman.

Weaver, P. A., & Resnick, L. B. (1979). The theory and practice of early reading: An introduction. In L. B. Resnick & P. A. Weaver (Eds.), *Theory and practice of early reading.* Hillsdale, NJ: Erlbaum.

Weil, M. L., and Murphy, J. (1982). *Instructional processes.* In H. E. Mitzel (Ed.), *Encyclopedia of Educational Research Fifth Edition.* New York: Macmillan.

Weiner, B. (1979). A theory of motivation for some classroom experiences. *Journal of Educational Psychology, 71,* 3–25.

Weiner, B. (1984). Principles for a theory of human motivation and their application within an attributional framework. In R. Ames & C. Ames (Eds.), *Research on motivation in education: Vol. 1, Student achievement* (pp. 15–38). San Diego: Academic Press.

Weiner, B. (1985). An attributional theory of achievement motivation. *Psychological Review, 92,* 548–573.

Weiner, B. (1986). *An attributional theory of motivation and emotion.* New York: Springer-Verlag.

Weiner, B. (1990). History of motivational research in education. *Journal of Educational Psychology, 82,* 616–622.

Weiner, B. (1992). Motivation. In M. Alkin (Ed.), *Encyclopedia of educational research* (6th ed.) (pp. 860–865). New York: Macmillan.

Weinstein, C. E., & Mayer, R. E. (1985). The teaching of learning strategies. In M. C. Wittrock (Ed.), *Handbook of research and teaching* (3rd ed.). New York: Macmillan.

Wertheimer, M. (1959). *Productive thinking.* New York: Harper & Row.

Wertsch, J. V. (1985). *Vygotsky and the social formation of mind.* Cambridge, MA: Harvard University Press.

Wertsch, J. V., & Stone, C. A. (1985). The concept of internalization in Vygotsky's account of the genesis of higher mental functions. In J. V. Wertsch (Ed.), *Culture, communication, and cognition: Vygotskian perspectives* (pp. 162–179). Cambridge, England: Cambridge University Press.

West, L. H. T., & Fensham, P. J. (1976). Prior knowledge or advance organizers affective variables in chemical learning. *Journal of Research in Science Teaching, 13,* 297–306.

West, L. H. T. & Pines, A. L. (Eds.) (1985). *Cognitive structure and conceptual change.* Orlando, FL: Academic Press.

West, R. F., & Stanovich, K. E. (1978). Automatic contextual facilitation in readers of three ages. *Child Development, 49,* 717–727.

Westfall, R. S. (1977). *The construction of modern science.* Cambridge, England: Cambridge University Press.

Whaley, J. F. (1981). Readers' expectations for story structures. *Reading Research Quarterly, 17,* 90–114.

Wheeler, A. E., & Kass, H. (1978). Student misconceptions in chemical equilibrium. *Science Education, 62,* 223–232.

White, A. G., & Bailey, J. S. (1990). Reducing disruptive behavior of elementary physical education students with sit and watch. *Journal of Applied Behavior Analysis, 3,* 353–359.

White, B. Y. (1984). Designing computer activities to help physics students understand Newton's laws of motion. *Cognition and Instruction, 1,* 69–108.

White, B. Y., & Frederiksen, J. R. (1998). Inquiry, modeling, and metacognition: Making science accessible to all students. *Cognition and Instruction, 16,* 3–118.

White, B. (1993). ThinkerTools: Causal models, conceptual change, and science education. *Cognition and Instruction, 10,* 1–100.

White, R., & Gunstone, R. (1992). *Probing understanding.* London: Falmer Press.

White, R. T., & Mayer, R. E. (1980). Understanding intellectual skills. *Instructional Science, 9,* 101–127.

Whitehead, A. N. (1929). *The aims of education.* New York: Macmillan.

Wiekart, D., Epstein, A., Schweinhant, L., & Bond, J. (1978). *The Ypsilanti preschool curriculum demonstration project: Preschool years and longitudinal results.* Ypsilanti, MI: High Scoped Educational Research Foundation.

Williams, J. P. (1994). Twenty years of research on reading: Answers and questions. In F. Lehr & J. Osborn (Eds.), *Reading, language, and literacy: Instruction in the twenty-first century* (pp. 59–73). Mahwah, NJ: Erlbaum.

Wineburg, S. S. (1996). The psychology of learning and teaching history. In D. C. Berliner & R. C. Calfee (Eds.), *Handbook of educational psychology* (pp. 423–437). New York: Macmillan.

Winne, P. H., Graham, L., & Prock, L. (1993). A model of poor reader's text-based inferencing: Effects of explanatory feedback. *Reading Research Quarterly, 28,* 53–66.

West, L. H. T. & Pines, A. L. (Eds.) (1985). *Cognitive structure and conceptual change.* Orlando, FL: Academic Press.

Wiser, M., & Amin, T. (2001). "Is heat hot?" Inducing conceptual change by integrating everyday and scientific perspectives on thermal phenomena. *Learning and Instruction, 11,* 331–355.

Wittrock, M. C. (1974). Learning as a generative activity. *Educational Psychologist, 11,* 87–95.

Wittrock, M. C. (1990). Generative processes of comprehension. *Educational Psychologist, 24,* 345–376.

Wittrock, M. C., Marks, C., & Doctorow, W. (1975). Reading as a generative process. *Journal of Educational Psychology, 67,* 484–489.

Wollman, W. T., & Lawson, A. E. (1978). The influence of instruction on proportional reasoning in seventh graders. *Journal of Research in Science Teaching, 15,* 227–232.

Wood, E., Pressley, M., & Winne, P. (1990). Elaborative interrogation effects on children's learning of factual content. *Journal of Educational Psychology, 82,* 741–748.

Woodring, P. (1958). Introduction. In W. James (Ed.), *Talks to teachers* (pp. 6–17). New York: Norton.

World Book Encyclopedia (1990). Chicago: Author.

Worthen, B. R. (1968). Discovery and expository task presentation in elementary mathematics. *Journal of Educational Psychology Monographs Supplement, 59,* (1, Pt. 2).

Yates, F. A. (1966). *The art of memory.* London: Routledge and Kegan Paul.

Yuill, N. M., & Oakhill, J. V. (1988). Effects of inference awareness training on poor reading comprehension. *Applied Cognitive Psychology, 2,* 33–45.

Zbrodoff, N. J. (1985). Writing stories under time and length constraints. *Dissertation Abstracts International, 46,* 1219A.

Zigler, E., & Muenchow, S. (1992). *Head start.* New York: Basic Books.

Zimmerman, B. J., & Martinez-Pons, M. (1990). Student differences in self-regulated learning: Relating grade, sex, and giftedness to self-efficacy and strategy use. *Journal of Educational Psychology, 82,* 51–59.

CREDITS AND ACKNOWLEDGMENTS

p. 23: Adapted from Katona, G. (1940). *Organizing and memorizing.* New York: Columbia University Press. Copyright 1940 Columbia University Press. Reprinted by permission.

p. 54: From Samuels, S. J. (1979, January). The method of repeated readings. *The Reading Teacher, 32,* 403–408. Reprinted with the permission of the International Reading Association and S. J. Samuels.

p. 58: From Tulving, E. & Gold, C. (1963). Stimulus information and contextual information as determinants of tachistoscopic recognition of words. *Journal of Experimental Psychology 66,* 322. Copyright 1963 by the American Psychological Association. Reprinted with permission.

p. 59: From West, R. F. & Stanovich, K. E. (1978). Automatic contextual facilitation in readers of three ages. *Child Development, 49,* 721. © Society for Research in Child Development, Inc. Reprinted by permission.

pp. 64 and 65: From McConkie, G. W. & Rayner, K. (1975). The span of effective stimulus during a fixation in reading. *Perception & psychophysics, 17,* 578–586. Reprinted by permission of Psychonomic Society Publications and G. W. McConkie.

p. 66: From Carpenter, P. A. & Just, M. A. (1981). Cognitive processes in reading: Models based on readers' eye fixations. In A. M. Lesgold & C. A. Perfetti (Eds.), *Interactive process in reading* (pp. 177–213). Copyright 1981 by Lawrence Erlbaum Associates, Inc. Reprinted by permission.

pp. 74 and 76–77: From Barlett, F. C. (1932). *Remembering: A study in experimental and social psychology.* Cambridge, England: Cambridge University Press. Copyright 1932 by Cambridge University Press. Reprinted with permission of Cambridge University Press.

p. 81: From Bransford, J. D. & Johnson, M. K. (1972). Contectual prerequisites for understanding: Some investigations of comprehension and recall. *Journal of Verbal Learning and Verbal Behavior, 61,* 722. Copyright 1972, Elsevier Science (USA),. Reproduced by permission of the publisher.

p. 82: From Pichert, J. & Anderson, R. C. (1977). Taking different perspectives on a story. *Journal of Educational Psychology, 69,* 309–315. Copyright © 1977 by the American Psychological Association. Reprinted by permission.

pp. 88, 93, and 94: From Brown, J. S. & Smiley, S. S. (1978). The development of strategies for studying texts. *Child Development, 49,* 1082. By permission of the Society for Research in Child Development.

p. 92: Excerpt from Appendix from Hyona, Jukka. (1994, January). Processing of topic shifts by adults and children. *Reading Research Quarterly, 29* (1), 76–90. Reprinted by permission of the International Reading Association.

p. 95: From Taylor, Barbara M., and Beach, Richard. (1984, Winter), The Effects of text structure instruction on middle-grade students' comprehension and production of expository text. *Reading Research Quarterly, 19* (2), 1340146. Reprinted by permission of the International Reading Association.

p. 106: From Rubman, C,.N., & Waters, H. S. (2000). A, B seeing: The role of constructive processes in children's comprehension monitoring. *Journal of Educational Psychology, 92,* 503–514.

pp 114–115: From Piaget J. (1955). *The language and thought of the child.* Cleveland: Meridian Books. Copyright 1955 Routledge.

p. 122: From Matsuhashi, A. (1982). Explorations in real-time production of written discourse. In M. Nystrand (Ed.), *What writers know: The language, process and structure of written discourse* (pp. 269–324). Copyright 1982, Elsevier Science (USA). Reproduced with the permission of the author.

p. 142: From Englert, C. S., Raphael, T. E. & Anderson, L. M. (1989). *Cognitive strategy instruction in writing project.* East Lansing, MI: Institute for Research on Teaching.

p. 156: From Lewis, A. B. (1989). Training students to represent arithmetic word problems. *Journal of Educational Psychology, 81,* 523. Copyright © 1989 by the American Psychological Association. Reprinted with permission.

pp. 160–61: From Hinsley, D. A. Hayes, J. R., & Simon, H. A. (1977). From words to equations: Meaning and representation in algebra word problems. In M. A. Just and P. A. Carpenter (Eds.), *Cognitive processes in comprehension* (pp. 89–106). Hillsdale, NJ: Erlbaum. By permission of publisher.

p. 163: From Mayer, R. E. (1982b). Memory for algebra story problems. *Journal of Educational Psychology, 74,* 199–218. Copyright © 1982 by the American Psychological Association. Adapted by permission.

p. 164: Adapted from Quilici, J. H. & Mayer, R. E. (1996). Role of examples in houw students learn to categorize statistics word problems. *Journal of Educational Psychology, 88,* 144–161.

p. 181: From *Thinking, problem solving, cognition* (2nd ed.) by Mayer © 1992 by W. H. Freeman and Company. Used with permission.

p. 182: From Groen, G. J., & Parkman, J. M. (1972). A chronometric analysis of simple addition. *Psychological Review, 97,* 329–343.

p. 185: From *The promise of cognitive psychology* by Mayer © 1981 by W. H. Freeman and Company. Used with permission.

pp. 192 and 193: Reprinted with permission from McCloskey, M., Caramazza, A., & Green, B. (1980). Curvilinear motion in the absence of external forces: Naïve beliefs about the motion of objects. *Science, 210,* 1139, 1140. Copyright 1980 American Association for the Advancement of Science.

pp. 196, and 198: From McCloskey, M. (1983) Intuitive physics. *Scientific American, 248,* 123, 126. Michael Goodman. © 1983. Scientific American. Reprinted by permission.

pp. 199, 200 and 201: Reprinted with permission from Clement, J. (1982). Students' preconceptions in introductory mechanics. *American Journal of Physics, 50,*

66–71. Copyright 1982 American Association of Physics Teachers.

p. 204: Chi, M. T. H. (2000). Self-explaining expository texts: the dual processes of generating inferences and repairing mental models. In R. Glaser (Ed.), *Advances in instructional psychology: Volume 5, Educational design and cognitive science* (pp. 161–238). Mahwah, NJ: Erlbaum.

p. 207: Adapted from Mayer, R. E. & Gallini, J. (1990). When is an illustration worth the thousand words? *Journal of Educational Psychology, V. 82,* 715–726. (Adapted from the *World Book Encyclopedia, Vol. 15,* p. 794, 1987, Chicago: World Book, Inc. Copyright 1990 by World Book, Inc. by permission of the publisher.)

pp. 210 and 212: From White, B. J. (1993). Thinker Tools: Causal models, conceptual change, and science education. *Cognition and Instruction, 10, 12.* Copyright 1993 by Lawrence Erlbaulm Associates, Inc. Reprinted by permission.

pp. 214, 215, 216, and 217: From Karplus, R., Karplus, E., Formisano, M. & Paulsen, A. (1979). Proptional reasoning and control variables in seven counties. In J. Lochhead & J. Clement (Eds). *Cognitive process instruction: Research on teaching thinking skills* (pp. 47–107). Philadelphia: Franklin Institute Press. Copyright 1979 by Lawrence Erlbaum Associates, Inc. Reprinted by permission.

p. 218: From Klahr, David (2000). *Exploring Science.* Cambridge, MA: MIT Press. Reprinted by permission. Copyright 2000 by MIT Press.

pp. 220, 221, and 222: From Dunbar, K. (1993). Concept discovery in a scientific domain. *Cognitive Science, 17,* 397–434. Copyright, Cognitive Science Society, Inc., used by permission.

p. 228: From *Thinking, problem solving, cognition* (2nd ed.) by Mayer © 1992 by W. H. Freeman and Company. Used wit permission.

p. 229: From Larkin, J. H. (1983). The role of problem representation in physics. In D. Gentner & A. L. Stevens (Eds.), *Mental modes* (pp. 75–980. Hillsdale, NJ: Erlbaum. Copyright 1983 by Lawrence Erlbaum Associates. Inc. Reprinted by permission.

p. 231: From Chi, Th.. H., Feltovich, P. J., & Glaser, R. (1981). Categorization and representation of physics problems. *Cognitive Science, 5,* 121–152.

p. 240: Adapted from Mayer, R. E. (1977). Incorporating problem solving into secondary school curricula. In G. D. Phye (Ed.) Handbook of Academic Learning (pp. 474–492). San Diego, CA: Academic Press.

pp. 242 and 243: From Thorndike, E. L. (1898). Animal intelligence: An experimental study of the associative processes in animals. *Psychological Review, Monograph Supplement,* 2 (8).

p. 244: Courtesy of Ralph Gerbrands Co., Arlington, Massachusetts.

p. 245: Modified from Skinner, B. F. (1938). *The behavior of organisms: An experimental analysis.* Englewood Cliffs, NJ: Prentice-Hall.

p. 248: From Sulzbacher, S. I. & Houser, J. E. (1968). A tactic to eliminate disruptive behaviors in the classroom: Group contingent consequences. *American Journal of Mental Deficiency, 73,* 88–90.

pp. 250 and 251: From O'Leary, K. D., Becker, W. C., Evans, M. B., & Saudargas, R. A. (1969). A token reinforcement program in a public school: A replication and systematic analysis. *Journal of Applied Behavior Analysis, 2,* 3–13. Copyright 1969 by the Society for the Experimental Analysis of Behavior, Inc.

p. 254: Adapted from Lepper, M. R., Greene, D., & Nisbett, R. E. (1973). Undermining children's intrinsic interest with external rewards: A test of the overjustification hypothesis. *Journal of Personality and Social Psychology, 28,* 129–137.

p. 258: Adapted from Trowbridge, M. H. & Cason, H. (1932). An experimental study of Thorndike's theory of learning, *Journal of General Psychology, 7,* 254–258. Published by Heldref Publications, 4000 Albemarle Street NW, Washington, DC 20016. Copyrightr © 1932.

p. 259: Adapted from Newell, K. M. (1974). Knowledge of results and motor learning. *Journal of Motor Behavior, 16,* 235–244. Published by Heldref Publications, 4000 Albemarle Street NW, Washington, DC 40016. Copyright © 1974.

p. 268 and 269: From Singley, M. K. & Anderson, J. R. (1989). *The transfer of cognitive skill.* Cambridge, MA: Harvard University Press. Copyright 1989 Harvard University Press. Reprinted by permission.

p. 283: Adapted from Bruner, J. S. & Kenney, H. (1966). Multiple ordering. In J. S. Bruner, R. R. Oliver, & P. M. Greenfield (Eds), *Studies in cognitive growth.* New York: Wiley.

p. 285: From Moreno, R. & Mayer, R. E. (1999). Multimedia-supported metaphors for meaning making in mathematics. *Cognition and Instruction, 17,* 215–248. Copyright 1999 Lawrence Erlbaum Associates. Reprinted by permission.

p. 289: Adapted from Kittel, J. E. (1957). An experimental study of the effect of external direction during learning on transfer and retention of principles. *Journal of Educational Psychology, 48,* 391–405.

p. 290: Adapted from Gagne, R. M. & Brown, L. T. (1961). Some factors in the programming of conceptual learning. *Journal of Experimental Psychology, 62,* 313–321.

pp. 295 and 296–97: From Fay, A. L. & Mayer, R. E. (1994). Benefits of teaching design skills before teaching LOGO computer programming: Evidence for syntax-independent learning. *Journal of Educational Computing Research, 11,* 187–210. Copyright 1994 Baywood Publishing Company. Reprinted by permission.

p. 299: Adapted from Roughhead, W. G. & Scandura, U. M. (1968). What is learned in mathematical discovery. *Journal of Educational Psychology, 59,* 283–289.

p. 300: Adapted from Mayer, R. E. & Greeno, J. G. (1972). Structural differences between learning outcomes produced by different instructional methods. *Journal of Educational Psychology, 63,* 165–173.

p. 302: From Moreno, R., Mayer, R. E., Spires, H., & Lester, J. C. (2001). The case for social agency in computer-based teaching: Do students learn more deeply when they interact with animated pedagogical agents? *Cognition and Instruction, 19.* Copyright 2001 Lawrence Erlbaum Associates. Reprinted by permission.

pp. 308 and 309: Adapted from Quilici, J. H. & Mayer, R. E. (1996). Role of examples in how students learn to categorize statistics word problems. *Journal of Educational Psychology, 88,* 144–161.

p. 311: Adapted from Cooper, G. & Sweller, J. (1987). The effects of schema acquisition and rule automation on mathematical problem-solving transfer. *Journal of Educational Psychology, 79,* 347–362.

pp. 314 and 315: Adapted from Paas, F. G. W. C. & van Merrienboer, J. J. G. (1994). Variability of worked examples and transfer of geometrical problem-solving skills: A cognitive load approach. *Journal of Educational Psychology, 86,* 122–133. Copyright © 1994 by the American Psychological Association. Adapted with permission.

pp. 316 and 317: Adapted from Reed, S. K., Dempster, A., & Ettinger, M. (1985). Usefulness of analogous solutions for solving algebra word problems. *Journal of Experimental Psychology: Learning, Memory, and Cognition, 11,* 106–125.

p. 318: Adapted from Chi, M. T. H., Bassok, M., Lewis, M. W., Reimann, P., & Glaser, R. (1989). Self-explanations: How students study and use examples in learning to solve problems. *Cognitive Science 13,* 145–182.

p. 322: From Burke, R. D. (1998). Representation, storage, and retrieval of tutorial stories in a social simulation. In R. C. Schank (Ed.), *Inside multimedia case based instruction* (pp. 175–284). Mahwah, NJ: Erlbaum. Copyright 1998 Lawrence Erlbaum Associates. Reprinted by permission.

pp. 328–29: Adapted from Clarke, A. (1977). *The encyclopedia of how it works.* New York: A&W.

p. 331: Adapted from Cook, L. K. & Mayer, R. E. (1998). Teaching readers about the structure of scientific text. *Journal of Educational Psychology, 80,* 448–456; Chambliss, M. J. & Calfee, R. C. (1998). *Textbooks for learning.* Oxford, England: Blackwell.

p. 335: Adapted from Boker, J. (1974). Immediate and delayed retention effects of interspersing questions in written instructional passages. *Journal of Educational Psychology, 66,* 96–98.

p. 336: Adapted from Mayer, R. E. (1975b). Different problem solving competencies established in learning computer programming with and without meaningful models. *Journal of Educational Psychology, 67,* 725–734.

p. 337: Adapted from Wood, E., Pressley, M., & Winne, P. (1990). Elaborative interrogation effects on children's learning of factual content. *Journal of Educational Psychology, 82,* 741–748.

pp. 342, 377 and 379: Adapted from Meyer, B. J. F., Brandt, D. H ., & Bluth, G. J. (1980). Use of top-level structure in text: Key for reading comprehension of ninth-grade students. *Reading Research Quarterly, 16,* 72–103.

pp. 344–45: From Liddie, W. (1977). *Reading for concepts.* New York: McGraw-Hill.

p. 345: Adapted from Loman, N. L. & Mayer, R. E. (1983). Signaling techniques that increase the understandability of expository prose. *Journal of Educational Psychology, 75,* 402–412.

p. 346: From Britton, B. K. & Gulgoz, S. (1991). Using Kintsch's computational model to improve instructional text: Effects of repairing inference calls on recall and cognitive structures. *Journal of Educational Psychology, 83,* 329–345.

pp. 349 and 350: Adapted from Mayer, R. E. (1983b), Can you repeat that? Qualitative and quantitative effects of repetition and advance organizers on learning from science prose, *Journal of Educational Psychology, 75,* 40–49.

p. 353: Adapted from Mayer, R. E. (1975). Information processing variables in learning to solve problems. *Review of Educational Research, 45,* 525–541.

p. 354: From *World Book Encyclopedia* (1991). Volume 15. Chicago: World Book, Inc. Copyright 1991 World Book, Inc. Reprinted by permission.

pp. 355 and 356: Adapted from Mayer, R. E. & Gallini, J. (1990). When is an illustration worth ten thousand words? *Journal of Educational Psychology, 82,* 715–726.

pp. 357 and 358: From Mayer, R. E. & Anderson, R. B. (1991). Animations need narrations: An experimental test of a dual-coding hypothesis. *Journal of Educational Psychology, 83,* 484–490.

p. 366: From Pressley, M. & Levin, J. R. (1978). Developmental constraints associated with children's use of the keyword method of foreign language vocabulary learning, *Journal of Experimental Child Psychology, 26,* 359–372. Art created by M. Pressley. © 1978 Elsevier Science (USA). Reproduced by permission of the publisher.

pp. 368 and 369: From Levin, J. R. McCormick, C. B., Miller, G. E., Berry, J. K. & Pressley, M. (1982). Mnemonic versus nonmnemonic vocabulary learning strategies for children. *American Educational Research Journal, 19,* 121–136.

pp. 372, 373 and 374: From Holley, C. D., Dansereau, D. F., McDonald, B. A., Garland, J.C., & Collins, K. W. (1979). Evaluation of a hierarchical mapping technique as an aid to prose processing. *Contemporary Educational Psychology, 4,* 227–237. © 1979 Elsevier Science (USA). Reproduced by permission of the publisher.

p. 375: Adapted from Chmielewski, T. L. & Dansereau, D. F. (1998). Enhancing the recall of text: Knowledge mapping training promotes implicit transfer. *Journal of Educational Psychology, 90,* 407–413.

p. 376: From Novak, J. D. & Gowin, D. B. (1984). *Learning how to learn.* New York: Cambridge University Press. Copyright 1984. Cambridge University Press. Reprinted with the permission of Cambridge University Press.

p. 377: From Meyer, B. J. F., Brandt, D. H., & Bluth, G. . (1980). Use of top-level structure in text: Key for reading comprehension of ninth-grade students. *Reading Research Quarterly, 16,* 72–103.

p. 378: Adapted from Meyer, B. J. F. (1975). *The organization of prose and its effects on memory*. Amsterdam: North-Holland; and Meyer, B. J. F. (1981). Basic research on prose comprehension: A critical review. In D. F. Fisher & C. W. Peters (Eds.), *Comprehension and the competent reader.* New York: Praeger.

pp. 382–83, 384 and 385: From Cook, L. K. & Mayer, R. E. (1988). Teaching readers about the structure of scientific text. *Journal of Educational Psychology, 80,* 448–456. Copyright © 1988 by the American Psychological Association. Reprinted with permission.

p. 385: Adapted from Kiewra, K. A., DuBois, N., Christian, D., McShane, A., Meyerhoffer, M., & Roskelley, D. (1991). Note-taking functions and techniques. *Journal of Educational Psychology, 83,* 240–245.

p. 388: Adapted from Peper, R. & Mayer, R. E. (1978). Note taking as a generative activity. *Journal of Educational Psychology, 70,* 514–522.

p. 389: Adapted from Doctorow, M., Wittrock, M. C., & Marks, C. (1978). Generative processes in reading comprehension. *Journal of Educational Psychology, 79,* 109–118.

p. 390: Adapted from Slotte, V. & Lonka, K. (1999). Review and process effects of spontaneous notetaking on text comprehension. *Contemporary Educational Psychology, 24,* 1–20.

p. 392: From King, A. (1992). Comparison of self questioning, summarizing, and notetaking-review as strategies for learning from lectures. *American Educational Research Journal, 29,* 303–323.

p. 394: From King, A., Staffieri, A., & Adelgais, A. (1998). Mutual peer tutoring: Effects of structuring tutorial interaction to scaffold peer learning. *Journal of Educational Psychology, 90,* 134–152.

p. 402: Adapted from Mayer, R. E. (1997). Incorporating problem solving into secondary school curricula. In G. D. Phye (Ed.), *Handbook of Academic Learning* (pp. 474–492). San Diego, CA: Academic Press.

p. 406: Adapted from Schoenfeld, A. H. (1979). Explicit heuristic training as a variable in problem solving performance. *Journal for Research in Mathematics Education, 10,* 173–187.

pp. 410 and 411: From Bloom, B. S. & Broder, L. J. (1950). *Problem-solving processes of college students: An exploratory investigation.* Chicago: University of Chicago Press. Copyright © 1950.

P. 419: Adapted from Olton, R. M. & Crutchfield, R. S. (1969). Developing the skills of productive thinking. In P. Mussen, J. Langer, & M. V. Covington (Eds.), *New directions in developmental psychology.* New York: Holt, Rinehart and Winston.

p. 423: Adapted from Adams, M. J. (1986). *Odyssey: A curriculum for thinking.* Watertown, MA: Charlesbridge Publishing. Copyright © Charlesbridge Publishing, 85 Main Street, Watertown, MN02472. Used with permission.

pp. 436 and 437: Adapted from Nunes, T., Schliemann, A. D., & Carraher, D. W. (1993). *Street mathematics and school mathematics.* Cambridge, England: Cambridge University Press. Reprinted with the permission of Cambridge University Press.

pp. 442–43: From Palinscar, A. S. (1986). Metacognitive strategy instruction. *Exceptional Children, 53,* 118–124. By permission of the Council for Exceptional Children.

p. 443: Adapted from Palinscar, A. S. & Brown, A. L. (1984). Reciprocal teaching of comprehension-fostering and monitoring strageties. *Cognition and Instruction, 1,* 117–175.

p. 446: Modified from Slavin, R. (1982). *Cooperative learning: Student teams.* Washington, DC: National Education Association. Copyright 1982 National Education Association Reprinted by permission.

p. 448: Based on Slavin, R. (1983b). *Cooperative learning.* New York: Longman.

pp. 451, 452 and 453: From Scardamalia, M., Bereiter, C., & Steinbach, R. (1984). Teachability of reflective processes in written composition. *Cognitive Science, 8,* 173–190.

p. 465: Based on Schiefele, U., (1992). Topic interest and levels of text comprehension. In K. A. Renninger, S. Hidi, & A. Krapp (Eds.), *The role of interest in learning and development* (pp. 151–182). Hillsdale, NJ: Erlbaum.

pp. 466 and 467: From Garner, R., Gillingham, M. G., & White, C. S. (1989). Effects of "seductive details" on macroprocessing and microprocessing in adults and children. *Cognition and Instruction, 6,* 41–57.

pp. 468 and 469: Adapted from Harp, S. F. & Mayer, R. E. (1997). The role of interest in learning from scientific text and illustrations: On the distinction between emotional interest and cognitive interest. *Journal of Educational Psychology, 89,* 82–102. Copyright © 1997 by the American Psychological Association. Adapted with permission.

p. 470: Adapted from Schunk, D. H. (1989). Self-efficacy and achievement behaviors. *Educational Psychology Review, 1,* 173–208.

p. 472: Based on Schunk, D. H. & Hanson, A. R. (1985). Peer models: Influences on children's self-efficacy and achievement. *Journal of Educational Psychology, 77,* 313–322.

p. 477: Based on Borkowski, J. G., Weyhing, R. S., & Carr, M. (1988). Effects of attributional retraining on strategy-based reading comprehension in learning-disabled students. *Journal of Educational Psychology, 80,* 46–53.

pp. 479, 480 and 481: Based on Graham, S. & Barker, G. P. (1990). The down side of help: An attributional-developmental analysis of helping behavior as low-ability cue. *Journal of Educational Psychology, 82,* 7–14.

AUTHOR INDEX

Ackerman, B. P., 58
Adams, J. A., 257, 258
Adams, M. J., 31, 34, 39, 43, 44, 45, 46, 49, 110, 413, 422, 423, 424
Adelgais, A., 393, 394
Agne, R., 213
Allington, R. L., 338
Ames, C., 482
Ames, R. E., 482
Amsel, E., 222
Anastasiow, N. J., 290
Anderson, J. R., 258, 268, 269, 270, 271
Anderson, L. M., 140, 142
Anderson, R. B., 356, 357, 358
Anderson, R. C., 59, 60, 82, 103
Anderson, R. G., 334
Anthony, H. M., 140
Applebee, A. N., 116
Arbitman-Smith, R., 421
Arntzen, O., 67
Ashby, J., 66
Ashcraft, M. H., 182
Atkinson, J. W., 365, 366, 461
Atkinson, R. C., 365
Ausubel, D. P., 203, 350, 351, 352

Bailey, J. S., 252
Baird, W., 465, 467
Baker, L., 103
Ball, D., 320
Balsley, Edyth, 47, 48
Bandura, A., 251, 470
Bangert-Drowns, R. L., 132
Barclay, C. R., 108
Barker, G. P., 478, 479, 480
Barnes, B. R., 351
Baron, J., 33, 34, 50, 51, 52
Barrows, H. S., 319
Bartlett, E. J., 129, 133, 134, 135, 136
Bartlett, F. C., 74, 75, 77, 110
Bassok, M., 315, 318, 391
Bayman, P., 293
Beach, R. W., 93, 95
Bean, T. W., 94
Beck, I. L., 62, 85, 86, 87
Becker, W. C., 249, 251
Beitzel, B. D., 367
Bereiter, C., 120, 122, 123, 127, 129, 130, 450, 451, 452, 453, 454
Berry, J. K., 367, 368, 369
Bibly, S. A., 290
Biddle, W. B., 334
Binder, K. S., 66
Binet, A., 403
Bisanz, G. I., 124
Bisbicos, E., 333
Blachman, B. A., 36, 42, 43
Blachowicz, C. L. Z., 57
Blagg, N., 421
Bloom, B. S., 408, 410, 411, 453
Blum, I. H., 55
Bluth, G. J., 342, 371, 375, 378, 380
Bobrow, D. G., 154
Boker, J., 334, 335
Borish, G. D., 290
Borkowski, J. G., 458, 477
Bradley, L., 32, 39, 40, 41, 42
Brandt, D. H., 342, 371, 375, 378, 380
Bransford, J. D., 81, 176, 421, 425
Brenner, M. E., 155, 304
Brewer, W. F., 201, 221
Britton, B. K., 128, 208, 343, 346, 347, 348
Broder, L. J., 408, 410, 411, 453
Bronowski, J., 194, 201
Brown, A. L., 80, 88, 89, 92, 93, 94, 100, 108, 110, 425, 440, 441, 443, 454
Brown, J. S., 184, 186, 439
Brown, L. T., 289, 290
Brownell, W. A., 279, 280
Bruce, B., 118
Bruer, J. T., 187
Bruner, J. S., 278, 279, 282, 283, 288
Bryan, W. L., 47, 48
Bryant, P., 32, 39, 40, 41, 42, 43, 52
Burke, R. D., 321, 322
Burns, M., 42
Burton, R. R., 184, 186
Bus, A. G., 42, 43
Busse, T. V., 413

Cable, G. W., 352
Caccamise, D. J., 124
Calfee, R. C., 50, 144, 331, 343
Calnan, M., 129
Cameron, J., 255
Campione, J. C., 80, 108
Capodilupo, S., 186
Caramazza, A., 192
Carey, S., 194, 201, 222, 224, 225, 226, 227
Carnine, D. W., 60, 61, 110
Carpenter, P. A., 32, 64, 66, 67
Carpenter, T. P., 283
Carr, M., 458, 477
Carraher, D. W., 431, 435, 436, 437
Carter, B., 38
Caruso, D. R., 401
Carver, R. P., 68, 69
Case, R., 186, 187
Cason, H., 257, 258
Catrambone, R., 173
Cattell, J. M., 50
Chall, J. S., 34, 43, 46, 49, 109
Chambliss, M. J., 331, 343
Champagne, A., 203
Chance, P., 424
Chapman, R., 50
Chase, W. G., 407
Chi, M. T. H., 204, 205, 230, 231, 315, 317, 318, 391
Chinn, C. A., 221
Chipman, S. F., 424
Chiu, M-H., 391
Chmielewski, T. L., 371, 372, 376
Clarke, A., 329
Clawson, E. U., 351
Clement, John, 153, 198, 199, 200, 201, 202, 408
Clymer, T., 52, 53
Cohen, A. D., 371
Cohen, H., 213
Cole, M., 433
Collins, A., 118, 439, 440, 452, 453
Collins, K. W., 371
Cook, L. K., 331, 376, 377, 383, 384, 385, 387
Cooper, G., 310, 311, 312
Corkill, A. J., 351, 352
Covington, M. V., 413, 416, 417
Cox, G. L., 95
Craig, R. C., 288
Crowder, R. G., 32, 63, 68, 69
Crutchfield, R. S., 265, 413, 419
Cubberly, E. P., 10
Cunningham, A. E., 42

Dalbey, J., 293
Dansereau, D. F., 371, 372, 374, 376
Davies, L. B., 413
Davis, G. A., 288
Davis, R. B., 400
Day, J. D., 80, 89, 94
Deci, E. L., 254, 255
De Corte, E., 166, 176
De Groot, A. D., 407, 458, 471, 472
de Leeuw, N., 391
Dempster, A., 172, 313, 315, 316, 317
Dennis-Rounds, J., 366
Derry, S. J., 350
Detterman, D. K., 401
Dewey, John, 6, 462, 463, 465, 467
Dienes, Z. P., 282
Dimitrakopoulov, A., 201, 203
DiVesta, F. J., 11, 12, 335
Doctorow, M., 59, 388, 389
Dogan, N., 128
Dominguez, J., 422
Dowhower, S. L., 55
Drake, M., 255
DuBois, N. F., 356
Duffy, S. A., 65
Dunbar, K., 219, 220, 221, 222
Durkin, D., 364

Ehri, L. C., 36, 39, 42, 43, 52, 54
Eisenberg, R., 255
Elliot-Faust, D. J., 107
Englert, C. S., 140, 141, 142, 143
English, L. D., 281
Erickson, G. L., 201
Essen, J., 129
Ettinger, M., 172, 313, 315, 316, 317
Evans, M. B., 249
Evans, R., 224
Eylon, B., 201, 224

Fairbanks, M. M., 62
Fay, A. L., 294, 295, 297
Feltovich, P. J., 230, 231
Fensham, P. J., 351
Feuerstein, R., 418, 419, 420
Fielding, L., 80, 109
Findell, B., 159, 176
Fischer, F. W., 38
Fisher, P., 57, 63, 66
Fitzgerald, J., 133, 138, 144
Fleisher, L. S., 55
Flesch, R. P., 45
Flower, L. S., 116, 117, 118, 119, 120, 125, 130, 137, 450
Flynn, J. R., 401
Ford, W. W., 281, 283
Formisano, M., 213
Francis, M., 137
Frase, L. T., 120
Frederiksen, J. R., 209, 211, 287
Freebody, P., 59
Freschi, R., 60, 61
Frost, J., 42
Fuson, K. C., 179

Gagne, R. M., 5, 18, 289, 290
Gal-Choppin, R., 201
Gallagher, M., 60
Gallimore, R., 412, 431, 432
Gallini, J., 207, 208, 354, 355, 356
Galton, F., 403
Gardner, H., 9, 403
Garland, J. C., 371
Garner, R., 466, 467
Garofalo, J., 174
Gentner, D., 118, 194, 206, 207
Gernsbacher, M. A., 79, 87, 90, 330

Gersten, R., 110
Gertzog, W. A., 194
Gijselaers, G., 319
Gillingham, M. G., 466, 467
Glaser, R., 230, 231, 315, 318, 391, 424
Glasman, L. D., 370
Glynn, S. M., 128, 208, 209, 343
Goelman, H., 122, 127, 129
Gold, C., 57, 58
Gordon, C., 82
Gorin, L., 105, 107, 108
Gormley, K., 83, 84
Goswami, U., 43, 52
Gough, P. B., 39
Gould, J. D., 118, 121, 127, 133
Gowin, D. B., 375, 377
Graesser, A. C., 79, 371
Graham, L., 101
Graham, S., 143, 144, 458, 478, 479, 480
Green, B., 192
Greene, D., 253, 254
Greeno, J. G., 153, 159, 165, 299, 300
Greer, B., 176
Griffin, P., 39, 42
Griffin, S. A., 186, 187
Griffiths, D., 213
Grinder, R. E., 11
Groen, G. J., 180, 182, 232
Groisser, D., 40
Grotzer, T. A., 424
Grouws, D. A., 155
Gulgoz, S., 343, 346, 347
Gunstone, R. F., 201, 202, 203

Ha, Y. W., 221
Haberlandt, K., 90, 91
Halldorson, M., 67
Halpern, D., 224
Halsford, G. S., 194
Hansen, J., 82, 97, 99
Hanson, A. R., 472, 473
Harp, S. F., 467, 468, 469
Harrington, H. L., 319
Harris, K. R., 143, 144
Harter, N., 47, 48
Hauft-Smith, K., 371
Hayes, J. R., 116, 117, 118, 119, 120, 125, 137, 159, 161, 234, 450
Haywood, C., 421
Hegarty, M., 153, 159, 165, 166
Heller, J., 153
Hendrix, G., 298
Herman, P. A., 59, 60
Hermann, G., 298
Herrnstein, R. J., 422
Hewson, P. W., 194
Hidi, S., 463, 465, 467, 482
Hiebert, J., 283
Hieser, J., 468
Hillman, D., 213
Hillocks, G., 138, 139
Hinsley, D., 159, 161, 162
Hoffman, M. B., 418
Hogaboam, T., 49, 53
Holley, C. D., 371, 372, 373, 374, 375
Honda, M., 224
Houser, J. E., 247, 248
Hsi, S., 301, 303, 400
Huey, E. B., 34, 36
Hull, C., 460, 461, 481
Hulme, C., 40
Hyona, J., 91, 92

Inhelder, B., 213, 222
Inman, W. E., 342
Ioannides, C., 201, 203
Itard, Dr. Jean-Marc, 2

Jacob, Francois, 221
James, William, 11
Jay, E., 224
Jenkins, E., 183
Jenkins, J. R., 55
Jensen, M., 418
Jeong, A., 294
Johnson, D. W., 447, 449
Johnson, N. S., 77, 79, 81
Johnson, R. E., 87
Johnson, R. T., 447, 449
Johnston, J. C., 50, 51
Jones, M. S., 367
Jordan, B., 438
Juel, C., 39, 40, 41
Just, M. A., 32, 64, 66, 67

Kameenui, E. J., 60, 61
Karplus, E., 213, 215, 217
Karplus, R., 213, 214, 216
Karweit, N. L., 447
Kass, H., 201
Katona, G., 22, 23, 24, 277
Kauffman, D. F., 356
Kearney, H., 194
Keavney, M., 255
Keisler, E. R., 288
Keizer, S., 319
Kellogg, R. T., 116, 118, 119, 124, 125, 131, 132
Kendler, H. H., 263
Kendler, T. S., 263
Kenney, H., 279, 282, 283
Kenney, P. A., 176
Kerr, S., 137
Kieran, C., 155
Kiewra, K. A., 356, 378, 385
Kile, R. S., 320
Kilpatrick, J., 159, 176
King, A., 389, 391, 392, 393, 394
Kintsch, W., 87, 95, 159, 286, 331, 469
Kittel, J. E., 288, 289
Klahr, D., 217, 218, 221
Klayman, J., 221
Klopfer, L., 203
Koestner, R., 255
Kohler, W., 277
Kolodiy, G., 213
Koskinen, P. S., 55
Kozulin, A., 421
Krapp, A., 463, 464, 482
Kreiger, L. E., 50
Krepelka, E. J., 413
Kroll, D. L., 174
Kuhn, D., 222, 224
Kurland, D. M., 293

LaBerge, D., 53
Lambert, N. M., 4, 129
Lampert, M., 320
Lane, H., 3
Larkin, J. H., 227, 229, 230, 231, 232
LaVancher, C., 391
Lave, J., 412, 431, 433, 438, 439, 440
Lawson, A. E., 213, 222, 223
Leder, G. C., 176
Lee, M., 294, 295
Lehrer, R., 177, 294
Leonhardt, T. M., 290
Lepper, M. R., 253, 254, 255
Lesgold, A. M., 33, 49
Lester, F. K., 174
Lester, J. C., 302, 303
Levin, B. B., 319, 320, 321
Levin, J. R., 354, 366, 367, 368, 369, 370
Levin, M. E., 367, 370
Lewis, A. B., 154, 155, 156, 165, 166, 315, 318, 391
Liberman, I. Y., 38
Liddie, W., 345
Limon, M., 205
Lindauer, B. K., 95, 96
Linn, M. C., 201, 224, 293, 301, 303, 400
Lipson, M.Y., 83, 85
Lochhead, J., 153, 408
Loftus, E. F., 154
Loman, N. L., 343, 345
Lonka, K., 389, 390
Lonn, S., 468
Lorch, E. P., 342, 343
Lorch, R. F., 341, 342, 343
Low, R., 167, 168
Loxterman, J. A., 85, 87
Lundberg, I., 42
Lundeberg, M. A., 319

Ma, L., 158
Machado, L. A., 422
Madsen, C. H., 251
Maher, C. A., 400
Main, G. C., 250
Mandler, J. M., 77, 79
Mansfield, R. S., 413, 414
Markman, E. M., 100, 102, 103, 105, 107, 108, 138
Marks, C., 59, 388, 389
Marr, M. B., 83, 84
Marsh, H. W., 470
Martinez, M. E., 401, 422, 424, 426
Martinez-Pons, M., 471
Matsuhashi, A., 121, 122
Mattingly, I. G., 36
Mautone, P., 343
Mayer, R. E., 5, 9, 12, 14, 17, 18, 19, 21, 22, 75, 87, 153, 159, 162, 163, 164, 165, 166, 171, 181, 185, 188, 194, 207, 208, 228, 284, 285, 286, 293, 294, 295, 297, 299, 300, 302, 303, 308, 309, 329, 331, 336, 343, 345, 349, 350, 351, 352, 353, 354, 355, 356, 357, 358, 376, 377, 383, 384, 385, 387, 388, 395, 402, 403, 408, 425, 467, 468, 469
McClelland, J. L., 51
McCloskey, M., 192, 193, 195, 196, 197, 198, 202
McCombs, B. L., 4
McConkie, G. W., 63, 64, 65, 87, 335
McCormick, C. B., 110, 366, 367, 368, 369
McCutchen, D., 137
McDermott, J., 227
McDermott, L. C., 201
McDonald, B. A., 371
McKenna, M. C., 46
McKeown, M. G., 62, 85, 86, 87
McKinnon, J. W., 213, 223
Meyer, B. J. F., 87, 89, 341, 342, 343, 371, 375, 376, 378, 379, 380
Miller, G. E., 366, 368, 369
Monk, C. A., 153, 165
Monod, Jacques, 221
Montessori, M., 281
Moreno, R., 284, 285, 286, 302, 303
Moser, H. E., 280
Mueller, S., 131, 132
Muenchow, S., 401, 426
Munro, B. C., 250
Muth, D., 128

Nagy, W. E., 56, 59, 60
Nathan, M. J., 159, 286
Nation, K., 40
Nelson, N., 144
Nemko, B., 55
Newbern, D., 371
Newell, K. M., 258, 259
Newman, S. E., 439
Nickerson, R. S., 416, 422, 424
Nisbett, R. E., 253, 254
Nold, E. W., 118
Norman, D. A., 364
Norwall, M. B., 370
Novak, J. D., 374, 375, 377
Novick, S., 201
Nunes, T., 431, 435, 436, 437

Nussbaum, J., 201
Nussinovitz, R., 201
Nystrand, M., 120, 126

Oakhill, J., 95, 98, 99
Okamoto, Y., 186
O'Leary, K. D., 249, 250, 251
O'Loughlin, M., 222
Olton, R. M., 265, 413, 419
Omanson, R. C., 62
Osborne, R. J., 201
Over, R., 167

Paas, F. G. W. C., 313, 314, 315
Pagnucco, J. R., 46
Paige, J. M., 157
Paivio, A., 365, 370
Palinscar, A. S., 80, 110, 425, 440, 441, 443, 454
Pany, D., 55
Papademetriou, E., 201, 203
Papert, S., 291, 292
Paris, S. G., 95, 96, 103
Parkman, J. M., 180, 182
Patel, V. L., 232
Paulsen, A., 213
Pauwels, A., 166
Pea, R. D., 293
Pearson, P. D., 60, 80, 82, 97, 99, 103, 104, 109
Pennington, B. F., 40
Peper, R., 387, 388
Perfetti, C. A., 33, 39, 49, 53, 62
Perkins, D. N., 173, 293, 424
Peterson, O., 42
Piaget, J, 114, 115, 213, 222
Pianko, S., 123, 133
Pichert, J., 82
Pierce, W. D., 255
Pintrich, P. R., 255, 458, 471, 472
Pollatsek, A., 32, 63, 64, 66
Polya, G., 169, 170, 171, 404, 405
Posner, G. J., 194, 195, 202, 205, 206
Presseisen, B. Z., 421
Pressley, M., 43, 46, 56, 57, 58, 97, 107, 109, 337, 364, 366, 367, 368, 369, 370, 390, 453
Prock, L., 101
Pyles, L. D., 371

Quilici, J. H., 163, 164, 308, 309
Quinlan, K. M., 25

Rand, Y., 418
Raney, G. E., 65
Raphael, T. E., 140, 142
Raugh, M. R., 365, 366
Rayner, K., 32, 63, 64, 65, 66, 335
Read, C., 127
Reed, S. K., 172, 173, 174, 175, 313, 315, 316, 317
Reicher, G. M., 50
Reichle, E. D., 63, 66
Renner, J. W., 213, 223
Renninger, K. A., 463, 482
Resnick, L. B., 14, 34, 188, 281, 283, 286
Revlin, R., 67
Reynolds, Will, 47, 48
Rice, G. E., 343
Richardson, K., 129
Richardson, V., 320
Rickards, J. P., 335
Rieben, L., 39
Riley, M., 153, 165
Rippa, S. A., 21
Robbins, C., 52
Roberts, K. T., 54
Robinson, C. S., 159
Robinson, D. H., 356
Robinson, F. P., 109
Rogers, T., 103, 104
Rogoff, B., 434, 438
Rosenshine, B. V., 80, 97, 109
Ross, B. H., 266
Ross, M., 254
Rothkopf, E. Z., 333, 334
Roughhead, W. G., 299
Royer, J. M., 352
Rubin, A., 118
Rubman, C. N., 105
Rumelhart, D. E., 77
Ryan, R. M., 255

Salomon, G., 173
Samuels, S. J., 53, 54, 55
Samuelstuen, M., 67
Sanchez, M., 422
Saudargas, R. A., 249
Sawyer, R. J., 143, 144
Scandura, J. M., 11, 299
Scardamalia, M., 120, 122, 123, 127, 129, 130, 450, 451, 452, 453, 454
Schank, R., 322, 323
Schiefele, U., 464, 465
Schliemann, A. D., 431, 435, 436, 437
Schloss, P. J., 251
Schoenfeld, A. H., 171, 173, 175, 176, 404, 406
Schuberth, R. E., 58
Schunk, D. H., 255, 469, 470, 472, 473
Schvaneveldt, R., 58
Schwartz, B. B., 286
Scott, J. A., 56, 59
Scribner, S., 129, 433
Segal, J. W., 424
Semlear, T., 58
Sereno, S. C., 63
Serpell, R., 434, 437
Shanahan, T., 144
Shankweiler, D., 38
Shavelson, R. J., 232, 233, 234, 470
Shepard, D. L., 110
Shulman, L. S., 25, 288
Siegler, R. S., 183, 186
Silver, E. A., 164, 176
Simon, D. P., 227
Simon, H. A., 157, 159, 161, 227, 234, 407
Sims, V., 171, 188
Sinatra, G. M., 85, 87
Singer, H., 34, 44, 45, 50, 67
Singley, M. K., 258, 268, 269, 270
Skinner, B. F., 244, 245, 246
Slavin, R. E., 444, 445, 446, 447, 448, 449
Slotte, V., 389, 390
Smiley, S. S., 88, 89, 92, 93, 94
Smith, E. E., 50, 424, 452
Smith, M. A., 251
Snitgen, D. A., 213, 222, 223
Snow, C., 42
Soloway, E., 153
Sovik, N., 67
Spearman, C., 407
Spector, J. E., 42
Spires, H., 302
Spoehr, K. T., 50, 58
Squire, J. R., 109
Staffieri, A., 393, 394
Stahl, S. A., 46, 62
Staley, R .K., 356
Stanovich, K. E., 40, 42, 53, 57, 58, 59
Stazyk, E. H., 182
Steenwyk, F. L., 94
Stein, B. S., 421
Steinbach, R., 450, 451, 452, 453
Steinberg, E. R., 119
Sternberg, R. J., 16, 17, 254, 403, 419, 421, 433
Stevens, A. L., 194
Stevens, D. D., 140
Stone, C. A., 432
Stotsky, S., 123
Strike, K. A., 194
Sulzbacher, S. I., 247, 248
Suppes, P., 154
Swafford, J., 159, 176
Sweller, J., 310, 311, 312, 356
Swets, J. A., 422

Tajika, H., 171, 188
Tamblyn, R., 319
Tamir, P., 201
Taylor, B. M., 89, 90, 93, 95
Taylor, J. J., 401
Tempelaar, S., 319
Tharp, R. G., 412, 431, 432
Thomas, D. R., 251
Thompson, A., 295
Thorndike, E. L., 6, 10, 21, 22, 25, 48, 188, 242, 243, 246, 256
Thorndyke, P. W., 77
Thurstone, L. L., 407
Torgesen, J. K., 36, 39, 40
Torney-Punta, J., 400
Trowbridge, D. E., 201
Trowbridge, M. H., 257, 258
Tulving, E., 57, 58
Unger, C., 224
Upton, L. R., 96

Van Haneghan, J., 176
van Ijzendoorn, M. H., 42, 43
van Merrienboer, J. J. G., 313, 314, 315
Venezky, R., 50
Verschaffel, L., 166, 176
Vosniadou, S., 103, 104, 105, 201, 203, 204
Voss, J. F., 124
Vye, N. J., 421
Vygotsky, Lev S., 431, 432, 433, 454

Wade, S. E., 467, 469
Wagner, R. K., 32, 36, 39, 40, 63, 68
Wagner, S., 155
Walters, R. H., 251
Waterman, D. A., 159
Waters, H. S., 105
Weaver, P. A., 34, 95
Weber, R., 338
Weiner, B., 460, 461, 475, 476
Weinstein, C. E., 395
Well, A. D., 64
Welsh, M. C., 40
Wenger, E., 412, 438, 439, 440
Wertheimer, M., 22, 276
Wertsch, J. V., 431, 432
West, L. H. T., 351
West, R. F., 57, 58, 59
Westfall, R. S., 194
Weyhing, R. S., 458, 477
Whaley, J. F., 79
Wheeler, A. E., 201
White, A. G., 252
White, B. Y., 207, 209, 210, 211, 212, 287
White, C. S., 466, 467
White, R. T., 201, 202
Williams, J. P., 46
Wilson, S. J., 335
Winne, P., 337
Winne, P. H., 98, 101
Winteler, A., 464
Wiser, M., 201
Wittrock, M. C., 19, 59, 201, 386, 388, 389
Wollman, W. T., 223
Woloshyn, V., 56, 57, 109, 364, 370, 390, 453
Wood, E., 337
Woodring, P., 10
Woodworth, R. S., 21

Yates, F. A., 365
Yeany, R. H., 208
Young, E., 159, 286
Youssef, M., 351
Yuill, N., 95, 98, 99

Zbrodoff, N. J., 123
Zigler, E., 401, 426
Zimmerman, B. J., 471

SUBJECT INDEX

Abstracting process, 319
Academic achievement
 cooperative learning and, 447
 individual interest and, 464–465
 motivation theory and, 461
 self-efficacy theory and, 472–475
Accommodative learning, 205–207
Activation theory, 221–222
Active learning, 471–472
Addition procedures, 182–183
Adjunct questions
 example, 332
 implications of, 338
 research on, 333–338
 theory, 333
Advance organizers
 example, 348–350
 implications of, 357–358
 research on, 351–357
 theory, 350–351
Adventures of Jasper Woodbury, The, 176, 177
Algebra story problems, 159
Algebra textbooks, 162
Ambiguous referencing, defined, 135
American Spelling Book, The, 44, 45
Analogical models, 207–208
Analogical reasoning, 281, 309, 323
Analogical transfer process, 171
Analogies, conceptual change with, 206
Anchored instruction, 177
ANIMATE program, 286
Animation, 356, 358
Apprenticeship
 cooperative learning and, 444–449
 overview of, 433
 participatory modeling and, 450–453
 reciprocal teaching and, 440–444
 traditional and cognitive, 437–440
Arithmetic
 concrete manipulatives in, 280
 materials for teaching, 281–282
 word problems, 165
Assisted performance, 412
Associative writing, 130
Attribution, 459, 460
 feedback hypothesis and, 478–481
 strategy training and, 476–477
 theory, 475–476
Automaticity effects/training
 decoding and, 46–50
 for recognizing letters, 52–55

Ball problem, 197–198
Basal readers, 45
Basal reading programs, 97–100
Base, defined, 206
Base problems, 171, 308, 319, 323
BASIC language, 293
Basic skills, 13, 14
Behavior, reward and, 253–254
Behaviorist approach, 6
Behaviorist theories
 of classroom management, 246–247
 of concept learning, 261–263
 of response learning, 256
 of reward, 252–253
 of skill learning, 267
BUGGY program, 184

Case-based learning
 factors in designing, 323
 interactive, 321–323
 introduction to, 319–320
 retrospective, 320–321
Cause/change problems, 165
Chain structures, 373
Children. *See also* Readers; Students
 comprehension monitoring of, 103–105
 developing metacognitive skills in, 108
 inference making development of, 96–97
 phoneme-trained, 41–42
 phonological awareness of, 38–39
 prose structure use by, 88–92
 topic shift effect on, 90–92
 vocabulary growth of, 56
Classification, defined, 331
Classroom
 activities, 252
 concept learning in, 260–261
 discussions, 87
 response learning in, 256
 skill learning in, 267
Classroom management
 contingency contracting and, 247–248
 introduction to, 246
 limitations of, 252
 theories, 246–247
 token economies and, 248–252
Cliff problem, 195–197
Cluster structures, 373
Coaching, defined, 440
Cognitive apprenticeship. *See* Apprenticeship
Cognitive approach, 7
Cognitive interest, 469
Cognitive processes
 in analogical thinking, 309
 decoding words and, 43–55
 inference making, 95–100
 involved in reading words, 32–36
 meaning access, 55–62
 metacognitive knowledge, 100–108
 phonological awareness, 36–43
 sentence integration, 62–69
 types of, 403
 using prior knowledge, 80–87
 using prose structure, 87–95
 in writing, 116–120
Cognitive Process Instruction (Clement), 408
Cognitive skills, 407
Cognitive Strategy Instruction in Writing (CSIW), 140–141, 143
Cognitive structure, 331
Cognitive theories
 of classroom management, 246–247
 of concept learning, 261–263
 of instruction, 329–332
 of motivation, 461
 of response learning, 256
 of reward, 252–254
 of skill learning, 267
Coherence, signaling and, 343, 347–348
Coin problem, 198–199
Collection, defined, 379
Combination problems, 165
Communication vs. composition, 120
Comparative organizers
 defined, 350
 for external connections, 351
Comparison
 defined, 379
 problems, 165
Comparison/contrast, defined, 331
Composition. *See* Writing process
Comprehension monitoring. *See also* Reading comprehension
 of children, 103–105
 defined, 100, 102
Computational expertise/skills
 feedback and, 258–259
 stages in development of, 179–180
Computational principles, 299
Computational problems, 158, 281–282
Computational procedures
 complex, 183–184
 training, 188
Computer applications
 concrete methods and, 284–287
 discovery methods and, 291–298
 inductive methods and, 301–303
Computers as Learning Partners (CLP), 303
Computer simulation, 321–323
Concept learning
 approaches to, 266
 in classroom, 260–261
 defined, 241
 implications of, 265–266
 research on, 263–265
 theories, 261–263
Concept mapping, 374–375, 377
Conceptual change, 194
 analogical models and, 207–208
 assimilative vs. accommodative learning and, 205–207
 instruction, 204
 promoting, 209–212, 235
Conceptual information, 343
Conceptual knowledge, 15
Concrete methods
 computer simulations and, 284–287

example, 278
implications of, 283
research on, 279–283
theories, 278–279
Concrete models
as advance organizers, 352–353
illustrations as, 353–357
Confirmation bias, 221
Consonants, phonic rules for, 53
Context effects, meaning access and, 57–58
Contextual approach, 8
Contingency contracting
costs of, 253–254
reinforcement theory and, 247–248
Control-of-variables task, 213, 215–218, 223
Cooperative incentive structure, 447
Cooperative learning
competitive environment and, 445–446
defined, 177
group learning and, 448–449
overview of, 444–445
student achievement and, 447–448
Cooperative task structure, 447, 448
Counting-all procedure, 179, 181, 183
Counting-on procedure, 179, 180, 181, 183
Covariance, defined, 379

Deciphering skills, 48
Declarative knowledge, 270
Decoding
automaticity effects and, 46–50
debate about, 43–46
defined, 33, 43
pronunciation strategy effects and, 51–52
training for, 52–55
word superiority effects and, 50–51
Decorative illustrations, 354
Deductive methods, 299–300
Deep questions, 464
Derived facts procedure, 179–180, 183
Description, defined, 379
Design-A-Plant game, 302–303
Diagramming steps, 156
Dienes blocks
for teaching numbers, 282
for teaching quadratic factoring, 282–283
Direct instruction approach, 56
Discovery methods
computer applications in, 291–298
example, 287
implications of, 290–291
research on, 288–290
theories, 287–288
Disruptive behaviors
defined, 248
number of, 248
percentage of, 250–251
rewards for reducing, 249–250
Distance-rate-time problems, 159–160, 162, 286
Drafts, polished vs. unpolished, 127–129
Drill-and-practice method, 13, 184, 186
Drive theories, 460–461

E. coli experiment, hypothesis creation and, 218–221
Edit/editor think-sheet, 141
Educational psychology
cautious optimism phase of, 11–12
central theme in, 6
contributions of, 24–26
defined, 4–5
naive optimism phase of, 10–11
paths for, 9–12
pessimism phase of, 11
reasons for decline of, 11
Educational Psychology (Ausubel), 203
Effort-based attributions, 459
Effort vs. interest, 461–463
Elaborative interrogation, 337
Electronic Laboratory Notebook, 301
Emotional interest, 469
English letter-sound combinations, 52–55
English vocabulary, teaching, 366–367
Enumeration
defined, 331
devices, 341
structure, 377, 384
Errors
detecting, 133, 134, 135
problem translation and, 155, 157
in relational statements, 153
Experience & Education (Dewey), 6
Explanative illustrations, 354, 355
Explanative text, 353
Expository instruction, 288, 290
Expository organizers
defined, 350
for prerequisite knowledge, 350–351
Expository prose, 373
Extradimensional shift task, 264
Extrinsic motivation, 459
Eye movements
during reading, 62–67
speed reading and, 68

Factual knowledge
expert/novice differences in, 228–229
for math problems, 152, 154
in physics expertise, 228
problem integration and, 158
problem translation and, 157
Feature detectors, 51
Feedback
classroom management and, 246–252
concept learning and, 260–266
law of effect and, 242–246
response learning and, 256–260
skill learning and, 267–271
views of, 241
Fixation duration, 63, 67
Fixation span, 63
Flynn effect, 401
Focal attention hypothesis, 54
Foreign language, teaching, 365–366
Formal discipline, 21–22
Formal tests, 436, 437
Frustrum problem, 169–171
Function indicators, 341

Generalization
defined, 331
prose structure, 377, 384
General transfer, 20–22
Generating process, 116, 125
Generative learning, 177
Generative strategies
defined, 386
implications of, 393–395
research on, 386–393
theory, 386
Geometry problems, 314
G-factors, 407
Global planning, 121, 123
Goal setting, 116, 120, 125
Gravity, misconception about, 201
Group learning, 448–449
Guided discovery methods, 288, 291–298

Hands-on-experience, 223, 234
Head Start, 401
Heterogeneous group, 448
Hierarchy structures, 373
How to Solve It (Polya), 169, 404
Human development, 3–4
Human faculty, 403
Hypothesis creation
scientific reasoning and, 218–221
teaching, 224–226
Hypothesis testing
scientific reasoning and, 213–218
teaching, 222–223

Ideational confrontation, 203
Illustrations
learning and, 355–356
types of, 354
Immersion approach, 56
Incidental learning, 333–334
Inconsistencies in stories
failure to recognize, 103–105
overview of, 100, 102
teaching children to detect, 105–108
Individual accountability, 448
Individual interest
defined, 463
motivation and, 463–465
Inductive methods
computer applications in, 301–303
example, 298
implications of, 300–301
research on, 298–300
theories, 298
Inference making
defined, 95
research on, 96–97
training issues, 97–100, 101
Informal tests, 436, 437
Information view, 241
Inhibition theory, 222
Instruction
automaticity training and, 52–55
cognitive theory of, 329–332
conceptual change promotion and, 209–212
confronting students' misconceptions and, 202–205
defined, 5
fostering scientific expertise and, 232–234
inference training and, 97–100

levels of guidance in, 288
phonological awareness training and, 40–43
planning and, 123–125
problem integration and, 166–169
problem translation skills and, 154–157
providing prior knowledge and, 85–87
reviewing process and, 137–138
scientific reasoning and, 221–226
solution planning and, 176–179
speed reading and, 67–69
summarization training and, 92–95
translation process and, 131–132
vocabulary training and, 58–62
Instructional methods
behaviorist approach, 6
cognitive approach, 7
contextual approach, 8
Instrumental enrichment
background, 417–419
description of, 420
evaluation of, 420–421
Integration process
advance organizers and, 350–351
learning strategies and, 362
Intellectual performance, 403
Intellectual testing, 407–408
Intentional learning, 333–334
Interactive case-based learning, 321–323
Interest, 458, 460
cognitive, 469
vs. effort, 461–463
emotional, 469
individual, 463–465
situational, 465–469
Interest and Effort in Education (Dewey), 462
Internalization process, 432
Intradimensional shift task, 263–264
Intrinsic motivation, 459
IQ scores, 401

Johnny Can't Read and What You Can Do About It (Flesch), 45
Journal of Educational Psychology, 10

Keyword method
story problems and, 174
for teaching foreign language, 365–366
Kinematics, defined, 227
Knowledge. *See also* Prior knowledge
acquisition, 12
construction, 12
as description vs. explanation, 194–195
kinds of, 15, 116
mapping, 371–374
structure test, 233–234
Knowledge telling, defined, 120, 450
Knowledge transforming, defined, 120, 450
Known facts procedure, 180, 183

Law of effect
defined, 243–244
Skinner theory, 244–246
Thorndike's theory, 242–243
Learner-centered approach, 2, 3
kinds of knowledge for, 15
memory system for, 15–17
Learners. *See* Students
Learning. *See also* Apprenticeship; Feedback
accommodative vs. assimilative, 205–207
active, 471–472
animation and, 356, 358
apprenticeship and, 433
based on effort or on interest, 461–469
cooperative, 444–449
deductive and inductive methods effect on, 299
defined, 5–6
discovery methods effects on, 290
by doing, 310–312, 314
from examples, 310–312, 314
group, 448–449
guidance during, 288–290, 332
illustrations and, 355–356
instructional methods and, 6–8
meaningful, 17–19
by memorizing, 22–24
with mnemonic strategies, 364–370
in and out of school, 434–437
signaling and, 341–348
with structure strategies, 370–385
transfer concept for, 19–22
by understanding, 23–24
using questions to guide, 394
views of, 12–14
Learning disabilities
inference training and, 98, 100–101
motivational training and, 477–478
Learning potential assessment device (LPAD), 418
Learning process
factors in, 8–9
memory system and, 15–17
Learning strategies
defined, 362
generative strategies, 386–395
mnemonic strategies, 364–370
overview of, 362–364
structure strategies, 370–385
Learning to read
decoding process and, 48–50
defined, 34
phonological awareness and, 39, 41
with and without attribution training, 478
Learning to Read: The Great Debate (Chall), 46
Learning to write. *See* Writing process
Legitimate peripheral participant, 439
Letter(s)
detectors, 51
phonics approach and, 43–44, 50
training for recognizing, 52–55
Levels effect, defined, 88
Linear writing process, 450
Linguistic knowledge
for math problems, 152
problem integration and, 158
problem translation and, 157
Literal error, 153, 154
Local planning, 121
Logical reasoning, 288–289
LOGO commands, 292, 294
LOGO environment, 291, 293, 304
Longhand writing, 132
Long-term memory, 16

Mapping methods, 371–376
Mapping process, 309, 319
Material rewards, 249
Mathemagenic activity, 386
Mathematical principles, 298–300
Mathematical reasoning, 289–290
Mathematics
concrete manipulatives in, 279–283
formal and informal, 435
pretest-to-posttest gains in, 447
Math problems
introduction to, 148, 152
problem integration and, 157–169
problem translation and, 152–157
procedure for solving, 404–406
skills needed for solving, 149–152
solution execution and, 179–188
solution planning and monitoring and, 169–179
Matrix group, 385
McGuffey Reders, 45
Meaning access
context effects and, 57–58
defined, 33, 55–57
training for increasing, 56, 58–62
Meaning-emphasis method, 44
Meaningful method, 276, 280
Mean pronunciation time, 49
Mediated learning experiences (MLE), 419
Mediationally deprived students, 419
Memorization
defined, 364
learning strategies and, 362
mnemonic strategies and, 364–370
Memory system, 15–17
Mental models, 331–332
Mental orthopedics, 403
Metacognitive knowledge
comprehension monitoring and, 100–108
defined, 100
Microworlds, 284, 287
Mindstorms (Papert), 291
Min model, 180, 182
Misconceptions
conceptual-change theory and, 194–195
confronting students', 202–205
research on, 195–202
Mixed transfer, 20, 22
Mnemonic strategies
defined, 364–365
implications of, 370
research on, 366–370
theory, 365
Modeling, defined, 440
Model students, 408, 410
Montessori materials, 281–282
Morse code, 47, 48
Motion, conception of, 195–201
Motivated Strategies for Learning Questionnaire (MSLQ), 458
Motivation
based on attributions, 475–481

based on interest, 461–469
based on self-efficacy, 469–475
defined, 460
research on, 460–461
reward and, 255
roots of, 459
views of, 459–460
Motor skill learning, 258–259
Multibase arithmetic blocks (MAB), 282

Narrative prose, 77–79
National Assessment of Educational Progress, 176
National Council of Teachers of Mathematics, 155
Negative-bias bug, 284
Negative transfer, 19
Neutral transfer, 19
New England Primer, The, 44
Nonlearners, 17
Nonreversal shift task, 264
Nonunderstanders, 17
Notetaking process, 386–390, 393
Number-line method, 155–156, 187–188
Numbers
Dienes blocks for teaching, 282
materials for teaching, 281–282

Odyssey course, 422–424
Organizational illustrations, 354, 355
Organization of Dots problems, 420
Organization process
learning strategies and, 362
signaling and, 341
Organize think-sheet, 141
Organizing process, 116, 120, 125
Outlining methods, learning with, 375–379
Overjustification, defined, 253

Parallelogram problem
concrete manipulatives for, 278
instruction methods for, 276–277
Participatory modeling
overview of, 450
writing process and, 450–453
Phoneme categorization, 38
Phoneme identity, 38
Phoneme isolation, 38
Phoneme substitution, 38
Phonics approach
pronunciation strategy effects and, 52
for reading, 43–44, 50
Phonological awareness
defined, 32, 36
development of, 38–40
tests of, 38–39
training, 40–43
Phonological awareness hypothesis, 39–40
Phonological decoding, 52
Physics
concepts, sample questions, 212
expert/novice differences in, 228–229
game for learning, 210
learners' misconceptions of, 195–202
problem, intuitive, 192–193
Place value concept, 281–282
Planning
defined, 120
instruction and, 123–125
research on, 121–123
for writing process, 116–117
Plan think-sheet, 141
Pointer words, defined, 341
Positive transfer, 19
Predict-observe-explain (POE) method, 202, 301
Pretests and posttests
participatory modeling and, 451–453
productive thinking program and, 418
for reading comprehension, 443
for scientific thinking, 226
for translation skills, 157
Prewriting activities, 124–125
Principles of Teaching (Thorndike), 6
Prior automatization theory, 410, 412
Prior knowledge
advance organizer and, 351
differences in amount of, 81–83
differences in the kinds of, 83–85
providing, 85–87
Problem(s)
cause/change, 165
combination, 165
of reading a word, 32–36
transfer, 310–316
triangle, 159–160
types, 160–163
ways of representing, 279
Problem-based learning, 319
Problem integration
defined, 157–159
example, 149–150
research on, 159–166
teaching, 166–169
Problem solvers
problem types and, 159–163
student schemas and, 163–164
successful vs. unsuccessful, 165–166
worked-out examples and, 315–318
Problem solving
deductive and inductive methods effect on, 300
elements of, 401–402
having sufficient information for, 166–167
heuristics, 171, 178
how to teach, 406, 408–410
implications for teaching, 412
instrumental enrichment program for, 417–421
notetaking process and, 388
overview of, 400–401
productive thinking program for, 413–417
project intelligence for, 421–424
solution plan for, 169–176
thinking skills instruction and, 424–426
transfer, 19, 172
what to teach in, 402–406
when to teach, 410–412
where to teach, 406–408
Problem translation
defined, 152
example, 149
research on, 153–154
teaching, 154–157
Procedural knowledge, 15, 270
Productive disposition, defined, 175
Productive thinking program
background, 413
description of, 413
evaluation of, 413–414, 416–417
Project intelligence
background, 421–422
description of, 422
evaluation of, 422–424
Pronunciation strategy effects, 51–52
Pronunciation time, mean, 49
Proportional reasoning task, 213–215, 223
Prose learning, 381
Prose structure
differences in use of, 88–89
inconsistency issues related to, 102–105
remembering important information in, 87–88
for science text, 382–383
summarization training and, 92–95
topic shift issues in, 90–92
types of, 377, 384
Psychology, evolution of role of, 9–12
Psychology and Pedagogy of Reading, The (Huey), 34
Punishment, reward and, 245–246
Pure discovery methods
computer programming and, 291–298
defined, 288
drawback of, 290

Quadratic factoring, teaching, 282–283
Questioning methods, 391–393

Readers
automaticity training for, 52–55
basal, 45
eye fixation of, 64–67
meaning access issues, 56–57
mean pronunciation time for, 49
prose structure use by, 88–92
teaching summarization skills to, 92–95
vocabulary training for, 58–62
Reader's perspective, defined, 80–81
Reading
eye movements during, 62–67
phonics approach for, 43–44
research, 34
skills, 39–40, 42
speed, 67–69
whole-word approach for, 44–46
words, 32–33
word superiority effect for teaching, 50–51
Reading comprehension
automaticity training and, 54
defined, 34
inference making for, 95–100
pretest-to-posttest gains in, 443
schema theory and, 76–79
skills needed for, 80
SQ3R approach for, 109–110
standardized tests and, 49
strategies, 441
using metacognitive knowledge for, 100–108
using prior knowledge for, 80–87

using prose structure for, 87–95
vocabulary training and, 58–62
Reading fluency
decoding words and, 43–55
defined, 34
phonological awareness and, 36–43
problem of reading a word and, 32–36
sentence integration and, 62–69
word meaning and, 55–62
Reading to learn, defined, 34
Reciprocal teaching
example, 442–443
overview of, 440–441
participatory modeling and, 451
reading comprehension and, 441, 444
Recognizing process, 309
Referent errors, 133, 134, 135
Reflection process, 117
Reflective writing process, 450
Regressive saccades, 63
Reinforcement theory, 245
classroom management and, 246
contingency contracting and, 247–248
token economies and, 248–252
Reinforcement view, 241
Relational statements, 153, 155
Relevance indicators, 341
Remedial students, 408, 410
Repeated readings method, 53–54
Representational illustrations, 354
Representational processes, 403
Response
cost procedure, 247
defined, 379
strengthening, 12
Response learning
in classroom, 256
defined, 241
feedback and, 241, 259–260
introduction to, 240
law of effect and, 242–246
research on, 256–259
theories, 256
Retention
advance organizers effects on, 350
signals for promoting, 343
Retention test, 17
keyword method strategy and, 366, 370
notetaking process and, 388–390, 393
Retrieval. *See* Known facts procedure
Retrospective case-based learning, 320–321
Reversal shift task, 263–264
Reviewing process
defined, 133
individual differences in, 134–137
instruction and, 137–138
making changes in, 133–134
for writing process, 117
Revision think-sheet, 141
Reward(s)
for classroom management, 249
costs of, 252–255
positive reinforcement concept and, 255–256
punishment and, 245–246
theories, 252–253
Rhetorical structures, 331
Rocket problem, 198, 200–201
Rote learners, 17
Rote method approach, 276

Saccade duration, 63
Saccade length, 63
Scaffolding, 440, 444
Schema
defined, 76
for narrative prose, 77–79
Schematic knowledge, 15
expert/novice differences in, 230–231
in physics expertise, 228
School mathematics, defined, 434
Science learning
building scientific knowledge for, 226–234
computer simulations in, 284–287
conceptual change and, 194, 205–212
discarding misconceptions in, 194–205
scientific reasoning and, 213–226
Scientific expertise
fostering, 232–234
novice and expert physicists and, 227–232
quantitative vs. qualitative differences and, 226–227
Scientific reasoning
as hypothesis testing vs. hypothesis creation, 213
research on, 213–221
survey about, 225
teaching, 221–224, 226
Seductive details hypothesis, 466–469
Selective combination process, 16–17
Selective comparison process, 17
Selective encoding process, 16
Self-concept, defined, 470
Self-efficacy, 458, 460
defined, 469–470
importance of, 470
theory, 470–471
Self-explanation
defined, 391
process, 205
Self-regulated strategy development (SRSD), 143–144
Self-repair process, 205
Semantic cues, 57
Semantic errors, 153, 154
Semantic knowledge, 15
expert/novice differences in, 229–230
in physics expertise, 228
Sensory memory, 15
Sentence context, word meaning and, 57
Sentence integration
defined, 33, 62
research on, 62–67
speed reading and, 67–69
Sentence wrap-up, defined, 66
Sequence
defined, 331
structure, 377, 384
S-factors, 407
Short-term memory (STM), 15–16
Signaling
example, 338–340
research on, 341–348
theory, 341
Simple addition, development of expertise for, 179–182
Situated learning theory, 431, 439
Situational interest
defined, 463
motivation and, 465–469
Situation models, 158, 159
Skill learning
in classroom, 267
cognitive, 270–271
defined, 241
research on, 268–270
theories, 267
Skinner boxes, 244–245
Social rewards, 249
Solution execution
defined, 179
example, 151–152
research on, 179–184
teaching for, 184–188
Solution plan(ning)
defined, 169
designing, 169–176
example, 150–151
teaching for, 176–179
Solution processes, 403
Sound units, 36, 38
Source problems, 319
Spatial learning strategy, 374
Specific transfer, 22
Speed reading, 67–69
SQ3R approach for reading, 109–110
Standardized tests, 49
Statistical principles, 299–300
Story
grammars, 77
problems, 159–165
writing, 144
Storyboard construction materials, 105–108
Storytelling problem, 114–116
Strategic knowledge, 15
expert/novice differences in, 231–232
in physics expertise, 228
Strategy training, 476–477
Street mathematics, defined, 435
Structural insight method, 276
Structure building
cognitive structure and, 331–332
defined, 329–330
how to guide, 332
Structure strategies
defined, 370–371
implications of, 379–385
research on, 371–379
theory, 371
Students. *See also* Apprenticeship; Problem solving
active learning and, 471–472
adjunct questions and, 333–338
advance organizers and, 351–357
attribution theory and, 475–481

dictation planning by, 121
mediationally deprived, 419
memory system of, 15–17
methods for teaching, 22–24
misconceptions, 195–202
mnemonic strategies for, 364–370
remedial vs. model, 408, 411
reviewing process for, 133–138
rhetorical structures and, 331
seductive detail hypothesis and, 466–469
self-efficacy theory and, 470–473
signaling and, 341–348
structure strategies for, 370–385
think-sheets for, 141–142
translation process for, 125–132
types of, 17
writing planning by, 121–125
Student schemas
differences in, 163–165
problem integration skills and, 166–169
for story problems, 159–163
Student Teams Achievement Divisions (STAD), 445, 448
Study strategy hypothesis, 471
Subordinate information, 89, 92
Subtraction bugs, 186
Subtraction procedure, 184–185
Summarization training, 92–95
Summarizing methods, 387–390
Summary statements, 341
Surface questions, 464
Symbol manipulation, 431
Syntactic cues, 57
Syntax errors, 133, 134

Talks to Teachers (James), 11
Target
defined, 206
problem, 308, 319, 323
Teacher(s)
attribution theory and, 478–481
background knowledge of text and, 87
learning metaphors used by, 13–14
Teaching. *See also* Feedback; Training
arithmetic, 280–282
computational problems, 281–282
concrete methods for, 278–287
detection of inconsistencies, 105–108
discovery methods for, 287–298
factors in, 8–9
foreign languages, 365–366
hypothesis creation, 224–226
hypothesis testing, 222–223
inductive methods for, 298–303
methods, 22–24
problem integration, 166–169
problem translation, 154–157
quadratic factoring, 282–283
reciprocal, 440–444
scientific expertise, 232–234
scientific reasoning, 221–224, 226
for solution planning, 176–179
within specific domains, 407–408
summarization skills, 92–95
Test(ing). *See also* Hypothesis testing
formal and informal, 436, 437
intellectual, 407–408
retention, 17
transfer, 17, 20, 356, 366, 370
Textbook lesson, how to improve, 328–329
Text interpretation, defined, 118
Text materials
detecting errors in, 133, 134, 135
mapping methods and, 371–375
questioning methods for, 391–393
summarizing methods for learning, 387–390
Text production, defined, 118
Theme-based learning, 319
ThinkerTools, 209–211
Thinking aloud
defined, 116
participatory modeling and, 451
problem solving skills and, 408
protocol, 116, 229
Thinking skills
process vs. product in, 408
programs, 402, 425
Think-sheets, 141–142
Three-column subtraction, 184–185
Time out concept, 247
Time-rate-distance word problems, 286
Token economies
classroom management and, 248–252
costs of, 254–255
Topic shift issues, 90–92
Top-level structures
defined, 375
identifying, 376–379
in prose learning, 381
summary of, 379
Training
attribution, 477, 478
automaticity, 52–55
computational procedures, 188
inference, 97–100, 101
phonological awareness, 40–43
in problem solving, 401–406
in productive thinking on creativity, 413–414, 419
reviewing process, 138
strategy, 476–477
summarization, 92–95
vocabulary, 58–62
Transfer concept
advance organizers and, 350–352
defined, 19
discovery methods effects on, 290
history of, 21–24
signaling and, 343
skill learning and, 270
testing for, 20
types of, 19
views of, 20–21
Transfer problems, 310–316
Transfer test, 17, 356, 366, 370
Translation process
constraints on, 126
defined, 125
individual differences in, 129–131
instruction and, 131–132
polished vs. unpolished drafts for, 127–129
relational statements and, 153
removing constraints on, 127
writing process and, 117
Translation skills, 157
Triangle problems, 159–160
Typographical cues, 341

Understanders, 17

Verbatim notes, 388–390
Videocases, learning from, 320–321
Vocabulary growth, approaches to, 56
Vocabulary training, 58–62
Vowels, phonic rules for, 53

Whole-word approach
for reading, 44–46
word superiority effects and, 50–51
Word(s)
decoding, 43–55
detectors, 51
reading tests, 41–43
recognition, 54
spelling tests, 41–43
teaching new, 60
Word meaning
meaning access and, 55–58
vocabulary training and, 58–62
Word problems
arithmetic, 165
problem solvers and, 166–168
solution planning and, 176–179
statistics, 163–164
Word processors, 131–132, 137
Worked-out examples
cognitive load reduction with, 312–313
example, 174
faster learning with, 310–312
increasing effectiveness of, 313–315
making better use of, 315–318
parts of, 309–310
using, 171–173
Writer-reader communication, 126
Writers
above-average vs. below-average, 135–137
errors detection by, 135
planning by, 123
translation process of, 129–131
Write think-sheet, 141
Writing process
analyzing, 116–118
instructional themes for, 119–120
model of, 117
participatory modeling and, 450–453
planning for, 120–125
reviewing process for, 133–138
student protocols and, 118–119
translating for, 125–132
Writing program
CSIW for, 140–143
instruction methods in, 138–140
strategy instruction in, 143–144

Yucatec midwives, apprenticeship of, 438

Zone of proximal development (ZPD), 432, 454